Twentieth-Century AMERICA

A Social and Political History

David Goldfield

Carl Abbott

Jo Ann E. Argersinger

Peter H. Argersinger

PEARSON
Prentice Hall

Upper Saddle River, NJ 07458

Library of Congress Cataloging-in-Publication Data

20th century America : a social and political history / David Goldfield . . . [et al.].
    p. cm
    Includes bibliographical references and index.
    ISBN 0-13-099514-2
      1. United States—History—20th century. 2. United States—Social conditions—
  20th century. 3. United States—Politics and government—20th century. I.
  Title: Twentieth century America. II. Goldfield, David R., 1944-

  E741.A14 2004
  973.91—dc22
                                  2004053511

Editorial Director: Charlyce Jones Owen
Executive Editor: Charles Cavaliere
Editorial Assistant: Shannon Corliss
Marketing Manager: Heather Shelstad
Marketing Assistant: Cherron Gardner
Managing Editor: Joanne Riker
Production Editor: Randy Pettit
Permissions Supervisor: Ronald Fox
Prepress and Manufacturing Buyer: Benjamin Smith
Interior Design: GGS Book Services, Atlantic Highlands
Cover Design: Kiwi Design
Cover Illustration/Photo: Erik Overbey Collection, University of South Alabama Archives
Composition: GGS Book Services, Atlantic Highlands

Credits and acknowledgments borrowed from other sources and reproduced, with permission, in this textbook appear on appropriate page within text (or on page 474).

Pearson Education LTD.
Pearson Education Australia PTY, Limited
Pearson Education Singapore, Pte. Ltd
Pearson Education North Asia Ltd
Pearson Education, Canada, Ltd
Pearson Educación de Mexico, S.A. de C.V.
Pearson Education-Japan
Pearson Education Malaysia, Pte. Ltd

ISBN 0-13-099514-2

CONTENTS

PREFACE

This book began with our students. The twentieth century is the time they entered the world, the time they are most familiar with, yet parts of which seem distant, even ancient to them. Their lives, who they are, where they live, and what they believe are most intimately connected with this century. Our objective is to render both the familiar and the distant events and people of the twentieth century accessible and connected to our students' lives today. The key to achieving that goal is a strong clear narrative. **Twentieth-Century America** is a compelling story of soaring ideals, incomparable tragedies, and perseverance; which is to say, the stuff of all human history. We try to tell this story in an engaging, forthright way, but we also provide students with an abundance of tools to help them absorb that story and put it in context. We introduce them to the concerns of the participants in America's history with primary source documents. The voices of contemporaries open each chapter, describing their own personal journeys toward fulfilling their dreams, hopes, and ambitions as part of the broader American journey. These voices provide a personal window on our nation's history, and the themes they express resonate throughout the narrative.

But if we wrote this book to appeal to our students, we also wrote it to engage their minds. We wanted to avoid academic trendiness, particularly the restricting categories that have divided the discipline of history over the last twenty years or so. We believe that the distinctions involved in the debates about multiculturalism and identity, between social and political history, between the history of the common people and the history of the elite, are unnecessarily confusing.

What we seek is integration—to combine political and social history, to fit the experience of particular groups into the broader perspective of the American past, to give voice to minor and major players alike because of their role in the story we have to tell.

APPROACH

In telling our story, we had some definite ideas about what we might include and emphasize that other texts do not—information we felt that the current and next generations of students will need to know about our past to function best in the society that emerged from the twentieth century.

Chronological Organization   A strong chronological backbone supports the book. We have found that the jumping back and forth in time characteristic of some textbooks confuses students. They abhor dates but need to know the sequence of events in history. A chronological presentation is the best way to be sure they do.

Geographical Literacy   We also want students to be geographically literate. We expect them not only to know what happened in American history, but where it happened as well. Physical locations and spatial relationships were often important in shaping historical events. The abundant maps in **Twentieth-Century America**—all numbered and called out in the text—are an integral part of our story.

Regional Balance   **Twentieth-Century America** presents balanced coverage of all regions of the country. In keeping with this balance, the South and the West receive more coverage in this text than in comparable books.

Point of View   **Twentieth-Century America** presents a balanced overview of the history of that century. But "balanced" does not mean bland. We do not shy away from definite positions on controversial issues, such as civil rights, military and foreign policy, feminism, the great waves of foreign migration, and cultural revolutions in music, fashion, and behavior. If students and instructors disagree, that's great. Discussion and dissent are important catalysts for understanding and learning.

Religion   Nor do we shy away from some topics that play relatively minor roles in other texts, like religion. Historians are often uncomfortable writing about religion and tend to slight its influence. This text stresses the importance of religion in twentieth-century American society as both a source of strength and a reflection of some of its more troubling aspects.

Historians mostly write for each other. That's too bad. We need to reach out and expand our audience. An American history text is a good place to start. Our students are not only our future historians, but more important, our future.

David Goldfield
Carl Abbott
Jo Ann E. Argersinger
Peter H. Argersinger

CHAPTER 1

THE AMERICAN JOURNEY IN 1900

New Industry

New Immigrants

Settling the Race Issue

New Cities

Attacking the American Indian Problem

An Emerging World Power

We were homeless, houseless, and friendless in a strange place. We had hardly money enough to last us through the voyage for which we had hoped and waited for three long years. We had suffered much that the reunion we longed for might come about; we had prepared ourselves to suffer more in order to bring it about, and had parted with those we loved, with places that were dear to us in spite of what we passed through in them, never again to see them, as we were convinced—all for the same dear end. With strong hopes and high spirits that hid the sad parting, we had started on our long journey. And now we were unexpectedly but surely . . . When my mother had recovered enough to speak, she began to argue with the *gendarme*, telling him our story and begging him to be kind. The children were frightened and all but I cried. I was only wondering what would happen. . . .

Here we had been taken to a lonely place; . . . our things were taken away, our friends separated from us; a man came to inspect us, as if to ascertain our full value; strange-looking people driving us about like dumb animals, helpless and unresisting; children we could not see crying in a way that suggested terrible things; ourselves driven into a little room where a great kettle was boiling on a little stove; our clothes taken off, our bodies rubbed with a slippery substance that might be any bad thing; a shower of warm water let down on us without warning. . . . We are forced to pick out our clothes from among all the others, with the steam blinding us; we choke, cough, entreat the women to give us time; they persist, "Quick! Quick!—or you'll miss the train!"—Oh, so we really won't be murdered! They are only making us ready for the continuing of our journey, cleaning us of all suspicions of dangerous sickness. Thank God! . . .

Oh, what solemn thoughts I had! How deeply I felt the greatness, the power of the scene! The immeasurable distance from horizon to horizon; . . . the absence of any object besides the one ship; . . . I was conscious only of sea and sky and something I did not understand. And as I listened to its solemn voice, I felt as if I had found a friend, and knew that I loved the ocean.

—Mary Antin

Mary Antin, *The Promised Land* (Boston: Houghton Mifflin Company, 1912), Chapter VIII.

MARY ANTIN, a thirteen-year-old Jewish girl from Russia, describes her family's perilous journey from the persecution of Jews in tsarist Russia to the ship that sailed from Hamburg, Germany, that would take her to Boston in far-away America. In 1894, Mary and her mother and sisters set out from their village to join her father in Boston.

Millions of European immigrants made similar journeys across the Atlantic (as did Chinese and Japanese immigrants, across the Pacific), a trip fraught with danger, unpredictable detours, occasional heartbreak, the sundering of family ties, and the fear of the unknown. So powerful was the promise of American life for the migrants that they willingly risked these obstacles to come to the United States. Mary wrote this extended letter to her uncle, who remained behind, during the first few months after her arrival in Boston. The letter was both a way of conveying the details of her family's exodus and of maintaining contact with a world and a family she had left behind.

Mary recalls the fear and frustration of being removed from the train at the Russian-German border by Russian police because of improper documents. Once her mother had settled the issue with the help of a local Jewish family, they reboarded the train to Berlin. Outside that city, they were once again removed from the train and, though they did not immediately understand what was happening, German authorities had arranged for a thorough cleansing and health inspection, since a cholera epidemic was raging in Russia. As the excerpt ends, you can sense Mary's exultation of joy and freedom as the ship leaves Hamburg for the open ocean and the place that lay beyond the horizon.

For Mary, America did indeed prove to be *The Promised Land*, as she entitled her emigration memoir, published in 1912. At the age of fifteen, she published her first poem in the *Boston Herald* and, after attending Barnard College in New York City, she wrote on immigrant issues, lectured widely, and worked for Theodore Roosevelt's Progressive party. She fought

Photographer Lewis Hine's portrait of a young Jewish woman arriving from Russia at Ellis Island 1905. Like hundreds of thousands of other immigrants who passed through the portals of New York harbor, this young woman's expression carries the hope, fear, and remembrance that touched her fellow wanderers as they embarked on their new life in America.

• CHRONOLOGY •

1886	American Federation of Labor is formed.
1887	Wanamaker's department store introduces a "bargain room," and competitors follow suit.
	Dawes Act is passed.
	Interstate Commerce Act is passed.
1890	Mississippi becomes the first state to restrict black suffrage with literacy tests.
	Government troops kill two hundred Sioux at Wounded Knee, South Dakota.
	Sherman Antitrust Act is passed.
	National American Woman Suffrage Association is organized.
1891	African-American physician Daniel Hale Williams establishes Provident Hospital, the nation's first interracially staffed hospital.
1892	General Electric opens the first corporate research and development division in the United States.

	Mining violence breaks out at Coeur d'Alene, Idaho.
	People's Party is organized.
1894	Pullman Sleeping Car Company strike fails.
	Immigration Restriction League is formed.
1895	American-born Chinese in California form the Native Sons of the Golden State to counter nativisim.
1896	In *Plessy v. Ferguson*, the Supreme Court permits segregation by law.
1897	George C. Tilyou opens Steeplechase Park on Coney Island in Brooklyn, New York.
1898	Congress passes the Erdman Act to provide for voluntary mediation of railroad labor disputes.
	Spanish-American War is fought.
	Hawaii is annexed.
	Anti-Imperialist League is organized.

against immigration restriction legislation and promoted public education as the main channel of upward mobility for immigrants. Though some have viewed her work as a bit too optimistic and perhaps naive, her own life is a strong testament of how a teenage girl moved from a medieval life in tsarist Russia to a career as a respected writer in the United States. Today, more than a century later, her story is being repeated by migrants from Latin America and Southeast Asia. They shared the same sorrows and hopes as Mary; they are the living reminders of our history as a nation of immigrants.

Mary and her family were part of a major transformation of life in the United States by 1900. As writer Henry Adams put it: "In the essentials of life . . . the boy of 1854 stood nearer the year one than to the year 1900." By 1900, the outlines of our nation today—its great, technologically advanced, and diverse cities, its emergence as a global power, and its efforts to address inequalities of race, income, and gender—were apparent. And those outlines set the nation apart from its nineteenth-century predecessor enough so that "boy" would find himself in another world in 1900.

Rapid industrial development, in addition to an upsurge in immigration, changed the nature of the country and the shape of its cities. Large factories staffed by semiskilled laborers displaced the skilled artisans and small shops that had dominated American industry in the nineteenth century. Industrial development also accelerated urbanization. Cities were, of course, nothing new on the American landscape, but this was an age of great cities. The proportion of the nation's population living in cities—swelled by migrants from the countryside and immigrants from Europe and Asia—increased from 20 to 40 percent, a rate of growth twice that of the population as a whole.

The changes in American life were exhilarating for some, tragic for others. New opportunities opened as old opportunities disappeared. Vast new wealth was created, but poverty increased, a dilemma that plagued governments, voluntary agencies, and religious organizations throughout the new century. New technologies eased life for some but left others untouched. The automobile, motion pictures, vacuum cleaners, and telephones scarcely existed before 1900 but changed lives dramatically after that date, altering courtship patterns, household chores, eating habits, and conversations. Imagine riding an elevator for the first time and wondering if the thing would suddenly drop or stall; imagine no longer living by the rhythm of the sun, now being able to turn on lights at any hour of the day or night; the convenience of indoor plumbing; the joys of listening to your favorite tunes on the phonograph; and sitting in a darkened theater enthralled by the flickering screen. Little wonder that young Mary seemed mesmerized by her new world; so were millions of other Americans.

KEY TOPICS

The technological and organizational innovations behind the emergence of large corporations and a new work force, and the response of government.

The impact of the new immigration.

The hardening of race relations and African-American migration.

New patterns of residence, consumption, and recreation in the industrial city.

The subjugation of Native Americans in the West.

Ideological assumptions of an emerging world power.

NEW INDUSTRY

Between 1870 and 1900, the United States transformed itself from an agricultural nation—a nation of farmers, merchants, and artisans—into the world's foremost industrial power, producing more than one-third of the world's manufactured goods. By the early twentieth century, factory workers made up one-fourth of the work force, and agricultural workers had dropped from a half to less than a third.

Inventing Technology: The Electric Age

By 1900, the electric age had dawned. Electricity freed manufacturers from dependence on water power. Factories no longer had to be located by rivers. They could be built anywhere accessible to the transportation system and a concentration of labor. Technology also enabled managers to substitute machines for workers, skewing the balance of power in the workplace toward employers. And it transformed city life, making available a host of new conveniences. By the early twentieth century, electric lights, appliances, ready-made clothing, and store-bought food eased middle-class life. Electric trolleys whisked clerks, salespeople, bureaucrats, and bankers to new urban and suburban subdivisions. Electric streetlights lit up city streets at night. Amusement parks drew crowds with mechanical attractions scarcely imaginable a generation earlier.

For much of the nineteenth century, the United States was dependent on the industrial nations of Europe for technological innovation. American engineers often went to England and Germany for education and training, and the textile industry, railroads, and the early steel industry benefited from German and Ewnglish inventions.

In the late nineteenth century, the United States changed from a technological borrower to a technological innovator. By 1910, a million patents had been issued in the United States, 900,000 of them after 1870. Elihu Thomson, a high school chemistry teacher in

Electricity conquered space and the night. The yellow glow of incandescent bulbs, the whiz of trolleys, and the rumble of elevated railways energize The Bowery, an emerging entertainment district in lower Manhattan at the end of the nineteenth century. *Source: W. Louis Sonntag, Jr., "The Bowery at Night, watercolor, 1895. Copyright Museum of the City of New York. 32.275.2*

Philadelphia who enjoyed dabbling in electricity, left teaching to devote himself full-time to his hobby. He purchased Thomas Edison's General Electric Company in 1892 and established the country's first corporate research and development division. His scientists produced what was then the most efficient light bulb design, and by 1914, General Electric was producing 85 percent of the world's light bulbs.

Following this precedent, other American companies established research and development laboratories. Standard Oil, U.S. Rubber, the chemical giant Du Pont, and the photographic company Kodak all became world leaders in their respective industries because of innovations their laboratories developed.

The Corporation and Its Impact

The process of invention that emerged in the United States gave the country a commanding technological lead. But the modernization of industry that made the United States the world's foremost industrial nation after 1900 reflected organizational as well as technological innovation. As industries sought efficient ways to apply technology and expand their markets within and beyond national borders, their work forces expanded, and their need for capital mounted. Coping with these changes required significant changes in corporate management, and entrepreneurs such as John D. Rockefeller in oil and Andrew Carnegie in steel captured large shares of their markets by consolidating operations and gobbling up smaller competitors. By 1890, Rockefeller's Standard Oil company controlled 90 percent of the nation's oil refining. By 1900, the Carnegie Steel Company (later U.S. Steel) was producing one-quarter of the country's steel.

The Changing Nature of Work

From the perspective of the workers, the growth of giant corporations was a mixed blessing. The corporations provided abundant jobs, but they firmly controlled working conditions. As late as the 1880s, shops of skilled artisans were responsible for most manufacturing in the United States. Since the midcentury, however, industrialists had been introducing ways to simplify manufacturing processes so they could hire low-skilled workers. This deskilling process accelerated in the 1890s in response to new technologies, new workers, and workplace reorganization. By 1906, according to a U.S. Department of Labor report, industrial labor had been reduced to minute, low-skilled operations, making skilled artisans obsolete.

Mechanization and technological innovation did not reduce employment, although they did eliminate some jobs, most of them skilled. On the contrary, the birth of whole new industries—steel, automobiles, electrical equipment, cigarettes, food canning, and machine tools—created a huge demand for workers. Innovations in existing industries, like railroads, similarly spurred job growth. The number of people working for U.S. railroads increased from eighty thousand to more than 1 million between 1860 and 1910.

Ironically, it was a shortage of skilled workers as much as other factors that encouraged industrialists to mechanize. Unskilled workers cost less than the scarce artisans. And with massive waves of immigrants arriving from Europe and Asia between 1880 and 1920 (joined after 1910 by migrants from the American South), the supply of unskilled workers seemed limitless.

To protect their interests some workers fitfully turned to organization. The American Federation of Labor (AFL) was organized in 1886, and other unions like the American Railway Union (ARU) also emerged briefly but, generally, with little success. The ARU, for example, was crushed in the great Pullman strike of 1894 by a combination of corporate and governmental power, expressed in strikebreakers, judicial injunctions, and military force.

Out on the Farm

Rural Americans, especially farmers, were also affected by corporate expansion. Rural migrants, attracted by the rise of industry and related occupations, far outnumbered foreign migrants in the nation's cities by 1900. The majority of Americans at the turn of the century remained in small towns and on farms; their lives began to change in important ways as their interdependence on railroads, industry, and cities increased. Western commercial farmers, for example needed the high demand of Eastern and Midwestern cities and the expanding world market. The rail network provided essential transportation for their crops; the nation's industrial sector produced necessary agricultural machinery. Banks and loan companies extended the credit and capital that allowed farmers to take advantage of mechanization and other new advances; and many other businesses graded, stored, processed, and sold their crops.

In the late 1880s, drought coincided with a slump in crop prices caused by surpluses and foreign competition. Squeezed between high costs for credit, transportation, and manufactured goods and falling agricultural prices, Western farmers faced disaster. They responded by lashing back at their points of contact with the new system. They especially condemned the railroads, believing that the companies exploited farmers' dependence on railroads by charging excessive and discriminatory freight rates.

Farmers also denounced the bankers and mortgage lenders who had provided the credit for them to acquire land, equipment, and machinery. When crops failed and prices fell, the debt burden proved calamitous for many farmers. Beginning in 1889, many Western farms were foreclosed. Joined by equally distressed Southern farmers, the Westerners mounted a third-party challenge in the early 1890s to compel government action, a challenge comparable to the workers' attempts to organize labor unions to defend their interests. Although the Populists, as they were called, had some success in gaining regulatory reforms in the West and South, their party had faded by 1900.

Government Responds

The concentration of American industry in the hands of a few powerful corporations alarmed many Americans, not just workers and farmers. Giant corporations threatened to restrict opportunities for small entrepreneurs like the shopkeepers, farmers, and artisans who abounded at midcentury. In the words of one historian, the corporations "seemed to signal the end of an open, promising America and the beginning of a closed, unhappier society." Impersonal and governed by profit, the modern corporation challenged the ideal of the self-made man and the belief that success and advancement would reward hard work. These concerns eventually prompted the federal and state governments to respond with antitrust and other regulatory laws.

Federal and state regulation of private enterprise represented a significant change for the role of government in American society. For the most part, government in the late nineteenth century was neither active nor productive by present standards. The receding government activism of the Civil War and Reconstruction years coincided with a resurgent belief in localism and **laissez-faire** politics. In addition, a Congress and presidency divided between the two major parties, a small and inefficient bureaucracy, and judicial restraints joined powerful private interests to limit the size and objectives of the federal government.

However, the rapid growth of great industrial corporations and their disruptive effects on traditional practices and values profoundly alarmed the public. Popular concern focused first on the nation's railroads, the preeminent symbol of big business. Both farm groups and business shippers complained of discriminatory rates levied by railroads. Consumers condemned the railroads' suppression of competition to maintain high rates. With the support of both major parties, Congress in 1887 passed the Interstate Commerce Act.

The act, among other provisions, prohibited discriminatory rates and established the **Interstate Commerce Commission (ICC)** to investigate and prosecute violations. The ICC was the first federal regulatory agency, but its powers were too limited to be effective. Senator Nelson Aldrich of Rhode Island, a leading spokesman for business interests, described the law as an "empty menace to great interests, made to answer the clamor of the ignorant." Presidents did little to enforce it, and railroads continued their objectionable practices.

Many people saw railroad abuses as indicative of the dangers of corporate power in general and demanded a broader federal response. As with railroad regulation, the first antitrust laws—laws intended to break up or regulate corporate monopolies—were passed by states. Exposés of the monopolistic practices of such corporations as Standard Oil forced both major parties to endorse national antitrust legislation during the campaign of 1888. In 1890, Congress enacted the Sherman Antitrust Act with only a single vote in opposition. But this near unanimity concealed real differences over the desirability and purpose of the law. Although it emphatically prohibited any combination in restraint of trade (any attempt to restrict competition), it was otherwise vaguely written and hence weak in its ability to prevent abuses. The courts further weakened the act, and presidents of both parties made little effort to enforce it. Essentially still unfettered, large corporations remained an ominous threat in the eyes of many Americans.

State governments were more active than the federal government. Considered closer and more responsible to the people, they had long exercised police powers and regulatory authority. They collected taxes for education and public works, and they promoted private enterprise and public health. Still, they did little by today's standards.

But state governments gradually expanded their role in response to the stresses produced by industrialization. Following the lead of Massachusetts in 1869, a majority of states had by the turn of the century created commissions to investigate and regulate industry. Public intervention in other areas of the industrial economy soon followed. One observer noted in 1887 that state governments enacted many laws and established numerous state agencies in "utter disregard of the laissez-faire principle." In Minnesota, for example, the state helped farmers by establishing a dairy commission, prohibiting the manufacture or sale of margarine, creating a bureau of animal industry, and employing state veterinarians. In the lumber industry, state officials oversaw every log "from the woods to the saw-mill." State inspectors examined Minnesota's steam boilers, oil production, and sanitary conditions. Other laws regulated railroads, telegraphs, and dangerous occupations, prohibited racial discrimination in inns, and otherwise protected the public welfare.

Not all such agencies and laws were effective, nor were all state governments as diligent as Minnesota's. Southern states, especially, lagged, and one Midwesterner complained that his legislature merely "meets in ignorance, sits in corruption, and dissolves in disgrace every two years." Still, the widening scope of state action represented a growing acceptance of public responsibility for social welfare and economic life and laid the foundation for more effective steps in the early twentieth century.

But even the rapid expansion of state and federal government regulation after 1900 did not resolve the conflicts of the workplace and boardroom. Issues such as competition, access, workers' rights, and corporate tactics and strategies continue to challenge governments into the twenty-first century even as the nature of the work force and technologies have changed in the interim.

These issues persist because, along with the belief that this is a nation of immigrants, Americans adhere to the ideal of opportunity, and translate "opportunity" almost always into economic prosperity. Journalist Herbert Croly put it this way in 1909: "The Promise of America has consisted largely in the opportunity which it offered of economic independence and prosperity. . . . The native American, like the alien immigrant, conceives the better future which awaits himself and other men in America as fundamentally a future in which economic prosperity will be still more abundant and still more accessible than it has yet been either here or abroad. . . . With all their professions of Christianity their national idea remains thoroughly worldly. . . . The Promise, which bulks so large in their patriotic outlook, is a promise of comfort and prosperity for an ever increasing majority of good Americans." Contrast Croley's optimism with a remark by a Pennsylvania coal miner a few years earlier that "The working people of this country . . . find monopolies as strong as government itself. They find capital as rigid as absolute monarchy. They find their so-called independence a myth." The history of American reform in the twentieth century is often a story of how these two visions could be reconciled, how the reality of the coal miner's life could approach the ideal of Croley's optimism.

NEW IMMIGRANTS

Still, Croley's ideal propelled the immigrant tide as Mary Antin's story relates. Though Mary and her family had no intention of returning to the Old World, Jewish immigrants were the exception in this regard. Wherever they came from, most migrants saw the ocean as

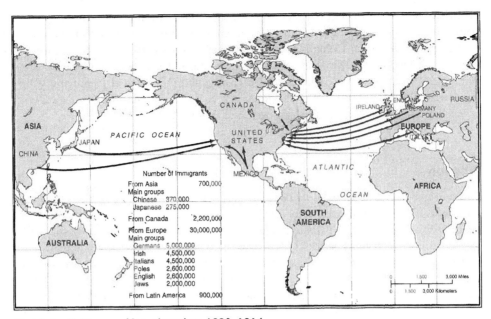

Number of Immigrants	
From Asia	700,000
Main groups	
Chinese	370,000
Japanese	275,000
From Canada	2,200,000
From Europe	30,000,000
Main groups	
Germans	5,000,000
Irish	4,500,000
Italians	4,500,000
Poles	2,600,000
English	2,600,000
Jews	2,000,000
From Latin America	900,000

MAP 1-1   Patterns of Immigration, 1820–1914
The migration to the United States was part of a worldwide transfer of population that accelerated with the Industrial Revolution and the accompanying improvement in transportation.

a two-way highway. They intended to stay only a year or two, long enough to earn money to buy land or, more likely, to enter a business back home and improve life for themselves and their families. Roughly half of all immigrants to the United States between 1880 and World War I returned to their country of origin. Some made several round trips. (see Map 1-1)

Most newcomers were young men. (Jews, again, were the exception: Reflecting their intention to stay in their new home, they tended to migrate in families.) Immigrants easily found work in the nation's booming cities. The quickest way to make money was in the large urban factories, with their voracious demands for unskilled labor. Except for the Japanese, few immigrants came to work on farms after 1880. By 1900, women began to equal men among all immigrant groups as young men who decided to stay sent for their families. In a few cases, entire villages migrated, drawn by the good fortune of one or two compatriots.

The Neighborhood

Immigrants did not live in homogeneous communities isolated from the rest of society. Rarely did a particular ethnic group comprise more than 50 percent of a neighborhood. These residential patterns persist in our cities today. The Chinese were the exception, but even the borders of Chinatowns usually overlapped with other neighborhoods. A particular apartment building might house families from Abruzzi in Italy, and Jews from Kiev might dominate a block of tenements in New York City's Lower East Side, but greater concentrations were rare. Even to call such districts "Jewish" or "Italian" distorts the reality. Most Italian immigrants identified not so much with Italy—which had only recently been unified—as with the village of their birth. Only with time did they come to see themselves as "Italian" in the way the rest of American society saw them. In much the same way today, native-born Americans tend to lump Latino immigrants into the category of "Hispanic," though immigrants from Colombia differ from their counterparts from Mexico, who, in turn are different from Cubans and Jamaicans, and so on. Still, increasing numbers of Latino immigrants have seen the economic and especially political benefits of identifying with a larger group that transcends national boundaries, in much the same way that Jews transcended national differences and Italians overcame regional distinctions.

The Job

If the neighborhood provided a familiar and supportive environment for the immigrant, work offered the ultimate reward for coming to America, as Croley predicted. All immigrants perceived the job as the way to independence and as a way out, either back to the Old World or into the larger American society. The type of work available to immigrants, then and now, depended on their skills, the local economy, and local discrimination. Mexican migrants to southern California, for example, concentrated in railroad construction. Mostly unskilled, they replaced Chinese laborers when the federal government excluded Chinese immigration after 1882. Mexicans built the interurban rail lines of Los Angeles in 1900 and established communities at their construction camps. Los Angeles businessmen barred Mexicans from other occupations. Similarly, Chinese immigrants were confined to work in laundries and restaurants within the boundaries of Los Angeles's Chinatown. There were no commercial laundries in China. Nor are Hispanic and Southeast Asian immigrants today trained in their native lands for hotel service, landscaping, or construction work. These are the service and industrial occupations where significant demands for low-skilled, low-wage labor exist.

The Japanese who came to Los Angeles around 1900 were forced into sectors of the economy native-born white people had either shunned or failed to exploit. The Japanese turned this discrimination to their benefit when they transformed the cultivation of market garden crops into a major agricultural enterprise. By 1904, Japanese farmers owned more than fifty thousand acres in California. George Shima, who came to California from Japan in 1889 with a little capital, made himself the "Potato King" of the Sacramento Delta. By 1913, Shima owned 28,000 acres of farmland.

Other ethnic groups in other parts of the country had to conform to similar constraints. Greeks in Chicago, for example, restricted to food services, established restaurants, fruit distributorships, and ice-cream factories throughout the city.

Stereotypes also channeled immigrants' work options, sometimes benefiting one group at the expense of another. Jewish textile entrepreneurs, for example, sometimes hired only Italians because they thought them less prone to unionization than Jewish workers. Other Jewish bosses hired only Jewish workers, hoping that ethnic loyalty would overcome the lure of the unions. Pittsburgh steelmakers preferred Polish workers to the black workers who began arriving in Northern cities in appreciable numbers after 1900. This decision began the decades-long tradition of handing down steel mill jobs through the generations in Polish families.

Jews alone among European ethnic groups found work almost exclusively with one another. Among the factors contributing to this pattern may have been the discrimination Jews faced in eastern Europe, the existence of an established Jewish community when they arrived, and their domination of the needle trades. Jews comprised three-quarters of the more than half-million workers in New York City's garment industry in 1910. Jews were also heavily concentrated in the retail trade.

Like their native-born counterparts, few married immigrant women worked outside the home, but unlike the native-born, many Italian and Jewish women did piecework for the garment industry in their apartments. Unmarried Polish women often worked in factories or as domestic servants. Japanese women, married and single, worked with their families on farms. Until revolution in China in 1911 began to erode traditional gender roles, married Chinese immigrant women typically remained at home.

The paramount goal for many immigrants was to work for themselves, rather than for someone else. Some immigrants, like George Shima, parlayed their skills and a small stake into successful businesses. Most new arrivals, however, had few skills, and no resources beyond their wits with which to realize their dreams. Major banks at the time were unlikely to extend even a small business loan to a budding ethnic entrepreneur. Family members and small ethnic-based community banks provided the initial stake for most immigrant businesses. Many of these banks failed, but a few survived and prospered. For example, the Bank of Italy, established by Amadeo Pietro Giannini in San Francisco in 1904, eventually grew into the Bank of America, one of the nation's largest financial institutions today.

Immigrants could not fully control their own destinies in the United States, any more than native-born Americans could. The vagaries of daily life, including death, disease, and bad luck, thwarted many immigrants' dreams. Hard work did not always ensure success. Add to these the difficulty of cultural adjustment to an unfamiliar environment, and the newcomers' confident hopes could quickly fade. Almost all immigrants, however, faced an obstacle that by its nature white native-born Americans did not. They faced it on the job, in the city at large, and even in their neighborhoods: the antiforeign prejudice of American nativism.

Nativism

Despite the openness of American borders in the nineteenth century, and contrary to the nation's reputation as a refuge from foreign persecution and poverty, immigrants have not always received a warm reception. Ben Franklin groused about the "foreignness" of German immigrants during the colonial era. From the 1830s to 1860, nativist sentiment, directed mainly at Irish Catholic immigrants, expressed itself in occasional violence and discrimination. Anti-immigrant sentiment gave rise to an important political party, the Know-Nothings in the 1850s. And, today, the attempts in California to limit the access of the children of illegal aliens to state services, and charges of some that immigrants take jobs away from native-born workers, and the concern that Spanish language and culture are "taking over" public schools and neighborhoods, resemble historic antiforeign sentiment or **nativism**. Much less evident today, is the crude "scientific" racism that characterized nativism a century ago when prominent educators, journalists, and politicians believed the new ethnic groups represented an inferior set of races. A prominent Columbia University professor wrote in 1887 that Hungarians and Italians were "of such a character as to endanger our civilization." Nine years later, the director of the U.S. Census warned that eastern and southern Europeans were "beaten men from beaten races. They have none of the ideas and aptitudes which fit men to take up readily and easily the problem of self-care and self-government." The result of unfettered migration would be "race suicide." Labor competition also contributed to the rise of anti-immigrant sentiment.

Immigrants and their organizations fought against these views through political pressure and also by "proving" their worth as new Americans. In 1895, a group of American-born Chinese in California formed a communal association called the Native Sons of the Golden State (a deliberate response to a nativist organization that called itself the Native Sons of the Golden West). Stressing the need to assimilate, the association's constitution declared, "It is

imperative that no members shall have sectional, clannish, Tong [a secret fraternal organiza-
tion] or party prejudices against each other. . . . Whoever violates this provision shall be
expelled." A guidebook written at the same time for immigrant Jews recommended that
they "hold fast," calling that attitude "most necessary in America. Forget your past, your customs, and your ideals. . . . A bit of advice to you: do not take a moment's rest. Run, do,
work, and keep your own good in mind." Although it is doubtful whether most Jewish
immigrants followed this advice in its entirety, it nonetheless reflects the way the pressure to
conform modified the cultures of all immigrant groups.

Assimilation connotes the loss of one culture in favor of another. The immigrant experience of the late nineteenth and early twentieth centuries might be described better as a process
of adjustment between old ways and new. It was a dynamic process that resulted in entirely
new cultural forms. It rarely followed a straight line toward or from the culture of origin. The
Japanese, for example, had not gone to Los Angeles to become truck farmers, but circumstances led them to that occupation, and they used their cultural heritage of hard work, strong
family ties, and sober living to make a restricted livelihood successful. Sometimes economics
and the availability of alternatives resulted in modifications of traditions that nonetheless maintained their spirit. In the old country, Portuguese held *festas* every Sunday honoring a patron
saint. In New England towns, they confined the tradition to their churches, instead of parading
through the streets. And instead of baking bread themselves, Portuguese immigrant women
were happy to buy all the bread they needed from local bakers.

In a few cases, the New World offered greater opportunities to follow cultural traditions
than the Old World. Young women who migrated from Italy's Abruzzi region to Rochester,
New York, found that it was easier to retain their Old World moral code in late-nineteenth-
century Rochester, where young men outnumbered them significantly. At the same time,
the enhanced economic prospects in Rochester enabled them to marry earlier than they
would have in their hometowns. It also allowed these young women to work outside the
home, something women rarely did in Abruzzi. Financial security allowed them to construct
the nuclear household that was the cultural ideal in the old country. In a similar way, Sicilians
who migrated to lower Manhattan discovered that ready access to work and relatively high
geographical mobility permitted them to live near and among their extended families much
more easily than they could in Sicily.

Despite the antagonism of native-born white people toward recent immigrants, the
greatest racial divide in America remained that between black and white, and red and
white. If we were a nation of immigrants, where did African Americans and Native
Americans fit into that "story"? To be sure, African Americans migrated from elsewhere, but
under such different circumstances from other immigrants that their experiences were distinctive. And, Native Americans, of course, predated European and African settlement by
centuries.

Early twentieth-century immigrants quickly caught on to these distinctions and
sought to assert their "whiteness" as a common bond with other European immigrant
groups and a badge of acceptance into the larger society. Nativists, however, often lumped
immigrants into the "black" category. The word *guinea*, for example, which originally
referred to African slaves, emerged as a derogatory epithet for Italians and, occasionally,
Greeks, Jews, and Puerto Ricans. When the Louisiana legislature debated disfranchisement in 1898, a lawmaker explained that "according to the spirit of our meaning when we
speak of 'white man's government,' Italians are as black as the blackest negro in existence."
For immigrants, therefore, becoming "white"—distancing themselves, both geographically
and culturally from African Americans—was often part of the process of adjusting to
American life, especially as increasing numbers of black Southerners began moving to
Northern cities.

SETTLING THE RACE ISSUE

A significant reason for this movement was the deteriorating conditions for African Americans in the South, where 90 percent of the nation's black population resided in 1900. If there was any group, with the possible exception of Native Americans, that was further from the "Promise of American Life," it was the former slave. Their journey, up from slavery to the status of full citizenship had stalled by 1900, especially, though not exclusively, in the South.

Black Aspirations and White Backlash

During the 1890s, a new generation of African Americans emerged in the South that demanded full participation in American society. As the young black editor of Nashville's *Fisk Herald* proclaimed in 1889, "We are not the Negro from whom the chains of slavery fell a quarter of a century ago. . . . We are now qualified, and being the equal of whites, should be treated as such." Charles Price, an educator from North Carolina, admonished colleagues in 1890, "If we do not possess the manhood and patriotism to stand up in the defense of . . . constitutional rights and protest long, loud and unitedly against their continual infringements, we are unworthy of heritage as American citizens and deserve to have fastened on us the wrongs of which many are disposed to complain."

For many in the generation of white Southerners who came of age in the same period, this assertiveness rankled. These young white people, raised on the myth of the Lost Cause—a heroic war of Southern independence to preserve a glorious civilization—were continually reminded of the heroism and sacrifice of their fathers during the Civil War. Confronted with what was, for many, worse conditions than their families had enjoyed before the war, they resented the changed status of black people. For them, African Americans replaced the Yankees as the enemy; they saw it as their mission to preserve white purity and dominance. Echoing these sentiments, David Schenck, a Greensboro, North Carolina, businessman, wrote in 1890 that "the breach between the races widens as the young free negroes grow up and intrude themselves on white society and nothing prevents the white people of the South from annihilating the negro race but the military power of the United States Government." Using the Darwinian language popular among educated white people at the time, Schenck concluded, "I pity the Negro, but the struggle is for the survival of the fittest race."

The South's deteriorating rural economy and the volatile politics of the early 1890s exacerbated the growing tensions between assertive black people and threatened white people. So too did the growth of industry and cities in the South. In the cities, black and white people came in close contact, competing for jobs and jostling each other for seats on streetcars and trains. Racist rhetoric and violence against black people accelerated in the 1890s.

Lynch Law

During 1892, a year of political agitation and economic depression, 235 **lynchings** occurred in the South. White mobs lynched nearly two thousand black Southerners between 1882 and 1903. During the 1890s, lynchings occurred at the rate of 150 a year. Most lynchers were working-class whites with rural roots, who were struggling in the depressed economy of the 1890s and enraged at the fluidity of urban race relations.

The silence or tepid disapproval of white leaders condoned this orgy of violence. The substitution of lynch law for a court of law seemed a cheap price to pay for white solidarity at a time when political and economic pressures threatened entrenched white leaders.

Lynching became a public spectacle; a ritual designed to reinforce white supremacy. Note the matter-of-face satisfaction of the spectators to this gruesome murder of a black man.

In 1893, Atlanta's Methodist bishop, Atticus G. Haygood, typically a spokesman for racial moderation, objected to the torture some white lynchers inflicted on their victims but added, "Unless assaults by Negroes on white women and little girls come to an end, there will most probably be still further displays of vengeance that will shock the world."

Haygood's comments reflect the most common justification for lynching—the presumed threat posed by black men to the sexual virtue of white women. Sexual "crimes" could include remarks, glances, and gestures. Yet only 25 percent of the lynchings that took place in the thirty years after 1890 had some alleged sexual connection. Lynchers did not carry out their grisly crimes to end a rape epidemic; they killed to keep black men in their place and to restore their own sense of manhood and honor.

Ida B. Wells, a black woman who owned a newspaper in Memphis, but who fled to Chicago in the 1890s when she condemned a brutal lynching in that city, admitted that she had lost her faith that education, wealth, and upright living guaranteed black people the equality and justice they had long sought. The reverse was true. The more black people succeeded the greater was their threat to white people.

Segregation By Law

Southern white lawmakers sought to cement white solidarity and ensure black subservence in the 1890s and early 1900s by instituting **segregation** by law and the **disfranchisement** of black voters. Racial segregation restricting black Americans to separate and rarely equal public facilities had prevailed nationwide before the Civil War. After 1870, the custom spread rapidly in Southern cities. In Richmond by the early 1870s, segregation laws required black people registering to vote to enter through separate doors and registrars to count their ballots separately. The city's prison and hospitals were segregated. So too were its horse-drawn railways, its schools, and most of its restaurants, hotels, and theaters.

During the same period, many Northern cities and states, often in response to protests by African Americans, were ending segregation. Massachusetts, for example, had passed the nation's first public accommodations law in May 1865, desegregating all public facilities. Cities such as New York, Cleveland, and Cincinnati desegregated their streetcars. Chicago, Cleveland, Milwaukee, and the entire state of Michigan desegregated their public school systems. Roughly 95 percent of the nation's black population, however, lived in the South. Integration in the North, consequently, required white people to give up very little to black people. And as African-American aspirations increased in the South during the 1890s as their political power waned, they became more vulnerable to segregation by law at the state level. At the same time, migration to cities, industrial development, and technologies such as railroads and elevators increased the opportunities for racial contact and muddled the rules of racial interaction.

Much of the new legislation focused on railroads, a symbol of modernity and mobility in the New South. The railroad segregation laws required the railroads to provide "separate but equal" accommodations for black passengers. Railroads balked at the expense involved in doing so and provided black passengers with distinctly inferior facilities. Many lines refused to sell first-class tickets to black people and treated them roughly if they sat in first-class seats or tried to eat in the dining car. In 1890, Homer Plessy, a black Louisianan, refused to leave the first-class car of a railroad traveling through the state. After being arrested, he filed suit, arguing that his payment of the first-class fare entitled him to sit in the same first-class accommodations as white passengers. He claimed that under his right of citizenship guaranteed by the Fourteenth Amendment, neither the state of Louisiana nor the railroad could discriminate against him on the basis of color. The Constitution, he claimed, was colorblind.

The U.S. Supreme Court ruled on the case, **Plessy v. Ferguson**, in 1896. In a seven-to-one decision, the Court held that Louisiana's railroad segregation law did not violate the Constitution as long as the railroads or the state provided equal accommodations for black passengers. The decision left unclear what "equal" meant. In the Court's view, "Legislation is powerless to eradicate racial instincts," meaning that segregation of the races was natural and transcended constitutional considerations. Such thinking was consistent with the scientific theories of the time that gave rise to nativist sentiment in the North against the new immigrants. The only justice to vote against the decision was John Marshall Harlan, a Kentuckian and former slave owner. In a stinging dissent, he predicted that the decision would result in an all-out assault on black rights. "The destinies of the two races . . . are indissolubly linked together," Harlan declared, "and the interests of both require that common government of all shall not permit the seed of race hate to be planted under the sanction of law."

Harlan's was a prophetic dissent. Both Northern and Southern states enacted new segregation laws in the wake of *Plessy v. Ferguson*, a decision that remained the law of the land until the *Brown* school desegregation decision of 1954. In practice, the separate facilities for black people these laws required, if provided at all, were rarely equal. A sense of futility, time, expense, and physical danger dissuaded black people from challenging the statutes. Protests in the press, appeals to white leaders, and occasional boycotts failed to stem the rising tide. By 1900, segregation by law extended to public conveyances, theaters, hotels, restaurants, parks, and schools. As cities boomed, African-American civil rights shrunk.

Disfranchisement

With economic and social segregation came political isolation in the South. The authority of post-Reconstruction Southern governments had rested on their ability to limit and control the black vote. Following the political instability of the late 1880s and the 1890s, however, white leaders determined to disfranchise black people altogether, thereby reinforcing white solidarity and eliminating the need to consider black interests. Obstacles loomed—the Fifteenth Amendment, which guaranteed freedmen the right to vote, and a Republican-dominated Congress—but with a national consensus emerging in support of white supremacy, they proved easy to circumvent.

The movement to reduce or eliminate the black vote in the South began in the 1880s and continued through the early 1900s. (See Overview table, "The March of Disfranchisement across the South, 1889–1908.") Democrats enacted a variety of measures to attain their objectives without violating the letter of the Fifteenth Amendment. They complicated the registration and voting processes. States enacted **poll taxes**, requiring citizens to pay to vote. They adopted the secret ballot, which confused and intimidated illiterate black voters accustomed to

• • • O V E R V I E W • • •

THE MARCH OF DISFRANCHISEMENT
ACROSS THE SOUTH, 1889–1908

YEAR	STATE	STRATEGIES
1889	Florida	Poll tax
1889	Tennessee	Poll tax
1890	Mississippi	Poll tax, literacy test, understanding clause
1891	Arkansas	Poll tax
1893, 1901	Alabama	Poll tax, literacy test, grandfather clause
1894, 1895	South Carolina	Poll tax, literacy test, understanding clause
1894, 1902	Virginia	Poll tax, literacy test, understanding clause
1897, 1898	Louisiana	Poll tax, literacy test, grandfather clause
1899, 1900	North Carolina	Poll tax, literacy test, grandfather clause
1902	Texas	Poll tax
1908	Georgia	Poll tax, literacy test, understanding clause, grandfather clause

using ballots with colors to identify parties. States set literacy and educational qualifications for voting or required prospective registrants to "interpret" a section of the state constitution. To avoid disfranchising poor, illiterate white voters with these measures, states enacted **grandfather clauses**, granting the vote automatically to anyone whose grandfather could have voted prior to 1867 (the year Congressional Reconstruction began). The grandfathers of most black men in the 1890s had been slaves, ineligible to vote.

Black people protested disfranchisement vigorously. When 160 South Carolina delegates gathered to amend the state constitution in 1895, the 6 black delegates among them mounted a passionate but futile defense of their right to vote. Black delegate W. J. Whipper noted the irony of white people clamoring for supremacy when they already held the vast majority of the state's elected offices. He also pointed out that African Americans voted responsibly where they had a majority and frequently elected white candidates. Robert Smalls, the state's leading black politician, urged delegates not to turn their backs on the state's black population. Such pleas fell on deaf ears.

A National Consensus on Race

How could the South get away with it? How could Southerners openly segregate, disfranchise, and lynch African Americans without a national outcry? Apparently the majority of Americans by 1900 subscribed to the notion that black people were inferior to white people and deserved to be treated as second-class citizens. Contemporary depictions of black people show scarcely human stereotypes: black men with bulbous lips and bulging eyes, fat black women wearing turbans and smiling vacuously, and black children contentedly eating watermelon or romping with jungle animals. These images appeared on cereal boxes, in advertisements, in children's books, in newspaper cartoons, and as lawn ornaments. Popular theater of the day featured white men in blackface cavorting in ridiculous fashion and singing songs such as "All Coons Look Alike to Me" and "I Wish My Color Would Fade." Immigrants from Europe took in these spectacles at vaudeville and minstrel shows and assumed the prevailing prejudices. Among the most widely read books of the era was *The Clansmen* (1905), a glorification of the rise of the Ku Klux Klan by Thomas Dixon, a North

Carolinian living in New York City. D.W. Griffith transformed *The Clansman* into an immensely popular motion picture epic under the title *Birth of a Nation* in 1915, a film, President Woodrow Wilson remarked, "written in lightning."

Intellectual and political opinion in the North bolstered Southern policy. So-called scientific racism purported to establish white superiority and black inferiority on biological grounds. Northern-born professional historians reinterpreted the Civil War and Reconstruction in the white South's favor. Historian William A. Dunning, the generation's leading authority on Reconstruction, wrote in 1901 that the North's "views as to the political capacity of the blacks had been irrational." Respected journals openly supported disfranchisement and segregation. The progressive journal *Outlook* hailed disfranchisement in 1904 because it made it "impossible in the future for ignorant, shiftless, and corrupt negroes to misrepresent their race in political action." Harvard's Charles Francis Adams Jr., chided colleagues who disregarded the "fundamental, scientific facts" that, he claimed, demonstrated black inferiority. The *New York Times*, summarizing this national consensus in 1903, noted that "practically the whole country" supported the "southern solution" to the race issue, because "there was no other possible settlement."

These views permeated Congress, which made no effort to block the institutionalization of white supremacy in the South. As a delegate at the Alabama disfranchisement convention of 1901 noted, "The race problem is no longer confined to the States of the South, [and] we have the sympathy instead of the hostility of the North."

By the mid-1890s, Republicans were so entrenched in the North and West that they did not need Southern votes to win presidential elections or to control Congress. Besides, business-oriented Republicans found common ground with conservative Southern Democrats on fiscal policy and foreign affairs. Their attention, diverted by economic problems and labor unrest, no longer rested on the South.

As the white consensus on race emerged, the status of African Americans slipped in the North as well as the South. Although no Northern states threatened to deny black citizens the right to vote, they did increase segregation. The booming industries of the North did not generally hire black workers. Antidiscrimination laws on the books since the Civil War went unenforced. In 1904, 1906, and 1908, race riots erupted in Springfield, Ohio; Greensburg, Indiana; and Abraham Lincoln's hometown of Springfield, Illinois, matching similar disturbances in Wilmington, North Carolina (1898) and Atlanta, Georgia (1906).

Response of the Black Community

American democracy had, it seemed, hung out a "whites only" sign by 1900. How could African Americans respond to the growing political, social, and economic restrictions on their lives? Given white America's hostility, protest proved ineffective, even dangerous. African Americans organized more than a dozen boycotts of streetcar systems in the urban South between 1896 and 1908 in an effort to desegregate them, but not one succeeded. The Afro-American Council, formed in 1890 to protest the deteriorating conditions of black life, accomplished little and disbanded in 1908. W.E.B. Du Bois organized an annual Conference on Negro Problems at Atlanta University beginning in 1896, but it produced no effective plan of action.

Leaving the South represented another, more realistic option, though relatively few African Americans exercised that right until after 1900. In 1879, Benjamin "Pap" Singleton, a Nashville real estate agent, led several thousand black migrants to Kansas. Henry McNeal Turner of Georgia, an African Methodist Episcopal (AME) bishop, promoted migration to Liberia, but only a few hundred made the trip in the late 1870s, Turner not included, and most of those returned disappointed. Most black people who moved in the 1890s stayed within the South, settling in places like Mississippi, Louisiana, and Texas, where they could find work with timber companies or farming new lands that had opened to cotton and rice cultivation.

Roots of the Great Migration

Nearly 90 percent of African Americans still lived in the South in 1900, most in rural areas. And by that time, many of these residents, strapped for cash and without land, had been drawn into a subservient position in a new labor system called **sharecropping**. The premise of this system was relatively simple: The landlord furnished the sharecroppers with a house, a plot of land to work, seed, some farm animals, and farm implements and advanced them credit at a store the landlord typically owned. In exchange, the sharecroppers promised the landlord a share of their crop, usually one-half. The croppers kept the proceeds from the sale of the other half to pay off their debts at the store and save or spend as they and their families saw fit. In theory, a sharecropper could save enough to secure economic independence.

But white landlords perceived black independence as both contradictory and subversive. With landlords holding the accounts at the store, black sharecroppers found that the proceeds from their share of the crop never left them very far ahead. In exchange for extending credit to sharecroppers, store owners felt justified in requiring collateral, but sharecroppers had no assets other than the cotton they grew. So Southern states passed crop lien laws, which gave the store owner the right to the following year's crop in exchange for the current year's credit. If the following year's harvest could not pay off the debt, the sharecropper sank deeper into dependence. Some found themselves in perpetual debt and worked as virtual slaves. They could not simply abandon their debts and go to another farm, because the new landlord would check their references. Those found to have jumped their debts could end up on a prison chain gang. Not all white landlords cheated their tenants, but given the sharecroppers' innocence regarding accounting methods and crop pricing, the temptation to do so was great. Thus weak cotton prices conspired with white chicanery to keep black people economically dependent.

Migration out of the South was one response to this situation. Between 1880 and 1900 black families began to move into the great industrial cities of the Northeast and Midwest. They were drawn by the same economic promise that attracted overseas migrants and were pushed by growing persecution in the South. They also responded to the appeals of black Northerners. As a leading black newspaper, the *Chicago Defender*, argued in the early 1900s, "To die from the bite of frost is far more glorious than at the hands of a mob. I beg you, my brother, to leave the benighted land." Job opportunities probably outweighed all other factors in motivating what became known as the **Great Migration**. Letters to the *Defender* spoke much less of the troubled life in the South than of the promise of a new, more productive life in the North.

In most Northern cities in 1900, black people typically worked as common laborers or domestic servants. They competed with immigrants for jobs, and in most cases they lost. Immigrants even claimed jobs that black workers once dominated, such as barbering and service work in hotels, restaurants, and transportation, much as Hispanic and Southeast Asian workers have assumed these positions in service employment in the twenty-first century.

Black women in particular had few options in the Northern urban labor force outside of domestic service, although they earned higher wages than they had for similar work in Southern cities. The retail and clerical jobs that attracted young working-class white women remained closed to black women. Employers rejected them for any job involving direct contact with the public. As one historian concluded, advertisers and corporate executives

An African-American religious meeting, New York City, early 1900s. Black migrants from the South found vibrant communities in Northern cities typically centered around black churches and their activities. Like immigrants from Asia and Europe, who sought to transplant the culture of their homelands within the urban United States, black migrants reestablished Southern religious and communal traditions in their new homes.

demanded "a pleasing physical appearance (or voice)—one that conformed to a native-born white American standard of female beauty [and served] as an important consideration in hiring office receptionists, secretaries, department store clerks, and telephone operators."

The lack of options black migrants confronted in the search for employment matched similar frustrations in their quest for a place to live. Even more than foreign immigrants, they were restricted to segregated urban ghettos. Small black ghettos existed in antebellum Northern cities. In 1860, four out of every five black residents of Detroit lived in a clearly defined district, for example. After the Civil War, black ghettos emerged in Southern and border cities. In Washington, D.C., black residents comprised nearly 80 percent of the population in a twenty-block area in the southwest quadrant of the city. In the 1890s, black people dominated an area east of downtown Atlanta known as Sweet Auburn, named after the avenue that cut through the neighborhood. As black migration to Northern cities accelerated after 1900, the pattern of residential isolation became more pronounced. The black districts in Northern cities were more diverse than those in Southern cities. Migration brought rural Southerners, urban Southerners, and West Indians together with the black Northerners already living there. People of all social classes lived in these districts.

The difficulties that black families faced to make ends meet paralleled in some ways those of immigrant working-class families. Restricted job options, however, limited the income of black families, even with black married women five times more likely to work than married white women. In black families, moreover, working teenage children were less likely than immigrant children to stay home and, therefore supplement the family income.

In the North as in the South, African Americans sought to counter the hostility of the larger society by building their own community institutions. An emerging middle-class leadership—including Robert Abbott, publisher of the *Chicago Defender*—sought to develop black businesses. Despite these efforts, chronic lack of capital kept black businesses mostly small and confined to the ghetto. Immigrant groups often pooled extended family capital resources or tapped ethnic banks. With few such resources at their disposal, black businesses failed at a high rate. Most black people worked outside the ghetto for white employers. Economic marginalization often attracted unsavory businesses—dance halls, brothels, and bars—to black neighborhoods. One recently arrived migrant from the South complained that in his Cleveland neighborhood, his family was surrounded by loafers, "gamblers [and] pocket pickers; I can not raise my children here like they should be. This is one of the worst places in principle you ever looked on in your life."

Other black institutions proved more lasting than black businesses. In Chicago in 1891, black physician Daniel Hale Williams established Provident Hospital, the nation's first inter-racially staffed hospital, with the financial help of wealthy white Chicagoans. Although it failed as an interracial experiment, the hospital thrived, providing an important training ground for black physicians and nurses.

The organization of black branches of the Young Men's and Young Women's Christian Association provided living accommodations, social facilities, and employment information for black young people. Many black migrants to Northern cities—perhaps a majority—were single, and the "Y" provided them guidance and a "home."

NEW CITIES

Despite the hardships associated with urban life, the American city continued to act, in the words of the contemporary novelist Theodore Dreiser, as a "giant magnet." No wonder; what an exciting place the city of 1900 proved to be; an electric environment filled with possibilities, inventions, innovations, and people of vast diversity. Few forgot their first entrance into one of these great turn-of-the-century cities and how, try as they might, they could not take it all in at once. When John Dewey first saw Chicago, the city exploding from the flatlands along Lake Michigan in 1894, he wrote excitedly to his wife in Michigan, "Chicago is the place to make you appreciate at every turn the absolute opportunity which chaos affords. . . . Every conceivable thing solicits you; the town seems filled with problems holding out their hands & asking somebody to please solve them—or else dump them in the Lake. I had no conception that things could be so much more phenomenal & objective than they are in a country village, & simply stick themselves at you, instead of leaving you to think about them. . . . [Y]ou can't really get rid of feeling here that there is a 'method' & if you could only get hold of it things could be so tremendously straightened out. . . . Think of all hell turned loose, & yet not hell any longer, but simply material for a new creation."

And creation occurred every few minutes it seemed. An urban explosion occurred during the late nineteenth century. In 1850, six cities had a population exceeding 100,000; by 1900, thirty-eight did; only 5 percent of the nation's population lived in cities of more than 100,000 inhabitants in 1850; by 1900, the figure was 19 percent. The nation's population tripled between 1860 and 1920, but the urban population increased ninefold. Of the 1,700 cities listed in the 1900 census, less than 2 percent even existed in 1800.

In Europe, a few principal cities, such as Paris and Berlin, absorbed most of the urban growth during this period. In the United States, by contrast, growth was more evenly distributed among many cities. In 1820, about 18 percent of the urban population of the United States lived in New York, the nation's largest city; by 1890, its share had fallen to

7 percent. Put another way, many U.S. cities experienced the pains of rapid growth and industrialization in the late nineteenth century.

Urban growth highlighted the growing divisions in American society, part of the "chaos" young Dewey noted. The crush of people and the emergence of new technologies expanded the city outward and upward as urban dwellers sorted themselves by social class and ethnic group. While the new infrastructure of water and sewer systems, bridges, and trolley tracks kept steel mills busy, it also fragmented the urban population by allowing settlements well beyond existing urban boundaries. The way people satisfied their needs for food, clothing, and shelter stimulated the industrial economy while distinguishing one class from another. Although urban institutions emerged to counter these divisive trends and apply some method to the madness Dewey discerned, they could not overcome them completely.

Centers and Suburbs

The centers of the country's great cities changed in scale and function in this era. Downtowns expanded up and out as tall buildings arose creating towering urban skylines. Residential neighborhoods were pushed out, leaving the center dominated by corporate headquarters and retail and entertainment districts. As retail and office uses crowded out dwellings from the city center, a new phenomenon emerged: the residential neighborhood. First the horse-drawn railway and, by 1900, the electric trolley, eased commuting for office workers. Some in the growing and increasingly affluent middle class left the crowded, polluted city altogether to live in new residential suburbs. These people did not abandon the city—they still looked to it for its jobs, schools, libraries, and entertainment—but they rejected it as a place to live, leaving it to the growing ranks of working-class immigrants and African Americans. This pattern contrasted with that of Europe, where the middle class remained in the city.

Consider the Russells of Short Hills, New Jersey. Short Hills lay 18 miles by railroad from New York City. William Russell; his wife, Ella Gibson Russell; and their six children moved there from Brooklyn in the late 1880s, seeking a "pleasant, cultured people whose society we could enjoy" and a cure for Russell's rheumatism. Russell owned and managed a small metal brokerage in New York and enjoyed gardening, reading, and socializing with his new neighbors. Ella Russell cared for their six children with the help of a servant and also found time for several clubs and charities.

The design of the Russells's home reflected the principles of Catharine Beecher and Harriet Beecher Stowe outlined in their suburban home bible, *American Woman's Home* (1869), still a standard reference in 1900. The kitchen, according to Beecher and Stowe, should be organized for expedience and hygiene. The home's utilities should be confined to a central core, freeing wall areas for other functions. The new technology of central heating made it unnecessary to divide a house into many small rooms, each with its own fireplace or stove. Taking advantage of this change, Beecher and Stowe recommended that a home's ground floor have fewer but larger rooms, to encourage the family to pursue their individual activities in a common space. Parlors and reception rooms disappeared, along with the rigid spatial segregation of the sexes. Such former standards as the children's wing, the male "smoking room," and the female parlor were not part of the new suburban home.

The once prevailing view that women were too frail for vigorous exercise was changing. Thus, the entire Russell family was to be found enjoying the tennis, swimming, and skating facilities on the grounds of the Short Hills Athletic Club. Because the community bordered on undeveloped woodland traversed by trails, "wheel clubs" appeared in the 1880s to organize families for bicycle outings.

The suburb underscored the growing fragmentation of life in and around American cities in 1900. Residence, consumer habits, and leisure activities reflected growing social and class divisions. Yet, at the same time, the growing materialism of American society promised a common ground for its disparate ethnic, racial, and social groups. Herbert Croly's "Promise of American Life," the fulfillment of economic aspirations, spurred the immigrant, the black migrants, and native-born city residents even if that promise remained elusive for some if not most of the hopefuls.

The New Middle Class

The new, great cities housed an expanded middle class, typified by the Russells, but including a broad range of "white-collar" office workers such as insurance agents, bank tellers, and legal assistants. Salespeople, factory supervisors, managers, civil servants, and technicians also swelled the middle class. Though relatively few followed the Russells out to the suburbs, they found new residential subdivisions within the city limits. These dwellings contrasted sharply with the crowded one- or two-room apartments that confined the working class.

A Consumer Society

The expanding urban middle class transformed America into a consumer society by 1900. In earlier times, land had been a symbol of prestige. Now it was things. And the new industries obliged with a dazzling array of goods and technologies to make life easier and allow more time for family and leisure.

By 1910, the new middle class lived in all-electric homes, with indoor plumbing and appliances unavailable twenty years earlier. A typical kitchen might include an electric coffeepot, a hot plate, a chafing dish, and a toaster. These items eased food preparation. The modern city dweller worked by the clock, not by the sun. One of the great wonders of New York after 1909 was the Metropolitan Life Insurance Company's giant clock, visible for blocks atop the tallest tower in the world. Time, as the company's salesmen would tell you, was on their side. The clock was not just a good metaphor for the insurance industry but for the great cities generally. Earnest young men with stopwatches patrolled factory floors, calculating worker movements and production quotas. Commuter railroads and, in a few cities, new subway systems proudly posted schedules, assuring commuters that they would all converge on downtown at the same time. A new phrase, the "rush hour," captured both the pace and the split-second timing required for the new order of things. Workers, blue- and white-collar alike, learned the regimen of time—when to report to work, when to take lunch, when to leave.

Time was money. Eating habits changed: Cold packaged cereals replaced hot meats at breakfast; fast lunches of Campbell's soup—"a meal in itself"—or canned stews weaned Americans from the heavy lunch. Jell-O appeared in the 1890s, touted as America's "most quick and easy" dessert. In Nashville at the same time, Joel Cheek ground and blended coffee beans in his store for customers' convenience. He convinced the city's Maxwell House Hotel to serve his new concoction, and in 1907, when President Theodore Roosevelt visited the hotel and drained his cup, he turned to Cheek and declared that the coffee was "good to the very last drop." A slogan and Maxwell House coffee were born.

Advertising played an important role in the consumer society. Advertisers told Americans what they wanted; they created demand and developed loyalty for brand-name products. In early-twentieth-century New York, a six-story-high Heinz electric sign was a sensation, especially the forty-foot-long pickle at its top.

The middle class liked anything that saved time: trolleys, trains, electric razors, vacuum cleaners. The telephone replaced the letter for everyday communication; it was quicker and less formal. By 1900, some 1.4 million phones were in service, and many middle-class homes had one. The new technology introduced new terms that reflected the pace of urban life: "I'll give you a buzz" or "Give me a ring."

The middle class liked its news in an easy-to-read form. Urban tabloids multiplied after 1880, led by Joseph Pulitzer's *New York World* and William Randolph Hearst's *New York Journal.* The newspapers organized the news into topical sections, used bold headlines and graphics to catch the eye, ran human interest stories to capture the imagination, inaugurated sports pages to attract male readers, and offered advice columns for women. And they opened their pages to a wide range of attractive advertising, much of it directed to women, who did about 90 percent of the shopping in American cities by 1900.

Although mainly middle class in orientation, the tabloid press drew urban society together with new features such as the comic strip, which first appeared in the 1890s, and the heart-rending personal sagas drawn from real life. Immigrants, who might have had difficulty reading small-type newspapers, received their initiation into the mainstream of American society through the tabloids.

In a similar manner, the department store, essentially a middle-class retail establishment, became one of the city's most democratic forums and the focus of the urban downtown after 1900. The department store also feminized downtown space in what had previously been a male-dominated domain. At first, most department-store customers were middle-class married women. Not expected to work and with disposable income and flexible schedules, these women had the means and time to wander department store aisles. The stores catered to their tastes—and the current emphasis on home and domesticity—with such items as prefabricated household furnishings, ready-made clothing, toys, and stationery.

Soon the spectacle and merchandise of the department store attracted shoppers from all social strata, not just the middle class. "The principal cause of the stores' success," one shopper explained in 1892, "is the fact that their founders have understood the necessity of offering a new democracy whose needs and habits" are satisfied "in the cheapest possible way," providing "a taste for elegance and comfort unknown to previous generations." Though many less affluent women came merely to "window-shop" (a new expression inspired by the large plate-glass display windows retailers installed in their stores to attract customers), some came to buy. After 1900, department stores increasingly hired young immigrant women to cater to their growing foreign-born clientele.

The department store was the turn-of-the-century shopping mall where young working-class people could "hang out." Mary Antin recalled how she and her teenage friends and sister would spend their Saturday nights in 1898 patrolling "a dazzlingly beautiful palace called a 'department store.' " It was there that Mary and her sister "exchanged our hateful homemade European costumes . . . for real American machine-made garments, and issued forth glorified in each other's eyes."

The Growth of Leisure Activities

By 1900, department stores were adding sporting goods sections, a reflection of the growth of leisure in urban society. And like other aspects of that society, leisure and recreation both separated and cut across social classes. The leisure activities of the wealthy increasingly removed them from the rest of urban society. For them, the good life required such prerequisites as a mansion on Fifth Avenue, carriages and horses for transportation, a pony for the younger children, a saddle horse for the older ones, and a yacht. As such sports as football became important extracurricular activities at Harvard, Yale, and other elite universities, intercollegiate games became popular occasions for the upper class to congregate and, not incidentally, to discuss business. For exercise and recreation, the elite gathered at the athletic clubs and country clubs that emerged as open spaces disappeared in the city. High fees and strict membership criteria kept these clubs exclusive. The first country club in the United States was founded in Brookline, Massachusetts, a Boston suburb, in 1882. Country clubs built golf courses for men and tennis courts primarily for women. The clubs offered a suburban retreat, away from the diverse middle- and working-class populations, where the elite could play in privacy.

Middle-class urban residents could not afford country clubs, but they rode electric trolleys to the end of the line to enjoy suburban parks and bicycle and skating clubs. Reflecting the emphasis on family togetherness in late-nineteenth-century America, both men and women participated in these sports. Bicycling in particular became immensely popular. New bikes cost at least $50, putting them beyond the reach of the working class.

If college football was the rage among the elite, baseball was the leading middle-class spectator sport. Organized baseball originated among the urban elite before the Civil War. The middle class took over the sport after the war. Baseball epitomized the nation's transition from a rural to an urban industrial society. Reflecting rural tradition, it was played on an expanse of green, usually on the outskirts of the city. It was leisurely; unlike other games, it had no time limit. Reflecting industrial society, however, it had clearly defined rules and was organized into leagues. Professional leagues were profit-making enterprises, and, like other enterprises, they frequently merged. Initially, most professional baseball games were played on weekday afternoons, making it hard for working-class spectators to attend. After merging with the American Association (AA) in 1883, the National League adopted some of the AA's innovations to attract more fans, including beer sales, cheap admission, and, despite the objections of Protestant churches, Sunday games.

The tavern, or saloon, was the workingman's club. Typically an all-male preserve, the saloon provided drink, cheap food, and a place for working men to read a newspaper, socialize, and learn about job opportunities. Advances in refrigeration in the 1870s allowed large breweries such as Anheuser-Busch and Pabst to distribute their product nationwide. Alcoholism was a severe problem in cities, especially, though not exclusively among working-class men, fueling the prohibition movement of the late nineteenth century.

Amusement parks, with their mechanical wonders were another hallmark of the industrial city. Declining trolley fares made these parks accessible to the working class around 1900. Unlike taverns, they provided a place for working-class men and women to meet and date.

The most renowned of these parks was Brooklyn's Coney Island. In 1897, George C. Tilyou opened Steeplechase Park on Coney Island. He brought an invention by George Washington Ferris—a giant rotating vertical wheel, equipped with swinging carriages—to the park from Chicago, and the Ferris wheel quickly became a Coney Island signature. Together with such attractions as mechanical horses and 250,000 of Thomas Edison's light bulbs, Steeplechase Park dazzled patrons with its technological wonders. It was quickly followed by Luna Park and Dreamland, and the Coney Island attractions became collectively known as "the poor man's paradise." Immigrant entrepreneurs, seeing a good thing, flocked to Coney Island to set up sideshows, pool halls, taverns, and restaurants. One German immigrant opened a small café serving sausages that he named "frankfurters" after his native Frankfurt. Locals called them "Coney Island hots" or "hot dogs" because they resembled the dachshund, a German-bred dog.

After 1900, the wonders of Coney Island began to lure people from all segments of an increasingly diverse city. Sightseers came from around the world. Notables such as Herman Melville, Mark Twain, and even Sigmund Freud (what did he think of Dreamland?) rubbed shoulders with factory workers, domestics, and department store clerks. In much the same manner, baseball was becoming a national pastime as games attracted a disparate crowd of people with little in common but their devotion to the home team.

Amusement for the masses. Better transportation, more leisure time, and disposable income fueled escapes such as Luna Park in Coney Island, Brooklyn, a place where people could come together and have fun in a relatively controlled environment.

Increasing materialism had revealed great fissures in American urban society by 1900, yet places like department stores, baseball parks, and amusement parks provided democratic spaces for some interaction. Newspapers and schools also offered diverse groups the vicarious opportunity to share similar experiences.

ATTACKING THE AMERICAN INDIAN PROBLEM

As urban residents fitfully came together in new places, one group of Americans moved further apart: the American Indian. Though the themes of displacement and dispossession existed almost from the initial contacts with Europeans, these accelerated in the late nineteenth century to the point where between 1887 and 1900, the amount of land held by Indians declined by more than half (see Map 1-2). The **Dawes Act**, passed in 1887, was primarily responsible for this situation. The Act divided tribal lands among individual Indians. Western settlers who had no interest in the Indians supported the law because it provided that reservation lands not allocated to individual Indians should be sold to white settlers.

The Dawes Act came in the midst of an attempt to modify, if not suppress Native American culture. Confined to reservations, Indians were a captive audience for white reformers who objected to the "pagan" practices of Indians and believed that native cultures inhibited the advance of the race. These reformers were well intentioned; indeed, they believed they were providing a simultaneous service in salvation and assimilation for the Native American. Protestant religious groups persuaded the Bureau of Indian Affairs to

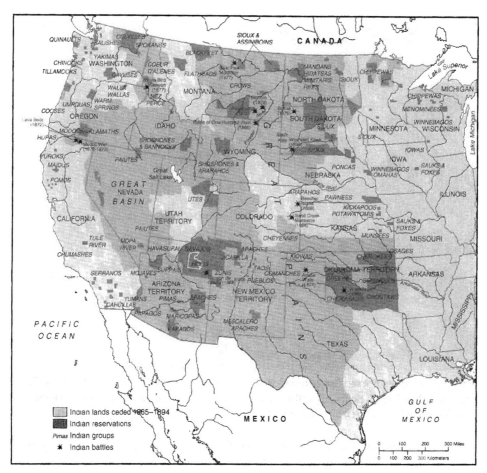

MAP 1-2 Indian Land Cessions, 1860–1894
As white people pushed into the West to exploit its resources, Indians were steadily forced to cede their lands. By 1900 they held only scattered parcels, often in areas considered worthless by white people. Restricted to these reservations, tribes endured official efforts to suppress Indian customs and values.

frame a criminal code prohibiting and penalizing tribal religious practices. Established in 1884, the code remained in effect until 1933. It was first invoked to ban the Sun Dance, the chief expression of Plains Indian religion. To enforce the ban, the government withheld rations and disrupted the religious ceremonies that transmitted traditional values. In 1890, to suppress the Ghost Dance religion, the army used artillery, firing exploding shells, and killed at least two hundred Sioux men, women, and children at Wounded Knee, South Dakota, in what became known as the **Wounded Knee Massacre**.

Missionaries attempted to convert Indians to Christianity but often found them reluctant to accept the creed of their conquerors. As one Crow Indian explained,

> We found there were too many kinds of religion among white men for us to understand, and that scarcely any two white men agreed which was the right one to learn. This bothered us a good deal until we saw that the white man did not take his religion any more seriously than he did his laws, and that he kept both of them just . . . to use when they might do him good in his dealings with strangers. These were not our ways. We kept the laws we made and lived our religion.

The government and religious groups also used education to eliminate Indian values and traditions. They isolated Indian children from tribal influences at off-reservation boarding

Zitkala-Sa's View of Americanization

Zitkala-Sa, or Red Bird, was an eight-year-old Sioux girl when she was taken from her South Dakota reservation in 1884 and placed in a Midwestern missionary school, where she encountered what she called the "iron routine" of the "civilizing machine." Here she recalls her first day at the school.

- What lessons were the missionaries trying to teach Zitkala-Sa by their actions?
- What lessons did Zitkala-Sa learn?

Soon we were being drawn rapidly away by the white man's horses. When I saw the lonely figure of my mother vanish in the distance, a sense of regret settled heavily upon me. . . . I no longer felt free to be myself, or to voice my own feelings. The tears trickled down my cheeks, and I buried my face in the folds of my blanket. Now the first step, parting me from my mother, was taken, and all my belated tears availed nothing. . . . Trembling with fear and distrust of the palefaces . . . I was as frightened and bewildered as the captured young of a wild creature. . . .

[At the missionary school,] the constant clash of harsh noises, with an undercurrent of many voices murmuring an unknown tongue, made a bedlam within which I was securely tied. And though my spirit tore itself in struggling for its lost freedom, all was useless. . . .

We were placed in a line of girls who were marching into the dining room. . . . A small bell was tapped, and each of the pupils drew a chair from under the table. Supposing this act meant they were to be seated, I pulled out mine and at once slipped into it from one side. But when I turned my head, I saw that I was the only one seated, and all the rest at our table remained standing. Just as I began to rise, looking shyly around to see how chairs were to be used, a second bell was sounded. All were seated at last, and I had to crawl back into my chair again. I heard a man's voice at one end of the hall, and I looked around to see him. But all others hung their heads over their plates. As I glanced at the long chain of tables, I caught the eyes of a paleface woman upon me. Immediately I dropped my eyes, wondering why I was so keenly watched by the strange woman. The

man ceased his mutterings, and then a third bell was tapped. Every one picked up his knife and fork and began eating. I began crying instead, for by this time I was afraid to venture anything more.

But this eating by formula was not the hardest trial in that first day. Late in the morning, my friend Judewin gave me a terrible warning. Judewin knew a few words of English; and she had overheard the paleface woman talk about cutting our long, heavy hair. Our mothers had taught us that only unskilled warriors who were captured had their hair shingled by the enemy. Among our people short hair was worn by mourners, and shingled hair by cowards!

. . . I remember being dragged out, though I resisted by kicking and scratching wildly. In spite of myself, I was carried downstairs and tied fast in a chair. I cried aloud, shaking my head all the while until I felt the cold blades of the scissors against my neck, and heard them gnaw off one of my thick braids. Then I lost my spirit. . . . My long hair was shingled like a coward's. In my anguish I moaned for my mother, but no one came to comfort me. Not a soul reasoned quietly with me, as my own mother used to do; for now I was only one of many little animals driven by a herder. . . .

I blamed the hard-working, well-meaning, ignorant [missionary] woman who was inculcating in our hearts her superstitious ideas. Though I was sullen in all my little troubles, as soon as I felt better I was . . . again actively testing the chains which tightly bound my individuality like a mummy for burial. . . .

Many specimens of civilized peoples visited the Indian school. The city folks with canes and eyeglasses, the countrymen with sunburnt cheeks and clumsy feet, forgot their relative social ranks in an ignorant curiosity. Both sorts of these Christian palefaces were alike astounded at seeing the children of savage warriors so docile and industrious. . . .

In this fashion many [whites] have passed idly through the Indian schools during the last decade, afterward to boast of their charity to the North American Indian. But few there are who have paused to question whether real life or long-lasting death lies beneath this semblance of civilization.

Source: Zitkala-Sa, "The School Days of an Indian Girl" (1900). Reprinted in *American Indian Stories* (Glorieta, NM: Rio Grande Press, 1976).

schools. Troops often seized Indian children for these schools, where they were confined until after adolescence. The schoolchildren were forced to speak English, attend Christian services, and profess white American values. (See "American Views: Zitkala-Sa's View of Americanization.")

Finally, the government and the religious reformers imposed the economic practices and values of white society on Indians. Government agents taught Indian men how to farm and distributed agricultural implements; Indian women were taught household tasks. These tactics reduced the status of Indian women, whose traditional responsibility for agriculture had guaranteed them respect and authority. Nor could men farm successfully on reservation lands that whites had already rejected as unproductive. Kiowa chief Little Mountain suggested that if the president wanted Indians to raise corn, he should send them land fit for corn production. Whites, however, believed that the real obstacle to economic prosperity for the Indians was their rejection of private property. The Indians' communal values, the reformers argued, inhibited the pursuit of personal success that lay at the heart of capitalism. As one Bureau of Indian Affairs official declared, Indians must be taught to be more "mercenary and ambitious to obtain riches."

Assimilation itself failed because most Indians clung to their own values and rejected as selfish, dishonorable, and obsessively materialistic those favored by whites. As Big Bear, a chief of the Otoe-Missouria, defiantly declared, "You cannot make white men of us. That is one thing you can't do." But if it was not yet clear what place Native Americans would have in America, it was at least clear by 1900 that they would no longer stand in the way of Western development.

AN EMERGING WORLD POWER

The nation's Indian policy evolved in the context of the United States' emergence as a world power by 1900, and some of the same religious, racial, and policy assumptions that informed government attitudes toward Native Americans guided the conduct of foreign affairs. These perspectives were paramount in the debate concerning entrance into the Spanish-American War in 1898 and its aftermath. They also played a role in subsequent foreign adventures, particularly in Latin America and involvement in World War I. Americans typically went into battle with sincere beliefs in the universal benefits of democracy and the Protestant faith, but often with incomplete or inaccurate understanding of the peoples we sought to liberate and convert. The crusading spirit brought to these enterprises was also evident in the nation's involvement in World War I and in the detachment or indifference with which Western European allies held those ideals. Americans still struggle with the notion of bringing these perfect beliefs to an imperfect world.

Still, the United States in 1900 was not necessarily an example of good intentions and bad results. There was much to commend the American experiment, even as citizens needed to travel further to attain the lofty ideals of its founding. The cities, where the promise of American life could be seen under the bright electric lights, even if immigrants and especially African Americans struggled to fulfill that promise, now held the nation's future, both in terms of the people who resided there and the aspirations they coveted. Despite the discomfort of many native-born Americans with the new order, the chaotic cities, the strange tongues, religious customs, and beliefs, they were typically not willing to allow prejudice to trump their pride in the nation's basic ideals of self-government and fair play. Though worker–management relations remained tense, in the new century safeguards increasingly emerged to protect the interests of working men and women. Though African Americans struggled against a regime of white supremacy in the South and racial prejudice undergirded by science in the North, they built communities and would eventually use the institutions and ideals of American society to secure meaningful and equal participation in the nation's life. Though nativist sentiment persisted and would flare during times of war, the sons and daughters of the early twentieth-century immigrants would eventually become full partners and fellow travelers in the American journey. This is not to say that some did not fall by the wayside, or that nativist sentiment and good-intentioned reforms to "assimilate" them did not burn or embarrass. But overall, their story is mainly a positive one, and one that portends well for the twenty-first century with the arrival of another wave of immigration that will undoubtedly change America as much as the earlier group transformed a small-town, overwhelmingly white and Protestant country into an urbanized, religiously and ethnically diverse nation.

Review Questions

1. Why were state governments more responsive to the impact of industrialization on American workers than the federal government?

2. How did Old World conditions influence Mary Antin's adjustment to American life? Would individuals from other immigrant groups express similar sentiments, or is Mary's reaction specific to her Jewish background?

3. The growing fragmentation of urban life reflected deep divisions in modern urban industrial society. At the same time, there were forces that tended to overcome these divisions. What were these forces, and were they sufficient to bridge the divisions?

4. Why did white Southerners find it necessary to severely restrict African-American voting rights and civil rights beginning in the 1890s?

5. What factors were most influential in the subjugation of American Indians?

6. What factors shaped American foreign policy in the late nineteenth century? How were they interrelated?

Key Terms

Dawes Act   *25*

Disfranchisement   *14*

Grandfather clauses   *16*

Great Migration   *18*

Interstate Commerce Commission (ICC)   *7*

Laissez-faire   *7*

Lynchings   *13*

Nativism   *11*

Poll taxes   *15*

Plessy v. *Ferguson*   *15*

Segregation   *14*

Sharecropping   *18*

Wounded Knee Massacre   *26*

Recommended Reading

Blumin, Stuart M. *The Emergence of the Middle Class: Social Experience in the American City, 1760–1900* (1989). Analyzes the key factors in the emergence of the urban middle class, especially in the late nineteenth century, and the impact of that class on urban society and culture.

Campbell, Charles S. *The Transformation of American Foreign Relations, 1865–1900* (1976). A comprehensive and cautious survey that provides many insights in U.S. foreign policy.

Daniels, Roger. *Coming to America: A History of Immigration and Ethnicity in American Life* (1990). The book's great virtue is its coverage of all immigrant groups; the discussion of Asian immigrants is especially good.

Hahn, Steven. *A Nation Under Our Feet: Black Political Struggles in the Rural South from Slavery to the Great Migration* (2003). A compelling account of how rural African-Americans became actively involved in Southern politics and how that participation transformed their identity.

Rabinowitz, Howard N. *Race Relations in the Urban South, 1865–1890* (1978). A fine survey of how African Americans built communities in the urban South despite the worsening racial situation after Reconstruction.

Williamson, Joel. *The Crucible of Race: Black–White Relations in the American South since Emancipation* (1984). An innovative work that details the racial attitudes of white Southerners and reveals how elites particularly used race to further political and social objectives.

Toward a Progressive Society

The Ferment of Reform

Reforming Industrial Society

Moral Crusades and Social Control

Conclusion

It was also my experience at Hull House that aroused my interest in industrial diseases. Living in a working-class quarter, coming in contact with laborers and their wives, I could not fail to hear tales of the dangers that workingmen faced, of cases of carbon monoxide gassing in the great steel mills, of painters disabled by lead palsy, of pneumonia and rheumatism among the men in the stockyards. Illinois then had no legislation providing compensation for accident or disease caused by occupation. (There is something strange in speaking of "accident and sickness compensation." What could "compensate" anyone for an amputated leg or a paralyzed arm, or even an attack of lead colic, to say nothing of the loss of a husband or son.) There was a striking occurrence about this time in Chicago which brought vividly before me the unprotected, helpless state of workingmen who were held responsible for their own safety.

A group of men were sent out in a tug to one of Chicago's pumping stations in Lake Michigan and left there while the tug returned to shore. A fire broke out on the tiny island and could not be controlled, the men had the choice between burning to death and drowning, and before rescue could arrive most of them were drowned. The contracting company, which employed them, generously paid the funeral expenses, and nobody expected them to do more. Widows and orphans must turn to the County Agent or private charity—that was the accepted way, back in the dark ages of the early twentieth century. William Hard, then a young college graduate living at Northwestern Settlement, wrote of this incident with a fiery pen, contrasting the treatment of the wives and children of these men whose death was caused by negligence with the treatment they would have received in Germany. His article . . . sent me to the Crerar Library to read everything I could on the dangers to industrial workers, and what could be done to protect them. But it was all German, or British, Austrian, Dutch, Swiss, even Italian or Spanish—everything but American. In those countries industrial medicine was a recognized branch of the medical sciences; in my own country it did not exist. When I talked to my medical friends about the strange silence on this subject in American medical magazines and textbooks, I gained the impression that here was a subject tainted with Socialism or with feminine sentimentality for the poor. . . .

Everyone with whom I talked assured me that the foreign writings could not apply to American conditions, for our workmen were so much better paid, their standard of living was so much higher, and the factories they worked in so much finer in every way than the European, that they did not suffer from the evils to which the poor foreigner was subject. That sort of talk always left me skeptical. It was impossible for me to believe that conditions in Europe could be worse than they were in the Polish section of Chicago, and in many Italian and Irish tenements, or that any workshops could be worse than some I had seen in our foreign quarters. And presently I had factual confirmation of my disbelief in the happy lot of the American worker. . . .

Professor Charles Henderson was teaching sociology in the University of Chicago. He had been much in Germany and had made a study of German sickness insurance for the working class. . . . Governor Deneen was then in office and Henderson persuaded him to appoint an Occupational Disease Commission, the first time a state had ever undertaken such a survey. . . . I was asked to do what I could as managing director of the survey, with the help of twenty young assistants, doctors, medical students, and social workers. . . .

It seemed far from a simple task. We could not even discover what were the poisonous occupations in Illinois. The Factory Inspector's office was blissfully ignorant, yet that was the only governmental body concerned with working conditions. There was nothing to do but begin with trades we knew were dangerous and hope that, as we studied them, we would discover others less well known. My field was to be lead. . . .

While we were visiting plants, we set our young assistants to reading hospital records, interviewing labor leaders and doctors and apothecaries in working class quarters, for we must unearth actual instances of poisoning if our study was to be of any value. . . .

It was pioneering, exploration of an unknown field. No young doctor nowadays can hope for work as exciting and rewarding. Everything I discovered was new and most of it was really valuable. . . .

Every article I wrote in those days, every speech I made, is full of pleading for the recognition of lead poisoning as a real and serious medical problem. It was easy to present figures demonstrating the contrast between lead work in the United States under conditions of neglect and ignorance, and comparable work in England and Germany, under intelligent control.

—Alice Hamilton

Alice Hamilton, *Exploring the Dangerous Trades: The Autobiography of Alice Hamilton* (Boston: Little, Brown, 1943).

ALICE HAMILTON'S recollection of her work to improve American industrial conditions in the early twentieth century illustrates important features of the **Progressive Era**, when many Americans attempted to reform the often harsh social and economic conditions fostered by rapid industrialization and urbanization. Women—often well educated like Hamilton, who was trained in pathology and bacteriology—were particularly instrumental in these efforts, which went far beyond simply reflecting any "feminine sentimentality for the poor."

European ideas and programs, as Hamilton found in industrial health, provided inspiration and precedents for American actions. Universities and their scholars, like Professor

Henderson, contributed mightily in addressing previously ignored problems, and governments like that of Illinois expanded their social responsibilities and undertook new initiatives. Some "progressives" like William Hard used their "fiery" pens to expose social problems requiring attention, others developed the careful tactics Hamilton followed in investigating, researching, and documenting problems and then working directly with governments to ameliorate them. Still others drew from their religious beliefs and moral indignation the burning desire to correct social injustices. Key agents of change were settlements, like the Northwestern Settlement where William Hard lived, or Hull House where Hamilton lived and established a well-baby clinic, investigated contagious diseases and the cocaine traffic, and launched city-wide movements to improve the health of the poor.

Hamilton's journey to reform and self-realization took her from a comfortable upbringing in Fort Wayne, Indiana into a world of poverty and public service in Chicago and on to professional achievements as a special investigator for the Department of Labor and as the first woman professor at Harvard University. Her report demonstrating that workers were casually exposed to disease and death in the workplace prompted Illinois in 1911 to pass an occupational disease law, requiring employers to provide safety measures and medical exams for endangered workers.

But industrial health was not at the forefront of progressivism and certainly did not define it. Indeed, in a sense, there was no "progressive movement," for progressivism had no unifying organization, central leadership, or consensus on objectives. Instead, it represented the coalescing of different and sometimes even contradictory movements that sought changes in American society. But reformers did share certain convictions. They believed that industrialization and urbanization had produced serious social disorders, from city slums to corporate abuses. They believed that new ideas and methods were required to correct these problems. In particular, they rejected the ideology of individualism in favor of broader concepts of social responsibility, and they sought to achieve social order through organization and efficiency. Finally, most progressives believed that government itself, as the organized agent of public responsibility, should address social and economic problems.

Other Americans dissented from these beliefs and strongly resisted the progressives' plans, including the employer who attacked Alice Hamilton, "this woman," for making "malicious and slanderous" reports when she detailed dangerous working conditions. The interaction among the reformers and the conflict with their opponents made the two decades before World War I a period of remarkable ferment and excitement. The progressives' achievements, and their failures, profoundly shaped America.

KEY TOPICS

The nature of progressivism.

Women and progressivism.

Expanding public responsibility through protective legislation and social insurance.

Regulating social behavior.

Religious influences in progressivism.

THE FERMENT OF REFORM

The diversity of progressivism reflected the diverse impulses of reform. Reformers responded to the tensions of industrialization and urbanization by formulating programs according to their own interests and priorities. Clergy and professors provided new ideas to

··· O V E R V I E W ···

MAJOR PROGRESSIVE ORGANIZATIONS AND GROUPS

GROUP	ACTIVITY
Social Gospel movement	Urged churches and individuals to apply Christian ethics to social and economic problems.
Muckrakers	Exposed business abuses, public corruption, and social evils through investigative journalism.
Settlement House movement	Attempted through social work and public advocacy to improve living and working conditions in urban immigrant communities.
National Consumers' League (1898)	Monitored businesses to insure decent working conditions and safe consumer products.
Women's Trade Union League (1903)	United workingwomen and their middle-class "allies" to promote unionization and social reform.
National Child Labor Committee (1904)	Campaigned against child labor.
Country Life movement	Attempted to modernize rural social and economic conditions according to urban-industrial standards.
National American Woman Suffrage Association	Led movement to give women the right to vote.
Municipal reformers	Sought to change the activities and structure of urban government to promote efficiency and control.
Conservationists	Favored efficient management and regulation of natural resources rather than uncontrolled development or preservation.

guide remedial action. Journalists exposed corporate excesses and government corruption and stirred public demand for reform. Business leaders sought to curtail disorder through efficiency and regulation, while industrial workers struggled to improve the horrible conditions in which they worked and lived. Women organized to protect their families and homes from threatening new conditions and even to push beyond their conventional focus on such domestic issues. Not all Americans joined in this reform ferment, and nearly every movement for change encountered fierce opposition. But in raising new issues and proposing new ideas, progressives helped America grapple with the problems of industrial society. (See the Overview table, "Major Progressive Organizations and Groups.")

The Context of Reform: Industrial and Urban Tensions

The origins of progressivism lay in the crises of the new urban-industrial order that emerged in the late nineteenth century. The severe depression and consequent mass suffering of the 1890s, the labor violence and industrial armies, the political challenges of Populism and an obviously ineffective government shattered the complacency many middle-class Americans had felt about their nation and made them aware of social and economic inequities that rural and working-class families had long recognized. Increasing numbers of Americans began to

• CHRONOLOGY •

1889	Jane Addams opens Hull House settlement in Chicago.		American Association for Labor Legislation is founded.
1893	Western Federation of Miners is organized.	1908	*Muller v. Oregon* upholds maximum workday for women.
1893–			
1898	Depression grips the nation.	1910	National Association for the Advancement of Colored People is organized.
1897	National Congress of Mothers is founded.		
1898	National Consumers' League is organized.	1911	Triangle Shirtwaist Fire kills 146 trapped workers.
1899	Illinois enacts first juvenile court law.		Wisconsin enacts first workers' compensation law.
	Anti-Cigarette League of America is established.		Missouri enacts first mothers' pension law.
1901	United States Steel Corporation is formed, the world's largest business at the time.	1912	Children's Bureau is established.
	New York Tenement House Law is enacted.	1914	Harrison Act criminalizes narcotics.
	Socialist Party of America is organized.	1915	National Birth Control League is formed.
1902	*McClure's* initiates muckraking journalism.	1916	Keating-Owen Act prohibits child labor.
1903	Women's Trade Union League is organized.	1917	Congress enacts literacy test for immigrants.
1904	National Child Labor Committee is formed.	1920	Eighteenth Amendment establishes national prohibition.
1905	Industrial Workers of the World is organized.		

question the validity of social Darwinism and the laissez-faire policies that had justified unregulated industrial growth. They began to reconsider the responsibilities of government and, indeed, of themselves for social order and betterment.

By 1900, a returning prosperity had eased the threat of major social violence, but the underlying problems intensified. Big business, which had disrupted traditional economic relationships in the late nineteenth century, suddenly became bigger in a series of mergers between 1897 and 1903, resulting in huge new business combinations. The formation in 1901 of the United States Steel Corporation, the world's largest firm, symbolized this development. Such giant corporations threatened to further squeeze opportunities for small firms and workers, dominate markets, and raise social tensions. They also inspired calls for public control.

Industrial growth affected factory workers most directly. Working conditions were difficult and often dangerous. Most workers still toiled nine to ten hours a day; steelworkers and textile employees usually worked twelve-hour shifts. Wages were minimal; an economist in 1905 calculated that 60 percent of all adult male breadwinners made less than a rock-bottom living wage. Family survival, then, often required women and children to work, often in the lowest-paid, most exploited positions. Southern cotton mills employed children as young as seven; coal mines paid twelve-year-old slate pickers thirty-nine cents for a ten-hour day. Poor ventilation, dangerous fumes, open machinery, and an absence of safety programs threatened not only workers' health but their lives as well. Such conditions were gruesomely illustrated in 1911 when a fire killed 146 workers, most of them young women, trapped inside the factory of the Triangle Shirtwaist Company in New York because management had locked the exits. The fire chief found "skeletons bending over sewing machines." The United States had the highest rate of industrial accidents in the world. Half a million workers were injured and thirty thousand killed at work each year. These terrible conditions cried out for reform.

Moreover, the increasing use of labor-saving machinery combined with growing immigration to assure a surplus of labor, which not only held wages down but raised the prospect of unemployment, intensified workers' sense of insecurity.

Other Americans saw additional social problems in the continuing flood of immigrants who were transforming America's cities. From 1900 to 1917, more than 14 million immigrants entered the United States, and most became urban dwellers. By 1910, immigrants and their children comprised more than 70 percent of the population of New York, Chicago, Buffalo, Milwaukee, and other cities. Most of the arrivals were so-called new immigrants from southern and eastern Europe, rather than the British, Irish, Germans, and Scandinavians who had arrived earlier from western and northern Europe. More than 3 million Italians disembarked; another 2.5 million newcomers came from the diverse nationalities of the Russian empire. Several hundred thousand Japanese also arrived, primarily in California, as did increasing numbers of Mexicans seeking work on the railroads or refuge from revolutionary turmoil at home. Crowding into urban slums, immigrants overwhelmed municipal sanitation, education, and fire protection services. Reacting to the poverty, congestion, and pollution, one Russian described his new life as "all filth and sadness."

Already disturbed by the effects of uncontrolled urbanization, many native-born Americans associated the immigrants with rampant urban crime and disease and with city bosses and government corruption. Ethnic prejudices abounded. Woodrow Wilson, then president of Princeton University, declared in 1902: "The immigrant newcomers of recent years are men of the lowest class from the South of Italy, and men of the meaner sort out of Hungary and Poland, men out of the ranks where there was neither skill nor energy, nor any initiative or quick intelligence." Americans of the Old Stock often considered the predominantly Catholic and Jewish newcomers a threat to social stability and cultural identity and so demanded programs to reform either the urban environment or the immigrants themselves.

Church and Campus

Many groups, drawing from different traditions and inspirations, responded to such economic and social issues. Reform-minded Protestant ministers were especially influential, creating the **Social Gospel Movement**. Appalled by urban chaos and the dismal lives of the poor, the Social Gospelers sought to introduce religious ethics into industrial relations and appealed to churches to meet their social responsibilities. Washington Gladden, a Congregational minister in Columbus, Ohio, was one of the earliest Social Gospelers. Shocked in 1884 by a bloody strike crushed by wealthy members of his own congregation, Gladden began a ministry to working-class neighborhoods that most churches ignored. He endorsed unions and workers' rights and proposed replacing a cruelly competitive wage system with profit sharing.

A more profound exponent of the Social Gospel was Walter Rauschenbusch, a Baptist minister who had served impoverished immigrants in New York's slums. In his books *Christianity and the Social Crisis* (1907) and *Christianizing the Social Order* (1912), he argued that Christians should work to build the Kingdom of God on earth by supporting social reform to alleviate poverty, slums, and labor exploitation. He attacked low wages for transforming workers "into lean, sallow, hopeless, stupid, and vicious young people, simply to enable some group of stockholders to earn 10 percent." Such ideas were popularized by Charles Sheldon, a Kansas minister whose book *In His Steps* sold 23 million copies and called on Americans to act in their daily lives as they believed Jesus Christ would in the same circumstances.

The Social Gospel was part of an emerging liberal movement in American religion. Scholars associated with this movement discredited the literal accuracy of the Bible and emphasized instead its general moral and ethical lessons. These modernists also abandoned theological dogmatism for a greater tolerance of other faiths and became more interested in social problems. To some extent, liberal Protestantism had its Jewish and Catholic counterparts.

Reform Judaism renounced certain ancient religious practices and favored adapting to American life; liberal Catholics urged their church to modernize its theological and social positions, especially by showing sympathy for labor unions. But most Jewish immigrants followed Old World habits, and liberal Catholicism was checked in 1907 when Pope Pius X condemned modernism for questioning the church's authority and conservatism. Thus the Social Gospel movement flowered among certain Protestant denominations, especially Episcopalians, Congregationalists, and Methodists. It climaxed in 1908 in the formation of the Federal Council of Churches of Christ in America. The Council, representing thirty-three religious groups, adopted a program entitled "The Church and Modern Industry" that endorsed welfare and regulatory legislation to achieve social justice. In pursuit of that program, the Council established a lobby in Washington to shape public policy. By linking reform with religion (as "Applied Christianity" in the words of Washington Gladden), the Social Gospel movement gave to progressivism a powerful moral drive that affected much of American life.

The Social Gospel movement helped to overcome older laissez-faire beliefs that the government should leave social and economic problems alone. It furnished reformers with a moral and ethical justification for government intervention to improve the social order. Scholars in the social sciences also gradually helped turn public attitudes in favor of reform by challenging the laissez-faire views of Social Darwinists and traditional academics. In *Applied Sociology* (1907), Lester Ward applied Darwinist reasoning in support of reform, calling for social progress through rational social planning and government intervention rather than through unrestrained and unpredictable competition. Sociology, Ward declared, should be "at once reformist and scientific." Economists also helped shape a reform Darwinism by rejecting laissez-faire principles in favor of state action to accomplish social evolution. Industrialization, declared economist Richard T. Ely, "has brought to the front a vast number of social problems whose solution is impossible without the united efforts of church, state, and science." In *The Theory of the Leisure Class* (1899) and *The Theory of Business Enterprise* (1904), Thorstein Veblen dismissed the classical belief in the justice of the market, described a disorderly economy that was socially determined, often through "predatory fraud," and insisted that efficiency and order required a more cooperative form of social organization.

Historians and other scholars who analyzed social and political processes also stressed the utility of purposeful action and government intervention in promoting desirable social change. In *The New History* (1912), James Harvey Robinson urged historians no longer to "catlogue mere names of persons and places which have not the least importance for the reader" but instead to "help us understand ourselves and our fellows and the problems and prospects of mankind." For Robinson, historical study could inspire reform, and he pointed out how expanding state powers in Europe had helped ameliorate social problems. Charles A. Beard was still more contemptuous of scholars studying "ancient devils, fog giants, [and] metaphysical dragons," and exhorted professors to use their scholarship to address contemporary social problems. The new social scientists thus not only provided a rationale for reform but, in their own activism in expert public service, a new mechanism for directing social change.

Muckrakers

Journalists also spread reform ideas by developing a new form of investigative reporting known as **muckraking**. Technological innovations that sharply reduced production costs had recently made possible the mass circulation of magazines, and editors competed to attract an expanding urban readership little interested in the staid periodicals of the past. Samuel S. McClure was the first to introduce promotional gimmicks and serialized popular fiction in *McClure's Magazine*; he then sent his reporters to uncover political and corporate corruption. Sensational exposés sold magazines, and soon *Collier's, Cosmopolitan, Everybody's,* and other journals began publishing investigations of business abuses, dangerous working conditions, and the miseries of slum life.

Muckraking articles inundated readers with facts and figures, names and dates, personalizing the impersonal forces reshaping America and making them starkly relevant to ordinary citizens. McClure and many of his writers genuinely hoped to stimulate reform; some publishers had only crudely commercial goals. In either event, muckraking aroused indignant public demands for reform. Lincoln Steffens detailed the corrupt links between "respectable" businessmen and crooked urban politicians in a series of articles called "The Shame of the Cities." Ida Tarbell revealed John D. Rockefeller's sordid construction of the Standard Oil monopoly. Muckraking novels also appeared. *The Octopus* (1901), by Frank Norris, dramatized the Southern Pacific Railroad's stranglehold upon California's farmers, and *The Jungle* (1906), by Upton Sinclair, exposed nauseating conditions in Chicago's meatpacking industry. Surveying the work of such muckrakers in 1906, one newspaper declared, "The public conscience has been awakened and wrong-doers have been stricken with wholesome fear. But henceforth the work of exposing evil must be transformed into a steady-going, constructive effort to prevent it."

The Gospel of Efficiency

Many progressive leaders believed that efficiency and expertise could control or resolve the disorder of industrial society. President Theodore Roosevelt (1901–1909)—who called muckrakers irresponsible radicals—spoke for more moderate reformers by praising "the gospel of efficiency." Like many other progressives, he admired corporations' success in applying management techniques to guide economic growth. Drawing from science and technology as well as from the model of the corporation, many progressives attempted to manage or direct change efficiently. They used scientific methods to collect extensive data and relied on experts for analysis and recommendations. "Scientific management," a revered concept often used interchangeably with "sound business management," seemed the key to eliminating waste and inefficiency in government, society, and industry alike. Rural reformers thought that "scientific agriculture" could bring prosperity to the impoverished Southern countryside; urban reformers believed that improvements in medical science and the professionalization of physicians through uniform state licensing standards could eradicate the cities' wretched public health problems.

Business leaders especially advocated efficiency, order, and organization. Industrialists were drawn to the ideas of Frederick Taylor, a proponent of scientific management, for cutting factory labor costs. Taylor proposed to increase worker efficiency through imposed work routines, speedups, and mechanization. Workers, Taylor insisted, should "do what they are told promptly and without asking questions. . . . It is absolutely necessary for every man in our organization to become one of a train of gear wheels." By assigning workers simple and repetitive tasks on machines, Taylorization made their skills expendable and enabled managers to control the production, pace of work, and hiring and firing of personnel. Stripped of their influence and poorly paid, factory workers shared little of the wealth generated by industrial expansion and scientific management. When labor complained of the adverse effects of the efficiency campaign, one business leader declared that unions failed "to appreciate the progressivism of the age."

Sophisticated managers of big business combinations saw some forms of government intervention as another way to promote order and efficiency. In particular, they favored regulations that could bring about safer and more stable conditions in society and the economy. Government regulations, they reasoned, could reassure potential consumers, open markets, mandate working conditions that smaller competitors could not provide, or impose systematic procedures that competitive pressures would otherwise undercut.

Labor Demands Its Rights

Industrial workers with different objectives also hastened the ferment of reform. Workers resisted the new rules of efficiency experts and called for improved wages and working conditions and reduced work hours. They and their middle-class sympathizers sought to achieve some of these goals through state intervention, demanding laws to compensate workers injured on the job, curb child labor, and regulate the employment of women. Sometimes they succeeded. After the Triangle Shirtwaist fire, for example, urban politicians with working-class constituencies created the New York State Factory Commission and enacted dozens of laws dealing with fire hazards, machine safety, and wages and hours for women.

Workers also organized unions to improve their lot. The American Federation of Labor (AFL), founded in 1886, grew rapidly during the Progressive Era, claiming four million members by 1920. Under the leadership of Samuel Gompers, the AFL concentrated on craft unionism, stressed practical "bread and butter" issues of higher wages and shorter hours, and fought for the basic rights to organize, bargain collectively, and strike. While aggressive in defending members' rights, it recruited mainly skilled workers, particularly native-born white males, and did little for workers in the mass production industries like steel, meatpacking, and textiles.

New unions sprang up to organize the factories and sweatshops where most immigrants and women worked. Despite strong employer resistance, the International Ladies Garment Workers Union (1900) and the Amalgamated Clothing Workers (1914) organized the garment trades, developed programs for social and economic reforms, and led their members— mostly young Jewish and Italian women—in spectacular strikes. The "Uprising of the

Labor agitation against low wages and poor working conditions sometimes brought support for remedial legislation, other times for state repression. State militia with fixed bayonets confront striking textile workers led by the Industrial Workers of the World in Lawrence, Massachusetts, in 1912.

20,000," a 1909 strike in New York City, included months of massive rallies, determined picketing, and police repression. One observer marveled at the women strikers' devotion to their union and their "emotional endurance, fearlessness, and entire willingness to face danger and suffering." Despite being badly beaten by strike breakers and police and unfairly fined and imprisoned by local courts, the women held out until they secured a 52-hour workweek and improved working conditions.

A still more radical union tried to organize miners, lumberjacks, and Mexican and Japanese farm workers in the West, black dockworkers in the South, and immigrant factory hands in New England. Founded in Chicago in 1905, the Industrial Workers of the World (IWW), whose members were known as **Wobblies**, rejected both the program and the tactics of the AFL, which they called the American Separation of Labor. Their objective was the abolition of the wage system and capitalism itself, to be achieved through industrial unionism, uniting all workers into One Big Union crossing all craft lines, and eventually a general strike. Their often flamboyant leaders included William "Big Bill" Haywood, whose "gigantic frame and one eye gave him the appearance of a sinister Cyclops," wrote Elizabeth Gurley Flynn, "but his face lit up with kindness in talks to workers." A fiery young orator, Flynn herself was another leading Wobbly, whom Haywood described as "the greatest woman agitator that the cause of those who toil with their hands has produced in a generation." The Wobblies used sit-down strikes, sit-ins, and mass rallies, tactics adopted by other industrial unions in the 1930s and the civil rights movement in the 1960s.

"Respectable people" considered the Wobblies violent revolutionaries. "Hanging is none too good for them," fumed a San Diego newspaper in 1912. "They are the waste material of creation and should be drained off into the sewer of oblivion." But most of the violence was committed against them, as private employers and public officials used every method, legal and illegal, in their efforts to destroy the IWW. When Wobblies struck against the silk mills in Paterson, New Jersey, for example, they were arrested, beaten, and imprisoned in such forceful repression that one journalist reported: "There's war in Paterson! But it's a curious kind of war. All the violence is the work of one side—the Mill Owners."

It was harder to suppress the issues raised by such strikes. "The struggle at Paterson is but one phase of the industrial problem that is characteristic of our times," declared the *Outlook*. Low wages, poor working conditions, corporate arrogance, and official inequities created dangerous social disruptions that had to be resolved. Labor unrest thus stimulated the reform impulse.

Extending the Woman's Sphere

Women reformers and their organizations played a key role in progressivism. Women responded not merely to the human suffering caused by industrialization and urbanization but also to related changes in their own status and role. By the early twentieth century, more women than ever before were working outside the home—in the factories, mills, and sweatshops of the industrial economy and as clerks in stores and offices. In 1910, more than a fourth of all workers were women, increasing numbers of them married. Their importance in the work force and participation in unions and strikes challenged assumptions that woman's "natural" role was to be a submissive housewife. Shrinking family size, labor-saving household equipment, and changing social expectations enabled middle-class women to find more time and opportunities to pursue activities outside the home. Better educated than previous generations, they also acquired interests, information, skills, and confidence relevant to a larger public setting.

The women's clubs that had begun multiplying in the late nineteenth century became seedbeds of progressive ideas in the early twentieth century. Often founded for cultural

Women's activism was critically important in reconstructing American life during the Progressive Era. Busily engaged in social housekeeping, Mother America uses corrective legislation to clean the dirty laundry of industrialization and injustice.

purposes, women's clubs soon adopted programs for social reform and gave their members a route to public influence. In 1914, an officer of the General Federation of Women's Clubs proudly declared that every cause for social reform had "received a helpful hand from the club-women." Generally, however, the clubs focused on public issues affecting women, home, and family, demanding protective laws, child labor laws, and consumer legislation.

Women also joined or created other organizations that pushed beyond the limits of traditional domesticity. "Woman's place is in the home," observed one progressive, but "no longer is the home encompassed by four walls." By threatening healthy and happy homes, urban problems required women to become "social housekeepers" in the community at large. The National Congress of Mothers, organized in 1897, worried about crime and disease and championed kindergartens, foster-home programs, juvenile courts, and compulsory school attendance.

Still more aggressive were the National Consumers' League, formed in 1898, and the Women's Trade Union League (WTUL; 1903), both of which organized women across class lines to promote social change. The National Consumers' League was led by the remarkable Florence Kelley, a socialist, lawyer, settlement worker, and industrial reformer who was unmatched, in the estimation of one colleague, in combining "knowledge of facts, wit, satire, burning indignation, prophetic denunciation—all poured out at white heat in a voice varying from flute-like tones to deep organ tones." The NCL tried to protect both women wage-earners and middle-class housewives by monitoring stores and factories to ensure decent working conditions and safe products. The WTUL, with branches in a number of cities, united working women and their self-styled middle-class "allies" both to unionize women workers and eliminate sweatshop conditions and to expand support for women's rights. Its greatest success came in the 1909 garment workers' strike when the "allies"—dubbed by one worker the "mink brigade"—assisted strikers with relief funds, bail money, food supplies, and a public relations campaign. This cooperation, declared one WTUL official, demonstrated the "sisterhood of women."

Although most progressive women stressed women's special duties and responsibilities as social housekeepers, others began to demand women's equal rights. In 1914, for example, critics of New York's policy of dismissing women teachers who married formed a group called the Feminist Alliance and demanded "the removal of all social, political, economic and other discriminations which are based upon sex, and the award of all rights and duties in all fields on the basis of individual capacity alone." With these new organizations and ideas, women gave important impetus and direction to the reform sentiments of the early twentieth century.

Trans-Atlantic Influences

A major source of America's progressive impulse lay outside its borders. European nations were already grappling with many of the same problems stemming from industrialization and urbanization, and they provided guidance, examples, and possible solutions. As one American observer said in 1915: What "the men and women who call themselves progressive . . . propose to do is to bring the United States abreast of Germany and other European countries in the matter of remedial legislation." Progressive reformers soon learned that the particular political, economic, and social structures of America required modifying, adapting, or even abandoning these imported ideas, but their influence was obvious.

University study in Europe taught Americans the limits of their traditional laissez-faire attitudes and the possibilities of state action. Trained in Germany, the economist Richard T. Ely returned to academic positions in America teaching that government "is the agency through which we must work." International influences were particularly strong in the Social Gospel movement, symbolized by William T. Stead, a British social evangelist whose idea of a "Civic Church" (a partnership of churches and reformers) captured great attention in the United States. Stead himself went to Chicago to promote "a broad and clear social programme," and his book, *If Christ Came to Chicago*, helped inspire Sheldon's *In His Steps*.

Muckrakers not only exposed American problems but looked for foreign solutions. *McClure's* sent Ray Stannard Baker to Europe in 1900 "to see why Germany is making such progress"; *Everybody's* sent Charles E. Russell around the world in 1905 to describe the social advances in Europe and New Zealand, which he called "this practical Utopia of the South Seas"; a third muckraking magazine reported extensively on what it termed "foreign experiment stations abroad."

Institutional connections also linked progressives with European reformers. The American Association for Labor Legislation, for example, was founded in 1905 as an offshoot of the International Association for Labor Legislation, founded in 1900 by French, Belgian, and German social economists. And the transatlantic movement of reform ideas and organizations flowed both ways: The National Consumers' League also began as a European import but eventually inspired affiliates of its own in France, Germany, and Switzerland.

By 1912, American consumer activists, trade unionists, factory inspectors, and feminists participated in regular international conferences on labor legislation, child welfare, social insurance, and housing reform and returned home with new ideas and strategies. State governments organized commissions to analyze European policies and agencies for lessons that might be applicable in the United States.

Socialism

The growing influence of socialist ideas also promoted the spirit of progressivism. Socialists never attracted a large following, but their criticism of the industrial economy gained increasing attention in the early twentieth century. American socialists condemned social and economic inequities, criticized limited government, and demanded public ownership of railroads, utilities, and communications in order to make America truly a democratic society. They also campaigned for tax reforms, better housing, factory inspections, and recreational facilities for all.

Muckrakers like Lincoln Steffens and Upton Sinclair were committed socialists, as were some Social Gospel ministers and labor leaders, but the most prominent socialist was the dynamic and engaging Eugene Debs. An Indiana labor leader who had converted to socialism while in prison for his role in the 1894 Pullman strike, Debs had an evangelical energy and a generous spirit. He decried what he saw as the dehumanization produced by industrial capitalism and hoped for an egalitarian society where everyone would have the opportunity "to develop the best there is in him for his own good as well as the good of society at large." Said one observer: "Debs has ten hopes to your one hope. He has ten loves to your one love. . . . When Debs speaks a harsh word it is wet with tears." Even a critical journalist concluded: "There was more of goodness in him than bubbled up in any other American."

In 1901, Debs helped organize the Socialist Party of America; thereafter he worked tirelessly to attract followers to a vision of socialism deeply rooted in American political and religious traditions. In the next decade, the party won many local elections, especially in Wisconsin and New York, where it drew support from German and Russian immigrants, and in Oklahoma, among poor tenant farmers. Socialism also was promoted by newspapers and magazines, including the *Appeal to Reason* in Girard, Kansas, which had a circulation of 500,000 by 1906. Convinced of the compatibility of socialism with basic American values like individualism, the *Appeal* proclaimed, "Socialism is coming. It's coming like a prairie fire and nothing can stop it."

Most progressives considered socialist ideas too drastic. Nevertheless, socialists contributed importantly to the reform ferment, not only by providing support for reform initiatives but often also by prompting progressives to push for some changes to undercut increasingly attractive radical alternatives.

Opponents of Reform

Not all Americans supported progressive reforms, and many people regarded as progressives on some issues opposed change in other areas. Social Gospeler Rauschenbusch, for instance, opposed expanding women's rights. More typically, opponents of reform held consistently traditional attitudes, like the conservatives who saw in feminism the orthodox bogies of "non-motherhood, free love, easy divorce, economic independence for all women, and other demoralizing and destructive theories."

Social Gospelers themselves faced opposition. Reacting to the rise of religious liberalism, Protestant traditionalists launched a conservative movement emphasizing what they termed fundamental beliefs. Particularly strong among evangelical denominations with rural roots, these **fundamentalists** stressed personal salvation rather than social reform. "To attempt reform in the black depths of the great city," said one, "would be as useless as trying to purify the ocean by pouring into it a few gallons of spring water." Indeed, the urban and industrial crises that inspired Social Gospelers to preach reform drove many evangelical leaders to endorse social and political conservatism. The most famous evangelist, the crude but spellbinding Billy Sunday, scorned all reforms but prohibition and denounced labor unions, women's rights, and business regulation as violating traditional values. Declaring that the Christian mission was only to save individual souls, he condemned the Social Gospel as "godless social service nonsense" and attacked its advocates as "infidels and atheists."

Business interests angered by exposés of corporate abuse and corruption attacked muckrakers. To capture public opinion, business groups like the American Bankers' Association accused muckrakers of promoting socialism. Major corporations like Standard Oil created public relations bureaus to improve their image and to identify business, not its critics, with the public interest. "The voice of the public," one press agent proclaimed, was "spoken through the Chamber of Commerce." Business also attacked muckrakers more directly. Advertising boycotts discouraged magazines from running critical stories, and credit restrictions forced some muckraking journals to suspend publication. By 1910, the heyday of muckraking was over.

Labor unions likewise encountered resistance. For a few years after 1898, leading industrialists followed the program of the National Civic Federation to promote industrial peace through trade agreements with unions, but by 1903 corporations launched an antiunion drive. Led by the National Association of Manufacturers, business groups denounced unions as corrupt and radical, hired thugs to disrupt them, organized strikebreaking agencies, and used blacklists to eliminate union activists. The antiunion campaign peaked in Ludlow, Colorado, in 1914. John D. Rockefeller's Colorado Fuel and Iron Company used armed guards and the state militia to shoot and burn striking workers and their families, eventually killing sixty-six men, women, and children. The courts aided employers by issuing injunctions against strikes and prohibiting unions from using boycotts, one of their most effective weapons. In the 1908 Danbury Hatters case (*Loewe v. Lawlor*), for example, the Supreme Court held that a boycott was a conspiracy in restraint of trade and thereby a violation of the Sherman Antitrust Act of 1890, a law presumably enacted to prevent corporate abuses; instead, individual union members were now liable to damage suits and the loss of their personal property, even home foreclosures.

Progressives campaigning for various forms of government intervention and regulation also met stiff resistance. Many Americans objected to what they considered unwarranted interference in private economic matters. Their political representatives were called the "Old Guard," implying their opposition to political and economic change. Again, the courts often supported these attitudes. In *Lochner v. New York* (1905), the Supreme Court even overturned a maximum-hours law on the grounds that it deprived employers and employees of their "freedom of contract"—incorrectly assuming that employers and individual workers possessed equal bargaining power in the workplace. (A dissenting judge criticized this decision as an unwarranted attempt to use the Constitution to protect laissez-faire, "an economic theory which a large part of the country does not entertain.") Progressives constantly had to struggle with such opponents, and progressive achievements were limited by the persistence and the influence of their adversaries.

REFORMING INDUSTRIAL SOCIETY

With their varied motives and objectives, progressives worked to transform society by improving living conditions, educational opportunities, family life, and social and industrial relations. They sought what they called "social justice," but their plans for social reform sometimes also smacked of social control—coercive efforts to impose uniform standards on a diverse population. Organized women dominated the movement to reform society but they were supported, depending upon the goal, by Social Gospel ministers, social scientists, urban immigrants, labor unions, and even some conservatives eager to regulate personal behavior.

Settlement Houses and Urban Reform

The spearheads for social reform were settlement houses, community centers in urban immigrant neighborhoods. Reformers created four hundred settlement houses, largely modeled after Hull House in Chicago, founded in 1889 by Jane Addams, after she had visited Toynbee Hall in London, the first settlement house. Settlement houses often reflected the ideals of the Social Gospel. "A simple acceptance of Christ's message and methods," wrote Addams, "is what a settlement should stand for." Yet most were secular institutions, avoiding religion to gain the trust of Catholic and Jewish immigrants. Some settlements, however, were openly religious,

The Flanner House, a black settlement house in Indianapolis, provided the black community with many essential services, including health care. In addition to this baby clinic, pictured in 1918, it established a tuberculosis clinic at a time when the city's public hospitals refused to treat black citizens afflicted with the disease.

like the Campbell House in Gary, Indiana, founded by the Methodist Women's Home Missionary Society not merely to aid but to convert and Americanize recent immigrants.

Other settlements were related to universities and drew upon their expanding social activism. Members of the faculty at the University of Chicago, for example, concerned about social unrest in the city, established a settlement house in the stockyards district. Mary McDowell moved from Hull House to become the director of the University of Chicago Settlement. After seven years of work, she concluded that "the Settlement brings to the University the problems of real life—vital problems that need the thinkers as well as the doers to solve them."

Most settlements were led and staffed primarily by middle-class young women, seeking to alleviate poverty and do useful, professional work when most careers were closed to them. Settlement work did not immediately violate prescribed gender roles because it initially focused on the "woman's sphere": family, education, domestic skills, and cultural "uplift." Thus settlement workers organized kindergartens and nurseries; taught classes in English, cooking, and personal hygiene; held musical performances and poetry readings; and sponsored recreation.

Their experiences in the slums, however, soon drew settlement workers into wider activities. However much they tried to help immigrants adapt to their new country's customs, they inevitably soon saw that the root problem for immigrants was widespread poverty that required more than changes in individual behavior. Unlike earlier reformers, they regarded many of the evils of poverty as products of the social environment rather than of moral weakness. Slum dwellers, Addams sadly noted, suffered from "poisonous sewage, contaminated water, infant mortality, adulterated food, smoke-laden air, juvenile crime, and unwholesome crowding." Thus settlement workers campaigned for stricter building codes to improve slums, better urban sanitation systems to enhance public health, public parks to revive the urban environment, and laws to protect women and children.

The problem of sanitation in the industrial city was obvious to all. While sanitary engineers used the gospel of efficiency in describing the problems of waste collection and disposal and proposed technical solutions, settlement workers started in the gutters. "It was not a delectable cause for a woman to embrace," conceded Mary McDowell of her campaign against the open garbage dumps and polluted sewers in the stockyards district, but it was necessary for public health and social progress. Drawing upon recent European innovations in waste disposal and using public pressure, McDowell became known as the "Garbage Lady back of the yards" for her success in improving Chicago's massive environmental problems. Settlement houses in Boston, New York, and other cities provided public health inspectors (Jane Addams herself served as garbage inspector for her ward), educated citizens about sanitation, and lobbied for fly and mosquito extermination and improved street-cleaning practices. McDowell and other settlement workers also organized women's groups to hold city cleanup campaigns, often lasting several weeks. Baltimore city officials attributed a sharp reduction in fires to the success of the Women's Civic League in removing rubbish, and other cleanup campaigns led to more effective sanitation ordinances.

Their crusade for housing reform also demonstrated the impact that social reformers often had on urban life. His work at the University Settlement in New York City convinced Lawrence Veiller that "the improvement of the homes of the people was the starting point for everything." Organizing pressure groups to promote tenement house reform, Veiller relied on settlement workers to help investigate housing conditions, prepare public exhibits depicting rampant disease in congested slums, and agitate for improvements. Based on their findings, Veiller drafted a new housing code limiting the size of tenements and requiring toilet facilities, ventilation, and fire protection. In 1901, the New York Tenement House Law became a model for other cities. To promote uniform building codes throughout the nation, the tireless Veiller founded the National Housing Association in 1910.

The famous photographer Lewis Hine used his camera to document child labor. The eight-year-old girl on the right in this 1911 photograph of women and children working in an Alabama canning factory had been shucking oysters for three years.

Protective Legislation for Women and Children

While settlement workers initially undertook private efforts to improve society, many reformers eventually concluded that only government power could achieve social justice. They demanded that state and federal governments protect the weak or disadvantaged. As Veiller insisted, it was "unquestionably the duty of the state" to enforce justice in the face of "greed on the part of those who desire to secure for themselves an undue profit."

Reformers especially sought to limit or outlaw child labor in order to promote healthy individual and social development. As they learned of children maimed or killed in industrial accidents or too weary from working all day in a factory to attend settlement activities, it was "inevitable," Addams said, "that efforts to secure a child labor law should be our first venture into the field of state legislation." The National Child Labor Committee, organized in 1904, led the campaign to curtail child labor. Reformers documented the problem with extensive investigations and also benefited from the public outrage stirred by socialist John Spargo's muckraking book *The Bitter Cry of the Children* (1906). In 1900, most states had no minimum working age; by 1914, every state but one had such a law. Effective regulation, however, required national action, for many state laws were weak or poorly enforced (see "American Views: Mother Jones and the Meaning of Child Labor in America").

AMERICAN VIEWS

Mother Jones and the Meaning of Child Labor in America

Born in Ireland in 1830, the legendary Mother Jones (Mary Harris Jones) became one of America's greatest social activists, organizing workers, participating in strikes, and protesting social and industrial conditions from the 1870s through the 1920s. Here she recounts one of her efforts to end child labor, one of the most persistent reform goals of the Progressive Era. Using the techniques of exposure and publicity characteristic of the period, and adroitly employing patriotic symbols and references, Jones skillfully raised troubling questions about the concepts of social and economic opportunity that many Americans associated with national development and identity.

How did Mother Jones gain public attention for the issue of child labor?

How did she invoke the treasured American concept of opportunity to gain support for her goal?

What did she argue was the relationship between child labor and the privileged status of other Americans?

How successful was her crusade against child labor?

In the spring of 1903 I went to Kensington, Pennsylvania, where 75,000 textile workers were on strike. Of this number at least 10,000 were little children. The workers were striking for more pay and shorter hours. Every day little children came into Union Headquarters, some with their hands off, some with the thumb missing, some with their fingers off at the knuckle. They were stooped little things, round shouldered and skinny. Many of them were not over ten years of age. . . .

We assembled a number of boys and girls one morning in Independence Park and from there we arranged to parade with banners to the court house where we would hold a meeting.

A great crowd gathered in the public square in front of the city hall. I put the little boys with their fingers off and hands crushed and maimed on a platform. I held up their mutilated hands and showed them to the crowd and made the statement that Philadelphia's mansions were built on the broken bones, the quivering hearts, and drooping heads of these children. That their little lives went out to make wealth for others. That neither state or city officials paid any attention to these wrongs. That they did not care that these children were to be the future citizens of the nation. . . .

(continued)

I called upon the millionaire manufacturers to cease their moral murders, and I cried to the officials in the open windows opposite, "Some day the workers will take possession of your city hall, and when we do, no child will be sacrificed on the altar of profit."

The reporters quoted my statement that Philadelphia mansions were built on the broken bones and quivering hearts of children. The Philadelphia papers and the New York papers got into a squabble with each other over the question. The universities discussed it. Preachers began talking. That was what I wanted. Public attention on the subject of child labor.

The matter quieted down for a while and I concluded the people needed stirring up again. . . . I decided to go with the children to see President Roosevelt to ask him to have Congress pass a law prohibiting the exploitation of childhood. I thought that President Roosevelt might see these mill children and compare them with his own little ones who were spending the summer at the seashore at Oyster Bay. . . .

All along the line of march the farmers drove out to meet us with wagon loads of fruit and vegetables. Their wives brought the children clothes and money. The interurban trainmen would stop their trains and give us free rides. . . .

Everywhere we had meetings, showing up with living children, the horrors of child labor. . . . [In New Jersey] I called on the mayor of Princeton and asked for permission to speak opposite the campus of the University. I said I wanted to speak on higher education. The mayor gave me permission. A great crowd gathered, professors and students and the people; and I told them that the rich robbed these little children of any education of the lowest order that they might send their sons and daughters to places of higher education. . . . And I showed those professors children in our army who could scarcely read or write because they were working ten hours a day in the silk mills of Pennsylvania. . . .

[In New York] I told an immense crowd of the horrors of child labor in the mills around the anthracite region and . . . I showed them Gussie Rangnew, a little girl from whom all the childhood had gone. Her face was like an old woman's. Gussie packed stockings in a factory, eleven hours a day for a few cents a day. . . . "Fifty years ago there was a cry against slavery and men gave up their lives to stop the selling of black children on the block. Today the white child is sold for two dollars a week to the manufacturers."

. . . . We marched down to Oyster Bay but the president refused to see us and he would not answer my letters. But our march had done its work. We had drawn the attention of the nation to the crime of child labor. And while the strike of the textile workers in Kensington was lost and the children driven back to work, not long afterward the Pennsylvania legislature passed a child labor law that sent thousands of children home from the mills, and kept thousands of others from entering the factory until they were fourteen years of age.

Source: The Autobiography of Mother Jones, 3rd (Chicago: Kerr Publishing Co., 1977).

Stiff resistance came from manufacturers who used child labor, conservatives who opposed government action as an intrusion into family life, and some poor parents who needed their children's income. But finally Congress in 1912 established the Children's Bureau to investigate the welfare of children. Julia Lathrop, from Hull House, directed the Bureau, the first government agency headed and staffed almost entirely by women. Lathrop and the Bureau lobbied Congress for several years and in 1916 saw the passage of the Keating-Owen Act, prohibiting the interstate shipment of goods manufactured by children. But the law was weaker than that of many states and did not cover most child workers. Even so, within a year the Supreme Court declared the measure unconstitutional.

Social reformers also lobbied for laws regulating the wages, hours, and working conditions of women and succeeded in having states from New York to Oregon pass maximum-hours legislation. After the Supreme Court upheld such laws in **Muller v. Oregon** (1908), thirty-nine states enacted new or stronger laws on women's maximum hours between 1909 and 1917. Fewer states established minimum wages for women. In 1912, Massachusetts created a commission with the power to recommend such wages, and within a year eight midwestern and western states authorized wage commissions to set binding rates. But 1913 was the peak year for such reform, and thereafter few other states followed these examples.

Protective legislation for women posed a troubling issue for reformers. In California, for example, middle-class clubwomen embraced the prevailing ideology of gender roles and favored protective legislation on grounds of women's presumed weakness. They wanted to preserve "California's potential motherhood." More radical progressives, as in the socialist-led Women's Trade Union League of Los Angeles, supported such legislation to help secure economic independence and equality in the labor market for women, increase the economic strength of the working class, and serve as a precedent for laws improving conditions for all workers.

Progressive Era lawmakers adopted the first viewpoint. They limited protective legislation to measures reflecting the belief that women needed paternalist protection, even by excluding them from certain occupations. Laws establishing a minimum wage for women, moreover, usually set a wage level below what the wage commissions reported as subsistence rates. Protective legislation thus assured women not economic independence but continued dependence upon husbands or fathers. In practice, then, the laws reinforced women's subordinate place in the labor force.

Protective legislation for male workers, as Alice Hamilton found, scarcely existed. Both lawmakers and judges rebuffed demands for the protection of all workers while approving reforms that endorsed inequality. Moreover, not only did industrialists oppose legislation establishing maximum hours and minimum wages for male workers but so did leaders of the American Federation of Labor, whose distrust of the state, often demonstrably under the influence of corporate interests, left them to seek such goals only through union not public action.

Only in particularly dangerous industries like mining and railroading did male workers gain much protection, due primarily to the relentless efforts of labor unions that broke from the conservative stance of the AFL. The Western Federation of Miners, formed in 1893, countered the mining corporations' indifference to safe working conditions by arguing that the extraordinary occupational hazards of underground work—cave-ins, explosions, great heat and fires, poisonous gases, silicosis and other diseases—required protective legislation. The union first denied that an eight-hour day was merely an economic issue by stressing the unquestionable health and safety aspects of long workdays. Union members drafted model legislation, launched petition campaigns, and testified at legislative hearings. In response, Utah in 1896 enacted an eight-hour law for mines and smelters, the nation's first such protection for male workers in the private sector. After the U.S. Supreme Court upheld this law in the landmark case *Holden* v. *Hardy* (1898), seven other Western mining states adopted similar measures, from Montana in 1901 to Colorado in 1913.

The Western Federation of Miners next sought legislation to eliminate occupational hazards, not merely to limit the time workers were exposed to them. By 1912 it had helped enact general safety laws for metal miners in six states, and four states from 1913 to 1917 also passed laws requiring changes in mining technology to prevent silicosis, which disabled and killed more miners than all accidents combined.

A more general movement to prevent occupational diseases made little headway. Between 1908 and 1912 the American Association for Labor Legislation (AALL) established a national commission on industrial hygiene, sponsored conferences on the subject, and drafted model legislation, particularly aimed at lead poisoning. Alice Hamilton's reports demonstrating that American factories had higher disease and death rates than European factories helped persuade seven states to pass occupational disease laws, requiring employers to provide medical exams and safety measures in certain occupations. But these laws were often weak and poorly enforced, and American delegates to an international conference on occupational diseases were embarrassed but not surprised when a Belgian physician declared: "It is well known that there is no industrial hygiene in the United States."

Social Insurance

Progressive reformers, drawing from differing perspectives, also developed legislation moving toward a rudimentary program of social insurance. These measures addressed the emerging problems of security in an industrial economy by proposing predictable and adequate public assistance to those made dependent by accident, illness, old age, unemployment, or death.

Workers' compensation, already widespread in Europe, was the earliest social insurance program in the United States. It was a specific response to the specific issue of industrial accidents, more common in America than elsewhere. Some were spectacular, like coal mining disasters that killed 361 in West Virginia and 239 in Pennsylvania; others regularly killed or incapacitated individual workers in a wide range of industries. Muckrakers drew public attention to the problem in articles like "Our Industrial Juggernaut," but workers and employers were already struggling over the issue. Traditionally, common law had held workers themselves primarily liable for injuries on the job, and the only recourse for the disabled worker or the surviving dependents of a deceased worker was to file a lawsuit seeking damages from the employer for negligence.

Courts typically favored employers, which spurred both workers and social reformers to demand a system providing greater assurance of compensation. At the same time, however, employers complained about the cost of litigation in "those damnable suits brought by the shyster lawyers," the increasing tendency of juries to side with crippled workers or impoverished widows, and the growing cost of liability insurance. Thus while industrialists strongly opposed legislation that would establish standards for wages, hours, and working conditions, many became willing to accept a compensation system that would not only limit their costs but increase worker efficiency and remove an important source of class conflict. The president of the National Association of Manufacturers soon endorsed workers' compensation as eliminating "the most fruitful source of worry, dissatisfaction, and friction to the employers and wage-workers." Politicians also favored workers' compensation laws as a way to dissuade workers' beliefs in a "grinding capitalism" and thereby gain "social peace and harmony."

Because so many groups saw advantages in workers' compensation, many states, beginning with Wisconsin in 1911, enacted such laws. But business goals more than social equity or the needs of injured workers shaped the final details of the legislation. Relieved of bitter litigation and public indignation over the treatment of injured workers, employers gained predictable costs, and their financial obligations (and workers' benefits) were limited by waiting periods, time limits, maximum allowances, and inadequate medical requirements. A 1922 study revealed that in no state did compensation cover more than one-fourth of the actual cost of injuries; workers, rather than employers, still bore the burden of industrial accidents.

A second step toward limited social insurance involved the movement to provide "mothers' pensions" to indigent widows with dependent children. Under nineteenth-century poor laws, local officials often sent such women to the almshouse and their children to orphan asylums. Drawing from idealized images of home and motherhood, the National Congress of Mothers argued that public pensions for widows with children would preserve the family home, enable "deserving" poor women to fulfill their maternal responsibilities, and prevent juvenile delinquency and social disorder. Other progressives favored mothers' aid as simply another means of dealing with a widespread poverty attributable more to social inequities than to personal failures. As one Kansas City reformer insisted, "If the poverty of the mother forces her to neglect her child the poverty should be removed and not the child." And in typical progressive rhetoric, a 1909 Conference on the Care of Dependent Children resolved, "the home should not be broken up for reasons of poverty, but only for considerations of inefficiency and immorality."

With little opposition, mothers' pensions were quickly authorized, beginning with Missouri in 1911 and reaching 39 states by 1919. Such assistance (soon called "aid to dependent children") was an important step in American social welfare, a recognition that public intervention was often necessary in an industrialized society. But as with workers' compensation, despite the inclusive rhetoric, the laws in practice were limited. While they provided grants to widows, most ignored deserted wives or mothers whose husbands were incapacitated and also restricted eligibility by residency, nationality, and property requirements. Most states also limited aid to "deserving" women who maintained a "suitable home," subjective phrases that allowed local administrators to deny or reduce pensions to those of different backgrounds, particularly immigrant or black women. Moreover, insufficient funding meant that even many eligible mothers received little or no assistance. Finally, local administration undercut the principle of public responsibility, as when county officials in southern Illinois simply refused to grant pensions at all. In short, despite their importance, mothers' pensions compromised the principle of social insurance—predictable and adequate income guarantees in response to specified risks—and failed to establish economic assistance apart from behavioral factors as an appropriate goal in itself.

Attempts by various reform groups to expand public social programs by establishing health and unemployment insurance and old-age pensions went nowhere. European nations began adopting compulsory old-age insurance in 1889, but in the United States opponents condemned state old-age pensions as the "counsel of despair," implying the failure of the nation's economic and social institutions. The Massachusetts Commission on Old Age, convened in 1910 to consider the subject, even rejected the idea of old-age pensions as "unAmerican" and subversive of "social progress."

Social justice reformers ridiculed this assumption that working-class Americans, through individual initiative, could themselves save for old age when their wages were so low that even during their working years they were "forever hovering on the brink of destitution, . . . forever underfed, usually badly housed." Indeed, a study of the aged in 1915 found the elderly living in a state of chronic "economic fear." Segments of the labor movement strongly supported attempts to establish old-age pensions, and the proposal drew heavy majorities in several Massachusetts cities in 1915, but only Arizona, strongly influenced by the Western Federation of Miners, enacted a state old-age pension plan to help the elderly poor at home instead of confining them to public poorhouses. Even this law of 1914 was promptly invalidated by the courts.

Plans for health insurance were still less successful, despite the uniform findings by several state investigations that the "facilities for medical care among wage earners are not satisfactory, whether considered from the standpoint of extent, cost, or proportion of persons receiving care in time of sickness." Labor unions cooperated with the AALL in proposing laws for health insurance, but even in New York and California, where success seemed most likely, a powerful alliance of insurance companies, physicians, druggists, and employers blocked their passage. Opponents denounced the very idea as "European paternalism run mad." The AALL complained of their "campaign of misrepresentation, hardly ever equalled in legislative campaigns in this country."

A similar fate met plans for the relief and prevention of unemployment. In the late nineteenth century, agrarian and labor radicals, most notably Populist Jacob Coxey in the 1890s, had unsuccessfully called for government public works programs for the unemployed during times of economic depression. Progressives developed more comprehensive plans by drawing from European precedents and emphasizing the impact of industrialization. Said John Andrews of AALL: "The time is past when the problem of unemployment could be disposed of either by ignoring it, as was the practice until recent years in America, or by attributing it to mere laziness and inefficiency. We are beginning to recognize that unemployment is not so much due to individual causes and to the shiftlessness of 'won't works,' as social and inherent in our present method of industrial organization."

Reasoning that if society were largely responsible for unemployment the government had to assume responsibility for its alleviation, the AALL proposed in 1913 that states rationalize the labor market through public employment exchanges and establish unemployment insurance. By 1915, two dozen states had some form of public employment offices, and numerous state legislatures considered insurance proposals drafted by AALL and labor representatives. But despite some popular support for unemployment insurance—in Massachusetts even the Republican party endorsed it—unrelenting employer opposition blocked any legislation. And AFL President Gompers, committed to union rather than government action, helped scuttle a Congressional proposal in 1916 to study unemployment insurance.

Compared to social insurance programs in western Europe, New Zealand, and Australia, the limited measures adopted in the United States were feeble responses to the social consequences of industrialization. As late as the 1920s, one European expert described the social insurance field in the United States as "practically untouched, irrelevant, and meaningless; a mirage." Business groups and other conservative interests had curbed the movement toward state responsibility for social welfare. Few more advances would come until the New Deal (1930s) and the Great Society (1960s), both heirs of progressivism in their commitment to governmental activism.

Making the State a Parent

The campaigns against child labor and for mothers' pensions were parts of a larger movement to recognize the needs of children and safeguard their interests. Another major objective, involving further expansion of state powers, was the establishment of a juvenile court system. Its advocates were prompted by a complex mix of ideas, hopes, and fears. Convinced that city conditions threatened both the proper physical and moral development of the young and thus social order itself, they believed that the state should exercise guardianship over troubled children and that social workers, sociologists, and psychologists could solve the problem of juvenile delinquency. In the nineteenth century the state had either to prosecute, sentence, and imprison youthful offenders just as it did hardened adult criminals or to simply release them. A separate juvenile court system would operate less rigidly in order to rehabilitate rather than punish or ignore wayward children.

The National Congress of Mothers (the forerunner of the Parent Teacher Association) and other women's groups assumed leadership in this movement. Said the nation's first juvenile court judge, Richard Tuthill of Chicago: "The women's clubs are the parents of all children. They have taught the state how to be a parent. . . . The women got the juvenile law passed." That first law, enacted by Illinois in 1899, established a juvenile court, a detention home, and a school for boys across the street from Hull House, with settlement workers helping to provide probation services. Ten states followed within five years, and by 1920 all but three states had established juvenile courts. The speed of this reform's adoption, said one New York official, "bears witness to its social need and constructive worth."

More a court of inquiry than of prosecution, the juvenile court neither followed formal rules of procedure, testimony, and evidence nor employed prosecutors, lawyers, and juries. Instead, juvenile court judges, often chosen for their empathetic qualities, exercised wide discretion in focusing on the character, lifestyle, and social environment of delinquents and not merely on the charges against them. Probation officers investigated the parents and home environment, provided judges with information to understand the personality and needs of the child, and supervised the delinquent afterwards.

Denver Judge Ben Lindsey became one of the most famous and influential juvenile court judges, rated in a 1914 poll as the eighth greatest American. Lindsey quickly concluded that the economic environment was at the root of delinquency. "The dependent and delinquent children who came into my court," he declared, "were made such by the hopeless economic conditions of their lives." Lindsey thus not only promoted the adoption of juvenile courts, as president of the International Juvenile Court Association, but he campaigned across the country for other reforms such as the eight-hour day—to "give the child's home a parent able to fulfil his parental duties"—and mothers' pensions—to "save the widows from starvation and the children from the streets." He drafted Colorado's child labor and child support laws, publicized the needs of underprivileged children, and raised funds to establish recreational facilities where children could play under the guidance of court officers. Although Denver's police commissioner thought that the "Kids' Judge" had "gone batty" at the prospect of children in jails, Lindsey had wide popular support in trying to improve the social and economic environment to aid children's development.

Still, in common with other juvenile court judges, Lindsey sometimes used his authority to send children to detention homes and reform schools. As one Minnesota judge declared in 1906, the court had to teach the child to behave properly "and if need be, to take him away from an immoral and vicious and criminal environment *even if it takes him away* from his parents, that he may be saved, even though they may be lost." Of course, the courts embodied middle-class conceptions of the "proper" behavior of both children and their parents. Thus probation officers (one of whom described popular dancing as the "ungraceful and unspeakable wrestling of the sexes") acted as the moral arbiters of the homes and lives of working-class and immigrant families, and judges not only sentenced burglars but scolded girls for their slang or makeup or because their dress broke "both hearts and laws." Even the sympathetic Judge Tuthill said the goal was to teach delinquents "the primary duty of obedience to authority" and their families the "lessons of cleanliness and decency." Thus the juvenile court systems sought both to help and reform working-class children and to protect the community from their "vicious habits and demoralizing associates."

Reshaping Public Education

Concerns about child labor and delinquency overlapped with increasing attention devoted to public schools. Beginning in the late nineteenth century, the rapid influx of immigrants, as well as the demands of the new corporate workplace, generated interest in education not only as a means of advancement but also as a tool for assimilation and the training of future workers. Middle-class women actively supported public school reforms. In 1900, for example, women's clubs in North Carolina launched a program to improve school buildings, increase teachers' salaries, and broaden the curriculum. Claiming efficiency and expertise, school administrators also pushed for changes, both to upgrade their own profession and to expand their public influence. And some intellectuals predicted that schools themselves could promote social progress and reform. Philosopher John Dewey sketched his plans for such progressive education in *The School and Society* (1899).

The modern urban public school system emerged between 1880 and 1920. Compulsory school attendance laws, kindergartens, age-graded elementary schools, professional training for teachers, vocational education, parent-teacher associations, and school nurses became standard elements in American education. School reformers believed in both the educational soundness of these measures and their importance for countering slum environments. The kindergarten served as a turn-of-the-century "head-start" program. As Jacob Riis contended, the kindergartner would "rediscover . . . the natural feelings that the tenement had smothered." Others supported the kindergarten as "the earliest opportunity to catch the little Russian, the little Italian, the little German, Pole, Syrian, and the rest and begin to make good American citizens of them." Further socialization came through vocational courses intended to instill discipline in poor students and prepare them to become productive adults.

Public education in the South lagged well behind that of the North. An educational awakening, supported by northern philanthropy and southern reformers, brought improvements after 1900. Per capita expenditures for education doubled, school terms were extended, thousands of new schoolhouses were erected, and high schools—virtually lacking before—spread across the region. But the South frittered away its limited resources on a segregated educational system that shortchanged both races. Black Southerners particularly suffered, for the new programs actually increased the disparity in funding for white and black schools. South Carolina spent twelve times as much per white pupil as per black pupil. Booker T. Washington complained in 1906 that the educational reforms meant "almost nothing so far as the Negro schools are concerned." As a northern critic observed, "To devise a school system which shall save the whites and not the blacks is a task of such delicacy that a few surviving reactionaries are willing to let both perish together."

Racism also underlay important changes in schooling of American Indians. The earlier belief that education would promote equality and facilitate assimilation increasingly gave way to a conviction that Indians were inferior and fit, at best, merely for manual labor. One speaker told the National Education Association in 1901 that those concerned with Indian education "can learn many things from the dealings of our southern friends with the plantation Negro." The plantation system, he maintained, was a "much more successful school for the training of a barbarous race than is the reservation." Such educators now rejected the notion of a common school education for Indian children in favor of manual training which would enable Indians to fill menial jobs and whites to "turn their attention to more intellectual employments." Educators also renounced the practice of integrating Indian children into previously all white classrooms, a policy begun in 1891. The superintendent of the Chilocco, Oklahoma, school believed the new commitment to practical vocational education "solved the Indian problem," but critics noted that limiting Indian children to a rudimentary and segregated education merely doomed them to the margins of American society.

Challenging Gender Restrictions

Most reformers held fairly conservative, moralistic views of sexuality and gender roles, but a small group of influential women sharply challenged conventional attitudes of the social role of women. In critiquing women's subordinate status in society and articulating the case for full female equality, these women began self-consciously to refer to themselves as "feminists." A group of writers, journalists, and labor leaders centered in New York City led in arguing that women's submergence in domesticity had to give way to opportunities for their personal freedom and self-development. The "problem of women's freedom," as lawyer and social reformer Crystal Eastman phrased it, was

> How to arrange the world so that women can be human beings, with a chance to exercise their infinitely varied gifts in infinitely varied ways, instead of being destined by the accident of their sex to one field of activity—housework and childraising. And second, if and when they choose housework and childraising, to have that occupation recognized by the world as work, requiring a definite economic reward and not merely entitling the performer to be dependent on some man.

Charlotte Perkins Gilman proposed an answer in *Women and Economics* (1898) and in her many subsequent writings and speeches. A communally organized society, with cooperative kitchens, nurseries, laundries, and housekeeping run by specialists, would free women from domestic drudgery and enable them to fulfill productive roles in the larger society while being happier wives and better mothers. Economic independence would permit women to "become humanly developed, civilized, and socialized."

Emma Goldman, a Russian immigrant, was more of an activist in seeking women's emancipation. A charismatic speaker (and celebrated anarchist), she delivered lectures attacking marriage as legalized prostitution rather than a partnership of independent equals and advocating birth control as a means to willing and "healthy motherhood and happy child-life." Most Americans opposed the radicalism of Goldman and Gilman, but the two raised important issues and shaped the context for others. "What you ask is so much worse than what we ask," a suffragist even told Gilman, "that they will grant our demands in order to escape yours."

Margaret Sanger, moreover, succeeded where Goldman could not in establishing the modern birth-control movement. Caught up in many of the reform efforts of the era—she was a public health nurse and an IWW organizer—Sanger soon made the struggle for reproductive rights her personal crusade. Her mother had died at forty-nine after eighteen pregnancies, and Sanger saw in New York's immigrant neighborhoods the plight of poor women worn out from repeated pregnancies or injured or dead from self-induced knitting-needle abortions. Despite federal and state laws against distributing or even discussing contraceptives, Sanger began promoting birth control as a way to avert such tragedies. In 1914, Sanger published a magazine, *Woman Rebel,* in which she argued, "A woman's body belongs to herself alone. It does not belong to the United States of America or any other government on the face of the earth." Prohibiting contraceptives meant "enforced motherhood," Sanger declared. "Women cannot be on an equal footing with men until they have full and complete control over their reproductive function."

Sanger's crusade attracted support from many women's and labor groups, but it also infuriated those who regarded birth control as a threat to the family and morality. Indicted for distributing information about contraception, Sanger fled to Europe. Other women took up the cause, forming the National Birth Control League in 1915 to campaign for the repeal of laws restricting access to contraceptive information and devices. They had little immediate success, but their cause would triumph in later generations.

Reforming Country Life

Although most progressives focused on the city, others sought to reform rural life, both to modernize its social and economic conditions and to integrate it more fully into the larger society. They worked to improve rural health and sanitation, to replace inefficient one-room country schools with modern consolidated ones under professional control, and to extend new roads and communication services into the countryside. To further these goals, President Theodore Roosevelt created the Country Life Commission in 1908. The country lifers had a broad program for social and economic change, involving expanded government functions, activist government agencies staffed by experts, and the professionalization of rural social services.

Agricultural scientists, government officials, and many business interests also sought to introduce industrial values into farming by promoting an efficient, scientific, and commercially oriented agriculture. A key innovation was the county agent system: the U. S. Department of Agriculture and business groups placed an agent in each county to teach farmers new techniques and encourage changes in the rural social values that had previously spawned the agrarian radicalism that most progressives decried. Farmers, it was hoped, would acquire new materialist values and learn "economy, order, . . . patriotism, and a score of other wholesome lessons," as one progressive put it in 1910. The Smith-Lever Act (1914) provided federal subsidies for county agents throughout the country. Its purpose, claimed Woodrow Wilson, was to produce "an efficient and contented population" in rural America.

Few rural people, however, welcomed these efforts. As one Illinois county agent said in 1915, "Farmers, as a whole, resent exceedingly those forces which are at work with missionary intent trying to uplift them." In some areas, said another observer, the county agent himself was regarded as "a sort of 'illegitimate child,' fathered by unhallowed business and left on the farmer's doorstep, certainly not wanted by many farmers." Most rural parents rejected school consolidation as meaning the loss of community control of education; complained one reformer, "'the little red schoolhouse' is evidently dearer to many than advanced theories of education." And farmers feared good roads would raise taxes and chiefly benefit urban business interests—"not the farmers," declared one in 1909, "but the automobile maker, banker, capitalist, and political office-seeker." In the end, most farmers believed that their problems stemmed not from rural life, but from industrial society and its nefarious trusts, banks, and middlemen. Rural Americans did not want their lives revolutionized. "The cases where much has been accomplished," lamented one Country Life reformer in 1913, "are the exception rather than the rule."

Even so, rural people were drawn into the larger urban-industrial society during the Progressive Era. Government agencies, agricultural colleges, and railroads and banks steadily tied farmers to urban markets. Telephones and rural free delivery (RFD) of mail, permanently established in 1902, lessened countryside isolation but quickened the spread of city values. Improved roads and the coming of the automobile eliminated many rural villages and linked farm families directly with towns and cities. Consolidated schools improved educational opportunities but in replacing one-room schools undermined rural neighborhoods and carried children out of their communities, eventually encouraging an ever-growing migration to the city.

MORAL CRUSADES AND SOCIAL CONTROL

Moral reform movements constituted an important aspect of progressivism. Although some appear anachronistic, misguided, or unduly coercive today, they generally reflected the progressive hope to protect people in a debilitating social environment. In practice, however, these efforts to shape society tended toward social control. Moreover, these efforts often meshed with the restrictive attitudes that more conservative Americans held on issues of race, religion, immigration, and morality. The result was widespread attempts to restrict certain groups and to control behavior.

Controlling Immigrants

Many Americans wanted to limit immigration for racist reasons. Nativist agitation in California particularly targeted Japanese immigrants. With the state's attorney general denouncing Japanese because of their "race undesirability" and the Asiatic Exclusion League, formed in 1905 and claiming over 100,000 members, demanding action, the California legislature unanimously called for the exclusion of Japanese immigrants. Such pressure prompted the federal government to secure restrictions on Japanese immigration in 1907. Californians, including local progressives, also hoped to curtail the increasing migration of Mexicans. A Stanford University researcher condemned Mexicans as an "undesirable class" compared to "the more progressive races," and in 1916 the Los Angeles County supervisors urged the federal government to deport Mexican immigrants.

Nationally, public debate focused on restricting the flow of new immigrants from southern and eastern Europe. Some labor leaders believed that mass immigration held down wages and impeded unionization; many sociologists thought it created serious social problems; other Americans disliked the newcomers on religious, cultural, or ethnic grounds. *The Menace*, a Missouri newspaper founded in 1911, soon had a million subscribers for its attack on Catholic immigrants, who it predicted would obstruct all progressive reform. Many restrictionists backed their prejudice with a distorted interpretation of Darwinism, labeling the Slavic and Mediterranean peoples "inferior races." Likening southern and eastern European immigrants to "the bubonic plague," one Texas congressman in 1912 called for "a quarantine" against all but "pure Caucasians."

As early as 1894, nativists had organized the Immigration Restriction League, which lobbied for a literacy test for admission, sure that it would "bear most heavily upon the Italians, Russians, Poles, Hungarians, Greeks, and Asiatics, and very lightly or not at all upon English-speaking immigrants or Germans, Scandinavians, and French." Several attempts to enact such a law failed, but after the United States Immigration Commission—established to investigate the impact of immigration on the nation—disparaged the new immigrants and recommended a literacy test in its 1911 report, Congress passed the restrictive measure in 1917.

Other nativists demanded the "Americanization" of immigrants already in the country. Fearing the newcomers as radicals, the Daughters of the American Revolution sought to inculcate loyalty, patriotism, and conservative values. Settlement workers and Social Gospelers promoted a gentler kind of Americanization by helping immigrants adapt to their new life with classes in English and home mission campaigns, but they too attempted to transfer their own values to the newcomers. The most prominent advocate of Americanization was a stereotypical progressive, Frances Kellor. She studied social work at the University of Chicago, worked in New York settlement houses, wrote a muckraking exposé of employment agencies that exploited women, and became director of the New York Bureau of Immigration. In 1915, she helped organize the National Americanization Committee and increasingly emphasized destroying immigrants' old-country ties and imposing an American culture.

Prohibition

Closely linked to progressives' worries about immigrants was their campaign for **prohibition**. The crusade against alcohol had begun in the nineteenth century, especially with the founding of the Woman's Christian Temperance Union in the 1870s. Under the leadership of Frances Willard, the WCTU invoked traditional domestic and religious concerns to campaign for restrictive liquor laws and support women's political activism. By the early twentieth century, not only had the WCTU become the largest organization of women in American history, with a quarter of a million members, but many other Americans had come to share its central objective. Certainly, the prohibition movement engaged many of the progressives' basic impulses. Social workers saw liquor as a cause of crime, poverty, and family violence; employers blamed it for causing industrial accidents and inefficiency; Social Gospel ministers condemned the "spirit born of hell" because it impaired moral judgment and behavior. But also important was native-born Americans' fear of the new immigrants—"the dangerous classes, who are readily dominated by the saloon." Many immigrants, in fact, viewed liquor and the neighborhood saloon as vital parts of daily life, and so prohibition became a focus of nativist hostilities, cultural conflict, and Americanization pressures. In the South, racism also figured prominently. Alexander McKelway, the southern secretary for the National Child Labor Committee, endorsed prohibition as a way to maintain social order and white supremacy. McKelway himself drank, but he helped organize the North Carolina Anti-Saloon League to deny alcohol to African Americans, whom he considered naturally "criminal and degenerate."

Protestant fundamentalists also stoutly supported prohibition, working through the Anti-Saloon League, founded in 1893. Their nativism and antiurban bias surfaced in demands for prohibition to prevent the nation's cities from lapsing into "raging mania, disorder, and anarchy." With most urban Catholics and Jews opposing prohibition—the Central Conference of American Rabbis denounced it as "born of fanaticism"—the Anti-Saloon League justified imposing its reform on city populations against their will: "Our nation can only be saved by turning the pure stream of country sentiment . . . to flush out the cesspools of cities and so save civilization from pollution."

With these varied motivations, prohibitionists campaigned for local and state laws against the manufacture and sale of alcohol. Beginning in 1907, they proved increasingly successful, especially in the South, Midwest, and Far West. Soon, twenty-six states had prohibition laws. But elsewhere prohibition was rejected by both legislatures and popular referenda, and some states, like Ohio in 1914, began to repeal their restrictive laws. So the Anti-Saloon League launched a skillful campaign to persuade Congress to adopt a constitutional amendment establishing national prohibition. In 1917, Congress approved the Eighteenth Amendment, which made prohibition the law of the land by 1920.

Less controversial was the drive to control narcotics, then readily available. Patent medicines commonly contained opium, heroin, and cocaine (popularly used for hay fever), and physicians known as "dope doctors" openly dispensed drugs to paying customers. Inaccurate assumptions that addiction was spreading in "the fallen and lower classes"—and particularly among black people and immigrants—prompted calls for restrictive legislation. In 1914, Congress passed the **Harrison Act**, prohibiting the distribution and use of narcotics for other than medicinal purposes.

The Devil's Toothpicks

Overlapping the campaigns against liquor and drugs was the widespread attempt to restrict or prohibit cigarettes. Again a complex coalition organized to support this goal: progressives interested in social efficiency and public health; evangelical Protestants alarmed by immorality; business leaders concerned with industrial productivity; and educators and physicians worried about mental and physical vitality.

Cigarettes were nearly unknown until James B. Duke mechanized their manufacture in the 1880s. For many years thereafter, cigarette smoking was largely confined to socially marginal groups such as immigrants from southern and eastern Europe (It was only Italians and Russians, said one critic, "who smoke cigarettes and they're no good anyhow"), young working-class men, "disreputable" women, and juvenile delinquents. The WCTU led the early attacks on cigarettes, staging public demonstrations, distributing literature in schools and churches, and lobbying legislatures for restrictive laws. In 1899 WCTU members led by Lucy Page Gaston organized the Anti-Cigarette League of America. The League sent recruiters across the nation, distributed pledge cards to school children, and reached out to church, fraternal, and business groups; by 1901 it had a remarkable 300,000 members. Gaston saw smoking as a sign of moral decay and denounced it as "offering burnt incense to Satan." She gained broader support for her efforts for state regulation of behavior by arguing that "tobacco fiends" were destined to be sick, addicted, criminally inclined, and dependent upon public support. The state had the obligation to intervene to protect both the smoker and society at large. Attributing so many social evils to the act of smoking enabled one moral reformer in North Carolina to predict that prohibiting cigarettes would "usher in the dawn of millennial peace and splendor in one full swoop."

Gaston's moral campaign against "the Devil's toothpicks" was joined by many Protestant organizations, some perhaps motivated by the Catholic practice of regularly hosting "smokers" in their parish halls. National organizations of Baptists, Methodists, and Presbyterians all condemned smoking in 1909, and Protestant service organizations like the Salvation Army and the YMCA endorsed anticigarette legislation as well.

Secular support came from health officials worried about heart disease, emphysema, and other illnesses. The Indiana State Health Commissioner went further and linked both insanity and "race deterioration" to cigarette smoking. Judge Ben Lindsey endorsed the Anti-Cigarette League, convinced from his work with juvenile delinquents that cigarettes led to alcohol, drugs, and crime. Fearing its impact on efficiency and productivity, business leaders like Henry Ford opposed cigarette smoking as "a plain business proposition," and many companies simply prohibited the practice among their employees. The business community, noted the *New York Times*, "didn't say: 'For the sake of your immortal soul, cut out the smoke.' It said: If you smoke, skidoo—no job for you." That approach convinced the *Times* that "the best reformer is not a reformer."

States began enacting restrictive laws, first prohibiting minors from buying cigarettes, then banning altogether the sale, manufacture, possession, or use of cigarettes. (Illinois's 1907 law prohibited only those cigarettes "containing any substance deleterious to health, including tobacco"). Municipalities also adopted ordinances ranging from prohibiting women from smoking in public to outlawing cigarette advertising. In New York, a Non-Smokers' Protective League was founded in 1911 and by 1913 it persuaded the state's Public Service Commission to prohibit smoking on railroads and streetcars.

Despite these successes, however, restrictive laws were rarely enforced and state laws were often repealed within a few years. Moreover, cigarette consumption actually grew steadily. By World War I, the anticigarette campaign would founder completely, one disappointed reformer conceding that "the 'coffin nails' have such a hold upon the American people that it is almost useless to oppose the habit."

Suppressing Prostitution

Reformers also sought to suppress the "social evil" of prostitution. Like crowded slums, sweatshops, and child labor, the "vice districts" where prostitution flourished were seen as part of the exploitation and disorder in the industrial cities. Women's low wages as factory workers and domestic servants explained some of the problem, as pointed out by a *McClure's* muckraking article entitled "The Daughters of the Poor." But nativism spurred public concern, as when New York officials insisted that most prostitutes and brothel owners, some of whom "have been seducers of defenseless women all their lives," were foreign born.

The response to prostitution was typical of progressivism: investigation and exposure, a reliance upon experts—boards of health, medical groups, clergy—for recommendations, and enactment of new laws. The New York City Committee of Fifteen, organized in 1900, investigated prostitution in response to complaints of clergymen and concerns about links among vice districts, urban political machines, and corrupt business interests. Its report dismissed as ineffective the European attempts to regulate prostitution. The progressive solution emerged in state and municipal action abolishing the "red light" districts previously tolerated and in a federal law, the Mann Act of 1910, prohibiting the interstate transport of women "for immoral purposes."

California provided other examples of progressives' interest in social control and moral reform. The state assembly, described by the *San Francisco Chronicle* as "a legislature of progressive cranks," prohibited gambling, cardplaying, and prizefighting. It also enacted the Red-Light Abatement Act and a University Dry Zone Act. Los Angeles—influenced by the aptly named Morals Efficiency League—banned premarital sex and introduced artistic censorship, banning Isadora Duncan's erotic dancing and Eugene O'Neill's play *Desire Under the Elms.* One critic in 1913 complained that the reformers' "frenzy of virtue" made "Puritanism . . . the inflexible doctrine of Los Angeles."

For Whites Only?

Racism permeated the Progressive Era. In the South, progressivism was built on the system of black disfranchisement and segregation established in the 1890s and early 1900s. Like most white Southerners, progressives believed that racial control was necessary for social order and that it enabled reformers to address other social problems. Such reformers also invoked racism to gain popular support for their objectives. In Georgia, for instance, child labor reformers warned that while white children worked in the Piedmont textile mills, black children were going to school: Child labor laws and compulsory school attendance laws were necessary to maintain white supremacy.

Governors Hoke Smith of Georgia and James Vardaman, "the White Chief," of Mississippi typified the link between racism and reform in the South. They supported progressive reforms ranging from child labor and prohibition to railroad regulation and direct primaries, but they also viciously attacked black rights. Their racist demagogy incited antiblack violence throughout the South. Anti-black race riots, like that produced in Atlanta by Smith's election in 1906, and lynching—defended on the floor of the U.S. Senate by a Southern progressive—were part of the system of racial control that made the era a terrible time for African Americans.

Even in the North, race relations deteriorated. Civil rights laws went unenforced, black customers were excluded from restaurants and hotels, and schools were segregated. A reporter in Pennsylvania found "this disposition to discriminate against Negroes has greatly increased within the past decade." Antiblack race riots exploded in New York in 1900 and Springfield, Illinois—Lincoln's hometown—in 1908.

Black Activism

But although most white progressives promoted or accepted racial discrimination and most black Southerners had to adapt to it, black progressive activism was growing. Even in the South, some African Americans struggled to improve conditions. In Atlanta, for example, black women created progressive organizations and established settlement houses, kindergartens, and day care centers. With public parks reserved for white people, the Gate City Day Nursery Association built and supervised a playground on the campus of Atlanta Baptist College. The women of the Neighborhood Union, organized in 1908, even challenged the discriminatory policies of Atlanta's board of education, demanding equal facilities and appropriations for the city's black schools. On a broader scale, in twenty-five cities from Richmond to San Antonio, blacks engaged in massive boycotts against segregated streetcars between 1900 and 1906. They had only limited success, but their efforts demonstrated a persisting commitment to reforming society.

In the North, African Americans more openly criticized discrimination and rejected Booker T. Washington's philosophy of accommodation. Ida Wells-Barnett, a crusading journalist driven from the South by white hostility to her antilynching campaign, settled in Chicago and became nationally prominent for her militant protests. She continued to denounce lynching but also expanded her reform activities, fighting fiercely against racial injustices, especially school segregation, agitating for woman suffrage and juvenile courts, and organizing kindergartens and settlement houses for Chicago's black migrants. A Danish observer in Chicago called her "the Jane Addams among the Negroes."

Still more important was W.E.B. Du Bois, who insisted upon equal opportunities for African Americans and campaigned tirelessly against all forms of racial discrimination. Du Bois had earned a Ph.D. in history from Harvard in 1895 and criticized Washington's philosophy in *The Souls of Black Folk* (1903), an eloquent analysis of the African-American experience. In 1905, he and other black activists met in Niagara Falls, Canada, to make plans to promote political and economic equality. In 1910, this **Niagara Movement** joined with a small group of white reformers, including Jane Addams and John Dewey, to organize the National Association for the Advancement of Colored People. The NAACP sought to overthrow segregation and establish equal justice and educational opportunities. As its director of publicity and research, Du Bois launched the influential magazine *The Crisis* to shape public opinion. "Agitate," he counseled, "protest, reveal the truth, and refuse to be silenced."

While the NAACP pursued legal challenges to city and state laws violating the constitutional rights of African Americans, another organization, the National Urban League, founded in 1911, developed programs to widen economic opportunities and improve social conditions for rural black migrants in northern cities. Each had limited success. The NAACP did persuade the Supreme Court to invalidate a Louisville, Kentucky, residential segregation law, but only by appealing to property rights rather than the principle of equal rights, and it failed repeatedly to secure the passage of a federal anti-lynching law. Even so, by 1918, growing black activism brought the NAACP 44,000 members in 165 branches. Two generations later, it would successfully challenge the racial discrimination that most early-twentieth-century white progressives either supported or tolerated.

CONCLUSION

In the early twentieth century, progressive reformers responded to the tensions of industrial and urban development by moving to change society and the role of the government. Rejecting an earlier emphasis on individualism and laissez-faire, they organized to promote social change and an interventionist state. Programs and laws to protect women, children, and injured workers testified to their compassion; the creation of new private organizations and public agencies indicated their interest in order and efficiency; investigations and reports, as muckrakers, social scientists, probation officers, or country lifers, reflected their optimism that harmful conditions, once exposed, could be corrected; campaigns against "social evils," whether perceived in drunkenness, prostitution, or "inferior" immigrants, illustrated their self-assured vision of the public good.

Women, in particular, played a major part in these efforts to reorganize society. While some defined their goals in terms of women's traditional concerns with family and moral issues, in pursuing those goals they nevertheless expanded their activities into new and important public roles. Others redefined their goals in light of urban industrialism and asserted leadership in broad areas of public policy. Feminism, socialism, a commitment to "social justice" for all, and other ideologies also prompted women's social activism.

Despite their efforts and their optimism, progressive reformers, both men and women, lost as many battles as they won. Social insurance programs were both inequitable and woefully undeveloped. Factory codes and child labor laws were both inadequate and poorly enforced. Actual working conditions for most wage earners in mines, mills, and factories were slow in showing real improvement. Troubling, too, were the progressives' frequent willingness to exclude African Americans from their efforts at social reform and their tendency at times to slide from social justice for all to social control of some Americans.

But the progressives had succeeded in advancing the two powerful ideas of positively addressing rather than passively witnessing social and economic inequities and expanding the scope of public responsibility and government action. And in their contested campaigns for improved housing, sanitation, labor legislation, and other social reforms, they invariably came to recognize the importance of political action. As the settlement worker Lillian Wald concluded, "When I went to New York, and was stirred to participate in community work . . . I believed that politics concerned itself with matters outside [women's] realm and experience. It was an awakening to me to realize that when I was working in the interests of those babies . . . I was really in politics." And just as obviously, political reform would be the next progressive campaign.

Review Questions

1. How did the progressive concern for efficiency affect social reform efforts, public education, government administration, and rural life?

2. Why did social reform and social control often intermingle in the Progressive Era? Can such objectives be separate?

3. What factors, old and new, stimulated the reform movements of progressivism?

4. How did the role of women change during the Progressive Era? How did that affect progressivism itself?

Key Terms

Fundamentalists *43*

Harrison Act *58*

Muckraking *37*

Muller v. *Oregon* *48*

Niagara Movement *61*

Progressive Era *32*

Prohibition *57*

Social Gospel Movement *36*

Wobblies *40*

Recommended Reading

Jane Addams, *Twenty Years at Hull House* (1910). Jane Addams's own classic story of settlement work.

Alan Dawley, *Struggles for Justice: Social Responsibility and the Liberal State* (1991). An important study that emphasizes the role of workers and women in promoting state activism.

William Deverell and Tom Sitton, *California Progressivism Revisited* (1994). A valuable collection of essays that examines the complex motivations underlying progressivism in California.

Steven J. Diner, *A Very Different Age: Americans of the Progressive Era* (1998). An engaging survey of the era, stressing social history.

Arthur S. Link and Richard L. McCormick, *Progressivism* (1983). A superb brief analysis of the complexities and scholarly interpretations of progressivism.

Upton Sinclair, *The Jungle* (1906). The most famous muckraking novel.

Robert Wiebe, *The Search for Order, 1877–1920* (1967). A masterful essay that emphasizes the organizational thrust of middle-class progressives.

PROGRESSIVE POLITICS: 1900–1916

Reforming Politics and Government

Theodore Roosevelt and the Progressive Presidency

Taft and the Tensions of Progressive Politics

Woodrow Wilson and Progressive Reform

Conclusion

Five thousand women, marching in the woman suffrage pageant yesterday, practically fought their way foot by foot up Pennsylvania avenue, through a surging mass of humanity that completely defied the Washington police, swamped the marchers, and broke their procession into little companies. The women, trudging stoutly along under great difficulties, were able to complete their march only when troops of cavalry from Fort Myer were rushed into Washington to take charge of Pennsylvania avenue. No inauguration has ever produced such scenes, which in many instances amounted to little less than riots. . . .

The parade in itself, in spite of the delays, was a great success. . . . As a spectacle the pageant was entrancing. Beautiful women, posing in classic robes, passed in a bewildering array, presenting an irresistible appeal to the artistic, and completely captivating the hundred thousand spectators who struggled for a view along the entire route.

Miss Margaret Foley, bearing aloft a large "Votes for Women" flag, and Mrs. G. Farquhar, carrying an American flag, led the procession. . . . After the float reading, "We Demand an Amendment to the United States Constitution Enfranchising the Women of This Country," came a body of ushers clad in light blue capes. . . . Two large floats . . . represented the countries in which women are working for equal rights, followed by a large body of women on foot dressed in street clothes, who bore the banners and pennants of scores of suffrage associations throughout the world. . . . The Homemakers . . . were dressed in long purple robes over their street clothes. Following them came a float, "In Patriotic Service," . . . and Miss Lillian Wald, the walking leader of a large body of women who followed the float, dressed as trained nurses, with gray caps and coats.

Miss Margaret Gage and Maurice Cohen, wearing college gowns with mortar boards, represented "Education," which was followed by nearly 1,000 women of the college section. . . . A group of young girls in blue capes represented the wage-earners, followed by "A Labor Story," which depicted the crowded condition of tenements, with women and children bending over sewing machines, dirty and disheveled, in squalid quarters. . . . [Then followed] the women in the government section, all wearing light blue capes, . . . the business women, dressed in similar manner, . . . the teachers, . . . the social workers, . . . the white and pink costumed delegation of "writers," . . . club women and women clergy.

The greatest ovation was given to "General" Rosalie Jones, who led her little band of hikers from New York over rough roads and through snow and rain to march for the "cause." . . .

But there were hostile elements in the crowd through which the women marched. . . . Passing through two walls of antagonistic humanity, the marchers for the most part kept their temper. They suffered insult and closed their ears to jibes and jeers. Few faltered, although several of the older women were forced to drop out from time to time.

The pageant moved up Pennsylvania avenue with great difficulty and surrounded with some danger. Crowds surged into the streets, completely overwhelming the police and stopping the pageant's progress. Mounted police charged into the crowds, but failed at times to drive them back, even with the free use of clubs. In more than an hour the pageant had moved only ten blocks.

Miss Inez Milholland, a New York society girl, mounted on her white horse and dressed as a herald, finally rode up beside a mounted policeman, and helped charge the crowd. Miss Milholland gesticulated and shouted at the crowd and rode her horse into it with good effect. . . .

When the surging multitude was driven back in one place it flowed back into the street at another. The pageant slowly moved along, sometimes not more than a dozen feet at a time. . . .

As a result of the unruly spirit of the biggest crowd that ever witnessed a parade on Pennsylvania avenue, or of the inactivity of the police, who seemed powerless to protect the marching suffragists, the Emergency Hospital last night was filled to overflowing. . . . While an automobile and ambulance and horse-drawn vehicle ran back and forth, with all the surgeons in the institution taking turns at riding on it, people who had fainted or been overcome by exhaustion, or crushed and trampled, were brought to the hospital.

Washington Post, March 4, 1913.

THESE JUMBLED news accounts from the *Washington Post* convey the excited reporters' views of the dramatic woman suffrage parade on March 3, 1913. But the women's difficult journey down Pennsylvania Avenue that day, suggestive of the much longer journey to achieve woman suffrage itself, demonstrated important characteristics of political life in the Progressive Era.

Political movements and campaigns challenged traditional institutions, relationships, and attitudes—here involving women's role in American politics—and often met strong, if not usually so violent, resistance. Progressives seeking political reforms organized their supporters across lines of class, education, occupation, geography, gender, and, at times, race and ethnicity—as the variety of groups in the suffrage parade demonstrated. Rather than rely solely on traditional partisan politics, reformers also adopted new political techniques, including lobbying and demonstrating, as nonpartisan pressure groups. Reform work begun at the local and state levels—where the suffrage movement had already met some success—inexorably moved to the national level as the federal government expanded its authority and became the focus of political interest. Finally, this suffrage demonstration revealed the exceptional diversity of the progressive movement, for the women marched, in part, against Woodrow Wilson, who had campaigned for the presidency as a progressive.

• CHRONOLOGY •

1898	South Dakota adopts initiative and referendum.		Pure Food and Drug Act is passed.
1900	Robert La Follette is elected governor of Wisconsin.	1908	William Howard Taft is elected president.
1901	President William McKinley is assassinated; Theodore Roosevelt becomes president.	1910	Ballinger-Pinchot controversy erupts.
	Socialist Party of America is organized.	1912	Progressive Party organizes and nominates Roosevelt.
	Galveston, Texas, initiates the city commission plan.		Woodrow Wilson is elected president.
1902	Antitrust suit is filed against Northern Securities Company.	1913	Sixteenth and Seventeenth Amendments are ratified.
	Mississippi enacts the first direct primary law.		Underwood-Simmons Tariff Act establishes an income tax.
	National Reclamation Act is passed.		Federal Reserve Act creates the Federal Reserve System.
	Roosevelt intervenes in coal strike.	1914	Federal Trade Commission is established.
1904	Roosevelt is elected president.	1916	Keating-Owen Act prohibits child labor.
1906	Hepburn Act strengthens the Interstate Commerce Commission.	1920	Nineteenth Amendment is ratified.
	Meat Inspection Act extends government regulation.		

Suffragists ultimately achieved their goal in the Progressive Era, as did other reformers seeking a variety of political objectives, ranging from restructuring municipal and state government to expanding popular influence within political bodies, both partisan and legislative; from expanding the reach of the federal government to restricting the role of political parties; from gaining office for themselves to denying victories for their opponents. Sometimes, however, those opponents claimed success, and sometimes progressives fought each other—all in a period of remarkable political creativity and conflict.

KEY TOPICS

Woman Suffrage and Electoral Reform.

Changes in Municipal and State Government.

The great woman suffrage parade leaves Capitol Hill and heads for the White House, March 3, 1913. Dramatic tactics and careful organizing like those that marked this parade helped secure reform in the Progressive Era.

New Political Leaders/New Political Styles.

Strengthening the Executive under Theodore Roosevelt.

Expanding Government's Regulatory Role.

Climax of Progressivism under Wilson.

REFORMING POLITICS AND GOVERNMENT

Progressives of all kinds clamored for the reform of politics and government, but as in the case of their desire to reform society, their political activism was motivated by different concerns and they sometimes pursued competing objectives. Many wanted to change procedures and institutions to promote greater democracy and responsibility. Others hoped to improve the efficiency of government, to eliminate corruption, or to increase their own influence. All justified their objectives as necessary to adapt the political system to the nation's new needs.

Woman Suffrage

One of the most important achievements of the era was woman suffrage. The right to vote had traditionally been restricted to men, a position the Supreme Court upheld in 1875 in ruling that the Constitution did not confer suffrage on women. The movement to establish woman suffrage had begun in the mid-nineteenth century, and by the 1890s several Western states had adopted the reform, enabling women to vote and a few to serve in elected office. For the most part, however, suffragists had been largely frustrated by the prevailing belief that women's "proper sphere" was the home and the family. Males dominated the public sphere, including voting. Woman suffrage, particularly when championed as a step toward women's equality, seemed to challenge the natural order of society, and it generated much opposition, not only among many men (New York Republican Senator Elihu Root maintained that by voting women would become "hard, harsh, unlovable, repulsive") but among traditionalist-minded women as well. "Housewives," announced the Women's Anti-Suffrage Association of Massachusetts, "you do not need a ballot to clean out your sink spout. A handful of potash and some boiling water is quicker."

Most women progressives viewed suffrage as the key issue of the period. Already taking active leadership in broad areas of public affairs—especially by confronting, investigating, and publicizing social problems and then lobbying legislators and other public officials to adopt their proposed solutions—they thought it ridiculous to be barred from the ballot box. But most of all, the vote meant power, both to convince politicians to take seriously their demands for social reforms and to participate fully in electoral as in other forms of politics, thereby advancing the status of women.

Under a new generation of leaders like the brilliant and charismatic Carrie Chapman Catt, suffragists adopted activist tactics to outflank their traditional opposition in the early twentieth century. Catt established "suffrage schools" to teach women the history of suffrage and to train them in lobbying, public speaking, and dealing with politicians and the press. Above all, she emphasized careful organizing down to the precinct level. Activists also employed newspapers and movies (including the popular "What 8,000,000 Women Want"), presented daily programs for workers' lunch hours, opened "suffrage shops" selling suffrage buttons, pencils, and even cigarettes, and arranged "suffrage tours" by automobile. They increasingly attracted workingwomen, but mass meetings and spectacular parades dramatized

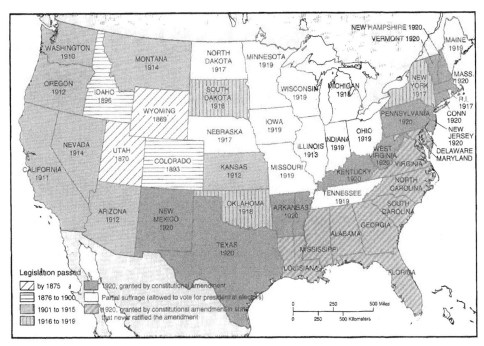

MAP 3-1 Woman suffrage in the United States before the ratification of the Nineteenth Amendment
Beginning with Wyoming in 1869, woman suffrage slowly gained acceptance in the West, but women in the South and much of the East got the ballot only when the Nineteenth Amendment was ratified in 1920.

the growing support for suffrage among women of all classes. By 1917, the National American Woman Suffrage Association had over 2 million members.

But some suffrage leaders shifted arguments as well as tactics to gain more support. They argued for woman suffrage within—not against—traditional ideas about women's role. Rather than insisting upon the "justice" of woman suffrage or emphasizing equal rights, they spoke of the special moral and maternal instincts women could bring to politics if allowed to vote. The suffrage movement now appeared less a radical, disruptive force than a vehicle for extending traditional female benevolence and service to society. Many suffragists, particularly among working-class groups, remained committed to the larger possibilities they saw in suffrage, but the new image of the movement increased public support by appealing to conventional views of women. Noted one Nebraska undergraduate, women students no longer feared "antagonizing the men or losing invitations to parties by being suffragists."

Gradually, the suffrage movement began to prevail (see Map 3-1). In 1910, Washington became the first state to approve woman suffrage since the mid-1890s, followed by California in 1911 and Arizona, Kansas, and Oregon in 1912. In 1913, Illinois became the first state east of the Mississippi River to adopt women suffrage, and New York then became the major target. But fearing that the state-by-state approach dissipated their energies and resources, suffragists also mounted national action, such as the dramatic inaugural parade in March 1913 described at the beginning of this chapter. The violence surrounding that event outraged public opinion, revived interest in a federal constitutional amendment to grant women the vote, and prompted women to send petitions and organize pilgrimages to Washington from across the country. In April, Alice Paul, who had organized the great parade, formed the Congressional Union (which became the National Woman's Party in 1916) to campaign for a federal amendment by constantly pressuring Congress and

President Wilson. More militant than Catt, Paul led suffragists in picketing the White House, the first group ever to do so. Nevertheless, Catt also persuaded NAWSA to adopt her "Winning Plan," a strategy to concentrate on achieving a federal amendment through aggressive nonpartisan lobbying at the national level. By 1919, thirty-nine states had established full or partial woman suffrage, and Congress finally approved an amendment. Ratified by the states in 1920, the **Nineteenth Amendment** marked a critical advance in political democracy.

Electoral Reform

Other electoral reforms changed the election process and the meaning of political participation. In the nineteenth century, parties had controlled not just campaigning but also voting itself, with each party printing its own distinctive ticket and using aggressive activists to distribute it at the polls, where voting was both open and supervised by other party officials. The first reform, the so-called **Australian ballot**, was adopted by most states during the 1890s or early in the new century. It provided for secret voting, freeing voters from intimidation and making vote buying and other corruption more difficult. It also replaced the individual party tickets with an official ballot listing all candidates and distributed by public officials. Parties and bosses thus lost much of their power over the voting process, and voters found it easier to vote independently. The Australian ballot led to quiet, orderly elections. One Cincinnati editor, recalling the "howling mobs" and chaos at the polls in previous elections, declared: "The political bummer and thug has been relegated to the background . . . while good citizenship . . . has come to the front."

Government responsibility for the ballot soon led to public regulation of other parts of the electoral process previously controlled by parties. Beginning with Mississippi in 1902, nearly every state provided for direct primaries to remove nominations from the boss-ridden caucus and convention system. Many states also enacted laws aimed at cleaning up campaign practices.

These reforms weakened the influence of political parties over the electoral process. Their decreasing ability to mobilize voters was reflected in a steady decline in voter participation, from 79 percent in 1896 to 49 percent in 1920. These developments had ominous implications, for parties and voting had traditionally linked ordinary Americans to their government. As parties slowly contracted, nonpartisan organizations and pressure groups, promoting narrower objectives, gained influence. Thus the National Association of Manufacturers (1895) and the United States Chamber of Commerce (1912) lobbied for business interests; the National Farmers Union (1902), for commercial agriculture; the American Federation of Teachers (1916), for professional educators. Many of these special-interest groups represented the same middle- or upper-class interests that had led the attack on parties. Their organized lobbying would give them greater influence over government in the future and contribute to a major twentieth-century trend: the declining popular belief in the value of voting or otherwise participating in politics.

More obviously, disfranchisement undermined American democracy. In the South, Democrats—progressive and conservative alike—eliminated not only black voters but also many poor white voters from the electorate through poll taxes, literacy tests, and other restrictions (see Chapter 1). Republicans in the North also tightened requirements for voting during this period, adopting educational or literacy tests in ten states, enacting strict registration laws, and gradually abolishing the right of aliens to vote. These restrictions reflected both the progressives' anti-immigrant prejudices and their obsessions with social control and with purifying politics and "improving" the electorate. Such electoral reforms reduced the political power of ethnic and working-class Americans, often stripping them of their political rights and means of influence.

Municipal Reform

Antiparty attitudes also affected progressives' efforts to reform municipal government, which they regarded as inefficient and corrupt, at least partly because of the power of urban political machines. Muckrakers had exposed crooked alliances between city bosses and business leaders that resulted in wasteful or inadequate municipal services. In some cities, urban reformers attempted to break these alliances and improve conditions for those suffering most from municipal misrule. For example, in Toledo, Ohio, Samuel "Golden Rule" Jones won enough working-class votes to be elected mayor four times despite the hostility of both major parties. Serving from 1897 to 1904, Jones opened public playgrounds and kindergartens, established the eight-hour day for city workers, and improved public services. Influenced by the Social Gospel, he also provided free lodging for the homeless and gave his own salary to the poor. Other reforming mayors also fought municipal corruption, limited the political influence of corporations, and championed public ownership of utilities.

Socialist mayors developed a distinct variety of urban reform. Socialists won hundreds of mayoral elections in the early twentieth century, often in small towns and cities, but also in several major cities. Milwaukee's Socialist mayor, Emil Seidel, pursued "sewer socialism," his program of achieving municipal ownership and better urban services. His working-class constituents benefited from municipal initiatives in housing and factory inspections, public employment and strike arbitration offices, and new public health measures. Also interested in administrative efficiency and reform, Seidel created a Bureau of Economy and Efficiency to oversee municipal government.

Another tool that some progressives advanced to address municipal problems was proportional representation, an electoral system that while preserving majority rule also enabled minority groups to win their fair share of seats on the city council. This reform was seen as both taking power from corrupt party bosses and guaranteeing democratic representation. The Proportional Representation League included on its governing council many of the most eminent progressives, including Jane Addams, Margaret Dreier Robins of the Women's Trade Union League, and the historian Charles A. Beard. A number of cities in the Midwest and West—including Ashtabula, Ohio; Kalamazoo, Michigan; Boulder, Colorado; and Sacramento, California—adopted proportional representation during the Progressive Era, but efforts in larger cities were usually frustrated.

More elitist progressives attempted to change the structure of urban government in other ways. Middle-class reformers worked to replace ward elections, which could be controlled by the neighborhood-based city machine, with at-large elections. To win citywide elections required greater resources and therefore helped swell middle-class influence at the expense of working-class wards. So did nonpartisan elections, which reformers introduced to weaken party loyalties.

Urban reformers developed two other structural innovations: the city commission and the city manager. Both attempted to institutionalize efficient, businesslike government staffed by professional administrators. As one municipal reformer maintained, "City business should be carried on by trained experts selected upon some other principle than popular suffrage." Galveston, Texas, initiated the city commission form in 1901 in response to a crisis in public services following a devastating tidal wave. Staunton, Virginia, appointed a professional city manager to run its government on a nonpartisan basis in 1908. Socialist mayors like Milwaukee's Seidel condemned the city commission and city manager plans for undermining democracy and popular government, but by 1920, hundreds of cities had adopted one of the new plans.

Business groups often promoted these reforms. In Des Moines, for example, the Commercial Club dominated the movement for the city commission in 1906, and its president declared that "the professional politician must be ousted and in his place capable businessmen chosen to conduct the affairs of the city." Again, then, reform in municipal government often shifted political power from ethnic and working-class voters, represented however imperfectly by partisan elections, to smaller groups with greater resources.

Progressive State Government

Progressives also reshaped state government. Some tried to democratize the legislative process, regarding the legislature—the most important branch of state government in the nineteenth century—as ineffective and even corrupt, dominated by party bosses and corporate influences. The Missouri legislature reportedly "enacted such laws as the corporations paid for, and such others as were necessary to fool the people." Populists had first raised such charges in the 1890s and proposed novel solutions: the **initiative** and the **referendum**. The initiative enabled reformers themselves to propose legislation directly to the electorate, bypassing an unresponsive legislature; the referendum permitted voters to approve or reject legislative measures. South Dakota Populists established the first system of "direct legislation" in 1898, and progressives adopted these innovations in twenty other states between 1902 and 1915.

Conservative opponents and procedural difficulties, however, often blocked these reforms. And the reforms could be turned against the progressives themselves. In the state of Washington in 1914, an initiative to establish an eight-hour workday was defeated by an electorate alarmed by conservative propaganda launched by business groups, and organized labor had to campaign against seven referendum measures, such as an antipicketing law, that conservative legislators had promoted. The head of the state federation of labor sadly concluded that the people could be "fooled and confused" when they voted directly on legislation.

Other innovations also expanded the popular role in state government. The **Seventeenth Amendment**, ratified in 1913, provided for the election of U.S. senators directly by popular vote instead of by state legislatures as the Constitution originally required. The legislative election of senators had not only been controlled by party bosses but was also often so corrupted by corporate interests that much of the public regarded the Senate itself as consisting of only "the instrumentalities and agents of corporations," as one reformer declared.

Beginning with Oregon in 1908, ten states adopted the **recall**, enabling voters to remove unsatisfactory public officials from office. Conservatives denounced the recall as radical and dangerous, but one California advocate defended it as a "desperate remedy for a desperate malady. It ranks next to revolution, an ultimate right possessed by all people of all nations."

Oregon also repeatedly considered adopting the reform of proportional representation for its legislature. The 1906 election seemed to demonstrate the need for it, as Republicans won 56 percent of the vote but captured fifty-nine of the sixty state representatives, leaving a large number of Democratic, Socialist, and Prohibitionist voters with little say in their own government. In 1908, Oregon's voters strongly approved an initiative legalizing proportional representation, but entrenched opponents subsequently managed to block the formal adoption of what the conservative *Portland Oregonian* termed the "most dangerous of all measures."

As state legislatures and party machines were curbed, dynamic governors gained greater importance. Robert La Follette in Wisconsin, Charles Evans Hughes in New York, Hiram Johnson in California, and other forceful governors emerged to push progressive programs into law. Elected governor in 1900, "Fighting Bob" La Follette was the prototype of the new governors, turning Wisconsin into "the laboratory of democracy" by his political skill and powerful personality. "His words bite like coals of fire," wrote one observer of La Follette's relentless agitation for reform. "He never wearies and he will not allow his audience to weary." Overcoming fierce opposition from "stalwart" Republicans, La Follette established direct primaries, railroad regulation, the first state income tax, workers' compensation, and other important measures before being elected to the U.S. Senate in 1906.

Robert M. LaFollette was a relentless campaigner for progressive reform. Under his leadership, noted Theodore Roosevelt, Wisconsin surpassed all other states "in securing both genuine popular rule and the wise use of the collective power of the people."

California's Governor Johnson was just as convinced of the correctness of his goals, attacking his political opponents as "depraved, corrupt, crooked, and putrescent." His speaking style, said one reporter, drove his audience "into almost a spiritual frenzy . . . rarely or never witnessed outside of religious meetings." Elected governor in 1910, he immediately pushed through a series of both labor and political reforms, including laws prohibiting child labor and mandating an eight-hour day for working-women and measures establishing the initiative, referendum, and recall (the last invoked in 2003 to remove Governor Gray Davis from office in favor of the actor Arnold Schwarzenegger). Johnson's continued domination of the legislature prompted the *Sacramento Bee* to observe: "The keynote to the action of the Legislature will be the Governor. Pretty much what he wishes done will be done, and little that he doesn't want done will be accomplished."

Progressive governors also stressed the values of efficiency and expertise in enhancing the regulatory power of state government. La Follette's great creation was the Legislative Reference Bureau, which was staffed by university professors to provide research and advice on public policy. He also used regulatory commissions to oversee railroads, banks, and other interests. Johnson was so committed to the scientific management of state affairs that one newspaper called him not a politician but "a crusader and an administrator." He sought efficiency through the innovative Board of Control, which reorganized and supervised public institutions and established new accounting and budgetary systems. Other new state agencies in California similarly relied on experts to investigate problems and supervise programs in conservation, working conditions, and social welfare. Hughes so vigorously expanded the supervisory authority of commissions in New York State that one political opponent complained of "government by commission."

Most other states followed suit, and expert commissions became an important feature of state government, gradually gaining authority at the expense not only of legislators but also of local officials. An observer in Virginia noted in 1912 that the emphasis on efficiency and expertise caused the government to "delegate all new functions, and some old ones, to state departments or commissions instead of to county officers."

"Experts" were presumed to be disinterested and therefore committed to the general welfare. In practice, however, regulators were subject to pressures from competing interest groups and hampered by limited information, and some commissions became captives of the very industries they were supposed to control. The problem would persist throughout the twentieth century. This irony was matched by the contradiction between the expansion of democracy through the initiative and referendum and the increasing reliance on non-elected professional experts to set and implement public policy. Such inconsistencies emphasize the complex mixture of ideas, objectives, and groups that were reshaping politics and government.

THEODORE ROOSEVELT AND THE PROGRESSIVE PRESIDENCY

When a crazed anarchist assassinated President William McKinley in 1901, Theodore Roosevelt entered the White House, and the progressive movement gained its most prominent national leader. Though only 42 years old, the nation's youngest president ever, Roosevelt had already had a remarkable career. The son of a wealthy New York family, he had entered Republican politics after graduating from Harvard in 1880. In turn, he had been a New York legislator, U.S. civil service commissioner, and assistant secretary of the Navy. After his well-publicized exploits in the Spanish-American War, he was elected governor of New York in 1898 and vice president in 1900. His public life was matched by an active private life, in which he both wrote works of history and obsessively pursued what he called the "strenuous life": boxing, wrestling, hunting, rowing, even ranching and chasing rustlers in Dakota Territory. His own son observed that Roosevelt "always wanted to be the bride at every wedding and the corpse at every funeral."

Roosevelt's frenetic activity, aggressive personality, and penchant for self-promotion worried some Americans when he ascended to the presidency. Mark Twain fretted that "Mr. Roosevelt is the Tom Sawyer of the political world of the twentieth century; always showing off; always hunting for a chance to show off; in his frenzied imagination the Great Republic is a vast Barnum circus with him for a clown and the whole world for audience." But Roosevelt's flamboyance and ambitions made him the most popular politician of the time and enabled him to dramatize the issues of progressivism and to become the first modern president.

TR and the Modern Presidency

Roosevelt rejected the limited role accepted by most presidents in the late nineteenth century. He believed that the president could do anything to meet national needs that the Constitution did not specifically prohibit. "Under this interpretation of executive power," he later recalled, "I did and caused to be done many things not previously done. . . . I did not usurp power, but I did greatly broaden the use of executive power." Indeed, the expansion of government power and its consolidation in the executive branch were among his most significant accomplishments.

Rather than deferring to Congress, which he regarded as slow and indecisive, Roosevelt exerted legislative leadership. He spelled out his policy goals in more than four hundred messages to Congress, sent drafts of bills to Capitol Hill, and intervened vigorously to win passage of "his" measures. Some members of Congress resented such "executive arrogance" and "dictatorship." Senator Orville Platt complained that Roosevelt tried "to force his views, instead of his recommendations, on Congress." Roosevelt generally avoided direct challenges to the conservative Old Guard Republicans who controlled Congress, but his activities helped shift the balance of power within the national government.

Roosevelt also reorganized the executive branch, extending its reach and shifting its emphasis. More than any of his predecessors, he believed in efficiency and expertise, which he attempted to institutionalize in special commissions and administrative procedures. To promote rational policymaking and public management, he staffed the expanding federal bureaucracy with able professionals. Here, too, he provoked opposition. The president, complained one Republican, was "trying to concentrate all power in Washington . . . and to govern the people by commissions and bureaus."

Finally, Roosevelt encouraged the development of a personal presidency by exploiting the public's interest in their exuberant young president. He established the first White House press room and skillfully handled the mass media. His endless and well-reported activities, from playing with his children in the White House to wrestling, hiking, and horseback riding with various notables, made him a celebrity—"TR" or "Teddy." The increasingly public dimension of the presidency not only kept TR in the spotlight that he craved but also enabled him to mold public opinion. He used the presidency as "the bully pulpit," speaking forcefully and directly to the nation. He wrote his own speeches, and his language conveyed his personality as well as his convictions.

Roosevelt and Labor

One sign of TR's vigorous new approach to the presidency was his handling of a coal strike in 1902. Fifty thousand members of the United Mine Workers Union walked off their jobs, demanding higher wages, an eight-hour day, and recognition of their union. The mine owners simply closed the mines, refused to negotiate, and waited for the union to collapse. But led by John Mitchell, the strikers held their ranks. The prospect of a freezing winter frightened consumers. Management's stubborn arrogance contrasted sharply with the workers' orderly conduct and willingness to negotiate and hardened public opinion against the owners. TR studied the strike closely, but his legal advisors told him the government had no constitutional authority to intervene.

As public pressure mounted, however, Roosevelt decided to act. He invited both the owners and the union leaders to the White House and declared that the national interest made government action necessary. Mitchell agreed to negotiate with the owners or to accept an arbitration commission appointed by the president. The owners, however, refused even to speak to the union leaders but instead denounced them as "a set of outlaws" and demanded that Roosevelt use the army to break the union, as President Grover Cleveland had done in the Pullman Strike in 1894.

Roosevelt was not a champion of labor, and in 1894 he had favored shooting the Pullman strikers. But as president, he believed his role was to mediate social conflict for the public good. Furious with the owners' "arrogant stupidity" and "insulting" attitude toward the presidency, Roosevelt announced that he would use the army to seize and operate the mines, not to crush the union. Questioned about the constitutionality of such an action, Roosevelt bellowed: "To hell with the Constitution when the people want coal." (Later, in his autobiography, TR more calmly explained that he had acted under "the Jackson-Lincoln theory of the presidency" because "occasionally great crises arise which call for immediate and vigorous executive action.") Reluctantly, the owners accepted the arbitration commission they had previously rejected. The commission gave the miners a 10 percent wage increase and a nine-hour day, but not the union recognition they wanted, and permitted the owners to raise coal prices by 10 percent.

Roosevelt's intervention, declared one newspaper, represented "a great personal triumph." TR described it as simply giving both labor and management a "square deal." It also set important precedents for an active government role in labor disputes and a strong president acting as a steward of the public. Although Roosevelt later angered labor by using troops in strikes in Colorado and Nevada and by issuing in 1903 an executive order mandating the "open shop" in government employment, he also enforced the eight-hour law on government works and supported Senator La Follette's successful effort to enact an employer's liability law for the District of Columbia.

Managing Natural Resources

In the second half of the nineteenth century, federal land policy had helped create farms and develop transportation, but it had also ceded to speculators and business interests much of the nation's forests, mineral deposits, waterpower sites, and grazing lands. Reckless exploitation of these resources alarmed a new generation that believed the public welfare required the **conservation** of natural resources through efficient and scientific management. Conservationists achieved early victories in the Forest Reserve Act (1891) and the Forest Management Act (1897), which authorized the federal government to withdraw timberlands from development and to regulate grazing, lumbering, and hydroelectric sites in the forests (see Map 3-2).

Roosevelt built upon these beginnings and his friendship with Gifford Pinchot to make conservation a major focus of his presidency. Pinchot, a Yale graduate from a wealthy and privileged background, had been trained abroad in French and German scientific forestry practices. Appointed in 1898 to head the new Division of Forestry (renamed the Forest Service in 1905), he brought rational management and regulation to resource development. Roosevelt admired what he called Pinchot's "tireless energy and activity, his fearlessness, . . . and his extraordinary efficiency." Those characteristics appeared to Pinchot's enemies as arrogance and ruthlessness, but Roosevelt identified with them, and the two became so close that the forester became known as the "crown prince" of the Roosevelt administration.

The conservation of natural resources fit Roosevelt's commitment to executive authority, informed by trained experts. Scientific management by professionals could benefit the national interest by preventing both waste and scarcity. In making decisions, TR proposed to use existing legislation "and then further to supplement it by Executive action." With Pinchot's advice and encouragement, TR used presidential authority to triple the size of the forest reserves to 150 million acres, set aside another 80 million acres valuable for minerals and petroleum, and establish dozens of wildlife refuges. When Congress curtailed Roosevelt's ability to establish additional national forests in 1907, he invoked the Antiquities Act of 1906 to continue his policies. That law, enacted in response to the looting of archaeological ruins in the Southwest, authorized the president to reserve public lands to protect and manage "objects of scientific or historic interest." Roosevelt seized upon its imprecise language, however, to circumvent Congress and exercise nearly unchecked discretion over the public domain. Most dramatically, he set aside 800,000 acres of the Grand Canyon as a national monument in 1908 and, on his last day in office in 1909, more than 600,000 acres in Washington state as the Mount Olympus National Monument. Pinchot also achieved a measure of discretion and autonomy for the Forest Service when its timber sales and grazing fees in the national forests made it less dependent on Congress for funding. Finally, when Roosevelt and Pinchot held a White House conservation conference of federal and state officials in 1908, Pinchot financed it from his personal fortune when Congress failed to appropriate funds for it. That conference led to the creation of the National Conservation Commission, forty-one state conservation commissions, and widespread public support for the conservation movement.

Not everyone, of course, agreed with TR's conservationist policies. Some favored **preservation**, hoping to set aside land as permanent wilderness, whereas Roosevelt simply favored a scientific and efficient, rather than uncontrolled, use of resources. Pinchot liked to rebut the preservationists by saying, "Wilderness is waste." Led by John Muir, a California

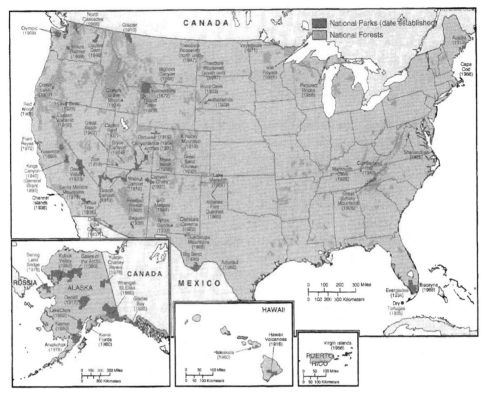

MAP 3-2 The growth of National Forests and National Parks
Rapid exploitation of the West prompted demands to preserve its spectacular scenery and protect its remaining forests. In 1872 Yellowstone became the first National Park, and the National Forest system began in the 1890s. Conservation became increasingly important during the Progressive Era but often provoked Western hostility.

naturalist and author who regarded nature as sacred, preservationists won some victories, helping establish several national parks, saving a stand of California's giant redwoods, and eventually creating the National Park Service in 1916.

There was considerable irony in the preservationist insistence upon wilderness, which often entailed further dispossession of American Indians. The leading figure in establishing Glacier National Park, for instance, wanted to preserve what he called the last remaining "wild and unknown portion" of America, and yet in his search for pristine landscapes in northern Montana George Bird Grinnell relied on Blackfeet guides and followed Indian trails through areas that he described as "absolutely virgin ground . . . with no sign of previous passage." Grinnell helped pressure the Blackfeet to give up some of their land to create the national park, though they reserved rights to continue using it for hunting, fishing, and timbering. Once the park was established, however, park officials eager to maintain its "original" wilderness condition prohibited hunting and excluded the Blackfeet from the land they depended upon. The tribe protested this "act of injustice," and the dispute has continued ever since. The creation of other parks similarly dispossessed Indians. The Shoshone were forced out of Yellowstone National Park, and Muir insisted that the tribes who had long lived in Yosemite had "no right place in the landscape" of that national park.

Other interests opposed both conservation and preservation. While some of the larger timber, mineral, and cattle companies supported federally supervised conservation programs as a way to achieve stability, avoid overproduction, and guarantee long-run profits, smaller Western entrepreneurs cared only about quick returns. Small ranchers in Colorado demonstrated their indifference to long-run issues and scientific expertise in a 1905 resolution against a federal management program to improve the grasslands and prevent overgrazing of the public range: "Resolved, that none of us know, or care to know, anything about grasses . . . outside of the fact for the present there are lots of them . . . and we are after getting the most of them while they last." At the same time, however, small ranchers feared that a system of leasing the land would drive them out of business and lead to the "grabbing up of practically all the public domain by cattle syndicates."

Many Westerners also resented having Easterners make key decisions about Western growth and saw conservation as a perpetuation of this colonial subservience. One Colorado Republican congressman denounced "goggle-eyed, bandy-legged dudes from the East and sad-eyed, absent minded professors and bugologists" for forcing conservation upon the West. Such attitudes prompted some Westerners to resist federal control of public resources. Many ranchers refused to pay grazing fees instituted by the Forest Service in 1906; in northwestern Colorado small stockraisers waged a war against rangers trying to enforce the law, stampeding cattle through their camps and even hiring gunmen to kill them. Elsewhere, arsonists set forest fires to protest the creation of forest reserves.

Not all federal policies for Western resource development and management generated Western opposition—or turned out as expected. Westerners were happy to take federal money for expensive irrigation projects that private capital would not undertake. They favored the 1902 National Reclamation Act sponsored by Francis Newlands of Nevada but pushed through Congress by Roosevelt. This act established what became the **Bureau of Reclamation**. Its engineers were to construct dams, reservoirs, and irrigation canals, and the government was to sell the irrigated lands to resident farmers in tracts no larger than 160 acres. The act helped shape the modern West through the forces of government power, expertise, and bureaucracy. By constructing massive dams and networks of irrigation canals, the Bureau reclaimed fertile valleys from deserts. Unfortunately, to promote economic development the Bureau did not enforce the 160-acre limitation or restrict the use of irrigation water to resident (not absentee) farmers. Rather than encouraging small family farms, then, the Bureau helped to create powerful corporate farms, exploiting both federal subsidies and migrant workers in the West. Reclamation projects also favored economic development over traditional ways of life. The modern system of reservoirs and canals created by Elephant Butte Dam in New Mexico destroyed the old irrigation ditches of small Hispanic farmers and turned them into agricultural laborers.

Exploiting Indian Land A second way in which Roosevelt's commitment to conservation and regional economic development pleased many Westerners involved the treatment of Indian reservation lands. In the nineteenth century, Indians had been forced onto reservations through intimidation or brutal warfare in order to open the remainder of the West to white settlement and development. Thereafter, the Dawes Severalty Act of 1887 had guided government Indian policy. The Dawes Act had two objectives. It sought to destroy Indian tribal structure and culture by allotting small parcels of tribal reservation lands to individual Indians in a misguided attempt to transform them into small capitalist farmers and facilitate their assimilation into the larger society. And it sought to wrest still more Indian land and resources for white exploitation by opening the unalloted reservation lands to white settlement. To protect Indians from immediate dispossession through trickery or manipulation, reservations were only gradually allotted and restrictions were placed on disposing of the allotments for twenty-five years. In the 1890s, Roosevelt had endorsed the dual objectives of the Dawes Act and rejected the notion, held by some "Eastern sentimentalists," that the Indians were being driven off the land they owned. "They did not own the land at all, in the white sense," he maintained; "they merely occupied it."

Theodore Roosevelt at the dedication ceremonies for Roosevelt Dam, part of the Bureau of Reclamation's Salt River Irrigation Project, Arizona, in 1911. Conservationists like Roosevelt advocated federally-funded water projects to promote efficient economic development of the American West.

As president, in his first message to Congress in 1901, Roosevelt praised the Dawes Act as "a mighty pulverizing engine" destroying Indian culture, but convinced of Indians' racial inferiority, he did not favor assimilation. Roosevelt's views were shared by Francis Leupp, a close friend he appointed as commissioner of Indian affairs. Chiefly concerned with the efficient economic development of the West rather than promoting independent tribal economies, both men supported efforts to make it easier for whites to gain control of Indian resources. Racism and a commitment to economic growth pushed aside any genuine concern for Indians or assimilation.

The first step was to speed up the allotment process. Despite Indian opposition, the government moved quickly to break up many reservations, ignoring treaties requiring tribal approval for land cessions and refusing to pay the asking price for Indian lands; instead individual land allotments were made to Indians and the remainder of the reservation opened to whites. The second step was to facilitate the acquisition of Indian allotments by local whites who would develop them. In 1906 Leupp persuaded Congress to pass the Burke Act, authorizing the elimination of many of the protective restrictions on allotments, which led to a large landless class among the Indians and to reservations checkered with non-Indian intrusions. More blatant was a second law, called by Indians the "Crime of 1908," which ended most restrictions on allotments in Oklahoma, where fraud, forgery, and criminal collusion by white lawyers, developers, and judges systematically placed Indian properties with farming, grazing, timber, and oil resources under white control.

Declaring Indians "grossly wasteful of their natural resources," Leupp also leased reservation lands to white business interests he regarded as more efficient. Mining companies received leases to prospect on previously closed tribal lands; sugar beet companies received leases in exchange for their pledge to employ Indian laborers. Declared Leupp: "Even the little papoose can be taught to weed the rows just as the pickaninny in the South can be used as a cotton picker." Working in the fields under white supervision, he maintained, would be better for Indians than "all the schools and all the philanthropic activities set afoot . . . by benevolent whites, if rolled into one and continued for a century." Indians would learn work habits while assisting regional economic development.

The Roosevelt administration also pursued conservation policies on Indian land, particularly by undertaking irrigation projects, often using tribal funds to do so despite Indian protests. Rather than helping the tribes, these ambitious projects favored whites by allocating the water to those judged most likely to make "efficient" and "beneficial use" of the precious resource in the arid West. By 1920, whites cultivated 50 percent more land on Indian irrigation projects than Indians did. The Bureau of Reclamation also developed irrigation projects at Indian expense. In the Southwest, for example, it channeled water to the growing city of Phoenix by transgressing the water rights of the Yavapais on their Arizona reservation. And although the Supreme Court ruled in 1908 that tribes retained absolute rights to reservation waters—in this case, the Bureau had illegally diverted the Milk River on the Montana reservation of the Gros Ventre—government agencies continued to approve and construct projects that drew off Indian rivers and inundated Indian land without benefiting the tribes.

Finally, Roosevelt also expanded federal management of reservation lands. He issued executive orders transferring control of millions of acres of timbered reservation land to the Forest Service in 1908, a step Secretary of Interior James Garfield defended as necessary "to improve the forest and yield the full market value of timber cut." Hastened land sales, huge irrigation projects, forestry management programs, and other federal policies put Indian resources in the service of regional economic development while helping make Indians dependent subjects rather than independent citizens.

Corporate Regulation

Nothing symbolized Roosevelt's active presidency better than his popular reputation as a "trustbuster." TR took office at a time of public anxiety about corporate power. Many Americans demanded that big business be broken up through strong enforcement of the Sherman Antitrust Act of 1890. Roosevelt, however, did not share their anxiety. On the contrary, he regarded the formation of large business combinations to be the result of a natural and beneficial process, but he understood the political implications of the public's concern. Although business leaders and Old Guard conservatives opposed any government intervention in the large trusts, Roosevelt knew better. "You have no conception of the revolt that would be caused if I did nothing," he said privately. To satisfy popular clamor, ensure social stability, and still retain the economic advantages he perceived in the efficiency and productivity of big modern corporations, TR proposed to "develop an orderly system, and such a system can only come through the gradually exercised right of efficient government control." Rather than invoking what he called "the foolish antitrust law," he favored government regulation to prevent corporate abuses and defend the public interest. "Misconduct," not size, was the issue. Roosevelt preferred to use government agencies, such as the Bureau of Corporations (1903), to work with corporations to avoid lawsuits, but at times he did take legal action against some "bad trusts."

In 1902, the Roosevelt administration filed its most famous antitrust suit against the Northern Securities Company, a holding company organized by J.P. Morgan to control the railroad network of the Northwest. For TR, this popular action had as much political as economic value. It was an assertion of government power that reassured a worried public and made corporate responsibility more likely. In 1904, the Supreme Court ordered the dissolution of the Northern Securities Company. Ultimately, Roosevelt brought forty-four antitrust suits against business combinations, but, except for a few like Standard Oil, which Roosevelt's

Roosevelt enjoyed this cartoon illustrating his distinction between good trusts, restrained by government regulations for public welfare, and bad trusts. On those he put his foot down.

investigators found operating illegal "monopolistic control . . . from the well of the producer to the door step of the consumer," he avoided the giant firms. Many of the cases had inconclusive outcomes, but Roosevelt was more interested in establishing a regulatory role for government than in breaking up big business.

The popularity of Roosevelt's action against the Northern Securities Company brought political benefits in the 1904 election, as did the public's fascination with his "personal presidency." (TR noted that during the campaign huge crowds came to "see the President as much as they would have come to see a circus.") By contrast the Democratic candidate, the colorless and conservative Judge Alton B. Parker, made little impact, and Roosevelt was elected with the largest popular majority ever polled to that time.

Roosevelt promptly responded to the growing popular demand for reform by pushing further toward a regulatory government. To complement his executive actions, he now proposed legislation "to work out methods of controlling the big corporations without paralyzing the energies of the business community." In 1906, Congress enacted three major regulatory laws: the Hepburn Act, the Pure Food and Drug Act, and the Meat Inspection Act. All three were compromises between reformers seeking serious government control of the industries and political defenders and lobbyists of the industries themselves.

To guarantee passage, Roosevelt supported what he characteristically saw as a moderate or balanced position. He demanded railroad regulation as the only way to avoid "an increase of the present evils on the one hand or a still more radical policy on the other." While abusive railroad practices prompted some to demand public ownership, TR sought to strengthen the Interstate Commerce Commission (ICC). The ICC had been established in 1887 as the first federal regulatory agency, but both the railroads and a conservative judiciary had blocked its efforts to prevent rebates, discriminatory rates, and pooling. The Hepburn Act enhanced the power of the ICC by authorizing it to set maximum railroad rates and extending its jurisdiction to include ferries, bridges, pipeline companies, and other businesses. It was a weaker law than many progressives had wanted; its own floor leader in the Senate described it as a "stupendous farce" prepared by railroad lawyers and with loopholes through which "a whole freight train" could be driven. Nevertheless, it marked the first time the federal government gained the power to set rules in a private enterprise.

The two other laws aimed at consumer protection in food and drugs. In part, this legislation reflected a public demand stimulated by muckraking exposés and sensational government investigations of industry abuses. Upton Sinclair's *The Jungle* (1906) graphically described the filth and disease in Chicago's meatpacking plants; a series of articles in *Collier's*

••• OVERVIEW •••

MAJOR LAWS AND CONSTITUTIONAL AMENDMENTS OF THE PROGRESSIVE ERA

LEGISLATION	EFFECT
Newlands Act (1902)	Provided for federal irrigation projects.
Hepburn Act (1906)	Strengthened authority of the Interstate Commerce Commission.
Pure Food and Drug Act (1906)	Regulated the production and sale of food and drug products.
Meat Inspection Act (1906)	Authorized federal inspection of meat products.
Sixteenth Amendment (1913)	Authorized a federal income tax.
Seventeenth Amendment (1913)	Mandated the direct popular election of senators.
Underwood-Simmons Tariff Act (1913)	Lowered tariff rates and levied the first regular federal income tax.
Federal Reserve Act (1913)	Established the Federal Reserve System to supervise banking and provide a national currency.
Federal Trade Commission Act (1914)	Established the FTC to oversee business activities.
Keating-Owen Act (1916)	Indirectly prohibited child labor.
Eighteenth Amendment (1919)	Instituted prohitibion.
Nineteenth Amendment (1920)	Established woman suffrage.

in 1905 reported that patent medicines were laced with alcohol, morphine, cocaine, opium, and other drugs, often producing unwitting alcohol and narcotic addiction rather than good health. Harvey Wiley, chief of the Bureau of Chemistry of the Department of Agriculture (the predecessor of the Food and Drug Administration) and long a critic of food adulteration, began in 1904 to publish the findings of his experiments with his Poison Squad, young men who agreed to serve as guinea pigs in the testing of food. The Poison Squad reports, indicating that as much as 20 percent of the food supply was adulterated, captivated and angered the public, inspiring poems, songs, gripping human interest stories, and demands for reform.

But many business leaders also supported government regulation, convinced that it would expand their markets by certifying the quality of their products and drive their smaller competitors out of business. Meatpacking companies, for example, worried especially about Germany's intention to close its markets to American processed meats; large pharmaceutical firms wanted to curtail the patent medicine companies that gave their industry such an unsavory reputation. Other businesses favored federal regulation as more rational and cost effective than complying with the many different pure food laws already adopted by most states by 1906. H.J. Heinz of the Heinz Ketchup Company was so committed to federal regulation that he appointed a staff to help Roosevelt and Congress draft the legislation and was credited by the Bureau of Chemistry with leading in reform "when government officials and legislators lagged."

The Meat Inspection Act and the Pure Food and Drug Act thus did extend government supervision and regulation over business to protect the public health and safety, but they also served some corporate purposes. Moreover, they required the government to assume the costs of inspection and allowed businesses to appeal decisions to the conservative courts.

Sinclair complained that the Meat Inspection Act aimed mostly to widen foreign markets for American meatpackers. Meat inspection, he declared, "is maintained and paid for by the people of the United States for the benefit of the packers; . . . men wearing the blue uniforms and brass buttons of the United States service are employed for the purpose of certifying to the nations of the civilized world that all the diseased and tainted meat which happens to come into existence in the United States of America is carefully sifted out and consumed by the American people." Indeed, later investigations revealed that little changed in the processing of canned meat, and of course nothing changed for the workers, Sinclair's major concern.

The food and drug measure was also rather weak, and lax enforcement further limited its effect. Roosevelt himself overrode scientific advice to permit questionable products to continue to be sold. Although some improvements were secured, including the elimination of cocaine from the soft drink Coca Cola, studies in the 1930s found that the production, advertising, and sale of worthless or even dangerous products persisted.

Despite the compromises and weaknesses in the three laws, TR was pleased. "Taken together," he contended, they marked "a noteworthy advance in the policy of securing federal supervision and control over corporations." Old Guard Republicans thought Roosevelt had extended government powers dangerously, one critic complaining that the new laws tended "toward the centralization of power in the United States and a corresponding decrease in the old time sovereignty of the states, or of the individual." In fact, however, Roosevelt's actual accomplishments had been relatively modest because of his need to compromise in Congress. As La Follette noted, Roosevelt's "cannonading filled the air with noise and smoke, which confused and obscured the line of action, but, when the battle cloud drifted by and the quiet was restored, it was always a matter of surprise that so little had really been accomplished."

Lurching to the Left?

In the final years of his administration, Roosevelt seemed to move to the left, convinced that his political responsibility was to lead the "ultraconservative" party of McKinley to a position of "progressive conservatism or conservative radicalism." His rhetoric was more radical than his actions, and he remained a staunch partisan, but his public advocacy of an expanded regulatory program increased stress on his party and forced other Republicans to decide how reformist they wanted the Grand Old Party (GOP) to be.

One area of popular concern that Roosevelt made a gesture of addressing was campaign financing. Many Americans were troubled by the increasing political influence of corporations, not only in legislation but also in election campaigns; the reality of popular democracy seemed threatened. The alliance between the business community and, in particular, the Republican party had been carefully nurtured by both partners and had conspicuously flowered in the 1896 and 1900 elections of President McKinley when corporate contributions helped shape the campaign against the reform crusades of Democrat William Jennings Bryan. In reaction, as early as 1897, states had begun to prohibit corporate campaign contributions. Roosevelt's 1904 election spurred interest in federal legislation.

Despite reservations about TR's regulatory ambitions, leading corporations like Standard Oil, J.P. Morgan and Company, and major insurance companies provided three-fourths of the Republican presidential campaign fund, and Roosevelt himself solicited corporate leaders for money. Democrats charged that corporations were financing Roosevelt's candidacy in exchange for immunity from antitrust suits. Roosevelt told the Republican national chairman to "say nothing" and to ignore press questions about the contributions.

But when a New York state investigation after the election revealed other troubling corporate campaign contributions—as well as bribery and payoffs to politicians—the resulting public outcry prompted Roosevelt to call for a ban on corporate political contributions. But he then showed little interest in the issue, and Congressional Republicans were able to delay and then weaken a Democratic bill before its passage in 1907. Republicans also defeated Democratic proposals to require political committees to disclose the size and source of campaign contributions, which reformers thought would drive corporations out of politics.

More bad publicity over corporate contributions to Republicans spurred Roosevelt to again call for reform, proposing in 1907 what he called a "very radical measure" for public financing of campaigns as a means to eliminate the need for parties to collect large campaign funds. But Roosevelt did not have such a bill introduced and actually worked to block Democratic bills to that effect. Instead he meant merely to float the idea to divert attention from another disclosure bill which was gaining in popularity. TR disingenuously warned that a disclosure law would "be obeyed only by the honest, and disobeyed by the unscrupulous, so as to act only as a penalty upon honest men." The head of the National Publicity Bill Organization, which led the campaign for disclosure laws, charged that Roosevelt had first "retarded the movement by his indifference and deliberate neglect" and then sabotaged it by proposing public financing of campaigning.

Only in 1911, when TR was no longer in office and Democrats and insurgent Republicans controlled Congress, were reformers able to end what one called "this farce of declaring for publicity and doing nothing for it." Then Congress finally passed a disclosure law and imposed limits on campaign spending. Public financing of campaigns remained unfulfilled.

Although partisanship drove Roosevelt in helping Republicans block campaign reform, he increasingly advocated other regulatory measures, calling for an eight-hour workday, stock market regulation, inheritance and income taxes, and the limitation of labor injunctions. Republican conservatives in Congress blocked such reforms, and tensions increased between the progressive and conservative wings of the party. Roosevelt's increasingly radical declarations brought business criticism as well. His demand for the adoption of the recall for judges, whose decisions against social legislation and labor rights he saw as recklessly endangering social stability, especially outraged his critics as itself destabilizing.

A financial panic and a recession in 1907 brought further polarization. Although the executive branch worked vigorously to resolve the financial crisis, many business leaders and conservatives contrived to blame Roosevelt's reform activities for undermining business confidence. Roosevelt struck back by charging that "speculation, corruption, and fraud" had provoked the depression, which "certain malefactors of great wealth" then manipulated to discredit his regulatory campaign to protect the public. In a spectacular message to Congress in January 1908, Roosevelt went further, denouncing by name corporate leaders and "purchased politicians" for persistently blocking reform measures "with every resource that bitter and unscrupulous craft could suggest and the command of almost unlimited money secure." Warning that "corrupt business and corrupt politics act and react with ever increasing debasement, one on the other," Roosevelt then repeated his demands for reform.

Although Midwestern progressives like La Follette supported Roosevelt's reform proposals, the party's conservative congressional leadership rebuffed them. "That fellow at the other end of the Avenue," growled Speaker of the House Joe Cannon, "wants everything, from the birth of Christ to the death of the devil." Roosevelt was just as dismissive of his opponents. "The ruling clique in the Senate, the House, and the National Committee, seem to regard every concession to decency as merely a matter of bargain and sale with *me*, which *I* must pay for in some way." Nearing the end of his term, Roosevelt had to leave the bitter impasse between the executive and Congress and the fierce division within the Republican party to be addressed by his successor to party and presidential leadership.

TAFT AND THE TENSIONS OF PROGRESSIVE POLITICS

Theodore Roosevelt handpicked his successor as president: a loyal lieutenant, William Howard Taft. A member of a prominent Ohio political family, Taft had a solid career as a federal judge, governor general of the Philippines, and TR's secretary of war. Later he would serve as chief justice of the United States. But if Roosevelt thought that Taft would be a successful president, pursuing progressive reform and holding the Republican party together, he was wrong. Taft's election as president in 1908 led to a Republican political disaster.

The Election of 1908

Roosevelt's intermittent interest in campaign reform did not extend to the nominating process, which to the dismay of many Republicans he manipulated to personally select the party's presidential nominee in 1908. And his choice of a successor, supposedly to pursue and promote "my policies," raised further questions about TR's commitment to reform rather than personal politics.

Senator La Follette and Governor Hughes were logical choices, but Roosevelt opposed the first as too radical ("exceeding the speed limit") and the second as too independent. His preference, astonishingly, was Elihu Root, his secretary of state but an arch conservative hostile to reform. Recognizing that Root was out of the question, TR settled on William Howard Taft, whom he liked personally and believed in broad accord with his policies. But Taft, too, was a conservative. He had supported TR's policies as a loyal lieutenant, but his own views had appeared more clearly in his earlier career as a judge, when he had earned the nickname of "Father of Injunctions" for his anti-union decisions.

Taft himself hoped Roosevelt would run again, thereby saving him from what he regarded as an unpleasant prospect. As he told a friend: "Any party which would nominate me would make a great mistake." But Roosevelt ruthlessly used his presidential patronage and influence to promote Taft's candidacy, promised the reluctant politician to eliminate other contenders ("I will break their necks with the utmost cheerfulness"), and carefully coached Taft on his public statements—all the while publicly denying he was controlling the process. The *Kansas City Times* ridiculed the charade:

> Says Roosevelt: "I announce no choice,
>
> To no man will I lend my voice,
>
> I have no private candidate,
>
> I care not whom you nominate—
>
> Just so it's Taft.
>
> The people are untrammeled, free,
>
> To pick out their own nominee,
>
> Far be it from me to dictate
>
> Who shall direct affairs of state—
>
> Just so it's Taft."

Roosevelt felt that he could not let the Republican convention choose its own nominee; that would produce a conservative who would not continue his policies. But while TR delivered the nomination to Taft, the convention otherwise remained under the control of the

Old Guard. It chose a conservative vice-presidential nominee and adopted a distinctly conservative platform. The *St. Louis Republic* sneered: "All the influences against which Roosevelt had pretended to be waging uncompromising war are satisfied with the Chicago ticket and platform."

One key plank of the platform was the focal point for a new element in national politics. Under increasing assault from anti-union employers using judicial injunctions against strikes and court decisions prohibiting union boycotts and restricting the right to organize (see Chapter 2), the American Federation of Labor (AFL) and the trade unions had turned to politics for relief. In 1906 the AFL presented its "Bill of Grievances" to Congress, demanding restrictions on judicial injunctions and the exemption of unions from the Sherman Antitrust Act, under which federal judges had sometimes ruled that unions were conspiracies in restraint of trade. When Congress rejected the demands, the AFL adopted an active "nonpartisan" political strategy, endorsing sympathetic candidates regardless of party and pressing both major parties to include labor planks in their platforms.

In 1908, the Republican national convention completely rejected the labor program, and under the influence of the National Association of Manufacturers it pointedly pledged to uphold "the authority and integrity of the courts." And while Roosevelt had previously denounced reactionary judges for their decisions against labor rights—by making workers' conditions "intolerable," he said, judges threatened to make a revolution "absolutely necessary"—Taft declared that he would "rather cut my hand off" than restrict judges' use of injunctions. AFL President Sam Gompers complained that organized labor had been "thrown down, repudiated, and relegated to the discard by the Republican party." The Democrats, by contrast, adopted six labor planks, including those calling for limitations on injunctions, an eight-hour workday for federal employees, and a Department of Labor. And they nominated William Jennings Bryan, who strongly endorsed labor's rights. As a consequence, the AFL supported Democratic candidates (Gompers denounced Taft as "the originator and specific champion" of "government by injunction"). In endorsing the Democratic party as more responsive than the Republicans, Gompers declared, "Labor does not become partisan to a political party but partisan to a principle." Nevertheless, labor increasingly aligned with the Democratic party, a trend that would grow more important as time passed.

The 1908 campaign illustrated the tensions of progressive politics in other ways as well. Taft himself conceded privately that many progressive Republicans regarded Bryan as "the legitimate successor of Roosevelt" in the fight for reform, and the Democratic platform endorsed popular election of senators, an income tax as a more equitable means of raising revenue, and tariff reduction. The Republican platform opposed the first two reforms and committed only to a revision of the tariff, without specifying a reduction. Nevertheless, the progressive Republicans had to trust in Taft for leadership. At the same time, conservative Republicans looked to the candidate for help in controlling the direction of the party after Theodore Roosevelt.

Campaign finance reform also intruded into the contest. The Republican convention had conspicuously rejected La Follette's proposed plank for the public disclosure of campaign expenditures, and the party again received large corporate donations, described by one conservative Republican senator as "like taking out an insurance policy." In an unprecedented move, Bryan reported the amount and sources of the Democratic campaign funds, which came from many small contributors (the Democrats had six times as many donors but only a third of the dollars of the Republicans).

Roosevelt worked hard to secure Taft's election, handling many political details himself, even revising Taft's speeches and urging the candidate, an indifferent campaigner, to be more active. Taft did win, but with only half of TR's 1904 majority, and Republicans lost a number of important congressional and gubernatorial elections. The new president would have to be skillful to maintain party unity and achieve a positive record. Gifford Pinchot observed that Taft faced "his new task with doubt and dread."

The Blundering President

Regarded even by his political opponents as competent and efficient as he entered the White House, the new president almost immediately earned the reputation of "Taft the blunderer." Prominent journalists dubbed him "the blundering politician," and one of his own closest colleagues concluded that he committed the most remarkable series of "colossal blunders" in American political history. A loyal lieutenant, Roosevelt ruefully concluded, did not necessarily make a good captain.

Taft's problems were many. Some involved his personality and limited political skills. Despite the widespread view, the 350-pound Taft was not particularly lazy—he obsessively played golf every day—but he certainly lacked political energy and interest. Even his wife expressed exasperation over his "unfortunate shortcoming of not knowing much and of caring less about the way the game of politics is played." He disliked discord and confrontations and shrank from making decisions, a trait that ironically encouraged the political conflict he hoped to avoid. Iowa Senator Jonathan Dolliver described Taft as a "large amiable island, surrounded entirely by persons who knew exactly what they wanted." To get away from Washington politics, he traveled frequently and took many lengthy vacations, directing the White House to not send him mail to his summer home in Massachusetts.

Taft also had a very different view of the presidency from that of his frenetic predecessor. He discouraged the personal presidency TR had encouraged and used so effectively. He thought dealing with the press both unpleasant and unnecessary and pursued what he called "nonpublicity." He ignored reporters' questions and objected to photographers. "Since Roosevelt," concluded one magazine in late 1909, "very little news has come out of the White House." As a consequence, however, Taft had no control over how his actions would be reported; denied presidential statements, official briefings, advice, or useful "leaks," the press often instead sought information from Taft's enemies.

Taft also ignored the symbolism of the presidency. He failed to appeal as a national leader for public support to overcome congressional opposition. He even refused to wave to the crowds that gathered to meet his train or watch his carriage rides in Washington. One observer noted that, after Roosevelt, the public expected more from a president; Taft "will be a dead card if he doesn't change."

Finally, Taft had a narrow view of presidential authority. He objected to Roosevelt's activism and regarded much of it as not merely in violation of procedures and tradition but, from his legalistic perspective, unwarranted by explicit constitutional provisions. Similarly, he held a more restricted view of the reach of national power. Not surprisingly, then, he had no grand visions or goals for his presidency.

Nevertheless, as president, Taft did preside over important progressive achievements. His administration pursued a more active and successful antitrust program than Roosevelt's. He supported additional regulatory legislation in the Mann-Elkins Act (1910), which extended the ICC's jurisdiction to telephone and telegraph companies. Taft set aside more public forest lands and oil reserves than Roosevelt had. He also supported a constitutional amendment authorizing an income tax, which went into effect in 1913 under the **Sixteenth Amendment**. One of the most important accomplishments of the Progressive Era, the income tax would provide the means for the government to expand its activities and responsibilities in the twentieth century.

Despite this record, however, Taft soon alienated progressives and floundered into a political morass. Complicating Taft's personality, limited political skills, and attitudes toward government was the ever-growing division within his Republican party. Midwestern reform Republicans, led by Wisconsin's La Follette, clashed with more conservative Republicans led by Senator Nelson Aldrich of Rhode Island. Where the reformers preferred lower tariffs, more vigorous government regulation, and political and economic reform, the Old Guard preferred to "stand pat." Politically inept, Taft was unable to mediate the conflicts between these two groups, and the party split apart.

Reformers wanted to restrict the power of the speaker of the House, "Uncle Joe" Cannon, a reactionary who systematically blocked progressive measures and loudly declared, "I am goddamned tired of listening to all this babble of reform." After seeming to promise support, Taft backed down when conservatives threatened to defeat important legislation. The insurgents in Congress eventually restricted the speaker's powers, but they never forgave what they saw as Taft's betrayal.

The tariff also alienated progressives from Taft. For decades, the Republican party had supported high tariffs to protect American industry from European competition, thereby promoting industrial growth but often allowing favored industries to garner high profits. While Democrats had generally favored lower tariffs, by the early twentieth century many Midwestern Republicans had also begun to advocate tariff reduction, some as a means to trim the power of big business, others as a way to curb a troublesome inflation. In 1908 Taft had campaigned for a lower tariff, and he summoned a special session of Congress to deal with the issue in 1909. But when Midwestern Republicans introduced tariff reform legislation, the president failed to support them, and Aldrich's Senate committee added 847 amendments, many of which raised tariff rates. Taft justified his inaction as avoiding presidential interference with congressional business, but his limited notion of presidential authority clashed with TR's example and the reformers' expectations. To save face, Taft tried to portray the Payne-Aldrich Tariff of 1909 as a major reform, further antagonizing progressives, who concluded that Taft had sided with the Old Guard against real change.

That perception solidified when Taft stumbled into a third political controversy, this one over conservation. Gifford Pinchot had become embroiled in a complex struggle over natural resources management with Richard Ballinger, Taft's secretary of the interior. Ballinger, a Seattle attorney closely tied to Western mining and lumbering interests, favored more private development of public lands than Pinchot did. When Pinchot challenged Ballinger's role in a questionable sale of public coal lands in Alaska to a J.P. Morgan syndicate, Taft upheld Ballinger and fired Pinchot. Despite the political implications, Taft insisted upon viewing the matter simply as an administrative issue: By attacking a cabinet secretary, Pinchot had violated the rule of direct-line authority. Indeed, Taft actually objected to Pinchot's methods more than his objectives. He had opposed the way Roosevelt and Pinchot had earlier used executive orders to circumvent Congress and now believed that Pinchot was "quite willing to camp outside the law to accomplish his beneficent programs." Moreover, hostile to media politics, Taft condemned Pinchot for running a "publicity machine" to criticize Ballinger. "We have a government of limited powers under the Constitution," Taft maintained, "and we have got to work out our problems on the basis of law. Now, if that is reactionary, then I am a reactionary." Nevertheless, progressives concluded that Taft had repudiated Roosevelt's conservation policies.

Progressives determined to replace Taft, whom they now saw as an obstacle to reform and denounced with increasing vigor. Stung by what he saw as unfair criticism, Taft responded in kind, criticizing the insurgent Republicans as "cantankerous, vicious, malignant . . . demagogues." In 1911, the National Progressive League organized to champion La Follette for the Republican nomination in 1912. Roosevelt rejected an appeal for support, convinced that a challenge to the incumbent president was both doomed and divisive. Besides, his own position was closer to Taft's than to what he called "the La Follette type of fool radicalism." But

Taft's political blunders increasingly angered Roosevelt. Condemning Taft as "disloyal to our past friendship . . . [and] to every canon of ordinary decency," TR began to campaign for the Republican nomination himself. With the party machinery controlled by the president, Roosevelt's supporters used primary elections to boost his chances. In thirteen state primaries, he won 278 delegates to only 46 for Taft. But most states did not then have primaries; that allowed Taft to dominate the Republican convention and win renomination. Roosevelt forces promptly formed a third party—the Progressive party—and nominated the former president. The Republican split almost guaranteed victory for the Democratic nominee, Woodrow Wilson.

WOODROW WILSON AND PROGRESSIVE REFORM

The growing pressures for reform called forth many new leaders. The one who would preside over progressivism's culmination, and ultimately its collapse, was Woodrow Wilson. Elected president in 1912 and 1916, he built upon previous progressive efforts and mediated among differing progressive views to achieve a strong reform program, further enlarge the power of the executive branch, and make the White House the center of national politics.

The Election of 1912

Despite the prominence of Roosevelt and La Follette, progressivism was not simply a Republican phenomenon. In Congress, Southern Democrats more consistently supported reform measures than Republicans did, and Democratic leader William Jennings Bryan surpassed Roosevelt as a persistent advocate of significant political and economic reform. As the Republicans quarrelled during Taft's administration, Democrats pushed progressive remedies and achieved major victories in the state and congressional elections of 1910. To improve the party's chances in 1912, Bryan announced he would step aside for new leadership. The Democratic spotlight shifted to the newly elected governor of New Jersey, Woodrow Wilson.

Born in Virginia as the son and grandson of Presbyterian ministers, Wilson combined a public eloquence that captured the imagination of millions with a cold personality that could repel even allies; he balanced a self-righteousness that led to stubborn inflexibility with an intense ambition that permitted the most expedient compromises. Wilson first entered public life as a conservative, steeped in the limited government traditions of his Southern upbringing and academic training. As president of Princeton University, beginning in 1902, he became a prominent representative of middle-class respectability and conservative causes. In 1910, New Jersey's Democratic bosses selected him for governor to head off the progressives, but, once in office, Wilson championed popular reforms and immediately began to campaign as a progressive for the party's 1912 presidential nomination.

Yet Wilson's progressivism differed from that of Roosevelt in 1912. TR remained committed to his presidential program, emphasizing a strong government that would regulate the new industrial society to promote economic and social order. He defended big business as inevitable and healthy provided that government control ensured that it would benefit the entire nation. Roosevelt called this program the **New Nationalism**, reflecting his belief in a powerful state and an overarching national interest. He also supported demands for popular issues of social welfare, including workers' compensation and the abolition of child labor.

Wilson was horrified by Roosevelt's vision. His **New Freedom** program rejected what he called TR's "regulated monopoly." Wilson wanted "regulated competition," with government's role limited to breaking up monopolies through antitrust action and preventing artificial barriers like tariffs from blocking free enterprise. Wilson opposed social welfare legislation as "paternalistic," reaching beyond the proper scope of the federal government, which he hoped to minimize. (This position, shot back the alarmed Roosevelt, meant the repeal of "every law for the promotion of social and industrial justice.")

Roosevelt's stance on social legislation attracted many women into political action. As Jane Addams observed, "their long concern for the human wreckage of industry has come to be considered politics." (See "American Views: Jane Addams and the Progressive Party.") The Progressive party also endorsed woman suffrage, accepted women as convention delegates, and pledged to assure women equal representation on party committees. The *New York Times* exaggerated in claiming that the 1912 campaign had become "feminized," but certainly women activists welcomed the opportunity of participating "in party affairs before the vote is won" and thereby "answering forcibly many of the objections to the vote" for women.

Of course, not all women supported Roosevelt and his Progressive party. His politics, like his presidency, were intensely personal and often opportunistic, and some progressives did not believe he was now sincere in demanding social reform. Said Jane Addams' friend, Anna Howard Shaw: "I wish I could believe he intended to do a single honest thing or that he would carry out a single plank in the platform if he were elected. . . . I cannot."

Unable to add progressive Democrats to the Republicans who followed him into the Progressive party, TR could not win despite his personal popularity. Other reform voters embraced the Socialist candidate, Eugene Debs. Calling for significant economic and political change, from government ownership of banks and railroads to restrictions on judicial power, Debs captured 900,000 votes—6 percent of the total, the Socialists' highest proportion of national votes ever. Taft, although now convinced that his former friend TR had become a "freak" unfit for public trust or office, played a small role in the campaign. "I might as well

---

AMERICAN VIEWS

Jane Addams and the Progressive Party

Jane Addams, the founder of Hull House in Chicago, was active not merely in a range of social reform movements but also in nearly all facets of progressive politics as well. An ardent suffragist, Addams seconded the presidential nomination of Theodore Roosevelt at the founding convention of the Progressive party in 1912, while a "Jane Addams Chorus" sang "Onward, Christian Soldiers" and "The Battle Hymn of the Republic." In this reminiscence from her second autobiography, Addams describes that convention and her part in the party's campaign of that year.

Why did settlement workers like Addams see the Progressive party as the climax to their struggle for social justice?

How did Addams's political interests fit into Roosevelt's program of the New Nationalism?

How does Addams's rhetoric reflect the moral impulses underlying much of progressive reform?

Why does Addams believe that women were attracted to the Progressive party?

It was in August, 1912, that the Progressive Party was organized.

Suddenly, as if by magic, the city of Chicago became filled with men and women from every state in the Union who were evidently haunted by the same social compunctions and animated by like hopes; they revealed to each other mutual sympathies and memories. They urged methods which had already been tried in other countries, for righting old wrongs and for establishing standards in industry. For three days together they defined their purposes and harmonized their wills into gigantic cooperation. . . .

They believed that the program of social legislation placed before the country by the Progressive Party was of great significance to the average voter quite irrespective of the party which might finally claim his allegiance.

The platform, in the hope that the political organization of the nation might never again get so far away from the life of the people, advocated equal suffrage, direct primaries, the initiative and referendum. . . . In spite of our belief in our leader [Theodore Roosevelt], I was there, and I think the same was true of many others, because the platform expressed the social hopes so long ignored by the politicians; although we appreciated to the full our good fortune in securing on their behalf the magnetic personality of the distinguished candidate. Perhaps we felt so keenly the uplifting sense of comradeship with old friends and coworkers not only because we had all realized how inadequate we were in small groups but because the very sentiments of compassion and desire for social justice were futile unless they could at last find expression as an integral part of . . . government. At any rate, it was evident that measures of industrial amelioration and demands for social justice, so long discussed by small groups, were at last thrust into the stern arena of political action. . . .

The Progressive Convention has been described many times, and perhaps never quite adequately. It was a curious moment of release from inhibitions, and it did not seem in the least strange that reticent men and women should speak aloud of their religious and social beliefs, confident that they would be understood. . . .

The women who identified themselves with the Progressive Convention inevitably experienced moments of heart searching and compunction. It is hard to understand it now, after we have possessed the ballot for a decade and have come to deem it a virtue "to enter politics," but at the moment we felt it necessary to give to the public our reasons for thus identifying ourselves with a political party. We said that when a great party pledges itself to the protection of children, to the care of the aged, to the relief of overworked girls, to the safeguarding of burdened men, it is inevitable that it should appeal to women and should seek to draw upon the great reservoir of their moral energy so long undesired and unutilized in practical politics; that one is the corollary of the other; a program of human welfare, the necessity for women's participation. . . .

The real interest in the measures advocated in the party platform came however during the campaign itself when it was possible to place them before many groups throughout the country. Sometimes the planks in our platform were sharply challenged, but more often regarded with approval and occasionally with enthusiasm. I recall a meeting in Leadville, Colorado, made up altogether of miners who were much surprised to find that politics had anything to do with such affairs. They had always supposed that hours of labor were matters to be fought for and not voted upon. It was very exhilarating to talk to them, and it seemed to me that I had never before realized how slow we had been to place the definite interests of the workingmen in such shape that they could be voted upon. As a campaign speaker I was sent from town to town in both Dakotas, in Iowa, Nebraska, Oklahoma, Colorado, Kansas, and Missouri. The comradeship which a like-minded group always affords, combined with the heartiness of western good will, kept my spirits at high tide in spite of the fatigue of incessant speaking. . . .

The campaign renewed one's convictions that if the community as a whole were better informed as to the ethical implications of industrial wrongs whole areas of life could be saved from becoming brutalized or from sinking into hard indifference. . . . At moments we believed that we were witnessing a new pioneering of the human spirit, that we were in all humility inaugurating an exploration into the moral resources of our fellow citizens.

Source: Jane Addams, *The Second Twenty Years at Hull-House.* (New York: The Macmillan Company, 1930.)

give up as far as being a candidate," he lamented. "There are so many people in the country who don't like me."

Wilson won an easy electoral college victory, though he received only 42 percent of the popular vote and fewer popular votes than Bryan had won in any of his three campaigns (see Map 3-3). Roosevelt came in second, Taft third. The disruption of the GOP also enabled

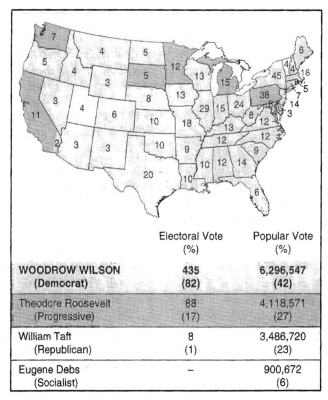

	Electoral Vote (%)	Popular Vote (%)
WOODROW WILSON (Democrat)	**435** **(82)**	**6,296,547** **(42)**
Theodore Roosevelt (Progressive)	88 (17)	4,118,571 (27)
William Taft (Republican)	8 (1)	3,486,720 (23)
Eugene Debs (Socialist)	–	900,672 (6)

MAP 3-3   The Election of 1912
The split within the Republican party enabled Woodrow Wilson to carry most states and become president even though he won only a minority of the popular vote.

the Democrats to gain control of Congress, giving Wilson the opportunity to enact his New Freedom program.

Implementing the New Freedom

As president, Wilson built on Roosevelt's precedent to strengthen executive authority. Recognizing the importance of the press, he instituted semiweekly news conferences, appointed a press secretary, and asked journalists to join him in a "partnership" in running the government. Yet Wilson was no more comfortable with reporters than Taft had been and while trying to control them for his own purposes was otherwise so evasive that one journalist concluded that "it was impossible to rely on anything he said. . . . He took such an intellectual pleasure in stating a thing so as to give the opposite impression to the fact . . . that one had to be constantly on the alert to keep from being misled." Thus although in the beginning Wilson effectively used the press to promote his program, he was eventually less able to do so, even in 1918 when he most needed to influence public opinion.

Wilson was more successful in bending the government to his will. He summoned Congress into special session in 1913 and delivered his message in person, the first president to do so since John Adams. Wilson proposed a full legislative program and worked forcefully to secure its approval, holding Congress in session for a year and a half—the longest session in history. He held regular conferences with Democratic leaders and had a private telephone line installed between the Capitol and the White House to keep tabs on congressional actions. When necessary to move Congress, he appealed to the public for support, ruthlessly used patronage, or compromised with conservatives. (One of Wilson's own cabinet members described him as "a man of high ideals but no principles.") "This Congress has a President on its back, driving it pitilessly," commented the *New York Times*. "Never were Congressmen driven so." With such methods and a solid Democratic majority, Wilson gained approval of important laws.

Wilson turned first to the traditional Democratic goal of reducing the high protective tariff, the symbol of special privileges for industry. "The object of the tariff duties henceforth laid," he announced, "must be effective competition." He forced through the **Underwood-Simmons Tariff Act** of 1913, the first substantial reduction in duties since before the Civil War. The act also levied the first income tax under the recently ratified Sixteenth Amendment. Conservatives condemned the "revolutionary" tax, but it was designed not to redistribute income but simply to compensate for lower tariff rates. The top tax rate paid by the wealthiest was a mere 7 percent. The greater importance of the income tax was its potential for expanding national authority.

Wilson next reformed the nation's banking and currency system, which was inadequate for a modernizing economy. The 1907 panic and a subsequent congressional investigation had dramatized the need for a more flexible and decentralized financial system. Wilson skillfully maneuvered a compromise measure through Congress, balancing the demands of agrarian progressives for government control with the bankers' desires for private control. The **Federal Reserve Act** of 1913 created twelve regional Federal Reserve Banks that, although privately controlled, were to be supervised by the Federal Reserve Board, appointed by the president. The law also provided for a flexible national currency and improved access to credit. Serious problems remained, but the new system promoted the progressive goals of order and efficiency and fulfilled Wilson's New Freedom principle of introducing limited government regulation in the public interest while preserving private business control.

Wilson's third objective in implementing the New Freedom was new antitrust legislation to fulfill his campaign pledge to break up monopolies. To this end, he initially supported the Clayton antitrust bill, which prohibited unfair trade practices and sharply restricted holding companies. But when business leaders and other progressives strenuously objected, Wilson reversed himself. Some protested the disruption of big business and its presumed benefits; others argued that it would be impossible to draft legislation anticipating every possible restraint of trade. Opting for continuous federal regulation rather than for the dissolution of trusts, Wilson endorsed the creation of the **Federal Trade Commission (FTC)** to oversee business activity and prevent illegal restrictions on competition.

The Federal Trade Commission Act of 1914 dismayed many of Wilson's early supporters because it departed from New Freedom concepts to embrace the New Nationalism's emphasis on positive regulation. Roosevelt's 1912 platform had proposed a federal trade commission; Wilson now accepted what he had earlier denounced as a partnership between trusts and the government that the trusts would dominate. Indeed, Wilson's conservative appointments to the FTC ensured that the agency would not seriously interfere with business, and by the 1920s the FTC had virtually become a junior partner of the business community.

The fate of the Clayton antitrust bill after Wilson withdrew his support reflected his new attitude toward big business. Congressional conservatives gutted the bill with crippling amendments before permitting it to become law in 1914. As one senator complained, "when the Clayton bill was first written, it was a raging lion with a mouth full of teeth. It has degenerated to a tabby cat with soft gums, a plaintive mew, and an anemic appearance. It is a sort of legislative apology to the trusts, delivered hat in hand, and accompanied by assurances that no discourtesy is intended."

The Clayton Act was also disappointing for labor. The AFL had continued its campaign against injunctions, with Gompers insisting that "popular government, democratic institutions, cannot exist together with the unlimited discretionary power of either a king or a judge."

A portrait of Woodrow Wilson by Edward Charles Tarbell. A strong president, Wilson led Congress to enact sweeping and significant legislation.

Although Wilson himself had little sympathy, the 1912 Democratic platform had reiterated the party's support for labor's goals, and under pressure he reluctantly added provisions to the Clayton bill seeming to exempt unions from antitrust prosecutions and to prohibit courts from issuing injunctions against workers peacefully engaged in meeting, picketing, striking, or boycotting. Gompers lauded the Clayton Act as labor's magna charta, but it actually added little substantive protection for unions and its ambiguous language ironically increased judges' discretionary authority to interpret legal constraints on union rights. As one observer concluded, the Clayton Act was designed to "please labor and yet make no change in the law." And, indeed, judges continued regularly to issue anti-union injunctions.

These measures of 1913–1914 indicate the limited nature of Wilson's vision of reform. In fact, he now announced that no further reforms were necessary—astonishing many progressives whose objectives had been completely ignored. Wilson refused to support woman suffrage and helped kill legislation abolishing child labor and expanding credits to farmers. And he seemed to undercut some of his own achievements when he appointed conservatives and corporate representatives to the new regulatory bodies ("a more reactionary Federal Reserve Board could not have been found with a fine-tooth comb," complained one Midwestern insurgent Republican).

Race relations provided a flagrant instance of Wilson's indifference to social justice issues. Raised in the South, he believed in segregation and backed the Southern Democrats in his cabinet when they introduced formal segregation within the government itself. Government offices, shops, restrooms, and restaurants were all segregated; employees who complained were fired. "When the Wilson Administration came into power," mourned one black editor, "it promised a 'new freedom' to all people, avowing the spirit of Christian Democracy. But on the contrary we are given a stone instead of a loaf of bread; we are given a hissing serpent rather than a fish." Federal officials in the South discharged black employees wholesale. One Georgia official promised there would be no more government jobs for African Americans: "A Negro's place is in the cornfield."

Surveying Wilson's course, the progressive journalist Herbert Croly expressed bewilderment: Wilson could not have concluded that all necessary reforms had been achieved "unless he had utterly misconceived the meaning and the task of American progressivism. . . . [Anyone] who seriously asserts that the fundamental wrongs of modern society can be easily and quickly righted as a consequence of a few laws passed . . . [by] a single Congress, casts suspicion either upon his own sincerity or upon his grasp of the realities of modern social and industrial life."

The Expansion of Reform

Wilson and the Democrats had won in 1912 only because the Republicans had split. In the 1914 elections the Democrats' majority in the House of Representatives was sharply reduced from 147 to 25. By 1916, Roosevelt had returned to the GOP, and Wilson realized that he had to attract some of TR's former followers. Wilson therefore abandoned his opposition to social and economic reforms aiding specific groups and promoted measures he had previously condemned as paternalistic and unconstitutional. But more than political expediency shaped Wilson's new course. He had also grown in the White House and now recognized that some problems could be resolved only by positive federal action. "Old political formulas," he said, "do not fit the present."

To assist farmers, Wilson convinced Congress to pass the Federal Farm Loan Act. This law, which Wilson himself had earlier rejected twice, provided federally financed, long-term agricultural credits. The Warehouse Act of 1916 improved short-term agricultural credit. The Highway Act of 1916 provided funds to construct and improve rural roads through the adoption of the "dollar-matching" principle by which the federal government would expand its power over state activities in the twentieth century.

Wilson and the Democratic Congress also reached out to labor. Reversing his earlier opposition to a child-labor law, Wilson now warned reluctant Southern Democrats that the party's electoral fortunes depended upon passing such a law, and he secured the enactment of the Keating-Owen Act prohibiting the interstate shipment of products made by child labor. In 1902, Wilson had denounced Roosevelt's intervention in the coal strike, but in 1916 he broke a labor-management impasse and averted a railroad strike by helping pass the Adamson Act establishing an eight-hour day for railway workers. Wilson also pushed the Kern-McGillicuddy Act, which achieved the progressive goal of a workers' compensation system for federal employees. Together, these laws marked an important advance toward government regulation of the labor market, and they helped consolidate labor support for the Democratic party.

Wilson also moved toward winning progressive support and promoting activist government when he nominated Louis Brandeis to the Supreme Court. Known as the "people's lawyer," Brandeis had successfully defended protective labor legislation before the conservative judiciary. The prospect that he would now join the bench outraged conservatives, including William Howard Taft, who denounced him as "a muckraker, an emotionalist . . . , a socialist." Brandeis was the first Jew nominated to the court, and anti-Semitism motivated some of his opponents. Wilson overcame a vicious campaign against Brandeis and secured his confirmation. The appointment of Brandeis, declared one reformer, "tends to restore faith in President Wilson."

By these actions, Wilson brought progressivism to a culmination of sorts and consolidated reformers behind him for a second term. Less than a decade earlier, Wilson the private citizen had assailed government regulation and social legislation; by 1916, he had guided an unprecedented expansion of federal power. His own transformation symbolized the development of progressivism itself.

CONCLUSION

The early twentieth century was a time of political ferment, as progressive reformers attempted to transform their government and the meaning of political participation. The creation of new agencies and political techniques indicated their creativity; campaigns to end political corruption, whether seen in urban machines or corporate influence, suggested their optimism; conflicts over the proper regulatory role of government revealed their own disagreements as well as the contrasting views of their opponents; dynamic leaders, both shaping and following public opinion, showed how perceptions of personal, partisan, and national interests could be conflated.

Progressive politics had its ironies and paradoxes. It called for democratic reforms—and did achieve woman suffrage, direct legislation, and popular election of senators—but helped disfranchise Southern blacks and Northern immigrants. It demanded responsive government but helped create bureaucracies and administrative agencies largely removed from popular control. It endorsed the regulation of business in the public interest but forged regulatory laws and commissions that tended to aid business. Some of the seeming contradictions reflected the persistent influence of traditional political attitudes and the necessity to accommodate conservative opponents; others revealed the progressives' own limitations in vision, concern, or nerve.

But both the successes and failures of progressivism revealed that the nature of politics and government had changed significantly. Americans had come to accept the principle that government action could resolve social and economic problems, and the role and power of government expanded accordingly. The emergence of an activist presidency, capable of developing programs, mobilizing public opinion, directing Congress, and taking forceful action, epitomized this key development.

These important features would be crucial when the nation became involved in World War I, which brought new challenges and dangers to the United States. The Great War would expose many of the limitations of progressivism and the naiveté of the progressives' optimism.

Review Questions

1. Why did the demand for woman suffrage provoke such determined support and such bitter opposition, as illustrated by the 1913 parade and riot in Washington, DC.?

2. How and why did the presidency change during the Progressive Era?

3. How did the progressive concern for efficiency affect government administration and electoral politics?

4. How and why did the relationship between business and government change during this time?

5. How did the role of women in politics change during the Progressive Era? How did that affect progressivism itself?

Key Terms

Australian ballot *68*

Bureau of Reclamation *76*

Conservation *74*

Federal Reserve Act *91*

Federal Trade Commission (FTC) *91*

Initiative *70*

New Freedom *87*

New Nationalism *87*

Nineteenth Amendment *68*

Preservation *74*

Recall *70*

Referendum *70*

Seventeenth Amendment *70*

Sixteenth Amendment *85*

Underwood-Simmons Tariff Act *91*

Recommended Reading

Kendrick A. Clements, *The Presidency of Woodrow Wilson* (1992). An excellent book that provides important new information on both Wilson and the presidency.

William Deverell and Tom Sitton, *California Progressivism Revisited* (1994). A valuable collection of essays that examines the complex motivations underlying progressivism in California.

Lewis L. Gould, *The Presidency of Theodore Roosevelt* (1991). A balanced and comprehensive account of TR's presidency.

Arthur S. Link and Richard L. McCormick, *Progressivism* (1983). A superb brief analysis of the complexities and scholarly interpretations of progressivism.

Upton Sinclair, *The Jungle* (1906). The most famous muckraking novel.

Robert Wiebe, *The Search for Order, 1877–1920* (1967). A masterful essay that emphasizes the organizational thrust of middle-class progressives.

CREATING AN EMPIRE: 1898-1917

Havana, Cuba

October 1901

When the Spanish-American war was declared the United States took a step forward, and assumed a position as protector of the interests of Cuba. It became responsible for the welfare of the people, politically, mentally, and morally. The mere fact of freeing the island from Spanish rule has not ended the care which this country should give. . . . The effect will be to uplift the people, gaining their permanent friendship and support and greatly increasing our own commerce. At present there are two million people requiring clothing and food, for but a small proportion of the necessaries of life are raised on the island. It is folly to grow food crops when sugar and tobacco produce such rich revenues in comparison. The United States should supply the Cubans with their breadstuffs, even wine, fruit, and vegetables, and should clothe the people. . . . The money received for their crops will be turned over in a great measure in buying supplies from the United States. . . .

Naturally the manufacturers of the United States should have precedence in furnishing machinery, locomotives, cars, and rails, materials for buildings and bridges, and the wide diversity of other supplies required, as well as fuel for their furnaces. With the present financial and commercial uncertainty at an end the people of the island will . . . come into the American market as customers for products of many kinds.

The meeting of the Constitutional Convention on November 5th will be an event in Cuban history of the greatest importance, and much will depend upon the action and outcome of this convention as to our future control of the island. . . . I considered it unwise to interfere, and I have made it a settled policy to permit the Cubans to manage every part of their constitution-making.

This has been due to my desire to prevent any possible charge of crimination being brought against the United States in the direction of their constitutional affairs. . . .

There is no distrust of the United States on the part of the Cubans, and I know of no widespread antipathy to this country, its people, or its institutions. There are, of course, a handful of malcontents, as there must be in every country. . . .

I could not well conceive how the Cubans could be otherwise than grateful to the United States for its efforts in their behalf. The reconstruction of the island has proceeded rapidly from the first, and I think the transformation is without any superior in the history of modern times. The devastation of the long war had left the island in an unparalleled condition when the United States interfered, and in the brief time since the occupation of the island by American troops the island has been completely rehabilitated—agriculturally, commercially, financially, educationally, and governmentally. This improvement has been so rapid and so apparent that no Cuban could mistake it. To doubt in the face of these facts that their liberators were not still their faithful friends would be impossible.

—General Leonard Wood

Major-General Leonard Wood, "The Future of Cuba," *The Independent* 54 (January 23, 1902): 193–194; and Wood, "The Cuban Convention," *The Independent* 52 (November 1, 1900): 265–266.

GENERAL LEONARD WOOD'S reports on Cuba, then under his control as military governor, captured the complex mixture of attitudes and motives that underlay the journey of the United States from a developing nation to a world power. Plans for economic expansion, a belief in national mission, a sense of responsibility to help others, scarcely hidden religious impulses and racist convictions—all combined in an uneasy mixture of self-interest and idealism. Such a variety of motives, to say nothing of the positive spin that Wood could impart to them, helped garner support for the new policies that the nation's leaders adopted, including extending American control over Cuba.

Wood himself had taken a symbolic journey in American expansionism. His earlier career had been on the American Southwestern frontier, with the troops chasing the Apache under Geronimo, but in 1898 he and Theodore Roosevelt formed the Rough Riders cavalry to participate in the Spanish-American War in Cuba. As Wood wrote on the transport ships headed for that Spanish colony: "This is the first great expedition our country has sent overseas and marks the commencement of a new era in our relations with the world." Upon Spain's surrender, Cuba came under United States military occupation, and Wood was appointed military governor of the island.

Wood's support for the war was reflected as well in his activities as a colonial administrator. Convinced of the superiority of American institutions, he favored their expansion. The United States had a responsibility, he believed, to uplift those less able. But expansion would promote American interests as well. Thus, Wood brought improved sanitation, schools, and transportation to Cuba, but he instituted these reforms through an authoritarian government and regarded Cubans as backward and incapable of self-government. And at the same time, he expected that American business interests would "naturally" be the beneficiaries of his reorganization of Cuban life. Thus Wood combined changes that satisfied paternalistic or humanitarian instincts with attempts to incorporate Cuba into America's new commercial empire, fulfilling the traditional colonial role of providing raw materials and serving as a market for American products and capital.

The tension between what one friend called the "righteous" and the "selfish" aspects of expanding American influence lay beneath the surface in Wood's reports. His claim that he

• CHRONOLOGY •

1887	United States gains naval rights to Pearl Harbor.		1904	United States acquires the Panama Canal Zone.
1890	Alfred Thayer Mahan publishes *The Influence of Sea Power upon History.*			Roosevelt Corollary is announced.
1893	Harrison signs but Cleveland rejects a treaty for the annexation of Hawaii.		1904–1905	Russo-Japanese War is fought.
1893–1897	Depression increases interest in economic expansion abroad.		1905	Treaty of Portsmouth ends the Russo-Japanese War through U.S. mediation.
1894–1895	Sino-Japanese War is fought.		1906	U.S. participates in Algeiras Conference.
1895	U.S. intervenes in Great Britain-Venezuelan boundary dispute.		1906–1909	United States occupies Cuba.
	Cuban insurrection against Spain begins.		1907–1908	Gentlemen's Agreement restricts Japanese immigration.
1896	William McKinley is elected president on an imperialist platform.		1909	United States intervenes in Nicaragua.
1898	Spanish-American War is fought.		1912–1933	United States occupies Nicaragua.
	Hawaii is annexed.		1914	Panama Canal opens.
	Anti-Imperialist League is organized.		1914–1917	United States intervenes in Mexico.
	Treaty of Paris is signed.		1915–1934	United States occupies Haiti.
1899–1902	Filipino-American War is fought.		1916–1924	United States occupies the Dominican Republic.
1899	Open Door note is issued.		1917	Puerto Ricans are granted U.S. citizenship.
	First Hague Peace Conference		1917–1922	United States occupies Cuba.
1901	Theodore Roosevelt becomes president.			
1903	Platt Amendment restricts Cuban autonomy.			
	Panama "revolution" is abetted by the United States.			

was not interfering with Cuba's constitutional convention was disingenuous, for he had already undertaken to limit those who could participate as voters or delegates and was even then devising means to restrict its autonomy. And in his repeated insistence that the Cubans were "grateful" for the intervention of "their faithful friends," the Americans, Wood obviously protested too much: Cubans, as well as Filipinos, Puerto Ricans, and others, rarely perceived American motives or American actions as positively as did Wood and other proponents of American expansion. Military victory in the Spanish-American War had provided the United States with an extensive empire, status as a world power, and opportunities and problems that would long shape American foreign policy.

KEY TOPICS

Why the United States became an imperial power in the 1890s.

The Spanish-American War and the colonial empire the United States gained as a result.

U.S. involvement in Asia, and the tensions with Japan that resulted.

U.S. predominance in the Caribbean and Latin America.

THE ROOTS OF IMPERIALISM

The United States had a long-established tradition of expansion across the continent. Through purchase, negotiation, or conquest, the vast Louisiana Territory, Florida, Texas, New Mexico, California, and Oregon had become U.S. territory. Indeed, by the 1890s, Republican Senator Henry Cabot Lodge of Massachusetts boasted that Americans had "a record of conquest, colonization, and territorial expansion unequalled by any people in the nineteenth century." Lodge now urged the country to build an overseas empire, emulating the European model of **imperialism** based on the acquisition and exploitation of colonial possessions. Other Americans favored a less formal empire, in which U.S. interests and influence would be assured through extensive trade and investments rather than through military occupation. Still others advocated a cultural expansionism in which the nation exported its ideals and institutions. All such expansionists could draw from many sources to support their plans. Some cited political, religious, and racial ideas; some were concerned with national security and power; others pointed to economic trends at home and abroad (see the Overview table, "Rationales for Imperialism").

Ideological Arguments

Scholars, authors, politicians, and religious leaders provided interlocking ideological arguments for the new imperialism. Some intellectuals, for example, invoked social Darwinism, maintaining that the United States should engage in a competitive struggle for wealth and power with other nations. "The survival of the fittest," declared one writer, was "the law of nations as well as a law of nature." As European nations expanded into Asia and Africa in the 1880s and 1890s, seeking colonies, markets, and raw materials, these advocates argued that the United States had to adopt similar policies to ensure national success.

Related to social Darwinism was a pervasive belief in racial inequality and, particularly, in the superiority of people of English, or Anglo-Saxon, descent. To many Americans, the

••• OVERVIEW •••

RATIONALES FOR IMPERIALISM

CATEGORY	BELIEFS
Racism and social Darwinism	Convictions that "Anglo-Saxons" were racially superior and should dominate other peoples, either to ensure national success, establish international stability, or benefit the "inferior" races by imposing American ideas and institutions on them.
Righteousness	The conviction that Christianity, and a supporting American culture, should be aggressively spread among the benighted peoples of other lands.
Mahanism	The conviction, following the ideas advanced by Alfred Thayer Mahan, that U.S. security required a strong navy and economic and territorial expansion.
Economics	A variety of arguments holding that American prosperity depended on acquiring access to foreign markets, raw materials, and investment opportunities.

industrial progress, military strength, and political development of England and the United States were proof of an Anglo-Saxon superiority that carried with it a responsibility to extend the blessings of their rule to less able people. John Fiske, a philosopher and historian, popularized these ideas in his oft-repeated lecture "Manifest Destiny." "The work which the English race began when it colonized North America," Fiske declaimed, "is destined to go on until every land on the earth's surface that is not already the seat of an old civilization shall become English in its language, in its religion, in its political habits and traditions, and to a predominant extent in the blood of its people." As a popular expression put it, colonialism was the "white man's burden," carrying with it a duty to aid and uplift other peoples. Such attitudes led some expansionists to favor imposing American ideas and practices on other cultures, regardless of those cultures' own values and customs. The political scientist John W. Burgess, for example, concluded that Anglo-Saxons "must have a colonial policy" and "righteously assume sovereignty" over "incompetent" or "barbaric races" in other lands.

Reflecting such aggressiveness, as well as Darwinian anxieties, some Americans endorsed expansion as consistent with their ideals of masculinity. Forceful expansion would be a manly course, relying upon and building strength and honor among American males. Men who would not shirk the challenges of empire would thereby improve their ability to compete in the international arena. "Pride of race, courage, manliness," predicted one enthusiast, would be both the causes and the consequences of assertive foreign policies.

American missionaries also promoted expansionist sentiment. Hoping to evangelize the world, American religious groups increased the number of Protestant foreign missions sixfold from 1870 to 1900. Women in particular organized foreign missionary societies and served in the missions. Missionaries publicized their activities throughout the United States, generating interest in foreign developments and support for what one writer called the "imperialism of righteousness." Abroad they pursued a religious transformation that often resembled a cultural conversion, for they promoted trade, developed business interests, and encouraged Westernization through technology and education as well as religion. Sometimes, as in the Hawaiian Islands, American missionaries even promoted annexation by the United States.

Indeed, the American religious press endlessly repeated the themes of national destiny, racial superiority, and religious zeal. The Reverend J. H. Barrows in early 1898 lectured on the "Christian conquest of Asia," suggesting that American Christianity and commerce would cross the Pacific to fulfill "the manifest destiny of the Christian Republic." Missionaries also contributed to the imperial impulse by describing their work, as Barrows did, in terms of the "conquest" of "enemy" territory. Thus, while missionaries were motivated by what they considered to be idealism and often brought real benefits to other lands, especially in education and health, religious sentiments reinforced the ideology of American expansion.

Strategic Concerns

Other expansionists were motivated by strategic concerns, shaped by what they saw as the forces of history and geography. America's location in the Western Hemisphere, its coastlines on two oceans, and the ambitions and activities of other nations, particularly Germany and Britain, convinced some Americans that the United States had to develop new policies to protect and promote its national security and interests. Alfred Thayer Mahan, a naval officer and president of the Naval War College, emphasized the importance of a strong navy for national greatness in his book *The Influence of Sea Power upon History*. To complement that navy, Mahan proposed that the United States build a canal across the isthmus of Panama to link its coasts, acquire naval bases in the Caribbean and the Pacific to protect the canal, and annex Hawaii and other Pacific islands to promote trade and service the fleet. The United States must "cast aside the policy of isolation which befitted her infancy," Mahan declared, and "begin to look outward."

Mahanism found a receptive audience, particularly among a group of nationalistic Republicans, predominantly from the Northeast. They included politicians like Henry Cabot Lodge and Theodore Roosevelt, journalists like Whitelaw Reid of the *New York Tribune* and Albert Shaw of the *Review of Reviews*, and diplomats and lawyers like John Hay and Elihu Root.

Conscious of European colonialism, such men favored imperial expansion, as Shaw wrote, "for the sake of our destiny, our dignity, our influence, and our usefulness." Roosevelt promoted Mahan's ideas when he became assistant secretary of the navy in 1897, but he was even more militaristic. Praising "the most valuable of all qualities, the soldierly virtues," Roosevelt declared in 1897: "No triumph of peace is quite so great as the supreme triumphs of war." One British observer concluded on the eve of the Spanish-American War that Mahan's influence had transformed the American spirit, serving "as oil to the flame of 'colonial expansion' everywhere leaping into life" (see American Views, "An Imperialist Views the World").

Even so, Mahan was not solely responsible for the large navy policy popular among imperialists. Its origins went back to 1881, when Congress established the Naval Advisory Board, which successfully lobbied for larger naval appropriations. An extensive program to replace the navy's obsolete wooden ships with modern cruisers and battleships was well under way by 1890 when the first volume of Mahan's book appeared. The United States soon possessed the formidable navy the expansionists wanted. This larger navy, in turn, demanded strategic bases and coaling stations. One writer indicated the circular nature of this development by noting in 1893 that Manifest Destiny now meant "the acquisition of such territory, far and near," that would secure "to our navy facilities desirable for the operations of a great naval power."

Economic Designs

One reason for the widespread support for a larger navy was its use to expand and protect America's international trade. Nearly all Americans favored economic expansion through foreign trade. Such a policy promised national prosperity: larger markets for manufacturers and farmers, greater profits for merchants and bankers, more jobs for workers. Far fewer favored the acquisition of colonies that was characteristic of European imperialism. Commercial, as opposed to colonial, goals were the primary objective. As one diplomat declared in 1890, the nation was more interested in the "annexation of trade" than in the annexation of territory.

The United States had long aggressively fostered American trade, especially in Latin America and East Asia. As early as 1844, the United States had negotiated a trade treaty with China, and ten years later a squadron under Commodore Matthew Perry had forced the Japanese to open their ports to American products. The dramatic expansion of the economy in the late nineteenth and early twentieth centuries caused many Americans to favor more government action to open foreign markets to American exports. Alabama Senator John Morgan had the cotton and textiles produced in the New South in mind when he warned: "Our home market is not equal to the demands of our producing and manufacturing classes and to the capital which is seeking employment. . . . We must either enlarge the field of our traffic, or stop the business of manufacturing just where it is." Woodrow Wilson echoed this persistent concern when he declared in 1912, "Our industries have expanded to such a point that they will burst their jackets if they cannot find a free outlet to the markets of the world. Our domestic markets no longer suffice. We need foreign markets."

Exports, particularly of manufactured goods, did increase greatly in the late nineteenth and early twentieth centuries. Still, periodic depressions fed these fears of overproduction. The massive unemployment and social unrest that accompanied these economic crises also provided social and political arguments for economic relief through foreign trade.

AMERICAN VIEWS

An Imperialist Views the World

Theodore Roosevelt, Henry Cabot Lodge, Alfred Thayer Mahan, and other influential imperialists frequently corresponded with one another, expressing their views forcefully if not always in depth. The following excerpts are from Roosevelt's private correspondence in 1897 while he was assistant secretary of the Navy and before the Spanish-American War began.

> In what ways does Roosevelt reflect the influence of Mahan?
>
> What is Roosevelt's view of war?
>
> How does Roosevelt view European nations?
>
> How does he view the independence of other nations in the Western Hemisphere?

I suppose that I need not tell you that as regards Hawaii I take your views absolutely, as indeed I do on foreign policy generally. If I had my way we would annex those islands tomorrow. If that is impossible I would establish a protectorate over them. I believe we should build the Nicaraguan canal at once, and in the meantime that we should build a dozen new battleships, half of them on the Pacific Coast; and these battleships should have a large coal capacity and a consequent increased radius of action. . . . I think President Cleveland's action [in rejecting the annexation of Hawaii] was a colossal crime, and we should be guilty of aiding him after the fact if we do not reverse what he did. I earnestly hope we can make the President [McKinley] look at things our way. Last Saturday night Lodge pressed his views upon him with all his strength.

I agree with all you say as to what will be the result if we fail to take Hawaii. It will show that we either have lost, or else wholly lack, the masterful instinct which alone can make a race great. I feel so deeply about it I hardly dare express myself in full. The terrible part is to see that it is the men of education who take the lead in trying to make us prove traitors to our race.

I fully realize the importance of the Pacific coast. . . . But there are big problems in the West Indies also. Until we definitely turn Spain out of those islands (and if I had my way that would be done tomorrow), we will always be menaced by trouble there. We should acquire the Danish Islands [in the West Indies], and by turning Spain out should serve notice that no strong European power, and especially not Germany, should be allowed to gain a foothold by supplanting some weak European power. I do not fear England; Canada is a hostage for her good behavior.

I wish we had a perfectly consistent foreign policy, and that this policy was that every European power should be driven out of America, and every foot of American soil, including the nearest islands in both the Pacific and the Atlantic, should be in the hands of independent American states, and so far as possible in the possession of the United States or under its protection.

To speak with a frankness which our timid friends would call brutal, I would regard a war with Spain from two standpoints: first, the advisability on the grounds both of humanity and self-interest of interfering on behalf of the Cubans, and of taking one more step toward the complete freeing of America from European dominion; second, the benefit done our people by giving them something to think of which isn't material gain, and especially the benefit done our military forces by trying both the Navy and the Army in actual practice. I should be very sorry not to see us make the experiment of trying to land, and therefore feed and clothe, an expeditionary force [on Cuba], if only for the sake of learning from our own blunders. I should hope that the force would have some fighting to do. It would be a great lesson, and we would profit much by it.

I wish there was a chance that the [U.S. battleship] *Maine* was going to be used against some foreign power; by preference Germany—but I am not particular, and I'd take even Spain if nothing better offered.

Source: The Letters of Theodore Roosevelt, ed. Elting E. Morison, (Cambridge, MA: Harvard University Press, 1951), Volume I.

In the depression of the 1890s, with the secretary of state seeing "symptoms of revolution" in the Pullman strike and Coxey's Army of unemployed workers (see Chapter 1), this interest in foreign trade became obsessive. More systematic government efforts to promote trade seemed necessary, a conclusion strengthened by new threats to existing American markets. In that tumultuous decade, European nations raised tariff barriers against American products, and Japan and the European imperial powers began to restrict commercial opportunities in the areas of China that they controlled. Many American leaders decided that the United States had to adopt decisive new policies or face economic catastrophe.

First Steps

Despite the growing ideological, strategic, and economic arguments for imperialism, the government interested itself only fitfully in foreign affairs before the mid-1890s. It did not pursue a policy of isolationism from international affairs, for the nation maintained normal diplomatic and trade ties and at times vigorously intervened in Latin America and East Asia. But U.S. officials were remarkably unconcerned with Europe (one secretary of state declared in 1885 that he had no interest in European affairs, which he regarded "with impatience and contempt"), and they were wholly indifferent to Africa, which the European powers were then carving up into colonies. Moreover, the government often deferred to the initiative of private interests, reacted haphazardly to outside events, and did little to create a professional foreign service. In short, much of American foreign policy remained undeveloped, sporadic, and impulsive.

American actions toward Hawaii, a key way station in the China trade, illustrated this situation. Although ruled by native monarchs, the islands came increasingly under U.S. influence as Americans arrived to establish sugar plantations and dominate the economy. Treaties in 1875 and 1887 integrated the islands into the American economy and gave the United States control over Pearl Harbor on the island of Oahu. In 1893 the American planters overthrew the queen and sought annexation to the United States. John Stevens, the American minister, ordered U.S. Marines to help the rebels, declared an American protectorate over the new Hawaii government, and wired Washington: "The Hawaiian pear is now fully ripe, and this is the golden hour for the United States to pluck it." A delegation from the new provisional government, containing no native Hawaiians, went to Washington to draft a treaty for annexation. President Benjamin Harrison signed the pact but could not get Senate approval before the new Grover Cleveland administration took office.

President Cleveland immediately called for an investigation of the whole affair. Soon convinced that "the undoubted sentiment of the people is for the Queen, against the provisional Government, and against annexation," Cleveland apologized to the queen for the "flagrant wrong" done her by the "reprehensible conduct of the American minister and the unauthorized presence on land of a military force of the United States." But the American-dominated provisional government refused to step down, and Cleveland's rejection of annexation set off a noisy, if inconclusive, debate in the United States.

Those who supported annexation saw it as merely part of a larger plan of expansion, the first step toward making the Pacific "an American ocean, dominated by American commercial enterprise for all time." Opponents maintained that the United States should not desert its traditional principles and "venture upon the great colonial system of the European powers."

Though opposed to annexing Hawaii, however, President Cleveland adopted an aggressive policy in Latin America that further excited public opinion over foreign issues. In 1895, he intervened in a boundary dispute between Great Britain and Venezuela over British Guiana. Cleveland was motivated not only by the long-standing U.S. goal of challenging Britain for Latin American markets but also by ever more expansive notions of the **Monroe Doctrine** and the authority of the United States. Secretary of State Richard Olney sent

COASTING.

As other imperial powers look on, the United States abandons its traditional principles to rush headlong into world affairs. Uncle Sam would not always find it a smooth ride.

Britain a blunt note (a "twenty-inch gun," Cleveland called it) demanding arbitration of the disputed territory and stoutly asserting American supremacy in the Western Hemisphere. Cleveland urged Congress to establish a commission to determine the boundary and enforce its decision by war if necessary. The astonished British ambassador reported an "extraordinary state of excitement into which the Congress of the United States and the whole country were thrown by the warlike Message . . . a condition of mind which can only be described as hysterical." As war fever swept the United States, Britain agreed to arbitration, recognizing the limited nature of the issue that so convulsed Anglo-American relations.

The United States' assertion of hemispheric dominance angered Latin Americans, and their fears deepened when the United States decided arbitration terms with Britain without consulting Venezuela, which protested before bowing to American pressure. The United States had intervened less to protect Venezuela from the British bully than to advance its own hegemony. The further significance of the Venezuelan crisis, as Captain Mahan noted, lay in its "awakening of our countrymen to the fact that we must come out of our isolation . . . and take our share in the turmoil of the world."

These bold steps in Hawaii and Venezuela indicated an increasing role for the United States in world affairs, but the nation had yet to adopt a consistent policy for expanding its influence. That would happen in the next few years.

THE SPANISH-AMERICAN WAR

The forces pushing the United States toward imperialism and international power came to a head in the Spanish-American War. The war had its origins in Cuba's quest for independence from the oppressive colonial control of Spain. The struggle activated Americans' long-standing interest in the island. Many sympathized with the Cuban rebels' yearning for freedom; others worried that disorder in Cuba threatened their own economic and political interests; and some thought that United States intervention would increase its influence in the Caribbean and along key Pacific routes to Asian markets. But few foresaw that the war that finally erupted in 1898 would dramatically change America's relationships with the rest of the world and give it a colonial empire.

The Cuban Revolution

In the nineteenth century, Cubans rebelled repeatedly against Spanish rule. One rebellion, the Ten Years' War from 1868 to 1878, had been brutally suppressed, but not before drawing American interest and sympathy. Cuba was the last major European colony in Latin America, with an economic potential that attracted American business interests and a strategic significance for any Central American canal. In the 1880s, Spanish control became increasingly harsh even while American investors expanded their economic influence in Cuba. Cuban discontent erupted again in 1895 when the Cuban patriot José Martí launched another revolt.

The rebellion was a classic guerrilla war in which the rebels controlled the countryside and the Spanish army the towns and cities. American economic interests were seriously affected, for both Cubans and Spaniards destroyed American property and disrupted American trade. The Cleveland administration, motivated as much by a desire to protect American property and establish a safe environment for further investments as by a concern for Cuban rights, urged Spain to adopt reforms. But the brutality with which Spain attempted to suppress the revolt promoted American sympathy for the Cuban insurgents. Determined to cut the rebels off from their peasant supporters, the Spaniards herded most civilians into "reconcentration camps," where tens of thousands died of starvation and disease.

Americans' sympathy was further aroused by the sensationalist **yellow press**. To attract readers and boost advertising revenues, the popular press of the day adopted bold headlines, fevered editorials, and real or exaggerated stories of violence, sex, and corruption. A circulation war between William Randolph Hearst's *New York Journal* and Joseph Pulitzer's *New York World* helped stimulate interest in Cuban war. "Blood on the roadsides, blood on the fields, blood on the doorsteps, blood, blood, blood! The old, the young, the weak, the crippled—all are butchered without mercy," the *World* feverishly reported of Cuba. "Is there no nation wise enough, brave enough to aid this blood-smitten land?" Failure to intervene to protect the innocent from Spanish lust and cruelty, insisted the yellow journalists, would be dishonorable and cowardly.

The nation's religious press, partly because it reflected the prejudice many Protestants held against Catholic Spain, also advocated American intervention. One religious newspaper endorsed an American war against Spain as God's instrument for attacking "that system of iniquity, the papacy." Another promised that if war came, "every Methodist preacher will be a recruiting officer" for the American military. The *Catholic Herald* of New York sarcastically referred to the "bloodthirsty preachers" of the Protestant churches, but such preachers undeniably influenced American opinion against Spain.

As the Cuban rebellion dragged on, more and more Americans advocated intervention to stop the carnage, protect U.S. investments, or uphold various principles. Expansionists like Roosevelt and Lodge clamored for intervention, but so did their opponents. Populists, for example, sympathized with a people seeking independence from colonial rule and petitioned Congress to support the crusade for Cuban freedom; conservative Democrats hoped that the excitement of intervention and war "might do much towards directing the minds of the people from imaginary ills, the relief of which is erroneously supposed to be reached by 'Free Silver.'" In the election of 1896, both major parties endorsed Cuban independence. The Democratic platform expressed "sympathy to the people of Cuba in their heroic struggle for liberty." The Republican platform not only wished Cubans success in "their determined contest for liberty" but urged intervention on the grounds that Spain was "unable to protect the property or lives of resident American citizens."

Growing Tensions

In his 1897 inaugural address, President William McKinley outlined an expansionist program ranging from further enlargement of the navy to the annexation of Hawaii and the construction of a Central American canal in Nicaragua, but his administration soon focused on Cuba. McKinley's principal complaint was that chronic disorder in Cuba disrupted America's investments and agitated public opinion. Personally opposed to military intervention, McKinley first used diplomacy to press Spain to adopt reforms that would settle the rebellion. Following his instructions, the U.S. minister to Spain warned the Spanish government that if it did not quickly establish peace, the United States would take whatever steps it "should deem necessary to procure this result." In late 1897, Spain modified its brutal military tactics and offered limited autonomy to Cuba, but Cubans insisted on complete independence, a demand that Spain refused to grant.

Relations between the United States and Spain deteriorated. In early 1898, the *New York Journal* published a private letter from the Spanish minister to the United States that mocked McKinley as "weak and a bidder for the admiration of the crowd." (The *Journal* called the letter "the worst insult to the United States in its history.") McKinley found more troubling the letter's intimation that Spain was not negotiating in good faith. Only days later, on February 15, 1898, the U.S. battleship *Maine* blew up in Havana harbor, killing 260 men. The Spaniards were not responsible for the tragedy, which a modern naval inquiry has attributed to an internal accident. But many Americans agreed with Theodore Roosevelt, the assistant secretary of the navy, who called it "an act of dirty treachery on the part of the Spaniards" and told McKinley that only war was "compatible with our national honor." Others demanded war, in the words of an Illinois politician, "if we would uphold our manhood." Cried another: "American manhood" required "avenging innocent blood." Thus understandings of appropriate male conduct also influenced decisions as to how the nation should act.

Popular anger was inflamed, but the sinking of the *Maine* by itself did not bring war, though it did restrict McKinley's options and pressure him to be more assertive toward Spain. One newspaper expressed its hope to see "any signs, however faint, of manhood in the White House." Other pressures soon began to build on the president. Increasingly, business interests favored war as less disruptive than a volatile peace that threatened their investments. Senator Lodge reported a consensus "that this situation must end. We cannot go on indefinitely with this strain, this suspense, and this uncertainty, this tottering upon the verge of war. It is killing to business." Further, McKinley feared that a moderate policy would endanger congressional candidates. Again Senator Lodge, although hesitant to suggest "war for political reasons," nevertheless advised McKinley, "If the war in Cuba drags on through the summer with nothing done, we shall go down in the greatest [election] defeat ever known."

At the end of March 1898 (when the French ambassador in Washington reported that "a sort of bellicose fury has seized the American nation"), McKinley sent Spain an ultimatum. He demanded an armistice in Cuba, an end to the reconcentration policy, and the acceptance of American arbitration, which implied Cuban independence. Desperately, Spain made concessions, abolishing reconcentration and declaring a unilateral armistice. But McKinley had already begun war preparations, withdrawing American diplomats from Cuba and Spain, ordering the navy to prepare for war, and drafting a war message for Congress. He submitted that message on April 11, asking for authority to use force against Spain "in the name of humanity, in the name of civilization, in behalf of endangered American interests." Congress declared war on Spain on April 25, 1898.

A few national leaders welcomed the war as a step toward imperialism, but there was little popular support for such a policy. Most interventionists were not imperialists, and Congress added the **Teller Amendment** to the war resolution, disclaiming any intention of annexing Cuba and promising that Cubans would govern themselves. Congress also refused to approve either a canal bill or the annexation of Hawaii. Nevertheless, the Spanish-American War did turn the nation toward imperialism.

War and Empire

The decisive engagement of the war took place not in Cuba but in another Spanish colony, the Philippines, and it involved the favored tool of the expansionists, the new navy (see Map 4-1). In 1897, McKinley had approved plans for an attack on the Philippines in the event of war with Spain. Once war was declared, Commodore George Dewey led the U.S. Asiatic squadron into Manila Bay and destroyed the much weaker Spanish fleet on May 1, 1898. This dramatic victory galvanized expansionist sentiment in the United States. The navy had long coveted Manila Bay as a strategic harbor, but other Americans, casting an eye on commercial opportunities in China, saw a greater significance in the victory. With Dewey's triumph, exulted one expansionist, "We are taking our proper rank among the nations of the world. We are after markets, the greatest markets now existing in the world." To expand this foothold in Asia, McKinley ordered troops to the Philippines, postponing the military expedition to Cuba itself.

Dewey's victory also precipitated the annexation of Hawaii, which had seemed hopeless only weeks before. Annexationists now pointed to the islands' strategic importance as steppingstones to Manila. "To maintain our flag in the Philippines, we must raise our flag in Hawaii," the *New York Sun* contended. McKinley himself privately declared, "We need Hawaii just as much and a good deal more than we did California. It is Manifest Destiny." In July, Congress approved annexation, a decision welcomed by Hawaii's white minority. Natives solemnly protested this step taken "without reference to the consent of the

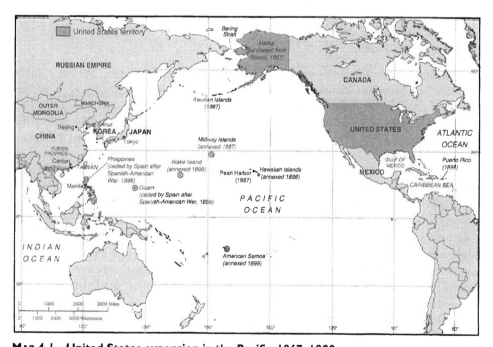

MAP 4-1 United States expansion in the Pacific, 1867–1899
Pursuing visions of a commercial empire in the Pacific, the United States steadily expanded its territorial possessions as well as its influence there in the late nineteenth century.

people of the Hawaiian Islands." Filipinos would soon face the same American imperial impulse.

Military victory also came swiftly in Cuba once the U.S. Army finally landed in late June. Victory depended largely on Spanish ineptitude, for the American army was poorly led, trained, and supplied. Troops had to fight with antiquated weapons and wear wool uniforms in the sweltering tropics. They were issued rotting and poisoned food by a corrupt and inefficient War Department. More than 5,000 Americans died of diseases and accidents brought on by such mismanagement; only 379 were killed in battle. State militias supplemented the small regular army, as did volunteer units, such as the famous Rough Riders, a cavalry unit of cowboys and Eastern dandies assembled by Leonard Wood and Theodore Roosevelt.

While the Rough Riders captured public attention, other units were more effective. The Tenth Negro Cavalry, for example, played the crucial role in capturing San Juan Hill, a battle popularly associated with the Rough Riders. One war correspondent wrote of the black soldiers' charge: "They followed their leaders up the terrible hill from whose crest the desperate Spaniards poured down a deadly fire of shell and musketry. They never faltered. . . . Their aim was splendid, their coolness was superb. . . . The war had not shown greater heroism." Nevertheless, the Rough Riders gained the credit, thanks in part to Roosevelt's self-serving and well-promoted account of the conflict, which one humorist proposed retitling *Alone in Cuba*.

U.S. naval power again proved decisive. In a lopsided battle on July 3, the obsolete Spanish squadron in Cuba was destroyed, isolating the Spanish army and guaranteeing its defeat. U.S. forces then seized the nearby Spanish colony of Puerto Rico without serious opposition. Humbled, Spain signed an armistice ending the war on August 12.

Americans were delighted with their military achievements, but the *Philadelphia Inquirer* cautioned, "With peace will come new responsibilities, which must be met. We have colonies to look after and develop."

The Treaty of Paris

The armistice required Spain to accept Cuban independence, cede Puerto Rico and Guam (a Pacific island between Hawaii and the Philippines), and allow the Americans to occupy Manila pending the final disposition of the Philippines at a formal peace conference. The acquisition of Puerto Rico and Guam indicated the expansionist nature the conflict had assumed for the United States. So did the postponement of the Philippine issue. McKinley knew that delay would permit the advocates of expansion to build public support for annexation. Because the U.S. Army did not capture Manila until after the armistice had been signed, he could not claim the islands by conquest, as Spain pointed out.

McKinley defended his decision to acquire the Philippines with self-righteous imperialist rhetoric, promising to extend Christian influence and American values. But he was motivated primarily by a determination to use the islands to strengthen America's political and commercial position in East Asia (see Map 4-2). Moreover, he believed the Filipinos poorly suited to self-rule, and he feared that Germany or Japan might seize the Philippines if the United States did not. Meeting in Paris in December, American and Spanish negotiators settled the final terms for peace. Spain agreed—despite Filipino demands for independence—to cede the Philippines to the United States.

The decision to acquire the Philippines sparked a dramatic debate over the ratification of the Treaty of Paris. Imperialists invoked the familiar arguments of economic expansion, national destiny, and strategic necessity while asserting that Americans had religious and racial responsibilities to advance civilization by uplifting backward peoples. The *United States*

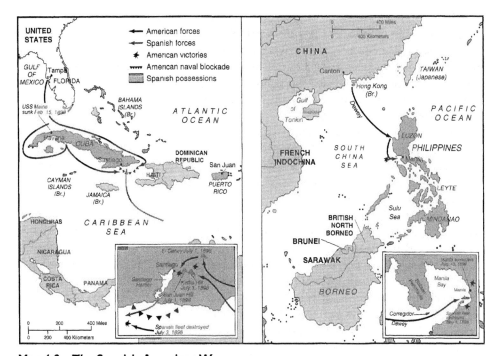

MAP 4-2   The Spanish-American War
The United States gained quick victories in both theaters of the Spanish-American War. Its naval power proved decisive, with Commodore Dewey destroying one enemy fleet in the Philippines and a second U.S. naval force cutting off the Spanish in Cuba.

Investor spoke for business leaders, for example, in demanding the Philippines as "a base of operations in the East" to protect American interests in China; other economic expansionists argued that the Philippines themselves had valuable resources and were a market for American goods or warned that "our commercial rivals in the Orient" would grab the islands if the United States did not. The *Presbyterian Banner* spoke for what it termed a nearly unanimous religious press in affirming "the desirability of America's retaining the Philippines as a duty in the interest of human freedom and Christian progress." The United States, it concluded, was "morally compelled to become an Asiatic power." Conveniently ignoring that most Filipinos were Catholic, the *Baptist Union* insisted: "The conquest by force of arms must be followed up by conquest for Christ." And some imperialists argued that conquering and holding the Philippines as colonies would create among Americans the "physical manhood" and "character of force" presumably necessary in the international Darwinian struggle.

Opponents of the treaty raised profound questions about national goals and ideals. They included such prominent figures as the civil service reformer Carl Schurz, steel baron Andrew Carnegie, social reformer Jane Addams, labor leader Samuel Gompers, and author Mark Twain. Their organizational base was the Anti-Imperialist League, which campaigned against the treaty, distributing pamphlets, petitioning Congress, and holding rallies. League members' criticisms reflected a conviction that imperialism was a repudiation of America's moral and political traditions embodied in the Declaration of Independence. The acquisition of overseas colonies, they argued, conflicted with the nation's commitment to liberty and its claim to moral superiority. They regarded as loathsome and hypocritical the transformation of a war to free Cuba into a campaign for imperial conquest and subjugation.

William Jennings Bryan ridiculed the imperialists' arguments of national destiny: "When the desire to steal becomes uncontrollable in an individual he is declared to be a kleptomaniac and is sent to an asylum; when the desire to grab land becomes uncontrollable in a nation we are told that the 'currents of destiny are flowing through the hearts of men.'" Some African Americans derided the rhetoric of Anglo-Saxon superiority that underlay imperialism and even organized the Black Man's Burden Association to promote Philippine independence.

But other arguments were less high-minded. Many anti-imperialists objected to expansion on the racist grounds that Filipinos were inferior and unassimilable. Gompers feared that cheap Asian labor would undercut the wages and living standards of American workers. The *San Francisco Call*, representing California-Hawaiian sugar interests, also wanted no competition from the Philippines.

The debate over the treaty became bitter. Furious at the opponents of empire, Roosevelt called them "little better than traitors." Carl Schurz responded that McKinley himself had earlier termed territorial annexation through conquest "a criminal act of aggression"; the president's seizure of the Philippines, Puerto Rico, and Hawaii, said Schurz, had perverted a legitimate concern for Cuba into "a war of selfish ambition and conquest."

Finally, on February 6, 1899, the Senate narrowly ratified the treaty. All but two Republicans supported the pact; most Democrats opposed it, although several voted for the treaty after Bryan suggested that approval was necessary to end the war and detach the Philippines from Spain. Thereafter, he hoped, a congressional resolution would give the Filipinos their independence. But by a single vote, the Republicans defeated a Democratic proposal for Philippine independence once a stable government had been established; the United States would keep the islands.

Bryan attempted to make the election of 1900 a referendum on "the paramount issue" of imperialism, promising to free the Philippines if the Democrats won. But other issues determined the outcome. Some of the most ardent anti-imperialists were conservatives who remained loyal to McKinley because they could not tolerate Bryan's economic policies. Republicans also benefited from the prosperity the country experienced under McKinley after the difficult 1890s, and they played on the nationalist emotions evoked by the war, especially by nominating the "hero of San Juan Hill," Theodore Roosevelt, for vice president. "If you choose to vote for America, if you choose to vote for the flag for which we fought," Roosevelt said, "then you will vote to sustain the administration of President McKinley." Bryan lost again, as in 1896, and under Republican leadership, the United States became an imperial nation.

IMPERIAL AMBITIONS: THE UNITED STATES AND EAST ASIA, 1899–1917

In 1899, as the United States occupied its new empire, Assistant Secretary of State John Bassett Moore observed that the nation had become "a world power. . . . Where formerly we had only commercial interests, we now have territorial and political interests as well." American policies to promote those expanded interests focused first on East Asia and Latin America, where the Spanish-American War had provided the United States with both opportunities and challenges. In Asia, the first issue concerned the fate of the Philippines, but looming beyond it were American ambitions in China, where other imperial nations had their own goals.

The Filipino-American War

Filipino nationalists, like Cuban insurgents, were already fighting Spain for their independence before the sudden American intervention. The Filipino leader, Emilio Aguinaldo, welcomed Dewey's naval victory as the sign of a de facto alliance with the United States; he then issued a declaration of independence and proclaimed the Philippine Republic. His own troops captured most of Luzon, the Philippines' major island, before the U.S. Army arrived. But the Filipinos' optimism declined as American officials acted in an increasingly imperious manner toward them, first refusing to meet with the "savages," then insisting that Filipino forces withdraw from Manila or face "forcible action," and finally dismissing the claims of Aguinaldo and "his so-called government." When the Treaty of Paris provided for U.S. ownership rather than independence, Filipinos felt betrayed. Mounting tensions erupted in a battle between American and Filipino troops outside Manila on February 4, 1899, sparking a long and brutal war.

Ultimately, the United States used nearly four times as many soldiers to suppress the Filipinos as it had to defeat Spain in Cuba and, in a tragic irony, employed many of the same brutal methods for which it had condemned Spain. Recognizing that "the Filipino masses are loyal to Aguinaldo and the government which he heads," U.S. military leaders adopted ever harsher measures, often directed at civilians, who were crowded into concentration camps in which perhaps 200,000 died. Americans often made little effort to distinguish between soldiers and noncombatants, viewing all Filipinos with racial antagonism. After reporting one massacre of a thousand men, women, and children, an American soldier declared, "I am in my glory when I can sight my gun on some dark skin and pull the trigger."

Before the military imposed censorship on war news, reporters confirmed U.S. atrocities; one wrote that "American troops have been relentless, have killed to exterminate men,

The Filipino-American War was documented extensively by photographers. "First position near Manila shows soldiers of the Twentieth Kansas Infantry Regiment deployed early in what would become a lengthy and brutal war.

women, and children, prisoners and captives, active insurgents and suspected people, from lads of 10 and up." A California newspaper defended such actions with remarkable candor: "There has been too much hypocrisy about this Philippine business. . . . Let us all be frank. WE DO NOT WANT THE FILIPINOS. WE DO WANT THE PHILIPPINES. All of our troubles in this annexation matter have been caused by the presence in the Philippine Islands of the Filipinos. . . . The more of them killed the better. It seems harsh. But they must yield before the superior race."

The overt racism of the war repelled African Americans. John Mitchell, a Virginia editor, condemned all the talk of "white man's burden" as deceptive rhetoric for brutal acts that could not be "defended either in moral or international law." Mitchell argued that white Southerners needed missionary work more than freedom-loving Filipinos. "With the government acquiescing in the oppression and butchery of a dark race in this country and the enslaving and slaughtering of a dark race in the Philippines," he concluded, "we think it time to call all missionaries home and have them work on our own people."

Other Americans also denounced the war. The Anti-Imperialist League revived, citing the war as proof of the corrosive influence of imperialism on the nation's morals and principles. Women figured prominently in mass meetings and lobbying efforts to have the troops returned, their moral stature further undercutting the rationale for colonial wars. Professors addressed antiwar rallies on college campuses. "Alas, what a fall," one University of Michigan professor told his audience. "Within the circuit of a single year to have declined from the moral leadership of mankind into the common brigandage of the robber nations of the world." By 1902, the realities of imperial policy—including American casualties—disillusioned most who had clamored to save Cuba.

By that time, however, the American military had largely suppressed the rebellion, and the United States had established a colonial government headed by an American governor general appointed by the president. Filipino involvement in the government was limited on educational and religious grounds. Compared to the Americans' brutal war policies, U.S. colonial rule was relatively benign, though paternalistic. William Howard Taft, the first governor general, launched a program that brought the islands new schools and roads, a public health system, and an economy tied closely to both the United States and a small Filipino elite. Independence would take nearly half a century.

China and the Open Door

America's determined involvement in the Philippines reflected its preoccupation with China. By the mid-1890s, other powers threatened prospects for American commercial expansion in China. Japan, after defeating China in 1895, annexed Taiwan and secured economic privileges in the mainland province of Fukien (Fujian); the major European powers then competed aggressively to claim other areas of China as their own **spheres of influence**, where they could dominate trade and economic development. In Manchuria, Russia won control of Port Arthur (Lüshun) and the right to construct a railway. Germany secured a ninety-nine year lease on another Chinese port and mining and railroad privileges on the Shandong Peninsula. The British wrung special concessions in Kowloon, opposite Hong Kong, and in other Chinese provinces, as well as a port facing the Russians in Manchuria. France gained a lease on ports and exclusive commercial privileges in southern China. The Chinese empress complained, "The various powers cast upon us looks of tiger-like voracity, hustling each other in their endeavors to be the first to seize upon . . . our territories."

These developments also alarmed the American business community. It was confident that given an equal opportunity, the United States would prevail in international trade because of its efficient production and marketing systems, but the creation of exclusive

A FAIR FIELD AND NO FAVOR.
UNCLE SAM: "I'm out for commerce, not conquest."

The United States usually preferred the "annexation of trade" to the annexation of territory. The Open Door policy promised to advance American commercial expansion, but Uncle Sam had to restrain other imperialists with colonial objectives.

spheres of influence would limit the opportunity to compete. In early 1898, business leaders organized the Committee on American Interests in China to lobby Washington to promote American trade in the shrinking Chinese market. The committee persuaded the nation's chambers of commerce to petition the McKinley administration to act. This campaign influenced McKinley's interest in acquiring the Philippines, but the Philippines, in the words of Mark Hanna, were only a "foothold"; China was the real target. The State Department soon reported that, given overproduction for the home market, "the United States has important interests at stake in the partition of commercial facilities in regions which are likely to offer developing markets for its goods. Nowhere is this consideration of more interest than in its relation to the Chinese Empire."

In 1899, the government moved to advance those interests. Without consulting the Chinese, Secretary of State John Hay asked the imperial powers to maintain an **Open Door** for the commercial and financial activities of all nations within their Chinese spheres of influence. Privately, Hay had already approved a plan to seize a Chinese port for the United States if necessary to join in the partition of China, but equal opportunity for trade and investment would serve American interests far better. It would avoid the expense of military occupation, avert further domestic criticism of U.S. imperialism, and guarantee a wider sphere for American business.

The other nations replied evasively, but Hay nonetheless announced that their acceptance of the Open Door was "final and definitive." In 1900, he seized an opportunity to extend the policy. An antiforeign Chinese nationalist movement known as the Boxers laid seige to the diplomatic quarters in Beijing. The defeat of the Boxer Rebellion by a multinational military force, to which the United States contributed troops, again raised the prospect of a division of China among colonial powers. Hay sent a second Open Door note, reaffirming "the principle of equal and impartial trade" while also calling for other nations to respect China's territorial integrity.

Despite Hay's notes, China remained a tempting arena for imperial schemes. But the Open Door became a cardinal doctrine of American foreign policy in the twentieth century, a means by which the United States sought to dominate foreign markets. The United States promoted an informal or economic empire, as opposed to the traditional territorial colonial empire that Americans preferred to identify with European powers. Henceforth, American economic interests expected the U.S. government to oppose any developments that threatened to close other nations' economies to American penetration and to advance "private enterprise" abroad.

Rivalry with Japan and Russia

At the turn of the twentieth century, both the Japanese and the Russians were more deeply involved in East Asia than was the United States. They expressed little support for the Open Door, which they correctly saw as favoring American interests over their own. But in pursuing their ambitions in China, the two came into conflict with each other. Alarmed at the threat of Russian expansion in Manchuria and Korea, Japan in 1904 attacked the Russian fleet at Port Arthur and defeated the Russians in Manchuria.

In this Russo-Japanese war, American sympathies lay with Japan, for the Russians were attempting to close Manchuria to foreign trade. President Theodore Roosevelt privately complained that a reluctant American public opinion meant that "we cannot fight to keep Manchuria open." He thus welcomed the Japanese attack in the belief that "Japan is playing our game." But he soon feared that an overwhelming Japanese victory could threaten American interests as much as Russian expansionism did and even "possibly mean a struggle between them and us in the future." Accordingly, he skillfully mediated an end to the war. In the Treaty of Portsmouth in 1905, Japan won control of Russia's sphere of influence in Manchuria, half the Russian island of Sakhalin, and recognition of its domination of Korea. For his role, TR won the Nobel Peace Prize (the first American to do so), but he especially welcomed the gains for U.S. prestige and national interest. Declared one London newspaper: "Mr. Roosevelt's success has amazed everybody."

This treaty marked Japan's emergence as a great power, but ironically, it worsened relations with the United States. Anti-American riots broke out in Tokyo. The Japanese people blamed Roosevelt for obstructing further Japanese gains and blocking a Russian indemnity that would have helped Japan pay for the war. Tensions were further aggravated by San Francisco's decision in 1906 to segregate Asian schoolchildren to avoid affecting the "youthful impressions" of white children. Japan regarded this as a racist insult, and Roosevelt worried that "the infernal fools in California" would provoke war. Finally he got the school order rescinded in exchange for his limiting Japanese immigration, which lay at the heart of California's hostility. Under the **Gentlemen's Agreement**, worked out through a series of diplomatic notes in 1907 and 1908, Japan agreed not to issue passports to workers coming to the United States, and the United States promised not to prohibit Japanese immigration overtly or completely.

Roosevelt also responded to the Japanese with military bluster. Already convinced that the United States needed a larger navy, commensurate with its new territorial responsibilities and commercial ambitions, he had persistently pushed a reluctant Congress to approve the construction of more battleships and armored cruisers. Tensions with Japan confirmed his conviction that "the American people must either build and maintain an adequate navy or else make up their minds definitely to accept a secondary position in international affairs, not merely in political, but in commercial matters." Both to encourage public support for his naval construction program and to demonstrate American power, Roosevelt sent the navy—freshly painted, it was dubbed the Great White Fleet—in a showy fourteen-month cruise around the world, stopping first in Japan. But the fleet's cruise only highlighted rather than resolving difficulties with Japan, which welcomed the fleet but refused to change its plans for Manchuria. Moreover, while Roosevelt took pride in the cruise, he had to outmaneuver a Congressional attempt to curtail it by cutting appropriations, a reminder that others did not fully share his commitment to an activist policy in world affairs.

To calm their mutual suspicions in East Asia, the United States and Japan adopted a series of agreements but failed to halt the deteriorating relationship. The Taft-Katsura Agreement (1905), the Root-Takahira Agreement (1908), and the Lansing-Ishii Agreement (1917) seemed to trade grudging American acceptance of Japan's special interests in

Manchuria and control of Korea for Japanese promises to respect American rule in the Philippines and maintain the Open Door in China. But these agreements were vague, if not contradictory, and produced discord rather than harmony between the two countries.

Increasingly, Japan began to exclude American trade from its territories in East Asia and to press for further control over China. Elihu Root, Roosevelt's secretary of state, insisted that the Open Door and American access be maintained but also asserted that the United States did not want to be "a protagonist in a controversy in China with Russia and Japan or with either of them." The problem was that the United States could not sustain the Open Door without becoming a protagonist in China. This paradox, and the unwillingness to commit military force, would plague American foreign policy in Asia for decades.

IMPERIAL POWER: THE UNITED STATES AND LATIN AMERICA, 1899–1917

In Latin America, where no major powers directly challenged American objectives as Japan and Russia did in Asia, the United States was more successful in exercising imperial power (see Map 4-3). In the two decades after the Spanish-American War, the United States intervened

MAP 4-3   The United States in the Caribbean
For strategic and economic reasons, the United States repeatedly intervened in the Caribbean in the first three decades of the twentieth century. Such interventions protected the U.S. claim of dominance but often provoked great hostility among Latin Americans.

• • • O V E R V I E W • • •

U.S. INTERVENTIONS IN LATIN AMERICA, 1891–1933

COUNTRY	TYPE OF INTERVENTION	YEAR
Chile	Ultimatum	1891–1892
Colombia	Military intervention	1903
Cuba	Occupation	1898–1902, 1906–1909, 1912 1917–1922
Dominican Republic	Military and administrative intervention	1905–1907
	Occupation	1916–1924
Haiti	Occupation	1915–1934
Mexico	Military intervention	1914 1916–1917
Nicaragua	Occupation	1912–1925, 1927–1933
Panama	Acquisition of Canal Zone	1904
Puerto Rico	Military invasion and territorial acquisition	1898

militarily in Latin America no fewer than twenty times to promote its own strategic and economic interests (see the Overview table, "U.S. Interventions in Latin America, 1891–1933"). Policymakers believed that these goals required restricting the influence of European nations in the region, building an isthmian canal under American control, and establishing the order thought necessary for American trade and investments to expand. Intervention at times achieved these goals, but it often ignored the wishes and interests of Latin Americans, provoked resistance and disorder, and created lasting ill will.

U.S. Rule in Puerto Rico

Well before 1898, expansionists had advocated acquiring Puerto Rico because of its strategic location in the Caribbean. During the Spanish-American War, Roosevelt urged Washington, "Do not make peace until we get" Puerto Rico. Military invasion and the Treaty of Paris soon brought the island under American control, with mixed consequences. A military government improved transportation and sanitation and developed public health and education. But to the dismay of Puerto Ricans, who had been promised that American rule would bestow "the advantages and blessings of enlightened civilization," their political freedoms were curtailed. "We have suffered everything. No liberty, no rights," said José Henna, a physician who had led resistance to Spanish colonialism. "We are Mr. Nobody from Nowhere."

In 1900, the United States established a civil government, but it was under U.S. control, and popular participation was even less than under Spain. In the so-called *Insular Cases* (1901), the Supreme Court upheld Congress's authority to establish an inferior status for Puerto Rico as an "unincorporated territory" without promise of statehood. Disappointed Puerto Ricans pressed to end this colonial status, some advocating independence, others statehood

Imperial Power: The United States and Latin America, 1899–1917   117

or merely greater autonomy. This division would continue throughout the twentieth century. In 1917, the United States granted citizenship and greater political rights to Puerto Ricans, but their island remained an unincorporated territory under an American governor appointed by the president.

Economic development also disappointed most islanders, for American investors quickly gained control of the best land and pursued large-scale sugar production for the U.S. market. The landless peasants struggled to survive as workers on large plantations. By 1929, the new governor—ironically, Theodore Roosevelt Jr.—found that under the domination of American capital, "poverty was widespread and hunger, almost to the verge of starvation, common." A subsequent investigation concluded that while "the influx of capital has increased the efficiency of production and promoted general economic development," the benefits had gone largely to Americans, not to ordinary Puerto Ricans, whose conditions were "deplorable." Increasingly, they left their homes to seek work in the United States.

Cuba as a U.S. Protectorate

Despite the Teller Amendment, the Spanish-American War did not leave Cuba independent. McKinley opposed independence and distrusted the Cuban revolutionaries. Many Americans considered the Cubans racial inferiors, and one U.S. general in Cuba snorted, "Why those people are no more fit for self-government than gun-powder is for hell." Accordingly, a U.S. military government was established in the island. Only in 1900, when the Democrats made an issue of imperialism, did the McKinley administration move toward permitting a Cuban government and withdrawing American troops. McKinley summoned a Cuban convention to draft a constitution under the direction of the American military governor, General Leonard Wood. Reflecting the continuing U.S. fear of Cuban autonomy, this constitution restricted suffrage on the basis of property and education, leaving few Cubans with the right to vote.

Even so, before removing its troops, the United States wanted to ensure its control over Cuba. It therefore made U.S. withdrawal contingent on Cuba's adding to its constitution the provisions of the **Platt Amendment**, drawn up in 1901 by the U.S. secretary of war. The Platt Amendment restricted Cuba's autonomy in diplomatic relations with other countries and in internal financial policies, required Cuba to lease naval bases to the United States, and most important, authorized U.S. intervention to maintain order and preserve Cuban independence. Cubans resented this restriction on their sovereignty. As General Wood correctly observed, "There is, of course, little or no independence left Cuba under the Platt Amendment."

Cubans quickly learned that harsh reality when the United States prevented Cuba from extending the same trade privileges to the British that U.S. merchants enjoyed. The Open Door would not apply in the Caribbean, which was to be an American sphere of influence. To preserve that influence, the United States sent troops into Cuba three times between 1906 and 1917 (Roosevelt admitted his recurrent itch to "wipe its people off the face of the earth"). The last occupation lasted six years. Meanwhile, American property interests in Cuba increased more than fourfold, and American exports to the island increased eightfold from 1898 to 1917.

During their occupations of Cuba, the Americans modernized its financial system, built roads and public schools, and developed a public health and sanitation program that eradicated the deadly disease of yellow fever. But most Cubans thought these material benefits did not compensate for their loss of political and economic independence. The Platt Amendment remained the basis of American policy toward Cuba until 1934.

The Panama Canal

The Spanish-American War intensified the long American interest in a canal through Central America to eliminate the lengthy and dangerous ocean route around South America. Its commercial value seemed obvious, but the war emphasized its strategic importance. McKinley declared that a canal was now "demanded by the annexation of the Hawaiian Islands and the prospective expansion of our influence and commerce in the Pacific."

Theodore Roosevelt moved quickly to implement McKinley's commitment to a canal after becoming president in 1901. He was convinced that a strong presidential role was at least as important in foreign affairs as in domestic politics. Neither Congress nor "the average American," he believed, took "the trouble to think carefully or deeply" about international affairs. Roosevelt's canal diplomacy helped establish the assertive presidency that has characterized U.S. foreign policy in the twentieth and early twenty-first centuries.

First, Roosevelt persuaded Britain to renounce its treaty right to a joint role with the United States in any canal venture. Britain's willingness reflected a growing friendship between the two nations, both wary of Germany's increasing aggressiveness. Where to build the canal was a problem. One possibility was Nicaragua, where a sea-level canal could be built. Another was Panama, then part of Colombia. A canal through Panama would require an elaborate system of locks, but the French-owned Panama Canal Company had been unsuccessfully trying to build a canal in Panama and was now eager to sell its rights to the project before they expired in 1904.

In 1902, Congress directed Roosevelt to purchase the French company's claims for $40 million and build the canal in Panama if Colombia ceded a strip of land across the isthmus on reasonable terms. Otherwise, Roosevelt was to negotiate with Nicaragua for the alternate route. In 1903, Roosevelt pressed Colombia to sell a canal zone to the United States for $10 million and an annual payment of $250,000. Colombia, however, rejected the proposal, fearing the loss of its sovereignty in Panama and hoping for more money. After all, when the Panama Canal Company's rights expired, Colombia could then legitimately collect the $40 million so generously offered the company.

Roosevelt was furious. After warning "those contemptible little creatures" in Colombia that they were "imperiling their own future," he began writing a message to Congress proposing military action to seize the isthmus of Panama. Instead of using direct force, however, Roosevelt worked with Philippe Bunau-Varilla, a

Theodore Roosevelt at the controls of a giant steam shovel during the construction of the Panama Canal in 1906. Roosevelt's aggressive acquisition of the Canal Zone and its subsequent control by the United States angered Panamanians for nearly a century.

French official of the Panama Canal Company, to exploit long-smoldering Panamanian discontent with Colombia. Roosevelt's purpose was to get the canal zone, Bunau-Varilla's, to get the American money. Roosevelt ordered U.S. naval forces to Panama; from New York, Bunau-Varilla coordinated a revolt against Colombian authority directed by officials of the Panama Railroad, owned by Bunau-Varilla's canal company. The bloodless "revolution" succeeded when U.S. forces prevented Colombian troops from landing in Panama, although the United States was bound by treaty to maintain Colombian sovereignty in the region. Bunau-Varilla promptly signed a treaty accepting Roosevelt's original terms for a canal zone and making Panama a U.S. protectorate, which it remained until 1939. Panamanians themselves denounced the treaty for surrendering sovereignty in the zone to the United States, but they had to acquiesce because their independence depended on American forces. The United States took formal control of the canal zone in 1904 and in a great feat of engineering completed construction of the Panama Canal in 1914.

Many Americans were appalled by what the *Chicago American* called Roosevelt's "rough-riding assault upon another republic over the shattered wreckage of international law and diplomatic usage." But others, as *Public Opinion* reported, wanted a "canal above all things" and were willing to overlook moral questions and approve the acquisition of the canal zone as simply "a business question." Roosevelt himself boasted, "I took the Canal Zone and let Congress debate," but his unnecessary and arrogant actions generated resentment among Latin Americans that rankled for decades.

The Roosevelt Corollary

To protect the security of the canal, the United States increased its authority in the Caribbean. The objective was to establish conditions there that would both eliminate any pretext for European intervention and promote American control over trade and investment. The inability of Latin American nations to pay their debts to foreign lenders raised the possibility of European intervention, as evidenced by a German and British blockade of Venezuela in 1903 to secure repayment of debts to European bankers. "If we intend to say hands off to the powers of Europe," Roosevelt concluded, "then sooner or later we must keep order ourselves."

In his 1904 annual message to Congress, Roosevelt announced a new policy, the so-called **Roosevelt Corollary** to the Monroe Doctrine. "Chronic wrongdoing," he declared, would cause the United States to exercise "an international police power" in Latin America. The Monroe Doctrine had expressed American hostility to European intervention in Latin America; the Roosevelt Corollary attempted to justify U.S. intervention and authority in the region. Roosevelt invoked his corollary immediately, imposing American management of the debts and customs duties of the Dominican Republic in 1905. Commercial rivalries and political intrigue in that poor nation had created disorder, which Roosevelt suppressed for both economic and strategic reasons. Financial insolvency was averted, popular revolution prevented, and possible European intervention forestalled.

Latin Americans vigorously resented the United States' unilateral claims to authority. By 1907, the so-called Drago Doctrine (named after Argentina's foreign minister) was incorporated into international law, prohibiting armed intervention to collect debts. Still, the United States would continue to invoke the Roosevelt Corollary to advance its interests in the hemisphere. As Secretary of State Elihu Root asserted, "The inevitable effect of our building the Canal must be to require us to police the surrounding premises." He then added, "In the nature of things, trade and control, and the obligation to keep order which go with them, must come our way."

THE BIG STICK IN THE CARIBBEAN SEA

The Roosevelt Corollary proclaimed the intention of the United States to police Latin America. Enforcement came, as this cartoon shows, with Roosevelt and subsequent presidents sending the U.S. Navy to one Caribbean nation after another.

Dollar Diplomacy

Roosevelt's successor as president, William Howard Taft, hoped to promote U.S. interests without such combative rhetoric and naked force. He proposed "substituting dollars for bullets"— using government action to encourage private American investments in Latin America to supplant European interests, promote development and stability, and gain profits for American bankers. Under this **dollar diplomacy**, American investments in the Caribbean increased dramatically during Taft's presidency from 1909 to 1913, and the State Department helped arrange for American bankers to establish financial control over Haiti and Honduras.

But Taft did not shrink from employing military force to protect American property or to establish the conditions he thought necessary for American investments. In fact, Taft intervened more frequently than Roosevelt had, with Nicaragua a major target. In 1909, Taft sent U.S. troops there to aid a revolution fomented by an American mining corporation and to seize the Nicaraguan customs houses. Under the new government, American bankers then gained control of Nicaragua's national bank, railroad, and customs service. To protect these arrangements, U.S. troops were again dispatched in 1912. To control popular opposition to the American client government, the marines remained in Nicaragua for two decades. Military power, not the social and economic improvement promised by dollar diplomacy, kept Nicaragua's minority government stable and subordinate to the United States.

Dollar diplomacy increased American power and influence in the Caribbean and tied underdeveloped countries to the United States economically and strategically. By 1913,

American investments in the region reached $1.5 billion, and Americans had captured more than 50 percent of the foreign trade of Costa Rica, Cuba, the Dominican Republic, Guatemala, Haiti, Honduras, Nicaragua, and Panama. But this policy failed to improve conditions for most Latin Americans. U.S. officials remained primarily concerned with promoting American control and extracting American profits from the region, not with the well-being of its population. One American diplomat, for instance, casually described a Guatemalan president in whose government San Francisco bankers had invested heavily under the premises of dollar diplomacy as a cruel despot who had "the good sense to be civil to our country and its citizens and to keep his cruelties . . . for home consumption." Not surprisingly, dollar diplomacy proved unpopular in Latin America.

Wilsonian Interventions

Taking office in 1913, the Democrat Woodrow Wilson repudiated the interventionist policies of his Republican predecessors. He promised that the United States would "never again seek one additional foot of territory by conquest" but would instead work to promote "human rights, national integrity, and opportunity" in Latin America. Wilson also named as his secretary of state the Democratic symbol of anti-imperialism, William Jennings Bryan. Their generous intentions were apparent when Bryan signed a treaty with Colombia apologizing for Roosevelt's seizure of the Panama Canal Zone in 1903.

Nonetheless, Wilson soon became the most interventionist president in American history, for a number of reasons. He agreed that the United States had to expand its exports and investments abroad and that U.S. dominance of the Caribbean was strategically necessary. He also shared the racist belief that Latin Americans were inferior and needed paternalistic guidance from the United States. In providing that guidance, through military force if necessary, Wilson came close to assuming that American principles and objectives were absolutes, that different cultural traditions and national aspirations were simply wrong. His self-righteousness and determination to transform other peoples' behavior led his policies to be dubbed "missionary diplomacy," but they also contained elements of Roosevelt's commitment to military force and Taft's reliance on economic power. An incredulous British editor soon concluded, "the Democrats have adopted bodily the foreign policy of the Republicans."

Caribbean Interventions In 1915, Wilson ordered U.S. Marines to Haiti. They went, explained Bryan, to restore order and preserve "American interests" that were "gravely menaced." The United States saved and even enhanced those interests by establishing a protectorate over Haiti and drawing up a constitution that increased U.S. property rights and commercial privileges. The U.S. Navy selected a new Haitian president, granting him nominal authority over a client government. Real authority, however, rested with the American military, which controlled Haiti until 1934, protecting the small elite who cooperated with foreign interests and exploited their own people. As usual, American military rule improved the country's transportation, sanitation, and educational systems, but the forced-labor program that the United States adopted to build such public works provoked widespread resentment. In 1919, marines suppressed a revolt against American domination, killing more than three thousand Haitians.

Wilson also intervened elsewhere in the Caribbean. In 1916, when the Dominican Republic refused to cede control of its finances to U.S. bankers, Wilson ordered the marines to occupy the country. The marines ousted Dominican officials, installed a military government to rule "on behalf of the Dominican government," and ran the nation until 1924. In 1917, the United States intervened in Cuba, which remained under American control until 1922.

Interfering with Mexico Wilson also involved himself in the internal affairs of Mexico. The lengthy dictatorship of Porfirio Díaz had collapsed in 1911 in revolutionary disorder. The popular leader Francisco Madero took power and promised democratic and economic reforms that alarmed both wealthy Mexicans and foreign investors, particularly Americans. In 1913, General Victoriano Huerta seized control in a brutal counterrevolution backed by the landed aristocracy and foreign interests. Most nations recognized the Huerta government, but Wilson, despite strong pressure from American investors, particularly John D. Rockefeller's oil companies, refused to do so. He was appalled by the violence of Huerta's power grab and was aware that opponents had organized to reestablish constitutional government.

Wilson hoped to bring the Constitutionalists to power and "to secure Mexico a better government under which all contracts and business and concessions will be safer than they have been." He authorized arms sales to their forces led by Venustiano Carranza; pressured Britain and other nations to deprive Huerta of foreign support; and blockaded the Mexican port of Vera Cruz. In April 1914 Wilson exploited a minor incident to have the marines attack and occupy Vera Cruz. This assault damaged his image as a promoter of peace and justice. One London editor, referring to "the sinister monstrosity of President Wilson's intervention," concluded "there has been nothing so cruelly immoral and so cynically cruel in the history of the world before." Street demonstrations erupted all over Latin America, and even Carranza and the Constitutionalists denounced the American occupation as unwarranted aggression. By August, Carranza had toppled Huerta, and Wilson shifted his support to Francisco ("Pancho") Villa, who seemed more susceptible to American guidance. But Carranza's growing popular support in Mexico and Wilson's preoccupation with World War I in Europe finally led the United States to grant de facto recognition to the Carranza government in October 1915.

Villa then began terrorizing New Mexico and Texas, hoping to provoke an American intervention that would undermine Carranza. In 1916, Wilson ordered troops under General John J. Pershing to pursue Villa into Mexico, leading Carranza to fear a permanent U.S. occupation of northern Mexico. Soon the American soldiers were fighting the Mexican army rather than Villa's bandits. On the brink of full-fledged war, Wilson finally ordered U.S. troops to withdraw in January 1917 and extended full recognition to the Carranza government. Wilson lamely defended these steps as showing that the United States had no intention of imposing on Mexico "an order and government of our own choosing." That had been Wilson's original objective, however. His aggressive tactics had not merely failed but had also embittered relations with Mexico.

PLAYING "AN EVER-GROWING PART": THE UNITED STATES AND EUROPE, 1900–1914

While the United States exerted its expanding power on Latin American nations and strove to increase its influence in Asia in the early twentieth century, it remained largely on the periphery of European affairs. But its triumph in the Spanish-American War had its consequences in Europe, too. As one London newspaper declared in 1898, "In the future America will play a part in the general affairs of the world such as she has never played before." And in 1908, a French author, in describing the United States as "a world power" with "commercial interests everywhere," predicted American intervention in "all those questions that hitherto have been arranged by agreement only among European powers." The United

States "is seated at the table where the great game is played, and it cannot leave it." And, indeed, the United States did take a larger role in Europe, but its traditional policy of non-involvement remained popular with many Americans and constituted an important restraint upon the new imperial power.

Responding to the war's lopsided outcome, European nations immediately began to adjust their policies to take into account the evident power of the United States. German officials even considered seeking an alliance in order to strengthen Germany in Europe. But Germany's rival, Great Britain, moved quickly to resolve all possible disputes with the United States and thereby establish a basis for long-term cooperation. Britain's strong support for the American annexation of the Philippines and its decision in 1901 to accede to American control of the projected isth-mian canal were early examples of its search for such a rapprochement. These steps not only abetted the expansionist ambitions of the United States but also enabled Britain to focus more of its attention and fleet on the North Atlantic against the growing German navy.

Still more obvious was Britain's 1903 role in settling a long-standing dispute about the boundary between Alaska and Canada, a member of the British Empire. The quarrel had heated up with gold discoveries in the area in 1899, and President Roosevelt rejected any compromise with Canada. He arranged for a commission of "impartial jurists of high repute" to decide the issue, but his appointees were ardent imperialists, including his close friend Senator Henry Cabot Lodge and his own secretary of war. Moreover, Roosevelt warned Britain that if the commission ruled in favor of Canada he would seize the disputed territory by military force. Regarding good relations with the United States as more impor-tant than the interests of Canada, the British commissioner voted with the Americans to award the area to the United States.

By 1905, only a decade after Britain and the United States seemed on the verge of war over Venezuela, the British foreign secretary could describe the preservation of Anglo-American friendship as a prime objective of British foreign policy, and diplomats of both countries agreed that their nations' interests were "absolutely identical and that the more closely we can work together, the better it will be for us and the world at large." In effect, Britain conceded the Western Hemisphere to the United States in exchange for possible assistance elsewhere, both in Asia and perhaps in Europe. Roosevelt also regarded the Anglo-American entente as a means to promote control of colonial areas, and when unrest oc-curred he defended British rule in India and Egypt as "a great advance for humanity . . . one of the mighty feats of civilization."

Crisis in Morocco In a significant step toward having the United States play what he called "an ever-growing part in the affairs of the world," Roosevelt assumed a prominent role in a serious European conflict over Morocco. Although his American critics objected that the Monroe Doctrine prohibited U.S. involvement in European politics, TR maintained that it was in the nation's interests "to keep matters on an even keel in Europe." The great European powers were aligning themselves into rival blocs: the Entente of Britain and France (and sometimes Russia) and the Alliance of Germany and Austria-Hungary (and sometimes Italy). France, supported by Britain, was attempting to secure control of Morocco, an effort challenged by Germany in 1905. As tensions grew and war seemed pos-sible, Germany approached Roosevelt for assistance, drawing a parallel between upholding the Open Door in China and in Morocco.

In 1906, Roosevelt helped arrange an international conference at Algeciras, Spain, to resolve the crisis. While he placated Kaiser Wilhelm II of Germany with flattery, Roosevelt instructed the American delegation to side with France and Britain and to insist upon "the Open Door, and for a policy which will create and foster civilization and trade within the Open Door." The Algeciras conference upheld France's claims to Morocco, which it soon expanded into a protectorate, and pledged to maintain an open door in Morocco, a pledge the United States would later use to insist upon securing petroleum and commercial opportunities. Roosevelt had helped preserve the balance of power in Europe while advancing what he saw as America's own interests. He took great pride in his accomplishment.

When the Senate considered the resultant treaty, however, many Senators objected to the involvement in European affairs as a violation of "the settled policy of this Government since its foundation." In supporting the treaty, administration officials had to minimize the political issues involved in the Algeciras conference and treaty and instead emphasize the importance of upholding the Open Door in Morocco. Even so, the Senate attached a reservation to the treaty declaring that its approval was "without purpose to depart from traditional American foreign policy."

Promoting Arbitration During this time of imperialist expansion and national rivalries, European nations persistently, if halfheartedly, sought ways to arrange for the peaceful settlement of international disputes. And the United States, where pacifists and peace organizations were both popular and influential, joined actively in these efforts.

In 1899, the United States met with twenty-five other nations in the Netherlands at the First Hague Peace Conference. It failed in its attempt to limit military and naval expenditures. (Admiral Mahan, an American delegate, did not help by remarking that the newly expanded role of the United States in the Pacific required a larger, not a smaller, navy.) But the conference did adopt rules to govern truces and the treatment of prisoners, and most importantly it created the Permanent Court of Arbitration, a panel of jurists to decide questions submitted to it. Conference participants did not bind themselves to use the court to settle their disputes, but Roosevelt soon persuaded Germany to submit the 1903 Venezuelan debt controversy to the international tribunal as a means to sustain the court and promote arbitration.

A few years later, President Roosevelt suggested holding a second Hague conference but acceded to the Russian tsar's desire to sponsor it, convinced that otherwise "there would be a feeling that I was posing too much as a professional peacemaker." TR worked closely with Britain and France preparing for the 1907 conference, but he distanced himself from the "peace men" like Andrew Carnegie and included none in the delegation to the "peace conference." Roosevelt certainly sought international stability, but he denounced those interested in "peace-at-any-price . . . who, whether from folly, from selfishness, from shortsightedness, or from sheer cowardice, rail at the manly virtues and fail to understand that righteousness is to be put before peace." Roosevelt favored limitation—but not reduction—of armaments and believed that "just at present the United States Navy is an infinitely more potent factor for peace than all the peace societies of every kind and sort."

Roosevelt succeeded in making the Second Hague Peace Conference a truly international affair by insisting that the nations of Latin America be invited, but he was unable to persuade the European powers to agree to limit military expenditures or to adopt rules restricting powerful new weapons such as submarines. Nor did the conference agree to American proposals for compulsory arbitration of most international disputes or to establish a genuine international court of justice (which finally emerged in 1920—after World War I—as the World Court). Even so, the Hague conference took an important step toward the codification of international law, and it led to another conference in 1909 which issued the Declaration of London codifying international law for maritime war and establishing the rights of neutral nations.

The United States continued to promote arbitration of international disputes after the Second Hague Conference. In the following year, Roosevelt and Root negotiated twenty-four bilateral arbitration treaties, under which each party agreed to submit many contested questions to the Hague Court. In 1910, President Taft, speaking at a peace meeting in

New York, proposed arbitration for all questions, and thereafter his administration negotiated general arbitration treaties with England and France. Under Woodrow Wilson, Secretary of State Bryan negotiated thirty conciliation, or "cooling off," treaties providing for submitting disputes to an international court.

However, public opinion and Senate opposition, rooted in more traditional perspectives toward the nation's involvement in world affairs, persistently restricted the effectiveness of these agreements. The treaties themselves provided for broad and numerous exceptions in the possible questions to be arbitrated and often did not require the disputants to accept the court's decisions. Moreover, the Senate invariably amended the treaties by providing for still more exceptions and reserving for itself the right to approve every particular agreement to arbitrate. Roosevelt complained that it was ridiculous to sign an arbitration treaty that effectively did no more than declare that arbitration might be accepted. Taft simply dropped his treaties (called by one critic another "blunder by the unhappy Taft administration") rather than ask the French and British governments to accept the crippling Senate amendments. Taft later quipped that he hoped "the senators might change their minds, or that the people might change the Senate; instead of which they changed me." The restrictive views held by the public and the Senate would shortly cause still greater difficulty for President Wilson.

Some of the irony of this persistent impasse was symbolized by Senator Henry Cabot Lodge, who regularly championed an imperial role for the United States while also speaking for those determined to maintain the traditional American isolationist stance toward European power politics. "In entangling alliances," he declared in discussing a proposed treaty a few years before World War I, "no man wants to engage this country; we have no concern with the wars of Europe."

CONCLUSION

By the time of Woodrow Wilson's presidency, the United States had been expanding its involvement in world affairs for half a century. Several themes had emerged from this activity: increasing American domination of the Caribbean, continuing interest in East Asia, the creation of an overseas empire, and the evolution of the United States into a major world power. Underlying these developments was an uneasy mixture of ideas and objectives. The American involvement in the world reflected a traditional, if often misguided, sense of national rectitude and mission. Generous humanitarian impulses vied with ugly racist prejudices as Americans sought both to help other peoples and to direct them toward U.S. concepts of religion, sanitation, capitalist development, and public institutions. American motives ranged from ensuring national security and competing with European colonial powers to the conviction that the United States had to expand its economic interests abroad. But if imperialism, both informal and at times colonial, brought Americans greater wealth and power, it also increased tensions in Asia and contributed to anti-American hostility and revolutionary ferment in Latin America. It also entangled the United States in the Great Power rivalries that would ultimately result in two world wars.

Review Questions

1. After the Spanish-American War, General Leonard Wood asserted that Cubans believed that their American "liberators" were "still their faithful friends." Why might Cubans not agree with Wood?

2. What factors, old and new, shaped American foreign policy at the end of the nineteenth century? How were they interrelated?

3. How were individual politicians and diplomats able to affect America's foreign policy? How were they constrained by government institutions, private groups, and public opinion?

4. To what extent was the United States' emergence as an imperial power a break from, as opposed to a culmination of, its earlier policies and national development?

5. How effective were U.S. interventions in Latin America? What were the objectives and consequences?

Key Terms

Dollar diplomacy *120*

Gentlemen's Agreement *114*

Imperialism *99*

Mahanism *101*

Monroe Doctrine *103*

Open Door *113*

Platt Amendment *117*

Roosevelt Corollary *119*

Spheres of influence *112*

Teller Amendment *106*

Yellow press *105*

Recommended Reading

Robert L. Beisner, *From the Old Diplomacy to the New, 1865–1900*, 2d ed. (1986). An excellent analysis of historiographical issues.

Charles S. Campbell, *The Transformation of American Foreign Relations, 1865–1900* (1976). A comprehensive and cautious survey that provides many insights in U.S. foreign policy.

Kristin L. Hoganson, *Fighting for American Manhood: How Gender Politics Provoked the Spanish-American and Philippine-American Wars* (1998). An innovative and provocative book showing how gender concerns influenced U.S. foreign policy.

Walter LaFeber, *The American Search for Opportunity, 1865–1913* (1993). A fascinating study documenting the disruptive international consequences of America's rise to world power.

Walter LaFeber, *The New Empire: An Interpretation of American Expansion, 1860–1898* (1963). An influential study that emphasizes economic factors on American foreign policy.

John L. Offner, *An Unwanted War: The Diplomacy of the United States and Spain over Cuba, 1895–1898* (1992). A revisionist account maintaining that conflict over Cuba was inevitable.

Louis A. Perez, Jr., *The War of 1898: The United States and Cuba in History and Historiography* (1998). A brief book that emphasizes how relations between Cuba and the United States shaped the war and its meaning.

David Pletcher, *The Diplomacy of Trade and Investment: American Economic Expansion in the Hemisphere* (1998). Stresses the complex but inconsistent and unsystematic nature of American economic expansion.

AMERICA AND THE GREAT WAR: 1914–1920

Waging Neutrality

Waging War in America

Waging War and Peace Abroad

Waging Peace at Home

Conclusion

I have been traveling for nearly three weeks through six Middle Western States, talking about the war, with all classes of people: farmers, labor leaders, newspaper editors, college professors, business men, and state officials. I have been trying to get at the bedrock sentiment of the people regarding it, and to set it down exactly as I find it.

Almost without exception, even among those who favor the war most vigorously, the people I have talked with have commented upon the lack of popular enthusiasm for the war. The more closely these people were connected with the farmers or the workingmen, the more sweeping and positive were their statements.

The attitude of the people is wholly different from what it was at the opening of our Spanish War in 1898. There are no heroic slogans, no boastfulness, no excitement, no glamour of war. There is still a great deal of haziness about the real issues and a great deal of doubt about how far America should go beyond mere defensive measures. One of the foremost political leaders of the West, himself an ardent supporter of the war, told me that if a secret ballot were taken as to whether American armies should be sent to France, the vote would be overwhelmingly against it. It is noteworthy, also, that the newspapers are full of a-b-c explanations of the reasons why we are at war and why we should go forward with it. . . . And finally, there are nowhere as yet any evidences of the passions and the hatred which war engenders. People do not hate Germans or Austrians or Turks; nor do they love the British.

On the other hand, if there is little enthusiasm, the people everywhere are taking the war as a grim necessity, feeling that they have been forced into it by events beyond their control, and they are going forward, more or less reluctantly, with the preparations; but they are really going forward. The draft was not popular; people wished it might have been done in some other way; and in some groups of population it was hated and feared, and yet, through all this country, there has been a won-derful and complete compliance with the law. In the same way the liberty loan is not popular. There is no popular rush to subscribe, and it has required an enormous amount of organization, advertis-ing, and pressure to sell the bonds, and yet they are being sold and will be sold. . . . And there have been no signs of any popular rush to enlist, and men have been obtained only by dint of the most vigorous advertising and pressure. It is significant also that more than half of those registered in Chicago are demanding exemption.

The only real enthusiasm that I could find was in such campaigns as that of the Red Cross, the Y.M.C.A., and here and there in work for the American Ambulance in France. The work of women everywhere for the Red Cross is remarkably organized and well supported. . . . Of the value of these activities, no matter what happens, the people are convinced.

This is as nearly a true statement of the general situation as I can make. I have met a good many men who think that this state of the popular mind, this deliberate and passionless method of doing what is regarded as a disagreeable duty, is the best possible method of getting into the great war. . . .

On the other hand, I met a good many people, especially among the leaders of war organiza-tions of various sorts, to whom the popular attitude is not only irritating but dangerous. They feel that the people are not fully awakened to the emergency, that they do not realize that the country is really at this moment at war, and that unless America meets with more enthusiasm and more speed the problems of raising money, producing food, and hurrying the training of men for armies in France the war may result in disaster.

—Ray Stannard Baker

Ray Stannard Baker, "West in Grim Business of War Without Passion," *St. Louis Post-Dispatch*, June 17, 1917.

RAY STANNARD BAKER, the famous journalist, thus described his journey across the Midwest in 1917, three years after World War I began in Europe and two months after the United States had joined the conflict by declaring war on Germany. Despite the official decision for war, the American people were reluctant participants, unconvinced that national interests were really involved. Instead, as Baker observed, they "seem to think that there was a fight between England and Germany with which Uncle Sam was not concerned in any way—but that he was simply an innocent bystander who happened to be in range and got hurt—quite as much by the fault of England as of Germany."

But as the perceptive Baker also discovered, the nation's leaders were determined to whip up popular support for the war effort through "organization, advertising, and pressure." The goal would be not only to train soldiers to fight in Europe but also to demonize Germany, mobilize the economy, and transform social attitudes within America itself.

This determination profoundly shaped the American wartime experience. Not only was the Great War the United States' first major military conflict on foreign soil, but it also changed American life. With economic management and social control considered essential to the war effort, government authority increased sharply. Business organizations, labor unions, farmers, ministers were all incorporated into the war effort. Women's organizational activities expanded dramatically beyond those noted by Baker and, in being focused broadly on the war effort, often developed in new and unexpected ways. Journalists, too, had their skills put to new and sometimes unfortunate uses; Baker himself, who had initilly opposed the war as a threat to all progress, eventually went to Europe to file confidential reports for the State Department and then to organize the Press Department and control news at the Versailles Peace Conference.

Many of the changes in American life, from increased efficiency to Americanization, often reflected prewar progressivism, and the war years did promote some reforms. But the war also diverted reform energies into new channels, subordinated generous impulses to those that were more coercive ("the passions and the hatred" which Baker found lacking in mid-1917 were soon widespread), and strengthened the conservative opposition to reform. The results were often reactionary and contributed to a postwar mood that not only curtailed further reform but also helped defeat the peace treaty upon which so much had been gambled.

KEY TOPICS

How sympathy for the Allies and outrage over German submarine warfare undermined U.S. neutrality during World War I.

Wilson's decision to join the conflict on the side of the Allies.

The reorganization of the U.S. economy and the challenge to civil liberties that resulted from the war effort.

Wilson's influence on the Versailles Treaty and his failure to gain its ratification in the U.S. Senate.

The postwar backlash.

• CHRONOLOGY •

1914	World War I begins in Europe.
	President Woodrow Wilson declares U.S. neutrality.
1915	Germany begins submarine warfare.
	Lusitania is sunk.
	Woman's Peace Party is organized.
1916	Gore-McLemore resolutions are defeated.
	Sussex Pledge is issued.
	Preparedness legislation is enacted.
	Woodrow Wilson is reelected president.
1917	Germany resumes unrestricted submarine warfare.
	The United States declares war on Germany.
	Selective Service Act establishes the military draft.
	Espionage Act is passed.
	Committee on Public Information, War Industries Board, Food Administration, and other mobilization agencies are established.
	American Expeditionary Force arrives in France.
	East St. Louis race riot erupts.
	Bolshevik Revolution occurs in Russia.
1918	Wilson announces his Fourteen Points.
	Sedition Act is passed.
	Eugene Debs is imprisoned.
	The United States intervenes militarily in Russia.
	Armistice ends World War I.
1919	Paris Peace Conference is held.
	Steel, coal, and other strikes occur.
	Red Scare breaks out.
	Prohibition amendment is adopted.
	Wilson suffers a massive stroke.
1920	Palmer Raids round up radicals.
	League of Nations is defeated in the U.S. Senate.
	Woman suffrage amendment is ratified.
	U.S. troops are withdrawn from Russia.
	Warren Harding is elected president.
1921	United States signs a separate peace treaty with Germany.

WAGING NEUTRALITY

Few Americans were prepared for the Great War that erupted in Europe in August 1914, but fewer still foresaw that their own nation might become involved in it. With near unanimity, they supported neutrality. But American attitudes, decisions, and actions, both public and private, undercut neutrality, and the policies of governments in Berlin, London, and Washington drew the United States into the war.

The Origins of Conflict

There had been plenty of warning. Since the 1870s, the competing imperial ambitions of the European powers had led to economic rivalries, military expansion, diplomatic maneuvering, and international tensions. A complex system of alliances divided the continent into two opposing blocs. In central Europe, the expansionist Germany of Kaiser Wilhelm II allied itself with the multinational Austro-Hungarian Empire. Confronting them, Great Britain and France formed alliances with tsarist Russia. A succession of crises threatened this precarious balance of power, and in May 1914 an American diplomat reported anxiously, "There is too much hatred, too many jealousies." He predicted "an awful cataclysm."

The cataclysm began a month later. On June 28, a Serbian terrorist assassinated Archduke Franz Ferdinand, the heir to the Austro-Hungarian throne, in Sarajevo. With Germany's support, Austria declared war on Serbia on July 28. Russia then mobilized its army against Austria to aid Serbia, its Slavic client state. To assist Austria, Germany declared war on Russia and then on Russia's ally, France. Hoping for a quick victory, Germany struck at France through neutral Belgium; in response, Britain declared war on Germany on August 4. Soon Turkey and Bulgaria joined Germany and Austria to form the **Central Powers**. The **Allies**—Britain, France, and Russia—were joined by Italy and Japan. Britain drew on its empire for resources, using troops from India, Canada, Australia, New Zealand, and South Africa. The war had become a global conflict, waged not only in Europe but also in Africa, the Middle East, and East Asia.

Mass slaughter enveloped Europe as huge armies battled to a stalemate. The British and French faced the Germans along a line of trenches stretching across France and Belgium from the English Channel to Switzerland. Little movement occurred despite great efforts and terrible casualties from artillery, machine guns, and poison gas. The British once suffered 300,000 casualties in an offensive that gained only a few square miles before being pushed back. Machine gunners went into shock at the carnage they inflicted. In the trenches, soldiers suffered in the cold and mud, surrounded by decaying bodies and human waste, enduring lice, rats, and nightmares and dying from disease and exhaustion. The belligerents subordinated their economies, politics, and cultures to military demands. The Great War, said one German soldier, had become "the grave of nations."

American Attitudes

Although the United States had also competed for markets, colonies, and influence, few Americans had expected this calamity. As one North Carolina congressman said, "This dreadful conflict of the nations came to most of us as lightning out of a clear sky." Most people believed that the United States had no vital interest in the war and would not become involved. "Our isolated position and freedom from entangling alliances," noted the *Literary Digest*, "inspire our press with the cheering assurance that we are in no peril of being drawn into the European quarrel." President Wilson issued a proclamation of neutrality and urged Americans to be "neutral in fact as well as in name . . . impartial in thought as well as in action."

However, neither the American people nor their president stayed strictly neutral. German Americans often sympathized with Germany, and many Irish Americans hoped for a British defeat that would free Ireland from British rule. But most Americans sympathized with the Allies. Ethnic, cultural, and economic ties bound most Americans to the British and French. Politically, too, most Americans felt a greater affinity for the democratic Western Allies—tsarist Russia repelled them—than for Germany's more authoritarian government and society. And whereas Britain and the United States had enjoyed a rapprochement since 1895, Germany had repeatedly appeared as a potential rival. Many Americans considered it a militaristic nation, particularly after it violated Belgium's neutrality.

Wilson himself admired Britain's culture and government and distrusted Germany's imperial ambitions. Like other influential Americans, Wilson believed that a German victory would threaten America's economic, political, and perhaps even strategic interests. "England is fighting our fight," he said privately. Secretary of State William Jennings Bryan was genuinely neutral, but most officials favored the Allies. Robert Lansing, counselor of the State Department; Walter Hines Page, the ambassador to England; and Colonel Edward House, Wilson's closest adviser on foreign affairs, assisted British diplomats, undercut official U.S. protests against British violations of American neutrality, and encouraged Wilson's suspicions of Germany. Early in the war, House wrote Page, "I cannot see how there can be any serious trouble between England and America, with all of us feeling as we do." House and Lansing assured the Allies privately that "we considered their cause our cause."

British propaganda bolstered American sympathies. British writers, artists, and lecturers depicted the Allies as fighting for civilization against a brutal Germany that mutilated nuns and babies. Although German troops, like most other soldiers, did commit outrages, they were not guilty of the systematic barbarity claimed by Allied propagandists. Britain, however, shaped America's view of the conflict. It cut the only German cable to the United States and censored war news to suit itself. German propaganda directed at American opinion proved so ineffectual that the German ambassador concluded it might as well be abandoned.

Sympathy for the Allies, however, did not mean that Americans favored intervention. The British ambassador complained that it was "useless" to expect any "practical" advantage from the Americans' sympathy, for they had no intention of joining the conflict. Indeed, few Americans doubted that neutrality was the appropriate course and peace the proper goal. The carnage in France solidified their convictions. Wilson was determined to pursue peace as long as his view of national interests allowed.

The Economy of War

Economic issues soon threatened American neutrality. International law permitted neutral nations to sell or ship war material to all belligerents, and, with the economy mired in a recession when the war began, many Americans looked to war orders to spur economic recovery. But the British navy prevented trade with the Central Powers. Only the Allies could buy American goods. Their orders for steel, explosives, uniforms, wheat, and other products, however, pulled the country out of the recession. One journalist rejoiced that "war, for Europe, is meaning devastation and death; for America a bumper crop of new millionaires and a hectic hastening of prosperity revival."

Other Americans worried that this one-sided war trade undermined genuine neutrality. Congress even considered embargoing munitions, but few Americans supported that idea. One financial journal declared of the Allied war trade: "We need it for the profits which it yields." Whatever its justification, however, the war trade strengthened U.S. ties with the

Allies and embittered the Germans. As the German ambassador noted, American industry was "actually delivering goods only to the enemies of Germany."

A second economic issue complicated matters. To finance their war purchases, the Allies borrowed from American bankers. Initially, Secretary of State Bryan persuaded Wilson to prohibit loans to the belligerents as "inconsistent with the true spirit of neutrality." But as the importance of the war orders to both the Allies and the American economy became clear, Wilson ended the ban. Secretary of the Treasury William McAdoo argued that it would be "disastrous" not to finance the Allies' purchases, on which "our prosperity is dependent." By April 1917, American loans to the Allies exceeded $2 billion, nearly one hundred times the amount lent to Germany. These financial ties, like the war trade they underwrote, linked the United States to the Allies and convinced Germany that American neutrality was only a formality.

The Diplomacy of Neutrality

This same imbalance characterized American diplomacy. Wilson insisted on American neutral rights but acquiesced in British violations of those rights while sternly refusing to yield on German actions. Wilson argued that while British violations of international law cost Americans property, markets, and time, German violations cost lives. As the *Boston Globe* noted, the British were "a gang of thieves" and the Germans "a gang of murderers. On the whole, we prefer the thieves, but only as the lesser of two evils."

When the war began, the United States asked belligerents to respect the 1909 **Declaration of London** on neutral rights. Germany agreed to do so; the British refused. Instead, skirting or violating established procedures, Britain instituted a blockade of Germany, mined the North Sea, and forced neutral ships into British ports to search their cargoes and confiscate material deemed useful to the German war effort. These British actions infringed U.S. trading rights. Wilson branded Britain's blockade illegal and unwarranted, but by October he had conceded many of America's neutral rights to avoid conflict with Britain. This concession reflected both Wilson's English sympathies, for he thought it unfair and unrealistic to demand that Britain abandon its most effective weapon, and the profitable war trade with the Allies. He was also convinced that the Allied cause was vital to America's interests.

The British then prohibited food and other products that Germany had imported during peacetime, thereby interfering further with neutral shipping. Even the British admitted that these steps had no legal justification, and one American official complained privately: "England is playing a . . . high game, violating international law every day." But when the Wilson administration finally protested, it undermined its own position by noting that "imperative necessity" might justify a violation of international law. This statement virtually authorized the British to violate American rights. In January 1915, Wilson yielded further by observing that "no very important questions of principle" were involved in the Anglo-American quarrels over ship seizures and that they could be resolved after the war.

This policy tied the United States to the British war effort and provoked a German response. With its army stalemated on land and its navy no match for Britain's, Germany decided in February 1915 to use its submarines against Allied shipping in a war zone around the British Isles. Neutral ships risked being sunk by mistake, partly because British ships illegally flew neutral flags. Germany maintained that Britain's blockade and the acquiescence of neutral countries in British violations of international law made submarine warfare necessary.

Submarines could not readily follow traditional rules of naval warfare. These rules had been drawn up for surface ships and required them to identify enemy merchant ships and ensure the safety of passengers before attacking. But small and fragile submarines depended on surprise attacks. They could not surface without risking disaster from the deck guns of Britain's armed merchant ships, and they were too small to rescue victims of their sinkings. Yet Wilson refused to see the "imperative necessity" in German tactics that he found in British tactics, and he warned that he would hold Germany responsible for any loss of American lives or property.

In May 1915, a German submarine sank a British passenger liner, the *Lusitania*. It had been carrying arms, and the German embassy had warned Americans against traveling on the ship, but the loss of life—1,198 people, including 128 Americans—caused Americans to condemn Germany. "To speak of technicalities and the rules of war, in the face of such wholesale murder on the high seas, is a waste of time," trumpeted one magazine. Yet only six of a thousand editors surveyed called for war, and even the combative Theodore Roosevelt estimated that 98 percent of Americans still opposed war. Wilson saw he had to "carry out the double wish of our people, to maintain a firm front in respect of what we demand of Germany and yet do nothing that might by any possibility involve us in the war."

That was difficult. Wilson demanded that Germany abandon its submarine campaign. His language was so harsh that Bryan resigned, warning that by requiring more of Germany than of Britain, the president violated neutrality and threatened to draw the nation into war. Bryan argued that "Germany has a right to prevent contraband from going to the Allies," and he protested Britain's use of American passengers as shields to protect contraband cargo. "This country cannot be neutral and unneutral at the same time," he declared. "If it is to be neutral it cannot undertake to help one side against the other." Bryan proposed prohibiting Americans from traveling on belligerent ships. His proposal gained support in the South and West, and Senator Thomas Gore of Oklahoma and Representative Jeff McLemore of Texas introduced it in congressional resolutions in February 1916.

Wilson moved to defeat the Gore-McLemore resolutions, insisting that they impinged on presidential control of foreign policy and on America's neutral rights. In truth, the resolutions abandoned no vital national interest while offering to prevent another provocative incident. Moreover, neither law nor tradition gave Americans the right to travel safely on belligerent ships. Wilson's assertion of such a right committed him to a policy that could only lead to conflict. Of the nation's "double wish," then, Wilson placed more priority on confronting what he saw as the German threat than on meeting the popular desire for peace.

Arguments over submarine warfare climaxed in April 1916. A German submarine torpedoed the French ship *Sussex*, injuring four Americans. Wilson threatened to break diplomatic relations if Germany did not abandon unrestricted submarine warfare against all merchant vessels, enemy as well as neutral. This threat implied war. Germany promised not to sink merchant ships without warning but made its **Sussex Pledge** contingent on the United States' requiring Britain also to adhere to "the rules of international law universally recognized before the war." Wilson's diplomatic victory, then, was hollow. Peace for America would depend on the British adopting a course they rejected. As Wilson saw it, however, "any little German lieutenant can put us into the war at any time by some calculated outrage." Wilson's diplomacy had left the nation's future at the mercy of others.

The Battle over Preparedness

The threat of war sparked a debate over military policy. Theodore Roosevelt and a handful of other politicians, mostly Northeastern Republicans convinced that Allied victory was in the national interest, advocated what they called **preparedness**, a program to expand the armed forces and establish universal military training. Conservative business groups also

A preparedness parade winds its way through Mobile, Alabama on July 4, 1916. By 1916, President Wilson, invoking the spirit of patriotism, had given his support to the preparedness program of military expansion. *Source: University of South Alabama Archives.*

joined the agitation. The National Security League, consisting of Eastern bankers and industrialists, combined demands for preparedness with attacks on progressive reforms.

But most Americans, certain that their nation would not join the bloody madness, opposed expensive military preparations. Many supported a large peace movement. Leading feminists like Jane Addams, Charlotte Perkins Gilman, and Carrie Chapman Catt formed the Woman's Peace Party in 1915, and other organizations like the American League to Limit Armaments also campaigned against preparedness. William Jennings Bryan denounced the militarism of Roosevelt as a "philosophy [that] can rot a soul" and condemned preparedness as a program for turning the nation into "a vast armory with skull and crossbones above the door." Most opponents agreed that military spending would undermine domestic reform and raise taxes while enriching arms merchants and financiers.

Wilson also opposed preparedness initially, but he reversed his position when the submarine crisis with Germany intensified. He also began to champion military expansion lest Republicans accuse him in the 1916 election of neglecting national defense. In early 1916, he made a speaking tour to generate public support for expanding the armed forces. Continuing opposition to preparedness, especially in the South and West, forced Wilson to drop his proposal for a national reserve force. Nevertheless, the National Defense Act and the Naval Construction Act increased the strength of the army and authorized a naval construction plan. Draped in the flag, Wilson marched at the head of a huge preparedness parade in Washington to celebrate the military program.

The Election of 1916

Wilson's preparedness plans stripped the Republicans of one issue in 1916, and his renewed support of progressive reforms (see Chapter 3) helped hold Bryan Democrats in line. Wilson continued his balancing act in the campaign itself, at first stressing "Americanism" and preparedness but then emphasizing peace. The slogan "He Kept Us Out of War" appealed to the popular desire for peace, and the Democratic campaign became one long peace rally. Wilson disliked the peace emphasis but exploited its political appeal. He warned, "The certain prospect of the success of the Republican party is that we shall be drawn, in one form or another, into the embroilments of the European war."

The Republicans were divided. They had hoped to regain their progressive members after Roosevelt urged the Progressive party to follow him back into the GOP. But many joined the Democratic camp, among them several Progressive party leaders who endorsed Wilson for having enacted the party's demands of 1912. Roosevelt's frenzied interventionism had also alienated many Midwestern Republicans opposed to preparedness and cost him any chance of gaining the nomination for himself. Instead, the GOP nominated Charles Evans Hughes, a Supreme Court justice and former New York governor. The platform denounced Wilson's "shifty expedients" in foreign policy and promised "strict and honest neutrality." Unfortunately for Hughes, Roosevelt's attacks on Wilson for not pursuing a war policy persuaded many voters that the GOP was a war party. The link with Roosevelt also kept Hughes from exploiting qualms about Wilson's own unneutrality. "If Hughes is defeated," wrote one observer, "he has Roosevelt to thank for it."

The election was the closest in decades (see Map 5-1). When California narrowly went for Wilson, it decided the contest. The results reflected sectional differences, with the South and West voting for Wilson and most of the Northeast and Midwest for Hughes. The desire for peace, all observers concluded, had determined the election.

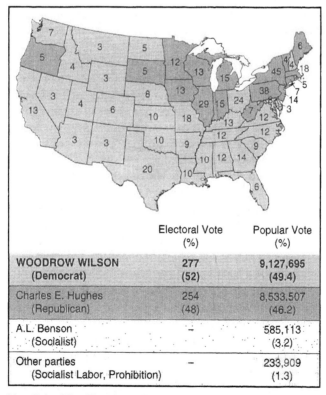

	Electoral Vote (%)	Popular Vote (%)
WOODROW WILSON (Democrat)	277 (52)	9,127,695 (49.4)
Charles E. Hughes (Republican)	254 (48)	8,533,507 (46.2)
A.L. Benson (Socialist)	–	585,113 (3.2)
Other parties (Socialist Labor, Prohibition)	–	233,909 (1.3)

MAP 5-1   The Election of Woodrow 1916
Woodrow Wilson won reelection in 1916—despite a reunified Republican party—by sweeping the South and West on campaign appeals to peace and progressive reform.

Descent into War

Still, Wilson knew that war loomed, and he made a last effort to avert it. In 1915 and 1916, he had tried to mediate the European conflict, using Colonel House as a secret intermediary. Now he again appealed for an end to hostilities. In January 1917, he sketched out the terms of what he called a "peace without victory." Anything else, he warned, would only lead to another war. The new world order should be based on national equality and **self-determination**, arms reductions, freedom of the seas, and an international organization to ensure peace. It was a distinctly American vision.

Neither the Allies nor the Central Powers were interested. Each side had sacrificed too much to settle for anything short of outright victory. Germany wanted to annex territory in eastern Europe, Belgium, and France and to take over Belgian and French colonies in Africa; Austria sought Balkan territory. The Allies wanted to destroy German military and commercial power, weaken the Austro-Hungarian Empire, take Germany's colonies in Africa, and supplant Turkish influence in the Middle East. One British leader denounced Wilson as "the quintessence of a prig" for suggesting that after three years of "this terrible effort," the two sides should accept American principles rather than their own national objectives. Wilson's initiative failed.

To break the deadlock, Germany decided to resume unrestricted submarine warfare. Such action seemed necessary: By 1917, nearly 700 German civilians died each day because of the British blockade, far more than the daily toll of British soldiers in the trenches. German generals believed that even if the United States declared war, it could do little more in the short run to injure Germany than it was already doing. German submarines, they hoped, would end the war by cutting the Allies off from U.S. supplies before the United States could send an army to Europe. On January 31, Germany announced its decision to unleash its submarines in a broad war zone.

Wilson was now virtually committed to a war many Americans opposed. He broke diplomatic relations with Germany and asked Congress to arm American merchant vessels. When the Senate refused, Wilson invoked an antipiracy law of 1819 and armed the ships anyway. Although no American ships had yet been sunk, he also ordered the naval gun crews to shoot submarines on sight. Wilson's own secretary of the navy warned that these actions violated international law and were a step toward war; Wilson called his policy "armed neutrality." Huge rallies across America demanded peace.

Yet several developments soon shifted public opinion. On March 1, Wilson released an intercepted message from the German foreign minister, Arthur Zimmermann, to the German minister in Mexico. It proposed that in the event of war between the United States and Germany, Mexico should ally itself with Germany; in exchange, Mexico would recover its "lost territory in Texas, New Mexico, and Arizona." The Zimmermann note produced a wave of hostility toward Germany and increased support for intervention in the war, especially in the Southwest which had opposed involvement. A revolution in Russia overthrew the tsarist regime and established a provisional government. Russia was now "a fit partner" for the United States, said Wilson. When submarines sank four American freighters in mid-March, anti-German feeling broadened.

On April 2, 1917, Wilson delivered his war message, declaring that neutrality was no longer possible, given Germany's submarine "warfare against mankind." To build support for joining a war that most people had long regarded with revulsion and as alien to American interests, Wilson set forth the nation's war goals as simple and noble. The United States would not fight for conquest or domination but for "the ultimate peace of the world and for the liberation of its peoples. . . . The world must be made safe for democracy." Interventionists were delighted with the decision for war but often distanced themselves from any goal other than promoting national interests. Some progressives who had opposed involvement were won over by Wilson's appeal to idealism.

But others in Congress attacked war. Senator Robert La Follette assailed Wilson's policies as unneutral. Senator George Norris of Nebraska condemned the economic motives for American belligerency, crying out, "We are going to war upon the command of gold." Ridiculing Wilson's advocacy of war as a means to promote democracy, House Democratic leader Claude Kitchin of North Carolina insisted that the American people opposed war and unsuccessfully urged holding a popular referendum on the question. After vigorous debate, the Senate passed the war resolution 82 to 6 and the House 373 to 50. On April 6, 1917, the United States officially entered the Great War, a war that Kitchin predicted would be "one vast drama of horrors and blood, one boundless stage upon which will play all the evil spirits of earth and hell."

WAGING WAR IN AMERICA

Mobilizing for military intervention was a massive undertaking. "It is not an army that we must shape and train for war," announced President Wilson; "it is a Nation." The government reorganized the economy to emphasize centralized management, developed policies to control public opinion and suppress dissent, and transformed the role of government itself. Mobilization often built on progressives' moralism and sense of mission and their work to resolve social and economic problems by government intervention. In other respects, however, the war experience undercut progressive achievements and withered the spirits of reformers. In many different ways, people on the home front—like soldiers in Europe—would participate in the Great War; all would find their lives changed.

Managing the War Economy

Surveying the nation's economy in May 1917, Secretary of War Newton Baker echoed Wilson. War no longer involved merely soldiers and weapons, he said. "It is the conflict of smokestacks now, the combat of the driving wheel and the engine." To harness those factories and machines for the war, federal and state governments developed a complex structure of agencies and controls for every sector of the economy, from industry and agriculture to transportation and labor (see the Overview table, "Major Government Wartime Agencies"). Supervised by the Council of National Defense, these agencies shifted resources to war-related enterprise, increased production of goods and services, and improved transportation and distribution.

The most important agency was the **War Industries Board (WIB)**, established in July 1917 to set industrial priorities, coordinate military purchasing, and supervise business. Led by financier Bernard Baruch, the WIB exercised unprecedented powers over industry by setting prices, allocating scarce materials, and standardizing products and procedures to boost efficiency. The number of sizes and styles of plows was reduced by 80 percent; the number of colors of typewriter ribbon dropped from 150 to 5. The WIB even specified how many trunks traveling salesmen could carry and how many stops elevators could make. Yet Baruch was not an industrial dictator; he aimed at business–government integration. The WIB promoted major business interests, helped suspend antitrust laws, and guaranteed huge corporate profits. So many business leaders became involved in the WIB that there was a popular outcry against business infiltration of the government, and one corporate executive admitted, "We

MAJOR GOVERNMENT WARTIME AGENCIES

AGENCY	PURPOSE
War Industries Board	Reorganized industry to maximize wartime production.
Railroad Administration	Modernized and operated the nation's railroads.
Food Administration	Increased agricultural production, supervised food distribution and farm labor.
National War Labor Board	Resolved labor-management disputes, improved labor conditions, and recognized union rights as means to promote production and efficiency.
Committee on Public Information	Managed propaganda to build public support for the war effort.

are all making more money out of this war than the average human being ought to." Some progressives began to see the dangers, and business leaders the advantages, of government economic intervention.

The **Railroad Administration** also linked business ambitions to the war economy. Under William McAdoo, it operated the nation's railroads as a unified system to move supplies and troops efficiently. Centralized management eliminated competition, permitted improvements in equipment, and brought great profits to the owners but higher prices to the general public. Progressive Republican Senator Hiram Johnson of California protested that the Railroad Administration was "outrageously generous to the railroads and shamefully unjust to the people."

Equally effective and far more popular was the **Food Administration**, headed by Herbert Hoover. Hoover had organized relief supplies for war-torn Belgium and now controlled the production and distribution of food for the United States and its allies. He persuaded millions of Americans to accept meatless and wheatless days so that the Food Administration could feed military and foreign consumers. Half a million women went door to door to secure food conservation pledges from housewives. City residents planted victory gardens in parks and vacant lots, and President Wilson even pastured sheep on the White House lawn.

Hoover also worked closely with agricultural processors and distributors, assuring profits in exchange for cooperation. Farmers profited from the war, too. To encourage production, Hoover established high prices for commodities, and agricultural income rose 30 percent. The federal and state governments also provided commercial farmers with sufficient farm labor despite the military draft and competition from high-wage war industries. The Food Administration organized the Woman's Land Army to work in the fields. Most states formed units of the Boys' Working Reserve for agricultural labor. Many Southern and Western states required "loafers" or "slackers" to work in agriculture. Agribusinesses in the Southwest persuaded the federal government to permit them to import Mexicans to work under government supervision and be housed in special camps.

The **National War Labor Board** supervised labor relations. In exchange for labor's cooperation, this agency guaranteed the rights of unions to organize and bargain collectively. With such support, unions sharply increased their membership. The labor board also encouraged improved working conditions, higher wages, and shorter hours. War contracts stipulated an eight-hour day, and by the end of the war, nearly half the nation's workers had achieved the forty-eight-hour week. Wages rose, too, but often only as fast as inflation. These improvements limited labor disputes during the war, and Secretary of War Baker praised labor as "more willing to keep in step than capital." But when unions like the Industrial Workers of the World did not keep in step, the government suppressed them.

Although these and other government regulatory agencies were dismantled when the war ended, their activities reinforced many long-standing trends in the American economy, from the consolidation of business to the commercialization of agriculture and the organization of labor. They also set a precedent for governmental activism that would prove valuable during the crises of the 1930s and 1940s.

Women and Minorities: New Opportunities, Old Inequities

The reorganization of the economy also had significant social consequences, especially for women and African Americans. In response to labor shortages, public officials and private employers exhorted women to join the work force—"For Every Fighter a Woman Worker" urged one poster. Women now took jobs previously closed to them. Besides farm work, they built airplanes, produced guns and ammunition, and manufactured tents and cartridge belts. More than 100,000 women worked in munitions plants and 40,000 in the steel industry. Women constituted 20 percent or more of all workers making electrical machinery, leather and rubber goods, and food. They operated drills and lathes, controlled cranes in steel mills, and repaired equipment in machine shops. "One of the lessons from the war," said one manufacturer, "has been to show that women can do exacting work." Harriot Stanton Blatch, a suffragist active in the Food Administration, estimated that a million women had replaced men in industry, where "their drudgery is for the first time paid for."

With women's labor crucial for the war effort, both government agencies and private industry recruited women for factory work. Here, four women, wearing "womanall" work-suits, pause at their jobs at the Westinghouse Electric Company in 1918.

Many working women simply shifted to other jobs where their existing skills earned better wages and benefits. The reshuffling of jobs among white women opened new vacancies for black women in domestic, clerical, and industrial employment. As black women replaced white women in the garment and textile industries, social reformers spoke of "a new day for the colored woman worker." But such optimism was unwarranted. Racial as well as gender segregation continued to mark employment, and wartime improvements were temporary. Federal efforts to prevent pay inequities and sexual harassment in the workplace were half-hearted and subordinated to the goals of efficiency and productivity. And, as one woman said of employers, "As usual, they did not want women to interfere in any way."

The war did help middle-class women reformers achieve two long-sought objectives: woman suffrage and prohibition. Women's support for the war effort prompted more Americans to support woman suffrage. Emphasizing the national cooperation needed to wage the war, one magazine noted that "arbitrarily to draw the line at voting, at a time when every man and woman must share in this effort, becomes an absurd anomaly." Even Woodrow Wilson finally endorsed the reform, terming it "vital to the winning of the war." Congress approved the suffrage amendment, which was ratified in 1920. The war also provided the final argument necessary for the adoption of prohibition, long advocated for other reasons. Convinced that abstaining from alcohol would save grain and make workers and soldiers more efficient, Congress also passed the prohibition amendment, which was ratified in 1919.

The war also changed the lives of African Americans. The demand for industrial labor caused a huge migration of black people from the rural South, where they had had little opportunity, few rights, and no hope. In Northern cities, they worked in shipyards, steel mills, and packing houses. Half a million African Americans moved North during the war, doubling and tripling the black populations of Chicago, Detroit, and other industrial cities.

Unfortunately, black people often encountered the kind of racial discrimination and violence in the North they had hoped to leave behind in the South. Fearful and resentful white people started race riots in Northern cities. In East St. Louis, Illinois, where thousands of black Southerners sought defense work, a white mob in July 1917 murdered at least thirty-nine black people, sparing, as an investigating committee reported, "neither age nor sex in their blind lust for blood." Others placed the tragedy in a larger context. The *Literary Digest* noted, "Race-riots in East St. Louis afford a lurid background to our efforts to carry justice and idealism to Europe." And Wilson was told privately that the riot was "worse than anything the Germans did in Belgium."

Financing the War

To finance the war, the government borrowed money and raised taxes. Business interests favored the first course, but Southern and Western progressives argued that taxation was more efficient and equitable and would minimize war profiteering. Conservative and business opposition to progressive taxation prompted California Senator Johnson to note, "Our endeavours to impose heavy war profit taxes . . . have brought into sharp relief the skin-deep dollar patriotism of some of those who have been loudest in declamations on war and in their demands for blood." Nevertheless, the tax laws of 1917 and 1918 established a graduated tax structure with increased taxes on large incomes, corporate profits, and wealthy estates. Conservative opposition, however, would frustrate progressives' hopes for permanent tax reforms.

The government raised two-thirds of the war costs by borrowing. Most of the loans came from banks and wealthy investors, but the government also campaigned to sell **Liberty Bonds** to the general public. Celebrities went to schools, churches, and rallies to persuade Americans to buy bonds as their patriotic duty. "Every person who refuses to subscribe," Secretary of the Treasury McAdoo told a California audience, "is a friend of Germany." Using techniques of persuasion and control from advertising and mass entertainment, the Wilson administration thus enlisted the emotions of loyalty, fear, patriotism, and obedience for the war effort.

Conquering Minds

The government also tried to promote a war spirit among the American people by establishing propaganda agencies and enacting legislation to control social attitudes and behavior. This program drew from the restrictive side of progressivism: its impulses toward social

SEND THE EAGLE'S ANSWER
MORE SHIPS
UNITED STATES SHIPPING BOARD   EMERGENCY FLEET CORPORATION

In World War I, mobilization of the home front was basic to military success. Government posters exhorted Americans to increase industrial and agricultural production, buy war bonds, and suppress dissent.

control, behavior regulation, and nativism. It also reflected the interests of more conservative forces. The Wilson administration adopted this program of social mobilization because many Americans opposed the war: German Americans with ethnic ties to the Central Powers; Irish Catholics and Russian Jews who condemned the Allies for persecution and repression; Scandinavian immigrants averse to military service; pacifists who recoiled from what Wilson himself called "the most terrible and disastrous of all wars"; radicals who denounced the war as capitalist and imperialist; and many others, especially among the rural classes of the South and Midwest, who saw no reason to participate in the distant war.

To rally Americans behind the war effort, Wilson established the **Committee on Public Information (CPI)** under the journalist George Creel. Despite its title, the CPI sought to manipulate, not inform, public opinion. Creel described his goal as winning "the fight for the minds of men, for the 'conquest of their convictions.' " The CPI flooded the country with press releases, advertisements, cartoons, and canned editorials. An average of six pounds of government publicity went each day to every newspaper in California, for example. The CPI made newsreels and war movies to capture public attention. It scheduled 75,000 speakers, who delivered a million speeches to 400 million listeners. Its women's division targeted American women in stereotyped emotional terms. It hired artists to draw posters, professors to write pamphlets in twenty-three languages, and poets to compose war poems for children.

Other government agencies launched similar campaigns. The Woman's Committee of the Council of National Defense established the Department of Educational Propaganda and Patriotic Education. Carrie Chapman Catt dropped her peace activism to head this bureau in the hope that the war effort would increase support for woman suffrage. The agency worked to win over women who opposed the war, particularly in the rural Midwest, West, and South. It formed women's speakers' bureaus, developed programs for community meetings at country schools, and distributed millions of pamphlets.

Government propaganda had three themes: national unity, the loathsome character of the enemy, and the war as a grand crusade for liberty and democracy. Obsessed with national unity and conformity, Creel promoted fear, hatred, and prejudice in the name of a triumphant

Americanism. Germans were depicted as brutal, even subhuman, rapists and murderers. The campaign suggested that any dissent was unpatriotic, if not treasonous, and dangerous to national survival. This emphasis on unreasoning conformity helped prompt hysterical attacks on German Americans, radicals, and pacifists.

Suppressing Dissent

The Wilson administration also suppressed dissent, now officially branded disloyalty. For reasons of their own, private interests helped shape a reactionary repression that tarnished the nation's professed idealistic war goals. The campaign also established unfortunate precedents for the future.

Congress rushed to stifle antiwar sentiment. The **Espionage Act** provided heavy fines and up to twenty years in prison for obstructing the war effort, a vague phrase but one "omnipotently comprehensive," warned one Idaho senator who opposed the law. "No man can foresee what it might be in its consequences." In fact, the Espionage Act became a weapon to crush dissent and criticism. In 1918, Congress passed the still more sweeping **Sedition Act**. Based on state laws in the West designed to suppress labor radicals, the Sedition Act provided severe penalties for speaking or writing against the draft, bond sales, or war production or for criticizing government personnel or policies. Congress emphasized the law's inclusive nature by rejecting a proposed amendment stipulating that "nothing in this act shall be construed as limiting the liberty or impairing the right of any individual to publish or speak what is true, with good motives, and for justifiable ends." Senator Hiram Johnson lamented: "It is war. But, good God, . . . when did it become war upon the American people?"

Postmaster General Albert Burleson banned antiwar or radical newspapers and magazines from the mail, suppressing literature so indiscriminately that one observer said he "didn't know socialism from rheumatism." Even more zealous in attacking radicals and presumed subversives was the reactionary Attorney General Thomas Gregory, who made little distinction between traitors and pacifists, war critics and radicals. Eugene Debs was sentenced to ten years in prison for a "treasonous" speech in which he declared it "extremely dangerous to exercise the right of free speech in a country fighting to make democracy safe in the world." By war's end, a third of the Socialist party's national leadership was in prison, leaving the party in shambles. Other notable radicals imprisoned included Ricardo Flores Magon, a Mexican-American labor organizer who was sentenced to twenty years for publishing antiwar material in his Los Angeles Spanish-language newspaper, *Regeneracion.*

Gregory also enlisted the help of private vigilantes, including several hundred thousand members of the reactionary American Protective League that sought to purge radicals and reformers from the nation's economic and political life. They wiretapped telephones, intercepted private mail, burglarized union offices, broke up German-language newspapers, harassed immigrants, and staged mass raids, seizing thousands of people they claimed were not doing enough for the war effort. Even George Creel conceded that "at all times their patriotism was a thing of screams, violence, and extremes, and their savage intolerances had the burn of acid."

State and local authorities also suppressed what they saw as antiwar, radical, or pro-German activities. They established 184,000 investigating and enforcement agencies known as councils of defense or public safety committees. They encouraged Americans to spy on one another, required people to buy Liberty Bonds, and prohibited teaching German in schools or using the language in religious services and telephone conversations (see American Views, "Mobilizing America for Liberty"). Indeed, suppression of all things German reached extremes. Germanic names of towns, streets, and people were changed; sauerkraut became liberty cabbage, and the hamburger, the liberty sandwich. In Tulsa, a member of the council

AMERICAN VIEWS

Mobilizing America for Liberty

The war years witnessed official and popular efforts to repress dissent and diversity. Much of this repression was aimed at America's immigrant groups and sought to create national unity through coercive Americanization that trampled on the rights and values that the nation claimed to be defending. The following is an official proclamation of Governor W. L. Harding of Iowa, issued on May 23, 1918.

What is the rationale for the governor's proclamation? What do you think of his interpretation of the constitutional guarantees of individual rights?

What other "inconvenience or sacrifice" might the proclamation impose on minorities?

How might the proclamation incite vigilantism?

The official language of the United States and the State of Iowa is the English language. Freedom of speech is guaranteed by federal and State Constitutions, but this is not a guaranty of the right to use a language other than the language of this country—the English language. Both federal and State Constitutions also provide that "no laws shall be made respecting an establishment of religion or prohibiting the free exercise thereof." Each person is guaranteed freedom to worship God according to the dictates of his own conscience, but this guaranty does not protect him in the use of a foreign language when he can as well express his thought in English, nor entitle the person who cannot speak or understand the English language to employ a foreign language, when to do so tends in time of national peril, to create discord among neighbors and citizens, or to disturb the peace and quiet of the community.

Every person should appreciate and observe his duty to refrain from all acts or conversation which may excite suspicion or produce strife among the people, but in his relation to the public should so demean himself that every word and act will manifest his loyalty to his country and his solemn purpose to aid in achieving victory for our army and navy and the permanent peace of the world. . . .

The great aim and object of all should be unity of purpose and a solidarity of all the people under the flag for victory. This much we owe to ourselves, to posterity, to our country, and to the world.

Therefore, the following rules should obtain in Iowa during the war:

First. English should and must be the only medium of instruction in public, private, denominational, or other similar schools.

Second. Conversation in public places, on trains, and over the telephone should be in the English language.

Third. All public addresses should be in the English language.

Fourth. Let those who cannot speak or understand the English language conduct their religious worship in their homes.

This course carried out in the spirit of patriotism, though inconvenient to some, will not interfere with their guaranteed constitutional rights and will result in peace and tranquility at home and greatly strengthen the country in battle. The blessings of the United States are so great that any inconvenience or sacrifice should willingly be made for their perpetuity.

Therefore, by virtue of authority in me vested, I, W. L. Harding, Governor of the State of Iowa, commend the spirit of tolerance and urge that henceforth the within outlined rules be adhered to by all, that petty differences be avoided and forgotten, and that, united as one people with one purpose and one language, we fight shoulder to shoulder for the good of mankind.

Source: B. F. Shambaugh, ed., *Iowa and War* (Iowa City: State Historical Society of Iowa, 1919).

of defense killed someone for making allegedly pro-German remarks. The council declared its approval, and community leaders applauded the killer's patriotism. A Midwestern official of the Council of National Defense noted, "All over this part of the country men are being tarred and feathered and some are being lynched. . . . These cases do not get into the newspapers nor is an effort ever made to punish the individuals concerned."

Members of the business community exploited the hysteria to promote their own interests at the expense of farmers, workers, and reformers. As one Wisconsin farmer complained, businessmen "now under the guise of patriotism are trying to ram down the farmers' throats things they hardly dared before." On the Great Plains from Texas to North Dakota, the business target was the Nonpartisan League, a radical farm group demanding state control or ownership of banks, grain elevators, and flour mills. Although the League supported the war, oversubscribed bond drives, and had George Creel affirm its loyalty, conservatives depicted it as seditious to block its advocacy of political and economic reforms, including the confiscation of large fortunes to pay for the war. Minnesota's public safety commission condemned members of the Nonpartisan League as traitors and proposed a "firing squad working overtime" to deal with them. Nebraska's council of defense barred League meetings. Public officials and self-styled patriots broke up the League's meetings and whipped and jailed its leaders.

In the West, business interests targeted labor organizations, especially the Industrial Workers of the World (IWW). In Arizona, for example, the Phelps-Dodge Company broke a miners' strike in 1917 by depicting the Wobblies as bent on war-related sabotage. A vigilante mob, armed and paid by the mining company, seized twelve hundred strikers, many of them Wobblies and one-third of them Mexican Americans, and herded them into the desert without food or water. Federal investigators found no evidence of sedition among the miners and reported that the company and its thugs had been inspired not by "patriotism" but by "ordinary strike-breaking motives." Corporate management was merely "raising the false cry of 'disloyalty' " to suppress workers' complaints.

Nonetheless, the government itself assisted the business campaign. It used the army to break loggers' support for the IWW in the Pacific Northwest, and it raided IWW halls across the country in September 1917. The conviction of nearly two hundred Wobblies on charges of sedition in three mass trials in Illinois, California, and Kansas crippled the nation's largest industrial union.

In the end, the government was primarily responsible for the war hysteria, regardless of how such fears were used. It encouraged suspicion and conflict by its own inflammatory propaganda, repressive laws, and violation of basic civil rights; by supporting extremists who used the war for their own purposes, and by not opposing mob violence against German Americans. This ugly mood would infect the postwar world.

WAGING WAR AND PEACE ABROAD

While mobilizing the home front, the Wilson administration undertook an impressive military effort to help the Allies defeat the Central Powers. Wilson also struggled to secure international acceptance for his plans for a just and permanent peace.

The War to End All Wars

When the United States entered the war, the Allied military position was dire. The losses from three years of trench warfare had sapped military strength and civilian morale. French soldiers mutinied and refused to continue an assault that had cost 120,000 casualties in five days; the German submarine campaign was devastating the British. On the eastern front, the Russian army collapsed, and the Russian government gradually disintegrated after the overthrow of the tsarist regime.

What the Allies needed, said French Marshal Joseph Joffre in April 1917, was simple: "We want men, men, men." In May, Congress passed the **Selective Service Act**, establishing conscription. More than 24 million men eventually registered for the draft, and nearly 3 million entered the army when their numbers were drawn in a national lottery. Almost 2 million more men volunteered, as did more than ten thousand women who served in the navy. Nearly one-fifth of America's soldiers were foreign-born (Europeans spoke of the "American Foreign Legion"); 367,000 were black. Many Indians served with distinction as well; in response, Indian veterans were made citizens in 1919, a status extended to all Indians five years later.

Civilians were transformed into soldiers in hastily organized training camps operated according to progressive principles. Prohibition prevailed in the camps; the poorly educated and largely working-class recruits were taught personal hygiene; worries about sin and inefficiency produced massive campaigns against venereal disease; and immigrants were taught English and American history. Some units were ethnically segregated: At Camp Gordon, Georgia, Italians and Slavs had separate units with their own officers. Racial segregation was more rigid, not only in training camps and military units but in assignments as well. The navy assigned black sailors to menial positions, and the army similarly used black soldiers primarily as gravediggers and laborers. But one black combat division was created, and four black regiments fought under French command. France decorated three of these units with its highest citations for valor. (White American officers urged the French not to praise black troops, treat black officers as equals, or permit fraternization.)

More than forty thousand women were recruited as noncombatant personnel, such as clerks, translators, and switchboard operators, thereby enabling more men to be assigned to combat duty. The navy awarded them equal rank with males performing the same tasks, and they were eligible after the war for veterans benefits. The army was a different story. Although serving in uniform and under military discipline, women had no formal military status, were ineligible for benefits, and often had their skills and contributions devalued. On the eve of a major battle in France, Merle Egan in the U.S. Army Signal Corps, working feverishly training soldiers to operate switchboards to help coordinate the massive military buildup, found that some resented taking instructions from a woman. But "when I reminded them that any soldier could carry a gun but the safety of a whole division might depend on the switchboard one of them was operating, I had no more trouble."

The first American troops landed in France in June 1917. This **American Expeditionary Force (AEF)** was commanded by General John J. Pershing, a career officer who had chased Pancho Villa across northern Mexico (see Chapter 4). A gruff stickler for discipline (Secretary of War Baker worried that a man who had his mind so much on buttons would not have time to think about how to win a war), Pershing wanted to train his soldiers for a full two years before committing them to battle in 1919, but the AEF was rushed across the Atlantic in order to revive the collapsing morale among the French. Private Leo Bailey recalled that few of his company had ever discharged a firearm of any kind. "To have sent us to the front at that time would have been murder," he said. "We were woefully ignorant of the basic principles of the soldier." Months of training, under French direction, then followed as the Americans learned about trench warfare: using bayonets, grenades, and machine guns and surviving poison gas attacks. Finally in October, the First Division, the Big Red One, moved into the trenches.

Full-scale American intervention began in the late spring of 1918 (see Map 5-2). General Tasker Bliss asked the French chief of staff: "Well, we have come over here to get killed. Where do you want to use us?" In June, the fresh American troops helped the French repulse a German thrust toward Paris at Château-Thierry. One soldier later recalled: "We saw the long lines of Marines leap from somewhere and start across the wheatfields. . . . As

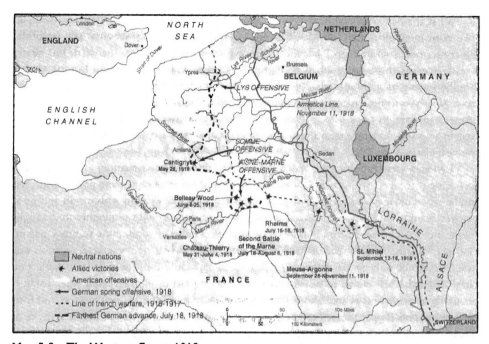

MAP 5-2   The Western Front, 1918
After three years of trench warfare, the arrival of large numbers of American troops in 1918 enabled the Allies to launch an offensive that drove back the Germans and forced an armistice.

the first wave disappeared over the crest we heard the opening clatter of dozens of machine guns that sprayed our advancing lines. Then we heard some shrieks that made our blood run cold. High above the roar of the artillery and the clatter of machine guns we heard the war cries of the Marines. . . . It seemed less than half an hour before all the machine guns had stopped firing." Further savage fighting at Belleau Wood blocked the Germans again, prompting a French officer to declare, "You Americans are our hope, our strength, our life." In July, the AEF helped defeat another German advance, at Rheims. The influx of American troops had tipped the balance toward Allied victory. By July 18, the German chancellor later acknowledged, "even the most optimistic among us knew that all was lost. The history of the world was played out in three days."

In July, Wilson also agreed to commit fifteen thousand American troops to intervene in Russia. Russia's provisional government had collapsed when the **Bolsheviks**, or communists, had seized power in November 1917. Under V. I. Lenin, the Bolsheviks had then signed an armistice with Germany in early 1918, which freed German troops for the summer offensive in France. The Allies' interventions were designed to reopen the eastern front and help overthrow the Bolshevik government. Lenin's call for the destruction of capitalism and imperialism alarmed the Allied leaders. One Wilson adviser urged the "eradication" of the Russian government. Soon American and British troops were fighting Russians in an effort to influence Russia's internal affairs. U.S. forces remained in Russia until 1920, even after Germany had surrendered in 1918. These military interventions failed, but they did promote lasting Russian distrust of the West.

The Allies were more successful on the western front. Having stopped the German offensive in July, they launched their own advance. The decisive battle began in late September when an American army over 1 million strong attacked German trenches in the Argonne Forest. Many Americans were still inexperienced; some had been drafted only in July and had spent more time traveling than training. One officer worried, "With their unfamiliarity with weapons, a gun was about as much use as a broom in their hands." Nevertheless, the Americans advanced steadily, despite attacks with poison gas and heavy artillery. Lieutenant Maury Maverick (later a Texas congressman) described the shelling: "We were simply in a big black spot with streaks of screaming red and yellow, with roaring giants in the sky tearing and whirling and roaring." An exploding shell terrified him: "There is a great swishing scream, a smash-bang, and it seems to tear everything loose from you. The intensity of it simply enters your heart and brain, and tears every nerve to pieces."

The battle for the Argonne raged for weeks. One German general reported that his exhausted soldiers faced Americans who "were fresh, eager for fighting, and brave," but he found their sheer numbers most impressive. Eventually, this massive assault overwhelmed the Germans. Despite severe casualties, the AEF had helped the British and French defeat the enemy. With its allies surrendering, its own army in retreat, and revolution breaking out among war-weary residents in its major cities, Germany asked for peace. On November 11, 1918, an armistice ended the Great War. More than 115,000 Americans were among the 8 million soldiers and 7 million civilians dead.

The Fourteen Points

The armistice was only a step toward final peace. President Wilson had already enunciated American war objectives on January 8, 1918, in a speech outlining what became known as the Fourteen Points. In his 1917 war message, Wilson had advocated a more democratic world system, and this new speech spelled out how to achieve it. But Wilson also had a political purpose. The Bolsheviks had published the Allies' secret treaties dividing up the expected economic and territorial spoils of war. Lenin called for an immediate peace based on the liberation of all colonies, self-determination for all peoples, and the rejection of annexations and punitive indemnities. Wilson's Fourteen Points reassured the Americans and Allies that they were fighting for more than imperialist gains and offered an alternative to what he called Lenin's "crude formula" for peace.

Eight of Wilson's points proposed creating new nations, shifting old borders, or assuring self-determination for peoples previously subject to the Austrian, German, or Russian empires. The point about Russia would haunt Wilson after the Allied interventions there began, for it called on all nations to evacuate Russian territory and permit Russia "an unhampered and unembarrassed opportunity for the independent determination of her own political development" under "institutions of her own choosing." Another five points invoked principles to guide international relations: freedom of the seas, open diplomacy instead of secret treaties, reduction of armaments, free trade, and the fair settlement of colonial claims. Wilson's fourteenth and most important point proposed a league of nations to carry out these ideals and ensure international stability.

Wilson and the German government had these principles in mind when negotiating the armistice. The Allies, however, had never explicitly accepted the Fourteen Points, and framing a final peace treaty would be difficult. While Wilson favored a settlement that would promote international stability and economic expansion, he recognized that the Allies sought "to get everything out of Germany that they can." Indeed, after their human and economic sacrifices, Britain and France wanted tangible compensation, not pious principles.

Convinced of the righteousness of his cause, Wilson decided to attend the peace conference in Paris himself, though no president had ever gone to Europe while in office. But Wilson weakened his position before he even set sail. First, he urged voters to support Democratic candidates in the November 1918 elections to indicate approval of his peace plans. But the electorate, responding primarily to domestic problems like inflation, gave the Republicans control of both houses of Congress. This meant that any treaty would have to be approved by Senate Republicans angry that Wilson had tried to use war and peace for partisan purposes. Second, Wilson refused to consult with Senate Republicans on plans for the peace conference and failed to name important Republicans to the Paris delegation. It would be Wilson's treaty, but Republicans would feel no responsibility to approve it.

The Paris Peace Conference

The peace conference opened on January 18, 1919. Meeting at the Palace of Versailles, the delegations were dominated by the principal Allied leaders themselves: Wilson of the United States, David Lloyd George of Britain, Georges Clemenceau of France, and Vittorio Orlando of Italy. The Central Powers and Bolshevik Russia were excluded. The treaty would be one-sided except to the extent that Wilson could insist on the liberal terms of the Fourteen Points against French and British intransigence. As Clemenceau remarked, "God gave us the Ten Commandments and we broke them. Mr. Wilson has given us the Fourteen Points. We shall see."

Wilson himself had broken two of the Fourteen Points before the conference began. He had acquiesced in Britain's rejection of freedom of the seas, and he had sent U.S. troops to intervene in Russia in violation of its right to self-determination.

For months, the conference debated Wilson's other goals and the Allies' demands for compensation and security. Lloyd George later commented, with reference to the self-righteous Wilson and the assertive Clemenceau, "I think I did as well as might be expected, seated as I was between Jesus Christ and Napoleon Bonaparte." Under protest, Germany signed the **Treaty of Versailles** on June 28, 1919. Its terms were far more severe than Wilson had proposed or Germany had anticipated. Germany had to accept sole responsibility for starting the war, which all Germans bitterly resented. It was required to pay huge

An exhuberant President Wilson greeting an enthusiastic Paris crowd with French President Poincaré in December 1918. Within a few months, the Paris Peace Conference would produce disillusionment, bickering, and a flawed treaty that did little to insure international peace and stability.

MAP 5-3   Europe and the Middle East After the Treaty of Versailles
World War I and the Treaty of Versailles rearranged the borders of Europe and the Middle East.
Germany, Russia, and the Austrian and Turkish empires all lost land, and new nations were recognized, but the principle of self-determination was only imperfectly observed.

reparations to the Allies; to give up land to France, Poland, Belgium, and Denmark; to cede its colonies; to limit its army and navy to small self-defense forces; to destroy military bases; and to promise not to manufacture or purchase armaments.

Wilson gained some acceptance of self-determination. As the German, Austro-Hungarian, Turkish, and Russian empires had collapsed at the end of the war, nationalist groups had proclaimed their independence. On one hand, the peace settlement formally recognized these new nation-states: Poland, Finland, Estonia, Latvia, and Lithuania in eastern Europe and Austria, Hungary, Czechoslovakia, and Yugoslavia in central Europe (see Map 5-3). On the other hand, France, Italy, Romania, and Japan all annexed territory regardless of the wishes of the inhabitants. Germans were placed under Polish control in Silesia and Czech control in Bohemia. Austrians were not allowed to merge with Germany. And the conference sanctioned colonialism by establishing a trusteeship system that enabled France, Britain, and Japan to take over German colonies and Turkish territory.

Moreover, Allied leaders endorsed the changes in eastern Europe in part because the new states there were anticommunist and would constitute a barrier against Bolshevism.

Indeed, the Allies at Versailles were preoccupied with Bolshevik Russia, which one of Wilson's aides called the "black cloud of the east, threatening to overwhelm and swallow up the world." Communist movements in early 1919 in Germany, Austria, and Hungary caused the Allies to fear that "the Russian idea was still rising in power," and they hoped to isolate and weaken Bolshevik Russia. Allied armies were in Russia during the peace conference, and Wilson and the other leaders agreed to provide further aid to fight the Bolsheviks. This hostility to Russia, like the punitive terms for Germany and the concessions to imperial interests, boded ill for a stable and just postwar order.

But Wilson hoped that the final section of the Versailles treaty would resolve the flaws of the agreement by establishing his great international organization to preserve peace: the **League of Nations**. The Covenant, or constitution, of the League was built into the treaty. Its crucial feature, Article Ten, bound the member nations to guarantee each other's independence, which was Wilson's concept of collective security. "At least," he told an aide, "we are saving the Covenant, and that instrument will work wonders, bring the blessing of peace, and then when the war psychosis has abated, it will not be difficult to settle all disputes that baffle us now." Sailing home, he mused: "Well, it is finished, and, as no one is satisfied, it makes me hope we have made a just peace; but it is all on the lap of the gods."

WAGING PEACE AT HOME

Wilson was determined to defeat opposition to the peace treaty. But many Americans were engaged in their own struggles with the new conditions of a nation suddenly at peace but riven by economic, social, and political conflict shaped by the war experience. Wilson's battle for the League of Nations would fail tragically. The other conflicts would rage until the election of 1920 restored a normalcy of sorts.

Battle over the League

Most Americans favored the Versailles treaty. A survey of fourteen hundred newspapers found fewer than two hundred opposed. Thirty-three governors and thirty-two state legislatures endorsed the League of Nations. But when Wilson called for the Senate to accept "the moral leadership . . . and confidence of the world" by ratifying the treaty, he met resistance. Some Republicans wanted to prevent the Democrats from campaigning in 1920 as the party responsible for a victorious war and a glorious peace, but most Republican opponents of the treaty raised serious questions, often reflecting national traditions in foreign relations. Nearly all Democrats favored the treaty, but they were a minority; some Republicans had to be converted for the treaty to be approved.

Progressive Republican senators, such as Robert La Follette and Hiram Johnson, led one group of opponents. Called the **Irreconcilables**, they opposed participation in the League of Nations, which they saw as designed to perpetuate the power of imperialist countries. Article Ten, they feared, would require the United States to help suppress rebellions in Ireland against British rule or to enforce disputed European borders. Johnson declared, "I am opposed to American boys policing Europe and quelling riots in every new nation's backyard." Most of the Irreconcilables gave priority to restoring civil liberties and progressive reform at home.

A larger group of opponents had reservations about the treaty's provisions. These **Reservationists** were led by Henry Cabot Lodge, the chair of the Senate Foreign Relations

Committee. They regarded Article Ten as eroding congressional authority to declare war. They also fretted that the League might interfere with domestic questions, such as immigration laws. Lodge held public hearings on the treaty to rouse and focus opposition. German Americans resented the war guilt clause; Italian and Polish Americans complained that the treaty did not satisfy the territorial ambitions of Italy and Poland; Irish Americans condemned the treaty's failure to give self-determination to Ireland. Many progressives also criticized the treaty's compromises on self-determination, reparations, and colonies. Linking these failures with Wilson's domestic policies, one former supporter concluded; "The administration has become reactionary, and deserves no support from any of us."

Lodge's own opposition was shaped by both partisanship and deep personal hostility. "I never expected to hate anyone in politics with the hatred I feel toward Wilson," Lodge confessed. Wilson reciprocated, and when Lodge proposed reservations or amendments to the treaty, Wilson refused to compromise. He proposed "a direct frontal attack" on his opponents. If they wanted war, he said, he would "give them a belly full." In early September 1919, Wilson set out across the country to win popular support for the League. In three weeks, he traveled eight thousand miles and delivered thirty-seven speeches.

In poor health following a bout with influenza, he collapsed in Pueblo, Colorado. Confused and in tears, Wilson mumbled to his secretary, "I seem to have gone to pieces." Taken back to Washington, Wilson on October 2 suffered a massive stroke that paralyzed his left side and left him psychologically unstable and temporarily blind. Wilson's physician and his wife, Edith Galt Wilson, kept the nature of his illness secret from the public, Congress, and even the vice president and cabinet. Rumors circulated that Edith Wilson was running the administration, but she was not. Instead, it was immobilized.

By February 1920, Wilson had partially recovered, but he remained suspicious and quarrelsome. Bryan and other Democratic leaders urged him to accept Lodge's reservations to gain ratification of the treaty. Wilson refused. Isolated and inflexible, he ordered Democratic senators to vote with the Irreconcilables against the treaty as amended by Lodge. On March 19, 1920, the Senate killed the treaty.

Economic Readjustment and Social Conflict

The League was not the only casualty of the struggle to conclude the war. Grave problems shook the United States in 1919 and early 1920. An influenza epidemic had erupted in Europe in 1918 among the massed armies. It now hit the United States, killing perhaps 700,000 Americans, far more than had died in combat. Frightened authorities closed public facilities and banned public meetings in futile attempts to stop the contagion.

Meanwhile, the Wilson administration had no plans for an orderly reconversion of the wartime economy, and chaos ensued. The secretary of the Council of National Defense later reported with but slight exaggeration, "The magnificent war formation of American industry was dissipated in a day; the mobilization that had taken many months was succeeded by an instantaneous demobilization." The government canceled war contracts and dissolved the regulatory agencies. Noting that "the war spirit of cooperation and sacrifice" had disappeared with the Armistice, Bernard Baruch decided to "turn industry absolutely free" and abolished the War Industries Board as of January 1, 1919. Other agencies followed in such haste that turmoil engulfed the economy.

The government also demobilized the armed forces. The army discharged 600,000 soldiers still in training camps; the navy brought AEF soldiers home from France so fast that it had to expand the troop fleet to four times its peak size during the war. With no planning or assistance, troops were hustled back into civilian life. There they competed for scarce jobs with workers recently discharged from the war industries.

As unemployment mounted, the removal of wartime price controls brought runaway inflation. The cost of food, clothing, and other necessities more than doubled over prewar rates. The return of the soldiers caused a serious housing shortage, and rents skyrocketed. Democratic leaders urged Wilson to devote less time to the League of Nations and more to the cost of living and the tensions it unleashed. Farmers also suffered from economic re-adjustments. Net farm income declined by 65 percent between 1919 and 1921. Farmers who had borrowed money for machinery and land to expand production for the war effort were left impoverished and embittered.

Women also lost their wartime economic advances. Returning soldiers took away their jobs. Male trade unionists insisted that women go back to being housewives. One New York union maintained that "the same patriotism which induced women to enter industry during the war should induce them to vacate their positions after the war." At times, male workers struck to force employers to fire women and barred women from unions in jobs where union membership was required for employment. Most women were willing to relinquish their jobs to veterans who had previously held them but objected to being displaced by men without experience. "During the war they called us heroines," one woman complained, "but they throw us on the scrapheap now." Indeed, state legislatures actually passed new laws pro-hibiting women from working in many of the occupations they had successfully filled dur-ing the war. By 1919, half of the women newly employed in heavy industry during the war were gone; by 1920, women constituted a smaller proportion of the work force than they had in 1910.

The postwar readjustments also left African Americans disappointed. During the war, they had agreed with W. E. B. Du Bois to "forget our special grievances and close our ranks shoulder to shoulder with our own white fellow citizens." Participation in the war effort, they hoped, might be rewarded by better treatment thereafter. African Americans had con-tributed to the fighting and home fronts. Now, the meagerness of their reward became clear.

Housing shortages and job competition interacted with racism in 1919 to produce race riots in 26 towns and cities, resulting in at least 120 deaths. In Chicago, 38 people were killed and more than 500 injured in a five-day riot that began when white thugs stoned to death a black youth swimming too near "their" beach. White rioters then fired a machine gun from a truck hurtling through black neighborhoods. But black residents fought back, no longer willing, the *Chicago Defender* reported, "to move along the line of least resistance as did their sires." The new militancy reflected both their experiences in the military and in industry and their exposure to propaganda about freedom and democracy. Racial conflict was part of a postwar battle between Americans hoping to preserve the new social relations fostered by the war effort and those wanting to restore prewar patterns of power and control.

Even more pervasive discontents roiled as America adjusted to the postwar world. More than 4 million angry workers launched a wave of 3,600 strikes in 1919. They were reacting not only to the soaring cost of living, which undermined the value of their wages, but also to employers' efforts to reassert their authority and destroy the legitimacy labor had won by its participation in the war effort. The abolition of government controls on industry enabled employers not only to raise prices but also to rescind their recognition of unions and re-impose objectionable working conditions. Employers also protected their rising profits by insisting that workers' wages remain fixed. In response, strikers demanded higher wages, better conditions, and recognition of unions and the right of collective bargaining.

The greatest strike involved the American Federation of Labor's attempt to organize steelworkers, who endured dangerous conditions and twelve-hour shifts. When the steel companies refused to recognize the union or even discuss issues, 365,000 workers went out on strike in September 1919. Strikers in Pennsylvania pointed out that they had worked "cheerfully, without strikes or trouble of any kind" during the war to "make the world safe for democracy" and that they now sought "industrial democracy." Employers hired thugs to beat the strikers, used strikebreakers to take their jobs, and exploited ethnic and racial divisions among them. To undercut support for the workers, management portrayed the strikers as disruptive radicals influenced by Bolshevism. After four months, the strike failed.

Employers used the same tactic to defeat striking coal miners, whose wages had fallen behind the cost of living. Refusing to negotiate with the United Mine Workers, coal operators claimed that Russian Bolsheviks financed the strike to destroy the American economy. Attorney General Mitchell Palmer secured an injunction against the strike under the authority of wartime legislation. Because the government no longer controlled coal prices or enforced protective labor rules, miners complained bitterly that the war had ended for corporations but not for workers.

Two municipal strikes in 1919 also alarmed the public when their opponents depicted them as revolutionary attacks on the social order. In Seattle, the Central Labor Council called a general strike to support 35,000 shipyard workers striking for higher wages and shorter hours. When 60,000 more workers from 110 local unions also walked out, the city ground to a halt. Workers behaved peacefully and protected public health and safety by operating garbage and fire trucks and providing food, water, and electricity. Nevertheless, Seattle's mayor, business leaders, and newspapers attacked the strikers as Bolsheviks and anarchists. Threatened with military intervention, the labor council called off the strike, but not before it had caused a public backlash against unions across the nation.

In Boston, the police commissioner fired police officers for trying to organize a union to improve their inadequate pay. In response, the police went on strike. As in Seattle, Boston newspapers, politicians, and business leaders attributed the strike to Bolshevism, although nothing indicated that the police wanted anything more than improved wages, conditions, and respect. Wilson denounced the Boston police strike as "a crime against civilization." Governor Calvin Coolidge mobilized the National Guard and gained nationwide acclaim when he stated, "There is no right to strike against the public safety by anybody, anywhere, anytime." The police were all fired; many of their replacements were war veterans.

The Red Scare

The strikes contributed to an anti-Bolshevik hysteria that swept the country in 1919. This **Red Scare** reflected fears that the Bolshevik revolution in Russia might spread to the United States. Steeped in the antiradical propaganda of the war years, many Americans were appalled by Russian Bolshevism, described by the *Saturday Evening Post* as a "compound of slaughter, confiscation, anarchy, and universal disorder." Their alarm grew in 1919 when Russia established the Third International to foster revolution abroad, and a few American socialists formed the American Communist party. But the Red Scare also reflected the willingness of antiunion employers, ambitious politicians, sensational journalists, zealous veterans, and racists to exploit the panic to advance their own purposes.

Fed by misleading reports about Russian Bolshevism and its influence in the United States, the Red Scare reached panic levels by mid-1919. Bombs mailed anonymously to several prominent people on May Day seemed proof enough that a Bolshevik conspiracy threatened America. The Justice Department, Congress, and patriotic organizations like the American Legion joined with business groups to suppress radicalism, real and imagined. The government continued to enforce the repressive laws against Wobblies, socialists, and other dissenters; a Minnesota senator warned that the nation was more imperiled than during the war itself. Indeed, Wilson and Attorney General Palmer called for more stringent laws and refused to release political prisoners jailed during the war. State governments harassed and arrested hundreds.

In a 1920 cartoon, "A. Mitchell Palmer Out for a Stroll," the *Chicago Tribune* lampooned the Attorney General for his repeated but unfounded warnings about Bolshevik threats in America. The postwar Red Scare weakened civil liberties, promoted nativist hostilities, and undermined reform.

Palmer created a new agency, headed by J. Edgar Hoover, to suppress radicals and impose conformity. Its war on radicalism became the chief focus of the Justice Department. As an ambitious and ruthless bureaucrat, Hoover had participated in the government's assault on aliens and radicals during the war. Now he collected files on labor leaders and other "radical agitators" from Senator La Follette to Jane Addams, issued misleading reports on communist influence in labor strikes and race riots, and contacted all major newspapers "to acquaint people like you with the real menace of evil-thinking, which is the foundation of the Red Movement." Indeed, the Justice Department itself promoted the Red Scare hysteria, which Palmer hoped would lead to his presidential nomination and Hoover hoped would enhance his own power and that of his bureau.

In November 1919, Palmer and Hoover began raiding groups suspected of subversion. A month later, they deported 249 alien radicals, including the anarchist Emma Goldman, to Russia. Rabid patriots endorsed such actions. One minister favored deporting radicals "in ships of stone with sails of lead, with the wrath of God for a breeze and with hell for their first port." In January 1920, Palmer and Hoover rounded up more than four thousand suspected radicals in thirty-three cities. Without warrants, they broke into union halls, club rooms, and private homes, assaulting and arresting everyone in sight. People were jailed without access to lawyers; some were beaten into signing false confessions. In Lynn, Massachusetts, thirty-nine people meeting to organize a bakery were arrested for holding a revolutionary caucus. Other arrests were just as outrageous, but the *Washington Post* clamored, "There is no time to waste on hairsplitting over infringement of liberty."

Other Americans began to recoil from the excesses and illegal acts. Assistant Secretary of Labor Louis Post stopped further deportations by demonstrating that most of the arrested were "working men of good character, who are not anarchists or revolutionists, nor politically or otherwise dangerous in any sense." They had been arrested, he said, "for nothing more dangerous than affiliating with friends of their own race, country, and language." Support for the Red Scare withered. Palmer's attempt to inflame public emotions to advance his own candidacy for the presidency backfired. When his predictions of a violent attempt to overthrow the government on May 1, 1920, came to naught, most Americans could see that no menace had ever existed. They agreed with the *Rocky Mountain News*: "We can never get to work if we keep jumping sideways in fear of the bewhiskered Bolshevik." Even one conservative Republican concluded that "too much has been said about Bolshevism in America." But if the Red Scare faded in mid-1920, the hostility to immigrants, organized labor, and dissent it reflected would endure for a decade. During the 1920s, the most acceptable forms of social change would be derived from technological and commercial innovations.

The Election of 1920

Palmer failed to win the Democratic nomination, but it would have been an empty prize anyway. The Democratic coalition that Wilson had cobbled together on the issues of progressivism and peace came apart after the war. Workers resented the administration's hostility to the postwar strikes. Ethnic groups brutalized by the Americanization of the war years blamed Wilson for the war or condemned his peace settlement. Farmers grumbled about wartime price controls and postwar falling prices. Wartime taxes and the social and economic turmoil of 1919–1920 alienated the middle class. Americans were weary of great crusades and social sacrifices; in the words of Kansas journalist William Allen White, they were "tired of issues, sick at heart of ideals, and weary of being noble." They yearned for what Republican presidential candidate Warren Harding of Ohio called "normalcy."

The Republican ticket in 1920 symbolized the reassurance of simpler times. Harding was a genial politician who in a lengthy career had devoted more time to golf and poker than to public policy. An Old Guard conservative, he had stayed with the GOP when Theodore Roosevelt led the progressives out in 1912. His running mate, Calvin Coolidge, governor of Massachusetts, owed his nomination to his handling of the Boston police strike.

Wilson called the election of 1920 "a great and solemn referendum" on the League of Nations, but such lofty appeals fell flat. Harding was ambiguous about the League, and the Democratic national platform endorsed it but expressed a willingness to accept amendments or reservations. The Democratic nominees, James Cox, former governor of Ohio, and the young Franklin D. Roosevelt, Wilson's assistant secretary of the navy, favored the League, but it was not a decisive issue in the campaign.

Harding won in a landslide reflecting the nation's dissatisfaction with Wilson and the Democratic party. "The Democrats are inconceivably unpopular," wrote Walter Lippmann, a prominent journalist. Harding received 16 million popular votes to Cox's 9 million. Running for president from his prison cell, Socialist Eugene Debs polled nearly a million votes. Not even his closest backers considered Harding qualified for the White House, but, as Lippmann said, the nation's "public spirit was exhausted" after the war years. The election of 1920 was "the final twitch" of America's "war mind."

CONCLUSION

The Great War disrupted the United States and much of the rest of the world. The initial American policy of neutrality yielded to sentimental and substantive links with the Allies and the pressure of German submarine warfare. Despite popular opposition, America joined the conflict when its leaders concluded that national interests demanded it. Using both military and diplomatic power, Woodrow Wilson sought to secure a more stable and prosperous world order, with an expanded role for the United States. But the Treaty of Versailles only partly fulfilled his hopes, and the Senate refused to ratify the treaty and its League of Nations. The postwar world order would be unstable and dangerous.

Participation in the war, moreover, had changed the American government, economy, and society. Some of these changes, including the centralization of the economy and an expansion of the regulatory role of the federal government, were already under way; some offered opportunities to implement progressive principles or reforms. Women's suffrage and prohibition gained decisive support because of the war spirit. But other consequences of the war betrayed both progressive impulses and the democratic principles the war was allegedly fought to promote. The suppression of civil liberties, manipulation of human emotions, repression of radicals and minorities, and exploitation of national crises by narrow interests helped disillusion the public. The repercussions of the Great War would linger for years, at home and abroad.

Review Questions

1. What might have been the consequences, positive and negative, if the "deliberate and passionless method of doing what is regarded as a disagreeable duty" that Ray Stannard Baker found in 1917 had continued to characterize the U.S. war effort?

2. What were the major arguments for and against U.S. entry into the Great War? What position do you find most persuasive? Why?

3. How and why did the United States shape public opinion in World War I? What were the consequences, positive and negative, of the propaganda of the Committee on Public Information, Food Administration, and other government agencies?

4. How did other groups exploit the war crisis and the government's propaganda and repression?

5. Evaluate the role of Woodrow Wilson at the Paris Peace Conference. What obstacles did he face? How successful was he in shaping the settlement?

6. Discuss the arguments for and against American ratification of the Treaty of Versailles.

Key Terms

Allies   *130*
American Expeditionary Force (AEF)   *145*
Bolsheviks   *146*
Central Powers   *130*
Committee on Public Information (CPI)   *141*
Declaration of London   *132*
Espionage Act   *142*
Food Administration   *138*
Irreconcilables   *150*
League of Nations   *150*
Liberty Bonds   *140*

National War Labor Board   *138*
Preparedness   *133*
Railroad Administration   *138*
Red Scare   *153*
Reservationists   *150*
Sedition Act   *142*
Selective Service Act   *145*
Self-determination   *136*
Sussex Pledge   *133*
Treaty of Versailles   *148*
War Industries Board (WIB)   *137*

Recommended Reading

Kendrick A. Clements, *The Presidency of Woodrow Wilson* (1992). The best single volume on the Wilson presidency.

Edward M. Coffman, *The War to End All Wars* (1968). A valuable study of the U.S. military role in World War I.

Robert H. Ferrell, *Woodrow Wilson and World War I, 1917–1921* (1985). A useful synthesis that emphasizes diplomatic issues.

D. Clayton James and Anne Sharp Wells, *America and the Great War, 1914–1920* (1998). A fine, succinct synthesis of recent scholarship.

David M. Kennedy, *Over Here: The First World War and American Society* (1980). Thorough and illuminating discussion of the impact of World War I on American society.

Robert K. Murray, *The Red Scare: A Study in National Hysteria, 1919–1920* (1955). An important early study that retains much value.

Ronald Schaffer, *America in the Great War: The Rise of the War Welfare State* (1991). An effective and provocative summary that illuminates the expanding role of government.

Robert H. Zieger, *America's Great War: World War I and the American Experience* (2000). A masterful account of the diplomatic, military, and domestic aspects of the war.

CHAPTER

6

TOWARD A MODERN AMERICA: THE 1920s

The Economy That Roared

The Business of Government

Cities and Suburbs

Mass Culture in the Jazz Age

Culture Wars

A New Era in the World?

Herbert Hoover and the Triumph of the New Era

Conclusion

Happy times were here again. American industry, adopting Henry Ford's policy of mass production and low prices, was making it possible for everybody to have his share of everything. The newspapers, the statesmen, the economists, all agreed that American ingenuity had solved the age-old problem of poverty. There could never be another depression. . . .

The war had done something to Henry, it had taught him a new way to deal with his fellow men. . . . He became more abrupt in his manner, more harsh in his speech. "Gratitude?" he would say. "There's no gratitude in business. Men work for money." . . . From now on he was a business man, and held a tight rein on everything. This industry was his, he had made it himself, and what he wanted of the men he hired was that they should do exactly as he told them. . . .

Every worker had to be strained to the uttermost limit, every one had to be giving the last ounce of energy he had in his carcass. . . . They were tired when they started in the morning, and when they quit they were grey and staggering with fatigue, they were empty shells out of which the last drop of juice had been squeezed. . . .

Henry Ford was now getting close to his two million cars a year goal. . . . From the moment the ore was taken out of the ship at the River Rouge plant [in Detroit], through all the processes turning it into steel and shaping it into automobile parts with a hundred-ton press, and putting five thousand parts together into a car which rolled off the assembly line under its own power—all those processes were completed in less than a day and a half!

Some forty-five thousand different machines were now used in the making of Ford cars, in sixty establishments scattered over the United States . . . Henry Ford was remaking the roads of America, and in the end he would remake the roads of the world—and line them all with filling stations and hot-dog stands of the American pattern.

—Upton Sinclair

Upton Sinclair, *The Flivver King: A Story of Ford–America* (Chicago: Charles H. Kerr Publishing Company, 1999).

UPTON SINCLAIR, one of America's most famous "muckraking" journalists, won his greatest recognition with the 1906 publication of his historical novel *The Jungle*, which graphically depicted the wretched conditions endured by Chicago's immigrant meat-packing workers. In *The Flivver King*, Sinclair again points up his extraordinary ability to weave together a dramatic and historical account of industrial America, particularly the rise of the automobile industry and the revolutionizing vision of Henry Ford—the entrepreneur who captured the American mind and symbolized modern America to the world.

"Machinery," proclaimed Henry Ford, "is the new Messiah." Others in the 1920s thought that Ford, too, deserved homage. "Just as in Rome one goes to the Vatican and endeavours to get audience of the Pope," noted one British observer, "so in Detroit one goes to the Ford Works and endeavours to see Henry Ford." Ford had introduced the moving assembly line at his automobile factory on the eve of World War I, and, by 1925, it was turning out a Model T car every ten seconds. Mass production was becoming a reality; in fact, the term originated in Henry Ford's 1926 description of the system of flow production techniques popularly called "Fordism." The system symbolized the nation's booming

Ford Motor Company's assembly line at its River Rouge plant in Detroit. The increasing mechanization of work, linked to managerial and marketing innovations, boosted productivity in the 1920s and brought consumer goods within the reach of far more Americans than before.
State Historical Society of Wisconsin

• CHRONOLOGY •

1915 Ku Klux Klan is founded anew.	Country Club Plaza in Kansas City opens.
1919 Volstead Act is passed.	**1923** Harding dies; Calvin Coolidge becomes president.
1920 Urban population exceeds rural population for the first time.	**1924** National Origins Act sharply curtails immigration.
Warren Harding is elected president.	Coolidge is elected president.
Prohibition takes effect.	**1925** Scopes trial is held in Dayton, Tennessee.
First commercial radio show is broadcast.	F. Scott Fitzgerald publishes *The Great Gatsby*.
Sinclair Lewis publishes *Main Street*.	**1927** Charles A. Lindbergh flies solo across the Atlantic.
1921 Sheppard-Towner Maternity and Infancy Act is passed.	**1928** Kellogg-Briand Pact is signed.
Washington Naval Conference limits naval armaments.	Herbert Hoover is elected president.
1922 Fordney-McCumber Act raises tariff rates.	**1929** Ernest Hemingway publishes *A Farewell to Arms*.
Sinclair Lewis publishes *Babbitt*.	

economy: In the 1920s, Europeans used the word Fordize as a synonym for Americanize. Ford coupled machines and technology with managerial innovations. He established the "five-dollar day," twice the prevailing wage in Detroit's auto industry, and slashed the workweek from forty-eight to forty hours. These changes, Ford argued, would reduce the costs of labor turnover and boost consumer purchasing power, leading to further profits from mass production.

The assembly line, however, alienated workers, and even Ford himself conceded that the repetitive operations of the assembly line were "so monotonous that it scarcely seems possible that any man would care to continue long at the same job." Ford first tried to adapt his mostly immigrant workers to these conditions through an Americanization program. His "Education Department" taught classes in English, sobriety, obedience, and industrial efficiency to the unskilled laborers entering the factory. After the course, they participated in a symbolic pageant: They climbed into a huge "melting pot," 15 feet across and 7 feet deep. After Ford managers stirred the pot with 10-foot ladles, the workers emerged wearing new clothes and waving American flags—new Americans made for the factory. As one Ford leader said, "As we adapt the machinery in the shop to turning out the kind of automobile we have in mind, so we have constructed our educational system with a view to producing the human product in mind."

When the labor market became more favorable to management in the early 1920s, Ford abolished the Education Department and relied on discipline to control workers. As Sinclair observed, after the Great War, Ford dismissed the role of "gratitude" in business and determined to keep "a tight rein on everything." To maximize profits and increase efficiency, Ford even prohibited talking, whistling, sitting, or smoking on the job. Wearing fixed expressions— "Fordization of the face"—workers could communicate only without moving their lips in the "Ford whisper." In keeping with the actions of other employers, Ford also joined the assault on labor organization, banning unions altogether and enlisting the aid of spies and informants to guard against their formation.

But even greater control and higher profits did not satisfy Henry Ford, for, like the 1920s itself, he remained conflicted about the progress he championed—the changes he saw and had helped facilitate. The automobile not only represented the new consumer culture, but it also transformed forever America and Americans themselves—highways, filling stations, and hamburger stands sprang up across the nation, and the car even altered the dating practices of young Americans, alarming some parents and community leaders about what they feared as "bedrooms on wheels." Cars and cigarettes were among the most intensively advertised goods in the 1920s, and for some they signaled rebellion and freedom. Women in short skirts and the rise of the Jazz Age—all contributed to what Ford saw as the evils of the "new America." Launching a "crusade" against this new direction toward which America was headed, Ford decided, according to Sinclair, that "what America needed was to be led back to its past." Embracing nativism and Protestantism, Ford, an ardent anti-Semite, targeted Jewish Americans in his diatribes, blaming them for radicalism and labor organization, and he singled out the "International Jew" for allegedly controlling the international financial community.

Henry Ford—and Fordism itself—thus reflected the complexity of the 1920s. Economic growth and technological innovation were paired with social conflict as traditions were destroyed, values were displaced, and new people were incorporated into a society increasingly industrialized, urbanized, and dominated by big business. Industrial production and national wealth soared, buoyed by new techniques and markets for consumer goods. Business values pervaded society and dominated government, which promoted business interests.

But not all Americans prospered. Many workers were unemployed, and the wages of still more were stagnant or falling. Farmers endured grim conditions and worse prospects. Social change brought pleasure to some and deep concern to others. City factories like the Ford Works attracted workers from the countryside, increasing urbanization; rapid suburbanization opened other horizons. Leisure activities flourished, and new mass media promoted modern ideas and stylish products. Workers would have to achieve personal satisfaction through consumption—and not production. But such experiences often proved unsettling, and some Americans sought reassurance by imposing their cultural or religious values on everyone around them. The tumultuous decade thus had many unresolved issues, much like the complex personality of Henry Ford himself. And Ford so dominated the age that when college students were asked to rank the greatest people of all time, Ford came in third—behind Christ and Napoleon.

KEY TOPICS

The American economy in the 1920s.

The cult of business.

Change and social dislocation.

Materialism and mass culture.

The groups excluded from the prosperity of the 1920s.

THE ECONOMY THAT ROARED

Following a severe postwar depression in 1920 and 1921, the American economy boomed through the remainder of the decade. Gross domestic product soared nearly 40 percent; output per worker-hour, or productivity, rose 72 percent in manufacturing; average per capita income increased by a third. Although the prosperity was not evenly distributed and some sectors of the economy were deeply troubled, most Americans welcomed the industrial expansion and business principles of the "New Era."

Boom Industries

Many factors spurred the economic expansion of the 1920s. The huge wartime and postwar profits provided investment capital that enabled business to mechanize. Mass production spread quickly in American industry; machine-made standardized parts and the moving assembly line increased efficiency and production. Businesses steadily adopted the scientific management principles of Frederick W. Taylor (see Chapter 2). These highly touted systems, though often involving little more than an assembly-line speedup, also boosted efficiency. The nation more than doubled its capacity to generate electricity during the decade, further bolstering the economy. In factories, electric motors cut costs and improved manufacturing; in homes, electricity spurred demand for new products. Henry Ford was right: Mass production and consumption went hand in hand. Although not one in ten farm families had access to electric power, most other families did by 1929, and many bought electric sewing machines, vacuum cleaners, washing machines, and other labor-saving appliances.

The automobile industry drove the economy. Its productivity increased constantly, and sales rose from about 1.9 million vehicles in 1920 to nearly 5 million by 1929, when 26 million vehicles were on the road. The automobile industry also employed one of every fourteen manufacturing workers and stimulated other industries from steel to rubber and glass. It created a huge new market for the petroleum industry and fostered oil drilling in Oklahoma, Texas, and Louisiana. It launched new businesses, from service stations (over 120,000 by 1929) to garages. It also encouraged the construction industry, a mainstay of the 1920s economy. Large increases in road building and residential housing, prompted by growing automobile ownership and migration to cities and suburbs, provided construction jobs, markets for lumber and other building materials, and profits.

New industries also sprang up. The aviation industry grew rapidly during the 1920s, with government support. The U.S. Post Office subsidized commercial air service by providing air-mail contracts to private carriers. Congress then authorized commercial passenger service over the mail routes, with regular traffic opening in 1927 between Boston and New York. By 1930, more than one hundred airlines crisscrossed America.

The Great War also stimulated the chemicals industry. The government confiscated chemical patents from German firms that had dominated the field and transferred them to such U.S. companies as DuPont. With this advantage, DuPont in the 1920s became one of the nation's largest industrial firms, a chemical empire producing plastics, finishes, dyes, and organic chemicals. It developed products for the commercial market: enamel for household appliances and automobile finishes, gasoline additives to eliminate engine knocks (many workers died from producing what the *New York World* called "loony gas"), rayon for women's clothing, cellophane to package consumer goods. Led by such successes, the chemicals industry became a $4 billion giant employing 300,000 workers by 1929.

The new radio and motion picture industries also flourished. Commercial broadcasting began with a single station in 1920. By 1927, there were 732 stations, and Congress created the Federal Radio Commission to prevent wave-band interference. The rationale for this agency, which was reorganized as the Federal Communications Commission (FCC) in 1934, was that the airwaves belong to the American people and not to private interests. Nevertheless, corporations quickly dominated the new industry. Westinghouse, RCA, and General Electric began opening strings of stations in the early 1920s. Large corporations also came to control radio manufacturing. Factory-made crystal radio sets became available in 1920, and some 5 million sets were sold by mid-decade. But corporate pressure and patent control eliminated more than 90 percent of the 750 manufacturers by 1927.

The motion-picture industry became one of the nation's five largest businesses, with twenty thousand movie theaters selling 100 million tickets a week. Hollywood studios were huge factories, hiring directors, writers, camera crews, and actors to produce films on an assembly-line basis. While Americans watched Charlie Chaplin showcase his comedic genius in such films as *The Gold Rush* (1925), such corporations as Paramount were integrating production with distribution and exhibition to maximize control and profit and eliminate independent producers and theaters. The advent of talking movies later in the decade brought still greater profits and power to the major studios, which alone could afford the increased engineering and production costs.

Corporate Consolidation

A wave of corporate mergers, rivaling that at the turn of the century, swept over the 1920s economy. Great corporations swallowed up thousands of small firms. Particularly significant was the spread of oligopoly—the control of an entire industry by a few giant firms. The number of automobile manufacturers dropped from 108 to 44, while only three companies—Ford, General Motors, and Chrysler—produced 83 percent of the nation's cars. Their large-scale, integrated operations eliminated competition from small firms. In the electric light and power industry, nearly four thousand local utility companies were merged into a dozen holding companies. Mergers also expanded oligopoly control over other industries. By 1929, the nation's two hundred largest corporations controlled nearly half of all nonbanking corporate wealth.

Oligopolies also dominated finance and marketing. Big banks extended their control through mergers and by opening branches. By 1929, a mere 1 percent of the nation's banks controlled half its banking resources. In marketing, national chain stores, such as A&P and Woolworth's, displaced local retailers. With fifteen thousand grocery stores and an elaborate distribution system, A&P could buy and sell goods for less than many corner grocers.

The corporate consolidation of the 1920s provoked little public fear or opposition. Independent retailers campaigned for local zoning regulations and laws to restrict chain stores, but for the most part, Americans accepted the idea that size brought efficiency and productivity.

Open Shops and Welfare Capitalism

Business also launched a vigorous assault on labor. In 1921, the National Association of Manufacturers organized an **open shop** campaign to break union-shop contracts, which required all employees to be union members. Denouncing collective bargaining as un-American, businesses described the open shop, in which union membership was not required and usually prohibited, as the "American plan." They forced workers to sign so-called **yellow-dog contracts** that bound them to reject unions to keep their jobs. Business also used boycotts to force employers into a uniform anti-union front. Bethlehem Steel, for example, refused to sell steel to companies employing union labor. Where unions existed, corporations tried to crush them, using spies or hiring strikebreakers.

Some companies advocated a paternalistic system called **welfare capitalism** as an alternative to unions. Eastman Kodak, General Motors, U.S. Steel, and other firms provided medical services, insurance programs, pension plans, and vacations for their workers and established employee social clubs and sports teams. These policies were designed to undercut labor unions and to persuade workers to rely on the corporation. Home-financing plans, for instance, increased workers' dependence on the company, and stock ownership plans inculcated business values among employees. Welfare capitalism, however, covered scarcely 5 percent of the work force and often benefited only skilled workers already tied to the company through seniority. Moreover, it was directed primarily at men. General Electric, for example, dismissed women workers when they married. Women rarely built up enough seniority to obtain vacations and pensions.

Corporations in the 1920s also promoted company unions, management-sponsored substitutes for labor unions, but company unions were usually forbidden to handle wage and hour issues. Their function was to implement company policies and undermine real unionism. General Electric's management reported that through its company union, "we have been able to educate and secure sympathy and support from a large body of employees who, under the old arrangement of bargaining with [AFL] craft unions, could not have been reached."

Partly because of these pressures, membership in labor unions fell from 5.1 million in 1920 to 3.6 million in 1929. But unions also contributed to their own decline. Conservative union leaders neglected ethnic and black workers in mass-production industries. Nor did they try to organize women, nearly one-fourth of all workers by 1930. And they failed to respond effectively to other changes in the labor market. The growing numbers of white-collar workers regarded themselves as middle class and beyond the scope of union action.

With increasing mechanization and weak labor unions, workers suffered from job insecurity and stagnant wages. Mechanization, *Fortune* concluded, meant that "from the purely productive point of view, a part of the human race is already obsolete." Unemployment reached 12 percent in 1921 and remained a persistent concern of many working-class Americans during the decade. And despite claims to the contrary, hours were long: The average workweek in manufacturing remained over fifty hours.

The promise of business to pay high wages proved hollow. Real wages (purchasing power) did improve, but most of the improvement came before 1923 and reflected falling prices more than it did rising wages. After 1923, American wages stabilized. Henry Ford made no general wage hike after 1919, although his workers would have needed an increase of 65 percent to recover the buying power they had enjoyed in 1914. Indeed, in 1928, Ford lowered wage rates. U.S. Steel also reduced weekly wages, even while its profits almost doubled between 1923 and 1929. The failure to raise wages when productivity was increasing threatened the nation's long-term prosperity. In short, rising national income largely reflected salaries and dividends, not wages.

Some workers fared particularly badly. Unskilled workers—especially southern and eastern Europeans, black migrants from the rural South, and Mexican immigrants—saw their already low wages decline relative to those of skilled workers. Southern workers earned much less than Northerners, even in the same industry, and women were paid much less than men, even for the same jobs. Male furniture assemblers, for example, earned 56 cents an hour; females, only 32 cents. Overall, the gap between rich and poor widened during the decade. By 1929, fully 71 percent of American families earned less than what the U.S. Bureau of Labor Statistics regarded as necessary for a decent living standard. The maldistribution of income meant that Americans would eventually be unable to purchase the products they made.

The expansion of consumer credit, rare before the 1920s, offered temporary relief by permitting consumers to buy goods over time. General Motors introduced consumer credit on a national basis to create a mass market for expensive automobiles. By 1927, two-thirds of automobiles were purchased on the installment plan. By 1929, providing consumer credit had become the nation's tenth largest business. Nevertheless, installment loans did not in the long run raise the purchasing power of an income; they simply added interest charges to the price of products.

Sick Industries

Despite the general appearance of prosperity, several "sick" industries dragged on the economy. Coal mining, textile and garment manufacturing, and railroads suffered from excess capacity (too many mines and factories), shrinking demand, low returns, and management–labor conflicts. For example, U.S. coal mines had a capacity of a billion tons, but scarcely half of that amount was needed because of increasing use of oil, natural gas, and hydroelectricity. Using company police, strikebreakers, and injunctions, mine operators broke the United Mine Workers and slashed wages by up to one-third. Unemployment in the industry approached 30 percent; by 1928, a reporter found "thousands of women and children literally starving to death" in Appalachia and the remaining miners held in "industrial slavery."

Similarly, the textile industry coped with overcapacity and declining demand by shifting operations from New England to the cheap-labor South, employing girls and young women for fifty-six-hour weeks at 18 cents an hour. Textile companies, aided by local authorities, suppressed strikes in Tennessee and North Carolina. Ella May Wiggins sang of the worries in the mills:

> How it grieves the heart of a mother,
> You every one must know.
> For we can't buy for our children,
> Our wages are too low.

Wiggins was murdered by company thugs, leaving behind five small children. The textile industry, despite substandard wages and repressive policies, remained barely profitable.

American agriculture never recovered from the 1921 depression. In 1919, gross farm income amounted to 16 percent of the national income; by 1929, it had dropped to half that. Agricultural problems did not derive from inefficiency or low productivity. Mechanization (especially more tractors) and improved fertilizers and pesticides helped to produce crop surpluses, but surpluses and shrinking demand forced down prices. After the war, foreign markets dried up, and domestic demand for cotton slackened. Moreover, farmers' wartime expansion left them heavily mortgaged in the 1920s. Small farmers, unable to compete with larger, better capitalized farmers, suffered most. Many lost their land and became tenants or farm hands. By 1930, only 57 percent of American farmers owned the land they worked, the lowest percentage ever.

Racial discrimination worsened conditions for black and Hispanic tenants, sharecroppers, and farm workers. In the South, black sharecroppers trapped in grinding poverty endured segregation, disfranchisement, and violence. Mexican immigrants and Hispanic Americans labored as migrant farm workers in the Southwest and California. Exploited by a contract labor system pervasive in large-scale agriculture, they suffered from poor wages, miserable living conditions, and racism that created, in the words of one investigation, "a vicious circle" from which "few can escape through their own efforts."

By the end of the 1920s, the average per capita income for people on the nation's farms was only one-fourth that of Americans off the farm. "Widespread agricultural disaster," warned one Iowa newspaper, was producing "a highly dangerous situation." Like textile workers in New England and the Piedmont and coal miners in Appalachia, rural Americans suffered in the 1920s.

THE BUSINESS OF GOVERNMENT

The Republican surge in national politics also shaped the economy. In the 1920 election, the Republican slogan was "Less government in business, more business in government." By 1924, Calvin Coolidge, the decade's second Republican president, proclaimed, "This is a business country . . . and it wants a business government." Under such direction, the federal government advanced business interests at the expense of other objectives (see American Views, "The Cult of Business").

AMERICAN VIEWS

The Cult of Business

During the 1920s, publicists and politicians joined manufacturers and merchants in proclaiming that business promoted not only material, but also social and even spiritual well-being. In his bestseller, *The Man Nobody Knows* (1924), advertising executive Bruce Barton portrayed Jesus Christ as the founder of modern business. The following excerpt from an article by Edward E. Purinton, a popular lecturer on business values and efficiency, makes even more extensive claims for business.

> How accurate are Purinton's claims of great opportunity in the corporate world of the 1920s? Of occupational mobility in the factory economy?
>
> What does this view of business imply about the role of government in American life?
>
> How do you think Protestant fundamentalists might have viewed the cult of business?

Among the nations of the earth today America stands for one idea: Business. National opprobrium? National opportunity. For in this fact lies, potentially, the salvation of the world.

Through business, properly conceived, managed, and conducted, the human race is finally to be redeemed. How and why a man works foretells what he will do, think, have, give, and be. And real salvation is in doing, thinking, having, giving, and being—not in sermonizing and theorizing . . .

What is the finest game? Business. The soundest science? Business. The truest art? Business. The fullest education? Business. The fairest opportunity? Business. The cleanest philanthropy? Business. The sanest religion? Business.

You may not agree. That is because you judge business by the crude, mean, stupid, false imitation of business that happens to be located near you.

The finest game is business. The rewards are for everybody, and all can win. There are no favorites—Providence always crowns the career of the man who is worthy. And in this game there is no "luck"—you have the fun of taking chances but the sobriety of guaranteeing certainties. The speed and size of your winnings are for you alone to determine . . .

The soundest science is business. All investigation is reduced to action, and by action proved or disproved. The idealistic motive animates the materialistic method. . . . Capital is furnished for the researches of "pure science"; yet pure science is not regarded pure until practical. Competent scientists are suitably rewarded—as they are not in the scientific schools . . .

The fullest education is business. A proper blend of study, work and life is essential to advancement. The whole man is educated. Human nature itself is the open book that all business men study; and the mastery of a page of this educates you more than the memorizing of a dusty tome from a library shelf. In the school of business, moreover, you teach yourself and learn most from your own mistakes. What you learn here you live out, the only real test.

The fairest opportunity is business. You can find more, better, quicker chances to get ahead in a large business house than anywhere else on earth. . . . Recognition of better work, of keener and quicker thought, of deeper and finer feeling, is gladly offered by the men higher up, with early promotion the rule for the man who justifies it. There is, and can be, no such thing as buried talent in a modern business organization. . . .

The sanest religion is business. Any relationship that forces a man to follow the Golden Rule rightfully belongs amid the ceremonials of the church. A great business enterprise includes and presupposes this relationship. I have seen more Christianity to the square inch as a regular part of the office equipment of famous corporation presidents than may ordinarily be found on Sunday in a verbalized but not vitalized church congregation . . . You can fool your preacher with a sickly sprout or a wormy semblance of character, but you can't fool your employer. I would make every business house a consultation bureau for the guidance of the church whose members were employees of the house . . .

The future work of the businessman is to teach the teacher, preach to the preacher, admonish the parent, advise the doctor, justify the lawyer, superintend the statesman, fructify the farmer, stabilize the banker, harness the dreamer, and reform the reformer.

Source: Edward E. Purinton, "Big Ideas from Big Business," *Independent*, April 16, 1921. National Weekly Corp., New York.

Republican Ascendancy

Republicans in 1920 had retained control of Congress and put Warren Harding in the White House. Harding was neither capable nor bright. One critic described a Harding speech as "an army of pompous phrases moving over the landscape in search of an idea." But he had a genial touch that contrasted favorably with Wilson. He pardoned Eugene Debs, whom Wilson had refused to release from prison, and he spoke out against racial violence. He also helped shape the modern presidency by supporting the Budget and Accounting Act of 1921, which gave the president authority over the budget and created the Budget Bureau and the General Accounting Office. Moreover, Harding recognized his own limitations and promised to appoint "the best minds" to his cabinet. Some of his appointees were highly accomplished, and two of them, Secretary of Commerce Herbert Hoover and Secretary of the Treasury Andrew Mellon, shaped economic policy throughout the 1920s.

A self-described progressive, dedicated to efficiency, Hoover made the Commerce Department the government's most dynamic office. He cemented its ties with the leading sectors of the economy, expanded its collection and distribution of industrial information, pushed to exploit foreign resources and markets, and encouraged innovation. His spreading influence led him to be called the secretary of commerce and "assistant secretary of everything else." Hoover's goal was to expand prosperity by making business efficient, responsive, and profitable.

One 1920s cartoon depicting a "View of Washington," showed Herbert Hoover everywhere at once. In fact, the talented and ambitious secretary of commerce was not a politician but a successful engineer, businessman, and administrator, who symbolized to many Americans the best of the New Era.

Andrew Mellon had a narrower goal. A wealthy banker and industrialist, he pressed Congress to reduce taxes on businesses and the rich. He argued that lower taxes would enable wealthy individuals and corporations to increase their capital investments, thereby creating new jobs and general prosperity. But Mellon's hope that favoring the rich would cause prosperity to trickle down to the working and middle classes proved ill-founded. Nevertheless, despite the opposition of progressives in Congress, Mellon succeeded in lowering maximum tax rates and eliminating wartime excess-profits taxes in 1921.

The Harding administration promoted business interests in other ways, too. The tariff of 1922 raised import rates to protect industry from foreign competition. High new duties on foreign aluminum, for instance, permitted manufacturers—including Mellon's own Alcoa Aluminum—to raise prices by 40 percent. But by excluding imports, high tariffs made it difficult for European nations to earn the dollars to repay their war debts to the United States. High rates also impeded American farm exports and raised consumer prices.

The Harding administration aided the business campaign against unions. Attorney General Harry Daugherty secured an injunction against a railroad strike in 1922 and promised to "use the power of the government to prevent the labor unions of the country from destroying the open shop."

The Republicans also curtailed government regulation. By appointing advocates of big business to the Federal Trade Commission, the Federal Reserve Board, and other regulatory agencies established earlier by the progressives, Harding made government the collaborator rather than the regulator of business. Progressive Republican Senator George Norris of Nebraska angrily asked, "If trusts, combinations, and big business are to run the government, why not permit them to do it directly rather than through this expensive machinery which was originally honestly established for the protection of the people of the country against monopoly?" Norris condemned the new appointments as nullifying "federal law by a process of boring from within" and as setting "the country back more than twenty-five years."

Finally, Harding reshaped the Supreme Court into a still more aggressive champion of business. He named the conservative William Howard Taft as chief justice and matched him with three other justices. All were, as one of them proclaimed, sympathetic to business leaders "beset and bedeviled with vexatious statutes, prying commissions, and government intermeddling of all sorts." The Court struck down much of the government economic regulation adopted during the Progressive Era, invalidated restraints on child labor and a minimum wage law for women, and approved restrictions on labor unions.

Government Corruption

The green light that Harding Republicans extended to private interests led to corruption and scandals. Harding appointed many friends and cronies, who saw public service as an opportunity for graft. Attorney General Daugherty's associates in the Justice Department took bribes in exchange for pardons and government jobs. The head of the Veterans Bureau went to prison for cheating disabled veterans of $200 million. Albert Fall, the secretary of the interior, leased petroleum reserves set aside by progressive conservationists to oil companies in exchange for cash, bonds, and cattle for his New Mexico ranch. Exposed for his role in the Teapot Dome scandal, named after a Wyoming oil reserve, Fall became the first cabinet officer in history to go to jail. Daugherty escaped a similar fate by destroying records and invoking the Fifth Amendment.

Harding was appalled by the scandals. "My God, this is a hell of a job!" he told William Allen White. "I have no trouble with my enemies . . . But my damned friends, . . . they're the ones that keep me walking the floor nights!" Harding died shortly thereafter, probably of a heart attack.

Coolidge Prosperity

On August 3, 1923, Vice President Calvin Coolidge was sworn in as president by his father while visiting his birthplace in rural Vermont, thereby reaffirming his association with traditional values. This image reassured Americans troubled by the Harding scandals. Coolidge's calm appearance hid a furious temper and a mean spirit.

Coolidge supported business with ideological conviction. He opposed the activist presidency of the Progressive Era, cultivating instead a deliberate inactivity calculated to lower expectations of government. He endorsed Secretary of the Treasury Mellon's ongoing efforts to reverse the progressive tax policies of the Wilson years and backed Secretary of Commerce Hoover's persistent efforts on behalf of the business community (although he privately sneered at Hoover as the "Wonder Boy").

Like Harding, Coolidge installed business supporters in the regulatory agencies. To chair the Federal Trade Commission he appointed an attorney who had condemned the agency as "an instrument of oppression and disturbance and injury instead of help to business." Under this leadership, the FTC described its new goal as "helping business to help itself"—which meant approving trade associations and agreements to suppress competition. This attitude, endorsed by the Supreme Court, aided the mergers that occurred after 1925. The *Wall Street Journal* crowed, "Never before, here or anywhere else, has a government been so completely fused with business."

And Coolidge confined the government's role to helping business. When Congress tried to raise farm prices through government intervention, Coolidge vetoed the measure as "preposterous" special-interest legislation. One economist said Coolidge's vetoes revealed "a stubborn determination to do nothing," but they revealed more. For on the same day that Coolidge vetoed assistance to farmers, he raised by 50 percent the tariff on pig iron, thereby increasing manufacturers' profits and farmers' costs for tools. Government action was acceptable for business but not for nonbusiness interests.

"Coolidge prosperity" determined the 1924 election. The Democrats, hopelessly divided, took 103 ballots to nominate the colorless, conservative Wall Street lawyer John W. Davis. His election prospects, Davis conceded, were less "than a snowball in hell." A more interesting opponent for Coolidge was Robert La Follette, nominated by discontented farm and labor organizations that formed a new Progressive party. La Follette campaigned against "the power of private monopoly over the political and economic life of the American people." The Progressive platform demanded government ownership of railroads and utilities, farm assistance, and collective bargaining. The Republicans, backed by immense contributions from business, denounced La Follette as an agent of Bolshevism. The choice, Republicans insisted, was "Coolidge or Chaos." Thus instructed, Americans chose Coolidge, though barely half the electorate bothered to vote.

The Fate of Reform

But progressive reform was not completely dead. Even Harding proposed social welfare measures, and, in the 1921 depression, he convened a conference on unemployment and helped spark voluntary relief. A small group in Congress, led by La Follette and George Norris, attacked Mellon's regressive tax policies and supported measures regulating agricultural processors, protecting workers' rights, and maintaining public ownership of a hydroelectric dam at Muscle Shoals, Alabama, that conservative Republicans wanted to privatize. Yet reformers' successes were few and often temporary.

The fate of women's groups illustrated the difficulties reformers faced in the 1920s. At first, the adoption of woman suffrage prompted politicians to champion women's reform issues. In 1920, both major parties endorsed many of the goals of the new **League of Women Voters**. Within a year, many states had granted women the right to serve on juries, several enacted equal pay laws, and Wisconsin adopted an equal-rights law. Congress passed the **Sheppard-Towner Maternity and Infancy Act**, the first federal social-welfare law, in 1921. It provided federal funds for infant and maternity care, precisely the type of protective legislation that the suffragists had described as women's special interest.

But thereafter women reformers gained little. As it became clear that women did not vote as a bloc but according to their varying social and economic backgrounds, Congress lost interest in "women's issues." In 1929, Congress killed the Sheppard-Towner Act. Nor could reformers gain ratification of a child-labor amendment after the Supreme Court invalidated laws regulating child labor. Conservatives attacked women reformers as "Bolsheviks."

Disagreements among women reformers and shifting interests also limited their success. Led by the National Woman's Party, some feminists campaigned for an Equal Rights Amendment. But other reformers feared that such an amendment would nullify the progressive laws that protected working women. Such reform organizations as the Consumers' League lost their energy and focus. The General Federation of Women's Clubs, always relatively conservative, promoted home economics and the use of electric appliances. Indeed, many younger women rejected the public reform focus of progressive feminists. The *Magazine of Business* even maintained that women valued the vacuum cleaner more than they did the vote. By 1927, the president of the Women's Trade Union League called the decade "hideous in the public life of our people and in the noisy flaunting of cheap hopes and cheaper materialism."

CITIES AND SUBURBS

The 1920 census reported that, for the first time, more Americans lived in urban than in rural areas. The trend toward urbanization accelerated in the 1920s as millions of Americans fled the depressed countryside for the booming cities. This massive population movement interacted with technological innovations to reshape cities, build suburbs, and transform urban life (see Map 6-1).

Expanding Cities

Urbanization affected all regions of the country. In absolute terms, the older industrial cities of the Northeast and upper Midwest grew the most, attracting migrants from the rural South and distressed Appalachia. New York remained the nation's foremost metropolis. All other major cities expanded—none more spectacularly than Detroit, which grew to 1.6 million people. The "Motor City" thrived on the booming automobile industry and related industries like glass manufacturing. Old trees and wide lawns gave way to multilane highways as apartment houses and parking lots obliterated old Detroit.

Rural Southerners also headed for Southern cities. In fact, the South was the nation's most rapidly urbanizing region. Migrants from the countryside poured into Atlanta, Birmingham, Memphis, and Houston. Little more than jungle before 1914, Miami became the fastest growing city in the United States during the 1920s—"the Magic City." Not all Southerners welcomed urban growth and the values it represented. The novelist Thomas Wolfe cautioned against boosters in Asheville, North Carolina, "who shout 'Progress Progress Progress'—when what they mean is more Ford automobiles, more Rotary Clubs,

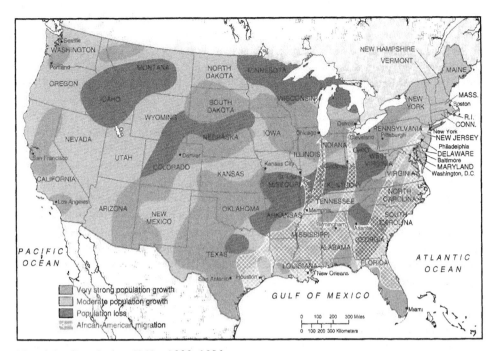

MAP 6-1   Population Shifts, 1920–1930
Rural Americans fled to the cities during the 1920s, escaping a declining agricultural economy to search for new opportunities. African Americans in particular left the rural South for Eastern and Midwestern cities, but the urban population also jumped in the West and in the South itself.

more Baptist Ladies Social unions. . . . We are not necessarily four times as civilized as our grandfathers because we go four times as fast in automobiles, because our buildings are four times as tall."

In the West, Denver, Portland, and Seattle (each a regional economic hub) and several California cities grew rapidly. Los Angeles grew by 115 percent and by 1930 was the nation's fifth largest city, with over 1.2 million people. Although it was the center of California's agricultural wealth and the motion-picture industry and one of the world's busiest ports, Los Angeles was also linked to the automobile industry. The southern California oil fields and the demand for gasoline made it the nation's leading refining center.

The population surge transformed the urban landscape. As land values soared, developers built skyscrapers, giving Cleveland, Kansas City, San Francisco, and many other cities modern skylines. By the end of the decade, American cities had nearly four hundred skyscrapers taller than 20 stories. The tallest, New York's 102-story Empire State Building, symbolized the urban boom.

The Great Black Migration

A significant feature of the rural-to-urban movement was the **Great Migration** of African Americans from the South. Like other migrants, they responded chiefly to economic factors. Southern segregation and violence made migration attractive, but job opportunities made it possible. Prosperity created jobs, and with the decline in European immigration, black workers filled the positions previously given to new immigrants. Though generally the lowest paid and least secure jobs, they were better than sharecropping in the rural South. Black men worked as unskilled or semiskilled laborers; black women became domestics in white homes.

The migrants often found adjustment to their new environment difficult. Southern rural black culture clashed with industrial work rhythms and discipline and with urban living. Still, more than a million and a half African Americans moved to northern cities in the 1920s.

There black ghettos usually developed, more because of prejudice than the wishes of the migrants. Although African Americans, like European immigrants, often wanted to live together to sustain their culture, racist restrictions meant that segregation, not congregation, most shaped their urban community. With thousands of newcomers limited to certain neighborhoods, housing shortages developed. Rapacious landlords charged ever-increasing rents for ever-declining housing. Rents doubled in New York's Harlem during the decade. In an example of the way racism exacerbated urban poverty, black workers earned less than working-class white workers but had to spend 50 percent more for housing. High rents and low wages forced black families to share inferior and unsanitary housing that threatened their health and safety. In Pittsburgh, only 20 percent of black houses had bathtubs, and only 50 percent had indoor toilets; in another city, an observer wrote that "the State would not allow cows to live in some of these apartments used by colored people." Continual migration disrupted efforts to develop a stable community; Harlem, said one social worker, was a "perpetual frontier."

However, the Great Migration also increased African Americans' racial consciousness, autonomy, and power. In 1928, for instance, black Chicagoans, using the ballot denied to African Americans in the South, elected the first black man to Congress since the turn of the century. Mutual-aid societies and fraternal orders proliferated. Churches were particularly influential. A reporter in 1926 counted 140 black churches in a 150-block area of Harlem. Most of these were "storefront churches" where "cotton-field preachers" provided an emotional and fundamentalist religion familiar to migrants from the rural South.

Another organization also appealed to poor black ghetto dwellers. The Universal Negro Improvement Association (UNIA), organized by Marcus Garvey, a Jamaican immigrant to New York, rejected the NAACP's goal of integration. A black nationalist espousing racial pride, Garvey exhorted black people to migrate to Africa to build a "free, redeemed, and mighty nation." In the meantime, he urged them to support black businesses. UNIA organized many enterprises, including groceries, restaurants, laundries, a printing plant, and the Black Star Steamship Line, intended as a commercial link between the United States, the West Indies, and Africa. UNIA attracted half a million members, the first black mass movement in American history. When Garvey was convicted of mail fraud and deported, however, the movement collapsed.

Racial pride also found expression in the **Harlem Renaissance**, an outpouring of literature, painting, sculpture, and music. Inspired by African-American culture and black urban life, writers and artists created works of power and poignancy. The poetry of Langston Hughes reflected the rhythm and mood of jazz and the blues. When a white patron complained that his writing was not "primitive" enough, Hughes responded, "I did not feel the rhythms of the primitive surging through me, and so I could not live and write as though I did. I was Chicago and Kansas City and Broadway and Harlem. And I was not what she wanted me to be." Other leading authors of the Harlem Renaissance who asserted their independence included Claude McKay, who wrote of the black working class in *Home to Harlem* (1928), Zora Neale Hurston, and James Weldon Johnson.

Barrios

Hispanic migrants also entered the nation's cities in the 1920s, creating their own communities, or barrios. Fifty thousand Puerto Ricans settled in New York, mostly in East ("Spanish") Harlem, where they found low-paying jobs. Far more migrants arrived from

Mexican Americans, like these farmworkers pitting apricots in Los Angeles County in 1924, often found jobs in the agribusiness enterprises of the Southwest but lived in barrios in the expanding cities of the region. More Mexicans than any other immigrants entered the United States in the 1920s.

Mexico. Although many of them worked as migrant farm laborers, they often lived in cities in the off-season. Others permanently joined the expanding urban economy in industrial and construction jobs. The barrios, with their own businesses, churches, and cultural organizations, created a sense of permanency.

These communities enabled the newcomers to preserve their cultural values and build social institutions, such as *mutualistas* (mutual aid societies), that helped them obtain credit, housing, and health care. But the barrios also reflected the hostility that Hispanics encountered in American cities, for racism often restricted them to such districts. The number of Mexicans in Los Angeles tripled during the 1920s to nearly 100,000, but segregation confined them to East Los Angeles. Other areas of the city, such as El Segundo and Lynwood, boasted of being "restricted to the white race" and having "no Negroes or Mexicans." Los Angeles maintained separate schools for Mexicans, and a social worker reported that "America has repulsed the Mexican immigrant in every step he has taken" toward integration. As new migrants streamed in, conditions in the barrios deteriorated, for few cities provided adequate public services for them. Denver's barrio was described in 1924 as an area "both God and Denver had forgotten" with "no paving, no sidewalks, no sewers."

Some Hispanics fought discrimination. *La Orden de Hijos de America* (the Order of the Sons of America), organized in San Antonio in 1921, campaigned against inequities in schools and the jury system. In 1929, it helped launch the larger League of United Latin American Citizens (LULAC), which would help advance civil rights for all Americans.

The Road to Suburbia

As fast as the cities mushroomed in the 1920s, the suburbs grew twice as fast. Park Ridge outside Chicago, Inglewood outside Los Angeles, Shaker Heights outside Cleveland, and many others expanded by 400 percent. New suburbs arose across the country. Fourteen hundred new subdivisions appeared in Los Angeles County during the 1920s; two-thirds of the new municipal incorporations in Illinois and Michigan were suburbs of Chicago, St. Louis, or Detroit. Some suburbs, such as Highland Park, where Henry Ford built his factory near Detroit, and Fairfield, Alabama, were industrial, but most were havens for the middle and upper classes.

Automobiles created the modern suburb. Nineteenth-century suburbs were small and linear, stretching along the street railway system. The new developments were sprawling and dispersed, for the automobile enabled people to live in formerly remote areas. A single-family house surrounded by a lawn became the social ideal, a pastoral escape from the overcrowded and dangerous city. Many suburbs excluded African Americans, Hispanics, Jews, and working-class people. Shaker Heights, for instance, limited land sales to white buyers and required expensive building materials and professional architects. Suburbanites of more modest means found homes in such places as Westwood, outside Chicago, the "World's Largest Bungalow Development."

Suburbanization and the automobile brought other changes. The government provided federal money to states to build highways, and by the end of the decade, road construction was the largest single item in the national budget. Autos and suburbs also stimulated the growth of new industries. In 1922, J.C. Nichols opened the Country Club Plaza, the first suburban shopping center, in Kansas City; it provided free off-street parking. Department stores and other large retailers began leaving the urban cores for the suburbs, where both parking and more affluent customers were waiting. Drive-in restaurants began with Royce Hailey's Pig Stand in Dallas in 1921. Two years later, the first fast-food franchise chain, White Castle, appeared, with its standardized menu and building, serving hamburgers "by the sack" to Americans in record numbers. Enjoying remarkable success, owners Walt Anderson and Billy Ingram described their volume of sales in one year: "Picture a line of buns, laid side by side, one hundred and sixty-three miles long, forty-one truckloads of hamburger, weighing two tons each, two carloads of onions, three carloads of pickles, ninety-six-hundred five gallon urns of coffee and you have an idea of the output of the White Castle System for the year 1925."

MASS CULTURE IN THE JAZZ AGE

The White Castle chain symbolized a new society and culture. Urbanization and the automobile joined with new systems of distributing, marketing, and communications to mold a mass culture of standardized experiences and interests. Not all Americans participated equally in the new culture, however, and some attacked it.

Advertising the Consumer Society

Advertising and its focus on increasing consumption shaped the new society. President Coolidge considered advertising "the most potent influence in adopting and changing the habits and modes of life, affecting what we eat, what we wear, and the work and play of the whole nation." A less complacent observer calculated that in 1925, nearly 50 percent more was spent "to educate consumers in what they may or may not want to buy" than on education from grade school through college.

Advertisers exhorted consumers via newspapers, billboards, streetcar signs, junk mail, radio, movies, and even skywriting. They sought to create a single market where everyone, regardless of region and ethnicity, consumed brand-name products. Advertisers attempted to stimulate new wants by ridiculing previous models or tastes as obsolete, acclaiming the convenience of a new brand, or linking the latest fashion with status or sex appeal. "If I wear a certain brand of underwear," observed one critic, "I have the satisfaction of knowing that my fellow-men not so fortunately clad are undoubtedly fouled swine."

The home became a focus of consumerism. Middle- and upper-class women purchased mass-produced household appliances, such as electric irons, toasters, vacuum cleaners, washing machines, and refrigerators. Working-class women bought packaged food, ready-made clothing, and other consumer goods to lighten their workload. Advertisers attempted to redefine the housewife's role as primarily that of a consumer, purchasing goods for her family. To promote sales of clothing and cosmetics, advertising depicted women as concerned with fashion, beauty, and sex appeal. It thus contributed to the declining interest in the larger social issues that the earlier women's movement had raised.

A shifting labor market also promoted mass consumption. The increasing number of white-collar workers had more time and money for leisure and consumption. Factory workers, whose jobs often provided little challenge, less satisfaction, and no prospect for advancement, found in consumption not only material rewards, but also, thanks to advertisers' claims, some self-respect and fulfillment as stylish and attractive people worthy of attention. Women clerical workers, the fastest-growing occupational group, found in the purchase of clothes and cosmetics a sign of social status and an antidote to workplace monotony. "People are seeking to escape from themselves," insisted a writer in *Advertising and Selling* in 1926. "They want to live in a more exciting world." Advertisers tried to portray popular fantasies rather than social realities.

Under the stimulus of advertising, consumption increasingly displaced the traditional virtues of thrift, prudence, and avoidance of debt. Installment buying became common. By 1928, fully 85 percent of furniture, 80 percent of radios, and 75 percent of washing machines were bought on credit. But with personal debt rising more than twice as fast as incomes, even aggressive advertising and the extension of credit could not indefinitely prolong the illusion of a healthy economy.

Leisure and Entertainment

During the 1920s, Americans also spent more on recreation and leisure, important features of the new mass society. Millions of people packed into movie theaters, whose ornate style symbolized their social importance. In Chicago, the Uptown boasted a four-thousand-seat theater, an infirmary, a nursery, and a restaurant; its turreted façade soared eight stories. Inside was a four-story lobby with twin marble staircases, crystal chandeliers, and an orchestra to entertain people waiting to enter. "It is beyond human dreams of loveliness," exclaimed one ad, "achieving that overpowering sense of tremendous size and exquisite beauty."

Movies helped spread common values and set national trends in dress, language, and behavior. Studios made films to attract the largest audiences and fit prevailing stereotypes. Cecil B. De Mille titillated audiences while reinforcing conventional standards with such religious epics as *The Ten Commandments* (1923) and *The King of Kings* (1927). Set in ancient times, such movies depicted both sinful pleasures and the eventual triumph of moral order. One Hollywood executive called for "passionate but pure" films that would give "the public all the sex it wants with compensating values for all those church and women groups."

Radio also helped to mold national popular culture. The first radio network, the National Broadcasting Company (NBC), was formed in 1926. Soon it was charging $10,000 to broadcast commercials to a national market. Networks provided standardized entertainment, personalities, and news to Americans across the nation. Radio incorporated listeners into a national society. Rural residents, in particular, welcomed the "talking furniture" for giving them access to the speeches, sermons, and business information available to city dwellers.

The phonograph, another popular source of entertainment, allowed families to listen to music of their choice in their own homes. The phonograph business boomed. Manufacturers turned out more than 2 million phonographs and 100 million records annually. Record companies promoted dance crazes, such as the Charleston, and developed regional markets for country, or "hillbilly," music in the South and West, as well as a "race market" for blues and jazz among the growing black and white urban population. The popularity of the trumpet player Louis Armstrong and other jazz greats gave the decade its nickname, the **Jazz Age**.

Jazz derived from African-American musical traditions. The Great Migration spread it from New Orleans and Kansas City to cities throughout the nation. Its improvisational and

Violinist Carroll Dickerson, at the Sunset Café in 1922, led one of the jazz bands that flourished in Chicago's many clubs, pointing out the central role of African Americans in the Jazz Age. *Variety* magazine dubbed Chicago the "hottest café town" in the United States but the Illinois Vigilance Association despaired that "in Chicago alone" it had "traced the fall of 1,000 girls . . . to jazz music" in just two years.

rhythmic characteristics differed sharply from older and more formal music and were often condemned by people who feared that jazz would undermine conventional restraints on behavior. One group in Cincinnati, arguing that the music would implant "jazz emotions" in babies, won an injunction against its performance near hospitals. Middle-class black Chicagoans frowned on jazz and favored "the better class of music." But conductor Leopold Stokowski defended jazz as the music of modern America: "Jazz has come to stay because it is an expression of the times, of the breathless, energetic, superactive times in which we are living; it is useless to fight against it."

Professional sports also flourished and became more commercialized. Millions of Americans, attracted by the popularity of such celebrities as Babe Ruth of the New York Yankees, crowded into baseball parks to follow major league teams. Ruth treated himself as a commercial commodity, hiring an agent, endorsing Cadillacs and alligator shoes, and defending a salary in 1932 that dwarfed that of President Hoover by declaring, "I had a better year than he did."

Large crowds turned out to watch such boxers as Jack Dempsey and Gene Tunney pummel each other; those who could not get tickets listened to radio announcers describe each blow. College football attracted frenzied followers among people with no interest in higher education. Universities built huge stadiums—Ohio State's had 64,000 seats. By 1929, the Carnegie Commission noted that the commercialization of college sports "overshadowed the intellectual life for which the university is assumed to exist."

Other crazes, from flagpole sitting to miniature golf, also indicated the spread of popular culture and its emphasis on leisure. Another celebrity who captured popular fascination was the aviator Charles Lindbergh, who flew alone across the Atlantic in 1927. In the *Spirit of St. Louis*, a tiny airplane built on a shoestring budget and nearly outweighed by the massive amount of fuel it had to carry, Lindbergh fought bad weather and fatigue for thirty-four hours before landing to a hero's welcome in Paris. Named its first "Man of the Year" by *Time*, one of the new mass-circulation magazines, Lindbergh won adulation and awards from Americans who still valued the image of individualism.

The New Morality

The promotion of consumption and immediate gratification weakened traditional self-restraint and fed a desire for personal fulfillment. The failure of wartime sacrifices to achieve promised glories deepened Americans' growing disenchantment with traditional values. The social dislocations of the war years and growing urbanization accelerated moral and social change. Sexual pleasure became an increasingly open objective. Popularization of Sigmund Freud's ideas weakened prescriptions for sexual restraint; the growing availability of birth-control information enabled women to enjoy sex with less fear of pregnancy; and movie stars, such as Clara Bow, known as "the It Girl," and Rudolph Valentino, flaunted sexuality to mass audiences. Traditionalists worried as divorce rates, cigarette consumption, and hemlines went up while respect for parents, elders, and clergy went down. A sociological study of Muncie, Indiana—the nation's "Middletown"—found that "religious life as represented by the churches is less pervasive than a generation ago."

Young people seemed to embody the new morality. Rejecting conventional standards, they embraced the era's frenzied dances, bootleg liquor, smoking, more revealing clothing, and sexual experimentation. They welcomed the freedom from parental control that the automobile afforded—although the car was hardly the "house of prostitution on wheels" that one critic called it. The "flapper"—a frivolous young woman with short hair and a skimpy skirt who danced, smoked, and drank in oblivious self-absorption—was a major obsession in countless articles, bearing such titles as "These Wild Young People" and "The Uprising of the Young." Few people were more alarmed than the president of the University of Florida. "The low-cut gowns, the rolled hose and short skirts are born of the Devil," he cried, "and are carrying the present and future generations to chaos and destruction." But feminists also condemned this symbol of changing standards. "It is sickening," Charlotte Perkins Gilman wrote in 1923, "to see so many of the newly freed abusing that freedom in mere imitation of masculine vice and weakness."

But the new morality was neither as new nor as widespread as its advocates and critics believed. Signs of change had appeared before the war in the popularity of new clothing fashions, social values, and public amusements among working-class and ethnic groups. And if it now became fashionable for the middle class to adopt such attitudes and practices, most Americans still adhered to traditional beliefs and values. Legislators in Utah and Virginia, for example, proposed laws requiring hemlines within three inches of the ankle and necklines within three inches of the throat. Moreover, as Gilman's comment suggests, the new morality offered only a limited freedom. It certainly did not promote social equality for women, who remained subject to traditional double standards, with marriage and divorce laws, property rights, and employment opportunities biased against them.

The Searching Twenties

Many writers rejected what they considered the materialism, conformity, and provincialism of the emerging mass culture. Their criticism made the postwar decade one of the most creative periods in American literature. The brutality and hypocrisy of the war stimulated their disillusionment and alienation. What Gertrude Stein called the "Lost Generation" considered, in the words of F. Scott Fitzgerald, "all Gods dead, all wars fought, all faiths in man shaken." Ernest Hemingway, wounded as a Red Cross volunteer during the war, rejected idealism in his novel *A Farewell to Arms* (1929), declaring that he no longer saw any meaning in "the words sacred, glorious, and sacrifice."

Novelists also turned their attention to American society. In *The Great Gatsby* (1925), Fitzgerald traced the self-deceptions of the wealthy. Sinclair Lewis ridiculed middle-class society and its narrow business culture in *Babbitt* (1922), whose title character provided a new word applied to the smug and shallow. In 1930, Lewis became the first American to win the Nobel Prize in literature.

Other writers condemned the mediocrity and intolerance of mass society. The critic Harold Stearns edited *Civilization in the United States* (1922), a book of essays. Its depiction of a repressive society sunk in hypocrisy, conformity, and materialism prompted his departure for Paris, where he lived, like Hemingway and Fitzgerald, as an expatriate, alienated from America. H.L. Mencken made his *American Mercury* the leading magazine of cultural dissenters. Conventional and conservative himself, Mencken heaped vitriol on the "puritans," "peasants," and "prehensile morons" he saw everywhere in American life.

When President Coolidge declined a request to exhibit American paintings in Paris by declaring that there were none, he seemed to confirm for the critics the boorishness of American society. But many of the critics were as self-absorbed as their targets. When the old progressive muckraker Upton Sinclair complained that he found nothing "constructive" in Mencken's voluminous writings, Mencken was delighted. "Uplift," he retorted, "has damn nigh ruined the country." Fitzgerald claimed to have "no interest in politics at all." Such attitudes dovetailed with the society they condemned.

CULTURE WARS

Despite the blossoming of mass culture and society in the 1920s, conflicts divided social groups. Some of these struggles involved reactions against the new currents in American life, including technological and scientific innovations, urban growth, and materialism. But movements to restrict immigration, enforce prohibition, prohibit the teaching of evolution, and even sustain the Ku Klux Klan did not have simple origins, motives, or consequences. The forces underlying the culture wars of the 1920s would surface repeatedly in the future (see the Overview table, "Issues in the Culture Wars of the 1920s").

Nativism and Immigration Restriction

For years, many Americans, from racists to reformers, had campaigned to restrict immigration. In 1917, Congress required immigrants to pass a literacy test. But renewed immigration after the war revived the anti-immigration movement, and the propaganda of the war and the Red Scare years generated public support for more restriction. Depicting immigrants as radicals, racial inferiors, religious subversives, or criminals, nativists clamored for congressional action. The Emergency Quota Act of 1921 reduced immigration by about two-thirds and established quotas for nationalities on the basis of their numbers in the United States in 1910. Restrictionists, however, demanded more stringent action, especially against the largely Catholic and Jewish immigrants from southern and eastern Europe. Coolidge himself urged that America "be kept American," by which he meant white, Anglo-Saxon, and Protestant.

Congress adopted this racist rationale in the **National Origins Act of 1924**, which proclaimed its objective to be the maintenance of the "racial preponderance" of "the basic strain of our population." This law restricted immigration quotas to 2 percent of the foreign-born

ISSUES IN THE CULTURE WARS OF THE 1920S

ISSUE	PROPONENT VIEW	OPPONENT VIEW
The new morality	Promotes greater personal freedom and opportunities for fulfilment.	Promotes moral collapse.
Evolutionism	A scientific advance linked to notions of progress.	A threat to religious belief.
Jazz	Modern and vital.	Unsettling, irregular, vulgar, and primitive.
Immigration	A source of national strength from ethnic and racial diversity.	A threat to the status and authority of old-stock white Protestants.
Great Migration	A chance for African Americans to find new economic opportunities and gain autonomy and pride.	A threat to traditional white privilege, control, and status.
Prohibition	Promotes social and family stability and reduces crime.	Restricts personal liberty and increases crime.
Fundamentalism	An admirable adherence to traditional religious faith and biblical injunctions.	A superstitious creed given to intolerant interference in social and political affairs.
Ku Klux Klan	An organization promoting community responsibility, patriotism, and traditional social, moral, and religious values.	A group of religious and racial bigots given to violent vigilantism and fostering moral and public corruption.
Mass culture	Increases popular participation in national culture; provides entertainment and relaxation.	Promotes conformity, materialism, mediocrity, and spectacle.
Consumerism	Promotes material progress and higher living standards.	Promotes waste, sterility, and self-indulgence.

population of each nationality as recorded in the 1890 census, which was taken before the mass immigration from southern and eastern Europe. Another provision, effective in 1929, restricted total annual immigration to 150,000, with quotas that nearly eliminated southern and eastern Europeans. The law also completely excluded Japanese immigrants.

Other actions targeted Japanese residents in America. California, Oregon, Washington, Arizona, and other Western states prohibited them from owning or leasing land, and in 1922, the Supreme Court ruled that, as nonwhites, they could never become naturalized citizens. A Japanese newspaper in Los Angeles criticized such actions as betraying America's own ideals. Dispirited by the prejudice of the decade, Japanese residents hoped for fulfillment through their children, the *Nisei*, who were American citizens by birth.

Ironically, as a U.S. territory, the Philippines was not subject to the National Origins Act, and Filipino immigration increased ninefold during the 1920s. Most Filipino newcomers became farm laborers, especially in California, or worked in Alaskan fisheries. Similarly, because the law did not apply to immigrants from the Western Hemisphere, Mexican immigration also grew. Nativists lobbied to exclude Mexicans, but agribusiness interests in the Southwest blocked any restrictions on low-cost migrant labor.

The Ku Klux Klan

Nativism was also reflected in the popularity of the revived Ku Klux Klan, the goal of which, according to its leader, was to protect "the interest of those whose forefathers established the nation." Although founded in Georgia in 1915 and modeled on its Reconstruction predecessor, the new Klan was a national, not only a Southern, movement and claimed several million members by the mid-1920s. Admitting only native-born white Protestants, the Klan embodied the fears of a traditional culture threatened by social change. Ironically, its rapid spread owed much to modern business and promotional techniques as hundreds of professional recruiters raked in hefty commissions selling Klan memberships to those hoping to defend their way of life.

In part, the Klan was a fraternal order, providing entertainment, assistance, and community for its members. Its picnics, parades, charity drives, and other social and family-oriented activities—perhaps a half-million women joined the Women of the Ku Klux Klan—sharply distinguished the organization from both the small, secretive Klan of the nineteenth century and the still smaller, extremist Klan of the later twentieth century. Regarding themselves as reformers, Klan members supported immigration restriction and prohibition.

But the Klan also exploited racial, ethnic, and religious prejudices and campaigned against many social groups and what it called "alien creeds." It attacked African Americans in the South, Mexicans in Texas, Japanese in California, and Catholics and Jews everywhere. A twisted religious impulse ran through much of the Klan's organization and activities. It hired itinerant Protestant ministers to spread its message, erected altars and flaming crosses at its meetings, and sang Klan lyrics to the tunes of well-known hymns. One Klan leader maintained that "the Klan stood for the same things as the Church, but we did the things the Church wouldn't do." This included publishing anti-Catholic newspapers, boycotting Catholic and Jewish businesses, and lobbying for laws against parochial schools and for compulsory Bible reading in the public schools. The Klan also resorted to violence. In 1921,

Appealing to traditional values and racist sentiments, the KKK also embraced the technological innovation and commercialism characteristic of the 1920s. Here two KKK members thrill a Klan gathering with their surprise landing in Dayton, Ohio, in 1924.

for example, a Methodist minister who belonged to the Klan murdered a Catholic priest on his own doorstep, and other Klansmen burned down Catholic churches. The leader of the Oregon Klan insisted that "the only way to cure a Catholic is to kill him."

To the Klan, Catholics and Jews symbolized not merely subversive religions, but also the ethnic diversity and swelling urban population that challenged traditional Protestant culture. To protect that culture, the Klan attempted to censor or disrupt "indecent" entertainment, assaulted those whom it accused of adultery, and terrorized doctors who performed abortions.

While the Klan's appeal seemed rooted in the declining countryside, it also attracted urban residents. Chicago had the largest Klan organization in the nation, with fifty thousand members, and Houston, Dallas, Portland, Indianapolis, Denver, and the satellite communities ringing Los Angeles were also Klan strongholds. Urban Klansmen were largely lower or lower middle class, many recently arrived from the country and retaining its attitudes; others were long-term urban residents who feared being marginalized by social changes, especially by competition from immigrants and new ideas.

The Klan also ventured into politics, with some success, but eventually it encountered resistance. In the North, Catholic workers disrupted Klan parades. In the South, too, Klan excesses provoked a backlash. After the Klan in Dallas flogged sixty-eight people in a "whipping meadow" along the Trinity River in 1922, respect turned to outrage. Newspapers demanded that the Klan disband, district attorneys began to prosecute Klan thugs, and in 1924 Klan candidates were defeated by a ticket headed by Miriam "Ma" Ferguson, whose gubernatorial campaign called for anti-Klan laws and for the loss of tax exemptions for churches used for Klan meetings. Elsewhere the Klan was stung by revelations of criminal behavior and corruption by Klan leaders, who had been making fortunes pocketing membership fees and selling regalia to followers. The Klan crusade to purify society had bred corruption and conflict everywhere. By 1930, the Klan had nearly collapsed.

Prohibition and Crime

Like the Klan, prohibition both reflected and provoked social tensions in the 1920s. Reformers had long believed that prohibition would improve social conditions, reduce crime and family instability, increase economic efficiency, and purify politics. They rejoiced in 1920, when the Eighteenth Amendment, prohibiting the manufacture, sale, or transportation of alcoholic beverages, took effect. Congress then passed the **Volstead Act**, which defined the forbidden liquors and established the Prohibition Bureau to enforce the law. But many social groups, especially among urban ethnic communities, opposed prohibition, and the government could not enforce the law where public opinion did not endorse it.

Evasion was easy. By permitting alcohol for medicinal, sacramental, and industrial purposes, the Volstead Act gave doctors, priests, and druggists a huge loophole through which to satisfy their friends' needs. Hearing that the use of sacramental wines increased by 800,000 gallons under Prohibition, one Protestant leader complained that "not more than one-quarter of this is sacramental—the rest is sacrilegious." City dwellers made "bathtub gin," and rural people distilled "moonshine." Scofflaws frequented the "speakeasies" that replaced saloons or bought liquor from bootleggers and rumrunners, who imported it from Canada, Cuba, or Mexico. The limited resources of the Prohibition Bureau often allowed bootleggers to operate openly. Dozens met publicly in a Seattle hotel in 1922 and adopted "fair prices" for liquor and a code of ethics "to keep liquor runners within the limits of approved business methods."

The ethics and business methods of bootleggers soon shocked Americans, however. The huge profits encouraged organized crime—which had previously concentrated on gambling and prostitution—to develop elaborate liquor distribution networks. Operating outside the law, crime "families" used violence to enforce contracts, suppress competition, and attack rivals. In Chicago, Al Capone's army of nearly a thousand gangsters killed hundreds. Using the profits from bootlegging and such new tools as the automobile and the submachine gun, organized crime corrupted city governments and police forces.

Gradually, even many "drys"—people who had initially favored prohibition—dropped their support, horrified by the boost the amendment gave organized crime and worried about a general disrespect for law that it promoted. A 1926 poll found that four-fifths of Americans wanted to repeal or modify prohibition, yet it remained in force because it was entangled in party politics and social conflict. Many rural, Protestant Americans saw prohibition as a symbolic cultural issue. As the comedian Will Rogers said, "Mississippi will vote dry and drink wet as long as it can stagger to the polls." Prohibition represented the ability of rural Protestants to control the newcomers in the expanding cities. Democrats called for repeal in their 1928 and 1932 platforms, and in 1933, thirty-six states ratified an amendment repealing what Herbert Hoover had called a "noble experiment."

Old-Time Religion and the Scopes Trial

Religion provided another fulcrum for traditionalists attempting to stem cultural change. Protestant fundamentalism, which emphasized the infallibility of the Bible, including the Genesis story of Adam and Eve, emerged at the turn of the century as a conservative reaction to religious modernism and the social changes brought by the mass immigration of Catholics and Jews, the growing influence of science and technology, and the secularization of public education. But the fundamentalist crusade to reshape America became formidable only in the 1920s.

Fundamentalist groups, colleges, and publications sprang up throughout the nation, especially in the South. The anti-Catholic sentiment exploited by the Klan was but one consequence of fundamentalism's insistence on strict biblical Christianity. A second was the assault on Darwin's theory of evolution, which contradicted literal interpretations of biblical Creation. The Southern Baptist Convention condemned "every theory, evolutionary or other, which teaches that man originated or came by way of lower animal ancestry." Fundamentalist legislators tried to prevent teaching evolution in public schools in at least twenty states. In 1923, Oklahoma banned textbooks based on Darwinian theory, and Florida's legislature denounced teaching evolution as "subversive." In 1925, Tennessee forbade teaching any idea contrary to the biblical account of human origins. The governor signed the law, saying that "there is a widespread belief that something is shaking the fundamentals of the country, both in religion and in morals. It is the opinion of many that an abandonment of the old-fashioned faith and belief in the Bible is our trouble."

Social or political conservatism, however, was not an inherent part of old-time religion. The most prominent anti-evolution politician, William Jennings Bryan, continued to campaign for political, social, and economic reforms. Never endorsing the Klan, he served on the American Committee on the Rights of Religious Minorities and condemned anti-Semitism and anti-Catholicism. Bryan feared that Darwinism promoted political and economic conservatism. The survival of the fittest, he complained, elevated force and brutality, ignored spiritual values and democracy, and discouraged altruism and reform. How could a person fight for social justice "unless he believes in the triumph of right?"

The controversy over evolution came to a head when the American Civil Liberties Union (ACLU) responded to Tennessee's violation of the constitutional separation of church and state by offering to defend any teacher who tested the anti-evolution law. John Scopes, a high school biology teacher in Dayton, Tennessee, did so and was arrested. Scopes's trial attracted national attention after Bryan agreed to assist the prosecution and Clarence Darrow, a famous Chicago lawyer and prominent atheist, volunteered to defend Scopes.

Millions of Americans tuned their radios to hear the first trial ever broadcast. The judge, a fundamentalist, sat under a sign urging people to "Read Your Bible Daily." He ruled that scientists could not testify in support of evolution: Because they were not present at the Creation, their testimony would be "hearsay." But he did allow Darrow to put Bryan on the stand as an expert on the Bible. Bryan insisted on the literal truth of every story in the Bible, allowing Darrow to ridicule his ideas and force him to concede that some biblical passages had to be construed symbolically. Though the local jury took only eight minutes to convict Scopes, fundamentalists suffered public ridicule from reporters, including H.L. Mencken, who sneered at the "hillbillies" and "yokels" of Dayton.

But fundamentalism was hardly destroyed, and anti-evolutionists continued their campaign. New organizations, such as the Bryan Bible League, lobbied for state laws and an anti-evolution amendment to the constitution. Three more states forbade teaching evolution, but by 1929 the movement had faltered. Even so, fundamentalism retained religious influence and would again challenge science and modernism in American life.

A NEW ERA IN THE WORLD?

Abroad, as at home, Americans in the 1920s sought peace and economic order. Rejection of the Treaty of Versailles and the League of Nations did not foreshadow isolationism. Indeed, in the 1920s, the United States became more deeply involved in international matters than ever before in peacetime. That involvement both produced important successes and sowed the seeds for serious future problems.

War Debts and Economic Expansion

The United States was the world's dominant economic power in the 1920s, changed by the Great War from a debtor to a creditor nation. The loans that the United States had made to its allies during the war troubled the nation's relations with Europe throughout the decade. American insistence on repayment angered Europeans, who saw the money as a U.S. contribution to the joint war effort against Germany. Moreover, high American tariffs blocked Europeans from exporting goods to the United States and earning dollars to repay their debts. Eventually, the United States readjusted the terms for repayment, and American bankers extended large loans to Germany, which used the money to pay reparations to Britain and France, whose governments then used the same money to repay the United States. This unstable system depended on a constant flow of money from the United States.

America's global economic role expanded in other ways as well. Exports, especially of manufactured goods, soared; by 1929, the United States was the world's largest exporter, responsible for one-sixth of all exports. American investment abroad more than doubled between 1919 and 1930. To expand their markets and avoid foreign tariffs, many U.S. companies became **multinational corporations**, establishing branches or subsidiaries abroad. Ford built assembly plants in England, Japan, Turkey, and Canada. International Telephone and Telegraph owned two dozen factories in Europe and employed more overseas workers than any other U.S. corporation.

Other companies gained control of foreign supply sources. American oil companies invested in foreign oil fields, especially in Latin America, where they controlled more than half of Venezuelan production. The United Fruit Company developed such huge operations in Central America that it often dominated national economies. In Costa Rica, the company had a larger budget than the national government.

Europeans and Latin Americans alike worried about this economic invasion; even Secretary of Commerce Herbert Hoover expressed concerns. Multinationals, he warned, might eventually take markets from American manufacturers and jobs from American workers. Business leaders, however, dismissed such reservations.

Hoover's concerns, moreover, did not prevent him from promoting economic expansion abroad. The government worked to open doors for American businesses in foreign countries, helping them to secure access to trade, investment opportunities, and raw materials. Hoover's Bureau of Foreign Commerce opened fifty offices around the world to boost American business. Hoover also pressed the British to give U.S. corporations access to rubber production in the British colony of Malaya. Secretary of State Charles Evans Hughes negotiated access to Iraqi oil fields for U.S. oil companies. The government also authorized bankers and manufacturers to form combinations, exempt from antitrust laws, to exploit foreign markets.

Rejecting War

Although government officials cooperated with business leaders to promote American strategic and economic interests, they had little desire to use force in the process. Popular reaction against the Great War, strengthened by a strong peace movement, constrained policymakers. Having repudiated collective security as embodied in the League of Nations, the United States nonetheless sought to minimize international conflict and promote its national security. In particular, the State Department sought to restrict the buildup of armaments among nations.

At the invitation of President Harding, delegations from nine nations met in Washington at the Washington Naval Conference in 1921 to discuss disarmament. The conference drafted a treaty to reduce battleship tonnage and suspend the building of new ships for a decade. The terms virtually froze the existing balance of naval power, with the first rank assigned to Britain and the United States, followed by Japan and then France and Italy. Japan and the United States also agreed not to fortify their possessions in the Pacific any further and to respect the Open Door in East Asia. Public opinion welcomed the treaty; the U.S. Senate ratified it with only one dissenting vote, and the 1924 Republican platform hailed it as "the greatest peace document ever drawn."

The United States made a more dramatic gesture in 1928, when it helped draft the Kellogg-Briand Pact. Signed by sixty-four nations, the treaty renounced aggression and outlawed war. Without provisions for enforcement, however, it was little more than symbolic. The Senate reserved the right of self-defense, repudiated any responsibility for enforcing the treaty, and maintained U.S. claims under the Monroe Doctrine. These limitations on the treaty, Senator Hiram Johnson noted, "have made its nothingness complete."

Managing the Hemisphere

Senate insistence on the authority of the Monroe Doctrine reflected the U.S. claim to a predominant role in Latin America. The United States continued to dominate the hemisphere to promote its own interests. It exerted its influence through investments, control of the Panama Canal, invocation of the Monroe Doctrine, and, when necessary, military intervention.

In response to American public opinion, the peace movement, and Latin American nationalism, the United States did retreat from the extreme gunboat diplomacy of the Progressive Era, withdrawing troops from the Dominican Republic and Nicaragua. Secretary of State Hughes assured Latin Americans that "we covet no territory; we seek no conquest; the liberty we cherish for ourselves we desire for others; and we accept no rights for ourselves that we do not accord to others." But Haiti remained under U.S. occupation throughout the decade, American troops stayed in Cuba and Panama, and the United States directed the financial policies of other Latin American countries. Moreover, it sent the Marines into Honduras in 1924 and back to Nicaragua in 1926. Such interventions could establish only temporary stability while provoking further Latin American hostility. "We are hated and despised," said one American businessman in Nicaragua. "This feeling has been created by employing American marines to hunt down and kill Nicaraguans in their own country."

Latin American resentment led to a resolution at the 1928 Inter-America Conference denying the right of any nation "to intervene in the internal affairs of another." The U.S. delegation rejected the measure, but the anger of Latin Americans prompted the Hoover Administration to decline support for the Roosevelt Corollary, and J. Reuben Clark, chief legal officer of the State Department, drafted the Clark Memorandum. Not published until 1930, this document stated that the Roosevelt Corollary was not a legitimate extension of the Monroe Doctrine and, thereby, helped prepare the way for the so-called Good Neighbor Policy toward Latin America. Still, the United States did not pledge nonintervention and retained the means, both military and economic, to dominate the hemisphere.

HERBERT HOOVER AND THE FINAL TRIUMPH OF THE NEW ERA

As the national economy steamed ahead in 1928, the Republicans chose as their presidential candidate Herbert Hoover, a man who symbolized the policies of prosperity and the New Era. Hoover was not a politician—he had never been elected to office—but a successful administrator who championed rational and efficient economic development. A cooperative government, he believed, should promote business interests and encourage corporations to form trade associations to assure stability and profitability. It should not regulate economic activities. Hoover's stiff managerial image was softened by his humanitarian record and his roots in rural Iowa.

The Democrats, by contrast, chose a candidate who evoked the cultural conflicts of the 1920s. Alfred E. Smith, a four-term governor of New York, was a Catholic, an opponent of prohibition, and a Tammany politician tied to the immigrant constituency of New York City. He had failed to gain the presidential nomination in 1924, when the party split over prohibition and the Klan, but in 1928 he won the dubious honor of running against Hoover. His nomination plunged the nation into the cultural strife that had divided the Democrats in 1924. Rural fundamentalism, anti-Catholicism, prohibition, and nativism were crucial factors in the campaign. The fundamentalist assault was unrelenting. Billy Sunday attacked Smith and the Democrats as "the forces of hell," and a Baptist minister in Oklahoma City warned his congregation, "If you vote for Al Smith, you're voting against Christ and you'll all be damned."

But Hoover was, in fact, the more progressive candidate. Sympathetic to labor, sensitive to women's issues, hostile to racial segregation, and favorable to the League of Nations, Hoover had always distanced himself from what he called "the reactionary group in the Republican party." By contrast, despite supporting state welfare legislation to benefit his urban working-class constituents, Smith was essentially conservative and opposed an active government. Moreover, he was as parochial as his most rural adversaries and never attempted to reach out to them. H.L. Mencken, who voted for Smith, nevertheless said of him, "Not only is he uninterested in the great problems facing the nation, but he has never heard of them." Smith himself responded to a question about the needs of the states west of the Mississippi by asking, "What states *are* west of the Mississippi?"

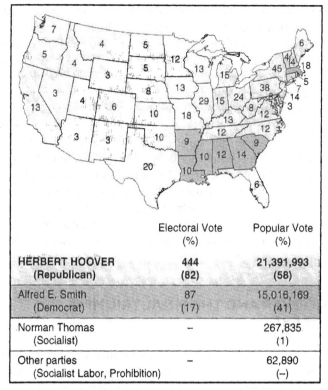

	Electoral Vote (%)	Popular Vote (%)
HERBERT HOOVER (Republican)	**444** **(82)**	**21,391,993** **(58)**
Alfred E. Smith (Democrat)	87 (17)	15,016,169 (41)
Norman Thomas (Socialist)	–	267,835 (1)
Other parties (Socialist Labor, Prohibition)	–	62,890 (–)

MAP 6-2   The Election of 1928
The cultural conflicts of the 1920s shaped the 1928 election.
Al Smith carried the largest cities, but Herbert Hoover swept most
of the rest of the nation, even attracting much of the usually
Democratic South.

Although many Americans voted against Smith because of his social background, those same characteristics attracted others. Millions of urban and ethnic voters, previously Republican or politically uninvolved, voted for Smith and laid the basis for a new Democratic coalition that would emerge in the 1930s. In 1928, however, with the nation still enjoying the economic prosperity so closely associated with Hoover and the Republicans, the Democrats were routed (see Map 6-2).

In his campaign, Hoover boasted that Republican policies could bring America to "the final triumph over poverty." But 1928 would be the Republicans' final triumph for a long time. The vaunted prosperity of the 1920s was ending, and the country faced a future dark with poverty.

CONCLUSION

The New Era of the 1920s changed America. Technological and managerial innovations produced giant leaps in productivity, new patterns of labor, a growing concentration of corporate power, and high corporate profits. Government policies from protective tariffs and regressive taxation to a relaxation of regulatory laws reflected and reinforced the triumphs of a business elite over traditional cautions and concerns.

The decade's economic developments, in turn, stimulated social change, drawing millions of Americans from the countryside to the cities, creating an urban nation, and fostering a new ethic of materialism, consumerism, and leisure and a new mass culture based on the automobile, radio, the movies, and advertising. This social transformation swept up many Americans but left others unsettled by the erosion of traditional practices and values. The concerns of traditionalists found expression in campaigns for prohibition and against immigration, the revival of the Ku Klux Klan, and the rise of religious fundamentalism. Intellectuals denounced the materialism and conformity they saw in the new social order and fashioned new artistic and literary trends.

But the impact of the decade's trends was uneven. Mechanization increased the productivity of some workers but cost others their jobs; people poured into the cities while others left for the suburbs; prohibition, intended to stabilize society, instead produced conflict, crime, and corruption; government policies advanced some economic interests but injured others. Even the notion of a "mass" culture obscured the degree to which millions of Americans were left out of the New Era. With no disposable income and little access to electricity, rural Americans scarcely participated in the joys of consumerism; racial and ethnic minorities were often isolated in ghettos and barrios; and many workers faced declining opportunities. Most ominous was the uneven prosperity undergirding the New Era. Although living standards rose for many Americans and the rich expanded their share of national wealth, more than 40 percent of the population earned less than $1,500 a year and fell below the established poverty level. The unequal distribution of wealth and income made the economy unstable and vulnerable to a disastrous collapse.

Review Questions

1. How did the automobile industry affect the nation's economy and society in the 1920s? In the excerpt from *The Flivver King*, how does Upton Sinclair illustrate the tension between workers and technology even as they both served Henry Ford's vision of mass production and mass consumerism?

2. What factors characterized the "boom industries" of the 1920s? The "sick industries"? How accurate is it to label the 1920s the "decade of prosperity"?

3. What were the underlying issues in the election of 1924? Of 1928? What role did politics play in the public life of the 1920s?

4. What were the chief points of conflict in the "culture wars" of the 1920s? What were the underlying issues in these clashes? Why were they so hard to compromise?

5. In what ways did the World War I experience shape developments in the 1920s?

6. What were the chief features of American involvement in world affairs in the 1920s? To what extent did that involvement constitute a new role for the United States?

Key Terms

Great Migration *171*
Harlem Renaissance *172*
Jazz Age *175*
League of Women Voters *170*
Multinational corporations *183*
National Origins Act of 1924 *178*
Nisei *179*

Open shop *163*
Sheppard-Towner Maternity and Infancy Act *170*
Volstead Act *181*
Welfare capitalism *163*
Yellow-dog contracts *163*

Recommended Reading

John Braeman, Robert Bremner, and David Brody, eds. *Change and Continuity in Twentieth Century America: The 1920s* (1968). Stimulating essays that cover important features of economic, social, and political history.

Warren I. Cohen, *Empire without Tears: America's Foreign Relations, 1921–1933* (1987). A splendid brief analysis of diplomatic and economic policy.

James J. Flink, *The Car Culture* (1975). The fascinating history of the automobile and its social impact.

Ellis W. Hawley, *The Great War and the Search for a Modern Order* (1979). A valuable survey emphasizing economic and organizational changes.

Sinclair Lewis, *Babbitt* (1922). An important novel of the 1920s that ridicules the empty business values of the booster society.

HERBERT HOOVER AND THE GREAT DEPRESSION: 1929–1933

CRASH!

Hard Times in Hooverville

Herbert Hoover and the Depression

Repudiating Hoover: The Election of 1932

Waiting for Roosevelt

Conclusion

I am sitting in the city free employment bureau. It's the women's section. We have been sitting here for four hours. We sit here every day, waiting for a job. There are no jobs. Most of us have had no breakfast . . .

We sit looking at the floor. No one dares think of the coming winter. Everyone is anxious to get work to lay something up for that long siege of bitter cold. But there is no work. Sitting in the room we all know it. That is why we don't talk much. There is a kind of humiliation in it. We look away from each other. We look at the floor. . . .

—Meridel LeSueur, "Women on the Breadlines," 1932.

"Meridel LeSueur: The Despair of Unemployed Women," from Susan Ware, *Modern American Women: A Documentary History* (New York: McGraw-Hill Higher Education, 2002), 145–146.

On April 27 [1933], according to the *New York Times*, Paul Schneider, aged forty-four, a sick and crippled Chicago school teacher, shot himself to death. His widow, left with three children, stated that he had not been paid for eight months. . . . Less than a month after Paul Schneider's discouragement drove him to suicide, the militant action of Chicago teachers—patient no more . . . resulted in the payment of $12,000,000 due them for the last months of 1932. Their pay for the five months of 1933 is still owed them. Five hundred of them are reported to be in asylums and sanitariums as a result of the strain. . . .

These are the conditions facing teachers fortunate enough to be employed. What of the unemployed? . . . "We are always hungry," wrote [one unemployed teacher]. "We owe six months rent. . . . We live every hour in fear of eviction. . . . My sister, a typist, and I . . . have been out of work for two years. . . . We feel discouraged . . . and embittered. We are drifting, with no help from anyone."

—Eunice Langdon

Eunice Langdon, "The Teacher Faces the Depression," *The Nation* 137 (August 16, 1933): 182–187.

MERIDEL LESUEUR and Eunice Langdon convey some of the trauma of the Great Depression, but no one voice can capture the traumatic experience of the Great Depression, when the American economy utterly collapsed, leaving millions of people jobless, homeless, or in constant fear of foreclosure, eviction, and even starvation. The decade of hard times constituted a journey into desperation and despair, and men, women, children everywhere saw their families and dreams shattered and felt the sting of humiliation as they stood in bread lines or begged for clothes or food scraps. The winter of 1932–1933 was particularly cruel: Unemployment soared and stories of malnutrition and outright starvation made headlines in newspapers throughout the nation. Hunger was so widespread in Kentucky and West Virginia that one relief committee limited its handouts to those who were at least 10 percent below their normal weight for their height. The school teacher who committed suicide lived in the city of Chicago where, that winter, half the people were without jobs, where half the city's property tax bills were left unpaid, and, most striking, where one newspaper declared "Starvation Hits 14,000."

Natural disaster accompanied the economic crisis in the drought-stricken states of the Great Plains and forced families to leave their farms. They packed up their meager belongings and took to the road to escape the darkened skies of the "Dust Bowl"—in search for anything better. Their story, best chronicled in John Steinbeck's novel *The Grapes of Wrath*, powerfully portrayed the Westward movement of these homeless migrants—"the path of people in flight"—as Steinbeck himself called it.

Their stories about their experiences in the Great Depression further underscored that the decade of hard times affected people differently. The collapse hit hardest those industries dominated by male workers, leaving mothers and wives with new roles as the family breadwinners, sometimes straining traditional family relationships and men's sense of purpose and respect. Some families drifted apart while others coped simply by making do. But the pressure for women—especially married women—to take on new economic responsibilities did not escape the wrath of the public. They were roundly condemned as "thieving parasites" and placed in the impossible position of being forced to work and told they should not hold jobs.

Race and ethnicity further complicated the problems of the jobless. Racial and ethnic preferences figured prominently in hiring and firing as well as the distribution of relief and other forms of assistance. Southern states routinely denied African Americans relief assistance as did Southwestern states for Hispanic Americans. City officials also discriminated against minority groups, firing them without cause to free up jobs for whites. In 1932, for example, Los Angeles fired Japanese-American transit workers and replaced them with less trained white Americans. The city of New Orleans not only fired its African-American workers but attempted to ban them completely from working on city-owned docks. And the governor of Colorado flouted the law by banning foreign labor in the entire state; officials were instructed to deport all Mexicans.

Hard times divided Americans along traditional lines of race, class, gender, and ethnicity and helped ensure that jobs and relief were granted on an unequal basis. Yet, Americans also united together, believing that community activism and self-help were necessary to combat the depression. President Hoover encouraged the virtue of self-reliance and called on the tradition of local responsibility for relief to assist the jobless. But as the depression deepened and the economy teetered on the edge of catastrophe, Hoover's policies and his advice became a source of public scorn and a symbol of governmental indifference.

KEY TOPICS

The stock market crash.

The Great Depression.

The experiences of the unemployed.

Hoover's voluntary remedies.

The Repudiation of Hoover and voluntarism.

The Election of Franklin D. Roosevelt.

CRASH!

The prosperity of the 1920s ended in a stock market crash that revealed the flaws honey-combing the economy. As the nation slid into a catastrophic depression, factories closed, employment and incomes tumbled, and millions lost their homes, hopes, and dignity. Some protested and took direct action; others looked to the government for relief.

The buoyant prosperity of the New Era, more apparent than real by the summer of 1929, collapsed in October when the stock market crashed. During the previous two years, the market had hit record highs, stimulated by optimism, easy credit, and speculators' manipulations. Political and business leaders had all predicted continued prosperity, and Hoover himself proclaimed in 1928, "We in America are nearer to the final triumph over poverty than ever before in the history of any land," adding that the "poorhouse is vanishing from among us." Stocks continued to rise in 1928 and the activity on Wall Street reached dizzying proportions. To account for the frenzy, one of the nation's most prominent psychologists explained that in a society of leisure and loose morals, "gambling in Wall Street is about the only thrill we have left." The market also captured international attention: The *London Daily Mail* reported that "Wall Street has become another world power, with more authority than the League of Nations. . . ."

But the market soon stuttered and then collapsed, as panicked investors dumped their stocks at any price. After having peaked in September 1929, the market began its tumble, and on Thursday, October 24, the volume of sales so clogged the system that the ticker tape was delayed by forty-eight minutes even before noon. In response, a group of leading financiers met during lunch at the House of Morgan across the street from the Stock Exchange; at the press conference afterwards, one banker dryly observed that "there has been a little distress selling on the Stock Exchange." The next day, President Hoover responded by pronouncing the economy "sound and prosperous. . . ." But on October 29, **Black Tuesday**," calamity struck, wiping out the previous year's gains in one day. Inside the Stock Exchange building, chaos ruled and brokers stood motionless or sobbing aloud; outside crowds of people gathered on Wall Street, many crying in disbelief and others praying for relief. It was a day of hysteria and incredulity as over $10 billion were lost in five hours of trading. Confidence in the economy disappeared, and the slide downward continued for months, and then years. It hit bottom in July 1932. By then, the stock of U.S. Steel had plunged from 262 to 22, Montgomery Ward, from 138 to 4. Much of the paper wealth of America had evaporated, and the nation sank into the Great Depression.

But the crash did more than expose the weaknesses of the economy. Business lost confidence and refused to make investments that might have brought recovery. Instead, banks called in loans and restricted credit, and depositors tried to withdraw their savings, which were uninsured. The demand for cash caused banks to fail, dragging the economy down further. And the Federal Reserve Board prolonged the depression by restricting the money supply.

From Panic to Depression

The Wall Street crash marked the beginning of the depression, but it did not cause it. The depression stemmed from weaknesses in the New Era economy. Most damaging was the unequal distribution of wealth and income. Workers' wages and farmers' incomes had fallen far behind industrial productivity and corporate profits; by 1929, the richest 0.1 percent of American families had as much total income as the bottom 42 percent. With more than half the nation's people living at or below the subsistence level, there was not enough purchasing power to maintain the economy. But an economy based on mass production required mass consumption.

A second factor was that oligopolies dominated American industries. By 1929, the 200 largest corporations (out of 400,000) controlled half the corporate wealth. Their power led to "administered prices," prices kept artificially high and rigid rather than determined by supply and demand. By not responding to purchasing power, this system not only helped bring on economic collapse but also dimmed prospects for recovery.

Weaknesses in specific industries combined with regional disparities to further unbalance the economy. Agriculture suffered from overproduction, declining prices, and heavy debt; so did the coal and textile industries. The New England shoemaking, textile, and shipbuilding industries, having never recovered from the postwar recession, sputtered to a halt. The South, in particular, suffered from desperate, rural poverty that was not offset by the economic growth of such cities as Atlanta and Houston in the 1920s. By the time of the stock market crash, in the entire Southern region, fewer than 500 people had incomes over $100,000, and 8.5 million black and white tenant farmers could barely feed their families. These difficulties left the economy dependent on a few industries for expansion and employment; they could not carry the burden. By 1929, fully one-fifth of the nation's industrial capacity remained unused. Even the automobile industry, which symbolized the New Era prosperity of the 1920s, fell victim to inadequate purchasing power at home and too few markets abroad. And offers to consumers to "buy on time" or through "installment credit"—essential to the 1920s economic expansion—ultimately proved unable to keep the auto industry alive. Banking presented other problems. Poorly managed and regulated, banks had contributed to the instability of prosperity; they now threatened to spread the panic and depression.

Another cornerstone of the twenties' prosperity—increased productivity through the increased reliance on technology—also led to the replacement of workers with machines. A study of unemployment in coal mining, railroads, and manufacturing found that more than 3.25 million workers had been replaced by machines during the 1920s, with over 1 million still unemployed by 1929. A 1932 report, authorized by President Hoover, focused concern on technological unemployment as well as the elimination of skilled workers no longer needed to perform unskilled, routinized labor on machines. Especially troublesome were the mass-production industries with high rates of job turnover and high rates of unemployment due to the introduction of new technologies and processes. The annual rate of unemployment in those sectors, according to the report, exceeded 10 percent between 1923 and 1928—the era of "Coolidge prosperity."

State and local fiscal policies also pointed to economic problems for the 1930s. The expansion of public education and road construction led to higher property taxes in communities throughout the nation, and although per capita tax collection at the federal level actually declined between 1920 and 1929, the tax burden in states and cities increased dramatically. Indeed, state and local taxes rose faster than personal incomes in the 1920s. Even before the stock market crash and subsequent depression, citizen groups had begun calling for fiscal restraint and balanced budgets at the state and local levels. Reports indicated the beginning of a decline in the real estate industry as early as 1926 and increasing property taxes added additional economic pressure. Homeowners and realtors organized to protest the increases in property taxes; still other citizens simply broke the law and refused to pay their property taxes. Tax delinquency rose in the 1920s, as certain communities witnessed the beginnings of a tax revolt. The Socialist mayor of Milwaukee, Daniel Hoan, denounced the formation of tax payer leagues as "tax dodgers," but in Chicago, the tax revolt resulted in a massive "tax strike," lasting from 1930 to 1933 that nearly bankrupted the city.

Government policies at the federal level also bore some responsibility for the crash and depression. Failure to enforce antitrust laws had encouraged oligopolies and high prices; companies created complex holding companies, selling large issues of stock and creating a pyramid of deception and fraud that collapsed during the stock market crash. The government's failure to regulate banking or the stock market also permitted financial recklessness and irresponsible speculation, and the Federal Reserve Bank did too little too late to combat the speculative craze that characterized the stock market. Even before the crash, bank failures had become commonplace, especially in the Midwest and Southeastern regions of the country. Moreover, the federal government was saddled with paying the debt incurred from World War I (about $24 billion), and interest rates on the national debt soared in the 1920s. Providing benefits for veterans and paying interest payments on the national debt accounted for half the federal budget throughout the decade. But new sources of revenue were not forthcoming. Instead, the government reduced tax rates on the wealthy, which further encouraged speculation on Wall Street and contributed to the maldistribution of income. Opposition to labor unions and collective bargaining helped keep workers' wages and purchasing power low. The absence of an effective agricultural policy and the high tariffs that inhibited foreign trade and reduced markets for agricultural products hurt farmers in the same way. In short, the same government policies that shaped the booming 1920s economy also pointed to economic disaster.

The Global Collapse

International economic difficulties spurred the depression as well. Shut out from U.S. markets by high tariffs, Europeans had depended on American investments to manage their debts and reparation payments from the Great War. The stock market crash dried up the flow of American dollars to Europe, causing financial panics and industrial collapse and making the Great Depression global. In turn, European nations curtailed their imports of American goods and defaulted on their debts, further debilitating the U.S. economy. Moreover, the industrialized nations of Western Europe were the prime markets for American goods, but not one European nation had recovered from the economic devastation caused by the Great War. Their economic problems were only exacerbated by America's imposition of high tariffs and the collective international decision to uphold the gold standard. Reliance on the gold standard did not bring the predicted economic stability but led instead to a form of economic nationalism among nations, as each attempted to preserve its gold supply and restrict imports. Not surprisingly, American exports fell by 70 percent from 1929 to 1932, and as foreign markets shrank, so did hopes for economic recovery.

The depression quickly became a worldwide disaster, as prices collapsed, wages declined, and unemployment soared, especially in the United States and in Germany. World trading came to a standstill; its volume plummeted by two-thirds between 1929 and 1933. The United States, which had replaced Britain as the world's leading creditor nation, rejected efforts among other countries to curtail high tariffs. Although France, Italy, and Australia also shied away from the proposed international moratorium of tariff increases, America even refused to send a delegation to a 1930 meeting, where the plan was to be finalized. Instead, the Republicans in Congress pushed through the **Smoot-Hawley** bill, raising tariffs to their highest level in American history. Over one thousand economists petitioned President Hoover not to sign the bill and one of his closest advisers, Thomas Lamont, a partner in J.P. Morgan, also appealed to Hoover to reject the tariff. "I almost went down on my knees," he later recalled, "to beg Herbert Hoover to veto that asinine Hawley-Smoot tariff. That act intensified nationalism all over the world." Hoover himself held many reservations about the proposed legislation, but still signed the bill into law. The law sent a signal to the rest of the world and within months, several nations, including Canada, Mexico, France, Spain, and New Zealand, responded by raising tariffs on American goods.

The growing international crisis threatened Germany's government, a prospect over which Hoover expressed alarm but little else, and led to the collapse of the gold standard in Great Britain the following year. Suspending the gold standard served to decrease the price of British exports and moderate Britain's economy's steady decline. Many countries followed the British example, but the United States held to the gold standard. The Federal Reserve system was forced to give up $755 million in gold in one month after Britain's decision, as banks in other countries converted dollars into gold. Foreign investors began withdrawing gold and dollars and domestic depositors also panicked: The result was a significant increase in bank failures in the United States. But Hoover remained firm in his commitment to the gold standard, and the Federal Reserve Bank raised the interest rate to protect America's gold supply. Higher rates, in turn, stymied domestic borrowing and investment, and the downward spiral in the United States proceeded apace.

HARD TIMES IN HOOVERVILLE

By early 1930, the effects of financial contraction were painfully evident. Factories shut down or cut back, and industrial production plummeted; by 1932, it was scarcely 50 percent of its 1929 level. Steel mills operated at 12 percent of capacity, auto factories, at 20 percent. Unemployment skyrocketed, as an average of 100,000 workers a week were fired in the first three years after the crash. By 1932, one-fourth of the labor force was out of work. In St. Louis, 75 percent of the workers in the building trades, a key sector of the 1920s economy, were jobless. Overall unemployment in Toledo reached 80 percent. The wages of those Americans lucky enough to work fell sharply. Personal income dropped by more than half between 1929 and 1932; by 1933, industrial workers had average weekly wages of only $16.73. Moreover, the depression began to feed on itself in a vicious circle: Shrinking wages and employment cut into purchasing power, causing business to slash production again and lay off workers, thereby further reducing purchasing power. Before his death in January 1933, Calvin Coolidge told a reporter that he held no hope for the American economy: "In other periods of depression, it has always been possible to see some things which were solid and upon which you could base hope. But as I look about, I now see nothing to give ground for hope, nothing of man."

The depression particularly battered farmers. Commodity prices fell by 55 percent between 1929 and 1932, stifling farm income. Cotton farmers earned only 31 percent of the pittance they had received in 1929. Unable to pay their mortgages, many farm families lost their homes and fields. "We have no security left," cried one South Dakota farm woman. "Foreclosures and evictions at the point of sheriff's guns are increasing daily." The land values of farms also dropped dramatically, and farmers were not even able to sell their homesteads to stave off foreclosure. Between 1920 and 1932, the average per-acre value declined from $69.31 to $29.68; the foreclosure rate jumped to 54.1 per thousand. In Iowa, the rate was 78.3 per thousand; one-third of the court cases in Iowa in 1933 dealt with foreclosures. Driven from their homes and their land, the dispossessed roamed the byways, highways, and railways of a troubled country.

Urban families were also evicted when they could not pay their rent. Some moved in with relatives; others lived in **Hoovervilles**—the name reflects the bitterness directed at the president—shacks where people shivered, suffered, and starved. Oklahoma City's vast Hooverville covered a hundred square miles; one witness described its hapless residents as squatting in "old, rusted-out car bodies," orange crates, and holes in the ground. The homeless in Seattle created a large and very visible Hooverville on the city's dock, dismaying

Homeless Americans gathered in squalid "Hoovervilles," like this one in Seattle, and struggled to survive.

Hands in their pockets, hungry men stand numbly in one of New York City's eighty-two breadlines. Said one observer: "The wretched men, many without overcoats or decent shoes, usually began to line up soon after six o'clock—in good weather or bad, rain or snow."

public officials twice who had the settlement burned down, but the homeless persisted. They were still there in 1934. In New York, "Hoovervilles" could be found throughout the city, and packing crates along with tin cans flattened and nailed to boards became homes to the down-and-out. One observer recalled daily passing a settlement of "tarpaper huts" which stretched a mile and a half along the Hudson in upper Manhattan, where "scores of families lived the lives of reluctant gypsies." In Chicago, in 1931, thousands of families were evicted; one municipal judge noted that he had an "average of four hundred cases a day. It was packed. People fainted, people cried." Forced into the streets, they slept where they could with only newspaper for cover. In the winter of 1931, one local reporter wrote of the irony of Chicago's "lovely Michigan Avenue bridge" where 20 feet below "are 2,000 homeless, decrepit, shivering men, wrapping themselves in old newspapers to keep from freezing, and lying down in the manure dust to sleep." Nearby, a social worker despaired at seeing a "crowd of some fifty men fighting over a barrel of garbage that had been set outside the backdoor of a restaurant. American citizens fighting for scraps of food like animals!"

Soup kitchens became standard features of the urban landscape, and lines of the hungry stretched for blocks. Reports of malnutrition became more frequent and deaths from starvation were reported in New York and Chicago. Despite efforts of parents, children were also victims. In Albany, New York, in 1932, a 10-year-old girl slumped over on her school desk and died from starvation. Widespread hunger and homelessness challenged the resources of relief agencies throughout the nation. Charities and local communities simply could not meet the massive needs, and neither the federal nor state governments had welfare or unemployment compensation programs. To survive, people planted gardens in vacant lots and back alleys and tore apart empty houses or tapped gas lines for fuel. In immigrant neighborhoods, social workers found a "primitive communism" in which people shared food, clothing, and fuel in the belief that "what goes around comes around." Few

Americans escaped hard times, but their experiences varied with their circumstances and expectations.

"Women's Jobs" and "Men's Jobs"

The depression affected wage-earning women in complex ways. Although suffering 20 percent unemployment by 1932, women were less likely than men to be fired. Gender segregation had concentrated women in low-paid service, sales, and clerical jobs that shrank less than the heavy industries where men predominated. But while traditional attitudes somewhat insulated working women, they also reinforced opposition to female employment itself, especially that of married women. As one Chicago civic organization complained, "They are holding jobs that rightfully belong to the God-intended providers of the household." Nearly every state considered restricting the employment of married women, and the city council of Akron, Ohio, resolved that public agencies and private employers should stop employing wives. Three-fourths of the nation's school systems refused to hire married women as teachers, and two-thirds dismissed female teachers who married. Many private employers, especially banks and insurance companies, also fired married women.

Firing women, however, rarely produced jobs for men because few men sought positions in the fields associated with women. Men did displace women as teachers, social workers, and librarians, but firing women simply aggravated the suffering of families already reeling from the depression. Disapproval of female employment implied that women did not deserve equal opportunities and probably stiffened the opposition to opening "men's jobs" to women when women were desperate for work. Accordingly, the depression merely aggravated traditional gender-based discrimination at the workplace, and women continued to be employed largely in such "female" occupations as domestic servants, garment workers, and laundresses. They worked long hours for little pay, earning only 50 cents for every dollar men received. One woman worker in Minneapolis who commented that she had "never been any good at housework" was refused factory work despite her experience. "Now," she added, "I got domestic work." But public hostility to wage-earning women did not deter women from taking jobs to help their families survive. Indeed, the proportion of married women in the work force increased in the 1930s—from 20 to 25 percent—and about one-third of working married women provided the sole support for their families.

Families in the Depression

"I have watched fear grip the people in our neighborhood around Hull House," wrote Jane Addams as the depression deepened in 1931 and family survival itself seemed threatened. Divorce declined because it was expensive, but desertion increased, and marriages were postponed. Birthrates fell. Fully one-quarter of women in their twenties did not have children during the depression—the lowest birthrate for any decade. Husbands and fathers, the traditional breadwinners, were often humiliated and despondent when laid off from work. One social worker observed in 1931: "Like searing irons, the degradation, the sheer terror and panic which loss of job brings, the deprivation and the bitterness have eaten into men's souls." Also that same year, a college professor wrote of his brother's suicide: He had been "utterly disheartened by his prolonged search for employment [and] went into a shabby hotel [where he] blew his brains out." He then added "after nearly thirty years of toil as a college professor, I myself had great difficulty in raising the money to pay for the modest kind of burial befitting the gentleman my brother was. I could not go to his funeral; I could not pay for both the burial expenses and the railway fare."

Unemployed men, sociologists reported, "lost much of their sense of time and dawdled helplessly and dully about the streets," dreading to return home. An unemployed Philadelphia man, according to his wife, was "always walking or looking [for work]. The places are so far apart that his feet get sore. . . . We had to put cotton in the heels of his shoes. Sometimes he don't know where he's walking." Still other out-of-work men left home to escape the sting of shame. As one New York man asked, "What's wrong with me, that I can't protect my own children?" Frustrated and hopeless, they wandered the streets by day, slept in wash rooms at railroad stations, and crowded around makeshift fires to stay warm. They lined up for soup or bread, often waiting for hours for their only meal of the day. Still others left their cities and communities altogether, riding the railways in search of anything. And the nation's transient population soared.

Women's responsibilities, by contrast, often grew. The number of female-headed households increased sharply. Not only did some women become wage earners, but their traditional role as homemakers also gained new significance. To make ends meet, many women sewed their own clothing, made underwear from flour sacks, and raised and canned vegetables, reversing the trend toward consumerism. Some also took on extra work at home. In San Antonio, one in every ten families had boarders, and in Alabama, housewives took in laundry at 10 cents for a week's washload. Garment manufacturers took advantage of women working in the home; some owners sent garments from New York to San Antonio, for the cheaper labor costs of Mexican-American women. Newspapers, magazines, and radio programs often minimized the hardships of women's increased responsibilities and instead celebrated their return to domesticity, encouraging women to become ever more efficient with their limited budgets.

The depression also affected children. Some parents sacrificed their own well-being to protect their children. One witness described "the uncontrolled trembling of parents who have starved themselves for weeks so that their children might not go hungry." But children felt the tension and fear, and many went without food. In New York City, 139 people, most of them children, died of starvation and malnutrition in 1933. Boys and girls stayed home from school and church because they lacked shoes or clothing; others gave up their plans for college. As hope faded, family conflicts increased. Some parents nagged their children, even considering them burdens. Many teenagers left home, either to escape parental authority or so that younger children would have more to eat. Labeled the "vast, homeless horde" by *Fortune* magazine, these **"juvenile transients"** suffered from starvation, exposure, illness, and accidents. The California Unemployment Commission concluded that the depression had left the American family "morally shattered. There is no security, no foothold, no future."

"Last Hired, First Fired"

The depression particularly harmed racial minorities. With fewer resources and opportunities, they were less able than other groups to absorb the economic pain. African Americans were caught in a double bind, reported a sociologist at Howard University in 1932: They were "the last to be hired and the first to be fired." Black unemployment rates were more than twice the white rate, reflecting increased job competition and persistent racism. In such cities as Charleston and Memphis, by 1930, unemployment rates for African Americans were 70 and 75 percent, respectively. Over half of Chicago's and nearly three-fourths of Detroit's African-American women were without work. Jobless white workers now sought the menial jobs traditionally reserved for black workers, such as street cleaning and domestic service. In Atlanta, white citizens paraded with banners denouncing the hiring of black workers "Until Every White Man Has a Job."

Racism also limited the assistance African Americans received. Religious and charitable organizations often refused to care for black people. Local and state governments set higher requirements for black people than for white people to receive relief and provided them with less aid. One Memphis resident saw the result of such policies: "Colored men and women with rakes, hoes, and other digging tools, with buckets and baskets, digging around in the garbage and refuse for food." In 1931, African-American women in Harlem joined together as the Harlem Housewives League to challenge the city's race-based inequalities in the distribution of relief. Out of work for longer periods of time and without even modest relief assistance, African Americans were forced to crowd together in already cramped apartments, while still paying exorbitant rents to white landlords. An African-American social worker described the despair and poverty of Harlem's residents who "lived in cellars and basements which had been converted into makeshift flats. Packed in damp, rat-ridden dungeons, they existed in squalor not too different from that of the Arkansas sharecroppers." On Chicago's South Side, one journalist found similar conditions, noting that relief workers "have come away so overwhelmed with horror that they have made efforts to have the whole place condemned—to the piteous distress of the occupants."

In addition to joblessness, African Americans were also confronted with disease and death at rates far higher than white Americans. Tuberculosis infected entire neighborhoods, and infant mortality rates were twice those of whites in a number of cities. In the South, racism and economic competition took on especially brutal features, and lynching increased in the early 1930s. In 1933 alone, twenty-four blacks were lynched. The depression, which not only increased racism and violence, also pushed families deeper into abject poverty. By 1932, most African Americans were suffering acute privation. "At no time in the history of the Negro since slavery," reported the Urban League, "has his economic and social outlook seemed so discouraging." African Americans were "hanging on by the barest thread."

Deportation and Discrimination

Hispanic Americans also suffered. As mostly unskilled workers, they faced increasing competition for decreasing jobs paying declining wages. They were displaced even in the California agricultural labor force, which they had dominated. By the mid-1930s, they made up only a tenth of the state's migratory labor force, which increasingly consisted of white people who had fled the South and the Great Plains. Other jobs were lost when Arizona, California, and Texas barred Mexicans from public works and highway construction jobs. Vigilantes threatened employers who hired Mexicans rather than white Americans.

The Great Depression made more desperate the plight of Hispanic Americans. This family of pecan shellers in San Antonio, Texas, labored by day for 5 cents and hour and rented this hovel for 50 cents per week.

Economic woes and racism drove nearly half a million Mexican immigrants and their American-born children from the United States in the 1930s. In 1931, President Hoover's Secretary of Labor, William N. Doak, denounced illegal aliens residing in the United States and affirmed his intention to deport them and free up jobs for American citizens. Local authorities in the Southwest, along with federal immigration officials, urged all Mexicans, regardless of their citizenship status, to return to Mexico. Some were unable to document their legal entry into the country; others feared more hostility and discrimination and simply left. To intimidate Mexicans and Mexican Americans, the U.S. Immigration Service led several raids, rounding up people and demanding proof of legal residency. Relief agencies in Los Angeles and San Antonio, already overwhelmed by demands for aid, responded to the federal raids by chartering buses and trains and offering all Mexicans free transportation to Mexico instead of relief assistance. In 1931, in Los Angeles, where 150,000 Mexican Americans resided, one official announced that tens of thousands of Mexicans "have been literally scared out of southern California." By 1933, Los Angeles county itself had sent fifteen trains filled with 12,000 Mexicans, who had been receiving relief, back to Mexico. By the end of decade, Los Angeles had lost about one-third of its Mexican population. Those who stayed faced all types of discrimination, including receiving much less relief assistance than the white jobless. Only the Catholic church provided relief to Mexicans in San Antonio. Fear of deportation kept many Mexican-American families from seeking relief or even health care in Texas.

Discontent in the Depression

Bewildered and discouraged, most Americans reacted to the crisis without protest. Influenced by traditional individualism, many blamed themselves for their plight. But others did act, especially to protect their families. Protests ranged from small desperate gestures like stealing food and coal to more dramatic deeds. Theft of food became more commonplace than either the police or store owners acknowledged. Newspapers rarely carried the stories and store owners feared that additional publicity would only encourage more looting of food. In Cleveland, one grocer was overwhelmed by a crowd of 6,000 when he advertised free food to the first 1,500 customers; the result was a riot ending in the arrest of 52 people. Homeowners tapped gas lines illegally to stay warm and coal miners secretly mined coal in mines, selling or bartering "bootlegged" coal for food. But the inability to feed their hungry families also drove others to more daring acts. In Louisiana, women seized a train to call attention to the needs of their families; in New Jersey, in the "bloodless battle of Pleasantville," one hundred women held the city council hostage to demand assistance.

Communists, socialists, and other radicals organized more formal protests. Communists led the jobless into "unemployment councils" that staged hunger marches, demonstrated for relief, and blocked evictions. Mothers facing eviction in Chicago told their children: "Run quick and find the Reds." Socialists built similar organizations, including Baltimore's People's Unemployment League, which had twelve thousand members. Such groups provided protection and assistance. However, local authorities often suppressed their protests. In 1932, police fired on the Detroit Unemployment Council as it marched to demand food and jobs, killing four marchers and wounding many more.

Rural protests also broke out. Again, communists organized some of them, as in Alabama, where the Croppers' and Farm Workers' Union mobilized black agricultural laborers in 1931 to demand better treatment. Mexican migrant workers responded to their exploitation by striking and thirty-seven violent agricultural strikes occurred in California alone in 1933. In the Midwest, the **Farmers' Holiday Association**, formed among family farmers in 1932, stopped the shipment of produce to urban markets, hoping to drive up prices and preclude bank foreclosures of their farms. Led by a charismatic Milo Reno, the farmers described their strike with the verse:

Let's call a "Farmers' Holiday"
A Holiday let's hold
We'll eat our wheat and ham and eggs
And let them eat their gold.

But a guerrilla war broke out as farmers blocked roads and halted freight trains, dumped milk in ditches, and fought bloody battles with deputy sheriffs and the state militia, who gassed the striking farmers. Midwestern farmers also tried to prevent foreclosure of their farms. In Iowa, farmers beat sheriffs and mortgage agents and nearly lynched a lawyer conducting foreclosure proceedings; in Nebraska, a Farmers' Holiday leader warned that if the state did not halt foreclosures, "200,000 of us are coming to Lincoln and we'll tear that new State Capitol Building to pieces."

HERBERT HOOVER AND THE DEPRESSION

The Great Depression challenged the optimism, policies, and philosophy that Herbert Hoover carried into the White House in 1929. The president took unprecedented steps to resolve the crisis but shrank back from the interventionist policies activists urged. Hoover depended on voluntary efforts to relieve the misery caused by massive unemployment. He created the President's Organization for Unemployment Relief to help raise private funds for voluntary relief agencies. Charities and local authorities, he believed, should help the unemployed; direct federal relief would expand government power and undermine the recipients' character. He vetoed congressional attempts to aid the unemployed. "The American way of relieving distress," said Hoover, was through "the voluntary agencies of self help in the community" (see the Overview table, "President Hoover's Responses to the Great Depression").

Self-Help, Popular Culture, and the Community

A long tradition of local responsibility for relief assistance combined with the commonly perceived virtue of self-help to define many communities' responses to the Great Depression throughout the nation. In 1930, President Hoover advised that each citizen should "maintain his self-reliance" and those who could help others should do so. And although hard times exacerbated all types of discrimination—dividing men and women, blacks and whites, and Hispanics and whites—they also united neighborhoods and communities, and people formed cooperatives for food and other forms of assistance. They held bake sales, sponsored bingo games, and sold raffle tickets to raise money for needy families. They also started barter clubs like the one in Seattle, where the Unemployed Citizens' League (UCL) collected 10,000 cords of wood, 8 train-car loads of fruits and vegetables, and 60 tons of fish for distribution to the needy. Calling themselves the "Republic of the Penniless," where "honorable employment was all that passed for currency," they constructed an elaborate system of labor in exchange for a variety of goods and also assisted the unemployed who were evicted

· · · OVERVIEW · · ·

PRESIDENT HOOVER'S RESPONSES TO THE GREAT DEPRESSION

ACTION	OBJECTIVE
Reaffirmed the traditional principles of voluntarism and self help to assist the jobless.	Instruct private agencies to handle the problem of unemployment relief, for governmental aid would be detrimental to the recipients' character.
Signed Hawley-Smoot Tariff into law (1930).	Provide protective support for U.S. products and encourage consumers to buy American goods.
Called on business leaders to maintain jobs and wages (1930).	Enlist the voluntary cooperation of the business community to combat the depression and unemployment by not reducing production, jobs, or wages.
Created the President's Emergency Committee for Employment (PECE) (1930).	Offer communities and citizens suggestions on how to reduce the hardship of joblessness through self-help projects.
Urged bankers to form the National Credit Corporation (1931).	Encourage bankers to lift themselves out of the banking crisis by setting aside funds to provide loans to struggling banks.
Established the President's Organization on Unemployment Relief (POUR) (1931).	Raise private dollars for relief and urge Americans to give generously to those without work.
Formed the Reconstruction Finance Corporation (1932).	Lend federal funds to banks, insurance companies, and railroads to enable "trickle-down" recovery; subsequently authorized to lend smaller amounts to states and localities for unemployment relief.

from their homes. Their efficiency and organization so impressed the city government that it joined together with the UCL to leverage the city's meager relief funds to help the jobless.

Working together and individually, many people aided the unemployed by collecting food scraps, providing assistance with rent monies, selling products door-to-door, and letting neighbors move into their homes and apartments. The Fuller Brush Company tapped part of that entrepreneurial energy, and door-to-door sales increased $1 million a year in the 1930s. But the organization of self-help groups proved more useful in assisting the unemployed, and citizen groups and charities joined forces in city after city to provide food for—and prevent eviction of—desperate families. Veterans in California organized and persuaded growers, dairies, and bakeries to donate surplus goods which they then distributed to those in need. Indeed, the number of self-help groups in Los Angeles County increased so rapidly that by 1933 a clearinghouse—the Unemployed Cooperative Relief Association—was established to coordinate activities. In Dayton, Ohio, African-American women organized a "production unit," making items from bread to clothing and using their small profits to purchase food for themselves and others in need. Unemployed groups also sprang up to assist each other in Philadelphia, Baltimore, Minneapolis, New York City, among many other cities and towns.

Still other jobless turned to apple selling, and the apple vendor became a symbol of the self-reliance championed by President Hoover. Indeed, Hoover made the startling claim that "many persons [had] left their jobs for the more profitable one of selling apples," a statement that certainly surprised the vendors themselves. But the apple-selling scheme had less to do with self-reliance and more with desperation and profit. Using the motto, "Buy an apple a day and eat the depression away," an association of apple shippers attempted to dispose of its surplus by shipping boxes of apples to major cities and promising the prospective vendors a profit of $1.85 on every box. But the plan did not work well for the sellers themselves, who often received much less, although many unemployed men attempted to make a go of it. New York City alone boasted 6,000 apple vendors and, despite their pitiful earnings, the U.S. Department of Labor excluded them from its count of the jobless.

The unemployed also tried even more desperate ventures and scams. They created illegal gambling halls and lottery games, and a number of jobless risked more than small change in the hope that their favorite numbers would solve their economic woes. The number of "loan sharks" multiplied in many of the poorest communities, and cash-starved residents mortgaged their futures by borrowing money for one more month of rent. Others preyed on the unemployed through pyramid schemes and phony investment opportunities. Chain letters flourished and people searched for any way to bring them better luck.

In many urban neighborhoods, victims of adversity turned to evangelical religion, flocking to revivalist meetings held in dilapidated houses, dank basements, and store-front churches. These "cult churches," as they were called, promised hope and salvation and were led by charismatic leaders, such as Daddy Grace of Baltimore, who delivered impassioned sermons. Both black and white urban residents found reassurance in their neighborhood ministries, where spiritual relief seemed to have boundless possibilities and where the vagaries of economic depression faded before the powers of personal redemption. More orthodox clergy decried the proliferation of these "depression churches," likening them to "weeds" that exploited the "baffled, miserable, and hopeless." But the members themselves celebrated their new churches as a source of joy and security and found among their leaders a level of personal engagement often missing in traditional congregations.

"Chronic unemployment," as the social workers called it, required, they insisted, social activities to cope with boredom and feelings of uselessness. And whether animated by despair or their experiences in the mass culture of the 1920s, people in the Great Depression filled movie theaters to watch musicals, westerns, and comedies, holding in special regard those movies featuring the decade's stars: Mickey Mouse, the Marx Brothers, and Shirley Temple. The zany antics of the Marx Brothers in such movies as *Monkey Business* (1931) and *Duck Soup* (1933) amused millions of Americans who were drawn to the exaggerated appearances of the thick-mustachioed Groucho, the frizzy-haired Harpo, and the wide-eyed Chico. Mae West also attracted viewers with her wisecracks and suggestive dress and other movie stars such as Fred Astaire and Ginger Rogers danced to the top of box office attractions.

Five thousand new films were produced by Hollywood in the 1930s, representing an important era for movie making. Some of the most popular movies echoed depression themes of the collapse of law and order and the corruption of society. Prohibition and the rise of organized crime helped produce a new film genre: the gangster movie. Edward G. Robinson in *Little Caesar* (1930) and James Cagney in *Public Enemy* (1931) portrayed criminals who became unconventional heroes to their audiences at a time of gangland violence and during an era of hard times with few opportunities for the down and out. The fearless self-reliance of such stars as Cagney appealed to Americans who celebrated his independence and persistence and welcomed his disdain for the hypocrisies of traditional business and politics.

Radio also flourished in the 1930s. The depression served to lower the price of radios substantially and led to the near collapse of Broadway—both developments meant more listeners and a greater variety of programming as a result of cheap talent eager for any job. In

1930, a radio cost on average $90; just two years later the price was only $42. Households owning a radio jumped from 13 million at the start of the decade to over 27 million at the end. Families routinely huddled around their sets to enjoy their favorite programs from the melodies of Bing Crosby to the thrilling drama of *The Shadow*. They followed the adventures of Dick Tracy and Superman and enjoyed the popular comedy variety show of Gracie Allen and George Burns. They relied on the radio for national news, soap operas, baseball games, and boxing matches. For younger Americans, *The Lone Ranger* became a special favorite.

Miniature golf became a new fad and sports, especially its heroes Knute Rockne, Babe Ruth, and Joe Louis, continued to excite enthusiastic fans. The home, too, became again a center for family leisure. Such board games as Monopoly, invented by an unemployed real estate salesperson, offered less expensive forms of entertainment as well as a commentary on business practices. Adults and children practiced new dance steps, including the jitterbug and the rhumba, and card playing and stamp collecting became popular hobbies.

Businesses and Bankers: Rejecting Voluntary Remedies

Hoover fought economic depression more vigorously than any previous president, but he believed that voluntary, private relief was preferable to federal intervention. The role of the national government, he thought, was to advise and encourage the voluntary efforts of private organizations, individual industries, or local communities. As secretary of commerce, Hoover had championed trade associations to achieve economic order and social progress. As president he persuaded Congress in 1929 to create the Federal Farm Board to promote voluntary agricultural cooperatives to raise farm income without government regulations. After the crash, he tried to apply this voluntarism to the depression.

Hoover first secured business leaders' pledges to maintain employment and wage levels. Assuring those key leaders that he was not interfering with business, Hoover explained that "it is a request from the government that you co-operate in prudent measures to solve a national problem." And although most corporations agreed to cooperate, they soon repudiated their pledges, slashed wages, and laid off workers. An official of the Bureau of Labor Statistics complained that business leaders "are hell-bent to get wages back to the 1913 level." Hoover himself said, "You know, the only trouble with capitalism is capitalists; they're too damn greedy." Still, he rejected government action.

But Hoover's brand of voluntarism differed from that of many major business and banking leaders, who described unemployment and economic downturns as inevitable phases of natural business cycles and not events requiring government action. Even his own secretary of the treasury, Andrew Mellon, had advised at the start of the depression: "Liquidate labor, liquidate stock, liquidate farmers, liquidate real estate." And in 1931 Albert Wiggin, head of the Chase National Bank of New York, told a Senate subcommittee investigating unemployment, "Human nature is human nature. Lives go on," adding that "you are always going to have . . . times that are prosperous and times that are not prosperous." An incredulous senator then asked, "You think, then, that the capacity for human suffering is unlimited?" Wiggin replied, "I think so." Hoover regarded such talk as economic fatalism; he rejected the inevitability of economic crises and declared, "I would remind these pessimists that exactly the same thing was once said of typhoid, cholera, and smallpox."

Hoover continued his quest to secure private assistance to shore up the economy, but his appeal to the banking community in 1931 encountered considerable resistance. Meeting with a selected group of bankers at the ornate home of the Secretary of Treasury Mellon, Hoover pressured them to create a special fund to help faltering banks. They agreed to do so only reluctantly, for as Hoover lamented, even those business leaders who denounced government interference in the economy still preferred "the government to do it." Establishing the **National Credit Corporation** with $500 million, the bankers provided loans to institutions at risk, but after helping only a few banks, they abandoned the program and again demanded federal action. Meanwhile, banks continued to close daily and the nation's financial system edged toward collapse.

To deal with the problem of unemployment through voluntary action, Hoover first created the **President's Emergency Committee for Employment (PECE)**—a board of thirty-two members charged to examine fully the dimensions of the problem. Without resources or authority, PECE limited its actions to modest suggestions of how citizens might help reduce the hardship of joblessness through home-improvement projects or other self-help initiatives. The following year, in 1931, Hoover established the **President's Organization on Unemployment Relief (POUR)**, headed by Walter S. Gifford, and instructed him to launch a major advertising campaign to raise private monies so that "the fear of cold and hunger will be banished from the hearts of thousands!" Issuing flyers and taking out advertisements in magazines and newspapers, the POUR campaign urged Americans to give generously to their local charities and portrayed the unemployed themselves as admirable patriots still committed to local responsibility and self-help. As one advertisement, picturing an unemployed man, explained: "Understand, we're not begging. We'd rather have a job than anything else you can give us. We're not scared either. If you think the good old U.S.A. is in a bad way more than temporarily, just try to figure out some other place you'd rather be." Gifford himself reflected and reinforced the administration's inability to grasp the scope of the problem; his response to the problem of inadequate relief for the jobless was to affirm that such assistance "was to be left squarely with the States, counties, and communities," and his solution to the depression was for "everybody [to] go back to work and have full pay for all jobs."

For ailing farmers, Hoover continued to press for the voluntary associations he had championed before the depression spread, but the economic realities of collapsing prices, mortgage foreclosures, and desperate farm families made his formula of organized self-help seem irrelevant. The Farm Board that he had created could not persuade farmers to form cooperative associations when prices were at rock bottom. Instead, the Board attempted to devise plans to provide farm relief, even including a plan that would pay farmers to reduce their acreage. But Hoover firmly rejected such an approach, arguing that it would require too much governmental intervention and inappropriately privilege farmers in the economy. Not even the Farm Holiday movement could stir Hoover to change his position.

The Failure of Voluntarism

The depression, then, rendered Hoover's beliefs meaningless. Even the conservative banking community called for governmental intervention. Private programs to aid the unemployed, moreover, scarcely existed. Only a few unions like the Amalgamated Clothing Workers had unemployment funds, and these were soon spent. Company plans for unemployment compensation covered less than 1 percent of workers, revealing the charade of the welfare capitalism of the 1920s. Some business leaders rejected any responsibility: "Even God Almighty never promised anybody that he should not suffer from hunger," snorted the president of the Southern States Industrial Council. Private charitable groups like the Salvation Army, church associations, and ethnic societies quickly exhausted their resources. The magazine *Judge* poked fun at relying on a system of barter to address the problem of unemployment, likening it to "giving somebody a pig and a couple of ducks they don't want in exchange for an overcoat that doesn't fit." By 1931, the director of Philadelphia's Federation of Jewish Charities conceded, "Private philanthropy is no longer capable of coping with the situation." Tens of thousands of Philadelphians, he noted, had been reduced to "the status of a stray cat prowling for food. . . . What this does to the innate dignity of the human soul is not hard to guess." Even the successful Unemployed Citizens League in Seattle conceded defeat by 1932 and demanded federal action: "We fail to understand how men in dominating political, financial, and industrial positions can ignore the necessity for fundamental change if the present worldwide breakdown is to be corrected."

In Detroit, Henry Ford—one of America's most popular symbols of prosperity and progress—also refused to follow Hoover's advice to maintain wages and jobs. During the 1920s, college students had ranked Ford third—after Christ and Napoleon—of the greatest people of all time (see "American Voices," Chapter 6); by 1932, however, Ford was publicly rebuked, as he laid off thousands of workers and forced the few remaining ones to work at breakneck speeds with their wages slashed to the barebones. One of the richest men in America, Ford disavowed any responsibility for assisting the unemployed. Responding to the local inability to provide relief and to Ford's especially harsh policies, the Communist-led Detroit Unemployed Council organized some three thousand marchers to protest at Ford's River Rouge plant. At the factory gate, police fired tear gas and then bullets at the marchers, leaving four dead and sixty wounded. Five days later at least fifteen thousand mourners walked with the four coffins, draped in red, and eulogies were delivered under a banner that proclaimed "Ford Gave Bullets For Bread." The *New York Herald Tribune* denounced the city's police for "using guns on an unarmed crowd, for viciously bad judgment and for the killing of four men." Henry Ford now symbolized the failure of private initiative and business responsibility to deal with the depression.

Nor could local governments cope, and their efforts declined as the depression deepened. New York City provided relief payments of $2.39 a week for an entire family, and other cities much less. By 1932, more than one hundred cities made no relief appropriations at all, and the commissioner of charity in Salt Lake City reported that people were sliding toward starvation. Only eight state governments provided even token assistance. Constitutional restrictions on taxes and indebtedness stopped some from responding to the relief crisis. Others lacked the will. Texas refused to issue bonds to fund relief (see American Views, "An Ohio Mayor on Unemployment and Relief").

AMERICAN VIEWS

An Ohio Mayor on Unemployment and Relief

Joesph Heffernan was the mayor of Youngstown, Ohio, when the nation sank into the Great Depression. Like other industrial cities, Youngstown soon confronted widespread unemployment and distress. In this document, written in 1932, Heffernan describes the obstacles he faced in responding to the suffering in Youngstown.

What would Heffernan think of President Hoover's belief that private charities and local authorities would provide unemployment relief?

What did Heffernan see as obstacles to a public response to the depression?

What did he fear would be the consequences of the failure to devise a rational and humane system of relief?

[In 1930] I asked for a bond issue of $1,000,000 for unemployment relief. Many leading business men went out of their way to show their disapproval. One of them . . . said to me: "You make a bad mistake in talking about the unemployed. Don't emphasize hard times and everything will be all right." An influential newspaper chastised me for "borrowing trouble"; the depression would be over, the editor maintained, before relief would be needed. . . . The gravity of the situation was so deliberately misrepresented by the entire business community that when the bond issue finally came to a ballot, in November 1930, it was voted down.

Thus we passed into the early days of 1931—fourteen months after the first collapse—with no relief in sight except that which was provided by the orthodox charities. Not a single move had been made looking toward action by a united community.

Strange as it may seem, there was no way in which the city government could embark upon a program of its own. We had no funds available for emergency relief, and without specific authorization from the people we could not issue bonds. . . .

As time went on, business conditions showed no improvement. Every night hundreds of homeless men crowded into the municipal incinerator, where they found warmth even though they had to sleep on heaps of garbage. In January 1931, I obtained the cooperation of the City Council to convert an abandoned police station into a "flop house." The first night it was filled, and it has remained filled ever since. I made a point of paying frequent visits to this establishment so that I could see for myself what kind of men these down-and-outers were, and I heartily wish that those folk who have made themselves comfortable by ignoring and denying the suffering of their less fortunate neighbors could see some of the sights I saw. There were old men gnarled by heavy labor, young mechanics tasting the first bitterness of defeat, clerks and white-collar workers learning the equality of misery, derelicts who fared no worse in bad times than in good, Negroes who only a short time before had come from Southern cotton fields, now glad to find any shelter from the cold, immigrants who had been lured to Van Dyke's "land of youth and freedom"—each one a personal tragedy, and all together an overwhelming catastrophe for the nation. . . .

This descent from respectability, frequent enough in the best of times, has been hastened immeasurably by two years of business paralysis, and the people who have been affected in this manner must be numbered in millions. This is what we have accomplished with our bread lines and soup kitchens. I know, because I have seen thousands of these defeated, discouraged, hopeless men and women, cringing and fawning as they come to ask for public aid. It is a spectacle of national degeneration. That is the fundamental tragedy for America. If every mill and factory in the land should begin to hum with prosperity tomorrow morning, the destructive effect of our haphazard relief measures would not work itself out of the nation's blood until the sons of our sons had expiated the sins of our neglect.

Even now there are signs of rebellion against a system so out of joint that it can only offer charity to honest men who want to work. Sometimes it takes the form of social agitation, but again it may show itself in a revolt that is absolute and final. Such an instance was reported in a Youngstown newspaper on the day I wrote these lines:—

Father of Ten Drowns Self

. . . Out of work two years, Charles Wayne, aged 57, father of ten children, stood on the Spring Common bridge this morning. . . . He took off his coat, folded it carefully, and jumped into the swirling Mahoning River. Wayne was born in Youngstown and was employed by the Republic Iron and Steel Company for twenty-seven years as a hot mill worker. "We were about to lose our home," sobbed Mrs. Wayne. "And the gas and electric companies had threatened to shut off the service."

Source: Joseph L. Heffernan, "The Hungry City: A Mayor's Experience with Unemployment," *Atlantic Monthly*, May 1932, pp. 538–540, 546.

Hoover blundered not in first relying on charities and local governments for relief but in refusing to admit that they were inadequate. Even his advisers warned that voluntarism and "individual initiative" had become obsolete. Both his vision and his efforts fell short. The noted Kansan and editor William Allen White observed "We can no longer depend on passing the hat, and rattling the tin cup. We have gone to the bottom of the barrel."

As the depression worsened, Hoover adopted more activist policies. He persuaded Congress to cut taxes to boost consumers' buying power, and he increased the public works budget. The Federal Farm Board lent money to cooperatives and spent millions trying to stabilize crop prices. Unable to control production, however, the board conceded failure by late 1931. More successful was the **Reconstruction Finance Corporation (RFC)**. Established in January 1932, the RFC lent federal funds to banks, insurance companies, and railroads so that their recovery could "trickle down" to ordinary Americans.

But Hoover still opposed direct aid to the general public, and he remained committed to balancing the budget. Throughout late 1931 and early 1932, faced with declining tax revenues, Hoover blocked additional funds for public works, affirming that a balanced budget was "the foundation of all public and private financial stability." Yet Hoover was ultimately forced to accept deficit financing as the depression deepened and tax revenues continued to decline; between 1931 and 1933, the national debt increased from $16 billion to $22.5 billion. Unwilling to spend more and still clinging to local responsibility for relief, Hoover vetoed as fiscally irresponsible a bill for federal relief when Congress finally addressed the issue early in 1932. Only after reducing considerably the proposed spending for public works did Hoover finally agree to sign a compromise bill—the Emergency Relief and Construction Act—which also enabled the RFC to lend small amounts to state and local governments for unemployment relief. *Fortune* magazine aptly referred to the act as "neither an adequate nor an impressive piece of legislation."

Not surprisingly, these programs satisfied few Americans. "While children starve," cried Pennsylvania's governor, Hoover "intends to let us have just as little relief as possible after the longest delay possible." Far more action was necessary, but Hoover remained committed to voluntarism and a balanced budget. The *New Republic* remarked in wonder: "Strangely enough, though he praises our government as representative and democratic, Mr. Hoover seems to regard most of the positive activities it might undertake as the intrusion of an alien sovereignty rather than the cooperative action of a people." Hoover's ideological limitations infuriated Americans who saw him as indifferent to their suffering and a reactionary protector of privileged business interests—an image his political opponents encouraged.

REPUDIATING HOOVER

The Bonus Army

Hoover's treatment of the **Bonus Army** symbolized his unpopularity and set the stage for the 1932 presidential election. In 1932, from 15,000 to 20,000 unemployed veterans of World War I from across the country gathered in Washington to demand payment of service bonuses not due them until 1945. Congress had passed the "bonus" bill in 1924, authorizing the special payment to the veterans, but in 1932, it refused to appropriate the millions of dollars needed for the early payment. The veterans' journey had begun in May in Portland, Oregon, when 300 jobless men jumped a train headed East; they called themselves the Bonus Expeditionary Force (BEF) and elected Walter W. Waters, a former sergeant, to head the delegation. They arrived in Washington about two weeks later and were assured of fair treatment by sympathetic Washington police. To support the BEF, other WWI veterans began streaming into nation's capital, some with their families, and all in desperate need of the promised bonus.

They had been traveling for weeks and were hungry and homeless and the city's police provided food for the veterans and allowed them to sleep in abandoned government buildings. They set up quasi-military encampments, with field kitchens and medical dispensaries, and the BEF's leaders went to Capitol Hill to lobby Congress for immediate passage of the payment. Their main camp, housing ten to fifteen thousand veterans and families, was a

Bonus Marchers battling police in Washington, DC, in 1932. Police and military assaults on these homeless veterans infuriated Americans and prompted Democratic Presidential nominee Franklin D. Roosevelt to declare, "Well, this will elect me."

shantytown erected on the marshy Anacostia Flats at the edge of Washington, where signs complaining about Hoover's indifference—he refused to meet with the BEF's leadership—were plentiful and visible. One read "Hard Times Are Still 'Hoovering' Over Us." Without adequate water and proper sanitation, the encampment was made worse when rain created large pools of mud and soaked the houses made from boxes and crates, but they persevered and took great strength from each other, sharing their past military experiences and recalling better times. Local merchants donated food and blankets, and the public's reaction to the BEF was largely one of sympathy. Still, the specter of such a large group of dirty and homeless families aroused concerns. When asked whether the crowd was dangerous, the head of Washington's police force responded, "Dangerous? No, except the danger of gradual rust and rot which attacks those with no occupation and no incentive. They are just middle-aged men out of a job."

Responding to the plight of the veterans, the House of Representatives in June passed a bill, providing for immediate payment of the bonus, but the next day the Senate rejected the proposal as too costly. Congress did authorize funds to provide veterans and their families transportation back home, but many stayed. Indeed, some bonus marchers occupied vacant buildings on Pennsylvania Avenue and their defiant mood, along with their pitiful presence just blocks from the Capitol building, troubled Hoover significantly. As a precaution, additional security measures were taken, including chaining the White House gates, barricading the executive mansion, and diverting traffic.

By late July, Hoover determined to evict the veterans. The Washington police bodily removed the veterans from the building, but a few skirmishes turned into an all-out riot, and police shot and killed two veterans. Hoover then directed General Douglas MacArthur to "surround the affected area and clear it without delay." But Hoover also urged MacArthur to give "every consideration and kindness" to all women and children. But MacArthur disobeyed Hoover's cautious orders and on July 28 led cavalry, infantry, tanks, and a mounted machine-gun squadron down Pennsylvania Avenue against the ragged Bonus Marchers. MacArthur also ignored the advice of his aide, Major and future president Dwight D. Eisenhower, who had counseled his commanding officer against partaking in a "street corner embroilment." Eisenhower's preference for restraint was also disregarded by another officer present, Major George S. Patton, who became personally angry at the behavior of the veterans and directed his soldiers to attack the crowd of men, women, and children with their swords flailing. Under MacArthur's command, the cavalry and infantry effectively drove out the veterans and their families, forcing them to flee for cover at the Anacostia encampment. Not content with the bloody evacuation of the veterans from the city's downtown vacant buildings, MacArthur's forces followed them across the Eleventh Street Bridge to their camp, setting it on fire and razing it to the ground. Flames, tear gas, and bayonets met fleeing families; two babies died from tear gas and one soldier put his bayonet through the leg of a young boy, who was trying to find his pet rabbit.

This assault provoked widespread outrage. "What a pitiful spectacle is that of the great American Government, mightiest in the world, chasing unarmed men, women, and children with army tanks," commented the *Washington News*. Republicans as well as Democrats roundly denounced Hoover for the attack: Republican Senator Bronson Cutting from New Mexico declared that the "use of federal troops against unarmed veterans, whether prompted by cowardice or stupidity, was an unpardonable outrage." Another senator wrote Hoover, decrying the unnecessary use of force and adding, "soup is cheaper than tear bombs and bread better than bullets in maintaining law and order in these times of depression, unemployment, and hunger." The administration tried to brand the Bonus Marchers as communists and criminals, but official investigations refuted such claims. The marchers were anxious and discouraged Americans, not revolutionaries, and if any criminals were among them, noted one critic, they were proportionately fewer than in President Harding's cabinet. The incident confirmed Hoover's public image as harsh and insensitive.

The Election of 1932

In the summer of 1932, with no prospects for victory, Republicans renominated Hoover. Confident Democrats selected Governor Franklin D. Roosevelt (FDR) of New York, who pledged "a new deal for the American people." A distant cousin of Theodore Roosevelt, FDR had prepared for the presidency. Born into a wealthy family in 1882, he had been educated at Harvard, trained in the law, and schooled in politics as a state legislator, assistant secretary of the navy under Wilson, and the Democratic vice-presidential nominee in 1920. In 1921, Roosevelt contracted polio, which paralyzed him from the waist down, leaving him dependent on braces or crutches. His struggle with this ordeal gave him greater maturity, compassion, and determination. His continued involvement in politics, meanwhile, owed much to his wife, Eleanor. A social reformer, she became a Democratic activist, organizing women's groups and campaigning across New York. In a remarkable political comeback, FDR was elected governor in 1928 and reelected in 1930.

The 1932 campaign gave scant indication of what Roosevelt's New Deal might involve. The Democratic platform differed little from that of the Republicans, and Roosevelt spoke in vague or general terms. He knew that the election would be a repudiation of Hoover more than an endorsement of himself. Still, observers gained clues from Roosevelt's record in New York, where he had created the first state system of unemployment relief and supported social welfare and conservation. More important was his outgoing personality, which radiated warmth and hope in contrast to Hoover's gloom. "If you put a rose in Hoover's hand," said one observer, "it would wilt." The overwhelming popular rejection of Hoover was palpable; when he campaigned, he was booed and hissed. The object of derision, Hoover grew reluctant even to leave the White House in the final days of the campaign. Public hostility and certain contempt faced him at every turn; indeed, on the last day of his presidential campaign, his motorcade was the target of a stink bomb. Hoover's failures, personal as well as political and economic, led to his repudiation and to a major shift in government policies.

WAITING FOR ROOSEVELT

The Worsening Depression

FDR carried every state south and west of Pennsylvania (see Map 7-1). It was the worst rout of a Republican candidate ever (except in 1912 when the party had split); Hoover even failed to carry a single rural county in his home state of Iowa. Yet the badly repudiated Hoover would remain president for four more months, as the Constitution then required. And in those four months of winter, the depression worsened, with rising unemployment, collapsing farm prices, and spreading misery. It was a time of unusually bitter cold in California, and blizzards blanketed areas with snow as far south as Atlanta, leaving a trail of sixty-five casualties. In Dayton, Ohio, the school week was reduced to three days because of limited funds; other schools shut down entirely—more than three hundred schools in Arkansas were forced to close. A million children went without education and teachers everywhere went without pay that winter. In Chicago, when teachers, unpaid for months, fainted in their classrooms from hunger, it symbolized the imminent collapse of the nation itself. Indeed, in that same city, the irony was not lost on the jobless who stood in line for soup at kitchens financed by

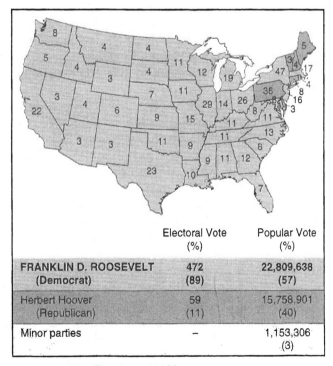

	Electoral Vote (%)	Popular Vote (%)
FRANKLIN D. ROOSEVELT (Democrat)	472 (89)	22,809,638 (57)
Herbert Hoover (Republican)	59 (11)	15,758,901 (40)
Minor parties	–	1,153,306 (3)

MAP 7-1   The Election of 1932
In the midst of the Great Depression, only the most rock-ribbed Republican states failed to turn to Franklin D. Roosevelt and the Democrats for relief. The election of 1932 was a landslide.

Al Capone but were unable to receive public assistance. *Fortune* magazine estimated that 28 percent of the nation's total population was without any income whatsoever.

Relief assistance became more scarce and private agencies shut their doors that cold winter rather than see the faces of people they could not help. But even in such desperate times, the stigma of relief remained. By the winter of 1932, only those who were completely destitute qualified to receive aid. They had to sell every personal item of value before qualifying for the smallest amount—never enough to pay the rent and buy food. Some ten states even barred relief recipients from voting. By 1932, even using such stringent standards, only about 25 percent of those eligible for relief were receiving it. Yet unemployment continue to climb; by March 1933, over 13 million Americans were without jobs.

Financial Collapse

Until his last day in office, Hoover remained convinced that the depression resulted from international problems of debt and trade, and as the nation moved toward catastrophe, Hoover focused more on foreign policy. In an unprecedented move, in late November 1932, the defeated Hoover invited the victorious Roosevelt to the White House to discuss the economic depression. Attempting to win Roosevelt's support for pursuing an extremely unpopular proposal—canceling war debts owed to the United States by European nations—Hoover lectured the new president on what he regarded as the foreign sources of the economic decline. But a wary Roosevelt had already determined that the causes of the depression were essentially domestic ones and was, in any case, reluctant to endorse a controversial issue supported by a totally discredited president. Hoover invited Roosevelt back to the White House in January 1933, but the relationship between these former friends had become frosty. Hoover had become more prickly and stubborn, ever sensitive to public criticism, and he regarded Roosevelt as intellectually shallow. Meanwhile, Roosevelt politely continued to reject Hoover's analysis of the depression and his efforts to resolve the international debt problem. After their second conversation, Hoover confided to an associate that he had spent his time in the meeting attempting to "educat[e] a very ignorant . . . well-meaning young man": Franklin Roosevelt.

The final blow to the economy came in February 1933 when panic struck the banking system. Nearly six thousand banks had already failed, robbing 9 million depositors of their savings. Desperate Americans rushed to withdraw their funds from the remaining banks, pushing them to the brink as well. They stood in long lines to withdraw their life savings, believing their money would be safer in any place other than a bank. Indeed, the public blamed bankers and business leaders for the economic failures, and the former heroes of the prosperity of the 1920s became the villains of the desperate 1930s. Senate investigations of Wall Street along with continued reckless, and occasionally illegal, practices of wealthy business leaders merely reaffirmed their public image as callous and greedy. With the federal government under Hoover immobilized, state governments shut the banks to prevent their failure. Just weeks before Roosevelt's inauguration, Hoover sent Roosevelt a lengthy handwritten letter that warned of impending economic catastrophe and even suggested that the bank crisis had resulted from the uncertainty caused by Roosevelt's election. (Roosevelt dismissed the letter as inappropriate and waited several weeks even before responding.)

Hoover's letter arrived three days after Roosevelt had been in Miami, greeting his supporters. On February 15, 1933, after speaking to the Miami crowd from an open car, Roosevelt was joined by Anton Cermak, the mayor of Chicago. Minutes later Cermak became the mistaken victim of an assassin's bullet aimed at the newly elected president. With remarkable calm, the unharmed Roosevelt held Cermak in his arms, demonstrating to Americans, according to his advisors, his capacity to remain in control during crisis situations. Roosevelt, one associate explained, held "nothing but the most complete confidence in his own ability to deal with any situation that might arise." Eleanor Roosevelt, too, observed that her husband's "reaction to any event was always to be calm. If it was something that was bad, he just became almost like an iceberg, and there was never the slightest emotion that was allowed to show."

By March, an eerie silence had descended on the nation. The American people were waiting for Roosevelt—his confidence and his promise—to deal with a collapsing nation. Outgoing President Hoover solemnly concluded, "We are at the end of our string."

CONCLUSION

The Great Depression took jobs, homes, and even hope away from many Americans. Families often tried to cope, but desertion often left homes broken and children in despair. Men, women, and children took to the roads in search of something better or to escape what they knew they no longer had. It was a time of hunger and hardship, and cities and communities throughout the nation were ill-prepared for the scope of the problem. Private charities attempted to maintain their role as relief givers, but they, too, were quickly overwhelmed. Most communities did not need the reminders from President Hoover to practice self-help and local responsibility. That had been the custom, and local officials and citizens cooperated in innumerable ways to help neighbors and struggling families.

But the depression also divided people, and traditional tensions based on gender, race, and ethnicity sharpened, resulting in discrimination in hiring, firing, and even the provision of unemployment relief. Mexican Americans were alternately frightened and deported; African Americans sank even lower in the depths of poverty, and even married women felt the pointed attacks of public hostility, as they were denied jobs and openly castigated.

For many, President Hoover's appeals to voluntarism and even his unprecedented steps in meeting the problem of unemployment—all seemed meaningless and ultimately even cruel. Business leaders ignored his pleas to maintain jobs and wages; bankers repudiated his efforts at self-help; and jobless Americans everywhere felt the pain of hunger and the sting of humiliation. Hoover continued to believe in an economic order where business, labor, and government operated cooperatively and orderly. Voluntary associations would bring progress and prosperity. These were the principles that had guided him in the 1920s as secretary of commerce and informed his own presidency, but in the 1930s, the nation neared catastrophe; the collapse of the banking system appeared imminent and political solutions were not forthcoming. Clinging, moreover, to the notion that the depression had its roots in the international economy, Hoover became still more rigid and uncompromising in his last days of office. His repudiation at the polls ended Hoover's career as a talented administrator and on an extremely bitter note of failure. Instead, the election of 1932 belonged to a new leader, whose personal warmth offered a welcoming change and whose promise of a "new deal" struck a resonant chord with Americans searching for change of any kind. Franklin D. Roosevelt would provide that change.

Review Questions

1. In "American Voices" at the beginning of this chapter, what were the effects of the depression and unemployment on men and women?

2. What were some of the causes of the Wall Street crash and what was the connection between the stock market collapse and the subsequent depression?

3. What were the major weaknesses in the economy and why did the depression become a global one?

4. How were the effects of unemployment and the depression shaped by gender, race, and ethnicity?

5. How did Americans respond to hard times?

6. Why did President Hoover's emphasis on voluntarism fail to resolve the problems of the Great Depression?

Key Terms

"Black Tuesday" *192*
Bonus Army *208*
Farmers' Holiday Association *200*
Hoovervilles *195*
"juvenile transients" *198*
National Credit Corporation *205*
President's Emergency Committee for Employment (PECE) *205*

President's Organization on Unemployment Relief (POUR) *205*
Reconstruction Finance Corporation (RFC) *208*
Smoot-Hawley Tariff *194*
Soup Kitchens *196*

Recommended Reading

Frank Freidel, *Franklin D. Roosevelt: A Rendezvous with Destiny* (1990). The best one-volume biography of FDR.

David Kennedy, *Freedom from Fear: The American People in Depression and War* (1999). The most recent and comprehensive survey of the period.

John Steinbeck, *The Grapes of Wrath* (1939). The classic novel of Dust Bowl migrants; still makes gripping reading.

Joan Hoff Wilson, *Herbert Hoover: Forgotten Progressive* (1975). An important account of Hoover's philosophy of government and society.

FRANKLIN D. ROOSEVELT, THE GREAT DEPRESSION, AND THE NEW DEAL: 1933–1939

Launching the New Deal

Consolidating the New Deal

The New Deal and American Life

Ebbing of the New Deal

Good Neighbors and Hostile Forces

Conclusion

Union Dues

President Roosevelt is a friend to the laboring' men,

Gives us the right to organize an' be real union men,

Union, union is all over the wide worl',

Back on the farm an' tobacco barns.

I'm glad I'm a union man: long may it live on.

I got the union blues, don't care where I go.

I got the union blues, don't care where I be.

It's good for you en' good for me;

I'm goin' down the road feelin' mighty glad,

I'm goin' down the road feelin' mighty glad,

The union is the best friend that labor ever had.

I'm goin' to write a letter, goin' to mail it in the month o' May

I'm goin' to write a letter, goin' to mail it this very day.

I'm goin' to thank the President for that seven-hour day.

I'm goin' to close my song, but won't close my mind,

I'm goin' to close my song, but won't close my mind—

That laboring' man was not left behind.

Coal miners' song; subsequently recorded by George Korson, *Coal Dust on the Fiddle* (1943). From www.historymatters.gmu.edu.

IN THE SUMMER of 1933, the signs were everywhere in the coal regions—on posters and billboards, in store windows: "The President wants you to join the union." In the 1920s, coal had been a sick industry, and its health had deteriorated with the onset of the Great Depression in 1929. Mounting unemployment and plummeting wages joined the industry's dangerous working conditions, arbitrary rules, and company domination. Membership in the United Mine Workers (UMW) had dropped from 400,000 in 1926 to barely 100,000 by 1933. Misery and hopelessness traveled in tandem. Yet now UMW officials spread the word that President Franklin Roosevelt favored the right to organize unions and bargain collectively.

The effect was electric. A UMW organizer in Pennsylvania found "a different feeling among the miners everywhere—they seem to feel that they are once more free men." In Kentucky, one organizer formed nine locals in a day, marveling that "the people have been so starved out that they are flocking into the Union by the thousands." Indeed, coal miners organized themselves spontaneously; union officials merely tried to keep up with the paperwork. The astonished governor of Pennsylvania told Roosevelt, "These people believe in you. . . . They trust you and all believe that you are working to get them recognition of the United Mine Workers of America."

The coal operators, accustomed to baronial control of the industry, vainly told their workers, "President Roosevelt is not an organizer for the United Mine Workers." But attitudes were changing. One organizer reported that whereas police had once chased union representatives out of Raton, New Mexico, "now the Mayor of the town gives us the city park for our meeting." Within two months, UMW membership numbered half a million.

Once organized, locals struck for union contracts and improved conditions. Some operators resisted, firing union leaders, recruiting strikebreakers, and employing police repression. When miners were shot, riots broke out. As one newspaper reported, "Miners' wives fought alongside their husbands, and sons joined with their fathers in battles with deputies." By September, the operators gave up, signing a contract that recognized the union, established a shorter work day, and improved wages and working conditions. As the *New Yorker* noted, "The defeated mine-owners agreed to all the things that deputy sheriffs usually shoot people for demanding." The miners and their families rejoiced in their victory, and they believed that President Roosevelt deserved credit for their hard won benefits and their new sense of respect and recognition. Miners everywhere expressed their sentiments in song; they used such songs as "Union Dues" to promote the union, rally their communities, sustain morale, and express their gratitude to their new president.

The union victory was not final, but these developments illustrated the forces that changed America in the 1930s. Responding to a crippling depression, the federal government—personalized by President Roosevelt—adopted an activist role in the economy and society. Its new reach seemed to extend everywhere—to the relief of those like the miners in Appalachia and the consternation of those like the coal operators. Federal activism restored hope and confidence for many Americans, often encouraging them to act for themselves.

The legislation that had spurred the miners' union drive was part of a massive and not always consistent program to promote economic recovery that in the process often promoted reform as well. The **New Deal**, as Roosevelt called his plan, achieved neither full recovery nor systematic reform, and its benefits were distributed unevenly. But it restored confidence to many Americans, permanently transformed the nation's responsibilities for the welfare of its citizens, and created a new coalition of political support in the Democratic party. The grateful union movement, for example, became an important part of Roosevelt's Democratic party. Franklin and Eleanor Roosevelt not only brought fresh hope to depression-weary Americans but also connected them to the White House as never before. By the end of the decade, President Roosevelt was proud of those changes and also frustrated by the persistence of hard times. But he was no longer worried that the economy—indeed the whole of society—teetered on the edge of catastrophe; his gaze now fixed abroad where even more ominous developments, he believed, threatened the nation's future and security.

KEY TOPICS

The Great Depression.

FDR's New Deal.

The New Deal and organized labor, minorities, women, and farmers.

FDR's Democratic coalition of reformers, labor, urban ethnic groups, white Southerners, Westerners, and African Americans.

The faltering of the New Deal.

Diplomacy in the Great Depression.

LAUNCHING THE NEW DEAL

In the midst of national anxiety, Franklin D. Roosevelt pushed forward an unprecedented program to resolve the crises of a collapsing financial system, crippling unemployment, and agricultural and industrial breakdown and to promote reform. The early New Deal achieved successes and attracted support, but it also had limitations and generated criticism that suggested the need for still greater innovations.

"Action Now!"

On March 4, 1933, Franklin Delano Roosevelt became president and immediately reassured the American people. He insisted that "the only thing we have to fear is fear itself—nameless, unreasoning, unjustified terror, which paralyzes needed efforts to convert retreat into advance." And he promised "action, and action now!" Summoning Congress, Roosevelt pressed forward on a broad front. In the first three months of his administration, the famous Hundred Days of the New Deal, the Democratic Congress passed many important laws (see the Overview table, "Major Laws of the Hundred Days").

Roosevelt's program reflected a mix of ideas, some from FDR himself, some from a diverse group of advisors, including academic experts dubbed the "brain trust," politicians, and social workers. It also incorporated principles from the progressive movement, precedents from the Great War mobilization, and even plans from the Hoover administration.

• CHRONOLOGY •

1932 Franklin D. Roosevelt is elected president.

1933 Emergency Banking Act is passed.

Agricultural Adjustment Administration (AAA) is created to regulate farm production.

National Recovery Administration (NRA) is created to promote industrial cooperation and recovery.

Federal Emergency Relief Act provides federal assistance to the unemployed.

Civilian Conservation Corps (CCC) is established to provide work relief in conservation projects.

Public Works Administration (PWA) is created to provide work relief on large public construction projects.

Civil Works Administration (CWA) provides emergency winter relief jobs.

Tennessee Valley Authority (TVA) is created to coordinate regional development.

1934 Securities and Exchange Commission (SEC) is established.

Indian Reorganization Act reforms Indian policy.

Huey Long organizes the Share-Our-Wealth Society.

Democrats win midterm elections.

1935 Supreme Court declares NRA unconstitutional.

National Labor Relations Act (Wagner Act) guarantees workers' rights to organize and bargain collectively.

Social Security Act establishes a federal social insurance system.

Banking Act strengthens the Federal Reserve.

Revenue Act establishes a more progressive tax system.

Resettlement Administration is created to aid dispossessed farmers.

Rural Electrification Administration (REA) is created to help provide electric power to rural areas.

Soil Conservation Service is established.

Emergency Relief Appropriation Act authorizes public relief projects for the unemployed.

Works Progress Administration (WPA) is created.

Huey Long is assassinated.

1936 Supreme Court declares Agricultural Adjustment Administration (AAA) unconstitutional.

Roosevelt is reelected president.

Sit-down strikes begin.

1937 Chicago police kill workers in Memorial Day Massacre.

FDR tries but fails to expand the Supreme Court.

Farm Security Administration (FSA) is created to lend money to small farmers to buy and rehabilitate farms.

National Housing Act is passed to promote public housing projects.

"Roosevelt Recession" begins.

1938 Congress of Industrial Organizations (CIO) is founded.

Fair Labor Standards Act establishes minimum wage and maximum hours rules for labor.

Roosevelt fails to "purge" the Democratic party.

Above all, the New Deal was a practical response to the depression. FDR had set its tone in his campaign when he declared, "The country needs, and, unless I mistake its temper, the country demands bold, persistent experimentation. . . . Above all, try something."

FDR first addressed the banking crisis. On March 5, he proclaimed a national bank holiday, closing all remaining banks. Congress then passed his Emergency Banking Act, a conservative measure that extended government assistance to sound banks and reorganized the weak ones. Prompt government action, coupled with a reassuring **fireside chat** over the radio by the president, restored popular confidence in the banks. When they reopened on March 13, deposits exceeded withdrawals. "Capitalism," said Raymond Moley of the brain trust, "was saved in eight days." In June, Congress created the **Federal Deposit Insurance Corporation (FDIC)** to guarantee bank deposits up to $2,500.

The financial industry was also reformed. The Glass-Steagall Act separated investment and commercial banking to curtail risky speculation. The Securities Act reformed the sale of stocks to prevent the insider abuses that had characterized Wall Street, and in 1934 the

• • • OVERVIEW • • •

MAJOR LAWS OF THE HUNDRED DAYS

LAW	OBJECTIVE
Emergency Banking Act	Stabilized the private banking system.
Agricultural Adjustment Act	Established a farm recovery program based on production controls and price supports.
Emergency Farm Mortgage Act	Provided for the refinancing of farm mortgages.
National Industrial Recovery Act	Established a national recovery program and authorized a public works program.
Federal Emergency Relief Act	Established a national system of relief.
Home Owners Loan Act	Protected homeowners from mortgage foreclosure by refinancing home loans.
Glass-Steagall Act	Separated commercial and investment banking and guaranteed bank deposits.
Tennessee Valley Authority Act	Established the TVA and provided for the planned development of the Tennessee River Valley.
Civilian Conservation Corps Act	Established the CCC to provide work relief on reforestation and conservation projects.
Farm Credit Act	Expanded agricultural credits and established the Farm Credit Administration.
Securities Act	Required full disclosure from stock exchanges.
Wagner-Peyser Act	Created a U.S. Employment Service and encouraged states to create local public employment office.

Securities and Exchange Commission (SEC) was created to regulate the stock market. Two other financial measures in 1933 created the Home Owners Loan Corporation and the Farm Credit Administration, which enabled millions to refinance their mortgages.

Creating Jobs

Roosevelt also provided relief for the unemployed. The Federal Emergency Relief Administration (FERA) furnished funds to state and local agencies. Harry Hopkins, who had headed Roosevelt's relief program in New York, became its director and one of the New Deal's most important members. FERA spent over $3 billion before it ended in 1935, and by then Hopkins and FDR had developed new programs that provided work rather than just cash. Work relief, they believed, preserved both the skills and the morale of recipients. In the winter of 1933–1934, Hopkins spent nearly $1 billion to create jobs for 4 million men and women through the Civil Works Administration (CWA). The CWA hired laborers to build roads and airports, teachers to staff rural schools, and singers and artists to give public performances. The Public Works Administration (PWA) provided work relief on useful projects to stimulate the economy through public expenditures. Directed by Harold Ickes, the PWA spent billions from 1933 to 1939 to build schools, hospitals, courthouses, dams, and bridges.

One of FDR's personal ideas, the Civilian Conservation Corps (CCC), combined work relief with conservation. Launched in 1933, the CCC employed 2.5 million young men to work on reforestation and flood control projects, build roads and bridges in national forests and parks, restore Civil War battlefields, and fight forest fires. The men lived in isolated CCC camps and earned $30 a month, $25 of which had to be sent home. "I'd go anywhere," said

A coal miner greeting Franklin D. Roosevelt in West Virginia in 1932. Roosevelt's promise of a New Deal revived hope among millions of Americans trapped in hard times.

one Baltimore applicant. "I'd go to hell if I could get work there." One of the most popular New Deal agencies, the CCC lasted until 1942.

Helping Some Farmers

Besides providing relief, the New Deal promoted economic recovery. In May 1933, Congress established the Agricultural Adjustment Administration (AAA) to combat the depression in agriculture caused by crop surpluses and low prices. The AAA subsidized farmers who agreed to restrict production. The objective was to boost farm prices to parity, a level that would restore farmers' purchasing power to what it had been in 1914. In the summer of 1933, the AAA paid Southern farmers to plow up 10 million acres of cotton and Midwestern farmers to bury 9 million pounds of pork. Restricting production in hard times caused public outrage. "Farmers are not producing too much," said one critic. "What we have overproduction of is empty stomachs and bare backs." Secretary of Agriculture Henry Wallace defended production controls as analogous to corporations maximizing profits: "Agriculture cannot survive in a capitalistic society as a philanthropic enterprise."

Agricultural conditions improved. Farm prices rose from 52 percent of parity in 1932 to 88 percent in 1935, and gross farm income rose by 50 percent. Not until 1941, however, would income exceed the level of 1929, a poor year for farmers. Moreover, some of the decreased production and increased prices stemmed from devastating droughts and dust storms on the Great Plains. The AAA itself harmed poor farmers while aiding larger commercial growers. As Southern planters restricted their acreage, they dismissed tenants and sharecroppers, and with AAA payments, they bought new farm machinery, reducing their need for farm labor. A reporter in 1935 found thousands of sharecroppers "along the highways and byways of Dixie, . . . lonely figures without money, without homes, and without hope." Thus, while big

New Deal agricultural programs stabilized the farm economy, but not all farmers benefited. Landowners who received AAA payments evicted these black sharecroppers huddled in a makeshift roadside camp in Missouri in 1935.

producers moved toward prosperity, many small farmers were forced into a pool of rural labor for which there was decreasing need or into the cities, where there were no jobs.

The Supreme Court declared the AAA unconstitutional in 1936, but new laws established the farm subsidy program for decades to come. Increasing mechanization and scientific agriculture kept production high and farmers dependent on government intervention.

The Flight of the Blue Eagle

The New Deal attempted to revive American industry with the National Industrial Recovery Act (NIRA), which created the National Recovery Administration (NRA). The NRA sought to halt the slide in prices, wages, and employment by suspending antitrust laws and authorizing industrial and trade associations to draft codes setting production quotas, price policies, wages and working conditions, and other business practices. The codes promoted the interests of business generally and big business in particular, but Section 7a of the NIRA guaranteed workers the rights to organize unions and bargain collectively—a provision that John L. Lewis of the United Mine Workers called an Emancipation Proclamation for labor.

Hugh Johnson became director of the NRA. He persuaded business leaders to cooperate in drafting codes and the public to patronize participating companies. The NRA Blue Eagle insignia and its slogan "We Do Our Part" covered workplaces, storefronts, and billboards. Blue Eagle parades marched down the nation's main streets and climaxed in a massive demonstration in New York City.

Support for the NRA waned, however. Corporate leaders used it to advance their own goals and to discriminate against small producers, consumers, and labor. Minnesota's Governor Floyd Olson condemned the dominance within the NRA of the same selfish business interests he saw as responsible for the depression: "I am not satisfied with hanging a laurel wreath on burglars, thieves, and pirates and calling them code authorities."

Businesses also violated the labor rights specified in Section 7a. Defiant employers viewed collective bargaining as infringing their authority. Employers even used violence to smother unions. The NRA did little to enforce Section 7a, and Johnson—strongly probusiness—denounced all strikes. Workers felt betrayed.

Roosevelt tried to reorganize the NRA, but the act remained controversial until the Supreme Court declared it unconstitutional in 1935.

Critics Right and Left

The early New Deal had not ended the depression. Recovery was fitful and uneven; millions of Americans remained unemployed. Nevertheless, the New Deal's efforts to grapple with problems, its successes in reducing suffering and fear, and Roosevelt's own skills carried the Democratic party to victory in the 1934 elections. But New Deal policies also provoked criticism, from both those convinced that too little had been achieved and those alarmed that too much had been attempted.

Despite the early New Deal's probusiness character, conservatives complained that the expansion of government activity and its regulatory role weakened the autonomy of American business. They also condemned the efforts to aid nonbusiness groups as socialistic, particularly the "excessive" spending on unemployment relief and the "instigation" of labor organizing. By 1934, as *Time* magazine reported, "Private fulminations and public carpings against the New Deal have become almost a routine of the business day." Industrialists and bankers organized the American Liberty League to direct attacks on the New Deal. The league distributed over 5 million copies of two hundred different pamphlets; it also furnished editorials and news stories to newspapers. These critics attracted little popular support, however, and their selfishness antagonized Roosevelt.

More realistic criticism came from the left. In 1932, FDR had campaigned for "the forgotten man at the bottom of the economic pyramid," and some radicals argued that the early New Deal had forgotten the forgotten man. Communists and socialists focused public attention on the poor, especially in the countryside. In California, Communists organized Mexican, Filipino, and Japanese farm workers into their Cannery and Agricultural Workers Union; in Arkansas and Tennessee, socialists in 1934 helped organize sharecroppers into the Southern Tenant Farmers Union, protesting the "Raw Deal" they had received from the AAA. Both unions encountered violent reprisals. Growers killed three picketers in California's San Joaquin Valley; in Arkansas, landlords shot union organizers and led vigilante raids on sharecroppers' shacks. This terrorism, however, created sympathy for farmworkers.

Even without the involvement of socialists or communists, however, labor militancy in 1934 pressed Roosevelt. Workers acted as much against the failure of the NRA to enforce Section 7a as against recalcitrant corporations. The number of workers participating in strikes leaped from 325,000 in 1932 (about the annual average since 1925) to 1.5 million in 1934. From dockworkers in Seattle and copper miners in Butte to streetcar drivers in Milwaukee and shoemakers in Boston, workers demanded their rights. Textile workers launched the largest single strike in the nation's history, shutting down the industry in twenty states.

Rebuffing FDR's pleas for fair treatment, employers moved to crush the strikes, often using complaisant police and private strikebreakers. In Minneapolis, police shot sixty-seven teamsters, almost all in the back, as they fled an ambush arranged by employers; in Toledo, company police and National Guardsmen attacked autoworkers with tear gas, bayonets, and rifle fire; in the textile strike, police killed six picketers in South Carolina, and soldiers wounded another fifty in Rhode Island. At times, the workers held their ground, and they often attracted popular support, even in general strikes that paralyzed such major cities as San Francisco. But against such powerful opponents, workers needed help to achieve their rights. Harry Hopkins and other New Dealers realized that labor's demands could not be ignored.

Popular discontent was also mobilized by four prominent individuals who demanded government action to assist groups neglected by the New Deal. Representative William Lemke of North Dakota, an agrarian radical leader of the Nonpartisan League, called attention to rural distress. Lemke objected to the New Deal's limited response to farmers crushed by the depression. In his own state, nearly two-thirds of the farmers had lost their land through foreclosures. The AAA's strategy of simply restricting production, he thundered, was an "insane policy in the midst of hunger, misery, want, and rags."

Francis Townsend, a California physician, proposed to aid the nation's elderly, many of whom were destitute. The Townsend Plan called for a government pension to all Americans over the age of 60, provided they would retire from work and spend their entire pension. This scheme promised to extend relief to the elderly, open jobs for the unemployed, and stimulate economic recovery. Townsend attracted people who, in his words, "believe in the Bible, believe in God, cheer when the flag passes by, the Bible Belt solid Americans." Over five thousand Townsend Clubs lobbied for government action to help the elderly poor.

Father Charles Coughlin, a Catholic priest in the Detroit suburb of Royal Oak, threatened to mobilize another large constituency against the limitations of the early New Deal. Thirty million Americans listened eagerly to his weekly radio broadcasts that mixed religion with anti-Semitism and demands for social justice and financial reform. Coughlin had condemned Hoover for assisting banks but ignoring the unemployed, and initially he welcomed the New Deal as "Christ's Deal." But after concluding that FDR's policies favored "the virile viciousness of business and finance," Coughlin organized the National Union for Social Justice to lobby for his goals. With support among lower-middle-class, heavily Catholic, urban ethnic groups, Coughlin posed a real challenge to Roosevelt's Democratic party.

Roosevelt found Senator Huey P. Long of Louisiana still more worrisome. Alternately charming and autocratic, Long had modernized his state with taxation and educational reforms and an extensive public-works program after his election as governor in 1928. Moving to the Senate and eyeing the White House, Long proposed more comprehensive social-welfare policies than the New Deal had envisaged. In 1934, he organized the Share-Our-Wealth Society. His plan to end poverty and unemployment called for confiscatory taxes on the rich to provide every family with a decent income, health coverage, education, and old-age pensions. Long's appeal was enormous. Within months, his organization claimed more than 27,000 clubs and 7 million members.

These dissident movements raised complex issues and simple fears. They built on concerns about the New Deal, both demanding government assistance and fretting about government intrusion; their programs were often ill defined or impractical—Townsend's plan would cost more than half the national income; and some of the leaders, like Coughlin and Long, approached demagoguery. Nevertheless, their popularity warned Roosevelt that government action was needed to satisfy reform demands and assure his reelection in 1936.

CONSOLIDATING THE NEW DEAL

Responding to the persistence of the depression and political pressures, Roosevelt in 1935 undertook economic and social reforms that some observers have called the Second New Deal. The new measures shifted the relative weights accorded to the constant objectives of recovery, relief, and reform. Nor did FDR's interest in reform simply reflect cynical politics. He had frequently championed progressive measures in the past, and many of his advisers had deep roots in reform movements. After the 1934 elections gave the president an even more Democratic Congress, Harry Hopkins exulted: "Boys—this is our hour. We've got to get everything we want—a works program, social security, wages and hours, everything—now or never."

Weeding Out and Lifting Up

"In spite of our efforts and in spite of our talk," Roosevelt told the new Congress in 1935, "we have not weeded out the overprivileged and we have not effectively lifted up the underprivileged." To do so, he developed "must" legislation, to which his allies in Congress added. One of the new laws protected labor's rights to organize and bargain collectively. Drafted by Senator Robert Wagner of New York to replace Section 7a, it received Roosevelt's endorsement only after it was clear that both Congress and the public favored it. The Wagner National Labor Relations Act, dubbed "Labor's Magna Carta," guaranteed workers' rights to organize unions and forbade employers to adopt unfair labor practices, such as firing union activists and forming company unions. The law also set up the National Labor Relations Board (NLRB) to enforce these provisions, protect workers from coercion, and supervise union elections.

Social Security Of greater long-range importance was the Social Security Act. Other industrial nations had established national social-insurance systems much earlier, but only the Great Depression moved the United States to accept the idea that the federal government should protect the poor and unemployed. Even so, the law was a compromise, framed by a nonpartisan committee of business, labor, and public representatives and then weakened by congressional conservatives. It provided unemployment compensation, old-age pensions, and aid for dependent mothers and children and the blind.

The conservative nature of the law appeared in its stingy benefit payments, its lack of health insurance, and its exclusion of more than one-fourth of all workers, including many in desperate need of protection, such as farm laborers and domestic servants. Moreover, unlike programs in other nations, the old-age pensions were financed through a regressive payroll tax on both employees and employers rather than through general tax revenues. Thus the new system was more like a compulsory insurance program. Roosevelt conceded as much but defended the taxes on workers as a tactic to protect the reform itself: "We put those payroll contributions there so as to give the contributors a legal, moral, and political right to collect their pensions and their unemployment benefits. With those taxes in there, no damn politician can ever scrap my social security program."

Roosevelt was justifiably proud. Despite its weaknesses, the Social Security Act was one of the most important laws in American history. It provided, he pointed out, "at least some measure of protection to the average citizen and to his family against the loss of a job and against poverty-ridden old age." Moreover, by establishing federal responsibility for social welfare, it inaugurated a welfare system that subsequent generations would expand.

Money, Tax, and Land Reform Another reform measure, the Banking Act of 1935, increased the authority of the Federal Reserve Board over the nation's currency and credit system and decreased the power of the private bankers whose irresponsible behavior had contributed to the depression and the appeal of Father Coughlin. The Revenue Act of 1935, passed after Roosevelt assailed the "unjust concentration of wealth and economic power,"

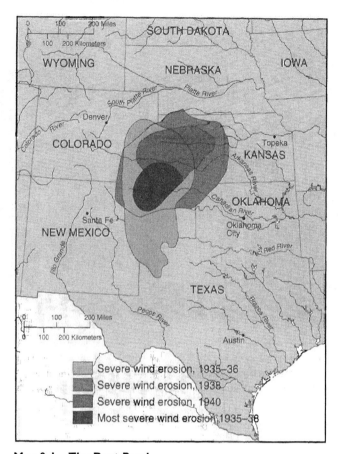

MAP 8-1   The Dust Bowl
Years of overcultivation, drought, and high winds created the Dust Bowl, which most severely affected the Southern Great Plains. Federal relief and conservation programs provided assistance, but many residents fled the area, often migrating to California.

provided for graduated income taxes and increased estate and corporate taxes. Opponents called it the Soak the Rich Tax, but with its many loopholes, it was scarcely that and was certainly not a redistributive measure such as Huey Long had proposed. Nevertheless, it set a precedent for progressive taxation and attracted popular support.

The Second New Deal also responded belatedly to the environmental catastrophe that had turned much of the Great Plains from Texas to the Dakotas into a "Dust Bowl" (see Map 8-1). Since World War I, farmers had stripped marginal land of its native grasses to plant wheat. When drought and high winds hit the plains in 1932, crops failed, and nothing held the soil. Dust storms blew away millions of tons of topsoil, despoiling the land and darkening the sky a thousand miles away. Families abandoned their farms in droves. Many of these poor "Okies" headed for California, their plight captured in John Steinbeck's novel *The Grapes of Wrath* (1939).

In 1935, Roosevelt established the Resettlement Administration to focus on land reform and help poor farmers. Under Rexford Tugwell, this agency initiated soil erosion projects and attempted to resettle impoverished farmers on better land, but the problem exceeded its resources. Congress moved to save the land, if not its people, by creating the Soil Conservation Service in 1935.

A symbol of progress and prosperity in the 1920s, automobility became something very different in the Great Depression. People fleeing the Dust Bowl, such as this family in Oklahoma, packed up their few tattered possessions and headed for California in hopes of getting a "little bit of this good dirt" for their own.

Expanding Relief

If reform gained priority in the Second New Deal, relief remained critical. With millions still unemployed, Roosevelt pushed through Congress in 1935 the Emergency Relief Appropriation Act, authorizing $5 billion—at the time the largest single appropriation in history—for emergency public employment. Roosevelt created the Works Progress Administration (WPA) under Hopkins, who set up work relief programs to assist the unemployed and boost the economy. Before its end in 1943, the WPA gave jobs to 9 million people (more than a fifth of the labor force) and spent nearly $12 billion. Three-fourths of its expenditures went on construction projects that could employ manual labor: The WPA built 125,000 schools, post offices, and hospitals; 8,000 parks; nearly 100,000 bridges; and enough roads and sewer systems to circle the earth thirty times. From New York City's La Guardia Airport to Atlanta's sewer system to irrigation ditches in the Far West, the WPA laid much of the basic infrastructure on which the nation still relies.

The WPA also developed work projects for unemployed writers, artists, musicians, and actors. "Why not?" said FDR. "They are human beings. They have to live." The Federal Writers' Project put authors to work preparing state guidebooks, writing historical pamphlets, and recording the memories of ex-slaves. The Federal Art Project hired artists to teach art in night schools, prepare exhibits at museums, and paint murals on post office walls. The Federal Theatre Project organized theatrical productions and drama companies that in four years played to 30 million Americans. The Federal Music Project hired musicians to collect and perform folk songs. These WPA programs allowed people to use their talents while surviving the depression, increased popular access to cultural performances, and established a precedent for federal support of the arts. "What has happened and in such a short time is almost incredible," said one reviewer. "From a government completely apathetic to art, we suddenly have a government very art conscious."

The National Youth Administration (NYA), another WPA agency, gave part-time jobs to students, enabling 2 million high school and college students to stay in school, learn skills, and do productive work. At the University of Nebraska, NYA students built an observatory; at Duke University, law student Richard M. Nixon earned 35 cents an hour doing research in the library. Lyndon Johnson, a Texas NYA official, believed that "if the Roosevelt administration had never done another thing, it would have been justified by the work of this great institution for salvaging youth."

The Roosevelt Coalition and the Election of 1936

The 1936 election gave Americans an opportunity to judge FDR and the New Deal. Conservatives alarmed at the expansion of government, business people angered by regulation and labor legislation, and wealthy Americans furious with tax reform decried the New Deal, but they were a minority. Even the presidential candidate they supported, Republican Governor Alf Landon of Kansas, endorsed much of the New Deal, criticizing merely the inefficiency and cost of some of its programs. (Roosevelt remarked whimsically that he thought he could defeat himself with such a campaign.) The New Deal's earlier critics on the left had also lost most of their following. The reforms of 1935 had undercut their arguments, and the assassination of Huey Long in the same year had removed their ablest politician. They formed the Union party and nominated William Lemke for the presidency, but they were no longer a threat.

The programs and politicians of the New Deal had created an invincible coalition behind Roosevelt. Despite ambivalence about large-scale government intervention, the New Deal's agricultural programs reinforced the traditional Democratic allegiance of white Southerners while attracting many Western farmers. Labor legislation clinched the active support of the nation's workers; Sidney Hillman of the Amalgamated Clothing Workers promised that his union would campaign for FDR "to see to it that we hold onto the gains labor has won." Middle-class voters, whose homes had been saved and whose hopes had been raised, also joined the Roosevelt coalition.

Urban ethnic groups, who had benefited from welfare programs and appreciated the unprecedented recognition Roosevelt's administration gave them also joined the coalition. FDR named the first Italian American to the federal judiciary, for example, and appointed five times as many Catholics and Jews to government positions as the three Republican

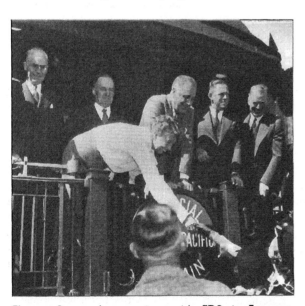

Eleanor Roosevelt campaigns with FDR in Fremont, Nebraska, in 1935. A visible activist for social and economic reform, she was also politically important in building the powerful Roosevelt coalition. "Previously," said the journalist Ruby Black, "a President's wife acted as if she didn't know that a political party existed."

presidents had during the 1920s. African Americans voted overwhelmingly Democratic for the first time. Women, too, were an important part of the Roosevelt coalition, and Eleanor often attracted their support as much as Franklin did. As one campaigner said to a roaring crowd in 1936, "Many women in this country when they vote for Franklin D. Roosevelt will also be thinking with a choke in the throat of Eleanor Roosevelt!"

This political realignment produced a landslide. Roosevelt polled 61 percent of the popular vote and the largest electoral college vote margin ever recorded, 523 to 8. Landon even lost Kansas, his own state, and Lemke received fewer than 900,000 votes. Democrats also won huge majorities in Congress. Roosevelt's political coalition reflected a mandate for himself and the New Deal; it would enable the Democrats to dominate national elections for three decades.

THE NEW DEAL AND AMERICAN LIFE

The landslide of 1936 revealed the impact the New Deal had on Americans. Industrial workers mobilized to secure their rights, women and minorities gained increased, if still limited, opportunities to participate in American society, and Southerners and Westerners benefited from government programs they turned to their own advantage. Government programs changed daily life, and ordinary people often helped shape the new policies.

Labor on the March

The labor revival in the 1930s reflected both workers' determination and government support. Workers wanted not merely to improve their wages and benefits but also to gain union recognition and union contracts to limit arbitrary managerial authority and achieve some control over the workplace. This larger goal provoked opposition from employers and their allies and required workers to organize, strike, and become politically active. Their achievement was remarkable.

The Second New Deal helped. By guaranteeing labor's rights to organize and bargain collectively, the Wagner Act sparked a wave of labor activism. But if the government ultimately protected union rights, the unions themselves had to form locals, recruit members, and demonstrate influence in the workplace.

At first, those tasks overwhelmed the American Federation of Labor (AFL). Its reliance on craft-based unions and reluctance to organize immigrant, black, and women workers left it unprepared for the rush of industrial workers seeking unionization. More progressive labor leaders saw that industrywide unions were more appropriate for unskilled workers in mass-production industries. Forming the Committee for Industrial Organization (CIO) within the AFL, they campaigned to unionize workers in the steel, auto, and rubber industries, all notoriously hostile to unions. AFL leaders insisted that the CIO disband and then in 1937 expelled its unions. The militants reorganized as the separate **Congress of Industrial Organizations**. (In 1955, the two groups merged as the AFL-CIO.)

The split roused the AFL to increase its own organizing activities, but it was primarily the new CIO that put labor on the march. It inspired workers previously neglected. The CIO's interracial union campaign in the Birmingham steel mills, said one organizer, was "like a second coming of Christ" for black workers, who welcomed the union as a chance for social recognition as well as economic opportunity. The CIO also employed new and aggressive tactics, particularly the sit-down strike, in which workers, rather than picketing outside the factory, simply sat inside the plant, thereby blocking both production and the use of strikebreakers. Conservatives were outraged, but Upton Sinclair said, "For seventy-five years big business has been sitting down on the American people, and now I am delighted to see the process reversed."

The CIO won major victories, despite bitter opposition from industry and its allies. The issue was not wages but labor's right to organize and bargain with management. Sit-down strikes paralyzed General Motors in 1937 after it refused to recognize the United Auto Workers. GM tried to force the strikers out of its Flint, Michigan, plants by turning off the heat, using police and tear gas, threatening strikers' families, and securing court orders to clear the plant by military force. But the governor refused to order National Guardsmen to attack, and the strikers held out, aided by the Women's Emergency Brigade, working-class women who picketed the building, heckled the police, and smuggled food to the strikers. After six weeks, GM signed a contract with the UAW. Chrysler soon followed suit. Ford refused to recognize the union until 1941, often violently disrupting organizing efforts.

Steel companies also used violence against unionization. In the Memorial Day Massacre in Chicago in 1937, police guarding a plant of the Republic Steel Company fired on strikers and their families, killing ten people as they tried to flee. Scores more were wounded and beaten in a police frenzy so violent that theaters refused to show a newsreel of the event. A Senate investigation found that Republic and other companies had hired private police to attack workers seeking to unionize, stockpiled weapons and tear gas, and corrupted authorities. The investigators concluded that "private corporations dominate their employees, deny them their constitutional rights, promote disorder and disharmony, and even set at naught the powers of the government itself." Federal court orders finally forced the companies to bargain collectively.

New Deal labor legislation, government investigations and court orders, and the federal refusal to use force against strikes helped the labor movement secure basic rights for American workers. Union membership leaped from under 3 million in 1932 to 9 million by 1939, and workers won higher wages, better working conditions, and more economic democracy.

Women and the New Deal

As federal programs proliferated in 1933, a Baltimore women's group urged the administration to "come out for a square and new deal for women." Although women did gain increased attention and influence, government and society remained largely bound by traditional values.

New Deal relief programs had a mixed impact on working women. Formal government policy required "equal consideration" for women and men, but local officials so flouted this requirement that Eleanor Roosevelt urged Harry Hopkins to "impress on state administrators that the women's programs are as important as the men's. They are so apt to forget us!" Women on relief were restricted to "women's work"—more than half worked on sewing projects, regardless of their skills—and were paid scarcely half what men received. WPA training programs also reinforced traditional ideas about women's work; black women, for example, were trained to be maids, dishwashers, and cooks. Although women constituted nearly one-fourth of the labor force, they obtained only 19 percent of the jobs created by the WPA, 12 percent of those created by the FERA, and 7 percent of those created by the CWA. The CCC excluded women altogether. Still, relief agencies provided crucial assistance to women in the depression.

Other New Deal programs also had mixed benefits for women. Despite demands by the League of Women Voters and the Women's Trade Union League for "equal pay for equal work and equal opportunity for equal ability regardless of sex," many NRA codes mandated lower wage scales for women than for men, which officials justified as reflecting "long-established customs." But by raising minimum wages, the NRA brought relatively greater improvements to women, who were concentrated in the lowest paid occupations, than to male workers. The Social Security Act did not cover domestic servants, waitresses, and women who worked in the home, but it did help mothers with dependent children.

Still more significant, the Social Security Act reflected and reinforced prevailing notions about proper roles for men and women. The system was based on the idea that men should be wage earners and women should stay at home as wives and mothers. Accordingly, if women worked outside the home and their husbands were eligible for benefits, those working women would not receive their own retirement pensions. And if women were without husbands but had children, welfare authorities removed them from work-relief jobs, regardless of whether they wanted to continue to work, and gave them assistance from the Aid to Dependent Children (ADC) program, which was also created under the Social Security Act. These new programs, then, while providing much needed assistance, also institutionalized a modern welfare system that segregated men and women in separate spheres and reaffirmed the then popular belief that the success of the family depended on that separation.

Women also gained political influence under the New Deal, although Molly Dewson, the director of the Women's Division of the Democratic party, exaggerated when she exclaimed, "The change from women's status in government before Roosevelt is unbelievable." Dewson herself exercised considerable political power and helped to shape the party's campaigns. Around Dewson revolved a network of women, linked by friendships and experiences in the National Consumers' League, Women's Trade Union League, and other progressive reform organizations. Appointed to many positions in the Roosevelt administration, they helped develop and implement New Deal social legislation. Secretary of Labor Frances Perkins was the first woman cabinet member and a key member of the network; other women were in the Treasury Department, the Children's Bureau, and relief and cultural programs.

Eleanor Roosevelt was their leader. Described by a Washington reporter as "a cabinet member without portfolio," she roared across the social and political landscape of the 1930s, pushing for women's rights, demanding reforms, traveling across the country, writing newspaper columns and speaking over the radio, developing plans to help unemployed miners in West Virginia and abolish slums in Washington, and lobbying both Congress and her husband. FDR used her as his eyes and ears and sometimes his conscience. He rebuffed her critics with a jaunty, "Well, that is my wife; I can't do anything about her." Indeed, Eleanor Roosevelt had become not merely the most prominent first lady in history but also a force in her own right and a symbol of the growing importance of women in public life.

Minorities and the New Deal

Despite the move of African Americans into the Democratic party, the New Deal's record on racial issues was limited. Although Roosevelt deplored racial abuses, he never pushed for civil rights legislation, fearing to antagonize the influential Southern Democrats in Congress whose support he needed. For similar reasons, many New Deal programs discriminated against African Americans. The CCC segregated black workers; NRA codes so often specified lower wages and benefits for black workers than for white workers or even excluded black workers from jobs that the black press claimed NRA stood for "Negro Run Around" or "Negroes Ruined Again." And racist officials discriminated in allocating federal relief. Atlanta, for instance, provided average monthly relief checks of $32.66 to white people but only $19.29 to black people.

However, disproportionately poor and unemployed African Americans did benefit from the New Deal's welfare and economic programs. W.E.B. Du Bois asserted that "large numbers of colored people in the United States would have starved to death if it had not been for the Roosevelt policies," adding that the New Deal served to sharpen their sense of the value of citizenship by making clear the "direct connection between politics and industry, between government and work, [and] between voting and wages." And key New Dealers campaigned against racial discrimination. Eleanor Roosevelt prodded FDR to appoint black officials, wrote articles supporting racial equality, and flouted segregationist laws. Attacked by white racists, she was popular in the black community. Harry Hopkins and Harold Ickes also promoted equal rights. Ickes, a former president of Chicago's NAACP chapter, insisted that African Americans receive PWA relief jobs in proportion to their share of the population and ended segregation in the Department of the Interior, prompting other cabinet secretaries to follow suit. As black votes in Northern cities became important, more pragmatic New Dealers also began to pay more attention to black needs.

African Americans themselves pressed for reforms. Civil rights groups protested discriminatory policies, including the unequal wage scales in the NRA codes and the CCC's limited enrollment of black youth. African Americans demonstrated against racial discrimination in hiring and their exclusion from federally financed construction projects.

In response, FDR took more interest in black economic and social problems. He prohibited discrimination in the WPA in 1935, and the NYA adopted enlightened racial policies. Roosevelt also appointed black people to important positions, including the first black federal judge. Many of these officials began meeting regularly at the home of Mary McLeod

With an appointment in the National Youth Administration, the educator Mary McLeod Bethune served as the highest-ranking African American woman in the Roosevelt administration. She advised FDR on all racial matters and envisioned "dozens of Negro women coming after me, filling positions of trust and strategic importance."

Bethune of the National Council of Negro Women. Dubbed the Black Cabinet, they worked with civil rights organizations, fought discrimination in government, influenced patronage, and stimulated black interest in politics.

The New Deal improved economic and social conditions for many African Americans. Black illiteracy dropped because of federal education projects, and the number of black college students and graduates more than doubled, in part because the NYA provided student aid to black colleges. New Deal relief and public health programs reduced black infant mortality rates and raised life expectancy rates. Conditions for black people continued to lag behind those for white people, and discrimination persisted, but the black switch to the Roosevelt coalition reflected the New Deal's benefits.

Native Americans also benefited from the New Deal. The depression had imposed further misery on a group already suffering from poverty, wretched health conditions (their life expectancy was the lowest of any group in the United States and their infant mortality rate the highest), and the nation's lowest educational level. Many New Deal programs had limited applicability to Indians, but the CCC appealed to their interests and skills. More than eighty thousand Native Americans received training in agriculture, forestry, and animal husbandry, along with basic academic subjects. CCC projects, together with those undertaken by the PWA and the WPA, built schools, hospitals, roads, and irrigation systems on reservations.

New Deal officials also refocused government Indian policy, which had undermined tribal authority and promoted assimilation by reducing Indian landholding and attacking Native American culture. Protests had been ignored. Appointed commissioner of Indian affairs in 1933, John Collier, a former social worker committed to reform, prohibited interference with Native American religious or cultural life, directed the Bureau of Indian Affairs to employ more Native Americans, and prevented Indian schools from suppressing native languages and traditions.

Collier also persuaded Congress to pass the Indian Reorganization Act of 1934, often called the Indians' New Deal. The act guaranteed religious freedom, reestablished tribal self-government, and halted the sale of tribal lands. It also provided funds to expand Indian landholdings, support Native American students, and establish tribal businesses. But social and economic problems persisted on the isolated reservations, and white missionaries and business interests attacked Collier's reforms as atheistic and communistic. And not all Native Americans supported Collier's reforms, asserting that he, too, stereotyped Indians and their culture and labeling his efforts as "back-to-the-blanket" policies designed to make Native American cultures historical commodities. Finally, Collier himself was disappointed by Congress' refusal to support his more radical proposals or to fund the economic programs designed to make Indians self-sufficient, acknowledging at the end of the decade that much more needed to be done for Native Americans (see American Views, "The Commissioner of the Bureau of Indian Affairs on the New Deal for Native Americans").

Hispanic Americans received less assistance from the New Deal. Its relief programs aided many Hispanics in California and the Southwest but ignored those who were not citizens. Moreover, local administrators often discriminated against Hispanics, especially by providing higher relief payments to Anglos. Finally, by excluding agricultural workers, neither the Social Security Act nor the Wagner Act gave Mexican Americans much protection or hope. Farm workers remained largely unorganized, exploited, and at the mercy of agribusinesses.

The New Deal: North, South, East, and West

"We are going to make a country," President Roosevelt declared, "in which no one is left out." And with that statement along with his belief that the federal government must take the lead in building a new "economic constitutional order," FDR ensured that his New Deal programs and policies fanned out throughout the nation, bolstering the stock market and banking in New York, constructing public housing for poor immigrant families and African Americans in most major cities, and building schools, roads, and bridges in all regions of the United States. Ironically, the New Deal also offered special benefits to the South, traditionally averse to government activism, and to the West, which considered itself the land of rugged individualism.

The New Deal's agricultural program boosted farm prices and income more in the South than any other region. By controlling cotton production, it also promoted diversification; its subsidies financed mechanization. The resulting modernization helped replace an

The Commissioner of the Bureau of Indian Affairs on the New Deal for Native Americans

John Collier, refomer and social worker, served as the Bureau of Indian Affairs (BIA) commissioner from 1933 until 1945. During his tenure, he radically transformed the agency—long known to be corrupt and hostile to Native Americans—into an organization committed to the preservation of tribal cultures and the restoration of Indian lands. Like other New Dealers, Collier attempted to use the power of the federal government to protect such groups as Native Americans, who had been without political power or economic influence. Collier was extraordinarily successful in promoting the restoration of tribal rights and autonomy and helped ensure that future generations of Native Americans could reclaim their lands. Yet, he was also frustrated by Congress' unwillingness to fund the programs he believed necessary for a genuine New Deal for Native Americans. In his 1938 annual report, he calls for greater economic support, arguing that it would be a good investment for the nation. Most important, even as he acknowledges that real changes have occurred since 1933, he also points up that there was still much to be done to achieve political autonomy and economic self sufficiency for American Indians.

How did Collier describe the treatment of Native Americans and why did white Americans regard Indians as a "problem" to be eliminated?

What were the new goals of the Bureau of Indian Affairs?

How did Collier regard the role of land in Native American society? Why?

What was the greatest challenge Collier saw for Native Americans in 1938?

For nearly 300 years white Americans, in our zeal to carve out a nation made to order, have dealt with the Indians on the erroneous, yet tragic, assumption that the Indians were a dying race—to be liquidated. We took away their best lands; broke treaties, promises; tossed them the most nearly worthless scraps of a continent that had once been wholly theirs. But we did not liquidate their spirit. The vital spark which kept them alive was hardy. So hard, indeed, that we now face an astounding and heartening fact.

Actually, the Indians, on the evidence of federal census rolls of the past eight years, are increasing almost twice the rate of the population as a whole.

With this fact before us, our whole attitude toward the Indians has necessarily undergone a profound change. Dead is the centuries-old notion that the sooner we eliminate this doomed race, preferably humanely, the better. . . . No longer can we naively talk of or think of the "Indian problem."

We, therefore, define our Indian policy somewhat as follows: So productively to use the moneys appropriated by the Congress for Indians as to enable them, on good, adequate land of their own, to earn decent livelihoods and lead self-respecting, organized lives in harmony with their own aims and ideals, as an integral part of American life. This will not happen tomorrow; perhaps not in our lifetime; but with the revitalization of Indian hope due to the actions and attitudes of this government during the last few years, that aim is a probability, and a real one. . . .

So intimately is all of Indian life tied up with the land and its utilization that to think of Indians is to think of land. The two are inseparable. Upon the land and its intelligent use depends the main future of the American Indian.

The Indian feels toward his land, not a mere ownership but a devotion and veneration befitting that what is not only a home but a refuge. . . . Not only does the Indian's major source of livelihood derive from the land but his social and political organizations are rooted in soil.

Since 1933, the Indian Service has made a concerted effort—an effort which is as yet but a mere beginning—to help the Indian to build back his landholdings to a point where they will provide an adequate basis for a self-sustaining economy, a self-satisfying social organization.

Source: John Collier, Annual Report of the Secretary of the Interior for the Fiscal Year Ended June 30, 1938. From www.historymatters.gmu.edu.

archaic sharecropping system with an emergent agribusiness. The rural poor were displaced, but the South's agricultural economy advanced.

The New Deal also improved Southern cities. FERA and WPA built urban sewer systems, airports, bridges, roads, and harbor facilities. Whereas Northern cities had already constructed such facilities themselves—and were still paying off their debts—the federal government largely paid for such modernization in the South, giving its cities an economic advantage.

Federal grants were supposed to be awarded to states in proportion to their own expenditures, but while Southern politicians welcomed New Deal funds—"I'm gonna grab all I can for the state of Texas," said Governor Lee O'Daniel—they refused to contribute their share of the costs. Nationally, the federal proportion of FERA expenditures was 62 percent; in the South, it was usually 90 percent and never lower than 73 percent. Virginia officials refused to provide even 10 percent, declaring, "It takes people a long time to starve." Some Southern cities and counties refused to contribute anything to relief, and Memphis spent less on relief—only 0.1 percent of its budget—than on maintaining public golf courses.

Federal money enabled Southern communities to balance their own budgets, preach fiscal orthodoxy, and maintain traditional claims of limited government. Federal officials complained of the South's "parasitic" behavior in accepting aid but not responsibility, and even Southerners acknowledged the hypocrisy of the region's invocation of state's rights. "We recognize state boundaries when called on to give," noted the *Houston Press*, "but forget them when Uncle Sam is doing the giving."

The federal government had a particularly powerful impact on the South with the **Tennessee Valley Authority (TVA)**, launched in 1933 (see Map 8-2). Coordinating activities across seven states, the TVA built dams to control floods and generate hydroelectric power, produced fertilizer, fostered agricultural and forestry development, encouraged conservation, improved navigation, and modernized school and health systems. Private utility companies denounced the TVA as socialistic, but most Southerners supported it. Its major drawback was environmental damage that only became apparent later. Over a vast area of the South, it provided electricity for the first time.

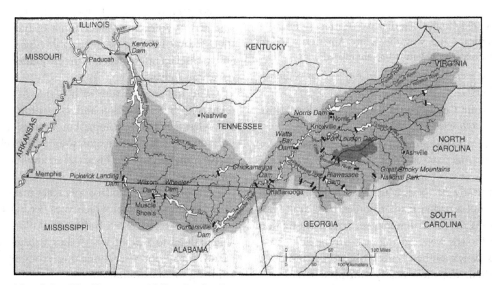

MAP 8-2 The Tennessee Valley Authority
By building dams and hydroelectric power plants, the TVA controlled flooding and soil erosion and generated electricity that did much to modernize a large region of the Upper South.

The New Deal further expanded access to electricity by establishing the Rural Electrification Administration (REA) in 1935. Private companies had refused to extend power lines into the countryside because it was not profitable, consigning 90 percent of the nation's farms to drudgery and darkness. The REA revolutionized farm life by sponsoring rural nonprofit electric cooperatives. By 1941, 35 percent of American farms had electricity; by 1950, 78 percent. By providing electric power to light and heat homes and barns, pump water, and run refrigerators, washing machines, and radios, one Arkansas newspaper concluded, the REA had made "a reality" of what had been only a "utopian dream."

The New Deal also changed the West. Westerners received the most federal money per capita in welfare, relief projects, and loans. Like Southerners, they accepted federal aid and clamored for more. Utah, which received the most federal relief funds per capita, was the nation's "prize 'gimme state,'" said one FERA official. Western farmers and cattle raisers were saved by federal payments, and even refugees from the Dust Bowl depended on relief assistance and medical care in federal camps.

The Bureau of Reclamation, established in 1902, emerged as one of the most important government agencies in the West. It built huge dams to control the Western river systems and promote large-scale development. The Hoover Dam on the Colorado River between Nevada and Arizona, completed in 1935; the Grand Coulee Dam on the Columbia River in Washington, finished in 1941; and other giant projects prevented flooding, produced cheap hydroelectric power, and created reservoirs and canal systems to bring water to farms and cities. By furnishing capital and expertise, the government subsidized and stimulated Western economic development, particularly the growth of agribusiness.

Westerners welcomed such assistance but rarely shared the federal goals of rational resource management. Instead, they often wanted to continue to exploit the land and resented federal supervision as colonial control. In practice, however, the government worked in partnership with the West's agribusinesses and timber and petroleum industries.

The New Deal and Public Activism

Despite Hoover's fear that government responsibility would discourage local initiative, the 1930s witnessed an upsurge in such activism. New Deal programs, in fact, often encouraged or empowered groups to shape public policy and social and economic behavior. Moreover, because the administration worried about centralization, some federal agencies fostered what New Dealers called "grass-roots democracy." The AAA set up committees totaling more than one hundred thousand people to implement agricultural policy and held referendums on crop controls; local advisory committees guided the various federal arts projects; federal management of the West's public grasslands mandated cooperation with associations of livestock raisers.

At times, local administration of national programs enabled groups to exploit federal policy for their own advantage. Wealthy planters shaped AAA practices at the expense of poor tenant farmers; local control of TVA projects excluded black people. But federal programs often allowed previously unrepresented groups to contest traditionally dominant interests. By requiring that public housing projects be initiated locally, for example, New Deal programs prompted labor unions, religious and civic groups, neighborhood associations, and civil rights groups to form associations to overcome the hostility of realty agents and bankers to public housing. Often seeing greater opportunities for participation and influence in federal programs than in city and state governments, such community groups campaigned to expand federal authority. In short, depression conditions and New Deal programs actually increased citizen involvement in public affairs.

EBBING OF THE NEW DEAL

After his victory in 1936, Roosevelt committed himself to further reforms. "I see one-third of a nation ill-housed, ill-clad, ill-nourished," he declared in his second inaugural address. "The test of our progress is not whether we add more to the abundance of those who have much; it is whether we provide enough for those who have too little." But determined opponents, continuing economic problems, and the president's own misjudgments blocked his reforms and deadlocked the New Deal.

Challenging the Court

Roosevelt regarded the Supreme Court as his most dangerous opponent. During his first term, the Court had declared unconstitutional several important measures. FDR complained that the justices held "horse-and-buggy" ideas about government that prevented the president and Congress from responding to changes. Indeed, most of the justices were elderly conservatives, appointed by Republicans and unsympathetic to an activist federal government. It seemed that the court would also strike down the Second New Deal.

Emboldened by the 1936 landslide, Roosevelt decided to restructure the federal judiciary. In early 1937, he proposed legislation authorizing the president to name a new judge for each one serving past the age of 70. Additional judges, he said, would increase judicial efficiency, but his real goal was to appoint new judges more sympathetic to the New Deal.

His court plan led to a divisive struggle. The proposal was perfectly legal: Congress had the authority, which it had used repeatedly, to change the number of judges on the Court. But Republicans and conservative Democrats attacked the plan as a scheme to "pack" the Court and subvert the separation of powers among the three branches of government. Some conservatives called the president a "dictator," but even many liberals expressed reservations about the plan or FDR's lack of candor in proposing it.

The Court itself undercut support for FDR's proposal by upholding the Social Security and Wagner Acts and minimum-wage legislation. Moreover, the retirement of a conservative justice allowed Roosevelt to name a sympathetic successor. Congress rejected Roosevelt's plan.

Roosevelt's challenge to the Court hurt the New Deal. It worried the public, split the Democratic party, and revived conservatives. Opponents promptly attacked other New Deal policies, from support for unions to progressive taxation. Henceforth, a conservative coalition of Republicans and Southern Democrats in Congress blocked FDR's reforms.

More Hard Times

A sharp recession, beginning in August 1937, added to Roosevelt's problems. The New Deal's deficit spending had reflected his desire to alleviate suffering, not a conviction that it would stimulate economic recovery. As the economy improved in 1936, Roosevelt decided to cut federal expenditures and balance the budget, but private investment and employment remained stagnant, and the economy plunged. A record decline in industrial production canceled the gains of the previous two years, and unemployment leaped from 7 million to 11 million within a few months. Republicans delighted in attacking the "Roosevelt recession," although it stemmed from retrenchment policies they themselves had advocated.

In 1938, Roosevelt reluctantly increased spending. His decision was based on the principles of British economist John Maynard Keynes. As Marriner Eccles of the Federal Reserve Board explained, the federal government had to serve as the "compensatory agent" in the economy: It should use deficit spending to increase demand and production when private investment declined and raise taxes to pay its debt and cool the economy when business activity became excessive. New appropriations for the PWA and other government programs revived the faltering economy, but neither FDR nor Congress would spend what was necessary to end the depression. Only the vast expenditures for World War II would bring full recovery.

Political Stalemate

The recession interrupted the momentum of the New Deal and strengthened its opponents. In late 1937, their leaders in Congress issued a "conservative manifesto" decrying New Deal fiscal, labor, and regulatory policies. Holding seniority in a Congress malapportioned in their favor, they blocked most of Roosevelt's reforms. None of his "must" legislation passed a special session of Congress in December. In 1938, Congress rejected tax reforms and reduced corporate taxes.

The few measures that passed were heavily amended. The Fair Labor Standards Act established maximum hours and minimum wages for workers but authorized so many exemptions that one New Dealer asked "whether anyone is subject to this bill." The Farm Tenancy Act established the Farm Security Administration to lend money to tenant farmers and agricultural laborers to acquire their own land, but appropriations were so limited that centuries would have been required to meet the need. The National Housing Act created the United States Housing Authority to finance slum clearance and public housing projects, but its total funds were less than what was needed to demolish tenements in New York City alone.

To protect the New Deal, Roosevelt turned again to the public, with whom he remained immensely popular. In the 1938 Democratic primaries, he campaigned against the New Deal's conservative opponents, but FDR could not transfer his personal popularity to the political newcomers he supported. What his foes attacked as a "purge" failed. Roosevelt lost further political leverage when the Republicans gained seventy-five seats in the House and seven in the Senate and thirteen governorships.

The 1938 elections did not repudiate the New Deal, for the Democrats retained majorities in both houses of Congress. But the Republican revival and the survival of the conservative Southern Democrats guaranteed that the New Deal had gone as far as it ever would. With Roosevelt in the White House and his opponents controlling Congress, the New Deal ended in political stalemate.

GOOD NEIGHBORS AND HOSTILE FORCES

Even before FDR's conservative opposition derailed the New Deal, the President felt the impact of congressional limitations in the area of foreign policy as well. Isolationists in Congress counseled against any U.S. involvement in world affairs and appealed to the growing national disillusionment with America's participation in the Great War to support their position.

Responding to the spreading popular belief that World War I had been fought to protect the fortunes of financiers and munitions makers, Republican Senator Gerald Nye established a committee in 1934 to investigate the origins of U.S. involvement in what many Americans termed the European War. For two years, the Nye Committee sensationally exposed the greed of big business and intimated that President Woodrow Wilson had gone to war to save profits for capitalists—and not democracy for the world. Jobless and homeless Americans reacted with anger to the committee's findings and public sentiment against fighting another "foreign" war hardened. Moreover, Roosevelt himself, although not an isolationist, believed that the gravity of the nation's economic depression warranted a primary focus on domestic recovery, and in the early years of his presidency, he took few international initiatives.

Those actions he did take related directly to salvaging America's desperate economy. As the depression worsened in 1933, American businesses searched for new markets throughout the world, and key business leaders informed FDR that they would welcome the opportunity to expand trade to the Soviet Union. Moscow was also eager to renew ties to the United States, and President Roosevelt extended formal recognition of the Soviet Union in November 1933. His decision was not without controversy; even his own mother denounced him for it. Still worse, the anticipated trade did not occur, although FDR believed that establishing diplomatic ties with the Soviets also served as a warning signal to Japan and its expansionist appetite.

Enhancing trade opportunities and rescuing the economy from the damage wrought by high tariffs figured prominently in Roosevelt's policies in the Western Hemisphere. In large measure, Roosevelt merely extended the Good Neighbor policy begun by President Herbert Hoover. Hoover had altered the U.S. policy of interventionism so that by the time he left office in March 1933, all U.S. troops had been removed from Latin America. Still, the Great Depression strained U.S.–Latin American relations, sending economic shock waves throughout Central and South America and, in several instances, helping propel to power ruthless dictators who ruled with iron fists and U.S. support. Moreover, although FDR continued the policy of military nonintervention, displeased with the 1933 election of a radical in Cuba as president, he supported a coup there, which resulted in the coming to power of the infamous dictator Fulgencio Batista; the Batista era lasted until it was overthrown by Fidel Castro in 1959.

Symbolic of "good neighbors," FDR visited the Caribbean in 1934, receiving an enthusiastic reception, and in 1936, he broke new ground by becoming the first U.S. president to sail to South America. He also worked to encourage trade by reducing tariffs. Between 1929 and 1933, the volume of trade worldwide had collapsed by 40 percent and American exports had plummeted by 60 percent. Eager to increase American exports, Secretary of State Cordell Hull, who, like Roosevelt himself, believed in the need for lower tariffs, finalized trade agreements with numerous Latin American nations that allowed "most favored nation" status and resulted in sharply increasing U.S. exports to its southern neighbors. Good neighbors were also good trading partners.

Neutrality and Fascism

Outside the hemisphere, during his first term as president, Roosevelt generally followed the policy of avoiding involvement in Europe's political, economic, and social problems. But the aggressive actions of Adolf Hitler in Germany ultimately led Roosevelt to a different position, and in the latter part of the decade, he faced the task of educating the American public, still resentful of U.S. participation in World War I, about the fascist danger that was spreading in Europe. Hitler came to power in 1933, shortly before FDR entered the White House, and he pledged to restore German pride and nationalism in the aftermath of the Versailles Treaty. As the leader of the National Socialist Workers Party—the Nazis—Hitler established a **fascist government**—a one-party dictatorship—closely aligned with corporate interests, committed to a "biological world evolution," and determined to establish a new empire, the Third Reich. He vowed to eliminate Bolshevik radicalism and purify the German "race" through the elimination of those he deemed undesirable, especially targeting the Jewish population—a group Hitler blamed for most, if not all, Germany's ills.

Others aided the spread of fascism. Italian leader Benito Mussolini, who had assumed power in 1922 and envisaged emulating the power and prestige of the Roman empire, brutally attacked Ethiopia in 1935. The following year, a young fascist military officer, Francisco Franco, led an uprising in Spain, and with the assistance of Italy and Germany, successfully ousted the Spanish Republicans by 1939 to create an authoritarian government. Meanwhile, Hitler implemented his plan of conquest: He remilitarized the Rhineland in 1936 and in 1938 he annexed Austria.

But the aggressive actions of Germany and Italy failed to eclipse American fears of being led into another European war. And Congress, too, made known its strong disinclination to get involved in international conflict by passing four Neutrality Acts designed to continue America's trade with its world partners but prohibit the president from taking sides in the mounting European crisis. The first act, passed in 1935, prohibited Americans from traveling to a war zone, banned loans to belligerent nations, and instituted an embargo on armaments to belligerents. The following year Congress extended the legislation for another year and then in 1937 made the neutrality prohibitions permanent, with the addition of a "cash-and-carry" provision that required belligerent nations to pay for American goods in advance of their shipment. President Roosevelt reluctantly signed the bill into law but continued to work to heighten public awareness of the dangers of Nazism.

Appeasement and More Neutrality After annexing Austria, Hitler pushed again in 1938 when he demanded the Sudetenland from Czechoslovakia. The French and the British refused to stand up to Hitler's insatiable reach, following instead a policy of appeasement. Meeting in Munich in September 1938, the leaders of England and France met with Hitler and Mussolini and abandoned their security obligations to the Czechs, yielding the Sudetenland to Hitler in exchange for a weak promise of no more annexations.

In America, too, the sentiment was for peace at all costs, and isolationism permeated the halls of Congress. Indeed, Hitler himself did not regard the United States as a threat to his expansionist plan: "America," he said in 1939, "is not dangerous to us." Hitler held FDR in low esteem and denounced America as a racially mixed nation of intellectual inferiors. "Transport a German to Kiev," Hitler declared, "and he remains a perfect German. But transplant him to Miami, and you make a degenerate out of him—in other words, an American." Isolationism also combined with anti-Semitism and with division among America's Jewish leadership to ensure that the United States would not become a haven for Jews suffering under Nazi brutality. News of Nazi atrocities against Austrian Jews in 1938 shocked the American press, and Hitler's violent pogrom, known as *Kristallnacht* (the Night of the Broken Glass), conducted against Jews throughout Germany in November 1938, added fresh proof of Nazi cruelty. Although the United States recalled its ambassador from Berlin to protest the pogrom (in response, Germany recalled its ambassador from Washington), the United States failed to alter its restrictive immigration quota system, the 1924 National Origins Act, to provide refuge for German Jews. Unchallenged, Hitler pressed on with his campaign of persecution and terror against what he termed "inferior races" and "anti-socials," herding Jews, Slavs, homosexuals, and handicapped citizens into concentration camps. As early as 1933, Hitler had established the first concentration camp at Dachau and by 1939, camps in Germany held over twenty-five thousand people.

As Europe edged closer to war, the relationship between the United States and Japan, periodically tense in the twentieth century, became more strained. Japan resented U.S. economic interests in East Asia and was offended by American immigration policy that excluded Japanese immigrants. The United States regarded Japan's desires for empire as threatening but also needed Japan as a trading partner, especially in the economically depressed 1930s. Consequently, in September 1931, when Japan seized Manchuria, the United States did little more than denounce the action. Again in 1937, when Japanese troops attacked Chinese forces north of Beijing in an effort to extend Japanese economic influence, and outright war began between Japan and China, the United States merely condemned the action. And although, that same year, President Roosevelt denounced "the epidemic of world lawlessness," indicting the aggressiveness of Italy, Germany, and Japan and calling for a "quarantine" of aggressors, he continued his policy of refusing to risk war with Japan.

Edging Toward Involvement

After the Munich agreement, President Roosevelt moved away from domestic reform toward preparedness for war, fearful that conflict in Europe was unavoidable and determined to revise the neutrality laws. In his State of the Union address in January 1939, FDR explained that "our neutrality laws" might "actually give aid to an aggressor and deny it to the victim." By the fall of that year, he had won support for eliminating the prohibition of arms and adding armaments to the list of cash-and-carry items—a revision that would enable the United States to provide important assistance to Britain and France in the winter of 1939–1940. Hitler's defiance of the Munich agreement and his conquest of all of Czechoslovakia by March 1939 merely anticipated his next move toward Poland later that summer and also convinced the British and the French that war was imminent.

CONCLUSION

The Great Depression and the New Deal mark a major divide in American history. The depression cast doubt on the traditional practices, policies, and attitudes that underlay not only the nation's economy but its social and political institutions and relationships as well. The New Deal failed to restore prosperity, but it did bring partial economic recovery. Moreover, its economic policies, from banking and securities regulation to unemployment compensation, farm price supports, and minimum wages, created barriers against another depression. The gradual adoption of compensatory spending policies also expanded the government's role in the economy. Responding to the failures of both private organizations and state and local governments, the federal government also assumed the obligation to provide social welfare. The New Deal established pensions for the elderly, aid for dependent mothers and children and the blind, public housing for the poor, and public health services. Although such programs were limited in scope and access, they helped establish a responsible government. "Better the occasional faults of a Government that lives in a spirit of charity," Roosevelt warned, "than the constant omission of a Government frozen in the ice of its own indifference."

Roosevelt also expanded the role of the presidency. As his White House took the initiative for defining public policy, drafting legislation, lobbying Congress, and communicating with the nation, it became the model for all subsequent presidents. Not only was the president's power increased, but Roosevelt also made the federal government, rather than state or local governments, the focus of public interest and expectations. Under Hoover, one secretary had handled all the White House mail; under FDR, a staff of fifty was overwhelmed.

Roosevelt and the New Deal also revitalized the Democratic party, drawing minorities, industrial workers, and previously uninvolved citizens into a coalition with white Southerners. The tensions in such a coalition sometimes prevented effective public policies, but the coalition made the Democrats the dominant national party.

Political constraints explained some of the New Deal's failures. Conservative Southern Democrats and Northern Republicans limited its efforts to curtail racial discrimination or protect the rural and urban poor. But Roosevelt and other New Dealers were often constrained by their own vision, refusing to consider the massive deficit spending necessary to end the depression or not recognizing the need to end gender discrimination. But if the New Deal did not bring the revolution its conservative critics claimed—it did not redistribute wealth or income—it did change American life.

By the end of the 1930s, as international relations deteriorated, FDR was already considering a shift, as he later said, from Dr. New Deal to Dr. Win-the-War. Reluctant to move beyond public opinion that did not want war and neutrality legislation that limited America's support of its allies, FDR cautiously led the nation toward war—this time against an enemy, he believed, far more threatening than even the Great Depression. Ironically, only then would President Roosevelt end the depression that had ravaged a nation for nearly a decade.

Review Questions

1. Describe the relief programs of the New Deal. What were they designed to accomplish? What were their achievements and their limitations?

2. What were the major criticisms of the early New Deal? How accurate were those charges?

3. How did the policies of the New Deal shape the constituency and the prospects of the Democratic party in the 1930s?

4. Describe the conflict between management and labor in the 1930s. What were the major issues and motivations involved? How did the two sides differ in resources and tactics, and how and why did these factors change over time?

5. How did the role of the federal government change in the 1930s? What factors were responsible for those changes?

6. What were Roosevelt's key international concerns at the end of the decade? What was the response of the American public and Congress to the prospect of U.S. involvement in war?

Key Terms

Congress of Industrial Organizations *228*
Fascist government *238*
Federal Deposit Insurance Corporation
  (FDIC) *218*
Fireside chat *218*

New Deal *217*
Securities and Exchange Commission
  (SEC) *219*
Tennessee Valley Authority (TVA) *234*

Recommended Reading

Paul Conkin, *The New Deal*, 3d ed. (1992). A brief and insightful critique of FDR's programs.

Steve Fraser and Gary Gerstle, eds., *The Rise and Fall of the New Deal Order, 1930–1980* (1989). A valuable collection of essays that surveys the New Deal and explores its legacy.

Frank Freidel, *Franklin D. Roosevelt: A Rendezvous with Destiny* (1990). The best one-volume biography of FDR.

David Kennedy, *Freedom from Fear: The American People in Depression and War* (1999). The most recent and comprehensive survey of the period.

William Leuchtenburg, *Franklin D. Roosevelt and the New Deal, 1932–1940* (1963). The best single-volume study of FDR's policies during his first two terms as president.

Harvard Sitkoff, ed., *Fifty Years Later: The New Deal Evaluated* (1985). The New Deal analyzed in an excellent selection of essays.

WORLD WAR II: 1939-1945

The Dilemmas of Neutrality

Holding the Line

Mobilizing for Victory

War and Peace

Conclusion

The scene [under the stadium] at The University of Chicago would have been confusing to an outsider, if he could have eluded the security guards and gained admittance. He would have seen only what appeared to be a crude pile of black bricks and wooden timbers. . . .

Finally, the day came when we were ready to run the experiment. We gathered on a balcony about 10 feet above the floor of the large room in which the structure had been erected. Beneath us was a young scientist, George Weil, whose duty it was to handle the last control rod that was holding the reaction in check. . . .

Finally, it was time to remove the control rods. Slowly, Weil started to withdraw the main control rod. On the balcony, we watched the indicators which measured the neutron count and told us how rapidly the disintegration of the uranium atoms under their neutron bombardment was proceeding.

At 11:35 A.M., the counters were clicking rapidly. Then, with a loud clap, the automatic control rods slammed home. The safety point had been set too low.

It seemed a good time to eat lunch. During lunch everyone was thinking about the experiment but nobody talked much about it.

At 2:30, Weil pulled out the control rod in a series of measured adjustments. Shortly after, the intensity shown by the indicators began to rise at a slow but ever-increasing rate. At this moment we knew that the self-sustaining [nuclear] reaction was under way.

The event was not spectacular, no fuses burned, no lights flashed. But to us it meant that release of atomic energy on a large scale would be only a matter of time.

—Enrico Fermi

December, 1942

Enrico Fermi, in *The First Reactor* (Washington, DC: U.S. Department of Energy, 1982), accessed at http://hep.uchicago.edu/cp.

ENRICO FERMI was describing the first controlled nuclear chain reaction—the critical experiment from which atomic weapons and atomic power would soon develop. Fermi himself had emigrated to escape the growing political repression of Fascist Italy. In 1938, he had received a Nobel Prize in physics. When he accepted the prize in Stockholm, Sweden, the family put secret plans into action and immigrated to the United States rather than returning to Italy. As the United States joined the ongoing global conflict of World War II, Fermi was placed in charge of nuclear fission research at the University of Chicago in 1942 and played a leading role in efforts to develop an atomic bomb. The following year found Fermi, other atomic scientists, and their families at Los Alamos, a science city that the government built hurriedly on a high plateau in northern New Mexico, where isolation was supposed to ensure secrecy and help the United States win the race with Nazi Germany to develop atomic weapons.

The instant city was a cross between a cheap subdivision and an army camp for deeply engaged but eccentric scientists. "I always pitied our Army doctors for their thankless job," Enrico's wife Laura Fermi later wrote: "They had prepared for the emergencies of the battlefields, and they were faced instead with a high-strung bunch of men, women, and children. . . . high-strung because we were too many of a kind, too close to one another, and we were all crackpots." Scientists spent their days designing a bomb that would change world politics and returned to dinners cooked on wood-burning stoves.

The Fermis were not the only family to give Los Alamos a multinational flavor. Laura remembered that it was "all one big family and all one big accent. . . . Everybody in science was there, both from the United States and from almost all European countries." British and Canadians worked alongside U.S. scientists. So did refugees from Europe who made Los Alamos the most distinguished collection of physicists in the world and contributed greatly to American victory (Laura Fermi later wrote about them in the book *Illustrious Immigrants*). Niels Bohr had fled Denmark to escape Nazi invasion. Edward Teller was a Hungarian who had studied in Germany. Hans Bethe had left Germany, and Stanislaus Ulam was the only member of his family to survive the Nazi conquest of Poland. Absent were scientists from the Soviet Union, which was bearing the worst of the fighting against Germany but was carefully excluded from the secret of the atomic bomb.

The internationalism of Los Alamos mirrored the larger war effort. Japan's attack on Pearl Harbor in December 1941 thrust the United States into a war that spanned the globe. U.S. allies against Japan in the Pacific and East Asia included Great Britain, Australia, and China. In Europe, its allies against Nazi Germany and Fascist Italy included Great Britain, the Soviet Union, and more than twenty other nations. The men and women racing to perfect the atomic bomb knew that victory was far from certain. Germany and Japan had piled one conquest on another since the late 1930s, and they continued to seize new territories in 1942. Allied defeat in a few key battles could have resulted in standoff or Axis victory. Not until 1944 did American economic power allow the United States and its allies to feel confident of victory. A new weapon might end the war more quickly or make the difference between victory and defeat.

The war's domestic impacts were as profound as its international consequences. The race to build an atomic bomb was only one part of a vast effort to harness the resources of the United States to the war effort. The war highlighted racial inequalities, gave women new opportunities, and fostered growth in the South and West. By devastating the nation's commercial rivals, compelling workers to retrain and factories to modernize, World War II left the United States dominant in the world economy. It also increased the size and scope of the federal government and built an alliance among the armed forces, big business, and science that helped shape postwar America.

KEY TOPICS

The reluctance of most Americans to get involved in World War II.

FDR's effort to support Britain and pressure Japan despite isolationism.

The nation's strategy for a two-front war against Germany and Japan.

The roles of the different allied nations in defeating Germany.

The social and economic transformation of the United States by the war.

The beginning of the Cold War and the emergence of the United States as a superpower.

THE DILEMMAS OF NEUTRALITY

Americans in the 1930s wanted no part of another overseas war. According to a Gallup Poll in 1937, 70 percent thought that the United States had made a mistake to fight in 1917. Despite two years of German victories and a decade of Japanese aggression against China, opinion polls in the fall of 1941 showed that a majority of voters still hoped to avoid war. President Roosevelt's challenge was to lead the United States toward rearmament and support for Great Britain and China without alarming a reluctant public.

The Roots of War

The roots of World War II can be found in the aftereffects of World War I. The peace settlement after that war created a set of small new nations in eastern Europe that were vulnerable to aggression from large neighbors such as Germany and the Soviet Union (officially the Union of Soviet Socialist Republics, or USSR). Italy and Japan thought that the Treaty of Versailles failed to recognize their stature as world powers. Many Germans were convinced that Germany had been betrayed rather than defeated in 1918. In the 1930s, economic crisis undermined an already shaky political order. Unemployment rose in every country and the level of international trade worldwide dropped by two-thirds. Economic hardship and political instability fueled the rise of right-wing dictatorships that offered territorial expansion by military conquest as the way to redress old rivalries, dominate trade, and gain access to raw materials.

Japanese internal propaganda in the 1930s stressed the need to rebuild Japan's greatness. Japanese nationalists believed that the United States, Britain, and France had treated Japan unfairly after World War I, despite its participation against Germany. They believed that Japan should expel the French, British, Dutch, and Americans from Asia and create a **Greater East Asia Co-Prosperity Sphere**, in which Japan gave the orders and other Asian peoples complied. Adding Manchuria to an East Asian empire that included Korea and Taiwan emboldened Japan's military in 1931. A full-scale invasion of China followed in 1937. Japan took many of the key cities and killed tens of thousands of civilians in the "rape of Nanking" but failed to dislodge the government of Jiang Jieshi (Chiang Kai-shek) and settled into a war of attrition.

Italian aggression embroiled Africa and the Mediterranean. The Fascist dictator Benito Mussolini had sent arms and troops to aid General Francisco Franco's right-wing rebels in Spain. The three-year civil war, which ended with Franco's victory in 1939, became a bloody testing ground for new German military tactics and German and Italian ambitions against democratic Europe.

In Germany, Adolf Hitler mixed the desire to reassert national pride and power after the defeat of World War I with an ideology of racial hatred. Coming to power by constitutional means in 1933, Hitler quickly consolidated his grip by destroying opposition parties and

• CHRONOLOGY •

1931	Japan invades Manchuria.
1933	Hitler takes power in Germany.
1935	Congress passes first of three Neutrality acts.
	Italy invades Ethiopia.
1936	Germany and Italy form the Rome-Berlin Axis.
	Civil war erupts in Spain.
1937	Japan invades China.
1938	Germany absorbs Austria.
	Munich agreement between Germany, Britain, and France.
1939	Germany and the Soviet Union sign a nonagression pact.
	Germany absorbs Czechoslovakia.
	Germany invades Poland; Great Britain and France declare war on Germany.
1940	Germany conquers Denmark, Norway, Belgium, the Netherlands, and France.
	Japan, Germany, and Italy sign the Tripartite Pact.
	Germany bombs England in the Battle of Britain.
	The United States begins to draft men into the armed forces.
	Franklin Roosevelt wins an unprecedented third term.
1941	The United States begins a lend-lease program to make military equipment available to Great Britain and later the USSR.
	The Fair Employment Practices Committee is established.
	Germany invades the Soviet Union.
	Roosevelt and Churchill issue the Atlantic Charter.
	Japan attacks U.S. military bases in Hawaii.
1942	American forces in the Philippines surrender to Japan.

President Roosevelt authorizes the removal and internment of Japanese Americans living in four western states.

Naval battles in the Coral Sea and off the island of Midway blunt Japanese expansion.

U.S. forces land in North Africa.

Soviet forces encircle a German army at Stalingrad.

The first sustained and controlled nuclear chain reaction takes place at the University of Chicago.

1943	U.S. and British forces invade Italy, which makes terms with the Allies.
	Racial conflict erupts in riots in Detroit, New York, and Los Angeles.
	The landing of Marines on Tarawa initiates the island-hopping strategy.
	U.S. war production peaks.
	Roosevelt, Churchill, and Stalin confer at Tehran.
1944	Allied forces land in Normandy.
	The U.S. Navy destroys Japanese sea power in the battles of the Philippine Sea and Leyte Gulf.
	The Battle of the Bulge is the last tactical setback for the Allies.
1945	Roosevelt, Stalin, and Churchill meet at Yalta to plan the postwar world.
	The United States takes the Pacific islands of Iwo Jima and Okinawa.
	Franklin Roosevelt dies; Harry S. Truman becomes president.
	Germany surrenders to the United States, Great Britain, and the USSR.
	The United Nations is organized at an international meeting in San Francisco.
	Potsdam Conference.
	Japan surrenders after the detonation of atomic bombs over Hiroshima and Nagasaki.

made himself the German Führer, or absolute leader. Proclaiming the start of a thousand-year Reich (empire), he combined the historic German interest in eastward expansion with a long tradition of racialist thought about German superiority. In the Nazi scheme, Germany and other northern European nations ranked above the Slavs of eastern Europe, who were to be pushed aside in order to provide more territory for a growing German population.

Special targets of Nazi hatred were Jews, who were prominent in German business and professional life but who soon faced persecution aimed at driving them from the country. In 1935, the "Nuremberg laws" denied civil rights to Jews and the campaign against them

The raspy-voiced Adolf Hitler had a remarkable ability to stir the German people. He and his inner circle made skillful use of propaganda, exploiting German resentment over the country's defeat in World War I and, with carefully staged mass rallies, such as this event in 1938, inspiring an emotional conviction of national greatness.

intensified. On November 9, 1938 in vicious attacks that became known as *Kristallnacht* (Night of the [Broken] Glass), Nazi thugs rounded up, beat, and murdered Jews, smashed property, and burned synagogues. The Nazi government began expropriating Jewish property and excluded Jews from most employment.

Germany and Italy formed the Rome-Berlin Axis in October 1936 and the Tripartite Pact with Japan in 1940, leading to the term **Axis Powers** to describe the aggressor nations. Political dissidents in all three nations had already been suppressed. Mussolini boasted of burying the "putrid corpse of liberty." Politicians in Japan feared assassination if they spoke against the army, and the Thought Police intimidated the public. Hitler's Germany, however, was the most repressive. The Nazi concentration camp began as a device for political terrorism, where socialists and other dissidents and "antisocials"—homosexuals and beggars—could be separated from "pure" Germans. In the camps, the inmates were overworked and abused. Hitler decreed that opponents should disappear into "night and fog." After conquering Poland, Nazi officials began to force Jews to wear yellow six-pointed stars. Homosexuals had to wear a pink triangle. Soon the systematic discrimination and concentration camps would evolve into massive forced labor camps and then into hellish extermination camps.

Hitler's War in Europe

After annexing Austria and Czechoslovakia through diplomatic bullying and uncontested coups, Germany demonstrated the worthlessness of the Munich agreement by invading Poland on September 1, 1939. Britain and France, Poland's allies, declared war on Germany but did nothing to stop the German war machine. Western journalists covering the three-week conquest of Poland coined the term *Blitzkrieg*, or "lightning war," to describe the German tactics. Armored divisions with tanks and motorized infantry quickly punched

MAP 9-1   Axis Europe, 1941, on the Eve of Hitler's Invasion of the Soviet Union

holes in defensive positions and raced forward 30 or 40 miles per day. Dive bombers blasted defenses. Portable radios coordinated the tanks, trucks, and motorcycles. Ground forces with horse-drawn artillery and supply wagons encircled the stunned defenders.

Hitler's greatest advantage was the ability to attack when and where he chose. From September 1939 to October 1941, Germany marched from victory to victory (see Map 9-1). Striking from a central position against scattered enemies, Hitler chose the targets and timing of each new front: eastward to smash Poland in September 1939; northward to capture Denmark and Norway in April and May 1940; westward to defeat the Netherlands, Belgium, and France in May and June 1940, an attack that Italy also joined; southward into the Balkans, enlisting Hungary, Romania, and Bulgaria as allies and conquering Yugoslavia and Greece in April and May 1941. Hitler also launched the Battle of Britain in the second half of 1940. German planes bombarded Britain mercilessly, in an unsuccessful effort to pound Britain into submission.

Hitler gambled once too often in June 1941. Having failed to knock Britain out of the war, he invaded the Soviet Union. The attack caught the Red Army off guard. The Nazis and Soviets had signed a nonagression pact in 1939, and the USSR had helped to dismember Poland. The Soviet dictator Joseph Stalin had disregarded warnings of a German buildup as a British attempt to goad him into war with Germany. Hitler hoped that smashing the USSR and seizing its vast resources would make Germany invincible. From June until December 1941, more than 4 million Germans, Italians, Hungarians, and Romanians pushed through Belarus, Ukraine, and western Russia. They encircled and captured entire Soviet armies. Before desperate Soviet counterattacks and a bitter winter stopped the German columns, they had reached the outskirts of Moscow and expected to finish the job in the spring.

Trying to Keep Out

"We Must Keep Out!" shouted the September 7, 1939, *Chicago Daily News*. As war erupted in Europe, most Americans wanted to avoid foreign quarrels. People who opposed intervention in the European conflict were sometimes called isolationists, but they considered themselves realists. Drawing their lessons from 1914–1918, they assumed that the same situation applied in 1939. For more than two years after the invasion of Poland, strong isolationist sentiment shaped public debate and limited President Roosevelt's ability to help Britain and its allies.

Much of the emotional appeal of neutrality came from disillusionment with the American crusade in World War I which had failed to make the world safe for democracy. Many opponents of intervention wanted the United States to protect its traditional spheres of interest in Latin America and the Pacific. The aviator Charles A. Lindbergh spoke for many when he argued that the best way to assure the safety of the United States was to conserve resources to defend the Western Hemisphere. Like George Washington, whose Farewell Address they quoted, they wanted to avoid becoming entangled in the perpetual quarrels of the European nations.

Congressional hearings by the Nye committee on munitions manufacturers and financiers had strengthened antiwar leanings. Between 1935 and 1937, Congress had passed five neutrality acts, which forbade arms sales and limited economic relations with nations at war. Other legislation prohibited loans to nations that had not paid their debts from World War I (including France and Great Britain). Noninterventionists spanned the political spectrum from left-leaning labor unions to such ultraconservative business tycoons as Henry Ford. The country's ethnic variety complicated U.S. responses. Nazi aggression ravaged the homelands of Americans of Polish, Czech, Greek, and Norwegian ancestry. In contrast, some Irish Americans, resentful of centuries of English rule of Ireland, applauded defeats that weakened Britain's empire. German Americans remembered the rabid anti-German sentiment of World War I and dreaded a second fight with Germany, while Mussolini had admirers among Italian Americans. Any move to intervene in Europe had to take these different views into account, meaning that Roosevelt had to move the United States slowly and carefully to the side of Britain.

Edging Toward Intervention

Despite the Nazi triumphs, nonintervention had direct emotional appeal. The case for supporting beleaguered Britain and China, by contrast, rested on such abstract values as the worth of free societies and free markets. Still, Roosevelt's appeals to democratic values gained support in 1939 and 1940. Radio broadcasts from England describing London under German bombing heightened the sense of imperiled freedom. The importance of open markets also bolstered interventionism. As Roosevelt pointed out, "Freedom to trade is essential to our economic life. We do not eat all the food we produce; we do not burn all the oil we can pump; we do not use all the goods we can manufacture." U.S. business leaders had little doubt that Axis victories would bring economic instability and require crushing defense budgets to protect "Fortress America."

Because 85 percent of the American people agreed that the nation should fight only if it was directly attacked, Roosevelt had to chip away at neutrality. The first step came in October 1939. A month-long congressional debate inspired millions of letters and telegrams in favor of keeping the arms embargo against warring nations. Nevertheless, the lawmakers reluctantly allowed arms sales to belligerent nations on a "cash-and-carry" basis, to avoid expanding European debts. In control of the Atlantic, France and Britain were the only expected customers. Meanwhile, the president helped Americans understand the connections between the wars in Europe and in East Asia. He popularized the expression, "the Second World War" and gradually convinced the nation that it faced a truly global challenge.

Isolationism and anti-Semitism help to explain why the United States accepted only a few thousand Jewish refugees. American law strictly limited the numbers of Europeans who could enter the United States, and Congress in 1939 declined to authorize the entry of 20,000 Jewish children above the quotas. Bureaucrats at the State Department blocked entry to "undesirables," such as left-wing opponents of Hitler, and were unsympathetic to Jewish refugees. In 1939, officials turned the passenger ship *St. Louis* away from Miami and forced its 950 German Jewish refugees back to Europe. FDR made small gestures, such as allowing fifteen thousand German and Austrian refugees, including many scientists and artists, to remain in the United States on visitor permits, but polls showed that the public supported restrictions on immigration. The consequences of these restrictions would prove tragic later in the war, as the Nazis began systematic genocide of European Jews.

The Collapse of France and U.S. Rearmament Despite the efforts of isolationists, in 1940 the United States edged close to involvement in the war. In May, the Roosevelt administration established the National Defense Advisory Commission and the Council of National Defense to deal with the strategic planning necessary to get the economy and the government prepared for war. The collapse of France in June 1940 scared Americans into rearming. The United States had a very powerful navy, but its land forces ranked only eighteenth in the world in size. However, the sudden defeat of France, which had survived four years of German attacks in World War I, made the new war seem far more serious. In the summer of 1940, Congress voted to expand the army to 2 million men, build 19,000 new war planes, and add 150 ships to the navy. Lawmakers approved the nation's first peacetime draft in September, requiring 16.5 million men between the ages of 21 and 35 to register for military service on October 16.

In the same month, the United States concluded a "destroyer deal" with Britain. The British were desperate for small, maneuverable warships to guard imports of food and war materials against German submarines. The Americans had long wanted additional air and naval bases to guard the approaches to North America. Roosevelt met both needs by trading fifty old destroyers for the use of bases on British territories in the Caribbean, Bermuda, and Newfoundland.

The Election of 1940 In the presidential election of 1940, however, foreign policy was secondary. Wendell Willkie, the Republican nominee, was a successful lawyer and utility executive who had fought the New Deal. Combining a homespun manner and a sharp mind, he differed from many in his party by sharing Roosevelt's belief in the importance of aid to Britain. The big campaign issue was therefore whether FDR's unprecedented try for a third term represented arrogance or a legitimate concern for continuity in a time of peril. The election was tighter than in 1932 or 1936, but Roosevelt received 55 percent of the vote. The president pledged that no Americans would fight in a foreign war. But if the United States were attacked, he said privately, the war would no longer be "foreign."

The Brink of War

After the election, FDR and his advisers edged the United States toward stronger support of Britain and put pressure on Japan. In January 1941, Roosevelt proposed the "lend-lease" program, which allowed Britain to "borrow" military equipment for the duration of the war. Roosevelt compared the program to lending a garden hose to a neighbor whose house had caught fire. Senator Robert Taft of Ohio countered that it was more like lending chewing gum, since you wouldn't want it back after it was used. Behind the scheme was Britain's inability to pay for American goods. "Well, boys," their ambassador explained to a group of reporters, "Britain's broke."

The **Lend-Lease Act** triggered intense political debate. The Committee to Defend America by Aiding the Allies argued the administration's position. In opposition, the strongly isolationist America First Committee claimed that lend-lease would allow the president to declare anything a "defense article." Their spokesperson, Charles Lindbergh, protested that the United States should not surrender weapons that it might need to defend itself. Congress finally passed the measure in March 1941, authorizing the president to lease, lend, or otherwise dispose of arms and other equipment to any country whose defense was considered vital to the security of the United States. The program proved invaluable in aiding Great Britain, to which the United States extended unlimited credit, and later in assisting the Soviet Union.

FDR soon began an undeclared war in the North Atlantic, instructing the navy to report sightings of German submarines to the British. In September, the U.S. destroyer *Greer* clashed with a German submarine. The encounter allowed Roosevelt to proclaim a "shoot on sight" policy for German subs and to escort British convoys to within 400 miles of Britain. In reply, German submarines torpedoed and damaged the destroyer *Kearny* on October 17 and sank the destroyer *Reuben James*, with the loss of more than one hundred lives, on October 30. After the attack on the *Reuben James*, Congress repealed parts of the Neutrality Act of 1939 to allow U.S. merchant ships to be armed and to carry munitions to Great Britain. The United States was now approaching outright naval war with Germany in the storm-churned waters of the Atlantic.

The Atlantic Charter With U.S. ships on a war footing in the North Atlantic, Roosevelt and the British prime minister, Winston Churchill, met secretly off Newfoundland in August 1941 to map out military strategy and goals for a postwar world. They agreed that the defeat of Germany was their first priority, and Japan was secondary. Their joint proclamation, known as the **Atlantic Charter**, provided a political umbrella for American involvement in the war. Echoing Woodrow Wilson, Roosevelt insisted on a commitment to oppose territorial change by conquest, to support self-government, to promote freedom of the seas, and to create a system of economic collaboration. Churchill signed to keep Roosevelt happy, but the document papered over sharp differences in U.S. and British expectations about the future of world trade and European colonial possessions.

Roosevelt's intent in the North Atlantic remains uncertain. Some historians think that he hoped the United States could support Britain short of war. Others believe that he accepted the inevitability of war but hesitated to outpace public opinion (the House of Representatives renewed the military draft in August 1941 by just one vote). In this second interpretation, FDR wanted to eliminate Hitler without going to war if possible, with war if necessary. "I am waiting to be pushed into the situation," he told his secretary of the treasury.

Events in the Pacific That final shove came in the Pacific rather than the Atlantic. In 1940, as part of its rearmament program, the United States decided to build a "two-ocean navy." This decision antagonized Japan, prodding it toward a war that most U.S. leaders hoped to postpone or avoid. Through massive investment and national sacrifice, Japan had achieved roughly 70 percent of U.S. naval strength by late 1941. However, America's buildup promised to reduce that ratio to only 30 percent by 1944. Furthermore, the United States was restricting Japan's vital imports of steel, iron ore, and aluminum in an effort to curb its military aggression. In July 1941, after Japan occupied French Indochina, Roosevelt froze Japanese assets in the United States, blocked shipments of petroleum products, and began to build up U.S. forces in the Philippines. These actions caused Japan's rulers to consider war against the United States while Japan still had a petroleum reserve. Both militarily and economically, it looked in Tokyo as if 1942 was Japan's last chance for victory.

The Japanese military made its choice in September. Unless the United States and Britain ended aid to China and acquiesced in Japanese dominance of southeast Asia—impossible conditions—war preparations would be complete in October. The Japanese General Staff defined its aims as "expelling American, Dutch, and British influences from East Asia, consolidating Japan's sphere of autonomy and security, and constructing a new order in greater East Asia." War planners never seriously considered an invasion of the United States or expected a decisive victory. They hoped that attacks on American Pacific bases would shock the United States into letting Japan have its way in Asia or at least win time to create impenetrable defenses in the central Pacific.

December 7, 1941

Since 1941, Americans have questioned Roosevelt's foreign policy. If he wanted an excuse for war, was the torpedoing of the *Reuben James* not enough? If he wanted to preserve armed neutrality, why threaten Japan by moving the Pacific fleet from California to Hawaii in 1940 and sending B-17 bombers to the Philippines in 1941? It now seems that Roosevelt wanted to restrain the Japanese with bluff and intimidation, so that the United States could focus on Germany, since the president and his advisors were nearly certain that defeating Hitler would require the United States's entry into the war. American moves were intended to be aggressive but measured in the Atlantic, firm but defensive in the Pacific. After July, however, Washington expected a confrontation with Japan over the oil fields and rubber plantations of Southeast Asia. Because the United States cracked Japanese codes, it knew by November that Japanese military action was imminent but expected the blow to come in Southeast Asia.

Instead, the Japanese navy launched a surprise attack on American bases in Hawaii. The Japanese fleet sailed a four-thousand-mile loop through the empty North Pacific, avoiding merchant shipping and American patrols. Before dawn on December 7, 1941, six Japanese aircraft carriers launched 351 planes in two bombing strikes on Pearl Harbor. Many islanders who saw the first wave roaring toward the U.S. bases thought they were witnessing especially realistic war games. As reports of the attack trickled in, the manager of a Honolulu radio station screamed over and over into the microphone: "This is no maneuver. This is the real McCoy!"

When the smoke cleared, Americans counted their losses: eight battleships, eleven other warships, and nearly all military aircraft damaged or destroyed, and 2,403 people killed. They could also count their good fortune. Dockyards, drydocks, and oil storage tanks remained intact because the Japanese admiral had refused to order a third attack. And the American aircraft carriers, at sea on patrol, were unharmed. They proved far more important than battleships as the war developed. Within hours, the Japanese attacked U.S. bases at Guam, Wake Island, and in the Philippines.

Speaking to Congress the following day, Roosevelt proclaimed December 7, 1941, "a date which will live in infamy." He asked for and got a declaration of war against Japan.

The Japanese attack on Pearl Harbor shocked the American people. Images of burning battleships confirmed the popular image of Japan as sneaky and treacherous and stirred a desire for revenge. The attack rendered the United States incapable of resisting Japanese aggression in Southeast Asia in early 1942, but it failed to achieve its goal of destryoing U.S. naval power in the Pacific.

Hitler and Mussolini declared war on the United States on December 11, following their obligation under the Tripartite Pact. On January 1, 1942, the United States, Britain, the Soviet Union, and twenty-three other nations subscribed to the principles of the Atlantic Charter and pledged not to negotiate a separate peace.

HOLDING THE LINE

When Japan was considering war with the United States and Great Britain in 1940, Admiral Isoroku Yamamoto, the chief of Japan's Combined Fleet, weighed the chances of victory: "If I am told to fight regardless of the consequences, I shall run wild for the first six months or a year, but I have utterly no confidence for the second or third year." The admiral was right. Japan's armies quickly conquered most of Southeast Asia; its navy forced the United States on the defensive in the central Pacific. As it turned out, Japan's conquests reached their limit after six months, but, in early 1942, it was far from clear that such would be the case. At the same time, in Europe, Allied fortunes went from bad to worse. Again, no one knew that German and Italian gains would peak at midyear. Decisive turning points did not come until

November 1942, a year after the United States had entered the war, and not until the middle of 1943 could the **Allies**—the United States, Britain, the Soviet Union, China, and other nations at war with Germany, Japan, and Italy—begin with confidence to plan for victory.

Stopping Germany

In December 1941, the United States plunged into a truly global war that was being fought on six distinct fronts (see Map 9-2). In North Africa, the British battled Italian and German armies that were trying to seize the Suez Canal, a critical transportation link to Asia. Along the 1,000 miles of the vast **Eastern Front**, Soviet armies held defensive positions as German forces, pushing deeply into Soviet territory, reached the outskirts of Moscow and Leningrad (St. Petersburg). In the North Atlantic, German submarines stalked merchant ships carrying supplies to Britain. In China, Japan controlled the most productive provinces but could not crush Chinese resistance, which was supported by supplies airlifted from British India over the high mountains of Burma ("the hump" to the aviators). In Southeast

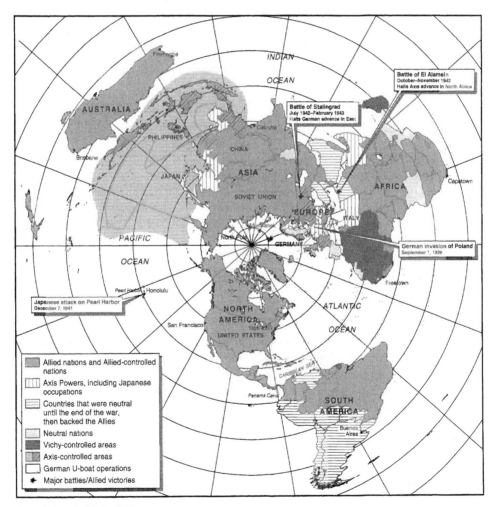

MAP 9-2 A Global War
World War II was truly a global war. As this map indicates, fighting engulfed both sides of the Eurasian continent and spread deep into the Atlantic, Pacific, and Indian oceans. The United States was the only major belligerent nation that was insulated from the battle fronts by two oceans.

Asia, Japanese troops attacked the Philippines, the Dutch East Indies (now Indonesia), New Guinea, Malaya, and Burma. In the central Pacific, the Japanese fleet faced the U.S. Navy.

Despite the popular desire for revenge against Japan, the Allies had already decided to defeat Germany first. The reasoning was simple: Germany, with its huge armies, massive industrial capacity, and technological expertise, was far stronger than Japan. Defeat of Japan would not assure the defeat of Germany, especially if it crushed the Soviet Union or starved Britain into submission. By contrast, a strategy that helped the Soviets and British survive and then destroyed German military power would doom Japan.

The Eastern Front and the Battle of Stalingrad The strategy recognized that the Eastern Front held the key to Allied hopes. In 1941, Germany had seized control of 45 percent of the Soviet population, 47 percent of its grain production, and more than 60 percent of its coal, steel, and aluminum industries. Hitler next sought to destroy the Soviet capacity to wage war. "Our aim," said the Führer Directive No. 41, "is to wipe out the entire defense potential remaining to the Soviets, and to cut them off. . . . from their most important centers of war industry." Hitler targeted southern Russia, an area rich in grain and oil. The German thrust in 1942 was also designed to eliminate the British from the Middle East.

The scheme was easier to plot on a map than to carry out in the fields of Russia. The German offensive opened with stunning success. Every day's advance, however, stretched supply lines. Tanks ran out of fuel and spare parts. The horses that pulled German supply wagons died for lack of food.

The turning point of the war in Europe came at Stalingrad (present-day Volgograd), an industrial center on the western bank of the Volga River. After initially aiming at the city, German armies had turned south toward Russian oil fields, leaving a dangerous strongpoint on their flank that the German command decided to capture. In September and October 1942, German, Italian, and Romanian soldiers fought their way house by house into the city. At night, the Soviets ferried their wounded across the Volga and brought in new ammunition. For both Hitler and Stalin, the city became a test of wills that outweighed even its substantial military importance.

The Red Army delivered a counterstroke on November 18 that cut off 290,000 Axis soldiers. Airlifts kept the Germans fighting for more than two additional months, but they surrendered in February 1943. This was the first German mass capitulation, and it came at immense human cost to both sides. The Soviet army suffered more deaths in this battle than the United States did in the entire war. Russians call the hills around Stalingrad "white fields" because human bones still turn up after spring thaws.

Behind the victory was an extraordinary revival of the Soviet capacity to make war. In the desperate months of 1941, the Soviets dismantled nearly three thousand factories and rebuilt them far to the east of the German advance in the midst of Siberian winter. As many as 25 million workers and their families followed the factories eastward. As the military took most able-bodied men, Soviet women tilled the fields and worked the machinery in the munitions plants. By the time the two armies clashed at Stalingrad, the Soviets were producing four times as many tanks and war planes as were the Germans, suggesting the outcome of the battles to come.

The Survival of Britain

After the failure of German air attacks in 1940, the British struggled to save their empire and supply themselves with food and raw materials. In World War I, German submarines (known as U-boats, from *Unterseeboot*) had nearly isolated Great Britain. In 1940 and 1941, they tried again. From bases in France, greatly improved U-boats intercepted shipments of oil from Nigeria, beef from Argentina, minerals from Brazil, and weapons from the United States. Through the end of 1941, German "tonnage warfare" sank British, Allied, and neutral merchant vessels faster than they could be replaced.

The Battle of the Atlantic The British fought back in what became known as the **Battle of the Atlantic**. Between 1939 and 1944, planning and rationing cut Britain's need for imports in half. At sea, the British organized protected convoys. Merchant ships sailing alone were defenseless against submarines. Grouping the merchant ships with armed escorts "hardened" the targets and made them more difficult to find in the wide ocean. Roosevelt's destroyer deal of 1940 and U.S. naval escorts in the western Atlantic in 1941 thus contributed directly to Britain's survival.

Nevertheless, German submarines dominated the Atlantic in 1942. U-boats operated as far as the Caribbean and the Carolinas, where the dangerous Cape Hatteras forced coastal shipping out to sea. In June 1942, U-boats sank 144 ships, and U-boats operating in "wolf-packs" continued to decimate convoys into 1943. The balance shifted only when Allied aircraft began to track submarines with radar, spot them with searchlights as they maneuvered to the surface, and attack them with depth charges. New sonar systems allowed escort ships to measure submarines' direction, speed, and depth. By the spring of 1943, American shipyards were also launching ships faster than the Germans could sink them.

British ground fighting in 1942 centered in North Africa, where the British operated out of Egypt and the Italians and Germans from the Italian colony of Libya. By October 1942, Field Marshal Erwin Rommel's German and Italian forces were within striking distance of the Suez Canal. At El Alamein, however, General Bernard Montgomery forced the enemy to retreat in early November and lifted the danger to the Middle East.

Retreat and Stabilization in the Pacific

Reports from eastern Asia after Pearl Harbor were appalling. The Japanese attack on the Philippines (Map 9-3) had been another tactical surprise that destroyed most American air power on the ground and isolated U.S. forces. In February, a numerically inferior Japanese force seized British Singapore, until then considered an anchor of Allied strength, and then pushed the British out of Burma. In a three-month siege, they overwhelmed Filipino and U.S. defensive positions on the Bataan peninsula outside Manila; thousands of their captives died of maltreatment on their way to prisoner-of-war camps in what is remembered as the Bataan Death March. On May 6, the last American bastion, the island fortress of Corregidor in Manila Bay, surrendered. The Japanese fleet was virtually undamaged at the end of April, and the Japanese army was triumphant in conquest of European and American territories in Southeast Asia.

The Battles of the Coral Sea and Midway The first check to Japanese expansion came on May 7–8, 1942, in the Battle of the Coral Sea, where U.S. aircraft carriers halted a Japanese advance toward Australia and confirmed that the U.S. navy could fight effectively. In June, the Japanese struck at the island of Midway, 1,500 miles northwest of Honolulu. Their goal was to destroy American carrier forces. The plan included a diversionary invasion of the Aleutian Islands (the westernmost parts of Alaska) and a main assault on Midway, to draw the Americans into battle on Japanese terms. Having cracked Japanese radio codes, U.S. forces were aware of the plan and refused the bait. On the morning of June 4, the Japanese and American carrier fleets faced off across 175 miles of ocean, each sending planes to search the other out. U.S. Navy dive bombers found the Japanese fleet and sank or crippled three

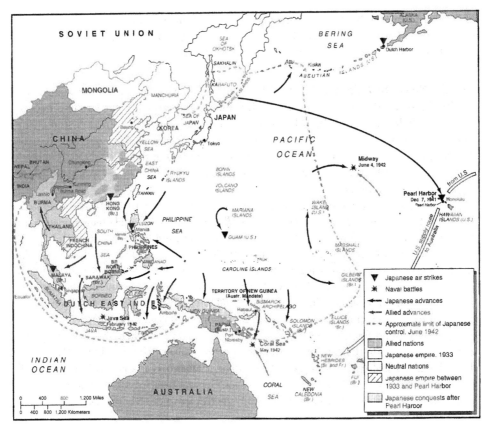

MAP 9-3   World War II in the Pacific, from Pearl Harbor to Midway
The first six months after the Japanese attack on Pearl Harbor brought a string of Japanese victories and conquests in the Pacific, the island southeast of Asia, and the British colonies of Malaya and Burma. Japan's advance was halted by a standoff battle in the Coral Sea, a decisive U.S. naval victory at Midway, and the length and vulnerability of Japanese supply lines to the most distant conquests.

aircraft carriers in five minutes; another Japanese carrier sank later in the day. The Battle of Midway ended Japanese efforts to expand in the Pacific.

MOBILIZING FOR VICTORY

News of the Japanese attack on Pearl Harbor shattered a bright Sunday afternoon. Twelve-year-old Jean Bartlett's family was headed to the movies when news of the attack came over the car radio. Elliott Johnson was eating in a Chinese restaurant in Portland, Oregon, when the proprietor burst from the kitchen with a portable radio; the line was two blocks long by the time he got to the marine recruiting office. In Cincinnati, the enormously popular Andrews Sisters found that no one had shown up for their Sunday matinee concert. "Where is Pearl Harbor?" Maxine Andrews asked the theater's doorman.

War changed the lives of most Americans for the next four years and for some forever. Millions of men and women served in the armed forces and millions more worked in defense factories. In order to keep track of this staggering level of activity, the number of civilian employees of the federal government quadrupled to 3.8 million, a much greater increase than during the New Deal. Meanwhile, youngsters saved tin foil, collected scrap metal, and followed the freedom-fighting stories of Wonder Woman in the comics. College science students were recruited to work at scientific espionage against the Nazis. The breadth of involvement in the war effort gave Americans a common purpose that softened the divisions of region, class, and national origin while calling attention to continuing inequalities of race.

Organizing the Economy

The need to fight a global war brought a huge expansion of the federal government. Congress authorized the president to reorganize existing government departments and to create new agencies. The War Manpower Commission allocated workers among vital industries and the military. The War Production Board invested $17 billion for new factories and managed $181 billion in war-supply contracts, favoring large existing corporations because they had experience in large-scale production.

The Office of Price Administration (OPA) fought inflation with price controls and rationing that began with tires, sugar, and coffee and eventually included meat, butter, gasoline, and shoes. "Use it up, wear it out, make it do or do without" was the OPA's slogan. Consumers used ration cards and ration stamps to obtain scarce products. By slowing price increases, the OPA helped to convince Americans to buy the war bonds that financed half the war spending. Americans also felt the bite of the first payroll deductions for income taxes as the government secured a steady of flow of revenue and soaked up some of the high wages that would have pushed inflation. In total, the federal budget in 1945 was $98 billion, eleven times as large as in 1939, and the national debt had increased more than sixfold.

Industry had reluctantly begun to convert from consumer goods to defense production in 1940 and 1941. By the time of the attack on Pearl Harbor, 25 percent of the national economy was devoted to military needs. Although corporations hated to give up the market for toasters and automobiles just as Americans had more money, the last passenger car for the duration of the war rolled off the assembly line in February 1942. Existing factories retooled to make war equipment, and huge new facilities turned out thousands of planes and ships. Baltimore, Atlanta, Fort Worth, Los Angeles, and Seattle became centers for aircraft production. New Orleans, Portland, and the San Francisco Bay area were shipbuilding centers. Henry J. Kaiser, who had helped to build vast projects such as the Grand Coulee Dam, turned out cargo ships by the thousands. One of the Kaiser shipyards built a Liberty ship (a standard-model cargo carrier) in ten and one-half days.

The United States applied mass production technology to

During the course of World War II, the government limited the consumption of a number of products to reserve supplies of products for the war effort and to prevent demand from pushing up the prices of scarce consumer goods. Shoppers, such as this woman at a grocery store counter, used ration stamps to obtain their share of controlled products.

aircraft production at a time when Japan was still building warplanes one at a time and Germany in small batches. The most spectacular example was the new Ford plant at Willow Run, Michigan, designed to adapt assembly-line approaches to manufacturing B-24 bombers. Where the typical automobile had 15,000 parts, a B-24 had 1,550,000. The assembly line itself was more than a mile long, starting with four separate tracks that gradually merged into one. By 1943, the plant was delivering ten planes a day. In factories all across the country, American aircraft workers were twice as productive as their German counterparts and four times more productive than Japanese.

Most defense contracts went to such established industrial states as Michigan, New York, and Ohio, but the relative impact was greatest in the South and West, where the war marked the takeoff of what Americans would later call the Sunbelt. Washington, DC, teemed with staff officers, stenographers, and other office workers who helped to coordinate the war effort. Albuquerque, New Mexico, more than doubled in population during the 1940s. War-boom cities, such as San Diego (up 92 percent in population in the 1940s) and Mobile (up 68 percent), bustled with activity and hummed with tension. Factories operated three shifts, movies ran around the clock, and workers filled the streets after midnight.

The hordes of war workers found housing scarce. Workers in Seattle's shipyards and Boeing plants scrounged for living space in offices, tents, chicken coops, and rooming houses where "hot beds" rented in shifts. The situation was similar in small towns, such as Seneca, Illinois, home to a company that normally made river barges. Between June 1942 and June 1945, it also built 157 specialized ships to land tanks in amphibious assaults. Thousands of new workers flocked to Seneca. They lined up three deep at the bars with their Friday paychecks. Residents would sometimes find a stranger rolled up in a blanket on their front porch.

The results of war production were staggering (see Figure 9-1). One historian estimates that 40 percent of the world's military production was coming from the United States by 1944. Equally impressive is the 30 percent increase in the productivity of U.S. workers between 1939 and 1945. Surging farm income pulled agriculture out of its long slump. The rich certainly got richer, but overall per capita income doubled, and the poorest quarter of Americans made up some of the ground lost during the Great Depression.

The Enlistment of Science

The war reached into scientific laboratories as well as shops and factories. "There wasn't a physicist able to breathe who wasn't doing war work," remembered Professor Philip Morrison. At the center of the scientific enterprise was Vannevar Bush, former dean at the Massachusetts Institute of Technology. As head of the newly established Office of Scientific Research and Development, Bush guided spending to develop new drugs, blood transfusion procedures, weapons systems, radar, sonar, and dozens of other military technologies. The scale of research and development dwarfed previous scientific work and set the pattern of massive federal support for science that continued after the war.

The most costly scientific effort was the development of radar, or radio detection and ranging devices. Building on British research on microwaves, the United States put $3 billion into the Radiation Laboratory at MIT. Increasingly compact and sophisticated radar systems helped defeat the German and Japanese navies and give the Allies control of the air over Europe. Radar research and engineering laid the basis for microwave technology, transistors, and integrated circuits developed after the war.

In the summer of 1945, *Time* magazine planned a cover story on radar as the weapon that won the war. However, the *Time* story was upstaged by the atomic bomb, the product of the war's other great scientific effort. As early as 1939, Albert Einstein had written to FDR about the possibility of such a weapon and the danger of falling behind the Germans. In late

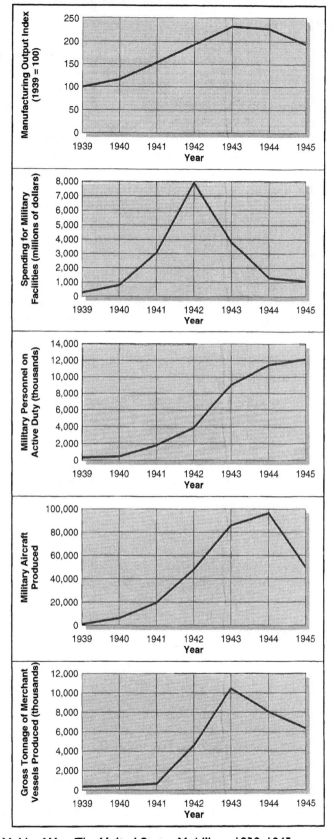

FIGURE 9-1   Making War: The United States Mobilizes, 1939–1945
The U.S. economic mobilization for World War II reached its peak in 1943, the year in which the Allies prepared for the offensives against Germany and Japan that they hoped would end the war. The number of men and women in uniform continued to grow until 1945.

1941, Roosevelt established what became known as the **Manhattan Project**. The work remained theoretical, however, until December 2, 1942, when scientists proved that it was possible to create and control a sustained nuclear reaction. Because Enrico Fermi was in charge of the experiment, the coded message of scientific discovery recalled the voyages of Columbus: "The Italian navigator has landed in the new world."

The Manhattan Project moved from theory to practice in 1943. The physicist J. Robert Oppenheimer directed the young scientists at Los Alamos in designing a nuclear-fission bomb. Engineers in other new science cities tried two approaches to producing the fissionable material. Richland, Washington, on the dusty banks of the Columbia River, burgeoned from a handful of peach farmers into a sprawling metropolis that supported the creation of plutonium at the Hanford Engineer Works. Oak Ridge, Tennessee, near Knoxville, was built around gaseous diffusion plants that separated rare and vital uranium-235 from the more common uranium-238. The two sites were chosen because of the proximity to hydroelectric power from new federal dams on the Columbia and Tennessee Rivers.

The Manhattan Project ushered in the age of atomic energy. Plutonium from Hanford fueled the first bomb tested at the Trinity site in New Mexico on July 16, 1945. The explosion astonished even the physicists; Oppenheimer quoted from Hindu scriptures as he tried to comprehend the results: "Now I am become Death, destroyer of worlds."

Men and Women in the Military

World War II required a more than thirtyfold expansion of the U.S. armed forces from their 1939 level of 334,000 soldiers, sailors, and marines. By 1945, 8.3 million men and women were on active duty in the army and army air forces and 3.4 million in the navy and Marine Corps, totals exceeded only by the Soviet Union. The military establishment was four times larger than that of World War I. Once in the military, sailors and GIs served an average of thirty-three months. In total, some 350,000 women and more than 16 million men served in the armed forces; 292,000 died in battle, 100,000 survived prisoner-of-war camps, and 671,000 returned wounded.

Most of the Americans in uniform served in support jobs that kept the war machine going. They repaired airplanes and built runways, tracked supplies, and counted coffins. The poet John Ciardi wrote out commendations for valor. Bill Mauldin drew cartoons for the Army newspaper *Stars and Stripes*. But for many readers, Mauldin's cartoon GIs, Willie and Joe, came to represent the experience of the front lines. As was true in wars through history, it was loyalty to the men in their own unit that kept fighting men steady. "The only thing that kept you going was your faith in your buddies," recalled a Marine from the Pacific theater. "You couldn't let 'em down. It was stronger than flag and country."

Twenty-five thousand American Indians served in the armed forces. Most were in racially integrated units, and Harvey Natcheez, of the Ute tribe, was the first American to reach the center of conquered Berlin. Because the Navajo were one of the few tribes that had not been studied by German anthropologists, the Army Signal Corps decided that their language would be unknown to the Axis armies. More than three hundred members of the tribe were "code-talkers" who served in radio combat-communication teams in the Pacific theater, transmitting vital information in Navajo.

Approximately 1 million African Americans served in the armed forces during World War II. African-American leaders had pressed for a provision in the Selective Service Act to bar discrimination "against any person on account of race or color." But as it had since the Civil War, the army organized black soldiers in segregated units and often assigned them to the more menial jobs, such as construction work, and excluded them from combat until manpower shortages forced changes in policy.

The average black soldier encountered discrimination on and off the base. Towns adjacent to army posts were sometimes open to white soldiers but off limits to blacks. At some Southern bases, German prisoners of war watched movies from the first rows along with white GIs while African-American soldiers watched from the back. Private Charles Wilson wrote President Roosevelt that Davis-Monthan Army Air Force Base in Tucson was color-coded: Barracks for African Americans were coated with black tar paper, and those for white soldiers sported white paint. Military courts were quick to judge and harsh to punish when black GIs were the accused. Despite the obstacles, all-black units, such as the 761st Tank Battalion and the 99th Pursuit Squadron, earned distinguished records. More broadly, the war experience helped to invigorate postwar efforts to achieve equal rights, as had also been true after World War I.

The nation had a different—but also mixed—reaction to the women who joined the armed forces as army and navy nurses and as members of the WACS (Women's Army Corps), WAVES (Navy), SPARS (Coast Guard), and Marine Corps Women's Reserve. The armed services tried not to change established gender roles. Military officials told Congress that women in uniform could free men for combat. Many of the women hammered at typewriters, worked switchboards, inventoried supplies. Others, however, worked close to combat zones as photographers, code analysts, and nurses who tended the ill and injured. WAC officers battled the tendency of the popular press to call females in the service "girls" rather than "women" or "soldiers" yet emphasized that military service promoted "poise and charm."

The greatest departure from expected roles was the work of the 1,074 members of the Women's Airforce Service Pilots (WASPS), a civilian auxiliary of the U.S. Army Air Forces. Many of the WASPS were women who had learned to fly as civilians. From 1942 to 1944, they ferried military aircraft across the United States, towed targets for antiaircraft practices, and tested new planes. Caro Bayley from Springfield, Ohio, lied about her height so that she could pilot B-25s and later flew high-hazard runs to test new radar systems. Nevertheless, WASPS were not allowed to carry male passengers, and the unit was dissolved when the supply of male pilots caught up with the demand.

The Home Front

The war inexorably penetrated everyday life. Residents in war-production cities had to cope with throngs of new workers. Especially in 1941 and 1942, many were unattached males—young men waiting for their draft call and older men without their families. They elbowed long-term residents in stores, snatched seats on the streetcars, and filled restaurants and theaters. Military and defense officials worried about sexually transmitted diseases and pressured cities to shut down their vice districts. At the same time, college officials scrambled to fill their classrooms, especially after the draft age dropped to 18 in 1942. Many colleges and universities responded to federal requests with special training programs for future officers and engineering and technical training for military personnel. Patricia Cain of Portland, Oregon, put off college to sign on as an electrician's helper in the shipyards. She remembered cartoons that asked; "What are you doing to help the war?" They showed women sipping tea, playing cards, and relaxing. "THIS?" And then a smiling woman worker with a lunch box, her hair tied up in a scarf, a large ship in the background, "Or THIS?"

Families in Wartime Americans put their lives on fast forward, as Judy Garland and Robert Walker did in the movie *The Clock* (1944). They played young people who meet in New York, fall in love, and are separated by the war in a matter of days. In real life, men and women often decided to beat the clock with instant matrimony. Couples who had postponed marriage because of the depression could afford to marry as the economy picked up. War intensified casual romances and heightened the appeal of marriage as an anchor in troubled times. Jewelers worried about running out of wedding rings. Altogether, the war years brought 1.2 million "extra" marriages, compared to the rate for the period 1920–1939.

The war's impact on families was gradual. The draft started with single men, then called up married men without children, and finally tapped fathers in 1943. Left at home were millions of "service wives," whose compensation from the government was $50 per month. Women who followed their husbands to stateside military posts and war factories often met cold welcomes from local residents. Harriet Arnow crafted a sensitive exploration of isolation from friends and family in her novel *The Dollmaker* about a Kentucky farm woman who accompanied her husband to a Detroit war plant.

The war had mixed effects on children. "Latchkey children" of working mothers often had to fend for themselves, but middle-class kids whose mothers stayed home could treat the war as an interminable scout project, with salvage drives and campaigns to sell war bonds. Children in the rural Midwest picked milkweed pods to stuff life jackets; in coastal communities, they participated in blackout drills. Seattle high schools set aside one class period a day for the High School Victory Corps, training boys as messengers for air-raid wardens, while girls knitted sweaters and learned first aid. Between the end of the school day and suppertime, children listened as Captain Midnight, Jack Armstrong, and Hop Harrigan ("America's ace of the airways") fought the Nazis and Japanese on the radio.

War Propaganda and Censorship The federal government tried to keep civilians of all ages committed to the war. It encouraged scrap drives and backyard victory gardens. The government also managed news about the fighting. Censors screened soldiers' letters. Early in the war, they blocked publication of most photographs of war casualties, although magazines such as *Life* were full of strong and haunting images. Worried about flagging commitment, censors later authorized photographs of enemy atrocities to motivate the public.

Government officials had a harder time controlling Hollywood. The Office of War Information wanted propaganda in feature films, but not so heavy-handed that it drove viewers from theaters. Officials told movie directors to tone down car chases because screeching tires implied wasted rubber. War films revealed the nation's racial attitudes, often drawing distinctions between "good" and "bad" Germans but uniformly portraying Japanese as subhuman and repulsive. The most successful films dramatized the courage of the Allies. *Mrs. Miniver* (1942) showed the British transcending class differences in their battle with the Nazis. *So Proudly We Hail* (1943) celebrated the heroism of navy nurses in the Pacific theater.

New Workers

As draft calls took men off the assembly line, women changed the composition of the industrial work force. The war gave them new job opportunities that were embodied in the image of Rosie the Riveter. Women made up one-quarter of West Coast shipyard workers at the peak of employment and nearly half of Dallas and Seattle aircraft workers. Most women in the shipyards were clerks and general helpers. The acute shortage of welders and other skilled workers, however, opened thousands of journeyman positions to them as well, work that was far more lucrative than waiting tables or sewing in a clothing factory. Aircraft companies, which compounded labor shortages by stubborn "whites only" hiring, developed new power tools and production techniques to accommodate the smaller average size of women workers, increasing efficiency for everyone along the production line.

By July 1944, fully 19 million women held paid jobs, up 6 million in four years. Women's share of government jobs increased from 19 to 38 percent and their share of manufacturing jobs from 22 to 33 percent. Mirroring the sequence in which the military draft took men, employers recruited single women before turning to married women in 1943 and 1944. Some women worked out of patriotism. Many others, however, needed to support their families and already had years of experience in the work force. As one of the workers recalled of herself and a friend, "We both had to work, we both had children, so we became welders, and if I might say so, damn good ones."

Americans did not know how to respond to the growing numbers of workingwomen. The country needed their labor, but many worried that their employment would undermine families. The federal government assisted female entry into the labor force by funding day-care programs that served 600,000 children. Employment recruitment posters showed strong, handsome women with rolled-up sleeves and wrenches in hand, but *Life* magazine reassured readers that women in factories could retain their sex appeal. Men and women commonly assumed that women would want to return to the home after victory; they were to work when the nation needed them and quit when the need was past.

Mexican-American workers made special contributions to the war effort. As defense factories and the military absorbed workers, western farms and railroads faced an acute shortage of workers. In the 1930s, western states had tried to deport Mexican nationals who were competing for scarce jobs. In 1942, however, the U.S. and Mexico negotiated the *bracero* program, under which the Mexican government recruited workers to come to the United States on six-to-twelve month contracts. More than two hundred thousand Mexicans worked on U.S. farms under the program, and more than one hundred thousand worked for western railroads. Although *bracero* workers still faced discrimination, the U.S. government tried to improve working conditions because it wanted to keep public opinion in Latin America favorable to the Allied cause.

The war was a powerful force for the assimilation of Native Americans. Forty thousand moved to off-reservation jobs; they were a key labor force for military supply depots throughout the West. The average cash income of Indian households tripled during the war. Many stayed in cities at its end. The stress of balancing tribal life and urban America is depicted in M. Scott Momaday's 1968 novel *House Made of Dawn*, which follows a World War II veteran as he moves between his home village in New Mexico and Los Angeles. The experience of the war accelerated the fight for full civil rights. Congress had made Indians citizens in 1924, in part to recognize their contributions in World War I, but several states continued to deny them the vote. Activists organized the National Congress of American Indians in 1944 and began the efforts that led the U.S. Supreme Court in 1948 to require states to grant voting rights.

African Americans, too, found economic advancement through war jobs. Early in the mobilization, labor leader A. Philip Randolph of the Brotherhood of Sleeping Car Porters worked with Walter White of the NAACP to plan a "Negro March on Washington" to protest racial discrimination by the federal government. To head off a major embarrassment, Roosevelt issued Executive Order 8802 in June 1941, barring racial discrimination in defense contracts and creating the **Fair Employment Practices Committee (FEPC)**; the order coined a phrase that reverberated powerfully through the coming decades: "No discrimination on grounds of race, color, creed, or national origin."

The FEPC's small staff resolved fewer than half of the employment discrimination complaints, and white resistance to black co-workers remained strong. In Mobile, New Orleans, and Jacksonville, agreements between shipyards and segregated unions blocked skilled black workers from high-wage jobs. Attempts to overturn discrimination could lead to violence. When the Alabama Dry Dock Company integrated its work force in May 1943, white workers rioted. Transportation workers in Philadelphia struck the following year to protest upgrading of jobs held by black workers. Nevertheless, African-American membership in labor unions doubled, and wartime prosperity raised the average black income from 41 percent of the white average in 1939 to 61 percent by 1950.

Clashing Cultures

As men and women migrated in search of work, they also crossed or collided with traditional boundaries of race and region. African-American migration out of the South accelerated in the early 1940s. Many of the migrants headed for well-established black neighborhoods in northern cities. Others created new African-American neighborhoods in western cities. White Southerners and black Northerners with different ideas of racial etiquette found themselves side by side in West Coast shipyards. In the Midwest, black migrants from the South and white migrants from Appalachia crowded into cities such as Cincinnati and Chicago, competing for the same high-wage jobs and scarce apartments.

Tensions between black and white residents exploded in at least fifty cities in 1943 alone. New York's Harlem neighborhood erupted in a riot after rumors of attacks on black servicemen. In Detroit, the issue was the boundary between white and black territories. In June 1943, an argument over the use of Detroit's Belle Isle Park set off three days of violence: Twenty-five black people and nine white people died in the most serious racial riot of the war.

Tensions were simultaneously rising between Mexican Americans and Anglos. As the Mexican community in Los Angeles swelled to an estimated four hundred thousand, newspapers published anti-Mexican articles. On June 6, 1943, off-duty sailors and soldiers attacked Latinos on downtown streets and invaded Mexican-American neighborhoods. The main targets were so-called *pachucos*—young Chicanos who wore flamboyant "zoot suits" with long, wide-shouldered jackets and pleated, narrow-cuffed trousers, whom the rioters considered delinquents or draft dodgers. The attacks dragged on for a week of sporadic violence against black people and Filipinos as well as Latinos.

Internment of Japanese Americans

On February 19, 1942, President Roosevelt issued Executive Order 9066, which authorized the secretary of war to define restricted areas and remove civilian residents who were threats to national security. The primary targets were 112,000 Japanese Americans in California and parts of Washington, Oregon, and Arizona. Japanese immigrants and their children in the western states had experienced forty years of hostility because of racial prejudice, fear of the growing power of Japan, and jealousy of their economic success as farmers and business owners. The outbreak of war triggered anti-Japanese hysteria and gave officials an excuse to take action against both enemy aliens (immigrants who retained Japanese citizenship) and their American-born children. As the U.S. general commanding on the

In 1942, the federal government removed Japanese Americans from parts of four western states and interned them in isolated camps scattered through the West.

West Coast put it, "A Jap is a Jap. It makes no difference whether he is an American citizen or not."

In the months after Pearl Harbor, some West Coast Japanese managed to move to other parts of the country, but most of them were unable to leave because of ties to families and businesses. At the end of April, Japanese in the coastal states were given a week to organize their affairs and report to assembly centers at fairgrounds and armories, where they were housed for several weeks before being moved again to ten internment camps in isolated locations in the western interior (see American Views, "The Internment of Japanese Americans in 1942"). Here, they were housed in tar-paper barracks, hemmed in by barbed wire fences, and guarded by military police. The victims reacted to the hardship and stress in different ways. Several thousand second-generation Japanese-Americans renounced their citizenship in disgust. But many others demonstrated their loyalty by cooperating with the authorities, finding sponsors who would help them move to other parts of the country, or joining the 442nd Regimental Combat Team, the most decorated American unit in the European war.

AMERICAN VIEWS

The Internment of Japanese Americans in 1942

In the spring of 1942, the U.S. Army ordered that Japanese Americans in four western states be relocated to internment camps distant from the Pacific Coast. Monica Itoe Stone describes the experience of her Seattle family as they were transferred to temporary quarters—at the state fairgrounds renamed "Camp Harmony" by the military—before they were moved again to Idaho.

How do the expectations of *issei* (immigrants who had been born in Japan) differ from those of *nisei* (their American-born children, including the author of this memoir)?

Why did the U.S. army wait five months after Pearl Harbor before beginning the internment?

Does the management of the assembly and internment suggest anything about stereotypes of Japanese Americans?

General DeWitt kept reminding us that E day, evacuation day, was drawing near. "E day will be announced in the very near future. If you have not wound up your affairs by now, it will soon be too late."

. . . On the twenty-first of April, a Tuesday, the general gave us the shattering news. "All the Seattle Japanese will be moved to Puyallup by May 1. Everyone must be registered Saturday and Sunday between 8 A.M. and 5 P.M.

Up to that moment, we had hoped against hope that something or someone would intervene for us. Now there was no time for moaning. A thousand and one details must be attended to in this one week of grace. Those seven days sputtered out like matches struck in the wind, as we rushed wildly about. Mother distributed sheets, pillowcases and blankets, which we stuffed into seabags. Into the two suitcases, we packed heavy winter overcoats, plenty of sweaters, woolen slacks and skirts, flannel pajamas and scarves. Personal toilet articles, one tin plate, tin cup and silverware completed our luggage. The one seabag and two suitcases apiece were going to be the backbone of our future home, and we planned it carefully.

Henry went to the Control Station to register the family. He came home with twenty tags, all numbered "10710," tags to be attached to each piece of baggage, and one to hang from our coat lapels. From then on, we were known as Family #10710.

[On the day set for relocation] we climbed into the truck. . . . As we coasted down Beacon Hill bridge for the last time, we fell silent, and stared out at the delicately flushed, morning sky of Puget Sound. We drove through bustling Chinatown, and in a few minutes arrived on the corner of Eighth and Lane. This area was ordinarily lonely and deserted but now it was gradually filling up with silent, labeled Japanese. . . .

(continued)

Finally at ten o'clock, a vanguard of Greyhound busses purred in and parked themselves neatly along the curb. The crowd stirred and murmured. The bus doors opened and from each, a soldier with rifle in hand stepped out and stood stiffly at attention by the door. The murmuring died. It was the first time I had seen a rifle at such close range and I felt uncomfortable. . . .

Newspaper photographers with flash-bulb cameras pushed busily through the crowd. One of them rushed up to our bus, and asked a young couple and their little boy to step out and stand by the door for a shot. They were reluctant, but the photographers were persistent and at length they got out of the bus and posed, grinning widely to cover their embarrassment. We saw the picture in the newspaper shortly after and the caption underneath it read, "japs good-natured about evacuation."

Our bus quickly filled to capacity. . . . The door closed with a low hiss. We were now the Wartime Civil Control Administration's babies.

About noon we crept into a small town. . . . and we noticed at the left of us an entire block filled with neat rows of low shacks, resembling chicken houses. Someone commented on it with awe, "Just look at those chicken houses. They sure go in for poultry in a big way here." Slowly the bus made a left turn, drove through a wire-fenced gate, and to our dismay, we were inside the oversized chicken farm. . . .

The apartments resembled elongated, low stables about two blocks long. Our home was one room, about 18 by 20 feet, the size of a living room. There was one small window in the wall opposite the one door. It was bare except for a small, tinny wood-burning stove crouching in the center. The flooring consisted of two by fours laid directly on the earth, and dandelions were already pushing their way up through the cracks. . . .

I stared at our little window, unable to sleep. I was glad Mother had put up a makeshift curtain on the window for I noticed a powerful beam of light sweeping across it every few seconds. The lights came from high towers placed around the camp where guards with Tommy guns kept a twenty-four hour vigil. I remembered the wire fence encircling us, and a knot of anger tightened in my breast. What was I doing behind a fence like a criminal? If there were accusations to be made, why hadn't I been given a fair trial? Maybe I wasn't considered an American anymore. My citizenship wasn't real, after all. Then what was I? I was certainly not a citizen of Japan as my parents were. On second thought, even Father and Mother. . . . had little tie with their mother country. In their twenty-five years in America, they had worked and paid their taxes to their adopted government as any other citizen.

Of one thing I was sure. The wire fence was real. I no longer had the right to walk out of it. It was because I had Japanese ancestors. It was also because some people had little faith in the ideas and ideals of democracy.

Source: Monica Itoe Sone, *Nisei Daughter* (Seattle: University of Washington Press, 1979).

Although the U.S. Supreme Court sanctioned the removals in *Korematsu* v. *United States* (1944), the nation officially recognized its liability with the Japanese Claims Act of 1948, for many internees had lost property that they had been powerless to protect. The nation acknowledged its broader moral responsibility in 1988, when Congress approved redress payments to each of the sixty thousand surviving evacuees.

The internment of West Coast Japanese contrasted with the treatment of Japanese Americans by the military government of Hawaii. Despite the greater threat that Japan posed to Hawaii than to California, local residents and officials avoided panic. Hawaii's long history as a multiethnic society made residents disinclined to look for a racial scapegoat. Less than 1 percent of Hawaii's Japanese-American population of 160,000 was interned. The treatment of mainland Japanese Americans also contrasted with the situation of German Americans and Italian Americans. The government interned approximately eleven thousand German nationals and German Americans who were explicitly seen as individual threats. Until November 1942, it imposed curfews and travel restrictions on Italians and Italian

Americans on the West Coast, but it interned fewer than two thousand. Both numbers were tiny fractions of the total populations.

The End of the New Deal

Roosevelt's New Deal ran out of steam in 1938. The war had reinvigorated his political fortunes by focusing national energies on foreign policy, over which presidents have the greatest power. Especially after the 1942 election left Congress in the hands of Republicans and conservative Southern Democrats, lawmakers followed the new tack. Conservative lawmakers ignored proposals that war emergency housing be used to improve the nation's permanent housing stock, abolished the National Resources Planning Board, curtailed rural electrification, and crippled the Farm Security Administration. Roosevelt himself declared that "Dr.-Win-the-War" had replaced "Dr. New Deal" at a 1943 press conference.

The presidential election of 1944 raised few new issues of substance. The Republicans nominated Governor Thomas Dewey of New York, who had made his reputation as a crime-fighting district attorney. The Democrats renominated Roosevelt for a fourth term. Missouri Senator Harry S Truman, a tough investigator of American military preparedness, replaced liberal New Dealer Henry Wallace as Roosevelt's running mate. The move appeased Southern Democrats and moved the ticket toward the political center.

The most important issue was a fourth term for Roosevelt. Supporters argued that the nation could not afford to switch leaders in the middle of a war, but Dewey's vigor and relative youth (he was twenty years younger than FDR) pointed up the president's failing health and energy. Voters gave Roosevelt 432 electoral college votes to 99, but the narrowing gap in the popular vote—54 percent for Roosevelt and 46 percent for Dewey—made the Republicans eager for 1948.

WAR AND PEACE

In January 1943, the U.S. War Department completed the world's largest office building, the Pentagon. The building housed 23,000 workers along 17.5 miles of corridors. It took three hundred telephone operators to direct the calls that came into the single Pentagon phone number for Secretary of War Henry Stimson, General George C. Marshall, and their thousands of subordinates. The building provided the space in which military planners could coordinate the tasks of raising and equipping the armed forces that would strike directly at Germany and Japan. Indeed, while Congress was chipping away at federal programs, the war effort was massively expanding the government presence in American life. The gray walls of the Pentagon symbolized an American government that was outgrowing its prewar roots.

Turning the Tide in Europe

The unanswered military question of 1942 and 1943 was when the United States and Britain would open a second front against Germany by attacking across the English Channel. U.S. leaders wanted to justify massive mobilization with a war-winning campaign and to strike across Europe to occupy the heart of Germany. Stalin needed a full-scale invasion of western Europe to divert German forces from the Eastern Front, where Soviet troops were inflicting 90 percent of German battle casualties.

The Allies spent 1943 hammering out war aims and strategies. Meeting in Casablanca in January 1943, Roosevelt and Churchill demanded the "unconditional surrender" of Italy, Germany, and Japan. The phrase meant that there would be no deals that kept the enemy governments or leaders in power and was an effort to avoid the mistake of ending World War I with Germany itself intact. Ten months later, the Allied leaders huddled again. Roosevelt and Churchill met with China's Jiang in Cairo and then flew on to meet Stalin in Tehran. Jiang and Stalin could not meet directly because the Soviet Union was neutral in the East Asian war. At Tehran, the United States and Britain promised to invade France within six months. "We leave here," said the three leaders, "friends in fact, in spirit, in purpose."

The superficial harmony barely survived the end of the war. The Soviets had shouldered the brunt of the war for nearly two-and-a-half years, suffering millions of casualties and seeing their nation devastated. Stalin and his generals scoffed at the small scale of early U.S. efforts. Roosevelt's ideal of self-determination for all peoples, embodied in the Atlantic Charter, seemed naive to Churchill, who wanted the major powers to carve out realistic spheres of influence in Europe. It was irrelevant to Stalin, who wanted control of eastern Europe.

The Campaign in North Africa The United States entered the ground war in Europe with Operation TORCH. Soon after the British victory at El Alamein, British and American troops under General Dwight Eisenhower landed in French Morocco and Algeria on November 8, 1942, against little opposition (see Map 9-4). These were territories that the Germans had left under a puppet French government after the French military collapsed in 1940. Despite the easy landings (French officials in Africa quickly switched sides), German troops that remained in North Africa taught U.S. forces hard lessons in tactics and leadership, but their stubborn resistance ended in May 1943, leaving all of Africa in Allied hands.

Eisenhower had already demonstrated his ability to handle the politics of military leadership, skills he perfected commanding a multinational army for the next two and one-half years. He also chose the right subordinates, giving operational command to Generals Omar Bradley and George Patton. Bradley was low-keyed and rock solid; to relax he worked algebra and calculus problems. Patton was a much flashier figure (he wore a pearl-handled revolver), with a mighty ego and a fierce commitment to victory.

The Invasion of Italy The central Mediterranean remained the focus of U.S. and British action for the next year. The British feared military disaster from a premature landing in western Europe and proposed strikes in southern Europe, which Churchill inaccurately called the "soft underbelly" of Hitler's empire. U.S. Army Chief of Staff George Marshall and President Roosevelt agreed to invade Italy in 1943, in part so that U.S. troops could participate in the ground fighting in Europe. Allied forces overran Sicily in July and August, but the Italian mainland proved more difficult. When Sicily fell, the Italian king and army forced Mussolini from power and began to negotiate peace with Britain and America (but not the Soviet Union). In September, the Allies announced an armistice with Italy, and Eisenhower's troops landed south of Naples. Germany responded by occupying the rest of Italy.

Just as American military planners had feared, the Italian campaign soaked up Allied resources. The mountainous Italian peninsula was one long series of defensive positions, and the Allies repeatedly bogged down. Week after week, the experience of GIs on the line was the same: "You wake up in the mud and your cigarettes are all wet and you have an ache in your joints and a rattle in your chest." Despite months of bitter fighting, the Allies controlled only two-thirds of Italy when the war there ended on May 1, 1945.

Soviet Advances and the Battle of Kursk Meanwhile, the Soviets recruited, rearmed, and upgraded new armies, despite enormous losses. They learned to outfight the Germans in tank warfare and rebuilt munitions factories beyond German reach. They also made good

MAP 9-4   World War II in Europe, 1942–1945
Nazi Germany had to defend it's conquests on three fronts. Around the Meditteranean, American and British forces pushed the Germans out of Africa and southern Italy, while guerrillas in Yugoslavia pinned down many German troops. On the Eastern Front, Soviet armies advanced hundreds of miles to drive the German Army out of the Soviet Union and eastern Europe. In June 1944, U.S. and British landings opened the Western Front in northern France for a decisive strike at the heart of Germany.

use of 17.5 million tons of U.S. lend-lease assistance. As Soviet soldiers recaptured western Russia and the Ukraine, they marched in 13 million pairs of American-made boots and ate U.S. rations (they called cans of Spam "second fronts"). They traveled in 78,000 jeeps and 350,000 Studebaker, Ford, and Dodge trucks. "Just imagine how we could have advanced from Stalingrad to Berlin without [lend-lease vehicles]," future Soviet Premier Nikita Khrushchev later commented.

The climactic battle of the German-Soviet war erupted on July 5, 1943. The Germans sent three thousand tanks against the Kursk Salient, a huge wedge that the Red Army had pushed into their lines. In 1941 and 1942, such a massive attack would have forced the Soviets to retreat, but now Soviet generals had prepared a defense in depth with three thousand tanks of their own. With 1 million men actively engaged on each side for more than two weeks, Kursk was the largest pitched battle of the war. It was a huge failure for Germany and marked the end of the last great German offensive, leaving Germany capable of a fighting retreat but too weak to have any hope of winning the war and expecting an American and British attack across the English Channel.

Operation OVERLORD

On **D-Day**—June 6, 1944—the western Allies landed on the coast of Normandy in northwestern France. Six divisions went ashore from hundreds of attack transports carrying four thousand landing craft, as vividly dramatized in the film *Saving Private Ryan*. Dozens of warships and twelve thousand aircraft provided support. One British and two American airborne divisions dropped behind German positions. When the sun set on the "longest day," the Allies had a tenuous toehold in France.

Americans had been waiting for the news. In Montgomery, Alabama, word of the invasion spread quickly by radio and then by extra editions of the newspaper. Flags appeared along the streets and traffic halted at 5:00 P.M. for buglers from nearby bases and the high school to sound the "call to the colors." At 6:00 P.M. all movie projectors were stopped to allow time for prayer.

The next few weeks brought limited success. The Allies secured their beachheads and poured more than a million men and hundreds of thousands of vehicles ashore in the first six weeks. However, the German defenders kept them pinned along a narrow coastal strip. **Operation OVERLORD**, the code name for the entire campaign across northern France, met renewed success in late July and August. U.S. troops improved their fighting skills through "experience, sheer bloody experience." They finally broke through German lines around the town of St.-Lô and then drew a ring around the Germans that slowly closed on the town of Falaise. The Germans lost a quarter of a million troops.

The German command chose to regroup closer to Germany rather than fight in France. The Allies liberated Paris on August 25; Free French forces (units that had never surrendered to the Nazis) led the entry. The drive toward Germany was the largest U.S. operation of the war. The only impediments appeared to be winter weather and getting enough supplies to the rapidly advancing armies.

The story was similar on the Eastern Front, where the Soviets relentlessly battered one section of the German lines after another. By the end of 1944, the Red Army had entered the Balkans and reached central Poland. With the end in sight, the Soviets had suffered as many as 27 million military and civilian deaths and sustained by far the heaviest burden in turning back Nazi tyranny.

Victory and Tragedy in Europe

In the last months of 1944, massive air strikes finally reduced German war production, which had actually increased during 1943 and much of 1944. The Americans flew daylight raids from air bases in Britain with heavily armed B-17s ("Flying Fortresses") and B-24s, ("Liberators") to destroy factories with precision bombing. On August 17, 1943, however, Germans shot down or damaged 19 percent of the bombers that attacked the aircraft factories of Regensburg and the ball-bearing factories of Schweinfurt. Air crews who were expected to fly dozens of missions could count the odds, and the Americans had to seek easier targets.

Gradually, however, the balance shifted. The new American P-51 escort fighter helped B-17s overfly Germany in relative safety after mid-1944. Thousand-bomber raids on railroads and oil facilities began to cripple the German economy. The raids forced Germany to devote 2.5 million workers to air defense and damage repair and to divert fighter planes from the front lines. The air raids cut German military production by one-third through 1944, destroyed the transportation system, and left Germany a set of isolated regions living off stockpiles of food and raw materials. Politics, rather than military need, governed the final great action of the European air war. British and U.S. bombers in February 1945 staged a terror raid on the nonindustrial city of Dresden, packed with refugees, filled with great art, and undefended by the Germans; a firestorm fueled by incendiary bombs and rubble from blasted buildings killed tens of thousands of civilians.

Out of the bombing raids that pitted pilots and crews against unseen enemies would come some of the most vivid efforts to relive and comprehend the experience of war. The movie *Twelve O'Clock High* (1949) focused on successive commanders of a U.S. bomber unit in Britain who became too involved with their men to function effectively. The literature of the bomber campaigns included antiwar novels like Joseph Heller's *Catch-22* (1961).

The Battle of the Bulge and the Collapse of Germany Even as the air bombardment intensified, Hitler struck a last blow. Stripping the Eastern Front of armored units, he launched twenty-five divisions against thinly held U.S. positions in the Ardennes Forest of Belgium on December 16, 1944. He hoped to split U.S. and British forces by capturing the Belgian port of Antwerp. The attack surprised the Americans, who had treated the Ardennes as a "ghost front," where nothing was going on. Taking advantage of snow and fog that grounded Allied aircraft, the Germans drove a 50-mile bulge into U.S. lines. Although Americans took substantial casualties, the German thrust literally ran out of gas beyond the town of Bastogne. The Battle of the Bulge never seriously threatened the outcome of the war, but pushing the Germans back through the snow-filled forest gave GIs a taste of the conditions that had marked the war in the Soviet Union.

The Nazi empire collapsed in the spring of 1945. American and British divisions crossed the Rhine in March and enveloped Germany's industrial core. The Soviets drove through eastern Germany toward Berlin. On April 25, American and Soviet Army troops met on the Elbe River. Hitler committed suicide on April 30 in his concrete bunker deep under devastated Berlin, which surrendered to the Soviets on May 2. The Nazi state formally capitulated on May 8.

The Holocaust The defeat of Germany revealed appalling evidence of the evil at the heart of the Nazi ideology of racial superiority. After occupying Poland in 1939, the Nazis also expanded concentration camps into forced-labor camps, where overwork, starvation, and disease killed hundreds of thousands of Jews, Gypsies, Poles, Russians, and others the Nazis classed as subhuman. As many as 7 million labor conscripts from both eastern and western Europe provided forced labor in fields, factories, mines, and repair crews, often dying on the job from overwork and starvation.

The "final solution" to what Hitler thought of as the "Jewish problem" went far beyond slave labor. The German army in 1941 had gained practice with death by slaughtering hundred of thousands of Jews and other civilians as it swept across Russia. In the fall of that year, Hitler decided on the total elimination of Europe's Jews. The elite SS, Hitler's personal army within the Nazi party, in 1942 set out to do his bidding. At Auschwitz, Treblinka, and several other death camps, the SS organized the efficient extermination of up to 6 million Jews and 1 million Poles, Gypsies, and others who failed to fit the Nazi vision of the German master race. Prisoners arrived by forced marches and cattle trains. Those who were not worked or starved to death were herded into gas chambers and then incinerated in huge crematoriums.

The evidence of genocide—systematic racial murder—is irrefutable. Allied officials had begun to hear reports of mass murder midway through the war, but inaccurate propaganda

The Nazi regime sent slave laborers who were too weak to continue working on its V-2 rocket projects to the Nordhausen concentration camp to die of starvation. When U.S. troops liberated the camp in April 1945, they found more than three thousand corpses.

about German atrocities in World War I made many skeptical. Moreover, the camps were located in the heart of German-controlled territory that Allied armies did not reach until 1945. At Dachau in southwestern Germany, American forces found 10,000 bodies and 32,000 prisoners near death through starvation. Soviet troops that overran the camps in Poland found even more appalling sights—gas chambers as big as barns, huge ovens, the dead stacked like firewood. For more than half a century, the genocide that we now call the **Holocaust** has given the world its most vivid images of inhumanity.

The Pacific War

In the Pacific, as in Europe, the United States used 1943 to probe enemy conquests and to build better submarines, bigger aircraft carriers, and superior planes. Washington divided responsibilities in the Pacific theater. General Douglas MacArthur operated in the islands that stretched between Australia and the Philippines. Admiral Chester Nimitz commanded in the central Pacific. The Allies planned to isolate Japan from its southern conquests. The British moved from India to retake Burma. The Americans advanced along the islands of the southern Pacific to retake the Philippines. With Japan's army still tied down in China, the Americans then planned to bomb Japan into submission.

Racial hatred animated both sides in the Pacific war and fueled a "war without mercy." Americans often characterized Japanese soldiers as vermin. Political cartoons showed Japanese as monkeys or rats, and some Marines had "Rodent Exterminator" stenciled on their helmets. In turn, the Japanese depicted themselves as the "leading race" with the duty to direct the rest of Asia. Japan treated Chinese, Filipinos, and other conquered peoples with contempt and brutality, and the record of Japanese atrocities is substantial. Japanese viewed

Americans as racial mongrels and called them demons. Each side expected the worst of the other and frequently lived up to expectations.

The Pacific campaigns of 1944 are often called **island hopping**. Planes from American carriers controlled the air, allowing the navy and land forces to isolate and capture the most strategically located Japanese-held islands while bypassing the rest. The process started in November 1943, when Marines took Tarawa. It worked to perfection with the assault on Saipan in June 1944. When the Japanese fleet challenged the attack, U.S. Navy flyers destroyed three aircraft carriers and hundreds of planes.

MacArthur used a version of the bypass strategy in the Solomon Islands and New Guinea, leapfrogging over Japanese strong points. The invasion of the Philippines repeated the approach by landing on Leyte, in the middle of the island chain. The Philippine campaign also destroyed the last offensive capacity of the Japanese fleet. In the Battle of Leyte Gulf, the U.S. military sank four Japanese battleships, four carriers, and ten cruisers. The Japanese home islands were left with no defensive screen against an expected invasion.

During 1943 and 1944, the United States also savaged the Japanese economy. Submarines choked off food, oil, and raw materials bound for Japan and island bases. By 1945, imports to Japan were one-eighth of the 1940 level. Heavy bombing of Japan began in early 1944, using the new long-range B-29. Japan's dense wooden cities were more vulnerable than their German counterparts, and Japanese air defenses were much weaker. A fire-bomb raid on Tokyo on the night of March 9, 1945, killed 124,000 people and left 1 million homeless; it was perhaps the single biggest mass killing of all time. Overall, conventional bombing destroyed 42 percent of Japan's industrial capacity. By the time the United States captured the islands of Iwo Jima and Okinawa in fierce fighting (April–June 1945) and neared the Japanese home islands, Japan's position was hopeless.

Searching for Peace

At the beginning of 1945, the Allies sensed victory. Conferring from February 4 to 11 in the Ukrainian town of Yalta, Roosevelt, Stalin, and Churchill planned for the postwar world. The most important American goal was to enlist the Soviet Union in finishing off the Pacific war. Americans hoped that a Soviet attack on Manchuria would tie down enough Japanese troops to reduce U.S. casualties in invading Japan. Stalin repeated his intent to declare war on Japan within three months of victory in Europe, in return for a free hand in Manchuria.

In Europe, the Allies had decided in 1944 to divide Germany and Austria into French, British, American, and Soviet occupation zones and to share control of Berlin. The Red Army already controlled Bulgaria, Romania, and Hungary, countries that had helped the Germans; Soviet officials were installing sympathetic regimes there. Soviet armies also controlled Poland. The most that Roosevelt could coax from Stalin were vague pledges to allow participation of noncommunists in coalition governments in eastern Europe. Stalin also agreed to join a new international organization, the United Nations (UN), whose foundations were laid at a conference in San Francisco in the spring of 1945. The new organization was intended to correct the mistakes of World War I, when the United States had stayed aloof from the League of Nations and had relied on the "parchment peace" of international treaties without mechanisms of enforcement. American leaders wanted the UN to provide a framework through which the United States could coordinate collective security against potential aggressors while retaining its own military strength as the primary means to preserve the peace.

Conservative critics later charged that the Allies "gave away" eastern Europe at the **Yalta Conference**. In fact, the Soviet Union gained little that it did not already control. In East Asia as well, the Soviets could seize the territories that the agreements granted them.

Roosevelt overestimated his ability to charm Stalin, but the Yalta talks could not undo the results of four years of fighting by the Soviet Army.

Truman and Potsdam On April 12, two months after Yalta, Roosevelt died of a cerebral hemorrhage. Harry Truman, the new president, was a shrewd politician, but his experience was limited; Roosevelt had not even told him about the Manhattan Project. Deeply distrustful of the Soviets, Truman first ventured into personal international diplomacy in July 1945 at a British-Soviet-American conference at Potsdam, near Berlin. Most of the sessions debated the future of Germany. The leaders endorsed the expulsion of ethnic Germans from eastern Europe and moved the borders of Poland 100 miles west into historically German territory. Truman also made it clear that the United States expected to dominate the occupation of Japan. Its goal was to democratize the Japanese political system and reintroduce Japan into the international community, a policy that succeeded. The **Potsdam Declaration** on July 26 summarized U.S. policy and gave Japan an opening for surrender. However, the declaration failed to guarantee that Emperor Hirohito would not be tried as a war criminal. The Japanese response was so cautious that Americans read it as rejection.

The Atomic Bomb Secretary of State James Byrnes now urged Truman to use the new atomic bomb, tested just weeks earlier. Japan's ferocious defense of Okinawa had confirmed American fears that the Japanese would fight to the death. Thousands of suicide missions by kamikaze pilots who tried to crash their planes into U.S. warships seemed additional proof of Japanese fanaticism. Prominent Americans were wondering if unconditional surrender was worth another six or nine months of bitter fighting. In contrast, using the bomb to end the conflict quickly would ensure that the United States could occupy Japan without Soviet participation, and the bomb might intimidate Stalin (see the Overview table, "The Decision to Use the Atomic Bomb"). In short, a decision not to use atomic weapons was never a serious alternative in the summer of 1945.

In early August, the United States dropped two of three available nuclear bombs on Japan. On August 6, at Hiroshima, the first bomb killed at least eighty thousand people and poisoned thousands more with radiation. A second bomb, three days later, at Nagasaki, took another forty thousand lives. Japan ceased hostilities on August 14 and surrendered formally on September 2. The world has wondered ever since whether the United States might have defeated Japan without resorting to atomic bombs, but recent research shows that the bombs were the shock that allowed the Emperor and peace advocates to overcome military leaders who wanted to fight to the death.

How the Allies Won

The Allies won with economic capacity, technology, and military skill. The ability to outproduce the enemy made victory certain in 1944 and 1945, but it was the ability to outthink and outmaneuver the Axis powers that staved off defeat in 1942 and 1943.

In the spring of 1942, an unbroken series of conquests had given the Axis powers control of roughly one-third of the world's production of industrial raw materials, up from only 5 percent in 1939. But while Germany and Japan struggled to turn these resources into military strength, the Soviet Union accomplished wonders in relocating and rebuilding its manufacturing capacity after the disasters of 1941. The United States, meanwhile, rearmed with astonishing swiftness, accomplishing in one year what Germany had thought would take three. By 1944, the United States was outproducing all of its enemies combined; over the course of the war, it manufactured two-thirds of all the war materials used by the Allies.

• • • O V E R V I E W • • •

THE DECISION TO USE THE ATOMIC BOMB

Americans have long argued whether the use of atomic bombs on the Japanese cities of Hiroshima and Nagasaki was necessary to end the war. Several factors probably influenced President Truman's decision to use the new weapon.

Military necessity	After the war, Truman argued that the use of atomic bombs was necessary to avoid an invasion of Japan that would have cost hundreds of thousand of lives. Military planners expected Japanese soldiers to put up the same kind of suicidal resistance in defense of the home islands as they had to American landings at the Philippines, Iwo Jima, and Okinawa. More recently, historians have argued that the Japanese military was near collapse and that an invasion would have met far less resistance than feared.
Atomic diplomacy	Some historians believe that Truman used atomic weapons to overawe the Soviet Union and induce it to move cautiously in expanding its influence in Europe and East Asia. Truman and his advisors were certainly aware of how the bomb might influence the Soviet leadership.
Domestic politics	President Roosevelt and his chief military advisers had spent billions on the secret atomic bomb project without the knowledge of Congress or the American public. The managers of the Manhattan Project may have believed that only proof of its military value would quiet critics and justify the huge cost.
Momentum of war	The United States and Britain had already adopted wholesale destruction of German and Japanese cities as a military tactic. Use of the atomic bomb looked like a variation on fire bombing, not the start of a new era of potential mass destruction. In this context, some historians argue, President Truman's choice was natural and expected.

The United States and the Soviet Union not only built more planes and tanks than the Axis nations, but they also built better ones. The Soviets developed and mass-produced the T-34, the world's most effective tank. American aircraft designers soon jumped ahead of the Germans, who were unable to update the designs that had given them the edge in the 1930s. The United States and Britain gained the lead in communication systems, radar, code-breaking capacity, and, of course, atomic weapons. Even behind the lines the Allies had the technical advantage. The U.S. and British forces that invaded France were fully motorized, and Soviet forces increasingly so, while the German army still depended on more than a million horses to draw supply wagons and artillery.

Superior technology had its great impact because the Allies learned hard lessons from defeat and figured out how to outfight the Axis. Hitler's generals outsmarted the Soviet military in 1941, Japan outmaneuvered the British and Americans in the first months of the Pacific war, and the German navy came close to squeezing the life from Great Britain in 1942. In 1943 and 1944, the tables were turned. The Russians reexamined every detail of their military procedures and devised new tactics that kept the vast German armies off guard and on the defensive. New ways to fight U-boats in the Atlantic devastated the German submarine service and staved off defeat. Americans in the Pacific utilized the full capacity of aircraft carriers, while Japanese admirals still dreamed of confrontations between lines of battleships.

Finally, the Allies had the appeal of democracy and freedom. The Axis nations were the clear aggressors. Germany and Japan made deep enemies by exploiting and abusing the people of the countries that they conquered, from Yugoslavia and France to Malaya and the Philippines, and incited local resistance movements. The Allies were certainly not perfect, but they fought for the ideals of political independence and were welcomed as liberators as they pushed back the Axis armies.

CONCLUSION

World War II changed the lives of tens of millions of Americans. It made and unmade families. It gave millions of women new responsibilities and then sent them back to the kitchen. It put money in pockets that had been emptied by the Great Depression and turned struggling business owners into tycoons. In war zones and behind the lines, it introduced millions of men and women in the armed forces to people and places outside the United States.

Whether on the home front or the fighting front, Americans knew that victory was uncertain. World War II adventure movies in which Americans always win leave the impression that triumph was necessary and inevitable. In fact, victory was the hard-fought result of public leadership and military effort. Under other leadership, the United States might have stood aside until it was too late to reverse the Axis conquest of Europe and East Asia. The collapse of the Soviet Union or failure of the North Atlantic convoy system might have made Germany unbeatable. In 1941 and 1942 in particular, Americans faced each day with fear and uncertainty.

The war unified the nation in new ways, while confirming old divisions. People of all backgrounds shared a common cause. Farm boys mixed with city slickers. Northerners with Southerners. "When I woke up the first morning on the troop train in Fulton, Kentucky," recalled one Midwesterner, "I thought I was in Timbuktu." The war narrowed the distance between native-born, small-town Americans and recent European immigrants from the big cities. The chasms between Protestant, Catholic, and Jewish Americans were far narrower in 1945 than they had been in 1940.

But nothing broke the barriers that separated white and black Americans. Unequal treatment in a war for democracy outraged black soldiers, who returned to fight for civil rights. The uprooting of Japanese Americans was another reminder of racial prejudice. After the war, however, memories of the contrast between the nation's fight against Axis tyranny and the unequal treatment of American citizens fueled a gradual shift of public attitudes that climaxed in the civil rights movements of the 1950s and 1960s.

The United States ended the war as the world's overwhelming economic power. It had put only 12 percent of its population in uniform, less than any other major combatant. For every American who died, twenty Germans and dozens of Russians perished. Having suffered almost no direct destruction, the United States was able to dictate a postwar economic trading system that favored its interests.

Nevertheless, the insecurities of the war years influenced the United States for decades. A nation's current leaders are often shaped by its last war. Churchill had directed strategy, and Hitler, Mussolini, and Truman had all fought in World War I and carried its memories into World War II. The lessons of World War II would similarly influence the thinking of presidents from Dwight Eisenhower in the 1950s to George Bush in the 1990s. Even though the United States ended 1945 with the world's mightiest navy, biggest air force, and only atomic bomb, the instability that had followed World War I made Western leaders nervous about the shape of world politics.

One result in the postwar era was conflict between the United States and the Soviet Union, whose only common ground had been a shared enemy. After Germany's defeat, their wartime alliance gave way to hostility and confrontation in the Cold War. At home, international tensions fed pressure for social and political conformity. The desire to enjoy the fruits of victory after fifteen years of economic depression and sacrifice made the postwar generation sensitive to perceived threats to steady jobs and stable families. For the next generation, the unresolved business of World War II would haunt American life.

Review Questions

1. What motivated German, Italian, and Japanese aggression in the 1930s? How did Great Britain, the USSR, and other nations respond to the growing conflict?

2. What arguments did Americans make against involvement in the war in Europe? Why did President Roosevelt and many others believe it necessary to block German and Japanese expansion? What steps did Roosevelt take to increase U.S. involvement short of war?

3. What was the military balance in early 1942? What were the chief threats to the United States and its allies? Why did the fortunes of war turn in late 1942?

4. Assess how mobilization for World War II altered life in the United States. How did the war affect families? How did it shift the regional balance of the economy? What opportunities did it open for women?

5. Did World War II help or hinder progress toward racial equality in the United States? How did the experiences of Japanese Americans, African Americans, and Mexican Americans challenge American ideals?

6. What factors were decisive in the defeat of Germany? How important were Soviet efforts on the Eastern Front, the bomber war, and the British-American landings in France?

7. What was the U.S. strategy against Japan, and how well did it work? What lay behind President Truman's decision to use atomic bombs against Japanese cities?

8. What role did advanced science and technology play in World War II? How did the scientific lead of the United States affect the war's outcome?

Key Terms

Allies *253*

Atlantic Charter *250*

Axis Powers *246*

Battle of the Atlantic *255*

Blitzkrieg *246*

D-Day *270*

Eastern Front *253*

Fair Employment Practices Committee *263*

Greater East Asia Co-Prosperity Sphere *245*

Holocaust *271*

Island hopping *273*

Lend-Lease Act *250*

Manhattan Project *260*

Operation OVERLORD *270*

Potsdam Declaration *274*

Yalta Conference *273*

Recommended Reading

Beth Bailey, and David Farber, *The First Strange Place: The Alchemy of Race and Sex in World War II Hawaii* (1992). Explores the effects of the war on American ideas about the proper roles of men and women, black people, white people, and Asian Americans.

Doris Kearns Goodwin, *No Ordinary Time: Franklin and Eleanor Roosevelt, the Home Front in World War II* (1994). Presents the tensions and crises of World War II through the daily lives of President Roosevelt and his wife Eleanor.

John Hersey, *Hiroshima* (1946). Recounts the atomic bombing through the eyes of victims and survivors.

John Keegan, *The Second World War* (1990). A comprehensive and readable account giving a strong sense of the relative importance of the various fronts.

William L. O'Neill, *A Democracy at War: America's Fight at Home and Abroad in World War II* (1993). Explores the choices that the United States made in mobilizing and conducting the war.

Martin J. Sherwin, *A World Destroyed: The Atomic Bomb and the Grand Alliance* (1975). Explains why American leaders never seriously considered alternatives to the atomic bomb.

Studs Terkel, *The Good War: An Oral History of World War II* (1984). Eloquent testimony about the effects of the war on both ordinary and extraordinary Americans.

CHAPTER

THE COLD WAR AT HOME AND ABROAD: 1946-1952

Launching the Great Boom

Truman, Republicans, and the Fair Deal

Confronting the Soviet Union

Cold War and Hot War

The Second Red Scare

Conclusion

My eyes popped when I got to town hall because the lobby and the stairs leading up to the hearing room were loaded with people. The upstairs hallway was jammed and the room was packed. People were standing along the walls. I remember there were a lot of children, toddlers—some in strollers—and many babies held by men and women. We expected there would be quite a turnout. But the extent of the crowd was a big surprise to me. . . . The meeting itself was rather brief. There were some speeches. No screaming and yelling the way people do at town meetings today. Everyone was quiet, anxious. I remember one guy in uniform, holding a baby, made a strong statement. These people were desperate. It was very moving. When the decision was announced, the crowd broke into applause.

Levittown was the last place on the planet I thought I would be living. But, as it turned out, we moved there because the house was such a good buy. . . . We loved living there. I came into work and told [*Newsday* managing editor Alan] Hathway that I would be eating crow for the rest of my days.

—Bernadette Rischer Wheeler

Bernadette Rischer Wheeler, in "Levittown at Fifty: Long Island Voices," at www.lihistory.com/specsec/hsvoices.htm; originally published in *Newsday*.

BERNADETTE WHEELER was a reporter for *Newsday*, the daily newspaper for the Long Island suburbs of New York, who covered the birth of the new community of Levittown. She remembers the meeting on May 21, 1947, when the local governing board approved construction of the new subdivision. The size of the crowd indicates the severity of the housing shortage after World War II and the intense desire of Americans to return to normal life. After years of hardship, they defined American ideals in terms of economic opportunity and the chance to enjoy national prosperity. Even President Truman replaced the model gun on his White House desk with a model plow. Over the next decade, the residents who moved to Levittown and thousands of other new subdivisions would start the baby boom and rekindle the economy with their purchases of automobiles, appliances, and televisions.

This compelling desire to enjoy the promise of American life after years of sacrifice helps to explain why Americans reacted so fiercely to new challenges and threats. They watched as congressional conservatives and President Truman fought over the fate of New Deal programs. More worrisome was the confrontation with the Soviet Union that was soon being called the **Cold War**. Triggered by the Soviet Union's imposition of Communist regimes throughout eastern Europe, the Cold War grew into a global contest in which the United States tried to counter Soviet influence around the world. By the time real war broke out in Korea in 1950, many Americans were venting their frustration by blaming international setbacks on internal subversion and by trying to root out suspected "reds."

The Cold War began in the late 1940s, but it would shape the United States and the world for another generation. Massive rearmament allowed U.S. presidents to act as international policemen in the name of democratic values—a vast change from earlier American goals to remain disengaged from the problems of other nations. Defense spending also reshaped American industry and helped stimulate twenty-five years of economic growth. The Cold War narrowed the range of political discussion, making many of the left-wing ideas of the 1930s taboo by the 1950s. It also made racial segregation and limits on immigration into international embarrassments and thus nudged the nation to live up to its ideals.

KEY TOPICS

Postwar shortages and the massive exit of women from the work force.

The beginning of a twenty-five-year economic boom.

The beginning of the postwar civil rights movement.

The origins of the Cold War.

The reelection of Harry Truman.

The Korean War and the nuclear arms race.

McCarthy and the second Red Scare.

LAUNCHING THE GREAT BOOM

In 1947, *The Best Years of Our Lives* swept seven Oscars at the Academy Awards. The immensely popular movie dealt with the problems of returning veterans as squarely as Hollywood could. It follows three veterans as they try to readjust to civilian life. The plot cuts between the personal problems of reconnecting with wives and sweethearts and the social challenge of finding meaningful work.

Behind the story line was nagging concern about the future. "Hard times are coming," one character predicts. When World War II ended, Americans feared that demobilization would bring a return of the inflation and unemployment that had followed World War I. Indeed, in the first eighteen months of peace, rising prices, strife between labor and management, and shortages of everything from meat to automobiles confirmed their anxiety. But in fact, 1947 and 1948 ushered in an economic expansion that lasted for a quarter century. The resulting prosperity would finance a military buildup and an activist foreign policy. It also supported continuity in domestic politics from the late 1940s to the mid-1960s.

Reconversion Chaos

Japan's sudden surrender took the United States by surprise. Plans called for a two-year phase-out of military spending, while gradually reintroducing veterans to the domestic economy. Now these plans were obsolete. The Pentagon, already scaling back defense spending, canceled $15 billion in war contracts in the first two days after Japanese surrender. Public pressure demanded that the military release the nation's 12 million servicemen and servicewomen as rapidly as possible. GIs in Europe and the South Pacific waited impatiently for their turn on slow, crowded troop ships and calculated their order of discharge according to length of time in uniform, service overseas, combat decorations, and number of children. Even at the rate of 25,000 discharges a day, it took a year to get veterans back to the States and civilian life.

Veterans came home to shortages of food in the grocery stores and consumer goods in the department stores. High demand and short supply meant inflationary pressure, checked temporarily by continuing the Office of Price Administration until October 1946. Meanwhile, producers, consumers, and retailers scrambled to evade price restrictions and scarcities. Farmers sold meat on the black market, bypassing the big packing companies for one-on-one deals at higher prices. Automobiles were especially scarce; the number of vehicles registered in the United States had declined by 4 million during the war. For the privilege of spending a few hundred dollars on a junker, consumers sometimes had to pay used-car dealers for such so-called accessories as $150 batteries and $100 lap robes.

A wave of strikes made it hard to retool factories for civilian products. Inflation squeezed factory workers, who had accepted wage controls during the war effort. Since 1941, prices had risen twice as fast as base wages. In the fall of 1945, more and more workers went on strike to redress the balance; the strikes interrupted the output of products from canned soup to copper wire. By January 1946, some 1.3 million auto, steel, electrical, and packinghouse workers were off the job. Strikes in these basic industries shut other factories down for lack of supplies. Presidential committees finally crafted settlements that allowed steel and auto workers to make up ground lost during the war, but they also allowed corporations to pass on higher costs to consumers. One Republican senator complained of "unionists who fatten themselves at the expense of the rest of us." Bill Nation, who inspected window moldings at a GM plant in Detroit, wondered who the senator was talking about. The strike gave him an hourly raise of 18 cents, pushing his weekly income to $59. After paying for food, housing, and utilities, Bill was left with $13.44 for himself, his wife, and five children to spend on clothes, comic books, and doctor bills.

Economic Policy

The economic turmoil of 1946 set the stage for two major and contradictory efforts to deal more systematically with peacetime economic readjustment. The Employment Act of 1946 and the Taft-Hartley Act of 1947 represented liberal and conservative approaches to the peacetime economy.

The Employment Act was an effort by congressional liberals to ward off economic crisis by fine-tuning government taxation and spending. It started as a proposal for a full-employment bill that would have committed the federal government to ensure everyone's "right to a useful and remunerative job." Watered down in the face of business opposition, it still defined economic growth and high employment as national goals. It also established the **Council of Economic Advisers** to assist the president. Even this weak legislation, putting the federal government at the center of economic planning, would have been unthinkable a generation earlier.

In the short term, the Employment Act aimed at a problem that did not materialize. Economists had predicted that the combination of returning veterans and workers idled by canceled defense work would bring depression-level unemployment of 8 to 10 million. In fact, more than 2 million women provided some slack by leaving the labor force outright. Federal agencies hastened their departure by publishing pamphlets asking men the pointed question, "Do you want your wife to work after the war?" In addition, consumer spending from a savings pool of $140 billion in bank accounts and war bonds created a huge demand for workers to fill. Total employment rose rather than fell with the end of the war, and unemployment in 1946–1948 stayed below 4 percent.

From the other end of the political spectrum, the **Taft-Hartley Act** climaxed a ten-year effort by conservatives to reverse the gains made by organized labor in the 1930s. The act passed in 1947 because of anger about continuing strikes. For many Americans, the chief culprit was John L. Lewis, head of the United Mine Workers, who had won good wages for coal miners with a militant policy that included wartime walkouts. In a country that still burned coal for most of its energy, the burly, bushy-browed, and combative Lewis was instantly recognizable, loved by his workers and hated by nearly everyone else. In April 1946, a forty-day coal strike hampered industrial production. The coal settlement was only days old when the nation faced an even more crippling walkout by railroad workers. Truman asked for the unprecedented power to draft strikers into the army; the threat undercut the union and led to a quick and dramatic settlement. Many middle-class Americans were convinced that organized labor needed to be curbed.

In November 1946, Republicans capitalized on the problems of reconversion chaos, labor unrest, and dissatisfaction with Truman. Their election slogan was simple: "Had enough?" The GOP won control of Congress for the first time since the election of 1928, continuing the political trend toward the right that had been apparent since 1938.

Adopted by the now firmly conservative Congress, the Taft-Hartley Act was a serious counterattack by big business against large unions. It outlawed several union tools as "unfair labor practices." It barred the closed shop (the requirement that all workers hired in a particular company or plant be union members) and blocked secondary boycotts (strikes against suppliers or customers of a targeted business). The federal government could postpone a strike by imposing a "cooling-off period," which gave companies time to stockpile their output. Officers of national unions had to swear that they were not Communists or Communist sympathizers, even though corporate executives had no similar obligation. The bill passed over Truman's veto.

The GI Bill

Another landmark law for the postwar era passed Congress without controversy. The Servicemen's Readjustment Act of 1944 was designed to ease veterans back into the civilian mainstream. Popularly known as the **GI Bill of Rights**, it was one of the federal government's most successful public assistance programs. Rather than pay cash bonuses to veterans, as after previous wars, Congress tied benefits to specific public goals. The GI Bill guaranteed loans of up to $2,000 for buying a house or farm or starting a business, a substantial sum at a time when a new house cost $6,000. The program encouraged veterans to attend college with money for tuition and books plus monthly stipends.

The GI Bill democratized American higher education by making college degrees accessible to men with working-class backgrounds. It brought far more students into higher education than could otherwise have enrolled. In the peak year of 1947, veterans made up half of all college students. "We're all trying to get where we would have been if there hadn't been a war," one veteran attending Indiana University told *Time* magazine. Veterans helped convert the college degree, once available primarily to the socially privileged, into a basic business and professional credential. However, an unfortunate side effect of the GI tide was to crowd women out of classrooms, although sixty thousand servicewomen did take advantage of educational benefits. Cornell University made room for veterans by limiting women to 20 percent of its entering class; the University of Wisconsin closed its doors to women from out of state. Women's share of bachelor's degrees dropped from 40 percent in 1940 to 25 percent in 1950.

College life in 1946 and 1947 meant close quarters. Universities were unequipped to deal with older or married students. Prefabricated apartments from the wartime atomic-energy project at Richland, Washington, were trucked to college campuses around the West to house newly enrolled veterans. Recycled Quonset huts became as much a part of campus architecture as gothic towers and ivy-covered halls. States rented surplus defense facilities for big-city extension campuses that would be easier for veterans to attend than traditional small-town universities. Many of these campuses evolved into major public universities, such as the University of Illinois at Chicago and Portland State University in Oregon.

Assembly-Line Neighborhoods

Americans faced a housing shortage after the war. In 1947, fully 3 million married couples were unable to set up their own households. Most doubled up with relatives while they waited for the construction industry to respond. Hunger for housing was fierce. Eager buyers lined up for hours and paid admission fees to tour model homes or to put their names in drawings for the opportunity to buy. When in 1946 the *Des Moines Register and Tribune* ran a fake apartment ad to check real-estate industry claims that the housing crisis was over, 351 people answered it. Fifty-six of them said that they lived in a hotel or rented room; 68 lived with parents.

The solution started with the federal government and its Veterans Administration (VA) mortgage program. By guaranteeing repayment, the VA allowed veterans to get home purchase loans from private lenders without a down payment. Neither the VA program nor the New Deal-era Federal Housing Administration (FHA) mortgage insurance program, however, could do any good unless there were houses to buy. Eyeing the mass market created by the federal programs, innovative private builders devised their own solution. In 1947, William Levitt, a New York builder who had developed defense housing projects, built two thousand rental houses for veterans on suburban Long Island. His basic house had 800 square feet of living space in two bedrooms, living room, kitchen, and bath, a 60-by-100-foot lot, and an unfinished attic waiting for the weekend handyman. It was only one-third the size of the typical new house fifty years later, but it gave new families a place to start. There were six thousand **Levittown** houses by the end of 1948 and more than seventeen thousand by 1951.

Other successful builders worked on the same scale. They bought hundreds of acres of land, put in utilities for the entire tract, purchased materials by the carload, and kept specialized workers busy on scores of identical houses. Floor plans were square, simple, and easy for semiskilled workers to construct. For the first time, kitchens across America were designed for preassembled cabinets and appliances in standard sizes. "On-site fabrication" was mass production without an assembly line. Work crews at the Los Angeles suburb of Lakewood started a hundred houses a day as they moved down one side of the street and back up the other, digging foundation trenches, pouring concrete, and working through the dozens of other stages of home building.

From 1946 through 1950, the federal government backed $20 billion in VA and FHA loans, approximately 40 percent of all home-mortgage debt. Housing starts neared 2 million in the peak year of 1950. New subdivisions were starting places for couples in their late twenties or early thirties making up for lost time on a tight budget. By the end of the 1940s, 55 percent of American households owned their homes. The figure continued to climb until the 1980s, broadening access to the dream of financial security for many families. All during this time, the suburban population grew much faster than the population of central cities, and the population outside the growing reach of metropolitan areas actually declined.

Isolation and Discrimination Unfortunately, the suburban solution to housing shortages also had costs. Vast new housing tracts tended to isolate women and children from traditional community life. They also did little to help African Americans. As the migration of black workers and their families to northern and western cities continued after the war, discrimination excluded them from new housing. As late as 1960, the 82,000 residents of Levittown had no African-American neighbors; not until 1957 did a black family move into a second Levittown near Philadelphia. Federal housing agencies and private industry worsened the problem by **redlining** older neighborhoods, which involved withholding home-purchase loans and insurance coverage from inner-city areas.

Public and private actions kept African Americans in deteriorating inner-city ghettos. When severe flooding in 1948 drove thousands of African Americans from leftover wartime housing in Portland, Oregon, for example, their only choice was to crowd into the city's small black neighborhood. Chicago landlords squeezed an estimated 27,000 black migrants per year into run-down buildings, subdividing larger apartments into one-room "kitchenette" units, with sinks and hot plates but no private bathrooms. One tenant commented that rats came "in teams." Families who tried to find new homes in white neighborhoods on the edge of black ghettos often met violence in the form of rocks thrown through their windows, firebombs, and angry white mobs.

Steps Toward Civil Rights

The problem of securing decent housing helped to motivate African Americans to demand full rights as citizens. The wartime experience of fighting for freedom abroad while suffering discrimination at home steeled a new generation of black leaders to reduce the gap between America's ideal of equality and its performance. As had also been true after World War I, some white Americans held the opposite view, hoping to reaffirm racial segregation. A wave of racist violence surged across the South after the war; special targets were black veterans who tried to register to vote. However, many white Americans felt uneasy about the contradiction between a crusade for freedom abroad and racial discrimination at home.

In this era of rapid change and racial tension, the Truman administration recognized the importance of securing civil rights for all Americans. Caught between pressure from black leaders and the fear of alienating southern Democrats, the president in 1946 appointed the Committee on Civil Rights, whose report developed an agenda for racial justice that would take two decades to put into effect. The NAACP had already begun a campaign of antisegregation lawsuits, which the Justice Department now began to support. The administration ordered federal housing agencies to modify their racially restrictive policies and prohibited racial discrimination in federal employment. Federal committees began to push for desegregation of private facilities in the symbolically important city of Washington, DC.

The president also ordered "equality of treatment and opportunity" in the armed services in July 1948. The army in particular dragged its feet, hoping to limit black enlistees to 10 percent of the total. Manpower needs and the record of integrated units in Korea from 1950 to 1953 persuaded the reluctant generals. Over the next generation, African Americans would find the military an important avenue for career opportunities.

Changes in national policy were important for ending racial discrimination, but far more Americans were interested in lowering racial barriers in professional team sports.

Jackie Robinson, the first black player in modern major league baseball, joined the Brooklyn Dodgers in 1947. He was both personally courageous and an outstanding player. Here he steals home against the Chicago Cubs in 1952.

Americans had applauded individual black champions, such as heavyweight boxer Joe Louis and sprinter Jesse Owens, but team sports required their members to travel, practice, and play together. The center of attention was Jack Roosevelt (Jackie) Robinson, a gifted African-American athlete, who opened the 1947 baseball season as a member of the Brooklyn Dodgers. Black baseball players had previously displayed their talents in the Negro leagues, but Robinson broke the color line that had reserved the modern major leagues for white players. His ability to endure taunting and hostility and still excel on the ball field opened the door for other African Americans and Latinos. In the segregated society of the 1940s, Robinson also found himself a powerful symbol of racial change.

Consumer Boom and Baby Boom

The housing boom was a product of both pent-up demand and a postwar "family boom." Americans celebrated the end of the war with weddings; the marriage rate in 1946 surpassed even its wartime high. Many women who left the labor force opted for marriage, and at increasingly younger ages. By 1950, the median age at which women married would be just over 20 years—lower than at any previous time in the twentieth century. Movies in the 1930s had abounded with independent career women. By the late 1940s, Hollywood reflected new attitudes and social patterns by portraying women as helpless victims or supportive wives and publicizing hard-edged stars, such as Joan Crawford, as homebodies at heart. The United States ended the 1940s with 7 million more married couples than at the decade's start.

New marriages jump-started the "baby boom," as did already married couples who decided to catch up after postponing childbearing during the war. In the early 1940s, an

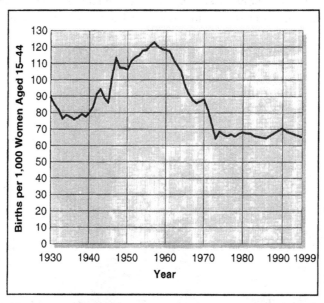

FIGURE 10-1 **The Postwar Baby Boom: The U.S. Birthrate. 1930–1995**
The baby boom after World War II was a product of high marriage rates and closely spaced children. The generation of Americans born between 1945 and 1960 has strongly affected American society and politics as its members have gone to school and college, entered the work force, started their own families, and begun to plan for retirement in the twenty-first century.

Americans were eager to enjoy the most modern appliances and houses. Manufacturers promoted streamlined kitchens to make life easier for housewives and their families.

average of 2.9 million children per year were born in the United States; in 1946–1950, the average was 3.6 million. Those 3.5 million "extra" babies needed diapers, swing sets, lunch boxes, bicycles, and schoolrooms (see Figure 10-1).

Fast-growing families also needed to stock up on household goods. Out of an average household income of roughly $4,000 in 1946 and 1947, a family of four had $300 to $400 a year for furnishings and appliances. A couple who studied *Consumer Reports* might equip its new Levittown kitchen with a Dripolator coffee maker for $2.45 and a Mirro-Matic pressure cooker for $12.95. The thrifty family could get along with a Motorola table radio in brown plastic for under $30; for $100, it could have a massive radio-phonograph combination in a four-foot console as the centerpiece of a well-equipped living room before the arrival of television.

TRUMAN, REPUBLICANS, AND THE FAIR DEAL

From new radios to new homes to new jobs, the economic gains of the postwar years propelled Americans toward the political center. After fifteen years of economic crisis and world war, they wanted to enjoy prosperity. They wanted to keep the gains of the New Deal, but without risking new experiments. William Levitt tried to humorously capture the American satisfaction with the fruits of free enterprise when he said in 1948 that "no man who owns his house and lot can be a Communist; he has too much to do."

Recognizing this attitude, Harry Truman and his political advisers tried to define policies acceptable to moderate Republicans as well as to Democrats. This project meant creating a bipartisan coalition to block Soviet influence in western Europe and defending the core of the New Deal's social and economic agenda at home.

This political package is known as the strategy of the "vital center," after the title of a 1949 book by Arthur Schlesinger Jr. The book linked anticommunism in foreign policy with efforts to enact inclusive social and economic policies to extend freedom abroad and at home at the same time. The vital center reflected the political reality of the Cold War years, when Democrats had to prove that they were tough on Communism before they could enact domestic reforms. The approach defined the heart of the Democratic Party for twenty years and found full expression in the administrations of John Kennedy (1961–1963) and Lyndon Johnson (1963–1969).

Truman's Opposition

Truman had unexpected luck in his campaign for a full term as president in 1948. Besides the Republicans, he faced new fringe parties on the far right and far left that allowed him to position himself in the moderate center. The blunt, no-nonsense Missourian entered the campaign an underdog, but, compared to his rivals, he soon looked like the country's best option for steering a steady course.

Truman's opponents represented the left-leaning American Progressive party, the **Dixiecrats** (officially the States' Rights Democrats), and the Republicans. The Progressive candidate was Henry Wallace, who had been FDR's vice president from 1941 to 1945 before being dumped in favor of Truman himself; more recently, he had been Truman's secretary of commerce. Dixiecrat Strom Thurmond, governor of South Carolina, had bolted the Democratic party over civil rights. The most serious challenger was the Republican Thomas Dewey, who had run against Roosevelt in 1944.

Wallace cast himself as the prophet for "the century of the common man." His background as a plant geneticist and farm journalist prepared him to deal with domestic policy but not with world affairs. After Truman fired him from the cabinet in 1946 for advocating a conciliatory stance toward the Soviet Union, Wallace went to Europe to praise the Soviet Union and to denounce U.S. foreign policy. On his return, enthusiastic college crowds raised his sights from "scaring the Democratic Party leftward" to running for president. Most liberal Democrats ran the other way when Wallace organized the Progressive party, leaving the Communist party to supply many of his campaign workers.

Wallace argued that the United States was forcing the Cold War on the Soviet Union and undermining American ideals by diverting attention from poverty and racism at home. He wanted to repeal the draft and destroy atomic weapons. His arguments had merit, for the United States was becoming a militarized society, but Wallace was the wrong person to change American minds. With his shy personality, disheveled appearance, and fanaticism about health food, he struck most voters as a kook rather than a statesman, and he made skepticism about the Cold War increasingly vulnerable to right-wing attack.

At the other political extreme were the Southerners who walked out when the 1948 Democratic National Convention called for full civil rights for African Americans. The raucous convention debate previewed the politics of the 1960s. Mayor Hubert Humphrey of Minneapolis challenged the Democratic party "to get out of the shadow of states' rights and walk forthrightly into the bright sunshine of human rights." His speech foreshadowed Humphrey's twenty years of liberal influence in the Democratic party, culminating in his presidential nomination in 1968.

When the angry Southerners met to nominate their own candidate, however, the South's important politicians stayed away. They had worked too long to throw away seniority and influence in Congress and the Democratic party. Major southern newspapers called the revolt futile and narrow-minded. Strom Thurmond claimed that the Dixiecrats were really trying to defend Americans against government bureaucracy, not fighting to preserve racial segregation, but few listened outside the deep South.

Tom Dewey, Truman's real opponent, had a high opinion of himself. He had been an effective governor of New York and represented the moderate eastern establishment within the Republican party. Fortunately for Truman, Dewey lacked the common touch. Smooth on the outside, he alienated people who should have been his closest supporters; as one political acquaintance put it, "You have to know Dewey really well to dislike him." He was an arrogant campaigner, refusing to interrupt his morning schedule to talk to voters. He acted like a snob and dressed like the groom on a wedding cake.

Dewey was also saddled with the results of the Republican-controlled "do-nothing" 80th Congress (1947–1948). Truman used confrontation with Congress to rally voters who had supported the New Deal. He introduced legislation that he knew would be ignored, and he used his veto even when he knew Congress would override it. All the while he was building a list of campaign issues by demonstrating that the Republicans were obstructionists. Vote for me, Truman argued, to protect the New Deal, or vote Republican to bring back the days of Herbert Hoover. After his nomination in July 1948, Truman called Congress back into session and challenged Republicans to pass a list of "must" bills on key issues. Congress did nothing, as he had expected, and Truman had more proof that the Republicans were all talk and no show.

Whistle-Stopping Across America

The 1948 presidential campaign mixed old and new. For the last time, a major candidate crisscrossed the nation by rail and made hundreds of speeches from the rear platform of trains. For the first time, national television broadcast the two party conventions, although the primitive cameras showed the handful of viewers little more than talking heads. The Republican campaign issued a printed T-shirt that read "Dew-It With Dewey," the earliest advertising T-shirt in the collections of the Smithsonian Institution.

Truman ran on both character and issues. He was a widely read and intelligent man who cultivated the image of a backslapper. "I'll mow 'em down. . . . and I'll give 'em hell," he told his vice-presidential running mate. Crowds across the country greeted him with "Give 'em hell, Harry!" He covered 31,700 miles in his campaign train and gave ten speeches a day. Republicans belittled the small towns and cities he visited, calling them "whistle stops." Democrats made the term a badge of pride for places like Laramie, Wyoming, and Pocatello, and Idaho.

Truman brought the campaign home to average Americans. He tied Dewey to inflation, housing shortages, and fears about the future of Social Security (an issue that Democrats would continue to use into the next century). In industrial cities, he hammered at the Taft-Hartley Act. In the West, he pointed out that Democratic administrations had built dams and helped turn natural resources into jobs. He called the Republicans the party of privilege and arrogance.

Harry Truman greets supporters and railroad workers in Pittsburgh at the start of an eighteen-state campaign tour in June 1948. Truman's grass-roots campaign and down-home style helped him pull out an unexpected victory in November 1948.

The Democrats, he said, offered opportunity for farmers, factory workers, and small business owners.

Truman got a huge boost from Dewey's unwillingness to fight. Going into the fall with a huge lead in the public opinion polls, Dewey sought to avoid mistakes. He failed to counter Truman's attacks and packed his speeches with platitudes: "Our streams abound with fish." "You know that your future is still ahead of you." The results astounded the pollsters, who had stopped sampling opinion in mid-October just as a swing to Truman gathered strength. Wallace and Thurmond each took just under 1.2 million votes. Dewey received nearly 22 million popular votes and 189 electoral votes, but Truman won more than 24 million popular votes and 303 electoral votes.

Truman's Fair Deal

Truman hoped to build on the gains of the New Deal. In his State of the Union address in January 1949, he called for a Fair Deal for all Americans. He promised to extend the New Deal and ensure "greater economic opportunity for the mass of the people." Over the next four years, however, conservative Republicans and southern Democrats forced Congress to choose carefully among Truman's proposals, accepting those that expanded existing programs but rejecting new departures. The result was a set of disconnected measures rather than the consistent program that Truman had advocated.

In the Housing Act of 1949, the federal government reaffirmed its concern about families who had been priced out of the private market. Passed with the backing of conservative Senator Robert Taft, "Mr. Republican" to his admirers, the act provided money for local housing agencies to buy, clear, and resell land for housing. The intent was to clear "substandard and blighted areas" and replace them with affordable modern apartments. The program never worked as intended because of scanty appropriations and poor design of the replacement housing, but it established the goal of decent housing for all Americans.

In 1950, Congress revitalized the weak Social Security program. Benefits went up by an average of 80 percent, and 10.5 million additional people received old-age and survivors' insurance. Most of the new coverage went to rural and small-town people, thus consolidating the broad support that has made it politically difficult to change Social Security ever since, even in the face of projected shortages in the twenty-first century.

Congress rejected other Fair Deal proposals that would remain on the national agenda for decades. A plan to alter the farm subsidy system to favor small farmers rather than agribusiness went nowhere. A Senate filibuster killed a permanent Fair Employment Practices Commission to fight racial discrimination in hiring, halting progress toward civil rights. The medical establishment blocked a proposal for national health insurance as "socialistic," leaving the issue to be revisited in the 1960s (with the passage of Medicare and Medicaid) and 1990s (with Bill Clinton's proposals for health-care reform). The overall message from Truman's second term was clear: Americans liked what the New Deal had given them but were hesitant about new initiatives.

CONFRONTING THE SOVIET UNION

In 1945, the United States and the Soviet Union were allies, victorious against Germany and planning the defeat of Japan. By 1947, they were engaged in a diplomatic and economic confrontation and soon came close to war over the city of Berlin. The business tycoon and presidential advisor Bernard Baruch characterized the conflict in April 1947 as a "cold war," and the newspaper columnist Walter Lippmann quickly popularized the term.

Over the next forty years, the United States and the Soviet Union contested for economic, political, and military influence around the globe. The heart of Soviet policy was control of eastern Europe as a buffer zone against Germany. The centerpiece of American policy was to link the United States, western Europe, and Japan into an alliance of overwhelming economic power. Both sides spent vast sums on conventional military forces and atomic weapons that held the world in a "balance of terror." They also competed for political advantage in Asia and Africa as newly independent nations replaced European colonial empires. For the United States, the Cold War was simultaneously an effort to promote democracy in Europe, maintain a strategically favorable military position in relation to the Soviet Union, and preserve its leadership of the world economy.

Each side in the Cold War thought the worst of the other. Behind the conflicts were Soviet insecurity about an aggressive West and American fear of Communist expansionism. Americans and Soviets frequently interpreted each other's actions in the most threatening terms, turning miscalculations and misunderstandings into crises. A U.S. public that had suffered through nearly two decades of economic depression and war reacted to international problems with frustration and anger. The emotional burdens of the Cold War warped and narrowed a generation of American political life around the requirements of anticommunism.

The End of the Grand Alliance

The Yalta Conference of February 1945 had recognized military realities by marking out rough spheres of influence. The Soviet defeat of Germany on the Eastern Front had made the Soviet Union the only military power in eastern Europe. The American and British attacks through Italy and France had made the Western allies dominant in western Europe and the Mediterranean. The Soviets, Americans, British, and French shared control of defeated Germany, each with its own occupation zone and its own sector of Berlin. The Western allies had the better of the bargain. Defeated Italy and Japan, whose reconstruction was firmly in Western hands, had far greater economic potential than had Soviet-controlled Bulgaria, Romania, or Hungary. In addition, the British, French, and American occupation zones in western Germany held more people and industrial potential than did the Russian zone in eastern Germany.

As the victorious powers tried to put their broad agreements into operation, they argued bitterly about Germany and eastern Europe. Was the Soviet Union to dominate eastern Europe, or was the region to be open to Western economic and political influence? For Poland, Truman and his advisors claimed that Yalta had assumed open elections on the American model. The Soviet Union saw Poland as the historic invasion route from the west; it claimed that Yalta had ensured that any Polish government would be friendly to Soviet interests and acted to guarantee that this would be so.

Facing Soviet intransigence over eastern Europe, Truman decided that the United States should "take the lead in running the world in the way the world ought to be run." One technique was economic pressure. The State Department "mislaid" a Soviet request for redevelopment loans. The United States and Britain objected to Soviet plans to take industrial equipment and raw materials from the western occupation zones in Germany, compensation that the Soviets thought they had been promised.

The United States also tried to involve the Soviet Union and eastern Europe in new international organizations. The Senate approved American membership in the newly organized United Nations (UN) with only two opposing votes, a sharp contrast to its rejection of the League of Nations in 1920. The Washington-based **International Monetary Fund (IMF)** and the **World Bank** were designed to revive international trade. The IMF stabilized national currencies against the short-term pressures of international trade. The World Bank drew on the resources of member nations to make economic development loans to governments for such projects as new dams or agricultural modernization. These organizations ensured that a reviving world economy would revolve around the industrial and technological power of the United States, and they continue to dictate economic policy of many developing nations into the twenty-first century.

In 1946, the United States also presented a plan in the United Nations to control atomic energy. Bernard Baruch suggested that an international agency should oversee all uranium production and research on atomic explosives. The Baruch plan emphasized enforcement and inspections that would have opened the Soviet nuclear effort to American interference, an unacceptable prospect for a nation trying to catch up with the United States by building its own atomic bombs. On-site inspection would remain a problem in arms control negotiations for the next half-century.

While UN delegates debated the future of atomic energy, American leaders were becoming convinced of Soviet aggressiveness. In February 1946, George Kennan, a senior American diplomat in Moscow, sent a "long telegram" to the State Department. He depicted a Soviet Union driven by expansionist Communist ideology. The Soviets, he argued, would constantly probe for weaknesses in the capitalist world. The best response was firm resistance to protect the western heartlands.

The British encouraged the same tough stand. Lacking the strength to shape Europe on its own, Great Britain repeatedly nudged the United States to block Soviet influence. Speaking at Westminster College in Missouri in March 1946, Winston Churchill warned that the Soviet Union had dropped an "Iron Curtain" across the middle of Europe and urged a firm Western response.

Churchill's speech matched the mood in official Washington. Truman's foreign-policy advisors shared the belief in an aggressive Soviet Union, and the president himself saw the world as a series of either–or choices. Administration leaders did not fear an immediate Soviet military threat to the United States itself, for they knew that World War II had exhausted the Soviet Union, but they also knew that the Soviets were strong enough to brush aside the U.S. occupation forces in Germany. Added to military apprehension were worries about political and economic competition. Communist parties in war-ravaged Europe and Japan were exploiting discontent. In Asia and Africa, the allegiance of nationalists who were fighting for independence from France, Great Britain, and the Netherlands remained in doubt. America's leaders worried that much of the Eastern Hemisphere might fall under Soviet control and turn its back on North America.

Were Truman and his advisors right about Soviet intentions? The evidence is mixed. In their determination to avoid another Munich, Truman and the "wise men" who made up his foreign-policy circle ignored examples of Soviet caution and conciliation. The Soviets withdrew troops from Manchuria in northern China and acquiesced in America's control of defeated Japan. They allowed a neutral but democratic government in Finland and technically free elections in Hungary and Czechoslovakia (although it was clear that Communists would do well there). They demobilized much of their huge army and reduced their forces in eastern Europe while expecting a falling out between capitalist Britain and the United States.

However, the Soviet regime also did more than enough to justify American fears. The Soviet Union could not resist exerting influence in the Middle East. It pressured Turkey to give it partial control of the exit from the Black Sea. It retained troops in northern Iran until warned out by the United States. The Soviets were ruthless in support of Communist control in eastern Europe in 1946 and 1947; they aided a Communist takeover in Bulgaria, backed a coup in Romania, and undermined the last non-Communist political opposition in Poland. U.S. policymakers read these Soviet actions as a rerun of Nazi aggression and determined not to let a new totalitarian threat undermine Western power.

The Truman Doctrine and the Marshall Plan

Whatever restraint the Soviet Union showed was too late or too little. Early in 1947, Truman and his advisors acted decisively. The British could no longer afford to back the Greek government that was fighting Communist rebels, and U.S. officials feared that a Communist takeover in Greece would threaten the stability of Italy, France, and the Middle East. Truman coupled his case for intervention in Greece with an appeal for aid to neighboring Turkey, which lived under the shadow of the Soviet Union. On March 12, he told Congress that the United States faced a "fateful hour." Taking the reported advice of Senator Arthur Vandenberg to "scare the hell out of the American people," he said that only the appropriation of $400 million to fight Communism in Greece and Turkey could secure the free world. Congress agreed, and the United States became the dominant power in the eastern Mediterranean.

Framing the specific request was a sweeping declaration that became known as the **Truman Doctrine**. The president pledged to use U.S. economic power to help free nations everywhere resist internal subversion or aggression. "It must be the policy of the United States," he said, "to support free peoples who are resisting attempted subjugation by armed minorities or by outside pressures. . . . I believe that our help should be primarily through economic and financial aid, which is essential to economic stability and orderly political processes."

Meanwhile, Europe was sliding toward chaos. Germany was close to famine after the bitter winter of 1946–1947. Western European nations were bankrupt and unable to import raw materials for their factories. Overstressed medical systems could no longer control diseases such as tuberculosis. Communist parties had gained in Italy, France, and Germany. Winston Churchill, again sounding the alarm, described Europe as "a rubble-heap, a charnel house, a breeding ground of pestilence and hate."

The U.S. government responded with unprecedented economic aid. Secretary of State George C. Marshall announced the European Recovery Plan on June 5, 1947. What the press quickly dubbed the **Marshall Plan** committed the United States to help rebuild Europe. The United States invited Soviet and eastern European participation, but under terms that would have reduced Moscow's control over its satellite economies. The Soviets refused, fearing that the United States wanted to undermine their influence; instead they organized their eastern European satellites in their own association for Mutual Economic Assistance, or Comecon, in 1949. In western Europe, the Marshall Plan was a success. Aid totaled $13.5 billion over four years. It met many of Europe's economic needs and quieted class conflict. Unlike the heavy-handed Soviet role in eastern Europe, the Marshall Plan expanded American influence through cooperative efforts. Because Europeans spent much of the aid on U.S. goods and machinery, and because economic recovery promised markets for U.S. products, business and labor both supported it. In effect, the Marshall Plan created an "empire by invitation," in which Americans and Europeans jointly planned European recovery.

Americans also micromanaged European policies. In Italy, for example, the United States forced the middle-of-the-road Christian Democrats to kick the Italian Communist party out of its governing coalition in return for more economic aid. In 1948, Marshall warned the Italians that aid would vanish if they voted the Communists into power. The State Department recruited Italian-American organizations to pressure relatives in Italy and was relieved when the Christian Democrats won.

U.S. policy in Japan followed the pattern set in Europe. As supreme commander of the Allied Powers, General Douglas MacArthur acted as Japan's postwar dictator. He tried to change the values of the old war-prone Japan through social reform, democratization, and demilitarization. At the end of 1947, however, the United States decided that democracy and pacifism could go too far. Policymakers were fearful of economic collapse and political chaos, just as in Europe. The "reverse course" in occupation policy aimed to make Japan an economic magnet for other nations in East Asia, pulling them toward the American orbit and away from the Soviet Union. MacArthur reluctantly accepted the new policy of "economic crank-up" by preserving Japan's corporate giants and encouraging American investment. At American insistence, the new Japan accepted American bases and created its own "self-defense force" (with no capacity for overseas aggression).

George Kennan summed up the new American policies in the magazine *Foreign Affairs* in July 1947. Writing anonymously as "X," Kennan argued that the Soviet leaders were committed to a long-term strategy of expanding Communism. The proper posture of the United States, he said, should be an equally patient commitment to "firm and vigilant **containment** of Russian expansive tendencies." Kennan warned that the emerging Cold War would be a long conflict, with no quick fixes.

Soviet Reactions

The bold American moves in the first half of 1947 put the Soviet Union on the defensive. In response, Soviet leaders orchestrated strenuous opposition to the Marshall Plan by French and Italian Communists. East of the Iron Curtain, Hungarian Communists expelled other political parties from a coalition government. Bulgarian Communists shot opposition leaders. Romania, Bulgaria, and Hungary signed defense pacts with the Soviet Union.

In early 1948, the Soviets targeted Czechoslovakia. For three years, a neutral coalition government there on the model of Finland had balanced trade with the West with a foreign policy friendly to the Soviet Union. In February 1948, while Russian forces assembled on the Czech borders, local Communists took advantage of political bumbling by other members of the governing coalition. Taking control of the government through a technically legal process, they pushed aside Czechoslovakia's democratic leadership and turned the nation into a dictatorship and Soviet satellite within a week.

Berlin in 1948 was still a devastated city. When the Soviet Union closed off ground access to the British, French, and American occupation zones, the city also became a symbol of the West's Cold War resolve. Allied aircraft lifted in food, fuel, and other essentials for West Berliners for nearly a year until the Soviets ended the blockade.

The climax of the Soviet reaction came in divided Berlin, located 110 miles inside the Soviet Union's East German occupation zone. The city was divided into one sector controlled by the Soviets and three others by the United States, Britain, and France. On June 4, 1948, Soviet troops blockaded surface traffic into Berlin, cutting off the United States, British, and French sectors. The immediate Soviet aim was to block Western plans to merge their three occupation zones into an independent federal republic (West Germany). Rather than abandon 2.5 million Berliners or shoot their way through, the Western nations responded to the **Berlin blockade** by airlifting supplies to the city. Planes landed every two minutes at Berlin's Tempelhof Airport. Stalin decided not to intercept the flights. After eleven months, the Soviets abandoned the blockade, making the Berlin airlift a triumph of American resolve.

American Rearmament

The coup in Czechoslovakia and the Berlin blockade shocked American leaders and backfired on the Soviets. The economic assistance strategy of 1947 now looked inadequate. Congress responded in 1948 by reinstating the military draft and increasing defense spending. Much of the money bought new war planes, as thrifty congressmen decided that air power was the easiest way for the United States to project its military power abroad.

The United States had already begun to modernize and centralize its national security apparatus, creating the institutions that would run foreign policy in the second half of the century. The National Security Act of July 1947 created the **Central Intelligence Agency (CIA)** and the **National Security Council (NSC)**. The CIA handled intelligence gathering and covert operations; the NSC assembled top diplomatic and military advisors in one committee. In 1949, legislation also created the Department of Defense to oversee the army, navy, and air force (independent from the army since 1947). The civilian secretary of defense soon emerged as a position with influence on foreign policy equal to that of the secretary of state. The new post of chairman of the joint chiefs of staff was supposed to coordinate the rival branches of the military.

In April 1949, ten European nations, the United States, and Canada signed the North Atlantic Treaty as a mutual defense pact. American commitments to the **North Atlantic Treaty Organization (NATO)** included military aid and the deployment of U.S. troops in western Europe. As Republican Senator Robert Taft warned in the ratification debate, NATO was the sort of "entangling alliance" that the United States had avoided for 160 years. It was also the insurance policy that western Europeans required if they were to accept the dangers as well as the benefits of a revived Germany, which was economically and militarily necessary for a strong Europe. In short, NATO was a sort of marriage contract between Europe and the previously standoffish United States. After 1955, its counterpart would be the **Warsaw Pact** for mutual defense among the Soviet Union and its European satellites (see Map 10-1).

Two years later, the United States signed similar but less comprehensive agreements in the western Pacific: the ANZUS Pact with Australia and New Zealand and a new treaty with the Philippines. The alliances reassured Pacific allies who were nervously watching the United States negotiate a unilateral peace treaty with Japan (ignoring the Soviet Union). The United States overcame opposition from nations that Japan had attacked in World War II by promising to assist their defense and maintaining military bases in Japan. Taken together, peacetime rearmament and mutual defense pacts amounted to a revolution in American foreign policy.

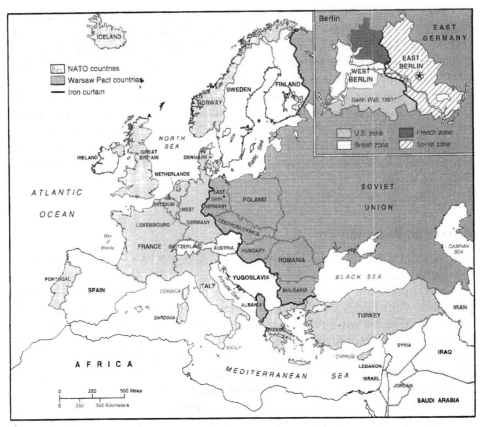

MAP 10-1   Cold War in Europe
In the late 1940s and 1950s, the Cold War split Europe into rigidly divided western and eastern blocs. Members of NATO allied with the United States to oppose Soviet expansion. The Soviet Union directed the military and foreign policies of members of the Warsaw Pact.

COLD WAR AND HOT WAR

The first phase of the Cold War reached a crisis in the autumn of 1949. The two previous years had seen an uneasy equilibrium in which American success in southern and western Europe and the standoff over Berlin (the blockade ended in May 1949) balanced the consolidation of Soviet power in eastern Europe. Now, suddenly, two key events seemed to tilt the world balance against the United States and its allies. In September, Truman announced that the Soviet Union had tested its own atomic bomb. A month later, the Chinese Communists under Mao Zedong (Mao Tse-tung) took power in China. The following summer, civil war in Korea sucked the United States into a fierce war with Communist North Korea and China. While Americans studied maps that showed communism spreading across Europe and Asia, their government accelerated a forty-year arms race with the Soviet Union.

The Nuclear Shadow

Experts in Washington had known that the Soviets were working on an A-bomb, but the news dismayed the average citizen. As newspapers and magazines scared their readers with artists' renditions of the effects of an atomic bomb on New York or Chicago, the shock tilted

Deciding on a Nuclear Arms Race

In 1950, the United States began work on a hydrogen (thermonuclear) bomb. The decision locked the United States and the Soviet Union into a nuclear arms race that lasted another forty years. In the first document reprinted here, an excerpt from a letter to President Truman written on November 25, 1949, Lewis Strauss, chairman of the Atomic Energy Commission, urged work on the H-bomb. In the second, scientist Edward Teller agreed. A refugee from Nazi-dominated Europe who had worked at Los Alamos, Teller remained an advocate of massive defense spending through the 1980s.

How did memories of World War II affect this Cold War decision?

How did U.S. policymakers evaluate the intentions of the Soviet Union?

Lewis Strauss, November 1949:

Dear Mr. President:

As you know, the thermonuclear (super) bomb was suggested by scientists working at Los Alamos during the war. . . . I believe that the United States must be as completely armed as any possible enemy. From this, it follows that I believe it unwise to renounce, unilaterally, any weapon which an enemy can reasonably be expected to possess. I recommend that the President direct the Atomic Energy Commission to proceed with the development of the thermonuclear bomb, at highest priority. . . .

Obviously the current atomic bomb as well as the proposed thermonuclear weapon are horrible to contemplate. All war is horrible. Until, however, some means is found of eliminating war, I cannot agree with those of my colleagues who feel that an announcement should be made by the President to the effect that the development of the thermonuclear weapon will not be undertaken by the United States at this time. This is because I do not think the statement will be credited in the Kremlin . . . and because primarily until disarmament is universal, our arsenal must be not less well equipped than with the most potent weapons that our technology can devise.

Edward Teller, March 1950:

President Truman has announced that we are going to make a hydrogen bomb. . . . The scientist is not responsible for the law of nature. It is his job to find out how these laws operate. . . . However, it is not the scientist's job to determine whether a hydrogen bomb should be constructed, whether it should be used, or how it should be used. This responsibility rests with the American people and their chosen representatives. Personally, as a citizen, I do not know in what other way President Truman could have acted. . . . To my mind we are in a situation no less dangerous than the one we were facing in 1939, and it is of the greatest importance that we realize it. We must realize. . . . that democracy will not be saved by ideals alone.

Source: Lewis L. Strauss, *Men and Decisions* (Garden City, NY: Doubleday & Co., 1962), pp. 219, 221–222, 228–229.

U.S. nuclear policy toward military uses. In 1946, advocates of civilian control had won a small victory when Congress gave control of atomic energy to the new Atomic Energy Commission (AEC). The AEC tried to balance research on atomic power with continued testing of new weapons. Now Truman told the AEC to double the output of fissionable uranium and plutonium for "conventional" nuclear weapons.

A more momentous decision soon followed. Truman decided in January 1950 to authorize work on the "super" bomb—the thermonuclear fusion weapon that would become the hydrogen bomb (H-bomb). The debate over the "super" pitted a cautious scientific advisory committee and J. Robert Oppenheimer against powerful political figures and a handful of scientists who believed, correctly, that the Soviets were already at work on a similar weapon. As would be true in future nuclear-defense debates, the underlying question was how much capacity for nuclear destruction was enough (see American Views, "Deciding on a Nuclear Arms Race").

Nuclear weapons proliferated in the early 1950s. The United States exploded the first hydrogen bomb in the South Pacific in November 1952. Releasing one hundred times the energy of the Hiroshima bomb, the detonation tore a mile-long chasm in the ocean floor. Great Britain became the third nuclear power in the same year. The Soviet Union tested its own hydrogen bomb only nine months after the U.S. test. Americans who remembered the attack on Pearl Harbor now worried that the Soviets might send fleets of bombers over the Arctic to surprise U.S. military forces and smash its cities into radioactive powder.

The nuclear arms race and the gnawing fear of nuclear war multiplied the apprehensions of the Cold War. Under the guidance of the Federal Civil Defense Administration, Americans learned that they should always keep a battery-powered radio and tune to 640 or 1240 on the AM dial for emergency information when they heard air raid sirens. Schoolchildren learned to hide under their desks when they saw the blinding flash of a nuclear detonation. Popular literature in the 1950s was filled with stories in which nuclear war destroyed civilization and left a handful of survivors to pick through the rubble.

More insidiously, nuclear weapons development generated new environmental and health problems. Soldiers were exposed to post-test radiation with minimal protection. Nuclear tests in the South Pacific dusted fishing boats with radioactivity and forced islanders to abandon contaminated homes. Las Vegas promoted tests in southern Nevada as tourist attractions, but radioactive fallout contaminated large sections of the West and increased cancer rates among "downwinders" in Utah. Weapons production and atomic experiments contaminated vast tracts in Nevada, Washington, and Colorado and left huge environmental costs for later generations (see Map 10-2).

MAP 10-2 The Landscape of Nuclear Weapons
The development and production of nuclear weapons was concentrated in the West and South. The World War II sites of Hanford, Los Alamos, and Oak Ridge remained active after the war. Workers at Savannah River, Rocky Flats, and Pantex produced nuclear materials. Scientists and engineers at Lawrence-Livermore and Sandia laboratories designed and assembled weapons that were tested at the Nevada Proving Grounds. Prospectors with Geiger counters swarmed over the canyons of southwestern Colorado and southeastern Utah in a uranium mining rush in the early 1950s.

The Cold War in Asia

Communist victory in China's civil war was as predictable as the Soviet nuclear bomb, but no less controversial. American military and diplomatic missions in the late 1940s pointed out that the collapse of Jiang Jieshi's Nationalist regime was nearly inevitable, given its corruption and narrow support. Nevertheless, Americans looked for a scapegoat when Jiang's anti-Communist government and fragments of the Nationalist army fled to the island of Taiwan off China's southern coast.

Advocates for Jiang, mostly conservative Republicans from the Midwest and West, were certain that Truman's administration had done too little. "China asked for a sword," complained one senator, "and we gave her a dull paring knife." Critics looked for scapegoats. Foreign service officers who had honestly analyzed the weakness of the Nationalists were accused of Communist sympathies and hounded from their jobs. The results were tragedy for those unfairly branded as traitors and damage to the State Department, a weakness that would haunt the United States as it became entangled in Southeast Asia in the 1950s and 1960s.

Mao's victory expanded a deep fissure between "Europe first" and "Asia first" approaches to American foreign policy. Both during and after World War II, the United States had made Europe its first priority. Strong voices, however, had persistently argued that America's future lay with China, Japan, and the Pacific nations. Influential senators claimed that the "loss of China" was the disastrous result of putting the needs of England and France above the long-term interests of the United States.

NSC-68 and Aggressive Containment

The turmoil of 1949 led to a comprehensive statement of American strategic goals. In April 1950, the State Department prepared a sweeping report known as **National Security Council Paper 68 (NSC-68)**. The document described a world divided between the forces of "slavery" and "freedom" and assumed that the Soviet Union was actively aggressive, motivated by greed for territory and a "fanatic faith" in Communism. To defend civilization itself, said the experts, the United States should use as much force as needed to resist Communist expansion anywhere and everywhere.

The authors of NSC-68 thought in terms of military solutions. Truman and his advisors in 1947 and 1948 had hoped to contain the Soviets by diplomacy and by integrating the economies of Europe and Japan with that of the United States. Now that the Soviets had the atomic bomb, however, the American atomic shield might be neutralized. Instead, NSC-68 argued that the United States needed to press friendly nations to rearm and to make its former enemies into military allies. It also argued that the nation needed expensive conventional forces to defend Europe on the ground and to react to crises as a "world policeman." NSC-68 thus advocated nearly open-ended increases in the defense budget (which, in fact, tripled between 1950 and 1954).

NSC-68 summed up what many people already believed. Although it was not a public document, its portrait of implacable Communist expansion would have made sense to most Americans; it certainly did to Harry Truman. The outbreak of war in Korea at the end of June 1950 seemed to confirm that Communism was a military threat. The thinking behind the report led the United States to approach the Cold War as a military competition and to view political changes in Africa and Asia as parts of a Soviet plan. The need for a flexible military response became the centerpiece of an American policy of active intervention that led eventually to the jungles of Vietnam in the 1960s. And the report's implied strategy of bankrupting the Communists through competitive defense spending helped destroy the Soviet Union at the end of the 1980s.

War in Korea, 1950–1953

The success of Mao and the Chinese Communists forced the Truman administration to define national interests in eastern Asia and the western Pacific. The most important U.S. interest was Japan, still an industrial power despite its devastating defeat. The United States had denied the Soviet Union any part in the occupation of Japan in 1945 and had shaped a more democratic nation that would be a strong and friendly trading partner. Protected by American armed forces, Japan would be part of a crescent of offshore strong points that included Alaska, the Philippines, Australia, and New Zealand.

Two questions remained at the start of 1950 (and were still troublesome at the turn of the century). One was the future of Taiwan and the remnants of Jiang's regime. Some American policymakers wanted to defend Jiang against the Communists. Others assumed that his tattered forces would collapse and allow Mao to complete the Communist takeover of Chinese territory. The other question was Korea, whose own civil war would soon bring the world to the brink of World War III.

The Korean peninsula is the closest point on the Asian mainland to Japan. With three powerful neighbors—China, Russia, and Japan—Korea had always had to fight for its independence. From 1910 to 1945, it had been an oppressed colony of the Japanese empire. As World War II ended, Soviet troops moved down the peninsula from the north and American forces landed in the south, creating a situation similar to that in Germany. The 38th parallel, which Russians and Americans set as the dividing line between their zones of occupation, became a de facto border. The United States in 1948 recognized an independent South Korea, with its capital at Seoul, under a conservative government led by Syngman Rhee. Rhee's support came from large landowners and from a police force trained by the Japanese before 1945. The Soviets recognized a separate North Korea, whose leader, Kim Il Sung, advocated radical social and political change. Both leaders saw the 38th parallel as a temporary barrier and hoped to unify all Koreans under their own rule. Each crushed political dissent and tried to undermine the other with economic pressure and commando raids.

As early as 1947, the United States had decided that Korea itself was not essential to American military strategy. Planners assumed that U.S. air power in Japan could neutralize unfriendly forces on the Korean peninsula. But Korea remained politically important as the only point of direct confrontation with the Soviet Union in Asia. In January 1950, Secretary of State Dean Acheson carefully excluded Korea from the primary "defensive perimeter" of the United States but kept open the possibility of international guarantees for Korean security.

On June 25, 1950, North Korea, helped by Soviet equipment and Chinese training, attacked South Korea, an act that started the **Korean War**, which lasted until 1953 (see Map 10-3). Truman and Acheson believed that Moscow lay behind the invasion. They worried that the attack was a ploy to suck America's limited military resources into Asia before a bigger war came in Europe or the Middle East. Republicans blamed Acheson's speech for inviting an invasion, but the war was really an intensification of an ongoing civil war that Stalin was willing to exploit. In fact, Kim originated the invasion plan and spent a year persuading Stalin to agree to it. Stalin hoped that the conquest of South Korea would force Japan to sign a favorable treaty with the USSR.

The explosion of a hot war after five years of world tension seemed to American leaders to demand a military response. As the South Korean army collapsed, Truman committed American ground troops from Japan on June 30. The United States also had the good fortune of securing an endorsement from the United Nations. Because the Soviet Union was boycotting the UN (hoping to force the seating of Mao's People's Republic of China in place of Jiang's government), it could not use its veto when the Security Council asked UN members to help South Korea. The Korean conflict remained officially a United Nations

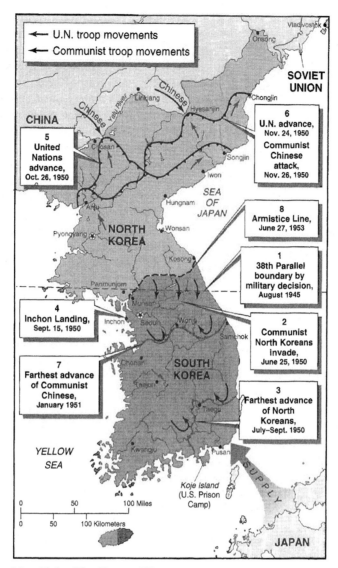

MAP 10-3   The Korean War
After rapid reversals of fortune in 1950 and early 1951, the war in Korea settled into stalemate. Most Americans agreed with the need to contain Communist expansion but found it deeply frustrating to fight for limited objectives rather than total victory.

action, although U.S. Generals Douglas MacArthur, Matthew Ridgway, and Mark Clark ran the show as the successive heads of the UN command.

The Politics of War

Fortunes in the first year of the Korean conflict seesawed three times. The first U.S. combat troops were outnumbered, outgunned, and poorly trained. They could not stop the North Koreans. By early August, the Americans clung to a narrow toehold around the port of Pusan on the tip of the Korean peninsula. As reinforcements arrived from the United States,

United Nation forces in Korea fought the weather as well as Communist North Koreans and Chinese. Baking summer heat alternated with fierce winters. Snow and cold were a major help to the Chinese when they surprised United States forces in November 1950 and drove American troops such as these southward.

however, MacArthur transformed the war with a daring amphibious counterattack at Inchon, 150 miles behind North Korean lines. The North Korean army was already overextended and exhausted. It collapsed and fled north.

The temptation to push across the 38th parallel and unify the peninsula under Syngman Rhee was irresistible. MacArthur and Washington officials disregarded warnings by China that it would enter the war if the United States tried to reunite Korea by force. U.S. and South Korean troops rolled north, drawing closer and closer to the boundary between North Korea and China.

Chinese forces attacked MacArthur's command in late October but then disappeared. MacArthur dismissed the attacks as a token gesture. In fact, they were a final warning. On November 26, the Chinese struck the overextended American columns. They had massed 300,000 troopswithout detection by American aviation. Their assault drove the UN forces into a two-month retreat that again abandoned Seoul.

Despite his glaring mistake, MacArthur remained in command until he publicly contradicted national policy. In March 1951, with the UN forces again pushing north, Truman prepared to offer a cease-fire that would have preserved the separate nations of South and North Korea. MacArthur tried to preempt the president by demanding that China admit defeat or suffer the consequences. He then published a direct attack on the administration's policy of limiting the Asian war to ensure the security of Europe.

President Truman had no choice. To protect civilian control of the armed forces, he relieved MacArthur of his command on April 11, 1951. The general returned to parades and a hero's welcome when he addressed a joint session of Congress. He quoted a line from an old barracks song: "Old soldiers never die; they just fade away." The song was soon heard on the radio, but Truman remained in charge of the war.

In Korea itself, U.S. and South Korean forces stabilized a strong defensive line that cut diagonally across the 38th parallel. Here the conflict settled into trench warfare. UN and Communist armies faced each other across steep bare hills that choked in clouds of summer dust and froze in winter. For two years, boredom alternated with fierce inch-by-inch battles for territory with such names as Heartbreak Ridge and Pork Chop Hill. The war's only glamour was in the air, where the arrival of new F-86 Saberjets in 1952 allowed American pilots to clear the skies of Chinese aviators in Russian-made MIG 15s.

Stabilization of the Korean front ushered in two years of truce negotiations beginning in July 1951, for none of the key actors wanted a wider war. The Chinese were careful to keep their war planes north of the ground combat zone. The Russians had stayed out of the war. The United States learned a painful lesson in 1950 and was willing to accept a divided Korea.

Negotiations stalled over thousands of Chinese prisoners of war who might not want to return to China. The political decision to turn free choice for POWs into a symbol of resistance to Communism left Truman's administration bogged down in a grinding war. Nearly half of the 140,000 U.S. casualties came after the truce talks started. The war was a decisive factor behind the Republican victory in the November 1952 elections and dragged on until June 1953, when an armistice returned the peninsula roughly to its prewar political division, a situation that has endured into the twenty-first century.

The blindly ambitious attack into North Korea was one of the great failures of intelligence and strategic leadership in American military history. Nearly everyone in Washington shared the blame for letting the excitement of battlefield victories obscure limited war aims. Civilian leaders could not resist the desire to roll back Communism. Truman hoped for a striking victory before the 1950 congressional elections. The Joint Chiefs of Staff failed to question a general with MacArthur's heroic reputation. MacArthur himself allowed ambition and wishful thinking to jeopardize his army.

Consequences of the Korean War The war in Korea was a preview of Vietnam fifteen years later. American leaders propped up an undemocratic regime to defend democracy. Both North Koreans and South Koreans engaged in savage political reprisals as the battlefront shifted back and forth. American soldiers found it hard distinguish between allied and enemy Koreans. American emphasis on the massive application of firepower led U.S. forces to demolish entire villages to kill single snipers. The air force tried to break North Korean resistance by pouring bombs on cities, power stations, factories, and dams; General Curtis Le May estimated that the bombings killed a million Koreans.

The Korean War had global consequences. It helped to legitimize the United Nations. In Washington, it confirmed the ideas underlying NSC-68, with its call for the United States to expand its military and to lead an anti-Communist alliance. Two days after the North Korean invasion, President Truman ordered the Seventh Fleet to protect the Nationalist Chinese on Taiwan, a decision that guaranteed twenty years of hostility between the United States and the People's Republic of China. In the same month, the United States began to aid France's struggle to retain control over its Southeast Asian colony of Indochina, which included Laos, Cambodia, and Vietnam.

In Europe, the United States now pushed to rearm West Germany as part of a militarized NATO and sent troops to Europe as a permanent defense force. It increased military aid to European governments and secured a unified command for the national forces allocated for NATO. The unified command made West German rearmament acceptable to France and the smaller nations of western Europe. Rearmament also stimulated German economic recovery and bound West Germany to the political and economic institutions of the North Atlantic nations. In 1952, the European Coal and Steel Community marked an important step toward economic cooperation that would evolve into the European Union by the end of the century. Dwight Eisenhower, who had led the Western allies in the invasion of France and Germany, became the new NATO commander in April 1951; his appointment symbolized the American commitment to western Europe.

THE SECOND RED SCARE

The Korean War reinforced the second Red Scare, an assault on civil liberties that stretched from the mid-1940s to the mid-1950s and dwarfed the Red Scare of 1919–1920. The Cold War fanned fears of Communist subversion on American soil. Legitimate concerns about espionage mixed with suspicions that Communist sympathizers in high places were helping

• • • O V E R V I E W • • •

THE SECOND RED SCARE

TYPE OF ANTI-COMMUNIST EFFORT	KEY TOOLS	RESULTS
Employee loyalty programs	U.S. attorney general's list of subversive organizations	Thousands of federal and state workers fired, careers damaged
Congressional investigations	HUAC McCarren Committee Army-McCarthy hearings	Employee blacklists, harassment of writers and intellectuals, Hollywood Ten
Criminal prosecutions	Trials for espionage and conspiracy to advocate violent overthrow of the U.S. government	Convictions of Communist Party leaders (1949), Alger Hiss (1950), and Rosenbergs (1951)

Stalin and Mao. The scare was also a weapon that the conservative wing of the Republican party used against men and women who had built Roosevelt's New Deal (see the Overview table, "The Second Red Scare").

Efforts to root out suspected subversives operated on three tracks. National and state governments established loyalty programs to identify and fire suspect employees. The courts punished members of suspect organizations. Congressional and state legislative investigations followed the whims of committee chairs. Anti-Communist crusaders often relied on dubious evidence and eagerly believed the worst. They also threatened basic civil liberties.

The Communist Party and the Loyalty Program

The Communist party in the United States was in rapid decline after World War II. Many intellectuals had left the party over the Nazi Soviet Pact in 1939. The wartime glow of military alliance with the Soviet Union helped the party recover to perhaps eighty thousand members—still fewer than one in every fifteen hundred Americans—but the postwar years brought a series of failures. In 1946, Walter Reuther defeated a Communist for the presidency of the huge United Auto Workers union, and other CIO unions froze Communists out of leadership positions. Communist support for Henry Wallace reduced the party's influence and separated it from the increasingly conservative mainstream of American politics.

Nevertheless, Republicans used Red-baiting as a campaign technique in 1944 and 1946, setting the stage for a national loyalty program. In 1944 they tried to frighten voters about "commydemocrats" by linking FDR, CIO labor unions, and Communism. Democrats slung their own mud by trying to convince voters that Hitler preferred the Republicans. Two years later, Republican campaigners told the public that the basic choice was "between Communism and Republicanism." Starting a thirty-year political career, a young Navy veteran named Richard Nixon won a southern California congressional seat by hammering on his opponent's connections to supposedly "Communist-dominated" organizations.

President Truman responded to the Republican landslide with Executive Order 9835 in March 1947, initiating a loyalty program for federal employees. Truman may have been trying to head off more drastic action by Congress. Nevertheless, Order 9835 was a blunt instrument. It authorized the attorney general to prepare a list of "totalitarian, Fascist, Communist, or subversive" organizations and made membership or even "sympathetic association" with such groups grounds for dismissal. The loyalty program applied to approximately 8 million Americans working for the federal government or defense contractors; similar state laws affected another 5 million.

Loyalty was a moving target. The attorney general's list grew by fits and starts, often with arbitrary additions. Many accusations were just malicious gossip, but allegations stayed in a worker's file even if refuted. Appointment to a new job in the federal government triggered a new investigation, in which officials might paw through the same old material. Many New Dealers and people associated with presumably liberal East Coast institutions were targets. An Interior Department official boasted that he had been especially effective in squeezing out graduates of Harvard and Columbia.

Federal employees worked under a cloud of fear. Would the cooperative store they had once patronized or the protest group they had joined in college suddenly appear on the attorney general's list? Would someone complain that they had disloyal books on their shelves? Loyalty boards asked about religion, racial equality, and a taste for foreign films; they also tried to identify homosexuals, who were thought to be targets for blackmail by foreign agents. The loyalty program resulted in 1,210 firings and 6,000 resignations under Truman and comparable numbers during Dwight Eisenhower's first term from 1953 to 1956.

Naming Names to Congress

Congress was even busier than the executive branch. The congressional hunt for subversives had its roots in 1938, when Congressman Martin Dies, a Texas Democrat, created the Special Committee on Un-American Activities. Originally intended to ferret out pro-Fascists, the Dies Committee evolved into the permanent **House Un-American Activities Committee (HUAC)** in 1945. It investigated "un-American propaganda" that attacked constitutional government.

One of HUAC's juiciest targets was Hollywood. In the last years before television, the movie industry stood at the height of its capacity to influence public opinion. In 1946, Americans bought an average of 90 million tickets every week. But Hollywood's reputation for loose morals, foreign-born directors, Jewish producers, and left-leaning writers aroused the suspicions of many congressmen. HUAC sought to make sure that no un-American messages were being peddled through America's most popular entertainment.

When the hearings opened in October 1947, studio executives, such as Jack Warner of Warner Brothers and Louis B. Mayer of MGM, assured HUAC of their anti-Communism. So did the popular actors Gary Cooper and Ronald Reagan. By contrast, eight screenwriters and two directors—the so-called Hollywood Ten—refused to discuss their past political associations, citing the free-speech protections of the First Amendment to the Constitution. HUAC countered with citations for contempt of Congress. The First Amendment defense failed when it reached the Supreme Court, and the Ten went to jail in 1950.

HUAC changed the politics of Hollywood. Before 1947, it had been fashionable to lean toward the left; even *The Best Years of Our Lives* contained criticism of American society. After the hearings, it was imperative to tilt the other way. Humphrey Bogart apologized for being a "dope" about politics. The government refused to let British-born Charlie Chaplin reenter the United States in 1952 because of his left-wing views. Other actors, writers, and directors found themselves on the Hollywood blacklist, banned from jobs where they might insert Communist propaganda into American movies.

At the start of 1951, the new Senate Internal Security Subcommittee joined the sometimes bumbling HUAC. The McCarran Committee, named for the Nevada senator who chaired it, targeted diplomats, labor union leaders, professors, and schoolteachers. Both committees turned their investigations into rituals. The real point was not to force personal confessions from witnesses but to badger them into identifying friends and associates who might have been involved in suspect activities.

The only sure way to avoid "naming names" was to respond to every question by citing the Fifth Amendment to the Constitution, which protects Americans from testifying against themselves. When the states adopted the Fifth Amendment in 1791, they wanted to protect citizens against false confessions coerced by intimidation and torture. The ordeal triggered by a congressional subpoena was certainly intimidating. Many Americans assumed that citing the amendment was a sure sign of guilt, not a matter of principle, and talked about Fifth Amendment Communists. "Taking the Fifth" could not protect jobs and reputations.

State legislatures imitated Congress by searching for "Reducators" among college faculty in such states as Oklahoma, Washington, and California. College presidents frequently fired faculty who took the Fifth Amendment. Harvard apparently used its influence to stay out of the newspapers, cutting a deal in which the FBI fed it information about suspect faculty, whom the university quietly fired. More common was the experience of the economics professor fired from the University of Kansas City after testimony before the McCarran Committee. He found it hard to keep any job once his name had been in the papers. A local dairy fired him because it thought its customers might be uneasy having a radical handle their milk bottles.

The moral dilemma posed by the investigations was revisited in 1954's Oscar-winning movie *On the Waterfront*. The director, Elia Kazan, and the scriptwriter, Budd Schulberg, had both "named names." They used the movie as a parable to justify their actions. The film's hero, played by Marlon Brando, agonizes about informing against corrupt officials in a dockworkers union. He finally speaks out at the urging of an activist priest. Most Americans called before HUAC and the McCarran Committee thought that Kazan and Schulberg had missed the point, for witnesses were usually being asked about previous political affiliations and beliefs, not current criminal activity.

Subversion Trials

In 1948, the Justice Department indicted the leaders of the American Communist party under the Alien Registration Act of 1940. Eleven men and women were convicted in 1949 of conspiring to advocate the violent overthrow of the United States government through their speech and publications. Some of the testimony came from Herbert Philbrick, an advertising manager and FBI informer who had posed as a party member. Philbrick parlayed his appearance into a bestseller entitled *I Led Three Lives* and then into a popular television series on which the FBI foiled Communist spies every Friday night.

The case of Alger Hiss soon followed. In 1948, a former Communist, Whittaker Chambers, named Hiss as a Communist, with whom he had associated in the 1930s. Hiss, who had held important posts in the State Department, first denied knowing Chambers but then admitted to having known him under another name. He continued to deny any involvement with Communists and sued Chambers for slander. As proof, Chambers gave Congressman Richard Nixon microfilms that he had hidden inside a pumpkin on his Maryland farm. Tests indicated that the "pumpkin papers" were State Department documents that had been copied on a typewriter that Hiss had once owned. With the new evidence, the Justice Department indicted Hiss for perjury—lying under oath. A first perjury trial ended in deadlock, but a second jury convicted Hiss in January 1950.

Hiss was more important as a symbol than as a possible spy. For more than forty years, the essence of his case was a matter of faith, not facts. Even his enemies agreed that any documents he might have stolen were of limited importance. What was important, they said, was the sort of disloyalty and "weak thinking" that Hiss represented. Moreover, his smugness as a member of the East Coast establishment enraged them. To his opponents, Hiss stood for every wrong turn that the nation had taken since 1932. In contrast, his supporters found a virtue in every trait that his enemies hated, from his refined taste to his education at Johns Hopkins University and Harvard Law School. Many supporters believed that he had been framed. Both sides claimed support from Soviet records that became public in the 1990s, but the weight of evidence is that he did pass information to the Soviets from the mid-1930s through 1945.

The case of Julius and Ethel Rosenberg represented a similar test of belief. In 1950, the British arrested nuclear physicist Klaus Fuchs, who confessed to passing atomic secrets to the Soviets when he worked at Los Alamos in 1944 and 1945. The "Fuchs spy ring" soon implicated the Rosenbergs, New York radicals of strong beliefs but limited sophistication. Convicted in 1951 of the vague charge of conspiring to commit espionage, they were sent to the electric chair in 1953 after refusing to buy a reprieve by naming other spies.

As with Alger Hiss, the government had a plausible, but not an airtight case. After their trial, the Rosenbergs became a cause for international protest. Their small children became pawns and trophies in political demonstrations, an experience recaptured in E.L. Doctorow's novel *The Book of Daniel* (1971). There is no doubt that Julius Rosenberg was a convinced Communist, and it is very likely that he was a minor participant in an atomic spy net, but Ethel Rosenberg was charged, in the words of FBI director J. Edgar Hoover, "as a lever" to pressure her husband into naming his confederates.

Senator McCarthy on Stage

The best-remembered participant in the second Red Scare was Senator Joseph McCarthy of Wisconsin. Crude, sly, and ambitious, McCarthy had ridden to victory in the Republican landslide of 1946. His campaign slogan, "Congress needs a tail gunner," claimed a far braver

Senator Joe McCarthy used press releases and carefully managed congressional committee hearings to attack suspected Communists, although he had almost no hard information. At the Army-McCarthy hearings in June, 1954 he clashed with attorney Joseph Welch. Here Welch listens as McCarthy points to Oregon on a map that supposedly showed Communist party organization in the United States.

war record than he had earned. He burst into national prominence on February 9, 1950. In a rambling speech in Wheeling, West Virginia, he latched on to the issue of Communist subversion. Although no transcript of the speech survives, he supposedly stated: "I have here in my hand a list of 205 that were known to the Secretary of State as being members of the Communist Party and who, nevertheless, are still working and shaping the policy of the State Department." In the following days, the 205 Communists changed quickly to 57, to 81, to 10, to 116.

McCarthy's rise to fame climaxed with an incoherent six-hour speech to the Senate. He tried to document the charges by mixing previously exposed spies with people who no longer worked for the government or who had never worked for it. Over the next several years, his speeches were aimed at moving targets, full of multiple untruths. He threw out so many accusations, true or false, that the facts could never catch up.

As politicians tried to figure out how to deal with McCarthy, the public heard the repeated accusations but not the lack of evidence. While some senators treated McCarthy as a crude outsider in their exclusive club, others embraced his message, and voters in 1950 turned against his most prominent opponents. Liberal politicians ran for cover; conservatives were happy for McCarthy to attract media attention away from HUAC and the McCarran Committee. In 1951, McCarthy even called George Marshall, then serving as secretary of defense, an agent of Communism. The idea was ludicrous. Marshall was one of the most upright Americans of his generation, the architect of victory in World War II, and a key contributor to the stabilization of Europe. Nevertheless, McCarthy was so popular that the Republicans featured him at their 1952 convention. That fall, the Republicans' presidential candidate, Dwight Eisenhower, appeared on the same campaign platform with McCarthy and conspicuously failed to defend George Marshall, who had been chiefly responsible for Eisenhower's fast-track career.

McCarthy's personal crudeness made him a media star but eventually undermined him. Given control of the Senate Committee on Government Operations in 1953, he investigated dozens of agencies from the Government Printing Office to the Army Signal Corps. Early in 1954, he began to harass the U.S. Army about the promotion of an army dentist with a supposedly subversive background. The confrontation turned into two months of televised hearings that revealed the emptiness of the charges. The cameras also put McCarthy's style on trial. "Have you no decency?" asked the army's lawyer, Joseph Welch, at one point.

The end came quickly. McCarthy's "favorable" rating in the polls plummeted. The comic strip *Pogo* began to feature a foolishly menacing figure with McCarthy's face named Simple J. Malarkey. The U.S. Senate finally voted 67 to 22 in December 1954 to condemn McCarthy for conduct "unbecoming a Member of the Senate." Until his death from alcoholism in 1957, he was an increasingly isolated figure, repudiated by the Senate and ignored by the media who had built him up.

Understanding McCarthyism

The antisubversive campaign that everyone now calls **McCarthyism**, however, died a slower death. Legislation, such as the Internal Security Act (1950) and the Immigration and Nationality Act (1952), remained as tools of political repression. HUAC continued to mount investigations as late as the 1960s.

Fear of Communist subversion reached deep into American society. In the early 1950s, Cincinnati's National League baseball team was phasing in a new double-play duo of second baseman Johnny Temple and shortstop Roy McMillan. The team was also trying out a new name, for it was important not to let the national game be tainted by Communism. Harking back to its origins as the Red Stockings, the team was now the "Redlegs," not the "Reds." The brief revision of baseball history was one example of how the fear of Communists spread from Washington through the grass roots. Cities and states required loyalty oaths from their employees; Ohio even required oaths from recipients of unemployment compensation.

In retrospect, at least four factors made Americans afraid of Communist subversion. One was a legitimate but exaggerated concern about atomic spies. A second was an undercurrent of anti-Semitism and nativism, for many labor organizers and Communist party members (like the Rosenbergs) had Jewish and eastern European backgrounds. Third was Southern and Western resentment of the nation's Ivy League elite. Most general, finally, was a widespread fear that the world was spinning out of control. Many people sought easy explanations for global tensions. It was basically reassuring if Soviet and Chinese Communist successes were the result of American traitors rather than of Communist strengths.

Partisan politics mobilized the fears and resentments into a political force. From 1946 through 1952, the conservative wing of the Republican party used the Red Scare to attack New Dealers and liberal Democrats. HUAC, the McCarran Committee, and McCarthy were all tools for bringing down the men and women who had been moving the United States toward a more active government at home and abroad. The Republican elite used McCarthy until this group won control of the presidency and Congress in 1952, and then it abandoned him.

The broader goal of the second Red Scare was conformity of thought. Many of the professors and bureaucrats targeted for investigation had indeed been Communists or interested in Communism, usually in the 1930s and early 1940s. Most saw it as a way to increase social justice, and they sometimes excused the failures of Communism in the Soviet Union. Unlike the handful of real spies, however, they were targeted not for actions but for ideas. The investigations and loyalty programs were efforts to ensure that Americans kept any left-wing ideas to themselves.

CONCLUSION

In the face of confrontation over Berlin, fighting in Korea, and growing numbers of nuclear weapons, the Cold War stayed cool because each side achieved its essential goals. The Soviet Union controlled eastern Europe, while the United States built increasingly strong ties with the NATO nations and Japan. Though the result was a stalemate that would last through the 1980s, it nevertheless absorbed huge shares of Soviet and American resources and conditioned the thinking of an entire generation.

The shift from prewar isolationism to postwar internationalism was one of the most important changes in the nation's history. To many of its advocates, internationalism represented a commitment to spread political democracy to other nations. As the 1950s and 1960s would show, the results often contradicted the ideal when the United States forcibly imposed its will on other peoples. Even as the results overseas fell short of the ideal, however, the new internationalism highlighted and helped change domestic racial attitudes.

The Truman years saw the implementation of a national security policy that dominated the next half-century. The armed forces were strong but subordinate to the civilian administration through the National Security Council and Department of Defense. The expansion of the close alliance between scientific research and defense needs that had begun with World War II augmented the national defense capacity. The United States led an international system of collective security based on mutual defense treaties, contributing financial assistance and sophisticated weapons while its allies helped to provide the military manpower.

These same years also brought increasing stability within the nation. The economic chaos of 1946 faded quickly. By identifying liberalism at home with anti-Communism abroad, Truman's efforts to define a vital center helped protect the New Deal. Americans in the early 1950s could be confident that New Deal and Fair Deal programs to expand economic opportunity and increase economic security were permanent, if incomplete, setting the stage for new social activism in the 1960s. If the Republicans had won in 1948, they might have dismantled the New Deal. By 1952, both presidential candidates affirmed the consensus that placed economic opportunity at the center of the national agenda. The suburban housing boom seemed to turn the dream of prosperity into reality for millions of families.

Despite the turmoil and injustice of the second Red Scare and deep worries about nuclear war, the United States emerged from the Truman years remarkably prosperous. It was also more secure from international threats than many nervous Americans appreciated. The years from 1946 to 1952 set the themes for a generation that believed that the United States could do whatever it set its mind to: end poverty, land an astronaut on the moon, thwart Communist revolutions in other countries. There was a direct line from Harry Truman's 1947 declaration that the United States would defend freedom around the world to John Kennedy's 1961 promise that the nation would bear any burden necessary to protect free nations from Communism. As the world moved slowly toward greater stability in the 1950s, Americans were ready for a decade of confidence.

Review Questions

1. As described in the opening of the chapter, what housing choices were available after World War II? How did these choices reshape American cities?

2. What were the key differences between Harry Truman and congressional Republicans about the legacy of the New Deal? Why did regulating labor unions become a central domestic issue in the late 1940s? Why did Truman manage to win the presidential election of 1948 despite starting as an underdog?

3. How did the postwar years expand opportunity for veterans and members of the working class? How did they limit opportunities for women? How did they begin to challenge racial inequities in American society? How did the postwar readjustment create a suburban society?

4. What foreign policy priorities did the United States set after 1945? To what extent did the United States achieve its most basic objectives? How did mutual mistrust fuel the origins and deepen the Cold War?

5. How did the Cold War change character in 1949 and 1950? What were key actions by the Soviet Union and China, and how did the United States respond? What was the effect of the chaotic fighting in Korea on U.S. domestic politics and diplomacy?

6. What factors motivated an increasingly frantic fear of domestic subversion in the late 1940s and early 1950s? Who were the key actors in the second Red Scare? What was its long-term impact on American society?

Key Terms

Berlin blockade *295*

Central Intelligence Agency (CIA) *295*

Cold War *280*

Containment *294*

Council of Economic Advisers *282*

Dixiecrats *288*

GI Bill of Rights *283*

House Un-American Activities Committee (HUAC) *305*

International Monetary Fund *292*

Recommended Reading

Paul Boyer, *By the Bomb's Early Light: American Thought and Culture at the Dawn of the Atomic Age* (1985). Examines the mixture of hopes and fears with which Americans greeted the arrival of the atomic age, giving detailed attention to popular culture as well as national policy.

Joseph C. Goulden, *The Best Years, 1945–1950* (1976). A very readable portrayal of the ways in which Americans adjusted to the postwar years, drawing heavily on contemporary magazine accounts.

Melvyn Leffler, *A Preponderance of Power: National Security, the Truman Administration, and the Cold War* (1992). Provides a balanced interpretation of responsibility for the Cold War in a detailed but readable account of American policy.

Samuel Lubell, *The Future of American Politics* (1952). An incisive analysis of the social forces that shaped the American political scene in the 1940s, giving insights that are still telling after more than four decades.

David McCullough, *Truman* (1992). A readable and sympathetic biography of the thirty-third president.

Victor Navasky, *Naming Names* (1980). The impact of HUAC on Hollywood and the entertainment industry, told by a strong opponent of the Committee.

Arnold Rampersad, *Jackie Robinson* (1997). Presents Jackie Robinson as a pioneer of racial integration on and off the ball field.

William Stueck, *Rethinking the Korean War: A New Diplomatic and Strategic History* (2002). An up-to-date analysis of the global impact of the war in Korea.

THE CONFIDENT YEARS: 1953-1964

The first day I was able to enter Central High School [in Little Rock, Arkansas, September 23, 1957], what I felt inside was terrible, wrenching, awful fear. On the car radio I could hear that there was a mob. I knew what a mob meant and I knew that the sounds that came from the crowd were very angry. So we entered the side of the building, very, very fast. Even as we entered there were people running after us, people tripping other people. . . . There has never been in my life any stark terror or any fear akin to that.

I'd only been in the school a couple of hours and by that time it was apparent that the mob was just overrunning the school. Policemen were throwing down their badges and the mob was getting past the wooden sawhorses because the police would no longer fight their own in order to protect us. So we were all called into the principal's office, and there was great fear that we would not get out of this building. We were trapped. And I thought, Okay, so I'm going to die here, in school. . . . Even the adults, the school officials, were panicked, feeling like there was no protection. . . . [A] gentleman, who I believed to be the police chief, said . . . "I'll get them out." And we were taken to the basement of this place. And we were put into two cars, grayish blue Fords. And the man instructed the drivers, he said, "Once you start driving, do not stop." And he told us to put our heads down. This guy revved up his engine and he came up out of the bowels of this building, and as he came up, I could just see hands reaching across this car, I could hear the yelling, I could see guns, and he was told not to stop. "If you hit somebody, you keep rolling, 'cause the kids are dead." And he did just that, and he didn't hit anybody, but he certainly was forceful and aggressive in the way he exited

this driveway, because people tried to stop him and he didn't stop. He dropped me off at home. And I remember saying, "Thank you for the ride," and I should've said, "Thank you for my life."
    —Melba Pattillo

Melba Pattillo Beals in Henry Hampton and Steve Frayer, eds., *Voices of Freedom: An Oral History of the Civil Rights Movement from the 1950s through the 1980s* (New York: Bantam, 1990).

MELBA PATTILLO was one of the nine African-American students who entered previously all-white Central High in the fall of 1957. Her enrollment in the high school, where she managed to last through a year of harassment and hostility, was a symbolic step in the journey toward greater racial equality in American society. School integration in Little Rock implemented the U.S. Supreme Court decision in the case of *Brown* v. *Board of Education* in 1954, which declared that racially segregated schools violated the mandate that all citizens receive equal protection of the law. The violence with which some white residents of Little Rock responded, and the courage of the students, marked one of the key episodes in the civil rights revolution that spanned roughly a decade from the *Brown* decision to the Voting Rights Act of 1965.

The struggle for full civil rights for all Americans was rooted in national ideals, but it was also shaped by the continuing tensions of the Cold War. President Dwight Eisenhower acted against his own inclinations and sent federal troops to keep the peace in Little Rock in part because he worried about public opinion in other nations. As the United States and the Soviet Union maneuvered for influence in Africa and Asia, domestic events sometimes loomed large in foreign relations. Few Americans questioned the rightness or necessity of contesting the Cold War—or of America's ultimate triumph. This consensus gave U.S. policy an overarching goal of containment but also narrowed American options by casting issues at home and abroad in terms of the U.S.–Soviet rivalry.

Melba Pattillo's life after Little Rock also reveals something about the increasing economic opportunities available to most Americans. She eventually graduated from San Francisco State University, earned a master's degree from Columbia University, and went on to a career as a television reporter and writer. San Francisco State, which was rapidly expanding on a new campus, was itself part of the great expansion of higher education that helped millions of Americans move into middle-class jobs and neighborhoods. The prosperous years from 1953 to 1964 spread the economic promise of the 1940s across American society. Young couples could afford large families and new houses. Labor unions grew conservative because cooperation with big business offered immediate gains for their members.

Despite challenges at home and abroad, Americans were fundamentally confident during the decade after the Korean War. They expected corporations to use scientific research to craft new products for eager customers. When the USSR challenged U.S. preeminence and launched the first artificial space satellite in 1957, Americans responded with shock followed by redoubled efforts to regain what they considered their rightful world leadership in science and technology.

KEY TOPICS

Affluence and conformity in the middle class during the 1950s.

The Cold War confrontation with the USSR during the Eisenhower and Kennedy administrations.

The struggle for African-American civil rights.

Lyndon Johnson and the Great Society.

• CHRONOLOGY •

1953 CIA backed coup returns the Shah, Reza Pahlevi, to power in Iran.

Soviet Union detonates hydrogen bomb.

1954 Vietnamese defeat the French; Geneva conference divides Vietnam.

United States and allies form SEATO.

Supreme Court decides *Brown v. Board of Education of Topeka*.

CIA overthrows the government of Guatemala.

China provokes a crisis over Quemoy and Matsu.

1955 Salk polio vaccine is announced.

Black citizens boycott Montgomery, Alabama, bus system.

Soviet Union forms the Warsaw Pact.

AFL and CIO merge.

1956 Interstate Highway Act is passed.

Soviets repress Hungarian revolt.

Israel, France, and Britain invade Egypt.

1957 U.S. Army maintains law and order in Little Rock after violent resistence to integration of Central High School.

Soviet Union launches *Sputnik*, world's first artificial satellite.

1958 United States and Soviet Union voluntarily suspend nuclear tests.

1959 Fidel Castro takes power in Cuba.

Nikita Khrushchev visits the United States.

1960 U-2 spy plane shot down over Russia.

Sit-in movement begins in Greensboro, North Carolina.

1961 Bay of Pigs invasion fails.

Kennedy establishes the Peace Corps.

Vienna summit fails.

Freedom rides are held in the Deep South.

Berlin crisis leads to construction of the Berlin Wall.

1962 John Glenn orbits the earth.

Cuban missile crisis brings the world to the brink of nuclear war.

Michael Harrington publishes *The Other America*.

1963 Civil rights demonstrations rend Birmingham.

Civil rights activists march in Washington.

Betty Friedan publishes *The Feminine Mystique*.

Limited Test Ban Treaty is signed.

Ngo Dinh Diem is assassinated in South Vietnam.

President Kennedy is assassinated.

1964 Civil Rights Act is passed.

Freedom Summer is organized in Mississippi.

Office of Economic Opportunity is created.

Gulf of Tonkin Resolution is passed.

Wilderness Act marks new direction in environmental policy.

1965 Medical Care Act establishes Medicare and Medicaid.

Elementary and Secondary Education Act extends direct federal aid to local schools.

Selma to Montgomery march climaxes era of nonviolent civil rights demonstrations.

Voting Rights Act suspends literacy tests for voting.

A DECADE OF AFFLUENCE

Americans in the 1950s believed in the basic strength of the United States. Television's General Electric Theater was third in the ratings in 1956–1957. Every week, its host, Ronald Reagan, a popular Hollywood lead from the late 1930s, stated, "At General Electric, progress is our most important product." It made sense to his viewers. Large, technologically sophisticated corporations were introducing new marvels: Orlon sweaters and Saran Wrap, long-playing records and Polaroid cameras. As long as the United States defended free enterprise, Reagan told audiences on national speaking tours, the sky was the limit.

Many Americans valued free enterprise and family life as part of the anti-Communist crusade. Social and intellectual conformity assured a united front. Congress established Loyalty Day in 1955. National leaders argued that strong families were bulwarks against

Communism and that churchgoing inoculated people against subversive ideas. Under the lingering cloud of McCarthyism, the range of political ideas that influenced government policy was narrower than in the 1930s and 1940s. Nevertheless, critics began to voice the discontents that exploded in the 1960s and 1970s.

What's Good for General Motors

Dwight Eisenhower presided over the prosperity of the 1950s. Both Democrats and Republicans had courted him as a presidential candidate in 1948. Four years later, he picked the Republicans because he wanted to make sure that the party remained committed to NATO and collective security in Europe rather than retreating into isolationism. He easily defeated the Democrat, Adlai Stevenson, the moderately liberal governor of Illinois. Stevenson was a thoughtful politician, a witty campaigner, and a favorite in academic circles. He also carried Truman's negative legacy of domestic policy confrontation, the hated war in Korea, and the "loss" of China, and he had no chance of winning.

Eisenhower and the Politics of the Middle Over the next eight years, Eisenhower claimed the political middle for Republicans. Publicists tried a variety of labels for his domestic views: "progressive moderation," "New Republicanism," "dynamic conservatism." Satisfied with postwar America, Eisenhower accepted much of the New Deal but saw little need for further reform. In a 1959 poll, liberals considered him a fellow liberal and conservatives thought him a conservative.

Eisenhower's first secretary of defense, "Engine Charlie" Wilson, had headed General Motors. At his Senate confirmation hearing, he proclaimed, "For years, I thought what was good for the country was good for General Motors and vice versa." Wilson's statement captured a central theme of the 1950s. Not since the 1920s had Americans been so excited about the benefits of big business. When *Fortune* magazine began in 1957 to publish an annual list of the 500 largest American corporations, it tapped a national fascination with America's productive capacity.

The New Prosperity The economy in the 1950s gave Americans much to like. Between 1950 and 1964, output grew by a solid 3.2 percent per year. Automobile production, on which dozens of other industries depended, neared 8 million vehicles per year in the mid-1950s; less than 1 percent of new car sales were imports.

American workers in the 1950s had more disposable income than ever before. Their productivity, or output per worker, increased steadily. Average compensation per hour of work rose faster than consumer prices in nine of eleven years from 1953 to 1964. Rising productivity made it easy for corporations to share gains with large labor unions. The steel and auto industries set the pace with contracts that gave their workers a middle-class way of life. In turn, labor leaders lost interest in radical changes in American society. In 1955, the older and politically more conservative American Federation of Labor absorbed the younger Congress of Industrial Organizations. The new AFL-CIO positioned itself as a partner in prosperity and foe of Communism at home and abroad.

For members of minority groups with regular industrial and government jobs, the 1950s were also economically rewarding. Industrial cities, such as Detroit, Dayton, and Oakland, offered them factory jobs at wages that could support a family. Black people worked through the Urban League, the National Association of Colored Women, and other race-oriented groups to secure fair employment laws and jobs with large corporations. Many Puerto Rican migrants to New York found steady work in the Brooklyn Navy Yard.

Mexican-American families in San Antonio benefited from maintenance jobs at the city's military bases. Steady employment allowed black people and Latinos to build strong community institutions and vibrant neighborhood business districts.

However, there were never enough family-wage jobs for all of the African-American and Latino workers who continued to move to northern and western cities. Many Mexican Americans were still migrant farm laborers and workers in nonunionized sweatshops. Minority workers were usually the first to suffer from the erosion of industrial jobs that began in the 1960s and black unemployment crept upward to twice the white rate.

Native Americans faced equally daunting prospects. To cut costs and accelerate assimilation, Congress pushed the policy of termination between 1954 and 1962. The government sold tribal land and assets, distributed the proceeds among tribal members, and terminated its treaty relationship with the tribe. Applied to such tribes as the Klamaths in Oregon and the Menominees in Wisconsin, termination gave thousands of Indians onetime cash payments but cut them adrift from the security of tribal organizations. The Bureau of Indian Affairs also encouraged Indians to move to large cities, but jobs were often unavailable. The new urban populations would nourish growing militancy among Native Americans in the 1960s and 1970s.

Beating Polio

When Dr. Jonas Salk announced an effective vaccine for polio on April 12, 1955, the United States gained a new hero. In the confident mid-1950s, the polio vaccine seemed another proof of American ability to improve the world.

Poliomyelitis, or infantile paralysis, attacks the nervous system; it can paralyze the legs or kill by short-circuiting muscles in the throat and chest. Before 1900, infants had often encountered the polio virus in their first months and developed lifelong immunity. In the twentieth century, cleaner houses and streets delayed contact with polio until the preschool years or later, when the disease could be devastating. The virus sometimes struck adults; it cost Franklin Roosevelt the use of his legs when he was in his thirties, but most victims were children.

Fear of polio had haunted American families after World War II. The disease killed fewer people than heart disease or cancer, but it seemed grossly unfair. Most Americans knew at least one child who hobbled through life on crutches and metal leg braces. Hospitals filled with new cases every summer—58,000 in 1952 alone. Many children clung to life inside iron lungs, metal cylinders that pumped air in and out of a hole in the throat.

Polio season peaked in July and August. Worried parents kept their children out of movie theaters and swimming pools, but the disease struck even the most careful families. One woman who grew up in the 1950s remembered: "Polio? That was the big fear when I was young. . . . I remember going to Dallas and seeing television for the first time. . . . Every day they would report 'another so many polio cases today.' "

Salk's announcement was welcome news. A generation later, President Ronald Reagan would list the polio vaccine with the steam engine and silicon chip as one of the great modern discoveries. By 2002, the number of new polio cases around the world had fallen to fewer than one thousand in only ten countries—not including the United States.

For Americans in the mid-1950s, the defeat of polio affirmed faith in the future. Everyday Americans had supported Salk's research through their contributions to the March of Dimes fund-raising appeals. Thousands of children had voluntarily participated in the field trials of the vaccine. The same scientific and technical know-how that corporations were using to craft new products, it seemed, could also belong to the nation as a whole for the benefit of all its people.

Reshaping Urban America

If Eisenhower's administration opted for the status quo on many issues, it nevertheless reshaped American cities around an agenda of economic development. In 1954, Congress transformed the public housing program into urban renewal. Cities used federal funds to replace low-rent businesses and run-down housing on the fringes of their downtowns with new hospitals, civic centers, sports arenas, office towers, and luxury apartments. Urban renewal temporarily revitalized older cities in the Northeast and Midwest that were already feeling the competition of the fast-growing South and West. *Fortune* in 1956 concluded that some of the largest cities were the best run—Cincinnati, New York, Philadelphia, Detroit, Milwaukee.

Only a decade later, the same cities would top the list of urban crisis spots, in part because of accumulating social costs from urban renewal. The bulldozers often leveled minority neighborhoods in the name of downtown expansion. Urban renewal displaced Puerto Ricans in New York, African Americans in Atlanta and Norfolk, Mexican Americans in Denver. Los Angeles demolished the seedy Victorian mansions of Bunker Hill, just northwest of downtown, for a music center and bank towers. A mile to the north was Chavez Ravine, whose Mexican-American population lived in substandard housing but maintained a lively community. When conservative opposition blocked plans for public housing, the residents were evicted, and Dodger Stadium was built. Here as elsewhere, urban showplaces rose at the expense of minority groups.

The Eisenhower administration also revolutionized American transportation. Americans had long dreamed of something better than two-lane highways that routed motorists through the stop-and-go traffic of cities and trapped them behind creeping trucks. By the early 1950s, they were fed up with roads designed for Model A Fords: They wanted to enjoy their new V-8 engines. The solution was the **Federal Highway Act of 1956**, creating a national system of interstate and defense highways. The legislation wrapped a program to build 41,000 miles of freeways in the language of the Cold War. The roads would be wide and strong enough for trucks hauling military hardware; they were also supposed to make it easy to evacuate cities in case of a Soviet attack.

Although the first interstate opened in Kansas in 1956, most of the mileage came in use in the 1960s and 1970s. Interstates halved the time of city-to-city travel. They were good for General Motors, the steel industry, and the concrete industry, because the roads were the construction equivalent of sixty Panama Canals. The highways promoted long-distance trucking at the expense of railroads. They also wiped out hundreds of homes per mile when they plunged through large cities. As with urban renewal, the bulldozers most often plowed through African-American or Latino neighborhoods, where land was cheap and white politicians could ignore protests. Some cities, such as Miami, used the highways as barricades between white and black neighborhoods.

Interstates accelerated suburbanization. The beltways or perimeter highways that began to ring most large cities made it easier and more profitable to develop new subdivisions and factory sites than to reinvest in city centers. Federal grants for sewers and other basic facilities further cut suburban costs. Continuing the pattern of the late 1940s, suburban growth added a million new single-family houses per year.

Comfort on Credit

Prosperity transformed spending habits. The 1930s had taught Americans to avoid debt. The 1950s taught them to buy on credit. Families financed their new houses with 90 percent Federal Housing Administration (FHA) mortgages and 100 percent Veterans Administration

(VA) mortgages. They filled the rooms by signing installment contracts at furniture and appliance stores and charging the drapes and carpeting on department-store credit cards. The value of consumer debt, excluding home mortgages, tripled from 1952 to 1964.

New forms of marketing facilitated credit-based consumerism. The first large-scale suburban shopping center was Northgate in Seattle, which assembled all the pieces of the full-grown mall—small stores facing an interior corridor between anchor department stores and surrounded by parking. By the end of the decade, developers were building malls with 1 million square feet of shopping floorspace. At the start of the 1970s, the universal credit card (Visa, MasterCard) made shopping even easier.

Surrounding the new malls were the servants and symbols of America's car culture. Whereas cities of the early twentieth century had been built around the public transportation of streetcars and subways, the 1950s depended on private automobiles. Interstate highways sucked retail business from small-town main streets to interchanges on the edge of town. Nationally franchised motels and fast-food restaurants sprang up along suburban shopping strips, pioneered by Holiday Inn (1952) and McDonald's (nationally franchised in 1955). By shopping along highways rather than downtown, suburban whites also opted to use places that minimized contact with people of other races.

More extreme than the mall were entirely new environments for high-intensity consumption and entertainment that appeared in the Southwest. Mobster Bugsy Siegel transformed Las Vegas with the Flamingo Hotel in 1947. Other hotel-casinos soon turned Vegas into a middle-class adult fantasy land. Disneyland was Las Vegas for the whole family, a walk-through fantasy designed to outperform wide-screen movies as a "real" experience. Opening in Orange County, California, in 1955, Disneyland offered a carefully tended environment that was as safe as a shopping mall and as artificial as Las Vegas—a never-ending state fair without the smells and dust.

The New 1950s Family

Family life in the Eisenhower years departed from historic patterns. Prosperity allowed children to finish school and young adults to marry right after high school. Young women faced strong social pressure to pursue husbands rather than careers; women went to college, people said, to get the "Mrs." degree rather than the B.A. In a decade when the popular press worried about "latent homosexuality," single men were also suspect. The proportion of single adults reached its twentieth-century low in 1960. At all social levels, young people married quickly and had an average of three children spaced closely together, adding to the number of baby boomers whose needs would influence American society for the rest of the century. Family activities replaced the street corner for kids and the neighborhood tavern for men. Strong families, said experts, defended against Communism by teaching American values.

The Impact of Television Television was made to order for the family-centered fifties. By 1960, fully 87 percent of households had sets. Previously popular entertainment had been a community activity: People saw movies as part of a group, cheered baseball teams as part of a crowd. TV was watched in the privacy of the home.

Television programming was up for grabs. Experts hoped that 90-minute dramas would elevate popular taste, but morning talk shows, quiz shows, and such puppet shows as *Howdy Doody* were common in the early days because they were cheap to produce. Variety hours recycled old vaudeville formats. Soap operas, fifteen-minute newscasts, and Saturday morning adventure shows were adapted straight from radio.

Situation comedies were the most successful programs. Viewers liked continuing characters who resolved everyday problems in half an hour. A few shows dealt with characters outside the middle-class mainstream, such as the bus driver and sewer worker played by Jackie Gleason and Art Carney on *The Jackie Gleason Show* and *The Honeymooners* (1952–1957). Most successful shows depicted the ideal of family togetherness. Lucille Ball and Desi Arnaz in *I Love Lucy* (1951–1955) started a family and left New York for suburbia. The families on *The Adventures of Ozzie and Harriet* (1952–1966), *Father Knows Best* (1954–1962), and *Leave It to Beaver* (1957–1962) were white, polite, and happy. The Nelsons, Andersons, and Cleavers bore northern European names and lived in single-family houses with friendly neighbors. Thousands of school-aged baby boomers wondered why their families didn't have good times like the families on the picture tube.

Stay-at-Home Moms and Working Women The 1950s extended the stay-at-home trend of the postwar years. Women in the fifties gave up some of their earlier educational gains. Their share of new college degrees and professional jobs fell. Despite millions of new electric appliances, the time spent on housework increased. Magazines proclaimed that proper families maintained distinct roles for dad and mom, who was urged to find fulfillment in a well-scrubbed house and children. While television programming helped limit women's roles by power of example, TV actresses assured readers that they were housewives first and career women second.

In fact, rather than allowing women to stay home as housewives, family prosperity in the 1950s often depended on their earnings. The number of employed women reached new highs. By 1960, nearly 35 percent of all women held jobs, including 7.5 million mothers with children under 17 (see Figure 11-1). The pressures of young marriages, large families, and economic needs interacted to erode some of the assumptions behind the idealized family and laid the groundwork for dramatic social changes in the 1960s and 1970s.

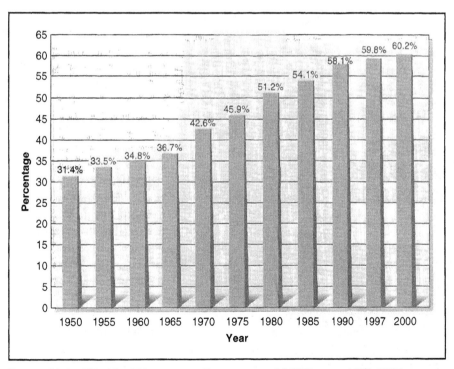

FIGURE 11-1   **Working Women as a Percentage of All Women, 1950–2000**
The proportion of American women who are part of the labor force (working or looking for work) has increased steadily since 1950, with the fastest increase between 1965 and 1985.

Inventing Teenagers

Teenagers in the 1950s joined adults as consumers of movies, clothes, and automobiles. Advertisers tapped and expanded the growing youth market by promoting a distinct "youth culture," an idea that became omnipresent in the 1960s and 1970s. While psychologists pontificated on the special problems of adolescence, many cities matched their high schools to the social status of their students: college-prep curricula for middle-class neighborhoods, vocational and technical schools for future factory workers, and separate schools or tracks for African Americans and Latinos. "Maturity" in middle-class high schools meant self-confidence and leadership; at vocational schools, it meant neatness and respect for authority. In effect, the schools trained some children to be doctors and officers and others to be mechanics and enlisted men.

All teenagers shared rock-and-roll, a new music of the mid-1950s that adapted black urban rhythm-and-blues for a white mass market. Rhythm-and-blues was the hard-edged and electrified offspring of traditional blues and gospel music. In turn, rock music augmented its black roots by drawing vitality from poor white Southerners (Buddy Holly, Elvis Presley), Hispanics (Richie Valens), and, in the 1960s, the British working class (the Beatles). Record producers played up the association between rock music and youthful rebellion. The 1955 movie *Blackboard Jungle* depicted juvenile delinquency to the music of Bill Haley's "Rock Around the Clock." Elvis Presley's meteoric career, launched in 1956 with "Heartbreak Hotel," depended on both his skill at blending country music with rhythm-and-blues and the sexual suggestiveness of his stage act.

Technological changes helped rock split off from adult pop music. Portable phonographs and 45-rpm records let kids listen to rock-and-roll in their own rooms. Car radios and transistor radios (first marketed around 1956) let disc jockeys reach teenagers outside the home. The result was separate music for young listeners and separate advertising for teenage consumers, the roots of the teenage mall culture of the next generation.

The raucous sounds and rebellious lyrics of early rock-and-roll gave adult authorities even more reason to emphasize social conformity. Schools, churches, and elected officials responded with

Movie actor James Dean died in an automobile accident shortly after completing *Rebel Without a Cause*. His tragic death and his depiction of alienated youth made him a symbol of dissatisfaction with the middle-class 1950s.

dress codes, campaigns against sinful comic books, and worry about juvenile delinquency. Young people responded by crowding movie theaters for *Rebel Without a Cause* (1955), in which James Dean played an anguished teenager in stifling suburbia.

Turning to Religion

Leaders from Dwight Eisenhower to FBI Director J. Edgar Hoover advocated churchgoing as an antidote for Communism. Regular church attendance grew from 48 percent of the population in 1940 to 63 percent in 1960. Moviegoers flocked to biblical epics: *The Robe* (1953), *The Ten Commandments* (1956), and *Ben-Hur* (1959). *Newsweek* talked about the "vast resurgence of Protestantism," and *Time* claimed that "everybody knows that church life is booming in the U.S."

The situation was more complex. Growing church membership looked impressive at first, but the total barely kept pace with population. In some ways, the so-called return to religion was new. Congress created new connections between religion and government when it added "under God" to the Pledge of Allegiance in 1954 and required currency to bear the phrase "In God We Trust" in 1955.

Radio and television preachers added a new dimension to religious life. Bishop Fulton J. Sheen brought vigorous anti-communism and Catholic doctrine to millions of TV viewers who would never have entered a Catholic church. Norman Vincent Peale blended popular psychology with Protestantism, presenting Jesus Christ as "the greatest expert on human nature who ever lived." His book *The Power of Positive Thinking* (1952) told readers to "stop worrying and start living" and sold millions of copies.

Another strand in the religious revival was found among revitalized evangelical and fundamentalist churches. During the 1950s, the theologically and socially conservative Southern Baptists passed the Methodists as the largest Protestant denomination. The evangelist Billy Graham continued the grand American tradition of the mass revival meeting. In auditoriums and stadiums, he preached personal salvation in words that everyone could understand. Graham was a pioneer in the resurgence of evangelical Christianity that gradually shifted the tone of American religious life by stressing an individual approach to belief and social issues. "Before we can solve the economic, philosophical, and political problems in the world," he said, "pride, greed, lust, and sin are going to have to be erased."

African-American churches were community institutions as well as religious organizations. With limited options for enjoying their success, the black middle class joined prestigious churches. Black congregations in northern cities swelled in the postwar years. Prestigious black churches thrived and often supported extensive social service programs. In southern cities, churches were centers for community pride and training grounds for the emerging civil rights movement.

The strength of religious belief across all segments of southern society would prove to be an important factor in promoting the progress of civil rights during the 1950s and 1960s. Black churches and the religious faith of thousands of black southerners were essential sources of the civil rights movement. At the same time, the beliefs of white evangelicals forced them to confront the contradictions between segregation and Christian teaching. The Southern Baptist Convention voted overwhelmingly in favor of peaceful segregation; Billy Graham in 1957 shared a pulpit with black civil rights leader Martin Luther King Jr. and insisted that all of his revival meetings be integrated.

Other important changes to come in American religion had their roots in the 1950s and early 1960s. Boundaries between many Protestant denominations blurred as church leaders emphasized national unity, paving the way for the ecumenical movement and denominational mergers. Supreme Court decisions sowed the seeds for later political activism among evangelical Christians. In *Engel* v. *Vitale* (1962), the Court ruled that public schools could not require children to start the school day with group prayer. *Abington Township* v. *Schempp* (1963) prohibited devotional Bible reading in the schools. Such decisions alarmed many evangelicals; within two decades, school prayer would be a central issue in national politics.

The Gospel of Prosperity

Writers and intellectuals often marveled at the prosperity of Eisenhower's America. For scholars and journalists who had grown up during the Great Depression, the lack of economic hardship was the big story. William H. Whyte Jr. searched American corporations for the changing character of the United States in *The Organization Man* (1956). The historian David Potter brilliantly analyzed Americans in *People of Plenty* (1954), contending that their national character had been shaped by the abundance of natural resources. In *The Affluent Society* (1958), economist John Kenneth Galbraith predicted that the challenge of the future would be to ensure the fair distribution of national wealth.

At times in these years, production and consumption even outweighed democracy in the American message to the world. Officially, the argument was that abundance was a natural byproduct of a free society. In fact, it was easy to present prosperity as a goal in itself, as Vice President Richard Nixon did when he represented the United States at a technology exposition in Moscow in 1959. The American exhibit included twenty-one models of automobiles and a complete six-room ranch house. In its "miracle kitchen," Nixon engaged Soviet Communist Party Chairman Nikita Khrushchev in a carefully planned "kitchen

The United States exhibit at a technology exposition in Moscow in 1959 displayed a wide range of American consumer goods, from soft-drink dispensers to sewing machines. It included a complete six-room ranch house with an up-to-date kitchen where, in a famous encounter dubbed the "kitchen debate," Vice President Richard Nixon and Soviet Communist Party Chairman Nikita Khrushchev disputed the merits of capitalism and Communism.

debate." The vice president claimed that the "most important thing" for Americans was "the right to choose": "We have so many different manufacturers and many different kinds of washing machines so that the housewives have a choice."

Khrushchev heard a similar message when he visited the United States in September 1959. His itinerary started with a helicopter ride over rush-hour Washington to show the ubiquity of individually owned automobiles. He went to a farm in Coon Rapids, Iowa, a machine shop in Pittsburgh, and Hollywood movie studios. Although Khrushchev never believed that ordinary workers had miracle kitchens, he returned to Moscow knowing that America meant "business."

The Underside of Affluence

The most basic criticism of the ideology of prosperity was the simplest—affluence concealed vast inequalities. Michael Harrington had worked among the poor before writing *The Other America* (1962). He reminded Americans about the "underdeveloped nation" of 40 to 50 million poor people who had missed the last two decades of prosperity. The poor were walled off in urban and rural backwaters. They were old people living on stale bread in bug-infested hotels. They were white families in the valleys of Appalachia, African Americans in city ghettos who could not find decent jobs, and Hispanic migrant workers whose children went for months without a glass of milk.

If Harrington found problems at the bottom of U.S. society, C. Wright Mills found dangers in the way that the Cold War distorted American society at the top. *The Power Elite* (1956) described an interlocking alliance of big government, big business, and the military. The losers in a permanent war economy, said Mills, were economic and political democracy. His ideas would reverberate in the 1960s during the Vietnam War.

Other critics targeted the alienating effects of consumerism and the conformity of homogeneous suburbs. Journalists indicted suburban society with coined terms like "slurb" and books like *The Crack in the Picture Window* (1957) and *The Split Level Trap* (1961). Sociologist David Riesman saw suburbia as the home of "other-directed" individuals who lacked inner convictions. Although much of the antisuburban rhetoric was based on intellectual snobbery rather than research, it represented significant dissent from the praise of affluence.

There was far greater substance to increasing dissatisfaction among women, who faced conflicting images of the perfect woman in the media. On one side was the comforting icon of Betty Crocker, the fictional spokeswoman for General Mills who made housework and cooking look easy. On the other side were sultry sexpots, such as Marilyn Monroe and the centerfold women of *Playboy* magazine, which first appeared in 1953. Women wondered how to be both Betty and Marilyn.

In 1963, Betty Friedan's book *The Feminine Mystique* recognized that thousands of middle-class housewives were seething behind their picture windows. It followed numerous articles in *McCall's*, *Redbook*, and the *Ladies' Home Journal* about the unhappiness of college-educated women who were expected to find total satisfaction in kids and cooking. Friedan repackaged the message of the women's magazines along with results of a survey of her Smith College classmates who were then entering their forties. What Friedan called "the problem that has no name" was a sense of personal emptiness. "I got up one morning," remembered Geraldine Bean, "and I got my kids off to school. I went in to comb my hair and wash my face, and I stood in front of the bathroom mirror crying . . . because at eight-thirty in the morning I had my children off to school. I had my housework done. There was absolutely nothing for me to do the rest of the day." She went on to earn a Ph.D. and win election to the board of regents of the University of Colorado.

Eventually, the critical analyses of Harrington, Mills, and Friedan would fuel radical political change; in the short run, they inspired radical art. New York and San Francisco had long sheltered cultural rebels who liked to confront the assumptions of mainstream Americans. The artsy bohemians of New York's Greenwich Village began to use Pop Art to satirize consumer culture. Meanwhile, the Beats came together in San Francisco, where poets, artists, and musicians drifted in and out of the City Lights bookstore. They attracted national attention in 1955 when Allen Ginsberg first chanted his poem "Howl" with its blistering attack on stifling materialism.

FACING OFF WITH THE SOVIET UNION

Americans got a reassuring new face in the White House in 1953, but not new policies toward the world. As had been true since 1946, the nation's leaders weighed every foreign policy decision for its effect on the Cold War. The United States pushed ahead in an arms race with the Soviet Union, stood guard on the borders of China and the Soviet empire, and judged political changes in Latin America, Africa, and Asia for their effect on the global balance of power.

U.S. and Soviet actions created a bipolar world that mimicked the effects of a magnet on a scattering of iron filings. The two poles of a magnet draw some filings into tightly packed clusters, pull others into looser alignments pointing toward one pole or the other, and leave a few in the middle unaffected. In the later 1950s and early 1960s, the United States and the USSR were the magnetic poles. Members of NATO, the Warsaw Pact, and other formal alliances made up the tight clusters. The Third World of officially uncommitted nations felt the influence of both blocs, sometimes aligning with one or the other and sometimes struggling to remain neutral.

Why We Liked Ike

In the late twentieth century, few leaders were able to master both domestic policy and foreign affairs. Some presidents, such as Lyndon Johnson, have been more adept at social problems than diplomacy. By contrast, Richard Nixon and George Bush were more interested in the world outside the United States.

Dwight Eisenhower was one of these "foreign-policy presidents." As a general, he had understood that military power should serve political ends. He had helped to hold together the alliance that defeated Nazi Germany and built NATO into an effective force in 1951–1952. He then sought the Republican nomination, he said, to ensure that the United States kept its international commitments. He sealed his victory in 1952 by emphasizing his foreign-policy expertise, telling a campaign audience that "to bring the Korean war to an early and honorable end . . . requires a personal trip to Korea. I shall make that trip . . . I shall go to Korea."

What makes Eisenhower's administration hard to appreciate is that many of its accomplishments were things that did not happen. Eisenhower refused to dismantle the social programs of the New Deal. He exerted American political and military power around the globe but avoided war. Preferring to work behind the scenes, he knew how to delegate authority and keep disagreements private.

In his "hidden-hand" presidency, Eisenhower sometimes masked his intelligence. It helped his political agenda if Americans thought of him as a smiling grandfather. The "Ike" whose face smiled from "I Like Ike" campaign buttons and who gave rambling, incoherent answers at White House press conferences knew exactly what he was doing—controlling information and keeping the opposition guessing. When his press secretary advised him to duck questions at one press conference, Ike replied, "Don't worry, I'll just confuse them." He was easily reelected in 1956, when Americans saw no reason to abandon competent leadership.

A Balance of Terror

The backdrop for U.S. foreign policy was the growing capacity for mutual nuclear annihilation. The rivalry between the United States and the USSR was therefore carried out within a framework of deterrence, the knowledge that each side could launch a devastating nuclear attack. The old balance of power had become a balance of terror.

The Eisenhower administration's doctrine of **massive retaliation** took advantage of America's superior technology while economizing on military spending. Eisenhower and his advisors worried that matching the land armies of China and the Soviet Union would inflate the role of the federal government in American society. Eisenhower compared uncontrolled military spending to crucifying humankind on a "cross of iron." "Every gun that is fired," he warned, "every warship launched, every rocket fired signifies . . . a theft from those who hunger and are not fed, those who are cold and not clothed." The administration concentrated military spending where the nation already had the greatest advantage—on atomic weapons. In response to any serious attack, the United States would direct maximum force against the homeland of the aggressor. Secretary of State Dulles called for "a maximum deterrent at a bearable cost." Reporters translated the policy as "more bang for the buck."

The massive-retaliation doctrine treated nuclear weapons as ordinary or even respectable. It put European and American cities on the frontline in the defense of Germany, for it meant that the United States would react to a Soviet conventional attack on NATO by dropping nuclear bombs on the Soviet Union, which would presumably retaliate in kind. The National Security Council in 1953 made reliance on "massive retaliatory damage" by nuclear weapons official policy.

The doctrine grew even more fearful as the Soviet Union developed its own hydrogen bombs. The chairman of the Atomic Energy Commission terrified the American people by mentioning casually that the Soviets could now obliterate New York City. Dozens of nuclear weapons tests in the late 1950s made the atomic threat immediate. So did signs for air-raid shelters posted on downtown buildings and air-raid drills that taught schoolchildren to duck under their desks if they saw the flash of an atomic bomb. Radioactivity carried by fallout from the tests appeared in milk supplies in the form of the isotope strontium 90. Stories about handfuls of survivors groping through the ruins of atomic war filled popular literature.

The Soviet Union added to worries about atomic war by launching the world's first artificial satellite. On the first Sunday of October 1957, Americans discovered that *Sputnik*—Russian for "satellite"—was orbiting the earth. The Soviets soon lifted a dog into orbit while U.S. rockets fizzled on the pad. Soviet propagandists claimed that their technological "first" showed the superiority of Communism, and Americans wondered if the United States had lost its edge. Schools beefed up science courses and began to introduce the "new math," Congress passed the National Defense Education Act to expand college and postgraduate education, and the new **National Aeronautics and Space Administration (NASA)** took over the satellite program in 1958.

The crisis was more apparent than real. Eisenhower had rejected the use of available military rockets for the U.S. space program in favor of developing new launch vehicles, and he overlooked the symbolic impact of *Sputnik*. He thus built himself into a political box, for the combination of Soviet rocketry and nuclear capacity created alarm about a missile gap. The Soviet Union was said to be building hundreds of intercontinental ballistic missiles (ICBMs) to overwhelm American air defenses designed to intercept piloted bombers. By the early 1960s, critics charged, a do-nothing administration would have put the United States

Schoolchildren in the 1950s regularly practiced taking cover in case of atomic attack. If there was warning, they were to file into interior hallways, crouch against the walls, and cover their heads with their jackets as protection from flying glass. If they saw the blinding flash of an atomic explosion without warning, they were to "duck and cover" under their school desks.

in peril. Although there was no such gap, Eisenhower was unwilling to reveal secret information that might have allayed public anxiety.

Containment in Action

Someone who heard only the campaign speeches in 1952 might have expected sharp foreign-policy changes under Eisenhower, but there was more continuity than change. John Foster Dulles, Eisenhower's secretary of state, had attacked the Democrats as defeatists and appeasers. He demanded that the United States liberate eastern Europe from Soviet control and encourage Jiang Jieshi to attack Communist China. Warlike language continued after the election. In 1956, Dulles proudly claimed that tough-minded diplomacy had repeatedly brought the United States to the verge of war: "We walked to the brink and looked it in the face. We took strong action." Critics protested that such "brinkmanship" endangered the entire world.

In fact, Eisenhower viewed the Cold War in the same terms as Truman. He worried about the "sullen weight of Russia" pushing against smaller nations and saw a world caught between incompatible values of freedom and communism, but caution replaced campaign rhetoric about "rolling back" Communism. Around the periphery of the Communist nations, from eastern Asia to the Middle East to Europe, the United States accepted the existing sphere of Communist influence but attempted to block its growth, a policy most Americans accepted.

The American worldview assumed both the right and the need to intervene in the affairs of other nations, especially countries in Latin America, Asia, and Africa. Policymakers saw these nations as markets for U.S. products and sources of vital raw materials. When political disturbances arose in these nations, the United States blamed Soviet meddling to justify U.S. intervention. If Communism could not be rolled back in eastern Europe, the CIA could still undermine anti-American governments in the Third World. The Soviets themselves took advantage of local revolutions, even when they did not instigate them; they thus confirmed Washington's belief that the developing world was a game board on which the superpowers carried on their rivalry by proxy.

Twice during Eisenhower's first term, the CIA subverted democratically elected governments that seemed to threaten U.S. interests. In Iran, which had nationalized British and U.S. oil companies in an effort to break the hold of Western corporations, the CIA in 1953 backed a coup that toppled the government and helped the young Shah, or monarch, gain control. The Shah then cooperated with the United States until his overthrow in 1979. In Guatemala, the leftist government was upsetting the United Fruit Company. When the Guatemalans accepted weapons from the Communist bloc in 1954, the CIA imposed a regime friendly to U.S. business.

For most Americans in 1953, democracy in Iran was far less important than ending the war in Korea and stabilizing relations with China. Eisenhower declined to escalate the Korean War by blockading China and sending more U.S. ground forces. Instead he shifted atomic bombs to Okinawa, only four hundred miles from China. The nuclear threat, along with the continued cost of the war on both sides, brought the Chinese to a truce that left Korea divided into two nations.

The following year, China began to shell the small islands of Quemoy and Matsu, from which the Nationalist Chinese on Taiwan were launching commando raids on the mainland. Again, Secretary Dulles rattled the atomic saber, and China stopped the attacks. Evidence now suggests that Washington misread the situation. Mao's "theatrical" shelling was a political statement, not a prelude to military assault. Stepping to the "brink of war" did not deter Chinese aggression, because China never planned to attack.

Halfway around the world, there was a new crisis when three American friends— France, Britain, and Israel—ganged up on Egypt. France was angry at Egyptian support for revolutionaries in French Algeria. Britain was even angrier at Egypt's nationalization of the British-dominated Suez Canal. And Israel wanted to weaken its most powerful Arab enemy. On October 29, 1956, Israel attacked Egypt. A week later, British and French forces attempted to seize the canal. The United States forced a quick cease-fire, partly to maintain its standing with oil-producing Arab nations. Because Egypt blocked the canal with sunken ships, the war left Britain and France dependent on American oil that Eisenhower would not provide until they left Egypt. Resolution of the crisis involved one of the first uses of peace-keeping troops under the United Nations flag.

In Europe, Eisenhower accepted the status quo because conflicts there could result in nuclear war. In 1956, challenges to Communist rule arose in East Germany, Poland, and Hungary and threatened to break up the Soviet empire. The Soviets replaced liberal Communists in East Germany and Poland with hard-liners. In Hungary, however, reformers took the fatal step of proposing to quit the Warsaw Pact. Open warfare broke out when the Soviet army rolled across the border to preserve the Soviet empire. Hungarian freedom fighters in Budapest used rocks and firebombs against Soviet tanks for several days, while pleading in vain for Western aid. NATO would not risk war with the USSR. Tens of thousands of Hungarians died, and 200,000 fled when the Soviets crushed the resistance.

Global Standoff

The Soviet Union, China, and the United States and its allies were all groping in the dark as they maneuvered for influence in the 1950s and 1960s. In one international crisis after another, each player misinterpreted the other's motivations and diplomatic signals. As documents from both sides of the Cold War become available, historians have realized what dangerously different meanings the two sides gave to confrontations between 1953 and 1964.

A good example was the U-2 affair of 1960, which derailed progress toward controlling the nuclear arms race. The Kremlin was deeply worried that West Germany and China might acquire atomic bombs. Washington wanted to reduce military budgets and nuclear fallout. Both countries voluntarily suspended nuclear tests in 1958 and prepared for a June 1960 summit meeting in Paris, where Eisenhower intended to negotiate a test ban treaty.

But on May 1, 1960, Soviet air defenses shot down an American U-2 spy plane over the heart of Russia and captured the pilot, Francis Gary Powers. The cover story for the U-2 was weather research, but the frail-looking black plane was a CIA operation. Designed to soar above the range of Soviet antiaircraft missiles, U-2s had assured American officials that there was no missile gap.

When Moscow trumpeted the news of the downing, Eisenhower took personal responsibility in hopes that Khrushchev would accept the U-2 as an unpleasant reality of international espionage. Unfortunately, the U-2 meant something very different to the Soviets, touching their festering sense of inferiority. They had stopped protesting the flights in 1957, because complaints were demeaning. The Americans thought that silence signaled acceptance. Khrushchev had staked his future on good relations with the United States; when Eisenhower refused to apologize in Paris, Khrushchev stormed out. Disarmament was set back for years because the two sides had such different understandings of the same events.

The most important aspect of Eisenhower's foreign policy was continuity. Despite militant rhetoric, the administration pursued containment as defined under Truman. The Cold War consensus, however, prevented the United States from seeing the nations of the developing world on their own terms. By viewing every independence movement and social revolution as part of the competition with Communism, American leaders created unnecessary problems. In the end, Eisenhower left troublesome and unresolved issues—upheaval in Latin America, civil war in Vietnam, tension in Germany, a nuclear arms race—for his successor, John Kennedy, who wanted to confront international Communism even more vigorously (see American Views, "Two Presidents Assess the Implications of the Cold War").

JOHN F. KENNEDY AND THE COLD WAR

John Kennedy was a man of contradictions. Many Americans recall his presidency (1961–1963) as a golden age, but we are more taken by his memory than we were by Kennedy himself. A Democrat who promised to get the country moving again, he presided over policies whose direction was set under Eisenhower. Despite stirring rhetoric about leading the nation toward a **New Frontier** of scientific and social progress, he recorded his greatest failures and successes in the continuing Cold War.

The Kennedy Mystique

Kennedy won the presidency over Richard Nixon in a cliffhanging election that was more about personality and style than about substance. Both candidates were determined not to yield another inch to Communism. The charming and eloquent Kennedy narrowly skirted scandal in his personal life. Well publicized as a hero from World War II, he tempered ruthless ambition with respect for public service. His forthright campaigning allayed voter concern about his Roman Catholicism. Nixon had wider experience and was a shrewd tactician, but he was also self-righteous and awkward. Eisenhower had wanted to drop Nixon as vice president in 1956 and gave him only lukewarm support in 1960—when a reporter asked Eisenhower to cite important decisions to which Nixon had contributed, Ike replied, "Give me a week and I might think of one."

Two Presidents Assess the Implications of the Cold War

In speeches two days apart in January 1961, outgoing President Dwight Eisenhower and incoming President John Kennedy offered contrasting interpretations of America's Cold War crusade. Eisenhower spoke with concern about the effects of defense spending on American society. Kennedy promised an unlimited commitment of resources to achieve national goals.

Why did Kennedy define the American mission to the world so broadly?

What changes in the 1950s led Eisenhower to warn about the dangers of pursuing that mission?

Do the selections show basic agreement or disagreement about the goals of national policy?

Dwight D. Eisenhower's Farewell Address, January 18, 1961

Our military organization today bears little relation to that known by any of my predecessors in peacetime. . . .

This conjunction of an immense military establishment and a large arms industry is new in the American experience. The total influence—economic, political, even spiritual—is felt in every city, every State house, every office of the federal government. We recognize the imperative need for this development. Yet we must not fail to comprehend its grave implications. . . .

In the councils of government, we must guard against the acquisition of unwarranted influence, whether sought or unsought, by the military-industrial complex. The potential for the disastrous rise of misplaced power exists and will persist.

We must never let the weight of this combination endanger our liberties or democratic processes. We should take nothing for granted. Only an alert and knowledgeable citizenry can compel the proper meshing of the huge industrial and military machinery of defense with our peaceful methods and goals.

John F. Kennedy
Inaugural Address, January 20, 1961

Let the word go forth from this time and place, to friend and foe alike, that the torch has been passed to a new generation of Americans—born in this century, tempered by war, disciplined by a hard and bitter peace, proud of our ancient heritage—and unwilling to witness or permit the slow undoing of those human rights to which this nation has always been committed, and to which we are committed today at home and around the world.

Let every nation know, whether it wishes us well or ill, that we shall pay any price, bear any burden, meet any hardship, support any friends, oppose any foe to assure the survival and the success of liberty.

Television was crucial to the outcome. The campaign featured the first televised presidential debates. In the first session, Nixon actually gave better replies, but his nervousness and a bad makeup job turned off millions of viewers, who admired Kennedy's energy. Nixon never overcame the setback, but the race was tight, with tiny margins in crucial states giving Kennedy the victory. His televised inauguration was the perfect setting for an impassioned plea for national unity: "My fellow Americans," he challenged, "ask not what your country can do for you—ask what you can do for your country."

Kennedy brought dash to the White House. His beautiful and refined wife, Jackie, made sure to seat artists and writers next to diplomats and businessmen at White House dinners. Kennedy's staff and large family played touch football, not golf. No president had shown such verve since Teddy Roosevelt. People began to talk about Kennedy's "charisma," his ability to lead by sheer force of personality. In fact, the image of a fit, vigorous man concealed the reality that he was battling severe physical ailments that demanded constant medical attention.

Behind the glamorous façade, Kennedy remained a puzzle. One day, Kennedy could propose the Peace Corps, which gave thousands of idealistic young Americans a chance to help developing nations; another day, he could approve plots to assassinate Fidel Castro.

Visitors who expected a shallow glad-hander were astonished to meet a sharp, hard-working man who was eager to learn about the world. One savvy diplomat commented, "I have never heard of a president who wanted to know so much."

Kennedy's Mistakes

Kennedy and Khrushchev perpetuated similar problems. Talking tough to satisfy their more militant countrymen, they pushed each other into corners, continuing the problems of mutual misunderstanding that had marked the 1950s. When Khrushchev promised, in January 1961, to support "wars of national liberation," he was really fending off Chinese criticism. But Kennedy overreacted in his first State of the Union address by asking for more military spending.

Three months later, Kennedy fed Soviet fears of American aggressiveness by sponsoring an invasion of Cuba. At the start of 1959, Fidel Castro had toppled corrupt dictator Fulgencio Batista, who had made Havana infamous for Mafia-run gambling and prostitution. Castro then nationalized American investments, and thousands of Cubans fled to the United States.

When fourteen hundred anti-Castro Cubans landed at Cuba's **Bay of Pigs** on April 17, 1961, they were following a plan from the Eisenhower administration. The CIA had trained and armed the invaders and convinced Kennedy that the landing would trigger spontaneous uprisings. But when Kennedy refused to commit American armed forces to support them, Cuban forces captured the attackers.

Kennedy followed the Bay of Pigs debacle with a hasty and ill-thought-out summit meeting with Khrushchev in Vienna in June. Poorly prepared and nearly incapacitated by agonizing back pain, Kennedy made little headway. Khrushchev saw no need to bargain and subjected him to intimidating tirades. "He just beat the hell out of me," Kennedy told a reporter. Coming after Kennedy's refusal to salvage the Bay of Pigs by military intervention, the meeting left the Soviets with the impression that the president was weak and dangerously erratic.

To exploit Kennedy's perceived vulnerability, the Soviet Union renewed tension over Berlin, deep within East Germany. The divided city served as an escape route from Communism for hundreds of thousands of East Germans. Khrushchev now threatened to transfer the Soviet sector in Berlin to East Germany, which had no treaty obligations to France, Britain, or the United States. If the West had to deal directly with East Germany for access to Berlin, it would have to recognize a permanently divided Germany. Kennedy sounded the alarm. He doubled draft calls, called up reservists, and warned families to build fallout shelters. Boise, Idaho, families paid $100 for a share in a community shelter with its own power plant and hospital. Outside New York, Art Carlson and his son Claude put up a prefabricated steel shelter in four hours; Sears planned to sell the same model for $700.

Rather than confront the United States directly, however, the Soviets and East Germans on August 13, 1961, built a wall around the western sectors of Berlin while leaving the access route to West Germany open. The **Berlin Wall** thus isolated East Germany without challenging the Western allies in West Berlin itself. In private, Kennedy accepted the wall as a clever way to stabilize a dangerous situation: "A wall," he said, "is a hell of a lot better than a war." Tensions remained high for months as the two sides tested each other's resolve. Berlin remained a point of East–West tension until East German Communism collapsed in 1989 and Berliners tore down the hated wall.

Getting into Vietnam

American involvement in Vietnam, located in Southeast Asia on the southern border of China, dated to the mid-1950s. Since the end of World War II, France had fought to maintain its colonial rule there against rebels who combined communist ideology with fervor for national independence under the leadership of Ho Chi Minh. The United States picked up three-quarters of the costs, but the French military position collapsed in 1954 after Vietnamese forces overran the French stronghold at Dien Bien Phu. The French had enough, and President Eisenhower was unwilling to join another Asian war. A Geneva peace conference "temporarily" divided Vietnam into a Communist north and a non-Communist south and scheduled elections for a single Vietnamese government.

The United States then replaced France as the supporter of pro-Western Vietnamese in the south. Washington's client was Ngo Dinh Diem, an anti-Communist from South Vietnam's Roman Catholic elite. U.S. officials encouraged Diem to put off the elections and backed his efforts to construct an independent South Vietnam. Ho meanwhile consolidated the northern half as a Communist state that claimed to be the legitimate government for all Vietnam. The United States further reinforced containment in Asia by bringing Thailand, the Philippines, Pakistan, Australia, New Zealand, Britain, and France together in the **Southeast Asia Treaty Organization (SEATO)** in 1954.

Another indirect consequence of the Vienna summit was growing American entanglement in South Vietnam, where Kennedy saw a chance to take a firm stand and reassert America's commitment to containment. In the countryside, Communist insurgents known as the **Viet Cong** were gaining strength. The anti-Communist leader, Diem, controlled the cities with the help of a large army and a Vietnamese elite that had worked with the French. The United States stepped up its supply of weapons and sent advisors, including members of one of Kennedy's military innovations, the Army Special Forces Group (Green Berets).

U.S. aid did not work. Despite overoptimistic reports and the help of sixteen thousand American troops, Diem's government by 1963 was losing the loyalty—the "hearts and minds"—of many South Vietnamese. North Vietnamese support for the Viet Cong canceled the effect of U.S. assistance. Diem courted a second civil war by violently crushing opposition from Vietnamese Buddhists. Kennedy's administration tacitly approved a coup on November 1 that killed Diem and his brother and installed an ineffective military junta.

Missile Crisis: A Line Drawn in the Waves

The escalating tensions of 1961 in Southeast Asia, the Caribbean, and Germany were a prelude to the crisis that came closest to triggering a nuclear war. In the summer of 1962, congressional Republicans had hounded Kennedy about the Soviet military presence in Cuba. On October 15, reconnaissance photos revealed Soviets at work on launching sites from which nuclear missiles could hit the United States. Top officials spent five exhausting and increasingly desperate days sorting through the options. Doing nothing was never considered: The missiles would be political disaster and a threat to national security. A full-scale invasion of Cuba was not feasible on short notice, and "surgical" air strikes were technically impossible. Either sort of military operation would kill hundreds of Soviet personnel and force Moscow to react. Secretary of Defense Robert McNamara suggested demanding removal of the missiles and declaring a naval "quarantine" against the arrival of further offensive weapons. A blockade would buy time for diplomacy.

Kennedy imposed the blockade in a terrifying speech on Monday, October 22. He emphasized the "deceptive" deployment of the Russian missiles and raised the specter of nuclear war. Americans would have been even more afraid had they known that some of the missiles were operational and that Soviets in Cuba were authorized to use them in self-defense. While Khrushchev hesitated, Soviet ships circled outside the quarantine line. On Friday, Khrushchev offered to withdraw the missiles in return for an American pledge not to invade Cuba. On Saturday, a second communication nearly dashed this hopeful opening by raising a new complaint about American missiles on the territory of NATO allies. The letter was the result of pressure by Kremlin hard-liners and Khrushchev's own wavering. Kennedy decided to accept the first letter and ignore the second. The United States pledged not to invade Cuba and secretly promised to remove obsolete Jupiter missiles from Turkey. Khrushchev accepted these terms on Sunday, October 28.

Why did Khrushchev risk the Cuban gamble? One reason was to protect Castro as a symbol of Soviet commitment to anti-Western regimes in the developing world. Americans hated the Castro government out of proportion to its geopolitical importance, but they rightly feared that Cuba would try to export revolution throughout Latin America. Kennedy had tried to preempt Castroism in 1961 by launching the **Alliance for Progress**, an economic development program for Latin America that tied aid to social reform. However, the United States had also orchestrated the Bay of Pigs invasion and funded a CIA campaign to sabotage Cuba. High American officials were not contemplating a full-scale invasion, but Castro and Khrushchev had reason to fear the worst.

Khrushchev also hoped to redress the strategic balance. As Kennedy discovered on taking office, the United States actually led the world in the deployment of strategic missiles. Intermediate-range rockets gave the USSR a nuclear club over western Europe, but in October 1962, the Soviet Union had fewer than fifty ICBMs to aim at the United States and China. The United States was creating a defensive triad of a thousand land-based Minuteman missiles, five hundred long-range bombers, and six hundred Polaris missiles on nuclear submarines targeted on the USSR. The strategic imbalance had sustained NATO during the Berlin confrontation, but forty launchers in Cuba with two warheads each would have doubled the Soviet capacity to strike at the United States.

Soviet missiles in Cuba thus flouted the Monroe Doctrine and posed a real military threat. Kennedy and Khrushchev had also backed each other into untenable positions. In September, Kennedy had warned that the United States could not tolerate Soviet offensive weapons in Cuba, never dreaming that they were already there. Had Khrushchev acted openly (as the United States had done when it placed missiles in Turkey), the United States would have been hard pressed to object under international law. By acting in secret and breaking previous promises, the Soviets outsmarted themselves. When the missiles were discovered, Kennedy had to act.

In the end, both sides were cautious. Khrushchev backed down rather than fight. Kennedy fended off hawkish advisors who wanted to destroy Castro. The world had trembled, but neither nation wanted war over "the missiles of October."

Science and Foreign Affairs

The two superpowers competed through science as well as diplomacy. When Kennedy took office, the United States was still playing catch-up in space technology. A Russian, Yuri Gagarin, was the first human to orbit the earth, on April 12, 1961. American John Glenn did not match Gagarin's feat until February 1962. Kennedy committed the United States to placing an American astronaut on the moon by 1970. The decision narrowed a multifaceted scientific and military program to a massive engineering project that favored the economic capacity of the United States.

The Soviet Union and the United States were also fencing about nuclear weapons testing. After the three-year moratorium, both resumed tests in 1961–1962. The United States started with underground tests to minimize fallout but then followed with atmospheric detonations. Renewed testing let the Russians show off huge hydrogen bombs with yields of 20 and 30 megatons—roughly one thousand times the power of the bombs dropped on Japan.

• • • OVERVIEW • • •

THE UNITED STATES AND THE SPACE RACE

YEAR	EVENT
1957	Soviets launch *Sputnik*, the first artificial satellite.
1961	Soviet cosmonaut Yuri Gagarin is the first human to orbit the earth.
	John Kennedy commits the United States to land a man on the moon by 1970.
1962	John Glenn is the first American to orbit the earth.
1966	*Gemini* capsules make the first rendezvous and dock in space.
1969	Neil Armstrong and Buzz Aldrin walk on the moon.
1972	Americans walk on the moon for the last time.
1973	Saturn rocket fuel tank is used as temporary orbiting space station, Skylab.
1975	U.S. *Apollo* and Soviet *Soyuz* spacecraft rendezvous and dock in orbit.
1981	First U.S. space shuttle is launched.
1986	Space shuttle *Challenger* crew of seven die when shuttle explodes after takeoff.
1988	Space shuttle flights resume.
1990	Hubble Space Telescope is launched into orbit.
2000	U.S. and Russian crew begins living aboard International Space Station.
2003	Space shuttle *Columbia* crashes on reentry.

Both nations worked on multiple targetable warheads, antiballistic missiles, and other innovations that might destabilize the balance of terror.

After the missile crisis showed his toughness, however, Kennedy had enough political maneuvering room to respond to pressure from liberal Democrats and groups like Women Strike for Peace and the Committee for a Sane Nuclear Policy by giving priority to disarmament. In July 1963, the United States, Britain, and the USSR signed the **Limited Test Ban Treaty** which outlawed nuclear testing in the atmosphere, in outer space, and under water, and invited other nations to join in. A more comprehensive treaty was impossible because the Soviet Union refused the on-site inspections the United States deemed necessary to distinguish underground tests from earthquakes. France and China, the other nuclear powers, refused to sign, and the treaty did not halt weapons development, but it was the most positive achievement of Kennedy's foreign policy and a step toward later disarmament treaties.

RIGHTEOUSNESS LIKE A MIGHTY STREAM: THE STRUGGLE FOR CIVIL RIGHTS

Supreme Court decisions are based on abstract principles, but they involve real people. One was Linda Brown of Topeka, Kansas, a third-grader whose parents were fed up with sending her past an all-white public school to attend an all-black school a mile away. The Browns volunteered to help the NAACP challenge Topeka's school segregation by trying to enroll Linda in their neighborhood school, beginning a legal case that reached the Supreme Court. Three years later, on May 17, 1954, the Court decided ***Brown v. Board of Education of Topeka***, opening a new civil rights era. The justices reversed the 1896 case of *Plessy* v. *Ferguson* by ruling that sending black children to "separate but equal" schools denied them equal treatment under the Constitution. Linda's mother heard about the decision on the radio while she was ironing and told her daughter when she got home from school; when Linda's father heard the news, his eyes filled with tears, and he said, "Thanks be to God."

The *Brown* decision made the growing effort to secure equal legal treatment for African Americans an inescapable challenge to American society. The first phase of the civil rights struggle built from the Supreme Court's decision in 1954 to a vast gathering at the Lincoln Memorial in 1963. In between, African Americans chipped away at the racial segregation of schools, universities, and public facilities with marches, boycotts, sit-ins, and lawsuits, forcing segregated communities to choose between integration and violent defiance. In the two years following the 1963 March on Washington, the federal government passed landmark legislation.

Getting to the Supreme Court

The *Brown* decision climaxed a twenty-five-year campaign to reenlist the federal courts on the side of equal rights (see the Overview table, "Civil Rights: The Struggle for Racial Equality"). The work began in the 1930s when Charles Hamilton Houston, dean of Howard University's law school, trained a corps of civil-rights lawyers. Working on behalf of the NAACP, he hoped to erode *Plessy* by suits focused on interstate travel and professional graduate schools (the least defensible segregated institutions, because states seldom provided alternatives). In 1938, Houston's student Thurgood Marshall, a future Supreme Court justice, took over the NAACP job. He and other NAACP lawyers such as Constance Baker Motley risked personal danger crisscrossing the South to file civil rights lawsuits wherever a local case emerged. In 1949, Motley was the first black lawyer to argue a case in a Mississippi courtroom since Reconstruction.

••• OVERVIEW •••

CIVIL RIGHTS: THE STRUGGLE FOR RACIAL EQUALITY

AREA OF CONCERN	KEY ACTIONS	RESULTS
Public school integration	Federal court cases	*Brown v. Board of Education of Topeka* (1954) Enforcement by presidential action, Little Rock (1957) Follow-up court decisions, including mandatory busing programs
Equal access to public facilities	Montgomery bus boycott (1955) Lunch counter sit-ins (1960) Freedom rides (1961) Birmingham demonstrations (1963) March on Washington (1963)	Civil Rights Act of 1964
Equitable voter registration	Voter registration drives, including Mississippi Summer Freedom Project (1964) Demonstrations and marches including Selma to Montgomery march (1965)	Voting Rights Act of 1965

The *Brown* case combined lawsuits from Delaware, Virginia, South Carolina, the District of Columbia, and Kansas. In each instance, students and families braved community pressure to demand equal access to a basic public service. Chief Justice Earl Warren brought a divided Court to unanimous agreement. Viewing public education as central for the equal opportunity that lay at the heart of American values, the Court weighed the consequences of segregated school systems and concluded that separate meant unequal. The reasoning fit the temper of a nation that was proud of making prosperity accessible to all.

Brown also built on efforts by Mexican Americans in the Southwest to assert their rights of citizenship. After World War II, Latino organizations such as the League of United Latin American Citizens battled job discrimination and ethnic segregation. In 1946, the federal courts had prohibited segregation of Mexican-American children in California schools. Eight years later, the Supreme Court forbade Texas from excluding Mexican Americans from juries. These cases provided precedents for the Court's decision in *Brown* and subsequent civil-rights cases.

Deliberate Speed

Racial segregation by law was largely a southern problem, the legacy of Jim Crow laws from early in the century. The civil rights movement therefore focused first on the South and allowed Americans elsewhere to think of racial injustice as a regional issue.

Southern responses to *Brown* emphasized regional differences. Few southern communities desegregated schools voluntarily, for to do so undermined the entrenched principle of a dual society. Their reluctance was bolstered in 1955 when the Supreme Court allowed segregated states to carry out the 1954 decision "with all deliberate speed" rather than immediately. The following year, 101 southern congressmen and senators issued the **Southern Manifesto**, which asserted that the Court decision was unconstitutional. President Eisenhower privately deplored the desegregation decision, which violated his sense of states' rights and upset Republican attempts to gain southern votes; he called both those who resisted the decision and those who wanted to enforce it "extremists."

Eisenhower's distaste for racial integration left the Justice Department on the sidelines. Courageous parents and students had to knock on schoolhouse doors, often carrying court orders. Responses varied: School districts in border states, such as Maryland, Kentucky, and Oklahoma, desegregated relatively peacefully. Further south, African-American children often met taunts and violence.

The first crisis came in Little Rock, Arkansas, in September 1957. The city school board admitted nine African Americans, including Melba Pattillo, to Central High, while segregationist groups, such as the White Citizens Council, stirred up white fears. Claiming to fear violence, Governor Orval Faubus surrounded Central High with the National Guard and turned the new

Elizabeth Eckford, one of the first black students to attend Central High in Little Rock, Arkansas, in 1957, enters the school amid taunts from white students and bystanders.

students away. Under intense national pressure, Faubus withdrew the Guard. When the black students entered the school, a howling mob forced the police to sneak the students out after two hours. Fuming at the governor's defiance of federal authority, which bordered on insurrection, Eisenhower reluctantly nationalized the National Guard and sent in the 101st Airborne Division to keep order. Eight of the students endured a year of harassment in the hallways of Central.

Virginians in 1958–1959 tried avoidance rather than confrontation. Massive resistance was a state policy that required local school districts to close rather than accept black students. When court orders to admit nineteen black students triggered the shutdown of four high schools and three junior highs in Norfolk, white parents tried to compensate with private academies and tutoring, but it was soon apparent that a modern community could not dismantle public education without becoming a laughingstock. Norfolk's leaders realized that no large business was going to locate in a city whose claim to fame was the "lost class of '59," and Virginia's elite privately welcomed federal court decisions that got them off the hook by striking down their own law.

Change came slowly to state universities. Border states desegregated colleges and professional schools with few incidents. Again, the story was different in the Lower South. In 1956, the University of Alabama admitted Autherine Lucy under court order but then expelled her before she could attend classes. In September 1962, James Meredith tried to enter the University of Mississippi, igniting a riot that the state refused to control. Because the governor directly defied the federal courts and broke promises to the administration, President Kennedy sent in the army. A year later, Governor George Wallace of Alabama grabbed headlines by "standing in the schoolhouse door" to prevent integration of the University of Alabama, gaining a national prominence that culminated in a third-party candidacy for president in 1968.

The breakthrough in school integration did not come until the end of the 1960s, when the courts rejected further delays, and federal authorities threatened to cut off education funds. As late as 1968, only 6 percent of African-American children in the South attended integrated schools. By 1973, the figure was 90 percent. Attention thereafter shifted to Northern communities, whose schools were segregated, not by law, but by the divisions between white and black neighborhoods and between white suburbs and multiracial central cities, a situation known as de facto segregation.

Public Accommodations

The civil rights movement also sought to integrate public accommodations. Most southern states separated the races in bus terminals and movie theaters. They required black riders to take rear seats on buses. They labeled separate restrooms and drinking fountains for "colored" users. Hotels denied rooms to black people, and restaurants refused them service.

The struggle to end segregated facilities started in Montgomery, Alabama. On December 1, 1955, Rosa Parks, a seamstress who worked at a downtown department store, refused to give up her bus seat to a white passenger and was arrested. Parks acted spontaneously, but she was part of a network of civil-rights activists who wanted to challenge segregated buses and was the secretary of the Montgomery NAACP. As news of her action spread, the community institutions that enriched southern black life went into action. The Women's Political Council, a group of college-trained black women, initiated a mass boycott of the privately owned bus company. Alabama State College professor Jo Ann Robinson worked through the night to mimeograph 52,500 flyers and enlisted students to spread them through the city. Martin Luther King Jr., a 26-year-old pastor, led the boycott. He galvanized a mass meeting with a speech that quoted the biblical prophet Amos: "We are determined here in Montgomery to work and fight until justice runs down like water, and righteousness like a mighty stream."

Montgomery's African Americans organized their boycott in the face of white outrage. A car pool substituted for the buses despite police harassment. As the boycott survived months of pressure, the national media began to pay attention. After nearly a year, the Supreme Court agreed that the bus segregation law was unconstitutional.

Victory in Montgomery depended on the steadfastness of African-American involvement. Leaders included Ralph Abernathy, other black preachers, and faculty members from Alabama State College. Participants cut across the class lines that had divided black Southerners. Success also revealed the discrepancy between white attitudes in the Deep South and national opinion. For white Southerners, segregation was a local concern best defined as a legal or constitutional matter. For other Americans, it was increasingly an issue of the South's deviation from national moral norms.

The Montgomery boycott won a local victory and made King famous, but it did not propel a wave of immediate change. King formed the **Southern Christian Leadership Conference (SCLC)** and sparred with the NAACP about community-based versus court-based civil-rights tactics, but four African-American college students in Greensboro, North Carolina, started the next phase of the struggle. On February 1, 1960, they put on jackets and ties and sat down at the segregated lunch counter in Woolworth's, waiting through the day without being served. Their patient courage brought more demonstrators; within two days, eighty-five students packed the store. Nonviolent sit-ins spread throughout the South.

The sit-ins had both immediate and long-range effects. In such comparatively sophisticated border cities as Nashville, Tennessee, sit-ins integrated lunch counters. Elsewhere, they precipitated white violence and mass arrests. Like soldiers on a battlefield, nervous participants in sit-ins and demonstrations drew strength from one another. "If you don't have courage," said one young woman in Albany, Georgia, "you can borrow it." King welcomed nonviolent confrontation. SCLC leader Ella Baker helped the students form a new organization, the **Student Nonviolent Coordinating Committee (SNCC)**.

The year 1961 brought "freedom rides" to test the segregation of interstate bus terminals. The idea came from James Farmer of the **Congress of Racial Equality (CORE)**, who copied a little-remembered 1947 Journey of Reconciliation that had tested the integration of interstate trains. Two buses carrying black and white passengers met only minor problems in Virginia, the Carolinas, and Georgia, but Alabamians burned one of the buses and attacked the riders in Birmingham, where they beat demonstrators senseless and clubbed a Justice Department observer. The governor and police refused to protect the freedom riders. The riders traveled into Mississippi under National Guard protection but were arrested at the Jackson bus terminal. Despite Attorney General Robert Kennedy's call for a cooling-off period, freedom rides continued through the summer. The rides proved that African Americans were in charge of their own civil rights revolution.

The March on Washington, 1963

John Kennedy was a tepid supporter of the civil rights movement and entered office with no civil rights agenda. He appointed segregationist judges to mollify Southern congressmen and would have preferred that African Americans stop disturbing the fragile Democratic party coalition. As Eisenhower did at Little Rock, Kennedy intervened at the University of Mississippi in 1962 because of a state challenge to federal authority, not to further racial justice.

In the face of slow federal response, the SCLC concentrated for 1963 on rigidly segregated Birmingham. April began with sit-ins and marches that aimed to integrate lunch counters, restrooms, and stores and secure open hiring for some clerical jobs. Birmingham's commissioner of public safety, Bull Connor, used fire hoses to blast demonstrators against buildings and roll children down the streets. When demonstrators fought back, his men chased them with dogs. Continued marches brought the arrest of hundreds of children. King's own "Letter from Birmingham City Jail" stated the case for protest: "We have not made a single gain in civil rights without determined legal and nonviolent pressure. . . . Freedom is never voluntarily given by the oppressor; it must be demanded by the oppressed."

The Birmingham demonstrations were inconclusive. White leaders accepted minimal demands on May 10 but delayed enforcing them. Antiblack violence continued, including a bomb that killed four children in a Birmingham church. Meanwhile, the events in Alabama had forced President Kennedy to board the freedom train with an eloquent June 11 speech and to send a civil-rights bill to Congress. "Are we to say . . . that this is the land of the free, except for Negroes, that we have no second-class citizens, except Negroes . . . ? Now the time has come for the nation to fulfill its promise."

On August 28, 1963, a rally in Washington transformed African-American civil rights into a national cause. A quarter of a million people, black and white, marched to the Lincoln Memorial. The day gave Martin Luther King Jr. a national pulpit. His call for progress toward Christian and American goals had immense appeal. Television cut away from afternoon programs for his "I Have a Dream" speech.

The March on Washington demonstrated the mass appeal of civil rights and its identification with national values. It also papered over growing tensions within the civil rights movement. John Lewis of SNCC wanted to challenge Kennedy for doing "too little, too late" but dropped the criticism under intense pressure. He was the only speaker at the march to talk about "black people" rather than "Negroes," an indication of growing militancy that split the civil-rights effort in the mid-1960s and moved younger African Americans, as well as Latinos and Native Americans, to emphasize their own distinct identities within American society.

"LET US CONTINUE"

The two years that followed King's speech mingled despair and accomplishment. The optimism of the March on Washington shattered with the assassination of John Kennedy in November 1963. In 1964 and 1965, however, President Lyndon Johnson pushed through Kennedy's legislative agenda and much more in a burst of government activism unmatched since the 1930s. Federal legislation brought victory to the first phase of the civil-rights revolution, launched the **War on Poverty**, expanded health insurance and aid to education, and opened an era of environmental protection.

Dallas, 1963

In November 1963, President Kennedy visited Texas to patch up feuds among Texas Democrats. On November 22, the president's motorcade took him near the Texas School Book Depository building in Dallas, where Lee Harvey Oswald had stationed himself at a window on the sixth floor. When Kennedy's open car swung into the sights of his rifle, Oswald fired three shots that wounded Texas Governor John Connally and killed the president. As doctors vainly treated the president in a hospital emergency room, Dallas police arrested Oswald. Vice President Lyndon B. Johnson (LBJ) took the oath of office as president on Air Force One while the blood-spattered Jacqueline Kennedy looked on. Two days later, as Oswald was being led to a courtroom, the Texas nightclub owner Jack Ruby killed Oswald with a handgun in full view of TV cameras.

After the assassination of John Kennedy in Dallas, Lyndon Johnson, with Jackie Kennedy looking on, took the oath of office as president aboard Air Force One at Love Field in Dallas.

Lee Oswald was a 24-year-old misfit. He had served in the Marines and worked maintaining U-2 spy planes before defecting to the Soviet Union, which he found to be less than a workers' paradise. He returned to the United States after three years with a Russian wife and a fervent commitment to Fidel Castro's Cuban revolution. It was later learned that he had tried to shoot a right-wing general in 1963. He visited the Soviet and Cuban embassies in Mexico City in September trying to drum up a job, but neither country thought him worth hiring.

Some Americans believe there is more to the story. Why? One possibility is the expectation that important events should have great causes. Oswald seems too insignificant to be responsible on his own for the murder of a charismatic president. The sketchy job done by the Warren Commission, appointed to investigate the assassination, also bred doubts in some minds. The commission hurried to complete its work before the 1964 election. It also sought to assure Americans that Kennedy had not been killed as part of a Communist plot. The Warren Commission calmed fears in the short run but left loose ends that have fueled conspiracy theories.

All of the theories remain unproved. Until they are, logic holds that the simplest explanation for cutting through a mass of information is usually the best. Oswald was a social misfit with a grievance against American society. Ruby was an impulsive man who told his brother on his deathbed that he thought he was doing the country a favor. Like presidents Garfield and McKinley before him, Kennedy died at the hands of one unbalanced man acting alone.

War on Poverty

Five days after the assassination, Lyndon Johnson claimed Kennedy's progressive aura for his new administration. "Let us continue," he told the nation, promising to implement Kennedy's policies. In fact, Johnson was vastly different from Kennedy. He was a professional politician who had reached the top through Texas politics and congressional infighting. As Senate majority leader during the 1950s, he had built a web of political obligations and friendships. Johnson's presence on the ticket in 1960 had helped to elect Kennedy by attracting southern voters, but the Kennedy entourage loathed him. He lacked Kennedy's polish and easy relations with the eastern elite. He knew little about foreign affairs but was a master of domestic politics.

Johnson's upbringing in rural Texas shaped a man who was endlessly ambitious, ruthless, and often personally crude, but also deeply committed to social equity. He had entered public life with the New Deal in the 1930s and believed in its principles. Johnson, not Kennedy, was the true heir of Franklin Roosevelt.

Johnson inherited a domestic agenda that the Kennedy administration had defined but not enacted. Kennedy's New Frontier had met the same fate as Truman's Fair Deal.

Initiatives in education, medical insurance, tax reform, and urban affairs had stalled or been gutted by conservatives in Congress.

Kennedy's farthest reaching initiative was rooted in the acknowledgment that poverty was a persistent American problem. Michael Harrington's study *The Other America* became an unexpected bestseller. As poverty captured public attention, Kennedy's economic advisors devised a community action program that emphasized education and job training, a national service corps, and a youth conservation corps. They prepared a package of proposals to submit to Congress in 1964 that downplayed the option of large-scale income transfers as politically unpopular. Instead, they focused on social programs to alter behaviors that were thought to be passed from generation to generation, thus following the American tendency to attribute poverty to the failings of the poor themselves.

Johnson made Kennedy's antipoverty package his own. Adopting Cold War rhetoric, he declared "unconditional war on poverty." The core of Johnson's program was the **Office of Economic Opportunity (OEO)**. Established under the direction of Kennedy's brother-in-law R. Sargent Shriver in 1964, the OEO operated the Job Corps for school dropouts, the Neighborhood Youth Corps for unemployed teenagers, the Head Start program to prepare poor children for school, and VISTA (Volunteers in Service to America), a domestic Peace Corps. OEO's biggest effort went to Community Action Agencies. By 1968, more than five hundred such agencies provided health and educational services. Despite flaws, the War on Poverty improved life for millions of Americans.

Civil Rights, 1964–1965

Johnson's passionate commitment to economic betterment accompanied a commitment to civil rights. In Johnson's view, segregation not only deprived African Americans of access to opportunity but also distracted white Southerners from their own poverty and underdevelopment. As he complained in a speech in New Orleans, southern leaders ignored the region's economic needs in favor of racial rabble-rousing.

One solution was the **Civil Rights Act of 1964**, which Kennedy had introduced but which Johnson got enacted. The law prohibited segregation in public accommodations, such as hotels, restaurants, gas stations, theaters, and parks, and outlawed employment discrimination on federally assisted projects. It also created the Equal Employment Opportunity Commission (EEOC) and included gender in list of categories protected against discrimination, a provision whose consequences were scarcely suspected in 1964.

Even as Congress was debating the 1964 law, **Freedom Summer** moved political power to the top of the civil-rights agenda. Organized by SNCC, the Mississippi Summer Freedom Project was a voter registration drive that sent white and black volunteers to the small towns and back roads of Mississippi. The target was a political system that used rigged literacy tests and intimidation to keep black Southerners from voting. In Mississippi in 1964, only 7 percent of eligible black citizens were registered voters.

Local black activists had laid the groundwork for a registration effort with years of courageous effort through the NAACP and voter leagues. Now an increasingly militant SNCC took the lead. The explicit goal was to increase the number of African-American voters. The tacit intention was to attract national attention by putting middle-class white college students in the line of fire. Freedom Summer gained sixteen hundred new voters and taught two thousand children in SNCC-run Freedom Schools at the cost of beatings, bombings, church arson, and the murder of three project workers.

Another outgrowth of the SNCC effort was the Mississippi Freedom Democratic party (MFDP), a biracial coalition that bypassed Mississippi's all-white Democratic party, followed state party rules, and sent its own delegates to the 1964 Democratic convention. To preserve party harmony, President Johnson refused to expel the "regular" Mississippi Democrats and offered instead to seat two MFDP delegates and enforce party rules for 1968. The MFDP walked out, seething with anger. Fannie Lou Hamer, a MFDP delegate who had already suffered in the struggle for voting rights, remembered, "We learned the hard way that even though we had all the law and all the righteousness on our side—that white man is not going to give up his power to us. We have to build our own power."

Freedom Summer and political realities both focused national attention on voter registration. Lyndon Johnson and Martin Luther King Jr. agreed on the need for federal voting legislation when King visited the president in December 1964 after winning the Nobel Peace Prize. For King, power at the ballot box would help black Southerners take control of their own communities. For Johnson, voting reform would fulfill the promise of American democracy. It would also benefit the Democratic party by replacing with black voters the white Southerners who were drifting toward anti-integration Republicans.

The target for King and the SCLC was Dallas County, Alabama, where only 2 percent of eligible black residents were registered, compared with 70 percent of white residents. Peaceful demonstrations started in January 1965. By early February, jails in the county seat of Selma held 2,600 black people whose offense was marching to the courthouse to demand the vote. The campaign climaxed with a march from Selma to the state capital of Montgomery. SNCC leader John Lewis remembered, "I don't know what we expected. I think maybe we thought we'd be arrested and jailed, or maybe they wouldn't do anything to us. I had a little knapsack on my shoulder with an apple, a toothbrush, toothpaste, and two books in it: a history of America and a book by [Christian theologian] Thomas Merton."

On Sunday, March 7, five hundred marchers crossed the bridge over the Alabama River, to meet a sea of state troopers. The troopers gave them two minutes to disperse and then attacked on foot and horseback "as if they were mowing a big field." The attack drove the demonstrators back in bloody confusion while television cameras rolled.

As violence continued, Johnson addressed a joint session of Congress to demand a voting rights law: "Our mission is at once the oldest and the most basic of this country: to right wrong, to do justice, to serve man." He ended with the refrain of the civil rights movement: "We shall overcome." By opening the political process to previously excluded citizens, the Voting Rights Act was as revolutionary and far reaching as the Nineteenth Amendment, guaranteeing women the right to vote, and the Labor Relations Act of 1935, which recognized labor unions as the equals of corporations.

Johnson signed the **Voting Rights Act** on August 6, 1965. The law outlawed literacy tests and provided for federal voting registrars in states where registration or turnout in 1964 was less than 50 percent of eligible population. It applied initially in seven southern states. Black registration in these states jumped from 27 percent to 55 percent within the first year. In 1975, Congress extended coverage to Hispanic voters in the Southwest. By the end of 1992, Virginia had elected a black governor, and nearly every southern state had elected black representatives to Congress. Less obvious but just as revolutionary were the thousands of black and Latino candidates, who won local offices, and the new moderation of white leaders, who had to satisfy black voters. In the long run, the Voting Rights Act climaxed the battle for civil rights and shifted attention to the continuing problems of economic opportunity and inequality.

War, Peace, and the Landslide of 1964

Lyndon Johnson was the peace candidate in 1964. Johnson had maintained Kennedy's commitment to South Vietnam. On the advice of such Kennedy holdovers as Defense Secretary Robert McNamara, he stepped up commando raids and naval shelling of North Vietnam, on the assumption that North Vietnam controlled the Viet Cong. On August 2, North Vietnamese torpedo boats attacked the U.S. destroyer *Maddox* in the Gulf of Tonkin while it was eavesdropping on North Vietnamese military signals. Two days later, the *Maddox* and the *C. Turner Joy* reported another torpedo attack (probably false sonar readings). Johnson ordered a bombing raid in reprisal and asked Congress to authorize "all necessary measures" to protect American forces and stop further aggression. Congress passed the **Gulf of Tonkin Resolution** with only two nay votes, effectively authorizing the president to wage undeclared war.

Johnson's militancy paled beside that of his Republican opponent. Senator Barry Goldwater of Arizona represented the new right wing of the Republican party, which was drawing strength from the South and West. A department-store heir, Goldwater wanted minimal government interference in free enterprise. As a former Air Force pilot, he also wanted aggressive confrontation with Communism. Campaign literature accurately described him as "a choice, not an echo." He declared that "extremism in the defense of liberty is no vice," raising visions of vigilantes and mobs. Goldwater's campaign made Johnson look moderate. Johnson pledged not "to send American boys nine or ten thousand miles from home to do what Asian boys ought to be doing for themselves" while Goldwater proposed an all-out war.

The election was a landslide. Johnson's 61 percent of the popular vote was the greatest margin ever recorded in a presidential election. Democrats racked up two-to-one majorities in Congress. For the first time in decades, liberal Democrats could enact their domestic program without begging votes from conservative Southerners or Republicans, and Johnson could achieve his goal of a **Great Society** based on freedom and opportunity for all.

The result was a series of measures that Johnson pushed through Congress before the Vietnam War eroded his political standing and distracted national attention. The National Endowment for the Arts and the National Endowment for the Humanities seemed noncontroversial at the time but would later become the focus of liberal and conservative struggles over the character of American life. The Wilderness Act (1964), which preserved 9.1 million acres from all development, would prove another political battlefield in the face of economic pressures in the next century.

The goal of increasing opportunity for all Americans stirred the president most deeply. As he told a July 1965 news conference, "When I was young, poverty was so common that we didn't know it had a name. An education was something that you had to fight for. . . . It is now my opportunity to help every child get an education, to help every Negro and every American citizen have an equal opportunity, to have every family get a decent home, and to help bring healing to the sick and dignity to the old."

The Elementary and Secondary Education Act was the first general federal aid program for public schools, allocating $1.3 billion for textbooks and special education. The Higher Education Act funded low-interest student loans and university research facilities. The Medical Care Act created **Medicare**, federally funded health insurance for the elderly, and **Medicaid**, which helped states offer medical care to the poor. The Appalachian Regional Development Act funded economic development in the depressed mountain counties of twelve states from Georgia to New York and proved a long-run success.

It is sometimes said that the United States declared war on poverty and lost. In fact, the nation came closer in to winning the war on poverty than it did the war in Vietnam. New or expanded social insurance and income support programs, such as Medicare, Medicaid, Social Security, and food stamps, cut the proportion of poor people from 22 percent of the American population in 1960 to 13 percent in 1970 (see Figure 11–2). Infant mortality dropped by a third because of improved nutrition and better access to health care for mothers and children. Taken together, the political results of the 1964 landslide moved the United States far toward the vision of an end to poverty and racial injustice.

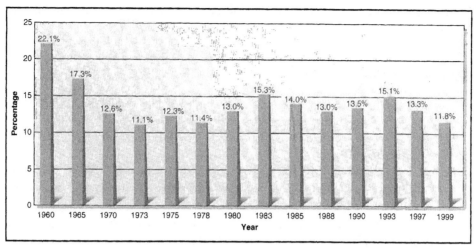

FIGURE 11-2   Poverty Rate, 1960–1999
With the improvement of federal health insurance, assistance for the elderly, and antipoverty programs, the proportion of Americans living in poverty dropped dramatically in the later 1960s. It began to inch upward again in the 1980s, when the priorities of the federal government shifted.
Data Source: Statistical Abstract of the United States.

CONCLUSION

The era commonly remembered as "the 1950s" stretched from 1953 to 1964. Consistent goals guided American foreign policy through the entire period, including vigilant anti-Communism and the confidence to intervene in trouble spots around the globe. At home, the Supreme Court's *Brown* decision introduced a decade-long civil rights revolution that reached its emotional peak with the March on Washington and its political climax with the Civil Rights Act (1964) and Voting Rights Act (1965). However, many patterns of personal behavior and social relations remained unchanged. Women faced similar expectations from the early fifties to the early sixties. Churches showed more continuity than change.

In retrospect, it is remarkable how widely and deeply the Cold War shaped U.S. society. Fundamental social institutions, such as marriage and religion, got extra credit for their contributions to anti-Communism. The nation's long tradition of home-grown radicalism was virtually silent in the face of the Cold War consensus. Even economically meritorious programs like more money for science and better roads went down more easily if linked to national defense.

But the consistency and stability of the 1950s were fragile. The larger world was too complex to fit forever within the narrow framework of bipolar conflict. American society was too disparate and dynamic for Cold War conformity. In the later 1960s and the 1970s, contradictions burst through the surface of the American consensus. Foreign competitors, resource scarcities, and environmental damage diminished economic abundance and sapped national confidence. Nations from Vietnam to Iran refused to cooperate with American plans for the world. Corrupt politicians threatened the constitutional order.

Under these pressures, the national consensus splintered after 1964. Some members of minority groups turned their back on integration. Some younger Americans dropped out of mainstream society to join the aptly named counterculture. Others sought the security of religious commitment and community. Perhaps most divisively, "hawks" battled "doves" over

Vietnam. If civil rights and the Cold War had been the defining issues for "the fifties," Vietnam would define "the sixties," which stretched from 1965 to 1974.

Review Questions

1. What were the sources of prosperity in the 1950s and 1960s? How did prosperity shape cities, family life, and religion? What opportunities did it create for women and for young people? How did it affect the American role in the world? Why did an affluent nation still need a war on poverty in the 1960s?

2. What assumptions about the Soviet Union shaped U.S. foreign policy? What assumptions about the United States shaped Soviet policy? What did American leaders think was at stake in Vietnam, Berlin, and Cuba?

3. Who initiated and led the African-American struggle for civil rights? What role did the federal government play? What were the goals of the civil rights movement? Where did it succeed, and in what ways did it fall short?

4. How did the growth of nuclear arsenals affect international relations? How did the nuclear shadow affect American politics and society?

5. In what new directions did Lyndon Johnson take the United States? Were there differences in the goals of the New Frontier and the Great Society?

6. Why was school integration the focus of such strong conflict? How did the work of Mexican Americans and African Americans support the same goal of equal access to education?

Key Terms

Alliance for Progress *332*
Bay of Pigs *330*
Berlin Wall *330*
Brown v. Board of Education of Topeka *333*
Civil Rights Act of 1964 *340*
Congress of Racial Equality (CORE) *337*
Federal Highway Act of 1956 *317*
Freedom Summer *340*
Great Society *342*
Gulf of Tonkin Resolution *342*
Limited Test Ban Treaty *333*
Massive retaliation *325*
Medicaid *342*
Medicare *342*

National Aeronautics and Space Administration (NASA) *325*
New Frontier *328*
Office of Economic Opportunity (OEO) *340*
Southeast Asia Treaty Organization (SEATO) *331*
Southern Christian Leadership Conference (SCLC) *337*
Southern Manifesto *335*
Student Nonviolent Coordinating Committee (SNCC) *337*
Viet Cong *331*
Voting Rights Act *341*
War on Poverty *338*

Recommended Reading

Michael Beschloss, *May-Day: Eisenhower, Khrushchev, and the U-2 Affair* (1986). The drama and confusion of the U-2 affair are used to interpret the meaning of the Cold War for the United States and the Soviet Union.

William Graebner, *Coming of Age in Buffalo* (1990). In words and pictures, places the complexity of teenage life in the 1950s within the American patterns of class and race.

David Halberstam, *The Fifties* (1993). Provides a readable and detailed account of political and social change.

Michael Harrington, *The Other America* (1962). Published early in the Kennedy years, an impassioned study that reminded Americans of continuing economic inequality and helped launch the War on Poverty.

Diane McWhurter, *Carry Me Home: Birmingham, Alabama: The Climactic Battle of the Civil Rights Revolution* (2000). A sweeping depiction of race relations in one of the nation's most divided cities.

Gerald Posner, *Case Closed* (1993). A detailed analysis of John Kennedy's death that refutes the most popular conspiracy theories.

Theodore White, *The Making of the President, 1960* (1961). A vivid account of the issues and personalities of the 1960 campaign.

Juan Williams, *Eyes on the Prize: America's Civil Rights Years, 1954–1965* (1988). A graphic and fast-moving account of the civil rights movement, written in conjunction with a PBS television series.

Tom Wolfe, *The Right Stuff* (1979). An irreverent account of the early years of the U.S. space program that captures the atmosphere of the 1950s and early 1960s.

SHAKEN TO THE ROOTS: 1965–1980

Contact light! O.K., engine stop. . . . Houston, Tranquility Base here. The Eagle has landed! . . .

We opened the hatch and Neil, with me as navigator, began backing out of the tiny opening [in the Lunar Module *Eagle*]. It seemed like a small eternity before I heard Neil say, "That's one small step for man. . . . one giant leap for mankind." In less than fifteen minutes I was backing awkwardly out of the hatch onto the surface to join Neil, who, in the tradition of all tourists, had his camera ready to photograph my arrival.

I took off jogging to test my maneuverability. The exercise gave me an odd sensation and looked even more odd when I later saw the films of it. With bulky suits on, we seemed to be moving in slow motion. . . . At one point, I remarked that the surface was "Beautiful, beautiful. Magnificent desolation." I was struck by the contrast between the starkness of the shadows and the desert-like barrenness of the rest of the surface. It ranged from dusty gray to light tan and was unchanging except for one startling sight: our LM sitting there with its black, silver and bright yellow-orange thermal coating shining brightly in the otherwise colorless landscape.

During a pause in experiments, Neil suggested we proceed with the flag. . . . To our dismay the staff of the pole wouldn't go far enough into the lunar surface. . . . I dreaded the possibility of the American flag collapsing into the lunar dust in front of the television camera.

Edgar Cortright, ed., *Apollo Expeditions to the Moon* (Washington, DC: NASA SP 350, 1975).

UZZ ALDRIN and Neil Armstrong, on July 20, 1969, completed the longest journey that any person had yet taken. Landing the *Apollo 11* lunar module on the surface of the moon climaxed a five-day trip across the quarter million miles separating the earth from the moon. Six and a half hours after the landing, Armstrong and Aldrin were the first humans to walk on the moon's surface.

The *Apollo 11* expedition combined science and Cold War politics. The American flag planted on the lunar surface was a symbol of victory in one phase of the space race between the United States and the Soviet Union. NASA had been working since 1961 to meet John F. Kennedy's goal of a manned trip to the moon before the end of the decade. The trial runs were *Apollo 8*, which sent American astronauts in orbit around the moon on Christmas Eve of 1968, and *Apollo 10* in May 1969. After the *Apollo 11* expedition, American astronauts made five more trips to the moon between 1969 and 1972, feats that helped restore the nation's standing as the world's scientific and technological leader.

Even with the excitement of *Apollo's* success, however, the United States was increasingly shaken and divided in the later 1960s and 1970s. The failure to win an easy victory in Vietnam eroded the nation's confidence and fueled bitter divisions about the nation's goals. Most Americans had agreed about the goals of the Cold War, the benefits of economic growth, and the value of equal opportunity. Stalemate in Southeast Asia, political changes in Third World countries, and an oil supply crisis in the 1970s challenged U.S. influence in the world. Frustrated with slow progress toward racial equality, many minority Americans advocated separation rather than integration, helping to plunge the nation's cities into crisis, while other Americans began to draw back from some of the objectives of racial integration.

Political scandals, summarized in three syllables as "Watergate," undercut faith in government. Fifteen years of turmoil forced a grudging recognition of limits to American military power, economic capacity, governmental prerogatives, and even the ideal of a single American dream.

KEY TOPICS

Vietnam, civil rights, and the unraveling of the national consensus.

The prolonged military struggle that resulted from Lyndon Johnson's decision to commit American forces to direct combat in Vietnam.

Growing opposition to the Vietnam War from 1965 to 1972.

The unraveling of the New Deal coalition beginning with the election of 1968.

Nixon's presidency and the Watergate scandal.

The growing militance of the struggle for civil rights among African Americans, Hispanic Americans, and Native Americans.

THE END OF CONSENSUS

Pleiku is a town in Vietnam 240 miles north of Saigon (now Ho Chi Minh City). In 1965, Pleiku was the site of a South Vietnamese army headquarters and American military base. At 2 A.M. on February 7, Viet Cong attacked the U.S. base, killing eight Americans and wounding a hundred. The national security advisor, McGeorge Bundy, in Saigon on a fact-finding visit; Ambassador Maxwell Taylor; and General William Westmoreland, the commander of U.S. forces in South Vietnam, all quickly recommended a retaliatory air strike against North

• CHRONOLOGY •

1962 Rachel Carson publishes *Silent Spring*.

Port Huron Statement launches Students for a Democratic Society.

1965 Congress approves Wilderness Act.

Malcolm X is assassinated.

Residents of Watts neighborhood in Los Angeles riot.

1967 African Americans riot in Detroit and Newark.

1968 Viet Cong launches Tet Offensive.

James Earl Ray kills Martin Luther King Jr.

Lyndon Johnson declines to run for reelection.

SDS disrupts Columbia University.

Sirhan Sirhan kills Robert Kennedy.

Peace talks start between the United States and North Vietnam.

Police riot against antiwar protesters during the Democratic National Convention in Chicago.

Richard Nixon is elected president.

1969 Neil Armstrong and Buzz Aldrin walk on the moon.

1970 United States invades Cambodia.

National Guard units kill students at Kent State and Jackson State Universities.

Earth Day is celebrated.

Environmental Protection Agency is created.

1971 *New York Times* publishes the secret "Pentagon Papers."

President Nixon freezes wages and prices.

"Plumbers" unit is established in the White House.

1972 Nixon visits China.

United States and Soviet Union adopt SALT I.

Operatives for Nixon's reelection campaign break into Democratic headquarters in the Watergate complex in Washington, D.C.

1973 Paris accords end direct U.S. involvement in South Vietnamese war.

United States moves to all-volunteer armed forces.

Watergate burglars are convicted.

Senate Watergate hearings reveal the existence of taped White House conversations.

Spiro Agnew resigns as vice president, is replaced by Gerald Ford.

Arab states impose an oil embargo after the third Arab-Israeli War.

1974 Nixon resigns as president, is succeeded by Gerald Ford.

1975 Communists triumph in South Vietnam.

United States, USSR, and European nations sign the Helsinki Accords.

1976 Jimmy Carter defeats Gerald Ford for the presidency.

1978 Carter brings the leaders of Egypt and Israel to Camp David for peace talks.

1979 SALT II agreement is signed but not ratified.

OPEC raises oil prices.

Three Mile Island nuclear plant comes close to disaster.

Iranian militants take U.S. embassy hostages.

1980 Iranian hostage rescue fails.

Soviet troops enter Afghanistan.

Ronald Reagan defeats Jimmy Carter for the presidency.

Vietnam. President Johnson concurred, and navy bombers roared off aircraft carriers in Operation FLAMING DART. A month later, Johnson ordered a full-scale air offensive code-named ROLLING THUNDER.

The attack at Pleiku triggered plans that were waiting to be put into effect since the Gulf of Tonkin resolution the previous summer. The official reason for the bombing was to pressure North Vietnam to negotiate an end to the war. As the South Vietnamese government lost control of the countryside, air strikes on North Vietnam looked like an easy way to redress the balance. In the back of President Johnson's mind were the need to prove his toughness and the mistaken assumption that China was aggressively backing North Vietnam.

The air strikes pushed the United States over the line from propping up the South Vietnamese government to leading the war effort. A president who desperately wanted a way out of Southeast Asia kept adding American forces. Eventually, the war in Vietnam would distract the United States from the goals of the Great Society and drive Johnson from office. It hovered like a shadow over the next two presidents, set back progress toward global stability, and divided the American people.

Deeper into Vietnam

Lyndon Johnson (LBJ) faced limited options in Vietnam (see Map 12-1). The pervasive American determination to contain Communism and Kennedy's previous commitments hemmed Johnson in. Advisors persuaded him that controlled military escalation—a middle course between withdrawal and all-out war—could secure Vietnam. They failed to understand the extent of popular opposition to the official government in Saigon and the willingness of North Vietnam to sacrifice to achieve national unity.

ROLLING THUNDER put the United States on the up escalator to war. Because an air campaign required ground troops to protect bases in South Vietnam, U.S. Marines landed on March 8. Over the next four months, General Westmoreland wore away Johnson's desire to contain American involvement. More bombs, a pause, an offer of massive U.S. aid—nothing brought North Vietnam to the negotiating table. Meanwhile, defeat loomed. Johnson dribbled in new forces and expanded their mission from base security to combat. On July 28, he finally gave Westmoreland doubled draft calls and an increase in U.S. combat troops from 75,000 to 275,000 by 1966 (see Figure 12-1).

Why did the United States escalate the war? According to one later argument, South Vietnam was a quagmire that dragged in a reluctant nation. Each step that the United States took to influence South Vietnamese politics and increase American military involvement made it more difficult to pull back. Events took on their own momentum and sucked the nation deeper into the Southeast Asian quicksand.

However, recent studies show that President Johnson and his advisors consciously chose war. They were haunted by memories of the Munich settlement of 1938 and believed in the "domino" theory which claimed that Communist success in one nation would inevitably topple adjacent nations. They had a faith in American military capacities and were committed to a doctrine of containment that was working in Europe (although it would prove to be irrelevant in Asia). With the encouragement of his highest advisors McGeorge Bundy, Secretary of State Dean Rusk, and Secretary of Defense Robert McNamara, President Johnson deliberately ignored a number of opportunities for a negotiated settlement, even after his landslide victory in 1964 gave him the political opportunity. He knew that a good outcome was questionable but opted for war in order to avoid the stigma of retreat.

Johnson's decision turned a South Vietnamese war into an American war. Secretary of Defense McNamara was clear about the change: "We have relied on South Vietnam to carry the brunt. Now we would be responsible for a satisfactory military outcome." At the end of 1967, American forces in South Vietnam totaled 485,000; they reached their maximum of 543,000 in August 1969.

The U.S. strategy on the ground was **search and destroy**. As conceived by Westmoreland, it used sophisticated surveillance and heavily armed patrols to locate enemy detachments, which could then be destroyed by air strikes, artillery, and reinforcements carried in by helicopter. The approach made sense when the opposition consisted of North Vietnamese troops and large Viet Cong units. It worked well in the sparsely populated Ia Drang Valley, where the First Air Cavalry chewed up North Vietnamese regulars in November 1965.

However, most opponents were not North Vietnamese divisions but were South Vietnamese guerrillas. The Viet Cong avoided "set-piece" battles. Instead, they forced the

MAP 12-1   The War in Vietnam

The United States attacked North Vietnam with air strikes but confined large-scale ground operations to South Vietnam and Cambodia. In South Vietnam, U.S. forces faced both North Vietnamese army units and Viet Cong rebels, all of whom received supplies by way of the so-called Ho Chi Minh Trail, named for the leader of North Vietnam. The coordinated attacks on cities and towns throughout South Vietnam during the Tet Offensive in 1968 surprised the United States.

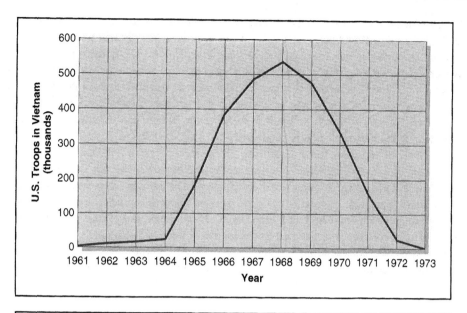

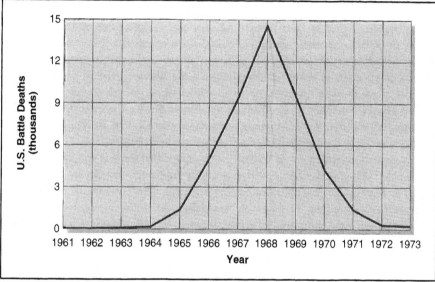

FIGURE 12-1   **The United States in Vietnam**

American involvement in Vietnam grew slowly in the Kennedy administration from 1961 to 1963, expanded rapidly under Lyndon Johnson from 1964 to 1968, and fell just as rapidly under Richard Nixon from 1969 to 1973. The "Nixon Doctrine" tried to substitute American weapons and equipment for American military personnel but failed to prevent a North Vietnamese victory in 1975 after United States withdrawal.

Data Source: Statistical Abstract of the United States.

United States to make repeated sweeps through farms and villages. The enemy were difficult for Americans to recognize among farmers and workers, making South Vietnamese society itself the target. The American penchant for massive firepower killed thousands of Vietnamese and made millions refugees. Because the South Vietnamese government was unable to secure areas after American sweeps, the Viet Cong often reappeared after the Americans had crashed through a district.

The American air war also had limited results. Pilots dropped a vast tonnage of bombs on the "Ho Chi Minh Trail," a network of supply routes from North Vietnam to South Vietnam through the mountains of neighboring Laos. Despite the bombing, thousands of workers converted rough paths into roads that were repaired as soon as they were damaged. Air assault on North Vietnam itself remained "diplomatic," intended to force North Vietnam to stop intervening in the South Vietnamese civil war. Since North Vietnam's leadership considered North and South to be one country, the American goal was unacceptable. Attacking North Vietnam's poorly developed economy, the United States soon ran out of targets. The CIA estimated that it cost nearly $10 to inflict every $1 of damage.

Despite the massive influx of American troops and firepower, the war was not winnable under conditions that the United States could accept. The United States wanted to engage in a limited war with a specific political goal of shoring up an independent South Vietnamese government. The Viet Cong and North Vietnam, in contrast, were fighting a total war of revolution and national liberation that continued struggles since the 1940s. There was no way for the United States to overcome this commitment without a level of mobilization that would have been impossible to sell to the American people.

Voices of Dissent

At home, protest against the war quickly followed the commitment of American combat forces. In the 1950s, dissenters on the left had been too intimidated by McCarthyism to protest overcommitment to the Cold War. Now a coalition of experienced antiwar workers and new college activists openly challenged the Cold Warriors. The first national antiwar march took place in Washington on April 17, 1965. Twenty-five thousand people picketed the White House, assembled at the Washington Monument for speeches by Senator Ernest Gruening of Alaska (one of the two dissenting votes on the Gulf of Tonkin Resolution) and African-American leaders, and walked up the Mall to the Capitol.

One group of opponents were "realists" who argued that the war was a mistake. Foreign policy expert Hans Morgenthau, for example, fully supported anti-Soviet containment in Europe but maintained that the United States had no vital interests in South Vietnam. Policymakers in Washington, he said, were misreading the situation, wasting American lives and resources, and weakening the American presence in regions such as Europe that were truly important to national security. Respected figures such as the Cold War strategist George Kennan joined in the dissent. Senator J. William Fulbright held well publicized hearings in 1966 and 1967, at which respectable critics of the war could state their case to a national audience, and published *The Arrogance of Power* (1967), a book that argued that even the United States needed to recognize limits on its vast political and military power.

If the realists thought that the United States was simply being stupid, more radical critics found the roots of the war in basic flaws in the American character and system. Novelist Norman Mailer compared the American military to big-game trophy hunters in Alaska in *Why Are We in Vietnam?* (1967). Others called the war an example of economic imperialism that showed the power of multinational corporations to control American foreign policy. A generation later, some of the same analysis would reappear in arguments against the North American Free Trade Agreement and the World Trade Organization.

From Protest to Confrontation In 1966 and 1967, antiwar activity changed from respectful protest to direct confrontations with what protesters called the "war machine." Protesters lay down in front of trains carrying munitions. Representatives of Women Strike for Peace journeyed to North Vietnam to explore possible solutions. Religious groups such

---

• • • OVERVIEW • • •

WHY WERE WE IN SOUTH VIETNAM?

American leaders offered a number of justifications for American military involvement in Vietnam. Here are some of the key arguments, with points that supported or questioned the explanation.

To Prop Up a Domino	Communist success in South Vietnam would undermine pro-American regimes in adjacent nations, which would topple like a row of dominoes.
Pro	The firm U.S. stand contributed to an anti-Communist coup in Indonesia in 1965 and encouraged pro-American interests in Thailand and the Philippines.
Con	Detailed knowledge of each nation in Southeast Asia shows that their own histories and internal issues were far more important in determining their futures than was American action in Vietnam.
To Contain China	China's Communist regime wanted to expand its control throughout Asia.
Pro	The People's Republic of China was hostile to the United States, as shown in the Korean War, and had a long history of trying to control Vietnam.
Con	North Vietnam had closer ties to the Soviet Union than to China and played the two Communist nations against each other to preserve its own independence from China.
To Defeat Aggression	South Vietnam was an independent nation threatened by invasion.
Pro	The major military threat to South Vietnam after 1965 came from the growing presence of the North Vietnamese army, and U.S. military intervention was necessary to counter that invasion.
Con	The conflict in South Vietnam originated as a civil war within South Vietnam. Moreover, South and North Vietnam were a single nation, artificially divided in 1954, so that North Vietnam was trying to reunify rather than invade South Vietnam.
To Protect Democracy	South Vietnam was a democratic nation that deserved American support.
Pro	South Vietnam had an emerging middle class and an opportunity to develop democratic institutions.
Con	South Vietnam was never a true democracy, ruled first by civilian dictator Ngo Dinh Diem and then a series of military strongmen.

---

as the American Friends Service Committee tried to dispense medical and humanitarian aid even-handedly in both North Vietnam and South Vietnam.

The tone of the debate became nastier. Johnson and his associates ridiculed dissenters (for example, Fulbright became "Halfbright" among the administration's inner circle). In turn, protesters chanted "Hey, hey, LBJ! How many kids did you kill today?" Much of the anger was directed at the military draft administered by the **Selective Service System**. In theory, the Selective Service picked the young men who could best serve the nation as soldiers and deferred induction of those with vital skills. As the war expanded, the administration tried to hold the allegiance of the middle class by finding ways to exempt their sons from service in Vietnam. Full-time college enrollment was good for a deferment; so was the right medical diagnosis from the right doctor. As a result, draftees and enlistees tended to be small-town and working-class youth. They were also young. The average GI in World War II had been in his mid-20s; the typical soldier in Vietnam was 19 or 20. Women who served as military nurses tended to come from the same small-town and working-class backgrounds where patriotism was unquestioned. The resentment created by the draft was an important wedge that began to erode the long-standing alliance between working-class Americans and the Democratic party.

Military service also deepened the gap between black and white Americans. The black community supplied more than its share of combat soldiers. In 1965, when African Americans made up 11 percent of the nation's population, 24 percent of the soldiers who died in Vietnam were black. This disparity forced the Defense Department to revise its combat assignments. Martin Luther King Jr. joined the protest in 1967. King called the war a moral disaster whose costs weighed most heavily on the poor and a new form of colonialism that was destroying Vietnamese society.

Draft resistance provided a direct avenue for protest against the war. Some young men burned the small paper cards that indicated their selective service classification, causing Congress to enact steep penalties for the act. Several thousand moved to Canada, to spend a decade or more in exile. Because of the well-publicized impact of the war on civilians and noncombatants, thousands of others described their religious and ethical opposition to war in applications for conscientious-objector classification. Much smaller numbers went to jail for refusing to cooperate in any way with the Selective Service System. And a handful of activists, including the Catholic priests Daniel Berrigan and Philip Berrigan, directly disrupted the operations of the draft by invading draft-board offices and trying to burn files or douse them with animal blood. Resistance mounted through the entire decade. By the end of 1969, over half the men drafted in California were refusing to show up, and prosecutions for draft evasion would peak in 1972 at nearly five thousand.

Antiwar protests were simultaneously symbolic and disruptive. Some activists dumped jars of animal blood over draft-board records. Others tried to block munitions trains. In October 1967, a hundred thousand people marched on the Pentagon and surrounded it with the light of burning draft cards. Some in front stuck flowers in the rifle barrels of the soldiers ringing the building; others kicked and spat. The troops and police cleared the grounds with tear gas and clubs.

The popular media portrayed the conflicting visions of the Vietnam war. Barry McGuire's song "Eve of Destruction" climbed the charts. Folksinger Phil Ochs sang "I Ain't Marching Anymore." "And it's one, two, three, what are we fighting for?" sang Country Joe and the Fish. Supporters countered with an aging John Wayne as a heroic American soldier saving South Vietnam in the movie *The Green Berets*. Country singer Merle Travis spoke for many small-town

Americans who supported the war in "Okie from Muskogee" (where they didn't burn draft cards).

New Left and Community Activism

The antiwar movement was part of a growing grass-roots activism that took much of its tone from the university-based **Students for a Democratic Society (SDS)**. The group was important for its ideas, not its size. Its Port Huron Statement, adopted in 1962, called for grass-roots action and "participatory democracy." Building on ideas of such 1950s dissenters as C. Wright Mills, SDS tried to harness youthful disillusionment about consumerism, racism, and imperialism. It wanted to counter the trends that seemed to be turning Americans into tiny cogs in the machinery of big government, corporations, and universities. SDS thought of itself as a "New Left" that was free from the doctrinal squabbles that hampered the old left of the 1930s and 1940s.

Many of the original SDS leaders were also participants in the civil rights movement. The same was true of Mario Savio, founder of the **Free Speech Movement (FSM)** at the University of California at Berkeley in 1964. Savio hoped to build a multi-issue "community of protest" around the idea of "a free university in a free society." FSM protests climaxed with a December sit-in that led to 773 arrests and stirred protest on other campuses.

What SDS wanted to do with its grass-roots organizing resembled the federal community-action programs associated with the war on poverty. The **Model Cities Program** (1966) invited residents of poor neighborhoods to write their own plans for using federal funds to improve local housing, education, health services, and job opportunities. Model Cities assemblies challenged the racial bias in programs like urban renewal and helped train community leaders.

In the 1970s and 1980s, when SDS was long gone and the Model Cities Program was fading, the lessons of grass-roots reform would still be visible in alternative organizations and political movements that strengthened democracy from the bottom up. Activists staffed food cooperatives, free clinics, women's health groups, and drug counseling centers across the country. Community-based organization was a key element in self-help efforts by African Americans, Asian Americans, and Latinos. Neighborhood associations and community-development corporations that provided affordable housing and jobs extended the "backyard revolution" into the 1980s and beyond. Social conservatives, such as anti-abortionists, used the same techniques on behalf of their own agendas.

The Feminist Critique

The growing dissatisfaction of many women with their domestic roles helped set the stage for a revived feminism that was another result of the ferment of the 1960s. Important steps in this revival included the Presidential Commission on the Status of Women in 1961; the addition of gender as one of the categories protected by the Civil Rights Act of 1964 (see Chapter 11); and creation of the National Organization for Women (NOW) in 1966.

Mainstream feminism targeted unequal opportunity in the job market. Newspapers in the early 1960s segregated help-wanted ads by sex, listing "Girl Friday" jobs in one column and professional work in another. College-educated baby boomers encountered "glass ceilings" and job discrimination, in which companies hired less qualified men who "needed the job" rather than more qualified women who supposedly did not. Throughout the mid-1960s and 1970s, activists battled to open job categories to women, who proved that they could indeed use tools, run computers, or pick stocks on Wall Street. They also battled for equal pay for everyone with equal qualifications and responsibilities.

Ms. magazine published its first issue in 1972. Edited by Gloria Steinem, the magazine attempted to bring a radical feminist message to a wide audience. Ms. emphasized the need for women to have equal access with men to education, health care, and employment and tried to help Americans rethink traditional gender roles.

Changes in sexual behavior paralleled efforts to equalize treatment in the workplace. More reliable methods of contraception, especially birth-control pills introduced in the early 1960s, gave women greater control over childbearing. In some ways a replay of ideas from the 1920s, a new sexual revolution eroded the double standard that expected chastity of women but tolerated promiscuity among men. Starting in the 1960s, women began to catch up to men by acting as if marriage was not necessary to sanction sexual relations. One consequence was a singles culture that accepted sexual activity between unmarried men and women.

More radical versions of the feminist message came from women who had joined the civil rights and antiwar movements only to find themselves working the copy machine and the coffeemaker while men plotted strategy. Radicals caught the attention of the national media with a demonstration against the 1968 Miss America pageant. Protesters crowned a sheep as Miss America and encouraged women to make a statement by tossing their bras and makeup in the trash.

Women's liberation took off as a social and political movement in 1970 and 1971 as influential books probed the roots of inequality between men's and women's opportunities. Women shared their stories and ideas in small "consciousness-raising" sessions. Ms. magazine gave the movement a national voice in 1972. Within a few years, millions of women had recognized events and patterns in their lives as discrimination based on gender. The feminist movement, and specific policy measures related to it, put equal rights and the fight against sexism (a word no one knew before 1965) on the national agenda and gradually changed how Americans thought about the relationships between men and women. Feminists focused attention on rape as a crime of violence and called attention to the burdens the legal system placed on rape victims. In the 1980s and 1990s, they also challenged sexual harassment in the workplace, gradually refining the boundaries between acceptable and unacceptable behavior.

Youth Culture and Counterculture

The popular context for the serious work of the New Left was the growing youth culture and **counterculture**, which drew most heavily from members of the college-bound or college-educated middle class. Millions of young people in the second half of the 1960s pursued traditional goals of jobs, families and military service, but millions more expressed their alienation from American society by sampling drugs or chasing the rainbow of a youth culture. Some just smoked marijuana, grew long hair, and listened to psychedelic rock—actions that could span class divisons. Others plunged into ways of life that scorned their middle-class backgrounds. The middle-aged and middle-class ignored the differences and dubbed the rebellious young "hippies."

The youth culture took advantage of the nation's prosperity. It was consumerism in a tie-dyed T-shirt. A high point was the 1969 Woodstock rock festival in New York State, a weekend of "sex, drugs, and rock-and-roll" for 400,000 young people. But Woodstock was an excursion, not a life-altering commitment. Members of the Woodstock Generation were consumers in a distinct market niche, dressing but not living like social reformers or revolutionaries. The musical *Hair* (1968) and the film *Easy Rider* (1969) harnessed their social ferment to the box office as mass culture absorbed the youth culture.

Within the youth culture was a smaller and more intense counterculture that added Eastern religion, social radicalism, and evangelistic belief in the drug LSD. The Harvard professor Timothy Leary and the writer Aldous Huxley claimed that hallucinogenic or psychedelic drugs, such as mescaline and LSD, would swing open the "doors of perception." Rock lyrics began to reflect the drug culture in 1966 and 1967, and young people talked about Leary's advice to "tune in, turn on, and drop out."

The mecca of the dropouts was San Francisco's Haight-Ashbury district. In the early 1960s, its cheap apartments had housed African Americans, beatniks, and homosexuals. Its radical atmosphere attracted a sudden influx of students and college dropouts in 1966. In 1967's "Summer of Love," the Haight was home to perhaps seven thousand permanent hippies and seventy thousand short-time visitors. "If you're going to San Francisco," said one song, "be sure to wear some flowers in your hair." Drugs and violence soon took over the streets, psychedelic businesses closed, and a respectable middle class bought the cheap real estate. Meanwhile, hippie districts sprang up around university campuses across the country.

The cultural rebels of the late 1950s and early 1960s had been trying to combine personal freedom with new social arrangements. Many hippies were more interested in altering their minds with drugs than with politics or poetry. Serious exploration of societal alternatives was left for the minority who devoted themselves to the political work of the New Left, communal living, women's liberation, and other movements.

Sounds of Change

The youth culture was shaped by films and philosophers, by pot and poets, but above all by music. Many changes in American society are mirrored in the abrupt shift from the complacent rock-and-roll of the early 1960s to the more provocative albums of mid-decade: Bob Dylan's *Highway 61 Revisited* (1965), the Beatles *Rubber Soul* (1965) and *Sergeant Pepper's Lonely Hearts Club Band* (1967), the Jefferson Airplane's *Surrealistic Pillow* (1967). The songs were still aimed at popular success, but the musicians were increasingly self-conscious of themselves as artists and social critics.

At the start of the decade, the African-American roots of rock-and-roll were unmistakable, but there was no social agenda. Elvis Presley and the Everly Brothers kept the messages personal, and there was no reason to anticipate any departure from popular music's normal concerns about love and loss. Music that criticized American society initially found a much smaller audience through the folk-music revival in a few big cities and university campuses. Folk singers, such as the long-established Pete Seeger and the younger Joan Baez, drew on black music, white country music, and old labor-organizing songs to keep alive dissenting voices.

Then, in an artistic revolution, the doors opened to a new kind of rock music. The Beatles capitalized on their immense popularity to begin a career of artistic experimentation.

They also opened the way for such hard-edged British bands as the Rolling Stones and The Who to introduce social criticism and class consciousness into rock lyrics. San Francisco's new psychedelic-rock scene took its name from drugs, such as LSD, and centered on shows at the Fillmore Auditorium, where performers in 1966 included the Jefferson Airplane, the Grateful Dead, and Buffalo Springfield. The Texan Janis Joplin came to San Francisco to draw on black musical styles after reading the Beat writers who had celebrated the city's jazz and racial openness.

Bob Dylan, a folksinger with an acoustic guitar, "went electric" at the Newport, Rhode Island, folk festival in 1965 and further transformed the music scene. Songs like "Blowin' in the Wind" and "Like a Rolling Stone" were personal and political at the same time; Dylan's music was musically exciting and socially critical in a way that expressed much of the discontent of American young people. Dylan paved the way for later singers like Bruce Springsteen and Kurt Cobain.

The transformation of rock in the mid-1960s invited far more explicit treatment of sex and illegal drugs than was previously accepted in pop music. Jim Morrison and The Doors, Lou Reed and the Velvet Underground, and Jimi Hendrix exploded onto the scene in 1967. Their driving rhythms and sexually aggressive stage personalities blended the tensions of big cities with influences from white rock-and-roll and black rhythm and blues. Hendrix spanned the greatest distance from ghetto blues clubs of the 1950s to the mass market of the late 1960s, with albums such as *Are Your Experienced* (1967). By 1972, both Morrison and Hendrix were dead of hard living and drug abuse. Meanwhile, *Rolling Stone* magazine had published its first issue in November 1967, giving the new sounds a forum for serious analysis.

Communes and Cults

Out of the half-secular, half-spiritual vision of the counterculture came people who not only dropped out of mainstream institutions but also tried to drop into miniature societies built on new principles. Thousands of Americans in the late 1960s and 1970s formed "intentional communities" or "communes," many as a response to the collapse of the Haight-Ashbury neighborhood into crime and drug abuse after 1967. Their members usually tried to combine individual freedom and spontaneity with cooperative living. Upper New England and the Southwest were commune country. The northern California coast and the Pacific Northwest were also attractive because of their fine climate for growing marijuana. Rural communes usually located on marginal land too poor to support commercial farming; members pored over *The Whole Earth Catalog* (1968) to figure out how to live on the land. There were also thousands of smaller and less conspicuous urban communes whose members occupied large old houses and tried to pursue experiments in socialism, environmentalism, or feminism.

A few communes followed coherent social theories, but many were free-form. It is easy to make fun of them in retrospect, with their tepees, log cabins, and eccentric architecture. Children ended up with off-the-tent names like Catnip, Psyche Joy, and Hummingbird. Adults practiced odd combinations of vegetarianism, Asian religion, and campfire singalongs. Communes were artificial families, financed by inheritances, food stamps, and handicraft sales, and they suffered from the same inequality between men and women that was fueling the feminist revolt. Like natural families, they were emotional hothouses; most collapsed because their members had incompatible goals.

Similar to communes but far more organized were exotic religious communities. Following an American tradition, they have offered tightly knit group membership and absolute answers to basic questions of human life. One of the most successful has been the Holy Spirit Association for the Unification of World Christianity (Unification Church), which Sun Myung Moon brought from Korea to the United States in 1973. Converts ("Moonies") have never numbered more than a few tens of thousands, but Moon amassed a huge fortune and dabbled in conservative politics.

Americans usually hear about cults only if they clash with authorities or end in disaster. Most tragic was the case of Jim Jones, who founded the People's Temple in California on a program of social justice but became increasingly dictatorial and abusive. He moved nearly a thousand followers to Guyana in South America and violently resisted authorities' efforts to penetrate his walls of secrecy. A congressional investigation of abuses within the colony led to the murder of Congressman Leo Ryan and mass suicide by nine hundred of Jones's followers, who drank cyanide-laced punch on November 18, 1978.

CITIES UNDER STRESS

In the confident years after World War II, big cities had an upbeat image. The typical movie with a New York setting opened with a shot of the towering Manhattan skyline and plunged into the bustling business or theater districts. By the 1970s, however, slums and squalid back streets dominated popular imagery. *The French Connection* (1971) followed a drug dealer from Fifth Avenue to empty and menacing warehouses. *Klute* (1971) and *Taxi Driver* (1976) took moviegoers through the twilight world of prostitution. *Blade Runner* (1982) showed a Los Angeles driven mad by corporate violence and social isolation. Such television cop shows as *Hill Street Blues* (1981–1987) and *Miami Vice* (1984–1990) repeated the message that cities had become places of random and frequent violence.

Diagnosing an Urban Crisis

Popular entertainment reflected Americans' growing discomfort with their cities. The nation entered the 1960s with the assumption that urban problems were growing pains. Exploding metropolitan areas needed money for streets, schools, and sewers. Politicians viewed the difficulties of central cities as byproducts of exuberant suburban growth that left outmoded downtowns in need of physical redevelopment. In mid-decade, however, TV networks and news magazines began to run stories about "Battlefield, USA" and "Crisis in the Cities" that described cities as sinking under racial violence, crime, and unemployment.

Central cities had a special burden in caring for the domestic poor. Baltimore had 27 percent of the Maryland population in 1970 but 66 percent of the state's welfare recipients. Boston had 14 percent of the Massachusetts population but 32 percent of the welfare clients. Impoverished, and often fragmented, families needed schools to serve as social-work agencies as well as educational institutions. Poor people with no other access to health care used city hospital emergency rooms as the family doctor.

Many urban problems were associated with the "second ghettos" created by the migration of 2.5 million African Americans from southern farms to northern and western cities in the 1950s and 1960s. At the start of World War II, black Americans had been much more rural than white Americans. By 1970, they were more urban. Fully one-third of all African Americans lived in the twelve largest cities, crowding into ghetto neighborhoods dating from World War II.

Postwar black migrants found systems of race relations that limited their access to decent housing, to the best schools, and to many unionized jobs. Many families also arrived just in time to face the consequences of industrial layoffs and plant closures in the 1970s and 1980s. Already unneeded in the South because of the mechanization of agriculture, the migrants found themselves equally unwanted in the industrial North, caught in decaying neighborhoods and victimized by crime.

The residential ghetto trapped African-American families who tried to follow the expectations of mainstream society. Because ghettos grew block by block, middle-class black families had to pioneer as intruders into white neighborhoods and then see ghetto problems crowd in behind them. Their children faced the seductions of the street, which became increasingly violent with the spread of handguns and trade in illegal drugs.

Central cities faced additional financial problems unrelated to poverty and race. Many of their roads, bridges, fire stations, and water mains were 50 to 100 years old by the 1960s and 1970s, and they were wearing out. Closure of the elevated West Side Highway along the Hudson River in Manhattan after huge chunks fell out of the roadway symbolized a spreading urban problem. Decay of urban utility and transportation systems was a byproduct of market forces and public policy. Private developers often borrowed money saved through Northeastern bank accounts, insurance policies, and pension funds to finance new construction in the suburbs and Sunbelt. The defense budget pumped tax dollars from the old industrial cities into the South and West.

High local taxes in older cities was one result, for the American system of local government demands that cities and the poor help themselves. By the early 1970s, the average resident of a central city paid roughly twice the state and local taxes per $1,000 of income as the average suburbanite. As Mayor Moon Laundreau of New Orleans commented, "We've taxed everything that moves and everything that stands still; and if anything moves again, we tax that, too."

Racial Rioting

African Americans and Hispanics who rioted in city streets in the mid-1960s were fed up with lack of job opportunities and with substandard housing and crime in their neighborhoods. Prominent black writers, such as James Baldwin in *The Fire Next Time* (1963), had warned of mounting anger. Suddenly the fires were real. Riots in Rochester, Harlem, and Brooklyn in July 1964 opened four years of racial violence. Before they subsided, the riots scarred most big cities and killed two hundred people, most of them African Americans.

The explosion of the Watts neighborhood in Los Angeles fixed the danger of racial unrest in the public mind. Trouble started on August 11, 1965, when a white highway-patrol officer arrested a young African American for drunken driving. Loud complaints drew a crowd, and the arrival of Los Angeles police turned the bystanders into an angry mob that attacked passing cars. Rioting, looting, and arson spread through Watts for two days until the National Guard cordoned off the trouble spots and occupied the neighborhood on August 14 and 15.

The outburst frightened white Americans. In most previous race riots, white residents had used violence to keep black residents "in their place." In Watts, African Americans were the instigators. The primary targets were the police and ghetto businesses that had reputations for exploiting their customers. The National Advisory Commission on Civil Disorders concluded in 1968 that most property damage was the "result of deliberate attacks on white-owned businesses characterized in the Negro community as unfair or disrespectful." In short, the riots were protests about the problems of ghetto life.

After Watts, Americans expected "long hot summers" and got them. Scores of cities suffered riots in 1966, including a riot by Puerto Ricans in Chicago that protested the same problems black people faced. The following year, the worst violence was in Newark, New Jersey, and in Detroit, where forty-three deaths and blocks of blazing buildings stunned television viewers.

Few politicians wanted to admit that African Americans and Hispanics had serious grievances. Their impulse was to blame riffraff and outside agitators—"lawbreakers and mad dogs," to quote California Governor Ronald Reagan. This theory was wrong. Almost all participants were neighborhood residents. Except that they were younger, they were representative of the African-American population, and their violence came from the frustration of rising expectations. Despite the political gains of the civil rights movement, unemployment remained high, and the police still treated all black residents as potential criminals. The urban riots were political actions to force the problems of African Americans onto the national agenda. "What are these people rioting about?" asked one resident. "They want recognition, and the only way they're going to get it is to riot."

Minority Separatism

Minority separatism tapped the same anger that fueled the urban riots. Separatists challenged the central goal of the civil rights movement, which sought full participation in American life. The phrase **Black Power** summed up the new alternative. The term came from frustrated SNCC leader Stokely Carmichael in 1966: "We've been saying freedom for six years—and we ain't got nothing. What we're going to start saying now is 'Black Power'!"

Black power translated many ways—control of one's own community through the voting machine, celebration of the African-American heritage, creation of a parallel society that shunned white institutions. At the personal level, it was a synonym for black pride. It propelled the successful political campaigns of Richard Hatcher in Gary, Indiana, and Carl Stokes in Cleveland, the first African Americans elected mayors of large northern cities.

Black Power also meant increased interest in the **Nation of Islam**, or Black Muslims, who combined a version of Islam with radical separatism. They called for self-discipline, support of black institutions and businesses, and total rejection of white people. The Nation of Islam appealed to blacks who saw no future in integration. It was strongest in northern cities, such as Chicago, where it offered an alternative to the life of the ghetto streets.

In the early 1960s, Malcolm X emerged as a leading Black Muslim. Growing up as Malcolm Little, he was a streetwise criminal until he converted to the Nation of Islam in prison. After his release, Malcolm preached that black Americans should stop letting white Americans set the terms by which they judged their appearance, communities, and accomplishments. He emphasized the African cultural heritage and economic self-help and proclaimed himself an extremist for black rights. In the last year of his life, however, he returned from a pilgrimage to Mecca willing to consider limited acceptance of white people. Rivals within the movement assassinated him in February 1965, but his ideas lived on in *The Autobiography of Malcolm X*.

The **Black Panthers** pursued similar goals. Bobby Seale and Huey Newton grew up in the Oakland, California, area and met as college students. They saw African-American ghettos as internal colonies in need of self-determination. They created the Panthers in 1966, began to carry firearms, and recruited Eldridge Cleaver as the group's chief publicist.

The Panthers asserted their equality. They shadowed police patrols to prevent mistreatment of African Americans and carried weapons into the California State Legislature in May 1967 to protest gun control. As Seale recalled, the goal was "to read a message to the world" and use the press to "blast it across the country." The Panthers also promoted community-based self-help efforts, such as a free breakfast program for school children and medical clinics, and ran political candidates. In contrast to the rioters in Watts, the Panthers had a political program, if not the ability to carry it through. The movement was shaken when Newton was convicted of manslaughter for killing a police officer, Cleaver fled to Algeria, and an unjustified police raid killed Chicago Panther leader Fred Hampton. Panther chapters imploded when they attracted thugs and shakedown artists as well as visionaries. Nevertheless, the Panthers survived as a political party into the 1970s. Former Panther Bobby Rush entered Congress in 1992.

Hispanic Activism in the Southwest Latinos in the Southwest developed their own "Brown Power" movement in the late 1960s. Led by Reies López Tijerina, Hispanics in rural New Mexico demanded the return of lands that had been lost to Anglo-Americans despite the guarantees of the Treaty of Guadalupe Hidalgo in 1848. Tijerina's "Letter from the Santa Fe Jail" denounced the "rich people from outside the state with their summer homes and ranches" and "all those who have robbed the people of their land and culture for 120 years." Mexican Americans in the 1970s organized for political power in southern Texas communities where they were a majority. In Denver, Rodolfo Gonzales established the Crusade for Justice. His "Plan for the Barrio" emphasized Hispanic cultural traditions, community control of schools, and economic development.

The best-known Hispanic activism combined social protest with the crusading spirit of earlier labor union organizing campaigns. César Chávez organized the multiracial United Farm Workers (UFW) among Mexican-American agricultural workers in California in 1965. Chávez was committed to both nonviolent action for social justice and the labor movement. UFW demands included better wages and safer working conditions, such as less exposure to pesticides. UFW Vice President Dolores Huerta spoke for the special needs of women who labored in the fields. Because farm workers were not covered by the National Labor Relations Act of 1935, the issue was whether farm owners would recognize the union as a bargaining agent and sign a contract. Chávez supplemented work stoppages with national boycotts against table grapes, lettuce, and certain brands of wine, making *la huelga* (the strike) into *la causa* for urban liberals. Rival organizing by the Teamsters Union and the short attention span of the national public gradually undermined the UFW's initial success. Nevertheless, Chávez's dogged toughness and self-sacrifice gave both Chicanos and the country a new hero.

Dolores Huerta and César Chávez confer at the 1973 convention of the United Farm Workers. Chávez and Huerta tried to build a union that welcomed workers of all ethnic backgrounds, but the UFW leaders were largely Hispanic, and the union took much of its symbolism from the Mexican heritage shared by most of its members.

Latino political activism had strong appeal for young people. Ten thousand young Chicanos stormed out of Los Angeles high schools in March 1968 to protest poor education and racist teachers. Some students organized as

Brown Berets to demand more relevant education and fairer police treatment. Many rejected assimilation in favor of community self-determination and began to talk about *la raza* (the people), whose language and heritage descended from centuries of Mexican history. "Chicano" itself was a slang term with insulting overtones that was now adopted as a badge of pride and cultural identity.

Native Americans Assert Their Identity Native Americans also fought both for equal access to American society and to preserve cultural traditions through tribal institutions. Congress in 1968 restored the authority of tribal laws on reservations. A few years later, it granted native Alaskans 40 million acres to settle claims for their ancestral lands. Legally sophisticated tribes sued for compensation and enforcement of treaty provisions, such as fishing rights in the Pacific Northwest. Larger tribes established their own colleges, such as Navajo Community College (1969) and Oglala Lakota College (1971). Navajo Community College, said its catalog, "exists to fulfill many needs of the Navajo people. . . . It provides a place where Navajo history and culture can be studied and learned; it provides training in the skills necessary for many jobs on the reservation which today are held by non-Navajos."

Native peoples analyzed their problems with their own writers and intellectuals. Vine Deloria Jr., in *Custer Died for Your Sins* (1969), spoke for a generation of Indians who wanted to control their own lives and ways of life. He argued against well-meaning efforts to apply standard antipoverty solutions to Indian communities because such programs undermined distinctive tribal cultures. He hoped that a united political front could help the tribes gain basic economic stability without bureaucratic intrusions. Meanwhile, novelist M. Scott Momaday's *House Made of Dawn* (1968) signaled a new generation of writers who would explore the challenges of finding self-respect and claiming the Indian heritage; among the new authors were James Welch in *Winter in the Blood* (1974) and Leslie Marmon Silko in *Ceremony* (1977).

Another development was a new media-oriented protest that asserted "Red Power." Native American students gained national attention by seizing the abandoned Alcatraz Island for a cultural and educational center (1969–1971). Indians in Minneapolis created the **American Indian Movement (AIM)** in 1968 to increase economic opportunity and stop police mistreatment. AIM participated in the cross-country Broken Treaties Caravan, which climaxed by its occupation of the Bureau of Indian Affairs in Washington in 1972. AIM also allied with Sioux traditionalists on the Pine Ridge Reservation in South Dakota against the tribe's elected government. In 1973, they took over the village of Wounded Knee, where the U.S. Army in 1890 had massacred three hundred Indians. They held out for seventy days before leaving peacefully. Since these events of the early 1970s, Indians have continued to assert their distinctiveness within American society.

The slogans of Black Power, Brown Power, and Red Power spanned goals that ran from civil rights to cultural pride to revolutionary separatism. They were all efforts by minorities to define themselves through their own heritage and backgrounds, not simply by looking in the mirror of white society. They thus questioned the American assumption that everyone wanted to be part of the same homogeneous society.

Suburban Independence: The Outer City

In the mid-1960s, the United States became a suburban nation. The 1970 census found more people living in the suburban counties of metropolitan areas (37 percent) than in central cities (31 percent) or in small towns and rural areas (31 percent). Just after World War II, most new suburbs had been bedroom communities that depended on the jobs, services, and shopping of central cities. By the late 1960s, suburbs were evolving into "outer cities," whose inhabitants had little need for the old central city. The *New York Times* in 1978 found that 40 percent of the residents of New York's Long Island and New Jersey suburbs visited the city fewer than three times a year, and most denied that they were part of the New York area. New residents in a suburban community had typically moved from other suburbs and felt no personal connection to or responsibility for old city neighborhoods. For them, suburban malls and shopping strips were the new American Main Street and suburban communities the new Middle America.

Suburban Economic Growth and Political Influence Suburbs captured most new jobs, leaving the urban poor with few opportunities for employment. In the fifteen largest metropolitan areas, the number of central city jobs fell by 800,000 in the 1960s, while the number of suburban jobs rose by 3.2 million. The shift from rail to air for business travel accentuated suburban job growth. Sales representatives and executives could arrive at airports on the edge of town rather than at railroad stations at the center and transact business without ever going downtown. The trend was first obvious at Chicago's O'Hare Airport in the 1960s; by the 1970s, every major airport had a fringe of hotels, office parks, and corporate offices. Around many cities, suburban retailing, employment, and services fused into so-called "edge cities." Examples are the Galleria Post Oak district in Houston and the Tysons Corner area in northern Virginia. Huge complexes of shopping malls, high-rise hotels, and glass-sided office buildings have far more space than old business districts in such cities as Fort Wayne and Wichita.

Suburban rings gained a growing share of public facilities intended to serve the entire metropolitan area. As pioneered in California, community colleges served the suburban children of the baby boom. Many of the new four-year schools that state university systems added in the 1960s and early 1970s were also built for suburbanites, from George Mason University and the University of Maryland Baltimore County in the Washington-Baltimore area to California State University campuses at Northridge and Fullerton. The California Angels in baseball and New York Islanders in hockey gave suburban regions exclusive claims to their own major league sports franchises.

Suburban political power grew along with economic clout. In 1962, the Supreme Court handed down a landmark decision in the case of **Baker v. Carr**. Overturning laws that treated counties or other political subdivisions as the units to be represented in state legislatures, *Baker* required that legislative seats be apportioned on the basis of population. This principle of "one person, one vote" broke the stranglehold of rural counties on state governments, but the big beneficiaries were not older cities, but fast-growing suburbs. By 1975, suburbanites held the largest block of seats in the House of Representatives—131 suburban districts, 130 rural, 102 central city, and 72 mixed. Reapportionment in 1982, based on the 1980 census, produced a House that was even more heavily suburban.

School Busing Controversies School integration controversies in the 1970s reinforced a tendency for suburbanites to separate themselves from city problems. In **Swann v. Charlotte-Mecklenburg Board of Education** (1971), the U.S. Supreme Court held that cross-town busing was an acceptable solution to the de facto segregation that resulted from residential patterns within a single school district. When school officials around the country failed to achieve racial balance, federal judges ordered their own busing plans. Although integration through busing occurred peacefully in dozens of cities, many white people resented the practice. Working-class students who depended on public schools found themselves on the front lines of integration, while many middle-class families switched to private education. For many Americans, the image of busing for racial integration was fixed in 1975, when white citizens in Boston reacted with violence against black students who were bused to largely white high schools in the South Boston and Charlestown neighborhoods. The goal of equal opportunity clashed with equally strong values of neighborhood, community, and ethnic solidarity.

Because the Supreme Court also ruled that busing programs normally stopped at school-district boundaries, suburbs with independent districts escaped school integration. One result was to make busing self-defeating, for it caused white families to move out of the integrating school district. Others placed their children in private schools, as happened frequently in the South. Busing also caused suburbanites to defend their political independence fiercely. In Denver, for example, a bitter debate lasted from 1969 until court-ordered busing in 1974. Byproducts included incorporation or expansion of several large suburbs and a state constitutional amendment that blocked further expansion of the city boundaries (and thus of the Denver school district).

THE YEAR OF THE GUN, 1968

Some years are turning points that force society to reconsider its basic assumptions. In 1914, the violence of World War I undermined Europe's belief in progress. In 1933, Americans had to rethink the role of government. In 1968, mainstream Americans turned against the war in Vietnam, student protest and youth counterculture turned ugly, and political consensus shattered.

The Tet Offensive

The longer the Vietnam War continued and the less interest that China or the Soviet Union showed in it, the less valid the conflict seemed to the American people. It looked more and more like a war for pride, not national security.

The Viet Cong's Tet Offensive on January 30, 1968, undermined that pride. At the end of 1967, U.S. officials were overconfidently predicting victory. They also fell for a North Vietnamese feint by committing U.S. forces to the defense of Khe Sanh, a strongpoint near the North–South border. The defense was a tactical success for the United States but thinned its forces elsewhere in South Vietnam. Then, at the beginning of Tet, the Vietnamese New Year, the Viet Cong attacked thirty-six of forty-four provincial capitals and the national capital, Saigon. They hit the U.S. embassy and reached the runways of Tan Son Nhut air base. If the United States was winning, the Tet offensive should not have been possible.

As a military effort, the attacks failed. U.S. and South Vietnamese troops repulsed the attacks and cleared the cities, but the offensive was a psychological blow that convinced the American public that the war was quicksand.

Television coverage of the Tet battles made the bad publicity worse. During World War II, officials had censored pictures from the front. Images from Vietnam went directly to the evening news; it was a "living room war." At least until Tet, the commentary from network news anchors had supported the American effort, but the pictures undermined civilian morale. Viewers could hear cigarette lighters clicking open to set villages in flames. A handful of images stayed in people's memories—a Buddhist monk burning himself to death in protest; a child with flesh peeled off by napalm; a South Vietnamese official executing a captive on the streets of Saigon.

In the wake of the Tet crisis, General Westmoreland's request for 200,000 more troops forced a political and military reevaluation. Clark Clifford, a dedicated Cold Warrior, was the new secretary of defense. Now he had second thoughts. Twenty "wise men"—the big names

GIs evacuate a wounded comrade from fighting near the border between Vietnam and Cambodia.

of the Cold War—told the president that the war was unwinnable on terms acceptable to America's allies and to many Americans. By devouring resources and souring relations with other nations, it endangered rather than enhanced American security. Most scholars have agreed with this assessment. The best option, the wise men told LBJ, was disengagement. "He could hardly believe his ears," Clifford remembered.

LBJ's Exit

The president was already in political trouble. After other prominent Democrats held back, Minnesota's liberal Senator Eugene McCarthy had decided to challenge Johnson in the presidential primaries. Because he controlled the party organizations in two-thirds of the states, Johnson did not need the primary states for renomination and ignored the first primary in New Hampshire. Enthusiastic college students staffed McCarthy's campaign. McCarthy won a startling 42 percent of the popular vote and twenty of twenty-four delegates in the New Hampshire primary. The vote was a protest against Johnson's Vietnam policy rather than a clear mandate for peace. As an unknown, McCarthy attracted voters who wanted the United States out of Vietnam and those who wanted all-out victory. Nevertheless, the vote proved that the political middle ground would no longer hold.

By showing Johnson's vulnerability, New Hampshire also drew Robert Kennedy into the race. The younger brother of the former president, Kennedy inspired both fervent loyalty and strong distaste. In the 1950s, he had worked for Senator Joe McCarthy and had been initially a reluctant supporter of civil rights during his brother's administration. He was arrogant and abrasive, but also bright and flexible. More than other mainstream politicians of the 1960s, he touched the hearts of Hispanic and African-American voters as well as the white working class. He had left his position as attorney general to win election to the Senate from New York in 1964. Now he put the Kennedy mystique on the line against a man whom he despised.

Facing political challenges and an unraveling war, on March 31, 1968, Johnson announced a halt to most bombing of North Vietnam, opening the door for peace negotiations that formally began in May 1969. He then astounded the country by withdrawing from the presidential race. It was a statesmanlike act by a man who had been consumed by a war he did not want, had never understood, and could not end. As he told an aide, the war made him feel like a hitchhiker in a hailstorm: "I can't run, I can't hide, and I can't make it stop." Hoping to save his domestic program, he served out his term with few friends and little credit for his accomplishments.

Red Spring

In the months that followed the Tet crisis, much of the industrial world was in ferment. Grass-roots rebellion shook the Soviet grip on eastern Europe. University students in Poland protested the stifling of political discussion. Alexander Dubček, the new leader of the Czech Communist party, brought together students and the middle class around reforms that caused people to talk about "Prague Spring"—a blossoming of democracy inside the Iron Curtain. In August, the Soviets sent in their tanks to crush the reforms and bring Czechoslovakia back into line.

Western Europe was also in turmoil. Students rioted in Italy and Berlin. Workers and students protested against the Franco regime in Spain. In Paris, student demonstrations against the Vietnam War turned into attacks on the university system and the French government. Students fought police in the Paris streets in the first days of May. Radical industrial workers called a general strike. The government nearly toppled.

Students at Columbia University in New York echoed Europe with their own rebellion. Columbia's African-American students and its SDS chapter had several grievances. One was the university's cooperation with the Pentagon-funded Institute for Defense Analysis. Another was its plan to build a gymnasium on park land that might better serve the residents of Harlem. Some students wanted changes in university policy, others a confrontation that would recruit new radicals. They occupied five university buildings, including the library and the president's office, for a week in April until police evicted them. A student strike and additional violence lasted until June. The "battle of Morningside Heights" (the location of Columbia) was tame when compared to the events in Warsaw or Paris, but it gave Americans a glimpse of the gap that divided radicalized students from national institutions.

Violence and Politics: King, Kennedy, and Chicago

Red Spring in France, Prague Spring in Czechoslovakia, and turmoil in New York were the background for the violent disruption of American politics through assassination and riot. On April 4, 1968, an ex-convict, James Earl Ray, shot and killed Martin Luther King Jr. as he stood on the balcony of a Memphis motel. King's death was the product of pure racial hatred, and it triggered a climactic round of violence in black ghettos. Fires devastated the West Side of Chicago and downtown Washington, D.C. The army guarded the steps of the Capitol, ready to protect Congress from its fellow citizens.

The shock of King's death was still fresh when another political assassination stunned the nation. On June 5, Robert Kennedy won California's primary election. He was still behind Vice President Hubert Humphrey in the delegate count but coming on strong. As Kennedy walked out of the ballroom at his headquarters in the Ambassador Hotel in Los Angeles, a Jordanian immigrant named Sirhan Sirhan put a bullet in his brain. Sirhan may have wanted revenge for America's tilt toward Israel in that country's victorious Six-Day War with Egypt and Jordan in 1967.

Kennedy's death ensured the Democratic nomination for Humphrey, a liberal who had loyally supported Johnson's war policy. After his nomination, Humphrey faced the Republican Richard Nixon and the Independent George Wallace. Nixon positioned himself as the candidate of the political middle. Wallace appealed to Southern whites and working-class Northerners who feared black militancy and hated "the ivory-tower folks with pointy heads."

Both got great help from the Democratic Convention, held in Chicago on August 26–29. While Democrats feuded among themselves, Chicago Mayor Richard Daley and his police department monitored antiwar protesters. The National Mobilization Committee to End the War in Vietnam drew from the New Left and from older peace activists—sober and committed people who had fought against nuclear weapons in the 1950s and the Vietnam War throughout the 1960s. They wanted to embarrass the Johnson-Humphrey administration by marching to the convention hall on nomination night. Mixed in were the Yippies. (The term supposedly stood for Youth International Party, but the idea of hippies making yippie! came first and the word later.) The Yippies planned to attract young people to Chicago with a promise of street theater, media events, and confrontation that would puncture the pretensions of the power structure. The first Yippie manifesto called for "rebels, youth spirits, rock minstrels, truth seekers, peacock freaks, poets, barricade jumpers, dancers, lovers, and artists" to turn Chicago into "Free America." To the extent they had a program, it was to use youth culture to attract converts to radical politics.

The volatile mix was ready for a spark. On August 28, the same night that Democratic delegates were nominating Humphrey, tensions exploded in a police riot. Protesters and Yippies had congregated in Grant Park, across Michigan Avenue from downtown hotels. Undisciplined police waded into the crowds with clubs and tear gas. Young people fought back with rocks and bottles. Television caught the hours of violence that ended when the National Guard separated police from demonstrators. On the convention floor, Senator Abraham Ribicoff of Connecticut decried "Gestapo tactics" on the streets of Chicago. Mayor Daley shouted back obscenities. For Humphrey, the convention was a catastrophe, alienating liberal Democrats and associating Democrats with disorder in the public mind.

The election was closer than Humphrey had any right to hope. Many Americans who liked Wallace's message were unwilling to vote for a radical third party. Nixon appealed to the white middle class and claimed that he had a secret plan to end the war. Humphrey picked up strength in October after he separated himself from Johnson's war policy. Election day gave Wallace 13.5 percent of the popular vote, Humphrey 42.7 percent of the popular vote and 191 electoral votes, and Nixon 43.4 percent of the popular vote and 301 electoral votes.

The Wallace candidacy was a glimpse of the future. The national media, getting only part of the story, saw Wallace in terms of bigotry and a backlash against civil rights. Many of Wallace's northern backers were unhappy with both parties. Liberal on economic issues but conservative on family and social issues, many of these working-class voters evolved into "Reagan Democrats" by the 1980s. In the South, Wallace was a transitional choice for conservative voters who would eventually transfer their allegiance from the Democratic to the Republican party.

NIXON AND WATERGATE

The new president was an unlikely politician, ill-at-ease in public and consumed by a sense of inferiority. A product of small-town California, he felt rejected by the eastern elite. After losing a 1962 race for governor of California, he announced that he was quitting politics and that the press would no longer have Dick Nixon "to kick around." In 1968, he skillfully sold a "new Nixon" to the media. Seven years later, the press was his undoing as it uncovered the Watergate scandal.

Nixon's painful public presence and dishonesty have tended to obscure his administration's accomplishments. He reduced tensions in the Cold War. He reluctantly upgraded civil rights enforcement, set goals for minority hiring by federal contractors, and presided over impressive environmental legislation.

Getting Out of Vietnam, 1969–1975

After 1968, things got worse in Southeast Asia before they got better. Nixon had no secret plan to end the war. Protests culminated in 1969 with the Vietnam Moratorium on October 15, when 2 million protesters joined rallies across the country. A month later, 500,000 demonstrators converged in Washington. Their presence made a deep impression on Nixon. Troops and barricades guarded the White House as the president and his staff spent days trying to counter the demonstrations.

Disaffection also mounted in Vietnam. Racial tensions sapped morale on the front lines. Nurses found their idealism strained as they treated young men maimed in thousands of nasty skirmishes in the jungles and mountains. Troops lost discipline, took drugs, and hunkered down waiting for their tours of duty to end. Soldiers "fragged" (killed) their own gung-ho or racist officers, and the high command had to adapt its code of justice to keep an army on the job.

Nixon and Vice President Spiro Agnew responded by trying to isolate the antiwar opposition, but Nixon also reduced the role of U.S. ground forces. He claimed that his policies represented "the great silent majority of my fellow Americans." Agnew blamed bad morale on journalists and intellectuals—on "nattering nabobs of negativism" and "an effete corps of impudent snobs." The administration arranged for a "spontaneous" attack by construction workers on antiwar protesters in New York. The hard-hat counterattack was a cynically manipulated symbol, but Nixon and Agnew tapped genuine anger about failure in Asia and rapid change in American society.

The New Left had already split into factions. Many activists continued to focus on peace work, draft resistance, and other efforts to link radical and liberal agendas. About a hundred angry SDS members, however, declared themselves the Weather Underground in 1969, taking their name from a Bob Dylan lyric ("You don't need a weatherman to know which way the wind blows"). They tried to disrupt Chicago and Washington with window-smashing "days of rage." Three Weatherpeople accidentally blew themselves up with a homemade bomb in New York in 1970. Others robbed a Boston bank to get money for the revolution. Still others bombed a University of Wisconsin building and killed a student.

"Vietnamization" and the Secret War Against Cambodia Nixon's secretary of defense, Melvin Laird, responded to the antiwar sentiment with "Vietnamization," withdrawing U.S. troops as fast as possible without undermining the South Vietnamese government. In July 1969, the president announced the **Nixon Doctrine**. The United States would help other countries fight their wars with weapons and money but not with soldiers. The policy substituted machines for men. Americans rearmed and expanded the South Vietnamese army and surreptiously bombed Communist bases in neutral Cambodia.

The secret war against Cambodia culminated with an invasion on April 30, 1970. Americans who had hoped that the war was fading away were outraged. Students shut down hundreds of colleges. At Kent State University in Ohio, the National Guard was called in to maintain order. Taunts, tossed bottles, and the recent record of violence put them on edge. On May 4, one unit unexpectedly fired on a group of nonthreatening students and killed four of them. At Jackson State University in Mississippi, two unsuspecting students were killed when troops fired on their dormitory.

Stalemate and Cease-fire   The Cambodian "incursion" extended the military stalemate in Vietnam to U.S. policy. Beginning in December 1969, a new lottery system for determining the order of draft calls by birthdate let two-thirds of young men know they would not be drafted. In December 1970, Congress repealed the Gulf of Tonkin Resolution and prohibited the use of U.S. ground troops outside South Vietnam. Cambodia, however, was already devastated. The U.S. invasion had destabilized its government and opened the way for the bloodthirsty Khmer Rouge, who killed millions of Cambodians in the name of a working-class revolution. Vietnamization continued; only ninety thousand U.S. ground troops were still in Vietnam by early 1972. A final air offensive in December smashed Hanoi into rubble and helped force four and a half years of peace talks to a conclusion.

The cease-fire began on January 27, 1973. It confirmed American withdrawal from Vietnam. North Vietnamese and Viet Cong forces would remain in control of the territory they occupied in South Vietnam, but they were not to be reinforced or substantially reequipped. The United States promised not to increase its military aid to South Vietnam. There were no solid guarantees for the South Vietnamese government. Immediately after coming to terms with North Vietnam, Nixon suspended the draft in favor of an all-volunteer military.

In 1975, South Vietnam collapsed. Only the American presence had kept its political, ethnic, and religious factions together. For the first two years after the Paris agreement, North Vietnam quietly rebuilt its military capacity. In the spring of 1975, it opened an offensive, and South Vietnamese morale evaporated. Resistance crumbled so rapidly that the United States had to evacuate its embassy in Saigon by helicopter while frantic Vietnamese tried to join the flight.

Coming to Terms with the Vietnam War

The United States withdrawal carried lingering moral responsibilities to both Vietnamese and Americans. Airlifts that accompanied U.S. evacuation brought out 100,000 Vietnamese most closely identified with the United States. They were followed by others who made their way to refugee camps in Thailand and by "boat people" who set out from Vietnam in small boats in hope of rescue. American veterans found a cool welcome; unlike the situation in 1945, few people at home wanted to remember the war. Veterans had to fight a long battle to get the government to admit that Agent Orange, a defoliant used to clear Vietnamese jungles, had serious effects on the health of those exposed. Meanwhile, members of the far right who had never accepted the failure of American aims in Vietnam played up frustration over the issue of MIAs (soldiers missing in action and unaccounted for who might still be prisoners of war).

It took time for artists and writers to come to terms with the experience of Vietnam. While the war was in progress, some of the most insightful analysis came from journalists such as Michael Herr in *Dispatches* (1968), Frances Fitzgerald in *Fire on the Lake* (1972), and Gloria Emerson in *Winners and Losers* (1976). Novelist Tom O'Brien depicted the senselessness of the war in *Going After Cacciato* (1978). Robert Stone drew the connection between the moral ambiguity of the war and the corruption of society at home through drugs and violence in *Dog Soldiers* (1974). The first serious movie about Vietnam was Robert Altman's *M.A.S.H.* in 1970. Supposedly set in a mobile army hospital during the Korean war, the film was a clearly pointed comment that highlighted the contradictions of the U.S. effort in Vietnam. When the television version of *M.A.S.H.* debuted in 1972, it strongly attacked military bureaucracy and incompetence. As the show continued into the 1980s, however, and the United States tried to leave Vietnam behind, the episodes lost much of their antimilitary edge and shifted to personal issues among characters. The visually stunning film *Apocalypse Now* (1979) tried to transform the war into an epic spectacle; it was full of vivid scenes but no compelling interpretation beyond the capacity of power to debase those who wield it. *Platoon* (1985) dealt on smaller scale with day-to-day terrors of countering guerilla warfare, but it was countered by Sylvester Stallone's cartoonish anti-Vietnamese heroics in *Rambo: Final Blood II* (1985).

Nixon and the Wider World

To his credit, Richard Nixon took American foreign policy in new directions even while he was struggling to escape from Vietnam and Cambodia. Like Dwight Eisenhower before him, Nixon's reputation as an anti-Communist allowed him to improve relations with China and the Soviet Union. Indeed, he hoped to distract the American people from frustration in Southeast Asia with accomplishments elsewhere.

Nixon and Henry Kissinger, his national security adviser (and, later, secretary of state), shared what they considered a realistic view of foreign affairs. For both men, foreign policy was not about crusades or moral stands. It was about the balance of world economic and military power and securing the most advantageous agreements, alliances, and military positions. In particular, they hoped to trade improved relations with China and the Soviet Union for help in settling the Vietnam War.

Since 1950, the United States had acted as if China did not exist, refusing economic relations and insisting that the Nationalist regime on Taiwan was the legitimate Chinese government. But the Republic of China was increasingly isolated within the Communist world. In 1969, it almost went to war with the Soviet Union. Nixon was eager to take advantage of Chinese-Soviet tension. Secret talks led to an easing of the American trade embargo in April 1971 and a tour of China by a U.S. table-tennis team. Kissinger then arranged for Nixon's startling visit to Mao Zedong in Beijing in February 1972.

Playing the "China card" helped to improve relations with the Soviet Union. The Soviets needed increased trade with the United States and a counterweight to China, the United States was looking for help in getting out of Vietnam, and both countries wanted to limit nuclear armaments. In 1969, the Senate came within one vote of stopping the development of defensive antiballistic missiles (ABMs). Opponents feared that strong antimissile defenses would encourage the idea that a nation could launch a first strike and survive the retaliation. Nixon treated the ABM program as a bargaining chip. Protracted negotiations led to arms agreements known as **SALT (Strategic Arms Limitation Treaty)** that Nixon signed in Moscow in May 1972. The agreements blocked creation of extensive ABM systems but failed to limit bombers, cruise missiles, or multiple independently targeted warheads on single missiles.

Diplomats used the French word **détente** to describe the new U.S. relations with China and the Soviet Union. Détente means an easing of tensions, not friendship or alliance. It facilitated travel between the United States and China. It allowed U.S. farmers to sell wheat to the Soviets. More broadly, détente implied that the United States and China recognized mutual interests in Asia and that the United States acknowledged the Soviet Union as an equal in world affairs. Détente made the world safer.

Courting Middle America

Nixon designed domestic policy to help him win reelection. His goal was to solidify his "Middle American" support. The strategy targeted the growing populations of the South and the suburbs, as well as blue-collar voters who were ready to abandon the Democrats for law-and-order Republicans.

The Nixon White House preferred to ignore troubled big cities. Spokesmen announced that the "urban crisis" was over and dismantled the urban initiatives of Johnson's Great Society, even though such programs as Model Cities had never been given enough money to work. Instead, Nixon tilted federal assistance to the suburbs. The centerpiece of his **New Federalism** was General Revenue Sharing (1972) which passed federal funds directly to local governments with no limits on use. By 1980, it had transferred more than $18 billion from the federal treasury to the states and more than $36 billion to local governments. Revenue sharing was a suburban-aid program. Its "no-strings" grants supplemented the general funds of every full-service government, whether a city of 2 million or a suburban town of 500.

Nixon pursued the southern strategy through the symbolism of Supreme Court nominations. His first nominees were Clement Haynsworth of Florida and G. Harrold Carswell of Alabama. Although the Senate rejected both as unqualified, the nominations nonetheless gave Nixon a reputation as a champion of the white South. He hoped to move cautiously in enforcing school desegregation, but a task force led by Secretary of Labor George Shultz crafted an approach that allowed substantial desegregation. In this instance, as elsewhere with his domestic policies, Nixon was inflammatory in speeches but moderate in action, increasing the funding of federal civil rights agencies.

Oil, OPEC, and Stagflation

One of the most troublesome domestic issues was inflation. The cost of living began to outpace wages in the late 1960s. Economists saw the situation as a classic example of "demand-pull" inflation, in which too many dollars from government and consumer spending were chasing too few goods and services. One of the causes was LBJ's decision to fight in Vietnam without tax increases until 1968. An income tax cut in 1969, supported by both parties, made the situation worse. Inflation eroded the value of savings and pensions. It also made U.S. goods too expensive for foreign buyers and generated a trade deficit that placed pressures on the international value of the dollar.

In August 1971, Nixon detached the dollar from the gold standard. The Treasury would no longer sell gold at $35 an ounce, a practice that had made the dollar the anchor around which other currencies fluctuated. The dollar could now float in value relative to other currencies, making U.S. exports more competitive but undercutting the nation's ability to lead global economic policy. Nixon took the action without consulting America's allies, even though it triggered drastic readjustments of international markets. It was an example of the political expediency with which he sometimes operated.

The U.S. economy took another hit from inflation in 1973–74. This time it was "cost-push" inflation, in which a price increase for one key product raises the cost of producing other items. The main cause was sharp increases in the price of energy, an input to every product and service. Angry at American support for Israel in the Arab-Israeli War of October 1973, Arab nations imposed an embargo on oil exports that lasted from October 1973 to March 1974. Gasoline and heating oil became scarce and expensive. Long lines at gas pumps and hurried rationing systems (such as allowing half the nation to buy gas on odd-numbered days and the other half on even-numbered days) panicked auto-dependent Americans. The shortages eased when the embargo ended, but the **Organization of Petroleum Exporting Countries (OPEC)** had challenged the ability of the industrial nations to dictate world economic policy.

Rising energy prices forced Americans to switch off unused lights, turn down thermostats, and put on sweaters. Consumers compared the efficiency ratings of appliances and the gas mileage of cars. Congress required states to enforce a fuel-saving highway speed limit of 55 miles per hour to get federal highway funds. Congress also enacted the first fuel economy standards for automobiles. The fuel efficiency of the average new car doubled from 14 miles per gallon in 1973 to 28 miles per gallon by the late 1980s, and more efficient imports captured a third of the U.S. car market by 1980.

While Nixon searched for short-term political advantage, underlying problems of the American economy went untreated. After thirty years at the top, the United States could no longer dominate the world economy by itself. The newly found power of OPEC was obvious. Just as important was the surging industrial capacity of Germany and Japan, which now had economies as modern as that of the United States. Declining rates of saving and investment in industrial capacity seemed to put the United States in danger of following the British road to economic obsolescence and second-level status. Indeed, a new term entered the popular vocabulary in 1971: *Stagflation* was the painful combination of stagnant economic growth, high unemployment, and inflation that matched no one's economic theory but everyone's daily experience.

Americans as Environmentalists

In the turbulent 1970s, Americans found one issue they could agree on, and resource conservation grew into a multifaceted environmental movement. Environmentalism dealt with serious problems. It was broad enough for both scientific experts and activists, for both Republican Richard Nixon and Democrat Jimmy Carter.

After the booming 1950s, Americans had started to pay attention to "pollution," a catchall for the damage that advanced technologies and industrial production did to natural systems. Rachel Carson's *Silent Spring* in 1962 pushed pollution onto the national agenda. Carson, a well-regarded science writer, described the side effects of DDT and other pesticides on animal life. In her imagined future, spring was silent because all the birds had died of pesticide poisoning. Other side effects of the industrial economy made headlines. An offshore oil well polluted the beaches of Santa Barbara, California, in 1969. Fire danced across the Cuyahoga River in Cleveland when industrial discharges ignited.

Environmentalism gained strength among Americans in 1970. On April 22, ten thousand schools and 20 million other people took part in Earth Day, an occasion first conceived by Wisconsin Senator Gaylord Nelson. Earth Day gained a grass-roots following in towns and cities across the country. New York closed Fifth Avenue to automobiles for the day. Companies touted their environmental credentials.

The American establishment had been looking for a safe and respectable crusade to divert the idealism and discontent of the 1960s. Now the mainstream media discovered the ravaged planet. So did a politically savvy president. An expedient pro-environmental stance might attract some of the antiwar constituency. Nixon had already signed the National Environmental Policy Act on January 1, 1970, and later in the year created the **Environmental Protection Agency (EPA)** to enforce environmental laws. The rest of the Nixon years brought legislation on clean air, clear water, pesticides, hazardous chemicals, and endangered species (see the Overview table, "The Environmental Decades") that made environmental management and protection part of governmental routine.

As Americans became more aware of human-caused environmental hazards, they realized that minority and low-income communities had more than their share of problems. In the Louisiana petrochemical belt along the Mississippi River, African Americans often lived downstream and downwind. Landfills and waste disposal sites were frequently located near minority neighborhoods. In Buffalo, white working-class residents near the Love Canal industrial site discovered in 1978 that an entire neighborhood was built on land contaminated by decades of chemical dumping. Activists sought to understand the health effects and

```
• • • O V E R V I E W • • •
```

THE ENVIRONMENTAL DECADES

ADMINISTRATION	FOCUS OF CONCERN	LEGISLATION
Johnson	Wilderness and wildlife	Wilderness Act (1964) National Wildlife Refuge System (1966) Wild and Scenic Rivers Act (1968)
Nixon	Pollution control and endangered environments	National Environmental Policy Act (1969) Environmental Protection Agency (1970) Clean Air Act (1970) Occupational Safety and Health Act (1970) Water Pollution Control Act (1972) Pesticide Control Act (1972) Coastal Zone Management Act (1972) Endangered Species Act (1973)
Ford	Energy and hazardous materials	Toxic Substances Control Act (1976) Resource Conservation and Recovery Act (1976)
Carter	Energy and hazardous materials	Energy Policy and Conservation Act (1978) Comprehensive Emergency Response, Compensation, and Liability Act (Superfund) (1980)

force compensation, paving the way for the Superfund cleanup legislation (see American Views, "Grass-roots Community Action").

From Dirty Tricks to Watergate

The **Watergate** crisis pivoted on Richard Nixon's character. Despite his solid political standing, Nixon saw enemies everywhere and overestimated their strength. Subordinates learned during his first administration that the president would condone dishonest actions— "dirty tricks"—if they stood to improve his political position. In 1972 and 1973, dirty tricks grew from a scandal into a constitutional crisis when Nixon abused the power of his office to cover up wrongdoing and hinder criminal investigations.

The chain of events that undermined Nixon's presidency started with the **Pentagon Papers**. In his last year as secretary of defense, Robert McNamara had commissioned a report on America's road to Vietnam. The documents showed that the country's leaders had planned to expand the war even while they claimed to be looking for a way out. In June 1971, one of the contributors to the report, Daniel Ellsberg, leaked it to the *New York Times*. Its publication infuriated Nixon.

In response, the White House compiled a list of journalists and politicians who opposed Nixon. As one White House staffer, John Dean, put it, the president's men could then "use the available federal machinery [Internal Revenue Service, FBI] to screw our political enemies." Nixon set up a special investigations unit in the White House. Two former CIA employees, E. Howard Hunt and G. Gordon Liddy, became the chief "plumbers," as the group was known because its job was to prevent leaks of information. The plumbers contributed to an atmosphere of lawlessness in the White House. They cooked up schemes to embarrass political opponents and ransacked the office of Ellsberg's psychiatrist.

AMERICAN VIEWS

Grass-roots Community Action

In the 1950s, a major chemical company closed a waste dump in Niagara Falls, New York. The site, known as Love Canal, was soon surrounded by a park, school, and hundreds of modest homes. Residents put up with noxious odors and seepage of chemical wastes until 1978, when they learned that the State Health Department was concerned about the health effects on small children and pregnant women. Over the next two years, residents battled state and federal bureaucracies and reluctant politicians for accurate information about the risks they faced and then for financial assistance to move from the area (often their homes represented their only savings). In October 1980, President Carter signed a bill to move all families permanently from the Love Canal area.

One of the leaders of the grass-roots movement was housewife Lois Gibbs. The following excerpts from her story show her increasing sophistication as a community activist, starting by ringing doorbells in 1978 and ending with national television exposure in 1980. Although the Love Canal case itself was unusual, community-based organizations in all parts of the country learned the tactics of effective action in the 1960s and 1970s.

> What public programs in the 1960s and 1970s gave citizens experience in grass-roots action?
>
> How might the Internet change the tactics of community organizing?

Knocking on Doors

I decided to go door-to-door with a petition. It seemed like a good idea to start near the school, to talk to the mothers nearest it. I had already heard that a lot of the residents near the school had been upset about the chemicals for the past couple of years. I thought they might help me. I had never done anything like this. . . . I was afraid a lot of doors would be slammed in my face, that people would think I was some crazy fanatic. But I decided to do it anyway. . . . and knocked on my first door. There was no answer. I just stood there, not knowing what to do. It

was an usually warm June day and I was perspiring. I thought: What am I doing here? I must be crazy. People are going to think I am. Go home, you fool! And that's just what I did.

It was one of those times when I had to sit down and face myself. I was afraid of making a fool of myself, I had scared myself, and I had gone home. When I got there, I sat at the kitchen table with my petition in my hand, thinking. Wait. What if people do slam doors in your face? People may think you're crazy. But what's more important—what people think or your child's health? Either you're going to do something or you're going to have to admit you're a coward and not do it. . . .

The next day, I went out on my own street to talk to people, I knew. It was a little easier to be brave with them. If I could convince people I knew—friends—maybe it would be less difficult to convince others. . . . I went to the back door, as I always did when I visited a neighbor. Each house took about twenty or twenty-five minutes. . . .

Phil Donahue and Political Action

The *Phil Donahue Show* called. They wanted us to appear on their June 18 show. The reaction in the office was different this time, compared to the show in October 1978. In October, everyone was excited. "Phil Donahue—wow!" Now, residents reacted differently. "Donahue. That's great press. Now we'll get the politicians to move!" . . . Now our people looked at the show as a tool to use in pushing the government to relocate us permanently. By this time we understood how politicians react to public pressure, how to play the political game. We eagerly agreed to go, and found forty other residents to go with us. . . .

[After arriving in Chicago] We then planned how we would handle the *Phil Donahue Show*. . . . We had to get the real issues across. Each resident was assigned an issue. One told of the chromosome tests. Another was to concentrate on her multiple miscarriages. Another was to ask for telegrams from across

(continued)

the country to the White House in support of permanent relocation. I coached them to get their point in, no matter the question asked. For example, if Donahue asked what you thought of the mayor, and your assignment was to discuss miscarriages, you should answer: "I don't like the mayor because I have had three miscarriages and other health problems, and he won't help us." Or; "My family is sick, and the mayor won't help us. That's why we need people to send telegrams to the White House for permanent relocation." . . . The residents were great! Each and every one followed through with our plan.

In July, I went on a speaking tour of California arranged by Jane Fonda and Tom Hayden. I visited many sites with problems similar to ours. I was able to give advice, based on our experiences. I told the leaders of each community that it wasn't hopeless that they could win. "Stick with it. We are!"

Source. Lois Marie Gibbs, as told to Murray Levine, *Love Canal: My Story* (Albany: State University of New York Press, 1982), pp. 12–13, 161–64.

Early in 1972, Hunt went to work for CREEP—the Committee to Re-Elect the President—while Liddy took another position on the presidential staff. CREEP had already raised millions from corporations and was hatching plans to undermine Democrats with rumors and pranks. Then, on June 17, 1972, five inept burglars hired with CREEP funds were caught breaking into the Democratic National Committee office in Washington's Watergate apartment building. The people involved knew that an investigation would lead directly to CREEP and then to the White House. Nixon felt too insecure to ride out what would probably have been a small scandal. Instead, he initiated a coverup. On June 23, he ordered his assistant H. R. Haldeman to warn the FBI off the case with the excuse that national security was involved. Nixon compounded this obstruction of justice by arranging a $400,000 bribe to keep the burglars quiet.

The coverup worked in the short run. As midlevel officials from the Justice Department pursued their investigation, the public lost interest in what looked more like slapstick than a serious crime. Nixon's opponent in the 1972 election was South Dakota Senator George McGovern, an impassioned opponent of the Vietnam War. McGovern was honest, intelligent, and well to the left on such issues as the defense budget and legalization of marijuana. He did not appeal to the white Southerners and blue-collar Northerners whom Nixon and Agnew were luring from the Democrats. An assassination attempt that took George Wallace out of national politics also helped Nixon win in a landslide.

The coverup began to come apart with the trial of the Watergate burglars in January 1973. Federal Judge John Sirica used the threat of heavy sentences to pressure one burglar into a statement that implied that higher-ups had been involved. Meanwhile, the *Washington Post* was linking Nixon's people to dirty tricks and illegal campaign contributions. The White House scrambled to find a defensible story. White House Counsel John Dean, who coordinated much of the effort, reported to Nixon in March that the scandal and coverup had become a "cancer on the presidency." Nixon was aware of many of the actions that his subordinates had undertaken. He now began to coach people on what they should tell investigators, claimed his staff had lied to him, and tried to set up Dean to take the fall.

In the late spring and early summer, attention shifted to the televised hearings of the Senate's Select Committee on Presidential Campaign Activities. Its chair was Sam Ervin of North Carolina, whose down-home style masked a clever mind. A parade of White House and party officials described their parts in the affair, often accusing each other and revealing the plumbers and the enemies list. The real questions, it became obvious, were what the president knew and when he knew it. It seemed to be John Dean's word against Richard Nixon's.

A bombshell turned the scandal into a constitutional crisis. A midlevel staffer told the committee that Nixon made tape recordings of his White House conversations. Both the

Senate and the Watergate special prosecutor, Archibald Cox, subpoened the tapes. Nixon refused to give them up, citing executive privilege and the separation of powers. In late October, after he failed to cut a satisfactory deal, he fired his attorney general and the special prosecutor. This "Saturday-night massacre" caused a storm of protest, and many Americans thought that it proved that Nixon had something to hide. In April 1974, he finally issued edited transcripts of the tapes, with foul language deleted and key passages missing; he claimed that his secretary had accidentally erased crucial material. Finally, on July 24, 1974, the U.S. Supreme Court ruled unanimously that Nixon had to deliver sixty-four tapes to the new special prosecutor.

Congress was now moving to impeach the president. On July 27, the House Judiciary Committee took up the specific charges. Republicans joined Democrats in voting three articles of impeachment: for hindering the criminal investigation of the Watergate break-in, for abusing the power of the presidency by using federal agencies to deprive citizens of their rights, and for ignoring the committee's subpoena for the tapes. Before the full House could vote on the articles of impeachment and send them to the Senate for trial, Nixon delivered the tapes. One of them contained the "smoking gun," direct evidence that Nixon had participated in the coverup on June 23, 1972, and had been lying ever since. On August 8 he announced his resignation, effective the following day.

Watergate was two separate but related stories. On one level, it was about individuals who deceived or manipulated the American people. Nixon and his cronies wanted to win too badly to play by the rules and repeatedly broke the law. Nixon paid for his overreaching ambition with the end of his political career; more than twenty others paid with jail terms.

On another level, the crisis was a lesson about the Constitution. The separation of powers allowed Congress and the courts to rein in a president who had spun out of control. The Ervin Committee hearings in 1973 and the House Judiciary Committee proceedings in 1974 were rituals to assure Americans that the system still worked. Nevertheless, the sequence of political events from 1968 to 1974 disillusioned many citizens.

The Ford Footnote

Gerald Ford was the first president who had not been elected as either president or vice president. Ford was Nixon's appointee to replace Spiro Agnew, who had resigned and pleaded no contest to charges of bribery and income tax evasion in 1973 as Watergate was gathering steam. Ford was competent but unimaginative. His first major act was his most controversial—the pardon of Nixon for "any and all crimes" committed while president. Since Nixon had not yet been indicted, the pardon saved him from future prosecution. To many Americans, the act looked like a payoff. Ford insisted that the purpose was to clear the decks so that the nation could think about the future rather than the past. That he also offered clemency to thousands of draft resisters substantiated his interpretation. However, the pardon increased cynicism about politics.

Ford's administration presided over the collapse of South Vietnam in 1975, but elsewhere in the world, détente continued. American diplomats joined the Soviet Union and thirty other European nations in the capital of Finland to sign the **Helsinki Accords**. The agreements called for increased commerce between the Eastern and Western blocs and for human rights guarantees. They also legitimized the national boundaries that had been set in eastern Europe in 1945.

At home, the federal government did little new during Ford's two and a half years in office. The economy slid into recession; unemployment climbed above 10 percent; inflation diminished the value of savings and wages. Ford beat back Ronald Reagan for the Republican presidential nomination, but he was clearly vulnerable.

His Democratic opponent was a political enigma. James Earl Carter Jr. had been a navy officer, a farmer, and the governor of Georgia. He was one of several new-style politicians who transformed southern politics in the 1970s. Carter and the others left race-baiting behind to talk like modern New Dealers, emphasizing that all white and black Americans needed better schools and economic growth. He appealed to Democrats as someone who could reassemble LBJ's political coalition and return the South to the Democratic party. In his successful campaign, Carter presented himself as an alternative to party hacks and Washington insiders.

JIMMY CARTER: IDEALISM AND FRUSTRATION IN THE WHITE HOUSE

Johnson and Nixon had both thought of themselves as outsiders even after nearly thirty years in national politics. Carter was the real thing, a stranger to the national policy establishment that revolves around Washington think tanks and New York law firms. As an outsider, Carter had one great advantage: freedom from the narrow mind-set of experts who talk only to each other. However, he lacked both the knowledge of key political players and the experience to resolve legislative gridlock.

The new president's personal background compounded his problems. Intellectuals found this devout Baptist hard to fathom. Labor leaders and political bosses did not know what to make of a deep Southerner. The national press was baffled. It was only after his presidency, when Americans took a clear look at Carter's moral character, that they decided they liked what they saw.

Even had he been the most skilled of politicians, however, Carter took office with little room to maneuver. Watergate bequeathed him a powerful and self-satisfied Congress and a combative press. OPEC oil producers, Islamic fundamentalists, and Soviet generals followed their own agendas. The American people themselves were fractionalized and quarrelsome, uneasy with the new advocacy of equality for women, uncertain as a nation whether they shared the same values and goals. Carter's attempt to govern like a preacher, with appeals to moral principles, did more to reveal divisions than establish common ground.

Carter, Energy, and the Economy

Carter was refreshingly low-key. After his inauguration, he walked from the Capitol to the White House, as Jefferson had. He preferred sweaters to tuxedos and signed official documents "Jimmy." He tended to tell the public what he thought rather than what pollsters said the people wanted to hear.

Carter's approach to politics reflected his training as an engineer. He was analytical, logical, and given to breaking a problem into its component parts. He was better at working with details than at defining broad goals. He filled his cabinet with experts rather than with political operators. He failed to understand the importance of personalities and was uncomfortable with compromise. He did not seem to understand the basic rules of Washington politics. For example, he and his cabinet officers developed policies and made appointments without consulting key congressional committee chairs.

The biggest domestic problem remained the economy, which slid into another recession in 1978. Another jump in oil prices helped make 1979 and 1980 the worst years for inflation in the postwar era. Interest rates surged past 20 percent as the Federal Reserve tried to reduce inflation by squeezing business and consumer credit. Carter himself was a fiscal conservative whose impulse was to cut federal spending. This course worsened unemployment and alienated liberal Democrats, who wanted to revive the Great Society.

Carter simultaneously proposed a comprehensive energy policy. He asked Americans to make energy conservation the moral equivalent of war—to accept individual sacrifices for the common good. Congress created the Department of Energy but refused to raise taxes on oil and natural gas to reduce consumption. However, the Energy Policy and Conservation Act (1978) did encourage alternative energy sources to replace foreign petroleum. Big oil companies poured billions of dollars into western Colorado to squeeze a petroleum substitute from shale. Solar energy research prospered. Breezy western hillsides sprouted "wind farms" to wring electricity out of the air.

However, antinuclear activism blocked one obvious alternative to fossil fuels. The antinuclear movement had started with concern about the ability of the Atomic Energy Commission to monitor the safety of nuclear power plants and about the disposal of spent fuel rods. In the late 1970s, activists staged sit-ins at the construction sites of nuclear plants. A near-meltdown at the Three Mile Island nuclear plant in Pennsylvania in March 1979 stalemated efforts to expand nuclear power capacity. Utilities were soon worrying about the costs of shutting down and dismantling their old nuclear plants rather than trying to build new ones.

When the OPEC price hikes undermined the inflation-fighting effort in the summer of 1979, Carter told the nation that a "moral and spiritual crisis" demanded a rebirth of the American spirit. He also proposed new steps to solve the energy crisis. The public did not know whether he had preached a sermon or given them marching orders. A cabinet reshuffle a few days later was supposed to show that he was firmly in charge. Instead, the media painted the president as inconsistent and incompetent.

Carter's problems were both personal and structural. In effect, opinion leaders by 1979 had decided that he was not capable of leading the nation and then interpreted every action as confirming that belief. There was also the practical problem of trying to hold the loyalty of Democratic liberals while attracting middle-of-the-road voters.

Closed Factories and Failing Farms

Ford and Carter both faced massive problems of economic transition that undercut their efforts to devise effective government programs. Here is how novelist John Updike described the fictional city of Brewer, Pennsylvania, at the start of the 1970s:

> Railroads and coal made Brewer. Everywhere in this city. . . . structures speak of expended energy. Great shapely stacks that have not issued smoke for half a century. . . . The old textile plants given over to discount clothing outlets teeming with a gimcrack cheer of banners FACTORY FAIR and slogans Where a Dollar Is Still a Dollar. . . . All this had been cast up in the last century by what now seem giants, in an explosion of iron and brick still preserved intact in this city where the sole new buildings are funeral parlors and government offices.

Updike's Brewer was like dozens of specialized industrial cities that fell behind a changing economic world in the 1970s and 1980s. Industrial decay stalked such "gritty cities" as Allentown, Pennsylvania; Trenton, New Jersey; and Gary, Indiana. Communities whose workers had made products in high volume for mass markets found that technological revolutions made them obsolete. When radial tires replaced bias-ply tires, Akron rubber workers paid the price. Merchants who replaced mechanical cash registers with electronic models left Dayton with block after block of outmoded factories. Asian steelmakers undercut the aging mills of Pittsburgh and Birmingham. Critics renamed the old manufacturing region of the Northeast and Middle West the Rustbelt in honor of its abandoned factories.

Similar stories of **deindustrialization** were playing out in small cities such as Springfield, Ohio, and large cities such as Cleveland. Springfield lost ten thousand manufacturing jobs and four thousand people during the 1970s, suffered unemployment of 17 percent, and needed $30 million in public subsidies to keep its largest factory going in 1982. Cleveland had built a century of prosperity on oil refining, steel, and metalworking; the metropolitan area had grown from 1.3 million in 1940 to 2.1 million in 1970. In the 1970s, however, it lost 165,000 people. As high-paying jobs in unionized industries disappeared, sagging income undermined small businesses and neighborhoods. Falling tax revenue brought the city to the verge of bankruptcy in 1978; bankers forced public service cuts and tax increases, which meant further job losses.

Plant closures were only one facet of business efforts to increase productivity by substituting machinery for employees. Between 1947 and 1977, American steelmakers doubled output while cutting their work force from 600,000 to 400,000. Lumber companies used economic recession in the early 1980s to automate mills and rehired only a fraction of their workers when the economy picked up. High interest rates in the early 1980s, the result of a ballooning federal deficit, attracted foreign investors and strengthened the dollar in relation to other currencies. A strong dollar made U.S. exports too expensive and foreign imports cheap, forcing American manufacturers to cut costs or perish.

Despite the despairing headlines, some older industries and their workers did find new roles in the sink-or-swim environment of technological and international competition. Buffalo, New York, lost much of its steel industry but retained smaller and more flexible factories making diverse products. The auto industry went through a similar cycle of crisis and response. Prosperity in the 1950s had led automobile executives to believe that they knew how to manipulate U.S. consumers. Booming imports of well-made Toyotas and Hondas and customer demand for smaller cars destroyed that complacency in the fuel-short 1970s. In response, Ford, Chrysler, and finally General Motors remade themselves on the Japanese model as lean and flexible manufacturers. They cast off old plants, workers, and executives, started over, often in new locations, and forced Japanese companies to shift production to U.S. localities and workers.

Parallel to the decline of heavy industry was the continuing transformation of American agriculture from small, family enterprises to corporate agribusinesses. Agriculture was a national success story in the aggregate, but one accompanied by many human and environmental costs. The early 1970s brought an unexpected boom in farming. Crop failures and food shortages around the world in 1972 and 1973 expanded markets and pushed up prices for U.S. farm products. For a few years, agriculture looked like the best way for the United States to offset the high cost of imported oil. But the boom was over by the 1980s, when global commodity prices slumped. Farmers found themselves with debts they could not cover. Farm bankruptcies in Iowa reached levels unseen since the 1930s, and rock stars staged "Farm Aid" concerts to raise money to fend off foreclosures.

The boom of the 1970s was thus a brief interruption in the long-term transformation of U.S. agriculture. The number of farms slid from 4 million in 1960 to 2.4 million in 1980 and 1.9 million in 2000. Many farmers sold out willingly, glad to escape from drudgery and financial insecurity. Others could not compete in an agricultural system that favored large-scale production by demanding large amounts of capital for equipment and fertilizer.

Corporate farming substituted capital investment for labor in the time-tested manner of industrial maturity. By the 1990s, the 600,000 largest farms and ranches were responsible for 94 percent of total production of U.S. farm products. Many of them were owned by large corporations that measured success by the bottom line rather than the stability of rural communities. Fewer than 2 percent of all American workers now make their living from farming, down from 8 percent in 1960.

Building a Cooperative World

Despite troubles on the home front, Carter's first two years brought foreign-policy successes that reflected a new vision of a multilateral world. As a relative newcomer to international politics, Carter was willing to work with African, Asian, and Latin American nations on a basis of mutual respect. He appointed Andrew Young—an African American from Georgia with long experience in the civil rights movement—as ambassador to the United Nations, where he worked effectively to build bridges to Third World nations.

An early result of the new approach was a decision to treat Panama as a nation, not a pocket colony. Following up on Republican initiatives, Carter's administration completed negotiations for two treaties about the status of the U.S.-run Panama Canal Zone and the American-managed Panama Canal. Carter considered the Canal Zone an unnecessary imperialist survivor and agreed to transfer control of the canal to Panama by 1999. Conservatives offered dire predictions of ruin for the canal and argued that the United States had every right to keep territory that it had seized at the start of the twentieth century. Against well-meaning advice to drop the treaties, Carter fought to a victory by one vote in the Senate in April 1978.

Carter's moral convictions were responsible for a new concern with human rights around the globe. He criticized the Soviet Union for preventing free speech and denying its citizens the right to emigrate, angering Soviet leaders, who didn't expect the human rights clauses of the Helsinki Accords to be taken seriously. Carter was also willing to criticize some (but not all) American allies. He withheld economic aid from South Africa, Guatemala, Chile, and Nicaragua, which had long records of human rights abuses. In Nicaragua, the change in policy helped left-wing Sandinista rebels topple the Somoza dictatorship.

The triumph of the new foreign policy was the **Camp David Agreement** between Egypt and Israel. Carter risked his reputation and credibility in September 1978 to bring Egyptian President Anwar al-Sadat and Israeli Prime Minister Menachem Begin together at Camp David, the presidential retreat. He refused to admit failure and dissuaded the two leaders from walking out. A formal treaty was signed in Washington on March 26, 1979. The pact normalized relations between Israel and its most powerful neighbor and led to Israel's withdrawal from the Sinai Peninsula. It was a vital prelude to further progress toward Arab-Israeli peace in the mid 1990s.

New Crises Abroad

The Cold War was a noxious weed that détente trimmed but did not uproot. In the last two years of Carter's administration, it sprang back to life around the globe and smothered the promise of a new foreign policy. The Soviets ignored the human rights provisions of the Helsinki Accords. Soviet advisors or Cuban troops intervened in African civil wars. At home, Cold Warriors who had never accepted détente found it easier to attack Carter than Nixon.

The Failure of SALT II Carter inherited negotiations for SALT II—a strategic arms-limitation treaty that would have reduced both American and Soviet nuclear arsenals—from the Ford administration. SALT II met stiff resistance in the Senate. Opponents claimed it would create a "window of vulnerability" in the 1980s that would invite the Soviets to launch a nuclear first strike. Carter tried to counter criticism by stepping up defense spending, starting a buildup that would accelerate under Ronald Reagan.

Hopes for SALT II vanished on January 3, 1980, when Soviet troops entered Afghanistan, a neutral Muslim nation on the southern border of the Soviet Union. Muslim tribespeople unhappy with modernization had attacked Afghanistan's pro-Communist government, which invited Soviet intervention. The situation resembled the American involvement in South

Vietnam. Similar, too, was the inability of Soviet forces to suppress the Afghan guerrillas, with their American weapons and control of the mountains. In the end, it took the Soviets a decade to find a way out.

The Iranian Hostage Crisis The final blow to Carter's foreign policy came in Iran. Since 1953, the United States had strongly backed Iran's monarch, Shah Reza Pahlevi. The Shah modernized Iran's economy but his feared secret police jailed and tortured political opponents. U.S. aid and oil revenues helped him build a large army, but the Iranian middle class despised his authoritarianism, and Muslim fundamentalists opposed the Westernizing influence of modernization. A revolution toppled the Shah at the start of 1979.

The upheaval installed a nominally democratic government, but the Ayatollah Ruhollah Khomeini, a Muslim cleric who hated the United States, exercised the real power. Throughout 1979, Iran grew increasingly anti-American. After the United States allowed the exiled Shah to seek medical treatment in New York, a mob stormed the U.S. embassy in Tehran on November 4, 1979, and took more than sixty Americans hostage. They demanded that Carter surrender the Shah.

Television brought pictures of blindfolded hostages and anti-American mobs burning effigies of Uncle Sam and wrapping American flags around garbage. The administration tried economic pressure and diplomacy, but Khomeini had no desire for accommodation. When Iran announced in April 1980 that the hostages would remain in the hands of the militants rather than be transferred to the government, Carter ordered an airborne rescue. Even a perfectly managed effort would have been difficult. The hostages were held in the heart of a city of 4 million hostile Iranians, hundreds of miles from the nearest aircraft carrier and thousands of miles from U.S. bases. Hampered by lack of coordination among the military services, the attempt misfired when three of eight helicopters malfunctioned and one crashed in the Iranian desert. The fiasco added to the national embarrassment. The United States and Iran finally reached agreement on the eve of the 1980 election. The hostages gained their freedom after 444 days, at the moment Ronald Reagan took office as the new president.

The hostage crisis consumed Jimmy Carter the way that Vietnam had consumed Lyndon Johnson. It gripped the public and stalemated other issues. For weeks, Carter limited public appearances to statements in the White House Rose Garden. The public blamed him for problems literally beyond his control, for failing to use military force, and then for using it and failing. Carter's tragedy was that "his" Iranian crisis was the fruit of policies hatched by the Eisenhower administration and pursued by every president since then, all of whom overlooked the Shah's despotic government because of his firm anti-Communism.

After thirty years in which the United States had viewed the entire world as a Cold War battlefield, Carter was willing to accept the developing world on its own terms. His human rights efforts showed that evangelical religious convictions could be tied to progressive aims. He wanted to avoid supporting oppressive regimes, but the past was too burdensome. Iranian rage at past policies of the sort Carter hoped to change destroyed his ability to direct a new course. After he left office, his continuing work for peace and humanitarian efforts would earn him the Nobel Peace Prize in 2002.

CONCLUSION

In the mid-1970s, Americans encountered real limits to national capacity. From 1945 to 1973, they had enjoyed remarkable prosperity. That ended in 1974. Long lines at gas stations showed that prosperity was fragile. Cities and regions felt the costs of obsolete industries. Environmental damage caused many Americans to reconsider the goal of economic expansion.

The nation also had to recognize that it could not run the world. American withdrawal from Vietnam in 1973 and the collapse of the South Vietnamese government in 1975 were defeats; the United States ended up with little to show for a long and painful war. SALT I stabilized the arms race, but it also recognized that the Soviet Union was an equal. The American nuclear arsenal might help deter a third world war, but it could not prevent the seizure of hostages in Iran.

These challenges came amid deep economic changes in the United States. The ways that Americans made their livings and the range of opportunities that they faced were in flux. The nation finished the 1970s more egalitarian than it had been in the early 1960s, but also more divided. More citizens had the opportunity to advance economically and to seek political power, but there were deepening fissures between social liberals and cultural conservatives, old and new views about roles for women, rich and poor, whites and blacks. In 1961, John Kennedy had called on his fellow citizens to "bear any burden, pay any price" to defend freedom. By 1980, the nation had neither the economic capacity to pay any price nor the unity to agree on what burdens it should bear.

Review Questions

1. Why did the United States fail to achieve its objectives in Vietnam? What factors limited President Johnson's freedom of action there? How did the Tet Offensive affect U.S. policy? How did antiwar protests in the United States influence national policy?

2. How did racial relations change between 1965 and 1970? What were the relationships between the civil rights movement and minority separatism? What were the similarities and differences among African-American, Latino, and Native American activism?

3. In what ways was 1968 a pivotal year for American politics and society?

4. What were the implications of détente? Why did the Cold War reappear in the late 1970s? How and why did U.S. influence over the rest of the world change during the 1970s?

5. How did Richard Nixon's political strategy respond to the growth of the South and West? How did it respond to the shift of population from central cities to suburbs?

6. How did the backgrounds of Presidents Johnson, Nixon, and Carter shape their successes and failures as national leaders?

7. What political and constitutional issues were at stake in the Watergate scandal? How did Watergate change American politics?

8. Why was the "space race" important for the United States? How did it strengthen the alliance among American science, government, and industry?

Key Terms

American Indian Movement (AIM) *363*
Baker v. Carr *364*
Black Panthers *361*
Black Power *361*
Camp David Agreement *381*
Counterculture *356*
Deindustrialization *380*
Détente *371*

Environmental Protection Agency *373*
Free Speech Movement (FSM) *355*
Helsinki Accords *377*
Model Cities Program *355*
Nation of Islam *361*
New Federalism *372*
Nixon Doctrine *369*

Recommended Reading

Tom Bates, *Rads: The 1970 Bombing of the Army Math Research Center at the University of Wisconsin and Its Aftermath* (1992). Bates attempts to use a specific episode to understand the collapse of the New Left.

David Caute, *Year of the Barricades* (1988). Tour the events of 1968 on both sides of the Atlantic.

Gloria Emerson, *Winners and Losers* (1976). The impact of the war in Vietnam on American society is told through the stories of individuals changed by the war.

David Farber, *Chicago '68* (1988); *Medium Cool* (1969), directed by Haskell Wexler. Farber's book contrasts the perspectives and language of city officials and protesters. Wexler's film captures the tension of Chicago in the hot summer through the eyes of a reporter.

David Halberstam, *October 1964* (1994). Halberstam uses the baseball season of 1964 and the World Series between the St. Louis Cardinals and New York Yankees to encapsulate the impacts of changing racial relations on American society.

Stanley Karnow, *Vietnam: A History* (1983). This comprehensive history of American involvement in Vietnam details the collapse of French rule and early U.S. relations with Vietnam.

Kim McQuaid, *The Anxious Years: America in the Vietnam-Watergate Era* (1989); John Morton Blum, *Years of Discord: American Politics and Society, 1961–1974* (1991); David Farber, *The Age of Great Dreams* (1994). McQuaid and Blum try to understand how the United States turned aside from the promise of the early 1960s. Farber offers a more positive assessment of many of the same developments.

CHAPTER 13

THE REAGAN REVOLUTION AND A CHANGING WORLD: 1981–1992

Reagan's Domestic Revolution

The Second (Short) Cold War

Growth in the Sunbelt

Values in Collision

Conclusion

The Khmer Rouge marched into the city [Phnom Penh, the capital of Cambodia], dressed in black. . . . Young Khmer Rouge [Marxist revolutionary] soldiers, eight or ten years old, were dragging their rifles, which were taller than them. . . . The whole city, more than two million people was forced out of their homes into the streets. My family walked until we reached Mao Tse-Tung Boulevard, the main boulevard in Phnom Penh. All the population of the city was gathered there. The Khmer Rouge were telling everyone to leave the city.

Although my two middle children were safe in France, my oldest and youngest daughters were close beside me. Parika was only seven. Mealy, who was nineteen, carried her infant son. I kept my children huddled together. As soon as a parent let go, a child would be lost in the huge crowd. . . . And the Khmer Rouge kept ordering everybody, "You must go forward." They shot their guns in the air. Even during the middle of the night the procession was endless. The Khmer Rouge kept shooting and we kept moving forward. . . .

Recently I saw the movie *Doctor Zhivago*, about the Russian Revolution. If you compare that to what happened in Phnom Penh, the movie is only on a very small scale. Even *Killing Fields* only gives you part of the idea of what happened in Cambodia. The reality was much more incredible. . . .

Each night, when we came back to the village from working in the fields, Mom would say, "Children, let's all go to sleep." She would quietly warn me that the wood had eyes and ears. She'd say, "It's nine o'clock now. Go to sleep. . . . There is nothing else to do but work. All the men are gone in our family." Mom was actually saying for the Khmer Rouge spies to hear, "They are only girls. Don't kill them. We are the only members left of the family." . . . We were lying to them about our identity. It was a horrible game.

If you hid your identity, that meant you wanted your past forgotten. We had changed from people who were intellectual, who used to think independently. . . . You became humiliated, allowed to live only as a slave. . . . We were accepted into the United States thanks to my husband's military service. . . . My daughters and I flew to the United States on July 4, 1979. . . . As we landed, I thought, "This is real freedom." . . .

I've found that America is a country where people have come from all over the world. You do your job, you get paid like anybody else, and you're accepted. But Cambodians I know in France, like my sister, feel differently. People are not accepted if they are not French. But in America you're part of the melting pot. . . . In 1983, I came to Los Angeles for my daughter Monie's wedding. I decided to stay. . . . Long Beach has the largest concentration of Cambodians in the country. I called the community center in Long Beach. They said they had no job openings. So I decided to get involved in running a store. . . . Donut shops are very American. . . .

All that refugees have is our work, our dreams. Do I still hurt from what happened in the past? When I opened my mouth to tell you my story, I don't know where my tears came from. . . . My daughters don't like to talk about the past in Cambodia. They want to forget and think about their future. They ask me why I would talk about the past with anybody. I said, "The past cannot be erased from my memory."

—Celia Noup

Celia Noup in Al Santoli, *New Americans: An Oral History* (New York, 1988).

CELIA NOUP taught school for twenty years in Cambodia, which borders on South Vietnam. In 1975, after a long civil war, the Communist Khmer Rouge insurgents took over Cambodia's capital, Phnom Penh, and forced its inhabitants into the countryside to work in the fields. Four years later, Noup managed to make her way to a refugee camp in neighboring Thailand and then to the United States. Here she joined hundreds of thousands of other refugees who arrived in the later 1970s and 1980s from war-devastated nations such as Cambodia, Vietnam, Laos, Ethiopia, and Afghanistan. Within a decade, she was working from 5:00 A.M. to 7:00 P.M. in her own donut shop near Los Angeles airport and worrying about helping her children buy houses.

Celia Noup's life shows some of the ways that new waves of immigration from Asia, Latin America, and Africa have changed the United States over the last generation. Immigrants fueled economic growth in the 1980s and 1990s with their labor and their drive to succeed in business. They revitalized older neighborhoods in cities from coast to coast and changed the ethnic mix of major cities. And they created new racial tensions that found their way into national political debates about immigration and into open conflict in places such as Miami and Los Angeles.

Noup's story is also a reminder of the drawn-out consequences of the U.S. involvement in Vietnam and the long shadow of the Cold War. The Cambodian civil war was fueled by reactions to the Vietnamese war and the American invasion of Cambodia in 1969. American refugee policy was humanitarian, but also political, opening the door to people fleeing Communist regimes but holding it shut against refugees from right-wing dictatorships. In Washington, foreign policy decisions in the 1980s started with the desire of a new administration to reaffirm American toughness after failures in Vietnam and ended with the astonishing evaporation of the Cold War.

By the end of Ronald Reagan's presidency (1981—1989), new rules governed domestic affairs as well as international relations. Since World War II, politics had followed a well-thumbed script. Lessons about full employment and social services that were accepted in 1948 still applied in 1968 or 1972. In the 1980s, however, Americans decided to reverse the growth of federal government responsibilities that had marked both Republican and Democratic administrations since the 1930s. By the 1990s, the center of U.S. politics had shifted substantially to the right, and even a "liberal" Democrat like Bill Clinton would sound like an Eisenhower Republican. The backdrop to the political changes were massive readjustments in the American economy that began in the 1970s with the decline of heavy industry and then continued to shift employment from factory jobs to service jobs in the 1980s (Celia's Noup's small shop was part of the service economy). The ideology of unregulated markets celebrated economic success and made "yuppies" or young urban professionals the center of media attention; some of the yuppies probably grabbed a donut on their way to catch a flight from Los Angeles to New York to help close a deal. But behind the lifestyle stories was a troubling reality: a widening gap between the rich and poor. The result by 1992 was a nation that was much more secure in the world than it had been in 1980, but also more divided against itself.

KEY TOPICS

Economic and social change during the Reagan administration.

The changing balance of American regions.

The rise of conservative thought.

The collapse of the Soviet Union and the end of the Cold War.

Instability and war in the Middle East.

Changes in the legal standing of women.

Conflict over family values and religious beliefs.

REAGAN'S DOMESTIC REVOLUTION

Political change began in 1980, when Ronald Reagan and his running mate George Bush rode American discontent to a decisive victory in the presidential election. Building on a conservative critique of American policies and developing issues that Jimmy Carter had placed on the national agenda, Reagan presided over revolutionary changes in American government and policies. He was a "Teflon president" who managed to take credit for successes but avoid blame for problems, and he rolled to a landslide reelection in 1984 and set the stage for George Bush's victory in 1988. The consequences of his two terms included an altered role for government, powerful but selective economic growth, and a shift of domestic politics away from bread-and-butter issues toward moral or lifestyle concerns.

An unresolved question is whether Ronald Reagan planned an economic revolution, or simply presided over changes initiated by others. Most memoirs by White House insiders suggest the latter; so do journalists who entitled books about the Reagan administration *Sleepwalking through History*, *The Acting President*, and *The Role of a Lifetime*. Even if Reagan was acting out a role that was scripted by others, however, he was a hit at the polling place. Americans, worried about inflation at home and declining power abroad, elected Reagan by voting *against* Jimmy Carter in 1980, but they enthusiastically voted *for* Reagan in 1984.

• CHRONOLOGY •

1973	*Roe v. Wade*: Supreme Court struck down state laws banning abortion in the first trimester of pregnancy.
1980	Ronald Reagan is elected president.
1981	Economic Recovery and Tax Act, reducing personal income tax rates, is passed.
	Reagan breaks strike by air traffic controllers.
	AIDS is recognized as a new disease.
1982	Nuclear freeze movement peaks.
	United States begins to finance Contra rebels against the Sandinista government in Nicaragua.
	Equal Rights Amendment fails to achieve ratification.
1983	Two hundred forty-one Marines are killed by a terrorist bomb in Beirut, Lebanon.
	Strategic Defense Initiative introduced.
	United States invades Grenada.
1984	Reagan wins reelection.
1985	Mikhail Gorbachev initiates economic and political reforms in the Soviet Union.
1986	Tax Reform Act is adopted.
1987	Congress holds hearings on the Iran-Contra scandal.
	Reagan and Gorbachev sign the Intermediate Nuclear Force treaty.
1988	George Bush is elected president.
1989	Communist regimes in eastern Europe collapse; Germans tear down Berlin Wall.
	Financial crisis forces federal bailout of many savings and loans.
	United States invades Panama to capture General Manuel Noriega.
1990	Iraq invades Kuwait; and the United States sends forces to the Persian Gulf.
	West Germany and East Germany reunite.
	Americans with Disabilities Act is adopted.
1991	Persian Gulf War: Operation Desert Storm drives the Iraqis from Kuwait.
	Soviet Union dissolves into independent nations.
	Strategic Arms Reduction Treaty (START) is signed.
1992	Acquittal of officers accused of beating Rodney King triggers Los Angeles riots.

Reagan's Majority

Ronald Reagan reinvented himself several times on his unusual journey to the White House. A product of small-town Illinois, he succeeded in Hollywood in the late 1930s as a romantic lead actor while adopting the liberal politics common at the time. After World War II, he moved rapidly to the political right as a spokesman for big business. For several years, he traveled the country under the sponsorship of the General Electric Company, giving a standard speech that extolled the virtues of free enterprise. He entered politics with a rousing conservative speech at the 1964 Republican convention and then accepted the invitation of wealthy California Republicans to run for governor in 1966. In two terms in that office, he offered little formal leadership but spoke for a state and then a nation that were drifting toward more conservative values and expectations.

With a common touch that made him a favorite for a sizable segment of the public, Reagan tapped into the nostalgia for a simpler America. Although he was 69 when elected, his status as a movie and television personality made him seem up-to-date. His Hollywood background made it easy for him to use popular films to make his points. He once threatened to veto legislation by challenging Congress with Clint Eastwood's "Make my day." Many blockbuster movies reinforced two of Reagan's messages. One was the importance of direct confrontation with bad guys ranging from terrorists (*Die Hard*) to drug dealers (*Lethal Weapon*). The second was the incompetence of government bureaucracies, whose elitist mistakes could only be set right by tough individuals, like the movie heroes Dirty Harry Callahan and John Rambo.

Some of Reagan's most articulate support came from anti-Communist stalwarts of both parties, who feared that the United States was losing influence in the world. Despite Jimmy Carter's tough actions in 1979 and 1980 and increased defense spending, such conservatives had not trusted him to do enough. The inability to free the hostages in Iran grated. The Panama Canal and SALT II treaties seemed to give away American power. Soviet military buildup, charged the critics, was creating a "window of vulnerability," a dangerous period when the Soviet Union might threaten the United States with a first strike by nuclear weapons.

Other Reagan voters directed their anger at government bureaucracies. Christian conservatives worried that social activists were using the federal courts to alter traditional values. Wealthy entrepreneurs from the fast-growing South and West believed that Nixon-era federal offices such as the Environmental Protection Agency and the Occupational Safety and Health Administration, were choking their businesses in red tape. Many of these critics had amassed new fortunes in oil, real estate, and retailing and hated the taxes that funded social programs. In many ways, the two groups were mismatched. Christian moralists had little in common with the high-rolling hedonists and Hollywood tycoons with whom Reagan rubbed shoulders, but they shared a deep distrust of the federal establishment.

Foreign policy activists and opponents of big government would have been unable to elect Reagan without disaffected blue-collar and middle-class voters who deserted the Democrats. Reagan's campaign hammered on the question, "Are you better off than you were four years ago?" Democrats faced a special dilemma with the deepening tension between working-class white voters and black voters. They needed both groups to win but found white blue-collar voters deeply alienated by affirmative action and busing for school integration. When pollsters read white Detroiters a statement from Robert Kennedy that called on Americans to recognize special obligations to black citizens who had endured racial discrimination, responses were vehement: "I can't go along with that!" "That's bull!" The same sorts of voters worried about inflation and blamed their difficulties on runaway government spending.

A further Democratic challenge was Ronald Reagan's personal appeal. The new president won over many Americans by surviving a 1981 assassination attempt in fine spirits. Reagan's popularity compounded the Democrats' inability to excite younger voters. The mid-1980s consistently showed that roughly two-thirds of people in their twenties and early thirties were choosing the Republicans as the party of energy and new ideas, leaving the Democrats to the middle-aged and elderly.

In the election of 1984, Democrats sealed their fate by nominating Walter Mondale, who had been vice president under Carter. Mondale was earnest, honest, and dull. Reagan ran on the theme, "It's Morning in America," with the message that a new age of pride and prosperity had begun. Mondale assumed that Americans cared enough about the exploding federal deficit that Reagan's defense spending had produced to accept an across-the-board tax increase. With the economy growing and inflation now in check, most voters did not want Mondale to remind them of long-range financial realities, and Reagan won reelection with 98 percent of the electoral votes. His election confirmed that the American public found conservative ideas increasingly attractive.

The New Conservatism

Reagan's approach to public policy drew on conservative intellectuals who offered a coherent critique of the New Deal-New Frontier approach to American government. Some of the leading figures were journalists and academics who had embraced the ideas of the vital center a generation earlier (see Chapter 10). Now they feared that the antiwar movement had undermined the anti-Communist stance and that social changes were corrupting main-stream values. *Commentary* magazine became a platform for these combative neoconservative arguments. *The Public Interest* was a new magazine for conservative or skeptical academic writers.

Downsizing the Great Society Worries about big government permeated the critique of domestic policy. Edward Banfield's radical ideas about the failures of the Great Society set the tone of the neoconservative analysis. In *The Unheavenly City* (1968), he questioned the basic idea of public solutions for social problems. He argued that inequality is based on human character and rooted in the basic structure of society; government action can solve only the problems that require better engineering, such as pollution control, better high-ways, or the delivery of explosives to military targets. Government's job, said Banfield, was to preserve public order, not to right wrongs or encourage unrealistic expectations.

Other conservative writers elaborated Banfield's ideas. The most influential was Charles Murray, whose 1984 book *Losing Ground* tried to do for neoconservative domestic policy what Michael Harrington's *The Other America* had done for liberal policy. Murray's basic argument was simple: Welfare assistance hurt more than it helped, by encouraging depen-dency and discouraging individual efforts at self-improvement. Despite massive antipoverty and welfare efforts since 1965, he contended, poverty, minority unemployment, and deviant behavior had increased rather than decreased. The blame, he said, must lie in welfare pro-grams themselves. Scholars have shown that Murray's book distorts the evidence and makes flawed arguments, but it had a major impact on political debates.

Free Market Utopians Another strand of conservative argument came from free market utopians. After years of stagflation, Americans were eager to hear that unleashing free mar-kets would trigger renewed prosperity. The *Wall Street Journal* evolved from a narrow busi-ness newspaper into a national conservative forum by devoting its editorial page to outspo-ken versions of neoconservatism. Politicians such as Congressman Jack Kemp built support for specific steps to cut economic regulation and encourage business enterprise.

The common themes of the conservative critique were simple: Free markets work bet-ter than government programs; government intervention does more harm than good; gov-ernment assistance may be acceptable for property owners, but it saps the initiative of the poor. In 1964, three-quarters of Americans had trusted Washington "to do what is right." By 1980, three-quarters were convinced that the federal government wasted tax money. The neoconservatives offered the details to support Reagan's own summary: "Government is not the solution to our problems; government is the problem." The cumulative effect of the neoconservative arguments was to trash the word "liberal" and convince many Americans that labor unions and minorities were "special interests," but that oil tycoons, defense con-tractors, and other members of Reagan's coalition were not.

The conservative cause found support in new "think tanks" and political lobbying orga-nizations. Many conservatives were convinced that university faculty members were hope-lessly liberal. In response, wealthy businesspeople funded alternative organizations, such as the Manhattan Institute, the Heritage Foundation, and the American Enterprise Institute, where conservative analysts could take the time to develop their own policy proposals and opinion pieces for newspapers. The cumulative effect was to shift the terms of political discussion substantially in a conservative direction between 1975 and 1990.

Conservative Political Tactics Conservatives promoted their ideology with new polit-ical tactics. Targeted mailings raised funds and mobilized voters with emotional appeals while bypassing the mass media, with their supposed preference for mainstream or liberal policies. Conservative organizers also knew how to use radio call-in shows to spread their message. Such appeals contrasted with the Democrats' reliance on more traditional ways to get out the vote through personal contacts and labor unions. Through the 1980s, Democrats repeatedly found themselves blindsided by creative Republican campaign tactics.

Reaganomics: Deficits and Deregulation

The heart of the 1980s revolution was the **Economic Recovery and Tax Act of 1981 (ERTA)**, which reduced personal income tax rates by 25 percent over three years. The explicit goal was to stimulate business activity by lowering taxes overall and slashing rates for the rich. Cutting the government's total income by $747 billion over five years, ERTA meant less money for federal programs and more money in the hands of consumers and investors to stimulate economic growth.

Reagan's first budget director, David Stockman, later revealed a second goal. ERTA would lock in deficits by "pulling the revenue plug." Because defense spending and Social Security were untouchable, Congress would find it impossible to create and fund new programs without cutting old ones. Compared with spending patterns in effect in 1980, the Reagan administration also shifted $70 billion per year from domestic to military programs. The first year's tax reductions were accompanied by cuts of $40 billion in federal aid to mass transit, school lunches, and similar programs. If Americans still wanted social programs, they could enact them at the local or state level, but Washington would no longer pay.

The second part of the economic agenda was to free capitalists from government regulations in the hope of increasing business innovation and efficiency. The **deregulation** revolution built on a head start from the 1970s. A federal antitrust case had split the unified Bell System of AT&T and its subsidiaries into seven regional telephone companies and opened long-distance service to competition. Congress also deregulated air travel in 1978. During the first forty years of commercial air service, the Federal Aviation Administration had matched airlines and routes (treating air service like a public utility); deregulation now allowed air carriers to start and stop service at will, resulting in cheaper and more frequent air service for major hubs and poorer and more expensive service for small cities. Economists tend to be satisfied that the net gains have outweighed the costs.

Environmental Regulation and Federal Lands Corporate America used the Reagan administration to attack environmental legislation as "strangulation by regulation." Reagan's new budgets sliced funding for the Environmental Protection Agency. Vice President Bush headed the White House Task Force on Regulatory Relief, which delayed or blocked regulations on hazardous wastes, automobile emissions, and exposure of workers to chemicals on the job.

Most attention, however, went to the controversial appointment of a Colorado lawyer, James Watt, as secretary of the interior. Watt had long worked to open up federal lands in the West to more intensive development. He was sympathetic to a Western movement known as the **Sagebrush Rebellion**, which wanted the vast federal land holdings in the West transferred to the states for less environmental protection and more rapid economic use. He once blamed air pollution on natural emissions from trees and compared environmentalists to Nazis and Bolsheviks. Federal resource agencies sold trees to timber companies at a loss to the Treasury, expanded offshore oil drilling, and expedited exploration for minerals.

Deregulation of the Banking Industry The early 1980s also transformed American financial markets. Savings and loans (S&Ls) had traditionally been conservative financial institutions that funneled individual savings into safe home mortgages. Under new rules, they began to compete for deposits by offering high interest rates and reinvested the money in much riskier commercial real estate. By 1990, the result was a financial crisis in which bad loans destroyed hundreds of S&Ls, especially in the Southwest. American taxpayers were left to bail out depositors to the tune of hundreds of billions of dollars to prevent a collapse of the nation's financial and credit system.

With the deregulation of financial markets, corporate consolidations and mergers flourished. Corporate raiders raised money with "junk bonds"—high-interest, high-risk securities—and snapped up profitable and cash-rich companies that could be milked of profits and assets. The merger mania channeled capital into paper transactions rather than investments in new equipment and products. Another effect was to damage the economies of small and middle-sized communities by transferring control of local companies to outside managers.

In the short term, the national economy boomed in the mid-1980s. Deregulated credit, tax cuts, and massive deficit spending on defense fueled exuberant growth. The decade as a whole brought nearly 20 million new jobs, especially for professional and managerial workers, office support staff, sales people, and workers providing personal services. Inflation dipped to 3 percent per year. The stock market mirrored the overall prosperity; the Dow Jones average of blue-chip industrial stock prices more than tripled from August 1982 to August 1987.

Crisis for Organized Labor

The flip side of the economic boom was another round in the Republican offensive against labor unions. Reagan set the tone when he fired more than eleven thousand members of the Professional Air Traffic Controllers Organization for violating a no-strike clause in their hiring agreements. He claimed to be enforcing the letter of the law, but the message to organized labor was clear. For many years, corporations had hesitated to hire permanent replacements for striking workers. With Reagan's example, large companies, such as Hormel and Phelps-Dodge, chose that option, undercutting the strike as an effective union strategy. During the Reagan administration, the National Labor Relations Board and other federal agencies also weakened collective bargaining by their interpretation of labor-management regulations.

Decline of Union Membership and Blue-collar Jobs Organized labor counted a million fewer members at the end of Reagan's administration in 1989 than in 1964, even though the number of employed Americans had nearly doubled. Many unions that had been the mainstays of the labor movement in the Roosevelt and Truman years found themselves in trouble, saddled with leaders who were unable to cope with the restructuring of the economy. As union membership declined and unions struggled to cope with the changing economy, corporations seized the opportunity to demand wage rollbacks and concessions on working conditions as trade-offs for continued employment, squeezing workers in one plant and then using the settlement to pressure another. Workers in the 1970s and 1980s faced the threat that employers might move a factory to a new site elsewhere in the United States or overseas. Or a company might sell out to a new owner, who could close a plant and reopen without a union contract. One 16-year-old described the changes in the grocery chain where her father worked for twenty-six years: "They're letting people go with no feelings for how long they've worked there, just lay 'em off. It's sad. He should be getting benefits after all these years and all the sacrifices he's made. Now they're almost ready to lay him off without a word."

Another cause for shrinking union membership was the overall decline of blue-collar jobs, from 36 percent of the American work force in 1960 to roughly 25 percent at the

The working-class family depicted on the television show *Roseanne* offered viewers a glimpse of the problems facing many Americans in an era of economic change marked by deindustrialization and the rise of service jobs.

end of the 1990s. Unionization of white-collar workers made up only part of the loss from manufacturing. Unions were most successful in recruiting government workers, such as police officers, teachers, and bus drivers. By the late 1980s, the American Federation of State, County, and Municipal Employees had twice the membership of the United Steel Workers. In the private sector, however, many white-collar jobs were in small firms and offices that were difficult to organize.

Impact of Economic Restructuring Popular culture's best take on the problems of blue-collar America was the television situation comedy *Roseanne* (1988–1997). Living in an industrial satellite of Chicago, Roseanne and Dan Conner struggle to raise a family on the income from a series of jobs as small business owner, assembly-line worker, waitress, and skilled laborer. The lifelong unionized factory job became a thing of the past as the shifting economy made it hard to accumulate savings and stay ahead of the financial crises of normal life, let alone keep kids in college. A telling statistic about the problems of the real equivalents of the "Conners" was the increase in personal bankruptcy filings from roughly 300,000 per year in the early 1980s to 1,200,000 per year by the later 1990s.

The community depicted in *Roseanne* represented the impacts of economic restructuring on the blue-collar success story of the 1950s and 1960s when increasing productivity, expanding markets for U.S. goods, and strong labor unions had made it possible for factory workers to enter the middle class. In an era of deindustrialization, however, companies replaced machine operators, assemblers, inspectors, and other production workers with more sophisticated machinery or shifted production to nonunion plants. The corporate merger mania of the 1980s added to instability when takeover specialists loaded old companies with new debt, triggering efforts to cut labor costs, sell off plants, or raid pension funds for cash to pay the interest. Manufacturing employment in the 1980s declined by nearly 2 million jobs, with the expansion of high-tech manufacturing concealing much higher losses in traditional industries. In sum, while corporate merger specialists steered their BMWs along the fast lane to success, displaced mill hands drove battered pickups along potholed roads to nowhere.

An Acquisitive Society

The new prosperity fueled lavish living by the wealthy and a fascination with the "lifestyles of the rich and famous." The television show of the same name, which premiered in 1984, offered its viewers glimpses of "champagne wishes" and "caviar dreams" as lived by entertainment stars and business tycoons. Prime time soap operas flourished, bringing to the small screen stories of intrigue among the rich folks of fast-growing Texas in *Dallas* (1978–1991), Colorado in *Dynasty* (1981–1989), and California in *Knots Landing* (1979–1993). With a few exceptions, even the "middle class" in television sitcoms enjoyed lives available only to the top 20 percent of Americans.

The national media in the early 1980s discovered "yuppies," or young urban professionals, who were both a marketing category and a symbol of social change. These upwardly mobile professionals supposedly defined themselves by elitist consumerism. Such middleline retailers as Sears had clothed Americans for decades and furnished their homes. With the help of catalog shopping, status-seeking consumers now flocked to such upscale retailers as Neiman-Marcus and Bloomingdale's. Yuppie as a marketing category meanwhile spawned variations, such as "buppie" for black urban professional. It was difficult for most Americans to feel much sympathy for the family in a *New York Times* profile in 1987 who had difficulty making ends meet on $600,000 a year.

Far richer than even such atypical yuppies were wheeler-dealers who made themselves into media stars of finance capitalism. The autobiography of Lee Iacocca, who had helped revive the fortunes of the Chrysler Corporation, was a bestseller in 1984, portraying the corporate executive as hero. *Forbes* magazine began to publish an annual list of the nation's four hundred richest people. The real-estate developer Donald Trump made himself a celebrity with a well-publicized personal life and a stream of projects crowned with his name: office tower, hotel, casino. Before he admitted to violating the law against profiting from insider information, the corporate-merger expert Ivan Boesky had told a business-school audience; "Greed is all right. . . . You shouldn't feel guilty," epitomizing an era of big business takeovers driven by paper profits rather than underlying economic fundamentals. Hollywood portrayed this era of corporate takeovers in the 1987 film *Wall Street*. The actor Michael Douglas plays Gordon Gekko, a Boesky-like character who mesmerizes an audience of shareholders when he intones, "Greed is good."

The superficial glamour of this era of acquisitiveness and corporate greed had its underside of loneliness and despair. Young novelists in the 1980s explored the emptiness of life among the privileged, repeating some of the themes of the 1920s in the process. Bret Easton Ellis in *Less Than Zero* (1985) dissected the despair and drug habits of college students from the affluent west side of Los Angeles. In *Bright Lights, Big City* (1986), Jay McInerney took on the same problems of glamour and depression among young professionals in New York, where the real incomes of people on the lower third of the economic ladder declined during the 1980s, while those of the top 10 percent rose by 40 percent. Novelist Tom Wolfe fictionalized the cold statistics in his bestselling novel *The Bonfire of the Vanities* (1987), depicting a New York where the art dealers and stockbrokers of glitzy Manhattan meet the poor of the devastated South Bronx only through an automobile accident to their mutual incomprehension and ruin.

New movements in popular music reacted to the acquisitive 1980s. Punk rock pared rock-and-roll to its basics, lashing out at the emptiness of 1970s disco sounds and the commercialization of youth culture. Punk music influenced grunge bands such as Nirvana, which expressed alienation from consumerism. Hip-Hop originated among African Americans and Latinos in New York, soon adding the angry and often violent lyrics of rap. Rap during the 1980s was about personal power and sex, but it also dealt with social inequities and deprivation and tapped some of the same anger and frustration that had motivated black power advocates in the 1960s. It crossed into the mainstream culture with the help of MTV, which had begun broadcasting in 1981, but it retained a hard-edged "attitude" that undercut any sense of complacency about an inclusive American society.

Poverty amid Prosperity

Federal tax and budget changes had different effects on the rich and poor (see Figure 13-1). Popular attention to the lifestyles of upscale Manhattan and Beverly Hills obscured the economic realities for many Americans. Those in the top fifth increased their share of after-tax income relative to everyone else during the 1980s, and the richest 1 percent saw their share of all privately held wealth grow from 31 percent to 37 percent. The 1981 tax cuts also came with sharp increases in the Social Security tax, which hit lower income workers the hardest. The tax changes meant that the average annual income of households in the bottom 20 percent *declined* and that many actually paid higher taxes.

The budget changes that fueled conspicuous consumption put pressure on American cities. Cities and their residents absorbed approximately two-thirds of the cuts in the 1981–1982 federal budget. Provisions for accelerated depreciation (tax write-offs) of factories and equipment in the 1981 tax act encouraged the abandonment of center-city factories in favor of new facilities in the suburbs. One result was a growing jobs-housing mismatch. There were often plenty of jobs in the suburbs, but the poorer people who most needed the jobs were marooned in city slums and dependent on public transit that seldom served suburban employers.

Federal tax and spending policies in the 1980s decreased the security of middle-class families. As the economy continued to struggle through deindustrialization, average wage rates fell in the 1980s when measured in real purchasing. The squeeze put pressure on traditional family patterns and pushed women who might otherwise have stayed home into the work force. Even with two incomes, many families found it hard to buy a house because of skyrocketing prices in urban markets and sky-high interest rates. The national home ownership rate actually fell for the first time in almost fifty years, from 66 to 64 percent of

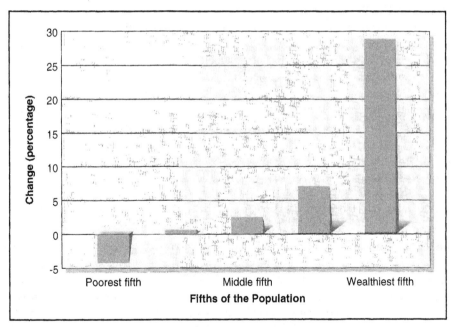

FIGURE 13-1 **Changes in Real Family Income, 1980–1990**
In the 1980s, the poor got poorer, the middle class made slight gains, and the most affluent 20 percent of the American people did very well. Tax changes that helped well-off households were one factor. Another factor was the erosion of "family-wage jobs" in manufacturing.

American households. Many Americans no longer expected to surpass their parents' standard of living.

Corporate Downsizing and White-collar Jobs Lower paying office jobs fell under the same sorts of pressure as factory jobs. Banks substituted ATMs for tellers, telephone companies replaced operators with automated information lines, and credit card companies computerized their operations to eliminate hand sorting of charge slips. Increasing numbers of clerical and office workers were "temps" who shifted from job to job. Organizations of all sorts, from corporations to universities, realized that a shift toward temporary and part-time workers not only kept wages low but also allowed less spending on health insurance and other benefits.

The chill of corporate "downsizing" hit white-collar families most heavily toward the end of the 1980s. Big business consolidations delivered improved profits by squeezing the ranks of middle managers as well as assembly-line workers. With fewer workers to supervise and with new technologies to collect and distribute information, companies could complete their cost cutting by trimming administrators. Takeovers sometimes meant the elimination of the entire management and support staff of target companies. In the 1950s, a college graduate could sign on with a large corporation like IBM or General Motors, advance through the ranks, and expect to retire from the same company. Now the expectation of a "job for life" looked dubious; AT&T, for one example, eliminated 76,000 jobs—one-fifth of its total—between 1985 and 1989. Those white-collar workers whose jobs survived clung to them more firmly than ever. The combined result was to clog the ladder of economic opportunity for college graduates, making the cab-driving Ph.D. and the *barrista* with the B.A. popular clichés.

Increase in the Poverty Rate At the lower end of the economic ladder, the proportion of Americans living in poverty increased. After declining steadily from 1960 to a low of 11 percent in 1973, the poverty rate climbed back to the 13 to 15 percent range. Although the economy in the 1980s created lots of new jobs, half of them paid less than poverty-level wages. Conservative critics began to talk about an underclass of Americans permanently outside the mainstream economy because of poor education, drug abuse, or sheer laziness. In fact, talk of an underclass was a way to avoid confronting the realities of limited economic opportunity. Most of the nation's millions of poor people lived in households with employed adults. In 1992, fully 18 percent of all full-time jobs did not pay enough to lift a family of four out of poverty, a jump of 50 percent over the proportion of underpaid jobs in 1981. One of the biggest barriers to better employment was not a disinterest in work, but rather the isolation of many job seekers in poverty neighborhoods without access to suburban jobs or the informal social networks that are the best way to find good employment.

The Wage Gap and the Feminization of Poverty Nor could most women, even those working full time, expect to earn as much as men. In the 1960s and 1970s, the average working woman earned just 60 percent of the earnings of the average man. Only part of the wage gap could be explained by measurable factors, such as education or experience. The gap narrowed in the 1980s, with women's earnings rising to 74 percent of men's by 1996 but falling back to 72 percent in 2000. About half of the change was the result of bad news, namely, a decline of earnings among men as high-wage factory jobs disappeared. The other half was the positive result of better educated younger women finding better jobs. Indeed, women took 56 percent of the four-year college degrees awarded in 1998 (up from 38 percent in 1960) and 43 percent of first professional degrees (up from 3 percent).

Nevertheless, the low earning capacity of women with limited education meant that women were far more likely than men to be poor. Women constituted nearly two-thirds of poor adults at the end of the 1980s. Only 6 percent of married-couple households were below poverty level, but 32 percent of households headed by a woman without a husband present were poor. The feminization of poverty and American reliance on private support for child rearing also meant that children had a higher chance of living in poverty than adults and that poor American children were worse off than their peers in other advanced nations.

Homelessness in America Falling below even the working poor were growing numbers of homeless Americans. Large cities have always had transient laborers, derelict alcoholics, and voluntarily homeless hobos. In the 1980s, several factors made homelessness more visible and pressing. A new approach to the treatment of the mentally ill reduced the population of mental hospitals from 540,000 in 1960 to only 140,000 in 1980. Deinstitutionalized patients were supposed to receive community-based treatment, but many ended up on the streets and in overnight shelters. New forms of self-destructive drug abuse, such as crack addiction, joined alcoholism. A boom in downtown real estate destroyed old skid-row districts with their bars, missions, and dollar-a-night hotels.

These factors tripled the number of permanently homeless people during the early and middle 1980s, from 200,000 to somewhere between 500,000 to 700,000. Twice or three times that many may have been homeless for part of a given year. For every person in a shelter on a given night, two people were sleeping on sidewalks, in parks, in cars, and in abandoned buildings. Because homeless people made middle-class Americans uncomfortable, it was reassuring to assume they were outsiders attracted by local conditions, such as tolerant attitudes (as some claimed in Seattle) or mild climate (as some claimed in Phoenix). In fact, few among the down-and-out have the resources to move from town to town. Bag ladies, panhandlers, working people, and yuppies were all parts of the same communities, neighbors in the broadest sense.

Consolidating the Revolution: George Bush

In 1988 George Bush, Reagan's vice president for eight years, won the presidential election with 56 percent of the popular vote and 40 out of 50 states. Bush's view of national and world politics reflected a background in which personal connections counted. He was raised as part of the New England elite, built an oil business in Texas, and then held a series of high-level federal appointments. As someone who had survived twenty years of bureaucratic infighting, his watchword was *prudence*. Using a comparison from baseball, Bush described himself as the sort of guy who would play the averages and "bunt 'em over" rather than go for the big inning.

Michael Dukakis, the Democratic nominee in 1988, was a dry-as-dust, by-the-numbers manager who offered the American people "competence." The Bush campaign director, Lee Atwater, looked for "hot-button" issues that could fit onto a 3-by-5 card. He found that Dukakis as governor of Massachusetts had delayed cleanup of Boston Harbor, favored gun control, and had vetoed a bill requiring schoolchildren to recite the Pledge of Allegiance (arguing correctly that it would be overturned in the courts). Even more damaging was that Massachusetts officials had allowed a murderer named Willie Horton a weekend furlough from prison, during which he had committed a brutal rape. Pro-Bush advertisements tapped into real worries among the voters—fear of crime, racial tension (Horton was black), worry about eroding social values. George Bush, despite his background in prep schools and country clubs, came out looking tough as nails, while the Democrats looked inept.

The ads locked Bush into a rhetorical war on crime and drugs that was his major domestic policy. Americans had good cause to be worried about public safety, but most were generally unaware that the likelihood of becoming the target of a violent crime had leveled off and would continue to fall in the 1990s or that crime was far worse in minority communities than elsewhere, in part due to gang- and drug-related activities.

The Bush administration stepped up the fight against illegal drugs and the federal drug-control budget tripled. In the early 1980s, a quarter of federal prison inmates were in jail for drug offenses. Longer sentences, mandatory jail time, and tougher parole terms for drug crimes pushed the proportion over 50 percent by 1990. The United States tried to stop the flow of cocaine by blockading its borders with airplanes, sea patrols, and specially trained dogs at airport customs lines. Casual and middle-class use of cocaine and marijuana began to decline in the mid-1980s. Drug use and drug sales were increasingly a problem of poor and minority neighborhoods.

George Bush believed that Americans wanted government to leave them alone. He ignored a flood of new ideas from entrepreneurial conservatives, such as Housing and Urban Development (HUD) Secretary Jack Kemp. The major legislation from the Bush administration were a transportation bill that shifted federal priorities from highway building toward mass transit and the **Americans with Disabilities Act** (1990) to prevent discrimination against people with physical handicaps.

The same attitude produced weak economic policies. The national debt had amounted to 50 percent of personal savings in 1980 but swelled to 125 percent by 1990. The massive budget deficits of the 1980s combined with growing trade deficits to turn the United States from an international creditor to a debtor nation. When Reagan took office, foreigners owed the United States and its citizens the equivalent of $2,500 for every American family. When Bush took office, the United States had used up its foreign assets and become the world's biggest debtor, with liabilities that averaged $7,000 per family. After pledging "no new taxes" in his campaign, Bush backed into a tax increase in 1990. The decision was in fact fiscally sound, correcting some of the effects of the 1981 tax cut, but voters found it hard to forget the president's waffling and attempts to downplay the importance of his decision.

The most conspicuous domestic event of the Bush administration—the "Rodney King riot" of April 1992 in Los Angeles—was a reminder of the nation's inattention to the problems of race and poverty. Rodney King was a black motorist who had been savagely clubbed and kicked by police officers while being arrested after a car chase on March 3, 1991. A nearby resident captured the beating on videotape from his apartment. Within two days, the tape was playing and replaying on national television. The grainy pictures shocked the nation and confirmed the worst black fears about biased police behavior. Early the next year, the four officers stood trial for unjustified use of force before a suburban jury. The televised trial and the unexpected verdict of not guilty on April 29 stirred deep anger that escalated into four days of rioting.

The disorder revealed multiple tensions among ethnic groups and was far more complex than the Watts outbreak of 1965. African Americans from south central Los Angeles participated, but so did Central American and Mexican immigrants in adjacent districts, who accounted for about one-third of the 12,000 arrests. The disorder spread south to Long Beach and north to the edge of upscale neighborhoods in Westwood and Beverly Hills. Rioters assaulted the downtown police headquarters, city hall, and the *Los Angeles Times* building. As in 1965, some targets were white passers-by and symbols of white authority. But members of competing minority groups were also victims as angry black people targeted hundreds of Korean-owned and Vietnamese-owned shops as symbols of economic discrimination. Four days of disorder left fifty-eight people dead, mostly African Americans and Latinos.

THE SECOND (SHORT) COLD WAR

Ronald Reagan entered office determined to reassert U.S. leadership in world affairs and not to lose the Cold War. He considered the Soviet Union not a coequal nation with legitimate world interests, but an "evil empire," like something from the *Star Wars* movies. After the era of détente, global tensions had started to mount in the late 1970s. They were soon higher than they had been since the 1960s. But by the end of Reagan's second term, unexpected changes were rapidly bringing the Cold War to an end, and George Bush faced a radically new set of foreign-policy issues.

Confronting the Soviet Union

Who renewed the Cold War after Nixon's diplomacy of détente and Carter's early efforts at negotiation? The Soviets had pursued military expansion in the 1970s, triggering the fear that they might stage a nuclear Pearl Harbor. The Soviet Union in 1980 was supporting Marxist regimes in civil wars in Angola, Ethiopia, Nicaragua, and especially Afghanistan, where its 1980 intervention led to a decade of costly and futile military occupation. Were these actions parts of a careful plan? Or did they result from the Cold War inertia of a rudderless nation that reacted to situations one at a time? Given the aging Soviet leadership and the economic weaknesses revealed in the late 1980s, it makes more sense to see the Soviets as muddling along rather than executing a well-planned global strategy.

On the American side, Reagan's readiness to confront "the focus of evil in the modern world" reflected the views of many conservative supporters that the Soviet Union was a monolithic and ideologically motivated foe bent on world conquest. In hindsight, some Reaganites claim that the administration's foreign policy and massive increases in defense spending were part of a deliberate and coordinated scheme to check a Soviet offensive and bankrupt the Soviet Union by pushing it into a new arms race. It is just as likely, however, that the administration's defense and foreign policy initiatives were a set of discrete but effective decisions.

The Reagan administration reemphasized central Europe as the focus of superpower rivalry, just as it had been in the 1950s and early 1960s. To counter improved Soviet armaments, the United States began to place cruise missiles and midrange Pershing II missiles in Europe in 1983. NATO governments approved the action, but it frightened millions of their citizens. By the mid-1980s, many Europeans saw the United States as the dangerous and aggressive force in world affairs and the Soviet Union as the voice of moderation—international attitudes that continue to this day.

The controversy over new missiles was part of new thinking about nuclear strategy. Multiple warheads on U.S. missiles already allowed Washington to target 25,000 separate places in the Soviet Union. National Security Directive D-13 (1981) set forth a new doctrine that it might be possible to fight and win a nuclear war, despite its enormous costs. A reactivated civil-defense program also suggested that the United States was serious about nuclear war. All Americans needed for survival, said one administration official, were "enough shovels" to dig fallout shelters.

Escalation of the nuclear arms race reinvigorated the antiwar and antinuclear movement in the United States as well as Europe. Drawing on the experience of the antiwar movement, the nuclear-freeze campaign caught the imagination of many Americans in 1981 and 1982. It sought to halt the manufacture and deployment of new atomic weapons by the great powers. The movement gained urgency when distinguished scientists argued that the smoke and dust thrown up by an atomic war would devastate the ecology of the entire globe by triggering "nuclear winter." Nearly a million people turned out for a nuclear-freeze rally in New York in 1982. Hundreds of local communities endorsed the freeze or took the symbolic step of declaring themselves "nuclear-free zones."

In response, Reagan announced the **Strategic Defense Initiative (SDI)** or "Star Wars" program in 1983. SDI was to deploy new defenses that could intercept and destroy ballistic missiles as they rose from the ground and arced through space. Ideas included super-lasers, killer satellites, and clouds of projectiles to rip missiles to shreds before they neared their targets. All of the technologies were untested; some existed only in the imagination. Few scientists thought that SDI could work. Many arms control experts thought that defensive systems were dangerous and destabilizing, because strong defenses suggested that a nation might be willing to risk a nuclear exchange. Nevertheless, President Reagan found SDI appealing, for it offered a way around the balance of terror.

Risky Business: Foreign-Policy Adventures

The same administration that sometimes seemed reckless in its grand strategy also took risks to assert U.S. influence in global trouble spots to block or roll back Soviet influence. Reagan asserted America's right to intervene anywhere in the world to support local groups who were fighting against Marxist governments. The assumption underlying this assertion, which later became known as the **Reagan Doctrine**, was that Soviet-influenced governments in Asia, Africa, and Latin America needed to be eliminated if the United States was to win the Cold War.

Nevertheless, Reagan kept the United States out of a major war and backed off in the face of serious trouble. Foreign interventions were designed to achieve symbolic victories rather than change the global balance of power. The exception was the Caribbean and Central America, the "backyard" where the United States had always claimed an overriding interest and where left-wing action infuriated Reagan's conservative supporters.

On October 25, 1983, for example, U.S. troops invaded the small independent Caribbean island of Grenada. A left-leaning government had invited Cuban help in building an airfield, which the United States feared would turn into a Cuban military base. Two thousand American troops overcame Cuban soldiers who were thinly disguised as construction workers, "rescued" American medical students, and put a more sympathetic and locally popular government in power.

Intervention and Covert Activities in Central America The Reagan administration attributed political turmoil in Central America to Soviet influence and to arms and agitators from Soviet-backed Cuba. Between 1980 and 1983, the United States sent more military aid to conservative governments and groups in Central America than it had during the previous thirty years. Indeed, Central America became the focus of a secret foreign policy operated by the CIA and then by National Security Council (NSC) staff, since a Democratic Congress was not convinced of the danger. The CIA and the NSC engaged not just in espionage but also in direct covert operations. The chief target was Nicaragua, the Central American country where leftist Sandinista rebels had overthrown the Somoza dictatorship in 1979. Reagan and his people were determined to prevent Nicaragua from becoming "another Cuba," especially when Sandinistas helped left-wing insurgents in neighboring El Salvador. In the early 1980s, Reagan approved CIA plans to arm and organize approximately 10,500 so-called Contras, from the remnants of Somoza's national guard. From bases in Honduras, the Contras harassed the Sandinistas with sabotage and raids. Reagan called the Contras "freedom fighters," listened to stories of their exploits, and hunched over maps to follow their operations in detail. Meanwhile, Americans with different views aided refugees from the war zones of Central America through the church-based sanctuary movement ("sanctuary" could imply both legal economic assistance and direct defiance of efforts to deport refugees).

The Reagan administration bent the law to support this covert effort to overthrow the Sandinista regime. An unsympathetic Congress blocked U.S. funding for the Contras. In response, CIA director William Casey directed Lieutenant Colonel Oliver North of the National Security Council staff to illegally organize aid from private donors. The arms pipeline operated until a supply plane was shot down in 1986. The Contras failed as a military effort, but the civil war and international pressure persuaded the Sandinistas to allow free elections that led to a democratic, centrist government.

The War Against Drugs The American war against drugs was simultaneously shaping U.S. policy in the Caribbean and straining relations with Latin America. The United States pressured South American nations such as Colombia and Peru to uproot coca plants grown by poor farmers. As president, George Bush also parlayed the war on drugs into war on Panama during his first year in office. General Manuel Noriega, the Panamanian strongman, had once been on the CIA payroll. He had since turned to international drug sales in defiance of United States antismuggling efforts. On December 20, 1989, American troops invaded Panama, hunted down Noriega, and brought him back to stand trial in the United States on drug-trafficking charges. A handful of Americans and thousands of Panamanians died, many of them civilians caught in crossfire.

Intervention in the Middle East If the results of intervention in Nicaragua and Panama were mixed, intervention in the Middle East was a failure. In 1982 Israel invaded Lebanon, a small nation to its north, to clear Palestinian guerrillas from its borders and to set up a friendly Lebanese government. The Israeli army bogged down in a civil war between Christian Arabs and Muslims. Reagan sent U.S. Marines to preserve the semblance of a Lebanese state and to provide a face-saving exit for Israel. Although the Marines arrived in Beirut to interpose themselves between Israeli tanks and the Lebanese, they remained on an ill-defined "presence mission" that angered Arabs and motivated terrorist actions against Israel and the United States among Islamic radicals. In October 1983, a terrorist car bomb killed 241 Marines in their barracks. The remainder were soon gone, confirming the Syrian observation that Americans were "short of breath" when it came to Middle East politics. The debacle in Lebanon undermined United States-backed peace initiatives in the Middle East. Continuing terrorist acts such as taking Americans hostage, bombing cruise ships, and sabotaging airliners were aimed at inhibiting U.S. support of Israel.

The Iran-Contra Affair Even less effective were the Reagan administration's secret efforts to sell weapons to Iran in return for Iranian help in securing the release of Americans held hostage by pro-Iranian Islamic radicals in Lebanon. The United States in 1985 joined Israel in selling five hundred antitank missiles to Iran, then embroiled in a long, bitter war with Iraq. The deal followed stern public pronouncements that the United States would never negotiate with terrorists—and considered Iran's religious leaders to be backers of international terrorism. It also violated this nation's official trade embargo against Iran that had been in place since the U.S. embassy seizure in 1980. In May 1986, National Security advisor Robert McFarlane flew to Iran for more arms-for-hostages talks, carrying a chocolate cake and a Bible autographed by Reagan to present to the Iranian leader Ayatollah Khomeini. The pro-Iranian radicals released several hostages, but others were soon taken. When the deals came to light in 1986 and Congressional hearings were held in the summer of 1987, Americans were especially startled to learn that Colonel North had funneled millions of dollars from the arms sales to the Nicaraguan Contras, in a double evasion of the law.

As had been true with Watergate, the Iran-Contra affair was a two-sided scandal. First was the blatant misjudgment of operating a secret, bumbling, and unlawful foreign policy that depended on international arms dealers and ousted Nicaraguan military officers. Second was a concerted effort to cover up the illegal and unconstitutional actions. North shredded relevant documents and lied to Congress. In his final report in 1994, Special Prosecutor Lawrence Walsh found that President Reagan and Vice President Bush were aware of much that went on and participated in efforts to withhold information and mislead Congress.

U.S. Policy in Asia American policy in Asia was a refreshing contrast with practices in Central America and the Middle East. In the Philippines, American diplomats helped push corrupt President Ferdinand Marcos out and opened the way for a popular uprising to put Corazon Aquino in office. Secretary of State George Shultz made sure that the United States supported popular democracy while reassuring the Philippine military. In South Korea, the United States similarly helped ease out an unpopular dictator by firmly supporting democratic elections that brought in a more popular but still pro-United States government.

Embracing Perestroika

Thaw in the Cold War started in Moscow. Mikhail Gorbachev became general secretary of the communist party in 1985, when the Soviet Union was trapped in the sixth year of its failed attempt to control Afghanistan. Gorbachev was the picture of vigor compared to his three elderly predecessors. A master of public relations who charmed western Europe's leaders and public, he was also a modernizer in a long Russian tradition that stretched back to Tsar Peter the Great in the eighteenth century. Gorbachev startled Soviet citizens by urging **glasnost**, or political openness with free discussion of issues and relaxation of controls on the press. He followed by setting the goal of **perestroika**, or restructuring of the painfully bureaucratic Soviet economy that was falling behind capitalist nations. His hope was that market-oriented reforms would help the Soviet Union keep up with the United States.

Gorbachev decided that he needed to reduce the crushing burden of Soviet defense spending if the Soviet Union was to have any chance of modernizing. During Reagan's second term, the Soviets offered one concession after another in a drive for arms control. They agreed to cut the number of land-based strategic weapons in half. They gave up their demand for an end to SDI research. In negotiations on conventional forces in Europe, they accepted bigger cuts for the Warsaw Pact nations than for NATO. They even agreed to on-site inspections to control chemical weapons.

Reagan had the vision (or audacity) to embrace the new Soviet position. He cast off decades of belief in the dangers of Soviet Communism and took Gorbachev seriously. One of his reasons for SDI had been his personal belief that the abolition of nuclear weapons was better than fine-tuning the balance of terror. Now he was willing to forget his own rhetoric. He frightened his own staff when he met with Gorbachev in the summer of 1986 and accepted the principle of deep cuts in strategic forces. Reagan explained that when he railed against the "evil empire," he had been talking about Brezhnev and the bad old days; Gorbachev and glasnost were different.

In the end, Reagan negotiated the **Intermediate Nuclear Force Agreement (INF)** over the strong objections of the CIA and the Defense Department. INF was the first true nuclear disarmament treaty (see the Overview table, "Controlling Nuclear Weapons: Four Decades of Progress"). Previous agreements had only slowed the growth of nuclear

CONTROLLING NUCLEAR WEAPONS: FOUR DECADES OF PROGRESS

Limiting the Testing of Nuclear Weapons	Limited Test Ban Treaty (1963)	Banned nuclear testing in the atmosphere, ocean, and outer space.
	Comprehensive Test Ban Treaty (1996)	Bans all nuclear tests, including underground tests. Rejected by U.S. Senate in 1999.
Halting the Spread of Nuclear Weapons	Nuclear Non-Proliferation Treaty (1968)	Pledged five recognized nuclear nations (United States, Soviet Union, Britain, France, China) to pursue disarmament in good faith, and 140 other nations not to acquire nuclear weapons.
	Strategic Arms Limitation Treaty (SALT I, 1972)	Limited the number of nuclear-armed missiles and bombers maintained by the United States and Soviet Union. Closely associated with United States-Soviet Union agreement to limit deployment of antiballistic missile systems to one site each.
	Strategic Arms Limitation Treaty (SALT II, 1979)	Further limited the number of nuclear-armed missiles and bombers. Not ratified but followed by Carter and Reagan administrations.
Reducing the Number of Nuclear Weapons	Intermediate Nuclear Force Agreement (1987)	Required the United States to eliminate 846 nuclear armed cruise missiles, and the Soviet Union to eliminate 1,846 SS-20 missiles.
	Strategic Arms Reduction Treaty (START I, 1991)	By July 1999, led to reductions of approximately 2,750 nuclear warheads by the United States and 3,725 warheads by the nations of the former USSR.
	Strategic Arms Reduction Treaty (START II, 1993)	Set further cuts in nuclear arsenals. Ratified by Russia in April 2000.

Data Source: Warhead data from Arms Control Association.

Mikhail Gorbachev and Ronald Reagan sign the Intermediate Nuclear Forces Treaty at the White House in 1987. The treaty marked a radical transformation in Reagan's approach to relations with the Soviet Union and lessened the military tension between NATO and the Soviet bloc in Europe.

weapons; they were "speed limits" for the arms race. The new pact matched Soviet SS-20s with American cruise missiles as an entire class of weapons that would be destroyed, with on-site inspections for verification.

Crisis and Democracy in Eastern Europe

President Bush loved to run the world by Rolodex. When someone's name came up at a formal dinner, he was likely to grab a phone and call the person up. When Congress was heading in the wrong direction, he started dialing senators and representatives. When a crisis threatened world peace, he would start chatting with presidents and prime ministers. He viewed diplomacy as a series of conversations and friendships among leaders, not the reconciliation of differing national interests.

As a believer in personal diplomacy, George Bush based much of his foreign policy on his changing attitudes toward Mikhail Gorbachev. He started lukewarm, talking tough to please the Republican right wing. Bush feared that Gorbachev, by instituting reforms that challenged the entrenched Communist party leaders, was being imprudent, one of the worst things Bush could say about another leader. Before 1989 was over, however, the president had decided that Gorbachev was OK. For the next two years, the United States pushed the prodemocratic transformation of Eastern Europe while being careful not to gloat in public or damage Gorbachev's position at home. He tried not to push the Soviet Union too hard and infuriate Russian hard-liners. "I don't want to do something that would inadvertently set back the progress," Bush said. Later asked whether the United States had a new foe after the end of the Cold War, Bush answered without hesitation; "The enemy is unpredictability. The enemy is instability."

The End of Communist Regimes in Eastern Europe The people of eastern Europe overcame both American and Soviet caution. Gorbachev had urged his eastern European allies to emulate perestroika to free their economies from stifling controls and proclaimed what his foreign ministry called the "Sinatra doctrine," alluding to the ballad, "My Way," popularized by Frank Sinatra. Each Communist nation could "do it its way" without fearing the Soviet tanks that had crushed change in Hungary in 1956 and Czechoslovakia in 1968. Instead of careful economic liberalization, the Warsaw Pact system collapsed. Poland held free elections in June 1989, Hungary adopted a democratic constitution in October, and prodemocracy demonstrations then forced out Communist leaders in other Eastern European countries. When East Germans began to flee westward through Hungary, the East German regime bowed to mounting pressure and opened the Berlin Wall on November 9. By the end of 1989, there were new democratic or non-Communist governments in Czechoslovakia, Romania, Bulgaria, and East Germany. These largely peaceful revolutions destroyed the military and economic agreements that had harnessed the satellites to the

Soviet economy (the Warsaw Pact and Comecon). The Soviet Union swallowed hard, accepted the loss of its satellites, and slowly withdrew its army from Eastern Europe.

German Reunification and the Dissolution of the Soviet Union Events in Europe left German reunification as a point of possible conflict. Soviet policy since 1945 had sought to prevent the reemergence of a strong, united Germany that might again threaten its neighbors. West German Chancellor Helmut Kohl removed one obstacle when he reassured Poland and Russia that Germany would seek no changes in the boundaries drawn after World War II. By July 1990, the United States and the Soviet Union had agreed that a reunited Germany would belong to NATO. The decision satisfied France and Britain that a stronger Germany would still be under the influence of the Western allies. In October, the two Germanies completed their political unification, although it would be years before their mismatched economies functioned as one. Reunification was the last step in the diplomatic legacy of World War II.

The final act in the transformation of the Soviet Union began with a failed coup against Mikhail Gorbachev in August 1991. The Soviet Union had held free elections in 1989. Now Gorbachev scheduled a vote on a new constitution that would decrease the power of the central Soviet government. Old-line Communist bureaucrats who feared the change arrested Gorbachev in his vacation house and tried to take over the government apparatus in Moscow. They turned out to be bumblers and drunks who had not secured military support and even failed to take over radio and television stations. Boris Yeltsin, president of the Russian Republic, organized the resistance. Muscovites flocked to support Yeltsin and defied tank crews in front of the Russian parliament building. Within three days, the plotters themselves were under arrest.

The wall that divided East from West Berlin from 1962 to 1989 was a hated symbol of the Cold War. When the Communist government of East Germany collapsed in November 1989, jubilant Berliners celebrated the opening of the wall and the reuniting of the divided city.

The coup hastened the fragmentation of the Soviet Union. Before the month was out, the Soviet parliament banned the Communist party. Gorbachev soon resigned. Previously suppressed nationalist feelings caused all of the fifteen component republics of the Soviet Union to declare their independence. The superpower Union of Soviet Socialist Republics ceased to exist. Russia remained the largest and strongest of the new states, followed by Ukraine and Kazakhstan.

The end of the Cold War leaves the historical assessment of the last half-century of U.S. foreign policy open to debate. Analysts agree that the relentless pressure of American defense spending helped bankrupt and undermine the Soviet Union. It is an open question whether this same American defense spending also weakened the United States's economy and its ability to compete in the world marketplace. Some scholars see the demise of the Soviet empire as ultimate justification for forty years of Cold War. Dissenters argue the opposite—that the collapse of European Communism shows that American leaders had magnified its threat. Before we can choose among differing views, we need to wait for scholars to explore Russian archives and develop a fuller history of Soviet Cold War policy to place alongside our understanding of U.S. policy (see the Overview table, "Why Did the Cold War End?").

• • • O V E R V I E W • • •

WHY DID THE COLD WAR END?

Commentators have offered a number of explanations for the rapid failure of the USSR and the collapse of Soviet power at the end of the 1980s. All of these factors made contributions to the complex unraveling of the Cold War.

Economic exhaustion	The United States in the late 1970s embarked on a great modernization and expansion of its military forces. The USSR exhausted its economy and revealed its technical backwardness by trying to keep pace. Gorbachev's policy of perestroika was an attempt to reduce the bureaucratic inertia of the economy.
Failure of leadership	The Soviet Union in the 1970s and early 1980s was governed by unimaginative bureaucrats. A closed elite that thought only of preserving their privileges and authority could not adapt to a changing world. The policy of glasnost was an effort to encourage new ideas.
Intervention in Afghanistan	The disastrous intervention in Afghanistan revealed the limits of Soviet military power. It alienated the large Muslim population of the USSR and brought disillusionment with the incompetence of its leaders.
Triumph of democratic ideas	As political discussion became more free, the appeal of democratic ideas took on its own momentum, especially in Eastern European satellite nations such as East Germany, Czechoslovakia, and Poland.
Power of nationalism	The collapse of the Soviet empire was triggered by the resurgence of national sentiments throughout the Soviet empire. National sentiments fueled the breakaway of the Eastern European satellite nations such as Hungary, Rumania, and Poland. Nationalism also broke up the USSR itself as fourteen smaller "socialist republics" declared independence of the Russian-dominated Union.

The Persian Gulf War

On August 2, 1990, President Saddam Hussein of Iraq seized the small neighboring oil-rich country of Kuwait. The quick conquest gave Iraq control of 20 percent of the world's oil production and reserves. President Bush demanded unconditional withdrawal, enlisted European and Arab allies in an anti-Iraq coalition, and persuaded Saudi Arabia to accept substantial U.S. forces for its protection against Iraqi invasion. Within weeks, the Saudis were host to tens of thousands of U.S. soldiers and hundreds of aircraft.

The background for Iraq's invasion was a simmering dispute over border oil fields and islands in the Persian Gulf. Iraq was a dictatorship that had just emerged from an immensely costly eight-year war with Iran. Saddam Hussein had depended on help from the United States and Arab nations in this war, but Iraq was now economically exhausted. Kuwait itself was a small, rich nation whose ruling dynasty enjoyed few friends but plenty of oil royalties. The U.S. State Department had signaled earlier in 1990 that it might support some concessions by Kuwait in the disputes. Saddam Hussein read the signal as an open invitation to do what he wanted; having been favored in the past by the United States, he probably expected denunciations but no military response.

The Iraqis gave George Bush a golden opportunity to assert America's world influence. The Bush administration was concerned that Iraq might target oil-rich Saudi Arabia. The importance of Middle Eastern oil helped enlist France and Britain as military allies and secure billions of dollars from Germany and Japan. Iraq itself had antagonized nearly all its neighbors. The collapse of Soviet power and Gorbachev's interest in cooperating with the United States meant that the Soviets would not interfere with U.S. plans.

Bush and his advisors offered a series of justifications for American actions. First, and most basic, were the desire to punish armed aggression and the presumed need to protect Iraq's other neighbors. In fact, there was scant evidence of Iraqi preparations against Saudi Arabia. The buildup of American air power plus the effective economic sanctions would have accomplished both protection and punishment. Sanctions and diplomatic pressure might also have brought withdrawal from most or all of Kuwait. However, additional American objectives—to destroy Iraq's capacity to create nuclear weapons and to topple Saddam's regime—would require direct military action.

The Persian Gulf itself offered an equally golden opportunity to the American and allied armed forces. Here were no tangled jungles, invisible guerrillas, or civilians caught in a civil war. The terrain was open and nearly uninhabited. The enemy had committed regular forces to traditional battle, where the superiority of American equipment and training would be telling. Indeed, the United States could try out the tactics of armored maneuver and close land-air cooperation that the Pentagon had devised to protect Germany against Soviet invasion.

Bush probably decided on war in October, eventually increasing the number of American troops in Saudi Arabia to 580,000. The United States stepped up diplomatic pressure by securing a series of increasingly tough United Nations resolutions that culminated in November 1990 with Security Council Resolution 678, authorizing "all necessary means" to liberate Kuwait. The president convinced Congress to agree to military action under the umbrella of the UN. The United States also ignored compromise plans floated by France and last-minute concessions from Iraq.

War began one day after the UN's January 15 deadline for Iraqi withdrawal from Kuwait. **Operation Desert Storm** opened with massive air attacks on command centers, transportation facilities, and Iraqi forward positions. The air war destroyed 40 to 50 percent of Iraqi tanks and artillery by late February. The attacks also seriously hurt Iraqi civilians by disrupting utilities and food supplies.

Americans found the **Persian Gulf War** fascinating. They bought millions of Middle East maps to follow the conflict. They watched CNN's live transmission of Baghdad under bombardment and stared at pictures of Patriot missiles presumably intercepting Iraqi Scud missiles. They read about Stealth fighter bombers that were invisible to radar and about precision-guided missiles (although most of the damage came from traditional bombing and low-tech A-10 antitank aircraft).

The forty-day rain of bombs was the prelude to a ground attack. Despite Saddam Hussein's threats that the coalition faced the "mother of all battles," the Iraqi military made the land war easy. They concentrated their forces near the Persian Gulf in Kuwait itself because they expected an amphibious landing near Kuwait City and a direct strike north along the coast. Instead, the allies moved 235,000 U.S., French, and British soldiers far into the interior. On February 24, 1991, these forces swept into Iraq in a great arc. Americans, Saudis, Syrians, and Egyptians advanced directly to liberate Kuwait. A cease-fire came one hundred hours after the start of the ground war. The Iraqis had been driven out of Kuwait, but the relatively slow advance of the left wing failed to prevent many of the Iraqi troops from escaping. Allied forces suffered only 240 deaths in action, compared to perhaps 100,000 for the Iraqis.

Bush directed Desert Storm with the "Vietnam syndrome" in mind, believing that Americans were willing to accept war only if it involved overwhelming U.S. force and ended quickly. The desire for a quick war, however, posed a problem. The United States hoped to replace Saddam Hussein without disrupting Iraqi society. Instead, the hundred-hour war incited armed rebellions in southern Iraq against Saddam by Shi'ite Muslims, a branch of Muslims who are a minority in that nation, and by ethnically distinct Kurds in the north. Because Bush and his advisors were unwilling to get embroiled in a civil war, they stood by while Saddam crushed the uprisings. In one sense, the United States won the war but not the peace. Saddam Hussein became a hero to many in the Islamic world simply by remaining in power. In another sense, Bush had accomplished exactly what he wanted: the restoration of the status quo. In 2002, however, President George W. Bush (the president's son, elected in 2000), made a change in the Iraqi regime a centerpiece of U.S. foreign policy.

GROWTH IN THE SUNBELT

The rise in the military and defense spending from the late 1970s through the early 1990s and the Persian Gulf War, was one of the most powerful sources of growth in the **Sunbelt**, the Southern and Western regions of the United States. Americans had discovered this "new" region in the 1970s. Kevin Phillips's book *The Emerging Republican Majority* (1969) first popularized the term "Sunbelt." Phillips pointed out that people and economic activity had been flowing southward and westward since World War II, shifting the balance of power away from the Northeast. Sections of the South and West, historically controlled from the Northeastern industrial core, have developed as independent centers of economic change.

The Sunbelt was a region of conservative voting habits where Republicans solidified their status as a majority party, a process continuing to the present. In the 1990s, the region's economic power was reflected in a conservative tone in both the Republican and Democratic parties and in the prominence of Southern political leaders. Indeed, the career of George Bush, who got his start in New England but gained his greatest success as a new Texan, epitomized the political trend toward the Sunbelt (see Map 13-1).

The rise of the Sunbelt, which is anchored by Florida, Texas, and California, reflected the leading economic trends of the 1970s and 1980s, including military spending, immigration

MAP 13-1 Fast-Growing and Shrinking Metropolitan Areas, 1900–2000
In the 1990s, boom cities were found in the Southeast, Southwest, and on the West Coast. In contrast, all of the large metropolitan areas that lost population were in Ohio, New York, or Pennsylvania, the area hardest hit by the decline of jobs in established manufacturing industries.

from Asia and Latin America, and recreation and retirement spending. Corporations liked the business climate of the South, which had weak labor laws, low taxes, and generally lower costs of living and doing business.

New factories dotted the Southern landscape, often in smaller towns rather than cities. General Motors closed factories in Flint, Michigan, but invested in a new Saturn plant in Spring Hill, Tennessee. In contrast to troubled industrial cities in the Northeast and Midwest, journalists and scholars found headlong prosperity in cities like Orlando, Charlotte, Atlanta, Dallas, and Phoenix. Houston, with sprawling growth, business spinoffs from NASA, and purring air conditioners, epitomized the booming metropolitan areas of the South and West. It was, said one reporter, "the place that scholars flock to for the purpose of seeing what modern civilization has wrought."

The Defense Economy

The Vietnam buildup and reinvestment in the military during the Carter (1977–1981) and Reagan (1981–1989) administrations fueled the growth of the Sunbelt. Over the forty years from the Korean conflict to the Persian Gulf War, the United States made itself the mightiest military power ever known. Military bases and defense contractors remolded the economic landscape, as mild winters and clear skies for training and operations helped the South and West attract more than 75 percent of military payrolls.

Big and small cities depended on defense spending. Southern California thrived on more than 500,000 jobs in the aircraft industry. Lockheed's huge Burbank plant drew thousands of families to the new suburbs of the San Fernando Valley; McDonnell-Douglas shaped the area around Los Angeles International Airport. Twelve thousand smaller firms and a third of the area's jobs depended on defense spending. A thousand miles away, visitors to Colorado

Springs could drive past sprawling Fort Carson and visit the new Air Force Academy, opened in 1958. Sunk deep from view was the North American Air Defense command post beneath Cheyenne Mountain west of the city. Malmstrom Air Force Base transformed Great Falls, Montana, from a manufacturing and transportation center into a coordinating center for Minuteman missiles targeted at Moscow and Beijing. Dark blue Air Force vans carried crews from Great Falls to missile sites dotted over a swath of rolling plains as vast as Maryland.

Defense spending underwrote the expansion of American science and technology. Nearly one-third of all engineers worked on military projects. Large universities, such as MIT, the University of Michigan, California Institute of Technology, and Stanford, were leading defense contractors. The modern electronics business started in New York, Boston and the San Francisco Bay area with research and development for military uses, such as guided-missile controls. California's Silicon Valley grew with military sales long before it turned to consumer markets. The space component of the aerospace industry was equally reliant on the defense economy, with NASA spending justified by competition with the USSR. NASA's centers were scattered across the South: launch facilities at the Kennedy Space Center in Cape Canaveral, Florida; research labs at Huntsville, Alabama; and Houston's Manned Spacecraft Center as the control center for the space exploration program.

New Americans

Few Americans anticipated the effects of the **Immigration and Nationality Act of 1965** which transformed the ethnic mix of the United States and helped to stimulate the Sunbelt boom. The new law initiated a change in the composition of the American people by abolishing the national quota system in effect since 1924. Quotas had favored immigrants from Western Europe and limited those from other parts of the world. The old law's racial bias contradicted the self-proclaimed role of the United States as a defender of freedom, and immigration reform was part of the propaganda battles of the Cold War. The new law gave preference to family reunification and welcomed immigrants from all nations equally. The United States also accepted refugees from Communist countries above the annual limits.

Immigration reform opened the doors to Mediterranean Europe, Latin America, and Asia. Legal migration to the United States surged from 1.1 million in 1960–1964 to nearly 4 million for 1990–1994. Nonlegal immigrants may have doubled the total number of newcomers in the 1970s and early 1980s. Not since World War I had the United States absorbed so many new residents from other countries. By the early 1990s, legal immigration accounted for 37 percent of all American population growth, compared with 10 percent before 1965. Meanwhile, over 2 million nonlegal immigrants had taken advantage of the Immigration Reform and Control Act of 1986 to legalize their presence in the United States.

Immigration changed the nation's ethnic mix. Members of officially defined ethnic and racial minorities accounted for 25 percent of Americans in 1990 and 30 percent in 2000. Roughly 28 million Americans had been born in other countries according to the 2000 census, or 10.4 percent of the population (see Table 13-1). This was lower than the high of 14.7 percent in 1910 but a great increase from the low of 4.7 percent in 1970. One-third of the foreign born were from Latin America and one-fourth were from Asia.

The largest single group of new Americans came from Mexico. The long shared border has facilitated easy movement from south to north. Especially in the border states of Texas, New Mexico, Arizona, and California, permanent immigrants have mingled with tourists, family members on visits, temporary workers, and other workers without legal permission to enter the United States. Mexican Americans in the later twentieth century were the largest minority group in many Southwestern and Western states. They were also transforming neighborhoods in Chicago and other Midwestern cities and changing everything from politics to the Catholic church.

TABLE 13.1

Major Racial and Ethnic Minorities in the United States

	1960 Population (in millions)	Percentage of total	2000 Population (in millions)	Percentage of total
American Indians	.5	0.3	2.5	0.9
Asians and Pacific Islanders	1.1	0.6	10.6	3.7
African Americans	18.9	10.5	34.7	12.3
Hispanics	not available		35.3	12.5

Source: United States Census Bureau

The East Coast has especially welcomed migrants from the West Indies and Central America. Many Puerto Ricans, who hold U.S. citizenship, came to Philadelphia and New York in the 1950s and 1960s. The 110th Street subway station in East Harlem marked the center of *El Barrio de Nueva York* for that city's 600,000 Puerto Ricans. Other countries sending large numbers of immigrants include Haiti, the Dominican Republic, Guatemala, Honduras, Nicaragua, El Salvador, and Jamaica. Cuban refugees from Castro's regime concentrated in Miami and in other major cities such as Chicago and New York.

Another great immigration has occurred eastward across the Pacific. Chinese, Filipinos, Koreans, Samoans, and other Asians and Pacific Islanders constituted only 6 percent of newcomers to the United States in 1965, but nearly half of all arrivals in 1990. The numbers of ethnic Chinese in the United States jumped from a quarter of a million in 1965 to 1,645,000 in 1990. Immigrants from Taiwan, Hong Kong, and the People's Republic created new Chinatowns in Houston and San Diego and crowded into the historic Chinatowns of New York and San Francisco.

The most publicized Asian immigrants were refugees from Indochina after Communist victories in 1975. The first arrivals tended to be highly educated professionals who had worked with the Americans. Another 750,000 Vietnamese, Laotians, and Cambodians arrived after 1976 by way of refugee camps in Thailand, as did Celia Noup. Most settled on the West Coast. The San Francisco Bay area, for example, had more than a dozen Vietnamese-language newspapers, magazines, and cable television programs. People in Silicon Valley knew Hewlett-Packard as "Little Vietnam" in the mid-1980s and Advanced Micro Devices as "Little Manila."

In addition to Southeast Asians, political conflicts and upheavals sent other waves of immigrants to the United States. Many Iranians fled the religious regime that took power in their country in the late 1970s, at the same time that Ethiopians were fleeing a nation shattered by drought, civil war, and doctrinaire Marxism. To escape repression in the Soviet Union, Jews and conservative Christians came to the United States in the 1980s, and the collapse of Communism in the Soviet Union opened the door for Russians, Ukrainians, Rumanians, and other eastern Europeans to emigrate to the United States in the 1990s.

Recent immigrants have found both economic possibilities and problems. On the negative side, legal and illegal immigration has added to the numbers of nonunion workers. By one estimate, two-thirds of the workers in the Los Angeles garment trade were undocumented immigrants. Most worked for small, nonunion firms in basements and storefronts, without health insurance or pensions. But a positive contrast was the abundance of opportunities for talent and ambition in the expanding economy of the mid-1980s and 1990s. The 130,000 Vietnamese immigrants of 1975 now have an average adjusted income above the national average. Asians and Pacific islanders by 2000 constituted 22 percent of students in California's public universities. Like earlier European immigrants, many newcomers have opened groceries, restaurants, and other businesses that serve their own group before expanding into larger markets. Juan Fernandez found it easier to set up a successful car repair shop in Gary, Indiana, than in Guadalajara, Mexico, because his fellow immigrants prefer a Spanish-speaking mechanic. Asian-born business owners have filled retail vacuums in central city neighborhoods abandoned by chain stores. One Korean told a typical story: "A friend of mine came over with his family. He invested a few dollars in a vegetable stand in downtown Manhattan. He and his sons got up early, went to the market early. . . . He took some of his earnings and invested in a candy store. Then he bought two more vegetable and fruit stands. . . . Their kids work hard too and they make a lot of money."

Old Gateways and New

The new immigration from Asia, Latin America, and the Caribbean had its most striking effects in coastal and border cities. New York again became a great mixing bowl of the American population. By 1990, some 28 percent of the population of New York City was foreign-born, compared to 42 percent at the height of European immigration in 1910. Journalist Andy Logan described the new immigrants' impact by the 1970s: "A third of the children now in the city's public schools are said to be the children of parents who were born in other countries. . . . Whole areas of the city, such as Washington Heights, in Manhattan, and Elmhurst, in Queens, would be half empty without the new arrivals." ZIP code 11373 in North Queens was reportedly the most diverse neighborhood in the world.

Just as important was the transformation of southern and western cities into gateways for immigrants from Latin America and Asia. Los Angeles emerged as "the new Ellis Island" that rivaled New York's historic role in receiving immigrants. As *Time* magazine put it in 1983, the arrival of more than 2 million immigrants in greater Los Angeles altered "the collective beat and bop of L.A." In 1960, a mere 1 percent of the Los Angeles County population was Asian and 11 percent was Hispanic. By 2000, the figures for a population of 9.5 million were 12 percent Asian and 45 percent Hispanic. The sprawling neighborhoods of East Los Angeles make up the second-largest Mexican city in the world. New ethnic communities appeared in Los Angeles suburbs: Iranians in Beverly Hills, Chinese in Monterey Park, Japanese in Gardena, Thais in Hollywood, Samoans in Carson, Cambodians in Lakewood. One hundred languages are spoken among students entering Los Angeles schools.

New York and Los Angeles are world cities as well as immigrant destinations. Like London and Tokyo, they are capitals of world trade and finance, with international banks and headquarters of multinational corporations. They have the country's greatest concentrations of international lawyers, accounting firms, and business consultants. The deregulation of international finance and the explosive spread of instant electronic communication in the 1980s confirmed their importance as global decision centers.

Similar factors turned Miami into the economic capital of the Caribbean. A quarter-million Cuban businessmen, white-collar workers, and their families had moved to the United States between 1959 and 1962 to escape Castro's new socialist government. New "freedom flights" carried 150,000 additional Cubans to the United States from 1966 to 1973 and a third round added 125,000 in 1980. Most of the newcomers stayed in south Florida. Cubans by the late 1970s owned about one-third of the area's retail stores and many of its other businesses. Their success in business made Miami a major Latino market and helped attract 2 million Latin American tourists and shoppers to its stores and hotels during the 1980s. Access to the Caribbean and South America also make Miami an international banking and commercial center with hundreds of offices for corporations engaged in U.S.-Latin American trade.

Cross-border communities in the Southwest, such as El Paso, Texas, and Juarez, Mexico, or San Diego, California, and Tijuana, Mexico, are "Siamese twins joined at the cash register."

Employees with work permits commute from Mexico to the United States. American popular culture flows southward. Bargain hunters and tourists pass in both directions. A shopping center near San Diego made 60 percent of its sales to Mexicans.

Both nations have promoted the cross-border economy. The Mexican government in the mid-1960s began to encourage a "platform economy" by allowing companies on the Mexican side of the border to import components and inputs duty-free as long as 80 percent of the items were reexported and 90 percent of the workers were Mexicans. The intent is to encourage American corporations to locate assembly plants south of the border. Such *maquila* industries can employ lower wage workers and avoid strict antipollution laws (leading to serious threats to public health on both sides of the border). From the Gulf of Mexico to the Pacific Ocean, eighteen hundred *maquiladora* plants employ half a million workers. North of the border, U.S. factories supply components under laws that mesh with the Mexican regulations.

The Graying of America

Retirees were another factor contributing to the growth of the Sunbelt. Between 1965 and 2000, the number of Americans aged 65 and over jumped from 18.2 million to 35 million, or 12.4 percent of the population. For the first time, most Americans could expect to survive into old age. The "young old" are people in their sixties and seventies who remain sharp, vigorous, and financially secure because of better private pensions, Social Security, and Medicare. The "old old" are the 9 million people in their eighties and nineties who often require daily assistance, although data show that improved medical services have made such Americans healthier and more self-sufficient than they were ten or twenty years ago.

Older Americans have become a powerful voice in public affairs. They tend to vote against local taxes but fight efforts to slow the growth of Social Security, even though growing numbers of the elderly are being supported by a relatively smaller proportion of working men and women. By the 1990s, observers noted increasing resentment among younger Americans, who fear that public policy is biased against the needs of men and women in their productive years. In turn, the elderly fiercely defend the programs of the 1960s and 1970s that have kept many of them from poverty. Protecting Medicare and Social Security was one of the Democrats' best campaign issues in 1996 and 2000, after Republicans suggested cuts in spending growth.

Retired Americans changed the social geography of the United States. Much growth in the South and Southwest has been financed by money earned in the Northeast and Midwest and transferred by retirees. Florida in the 1980s absorbed nearly 1 million new residents aged sixty or older. California, Arizona, Texas, the Carolinas, and the Ozark Mountains of Missouri and Arkansas have all attracted retirees, many of them in age-segregated communities such as Sun City near Phoenix.

VALUES IN COLLISION

In 1988, two very different religious leaders sought the presidential nomination. Pat Robertson's campaign for the Republican nomination tapped deep discontent with the changes in American society since the 1960s. A television evangelist, Robertson used the mailing list from his *700 Club* program to mobilize conservative Christians and pushed the Republican Party further to the right on family and social issues. Jesse Jackson, a civil-rights leader and minister from Chicago, mounted a grass-roots campaign with the opposite goal of moving the Democratic party to the left on social and economic policy. Drawing on his experience in the black civil rights movement, he assembled a "Rainbow Coalition" that included labor unionists, feminists, and others whom Robertson's followers feared. Both Jackson and Robertson used their powerful personalities and religious convictions to inspire support from local churches and churchgoers.

In diagnosing social ills, Robertson pointed to the problems of individual indulgence, while Jackson pointed to racism and economic inequality. Their sharp divergence expressed differences in basic values that divided Americans in the 1980s and beyond. In substantial measure, the conflicts were rooted in the social and cultural changes of the 1960s and 1970s that had altered traditional institutions, especially the 1950s ideal of a "Ward and June Cleaver" family. Changes in roles and expectations among women and new openness about gay and lesbian sexuality were particularly powerful in dividing American churches and politics.

Women's Rights and Public Policy

The women's liberation movement of the 1960s achieved important gains when Congress wrote many of its goals into law in the early 1970s. Title IX of the Educational Amendments (1972) to the Civil Rights Act prohibited discrimination by sex in any educational program receiving federal aid. The legislation expanded athletic opportunities for women and slowly equalized the balance of women and men in faculty positions. In the same year, Congress sent the Equal Rights Amendment (ERA) to the states for ratification. The amendment read, "Equal rights under the law shall not be denied or abridged by the United States or by any state on account of sex." More than twenty states ratified in the first few months. As conservatives who wanted to preserve traditional family patterns rallied strong opposition, however, the next dozen states ratified only after increasingly tough battles in state legislatures. The ERA then stalled, three states short, until the time limit for ratification expired in 1982.

Abortion Rights and the Conservative Backlash In January 1973, the U.S. Supreme Court expanded the debate about women's rights with the case of *Roe v. Wade*. Voting 7 to 2, the Court struck down state laws forbidding abortion in the first three months of pregnancy and set guidelines for abortion during the remaining months. Drawing on the earlier decision of *Griswold v. Connecticut*, which dealt with birth control, the Court held that the Fourteenth Amendment includes a right to privacy that blocks states from interfering with a woman's right to terminate a pregnancy. The Supreme Court later upheld congressional limitations on the use of federal funds for abortion in *Webster v. Reproductive Health Services* (1989) and allowed some state restrictions in *Planned Parenthood v. Casey* (1992). Nevertheless, the *Roe* decision remained in place.

These changes came in the context of increasingly sharp conflict over the feminist agenda. Both the ERA and *Roe* stirred impassioned support and equally passionate opposition. Behind the rhetoric were male fears of increased job competition during a time of economic contraction and concern about changing families. Also fueling the debate was a deep split between the mainstream feminist view of women as fully equal individuals and the contrary conservative belief that women had a special role as anchors of families, an updating of the nineteenth-century idea of separate spheres. For conservative politicians, the ERA was a good "wedge issue" that could help split religious conservatives from the Democratic party. The debate about abortion drew on the same issue of women's relationship to families but added strong religious voices, particularly the formal opposition of the Roman Catholic church to abortion. The arguments also tapped such deep emotion that the two sides could not even agree on a common language, juxtaposing a right to life against rights to privacy and freedom of choice.

Women in the Work Force The most sweeping change in the lives of American women did not come from federal legislation or court cases, but from the growing likelihood that a woman would work outside the home. In 1960, some 32 percent of married women were in the labor force; forty years later, 61 percent were working or looking for work (along with 69 percent of single women). Federal and state governments slowly responded to the changing demands of work and family with new policies such as a federal child-care tax credit.

More women entered the work force as inflation in the 1970s and declining wages in the 1980s eroded the ability of families to live comfortable lives on one income. Between 1979 and 1986, fully 80 percent of married households saw the husband's income fall in constant dollars. The result was headlined in the *Wall Street Journal* in 1994: "More Women Take Low-Wage Jobs Just So Their Families Can Get By."

A second reason for the increase in workingwomen from 29 million in 1970 to 66 million in 2000 was the broad shift from manufacturing to service jobs, reducing demand for factory workers and manual laborers and increasing the need for such "women's jobs" as data entry clerks, reservation agents, and nurses. Indeed, the American economy still divides job categories by sex. There was some movement toward gender-neutral hiring in the 1970s because of legal changes and the pressures of the women's movement. Women's share of lawyers more than quadrupled, of economists more than tripled, and of police detectives more than doubled. Nevertheless, job types were more segregated by sex than by race in the 1990s.

Coming Out

New militancy among gay men and lesbians drew on several of the social changes of the late 1960s and 1970s. Willingness to acknowledge and talk about nonstandard sexual behavior was part of a change in public values. Tactics of political pressure came from the antiwar and civil rights movements. The timing, with a series of key events from 1969 to 1974, coincided with that of women's liberation.

Gay activism spread from the biggest cities to smaller communities, from the coasts to Middle America. New York police had long harassed gay bars and their customers. When police raided Manhattan's Stonewall Inn in June 1969, however, patrons fought back in a weekend of disorder. The **Stonewall Rebellion** was a catalyst for homosexuals to assert themselves as a political force. San Francisco also became a center of gay life. Its large homosexual community dated to World War II, when gays discharged from the armed forces in the Pacific theater were processed out through San Francisco. Openly gay poets and artists were prominent in the city's avant-garde circles. By the late 1970s, the city had more than three hundred business and social gathering places identified as gay and lesbian.

With New Yorkers and San Franciscans as examples, more and more gay men and lesbians "came out," or went public about their sexual orientation. They published newspapers, organized churches, and lobbied politicians for protection of basic civil rights such as equal access to employment, housing, and public accommodations. They staged "gay pride" days and marches. In 1974, the American Psychiatric Association eliminated homosexuality from its official list of mental disorders.

The character of life in gay communities took an abrupt turn in the 1980s when a new worldwide epidemic began to have an impact on the United States. Scientists first identified a new disease pattern, **acquired immune deficiency syndrome (AIDS)**, in 1981. The name described the symptoms resulting from the human immunodeficiency virus (HIV), which destroys the body's ability to resist disease. HIV is transferred through blood and semen. In the 1980s, the most frequent American victims were gay men and intravenous drug users.

A decade later, it was clear that HIV/AIDS was a national and even global problem. By early in the twenty-first century, AIDS had been responsible for approximately 500,000 deaths in the United States, and transmission to heterosexual women was increasing. The U.S. Centers for Disease Control and Prevention estimated roughly forty thousand new cases of HIV infection per year in the late 1990s, bringing the total close to 800,000. Once a problem of big cities, HIV infection had spread to every American community and had helped to change American attitudes about the process of dying through the spread of hospices for the care of the terminally ill. Meanwhile, the toll of AIDS deaths in other parts of the world, particularly eastern Africa, dwarfed that in the United States and made AIDS a world health crisis.

HIV/AIDS triggers many of the same intense emotions as polio. It strikes people in their prime and gradually wastes their strength. Because it first seemed narrowly targeted at specific groups, the spread of the epidemic inspired intense anger among gays who believed

that straight society and government agencies were indifferent to their plight. The Aids Coalition to Unleash Power, or ACT UP, used aggressive and sometimes outrageous tactics to pressure the government to increase funding and speed the approval process for new drugs. According to AIDS researcher Anthony Fauci, AIDS activists changed the practice of medicine in the United States for the better by giving patients greater control of their own treatment.

At the same time, HIV/AIDS remains as daunting scientifically as it has been politically volatile. Even as new drugs extended survival rates and made the disease relatively manageable for hundred of thousands of U.S. victims, a preventive vaccine has been much more elusive than the polio vaccine. In 2002, the federal budget allocated $2.8 billion for HIV/AIDS research and another $10 billion for prevention and treatment programs in the United States and other nations, amounts vastly greater than the funds spent fighting polio. If Salk's success confirmed American confidence

The AIDS Quilt, displayed in Washington in October 1992, combined individual memorials to AIDS victims into a powerful community statement. The quilt project reminded Americans that AIDS had penetrated every American community.

in the 1950s, the global struggle against HIV and AIDS mirrors the complexity of the twenty-first century.

By the 1990s, Americans were accustomed to open discussion of gay sexuality, if not always accepting of its reality. Television stars and other entertainers could "come out" and retain their popularity. So could politicians in selected districts. Tony Kushner's drama *Angels in America* (1993) won national prizes for its intense exploration of the impact of AIDS on an ordinary American community. On the issue of gays in the military, however, Congress and the Pentagon were more cautious, accepting a policy that made engaging in homosexual acts, though not sexual orientation itself, grounds for discharge.

Churches in Change

Americans picture mining frontiers as rip-roaring places, where a handful of women hold the fort while the men work hard, drink deep, and carry on. Modern Grand Junction, Colorado, however, is far less exciting. Between 1980 and 1984, efforts to develop the oil-shale resources of western Colorado pushed the population of Grand Junction from sixty thousand to eighty thousand. Hopes were high and money was easy, but there was also a boom in religion. Newcomers to Grand Junction, a fast-changing city within a rapidly evolving society, searched for family stability and a sense of community by joining established congregations and organizing new churches. The telephone book in 1985 listed twenty-eight mainstream Protestant and Catholic churches, twenty-four Baptist churches (reflecting the Oklahoma and Texas roots of many oil workers), five more liberal churches (such as Unitarians), and more than fifty Pentecostal, Bible, and Evangelical churches. Nearly a dozen Christian schools supplemented the public schools.

Grand Junction's religious bent is typical of the contemporary United States, where religion is prominent in daily lives, institutions, and public policy debates. Americans take their search for spiritual grounding much more seriously than do citizens of other industrial nations. Roughly half of privately organized social activity (such as charity work) is church related. In the mid-1970s, 56 percent of Americans said that religion was "very important" to them, compared to only 27 percent of Europeans.

As the Grand Junction statistics also suggest, mainline Protestant denominations that traditionally defined the center of American belief struggled after 1970. The United Methodist Church, the Presbyterian Church U.S.A., the United Church of Christ, and the Episcopal Church battled internally over the morality of U.S. foreign policy, the role of women in the ministry, and the reception of gay and lesbian members. They were strengthened by the ecumenical impulse, which united denominational branches that had been divided by ethnicity or regionalism. However, they gradually lost their position among American churches, perhaps because ecumenism diluted the certainty of their message. Liberal Protestantism has also historically been strongest in the slow-growing Northeast and Midwest.

By contrast, evangelical Protestant churches have benefited from the direct appeal of their message and from strong roots in the booming Sunbelt. Members of evangelical churches (25 percent of white Americans) now outnumber the members of mainline Protestant churches (20 percent). Major evangelical denominations include Baptists, the Church of the Nazarene, and the Assemblies of God. Fundamentalists, defined by a belief in the literal truth of the Bible, are a subset of evangelicals. So are 8 to 10 million Pentecostals and charismatics, who accept "gifts of the spirit," such as healing by faith and speaking in tongues.

Outsiders know evangelical Christianity through "televangelists." Spending on religious television programming rose from $50 to $600 million by 1980. The "electronic church" built on the radio preaching and professional revivalism of the 1950s. By the 1970s, it reached 20 percent of American households. Americans everywhere recognized the Big Four. Oral Roberts had a television show and Oral Roberts University in Oklahoma. Pat Robertson had the Christian Broadcasting Network in Virginia. Jerry Falwell claimed leadership of the Moral Majority (see "American Views: The Religious Imperative in Politics"). Jim and Tammy Faye Bakker had grand plans for real-estate developments before their schemes collapsed in fraud.

Behind the glitz and hype of the television pulpit, evangelical churches emphasized religion as an individual experience focused on personal salvation. Unlike many of the secular and psychological avenues to fulfillment, however, they also offered communities of faith that might stabilize fragmented lives. The conservative nature of their theology and social teaching in a changing society offered certainty that was especially attractive to many younger families.

Another important change in national religious life has been the continuing "Americanization" of the Roman Catholic church following the Second Vatican Council in 1965, in which church leaders sought to respond to postwar industrial society. In the United States, Roman Catholicism moved toward the center of American life, helped by the popularity of John Kennedy and by worldly success that made Catholics the economic peers of Protestants. Even as the tight connection between Catholicism and membership in European immigrant communities gradually faded, Asian and Latino immigrants brought new vigor to many parishes and many inner-city churches have been centers for social action. Church practice lost some of its distinctiveness; celebrating Mass in English rather than Latin was an important move toward modernization, but it also sparked a conservative countereffort to preserve the traditional liturgy. Traditional and nontraditional Catholics also disagree about whether priests should be allowed to marry and make other adaptations to American culture.

Culture Wars

In the 1950s and 1960s, Americans argued most often over foreign policy, racial justice, and the economy. Since the 1980s, they have also quarreled over beliefs and values, especially as the patterns of family life have become more varied. In the course of these quarrels, religious belief has heavily influenced politics as individuals and groups try to shape America around their particular, and often conflicting, ideas of the godly society. One expert talks about a division between cultural liberals and conservatives, another about "culture wars" between progressivism and orthodoxy. Americans who are undogmatic in religion are often liberal in politics as well, hoping to lessen economic inequities and strengthen individual social freedom. Religious conservatism and political conservatism also tend to go together. To some degree, this cultural division runs all the way through American society, dividing liberal North from conservative South, cities from small towns, and college professors from Kiwanis Club members.

The division on social issues is related to theological differences within Protestantism. The "conservative" emphasis on personal salvation and the literal truth of the Bible also expresses itself in a desire to restore "traditional" social patterns. Conservatives worry that social disorder occurs when people follow personal impulses and pleasures. In contrast, the "liberal" or "modern" emphasis on the universality of the Christian message restates the Social Gospel with its call to build the Kingdom of God through social justice and may recognize divergent pathways toward truth. Liberals worry that greed in the unregulated marketplace creates disorder and injustice.

The cultural conflict also transcends the historic three-way division of Americans among Protestants, Catholics, and Jews. Instead, the conservative-liberal division now cuts through each group. For example, Catholic reformers, liberal Protestants, and Reform Jews

The Religious Imperative in Politics

The strong religious faith of many Americans frequently drives them to different stands on political issues. The first of these two documents, a letter by Jerry Falwell to potential supporters of the Moral Majority, reflects the politically conservative outlook of many evangelical Christians. Falwell is pastor of the Thomas Road Baptist Church in Lynchburg, Virginia. He founded the Moral Majority, a conservative religious lobbying and educational organization, in 1979 and served as its president until 1987, the year he wrote the letter reprinted here. The second document, from an open letter issued by the Southside United Presbyterian Church in Tucson in 1982, expresses the conviction of other believers that God may sometimes require civil disobedience to oppose oppressive government actions. The letter explains the church's reasons for violating immigration law to offer sanctuary to refugees from repressive Central American regimes supported by the United States.

> How do Falwell and the Southside Presbyterian Church define the problems that demand a religious response?
>
> Are there any points of agreement?
>
> How does each statement balance the claims of God and government?

From the Reverend Jerry Falwell:

I believe that the overwhelming majority of Americans are sick and tired of the way that amoral liberals are trying to corrupt our nation from its commitment to freedom, democracy, traditional morality, and the free enterprise system.

And I believe that the majority of Americans agree on the basic moral values which this nation was founded upon over 200 years ago.

Today we face four burning crises as we continue in this Decade of Destiny; the 1980s loss of our freedom by giving in to the Communists; the destruction of the family unit; the deterioration of the free enterprise system; and the crumbling of basic moral principles which has resulted in the legalizing of abortion, wide-spread pornography, and a drug problem of epidemic proportions.

That is why I went to Washington, D.C., in June of 1979, and started a new organization The Moral Majority.

Right now you may be wondering: "But I thought Jerry Falwell was the preacher on the Old-Time Gospel Hour television program?"

You are right. For over twenty-four years I have been calling the nation back to God from the pulpit on radio and television.

But in recent months I have been led to do more than just preach. I have been compelled to take action.

I have made the commitment to go right into the halls of Congress and fight for laws that will save America. . . .

I will still be preaching every Sunday on the Old-Time Gospel Hour and I still must be a husband and father to my precious family in Lynchburg, Virginia.

But as God gives me the strength, I must do more. I must go into the halls of Congress and fight for laws that will protect the grand old flag . . . for the sake of our children and grandchildren.

From Southside United Presbyterian Church.

We are writing to inform you that Southside Presbyterian Church will publicly violate the Immigration and Nationality Act, Section 274 (A). . . .

We take this action because we believe the current policy and practice of the United States Government with regard to Central American refugees is illegal and immoral. We believe our government is in violation of the 1980 Refugee Act and international law by continuing to arrest, detain, and forcibly return refugees to the terror, persecution, and murder in El Salvador and Guatemala.

We believe that justice and mercy require that people of conscience actively assert our God-given right to aid anyone fleeing from persecution and murder. . . .

We beg of you, in the name of God, to do justice and love mercy in the administration of your office. We ask that "extended voluntary departure" be granted to refugees from Central America and that current deportation proceedings against these victims be stopped.

Until such time, we will not cease to extend the sanctuary of the church. . . . Obedience to God requires this of us all.

Sources: Gary E. McCuen, ed., *The Religious Right* (G. E. McCuen Publishers, 1989), pp. 11–14; Ann Crittenden, *Sanctuary* (Weidenfeld and Nicolson, 1988), p. 74.

may find agreement on issues of cultural values despite theologies that are worlds apart. The same may be true of conservative Catholics, fundamentalist Protestants, and Orthodox Jews.

Conservatives have initiated the culture wars, trying to stabilize what they fear is an American society spinning out of control because of sexual indulgence. In fact, the evidence on the sexual revolution is mixed. Growing numbers of teenagers reported being sexually active in the 1970s, but the rate of increase tapered off in the 1980s. The divorce rate began to drop after 1980. Births to teenagers dropped after 1990, and the number of two-parent families increased. Sexual advice and self-help books proliferated, with such titles as *Open Marriage* (1972) and *The Joy of Sex* (1972), but most adults remained staid and monogamous, according to data from 1994. Perhaps the logical extension of reading about sex in the 1970s was an astonishing eagerness to talk about sex in the 1990s, a decade when soap opera story lines and talk shows covered everything from family violence to exotic sexual tastes.

The explosion of explicit attention to sexual behavior set the stage for religiously rooted battles over two sets of issues. One cluster revolves around so-called family values, questioning the morality of access to abortion, the acceptability of homosexuality, and the roles and rights of women. A second set of concerns has focused on the supposed role of public schools in undermining morality through sex education, unrestricted reading matter, nonbiblical science, and the absence of prayer. Opinion polls show clear differences among religious denominations on issues such as censorship of library books, acceptability of racially segregated neighborhoods, freedom of choice in terminating pregnancy, and homosexuality.

Not all issues of the culture wars carry the same weight. Censorship of art exhibits and library collections has mostly been an issue for political grandstanding. U.S. senators grabbed headlines in 1989 by attacking the National Endowment for the Arts for funding "obscene" art, but a local jury in Cincinnati later proved tolerant of sexually explicit images in a photographic exhibition. Efforts to restrict legal access to abortion mobilized thousands of "right to life" advocates in the late 1980s and early 1990s, but illegal acts remained the work of a radical fringe.

A culturally conservative issue with great popular appeal in the early 1990s was an effort to prevent states and localities from protecting homosexuals against discrimination. Under the slogan "No special rights," antigay measures passed in Cincinnati, Colorado, and communities in Oregon in 1993 and 1994, only to have the Supreme Court overturn the Colorado law in *Romer v. Evans* (1996). It is important to note that public support for lesbian and gay civil rights varies with different issues (strong support for equal employment opportunity, much less for granting marriage rights to same-sex couples) and whether the issues are framed in terms of specified rights for gays or in terms of the right of everyone, including gays, to be free from government interference with personal decisions, such as living arrangements and sexual choices.

CONCLUSION

Americans entered the 1980s searching for stability. The 1970s had brought unexpected and uncomfortable change. Soviet actions in Asia and Africa seemed to be destabilizing the world. The memory of defeat in Vietnam left a bitter taste, and hostages in Tehran seemed to signal the end to America's global postwar dominance. Energy crises, inflation, and boarded-up factories eroded purchasing power and undermined confidence in the future. Traditional values seemed under siege. Ronald Reagan's presidential campaign played to these insecurities by promising to revitalize the older ways of life and restore the United States to its former influence.

Taken as a whole, the years from 1981 through 1992 brought transformations that redirected the course of American life. Because many changes were associated with national policy choices, it is fair to call this the era of the Reagan revolution. The astonishing collapse of the Soviet Union ended forty years of Cold War. New political leadership in Washington reversed the fifty-year expansion of federal government programs to deal with economic and social inequities. Prosperity alternated with recessions that shifted the balance between regions. The stock market rode a roller coaster, familiar corporate names vanished, and the national media made temporary heroes of business tycoons.

Economic inequality increased after narrowing for a generation at the same time that more and more leaders proclaimed that unregulated markets could best meet social needs. Middle-class Latinos and African Americans made substantial gains while many other minority Americans sank deeper into poverty.

At the same time, it is important to recognize that every revolution has its precursors. Intellectuals had been clarifying the justifications for Reagan administration actions since the 1960s. The Reagan-Bush years extended changes that had begun in the 1970s, particularly the conservative economic policies and military buildup of the troubled Carter administration. In retrospect, the growing weakness of the USSR should also have been apparent in the same decade, had not the United States been blinded by its fear of Communist power. Intervention in the Persian Gulf amplified American policies that had been in place since the CIA intervened in Iran in 1953. The outbreak of violence in Los Angeles after the Rodney King verdict showed that race relations were as tense as they had been in the 1960s.

In 1992, the United States stood as the undisputed world power. Its economy was poised for a surge of growth at the same time that rivals such as Japan were mired in economic crisis. It was the leader in scientific research and the development of new technologies. Its military capacities far surpassed those of any rival and seemed to offer a free hand in shaping the world—capacities that would be tested and utilized in the new century.

Review Questions

1. Is it accurate to talk about a Reagan revolution in American politics? Did Reagan's presidency change the economic environment for workers and business corporations? How did economic changes in the 1980s affect the prospects of the richest and poorest Americans?

2. How did American ideas about the proper role of government change during the 1980s? What were the basis of these changes?

3. What caused the breakup of the Soviet Union and the end of the Cold War? Did U.S. foreign policy under Reagan and Bush contribute significantly to the withdrawal of Soviet power from eastern Europe? Did the collapse of the USSR show the strength of the United States and its allies or the weakness of Soviet Communism?

4. How did the United States use military force during the Reagan and Bush administrations? Did military actions achieve the expected goals?

5. What were some of the important economic trends that shifted American growth toward the Sunbelt (South and West)? How has immigration from other nations affected the different American regions?

6. What changes in family roles and sexual behavior became divisive political issues? How have churches responded to cultural changes? What are some of the ways in which churches and religious leaders have tried to influence political decisions?

7. How did U.S. military involvement in Southeast Asia in the 1960s continue to affect American society for decades to come?

Key Terms

Acquired immune deficiency syndrome (AIDS) *415*

Americans with Disabilities Act *398*

Deregulation *391*

Economic Recovery and Tax Act of 1981 (ERTA) *391*

Glasnost *402*

Immigration and Nationality Act of 1965 *410*

Intermediate Nuclear Force Agreement (INF) *402*

Operation Desert Storm *407*

Persian Gulf War *408*

Perestroika *402*

Reagan Doctrine *400*

Roe v. Wade *414*

Sagebrush Rebellion *391*

Stonewall Rebellion *415*

Strategic Defense Initiative (SDI) *400*

Sunbelt *408*

Recommended Reading

Elijah Anderson, *Streetwise: Race, Class, and Change in an Urban Community* (1990). This is a deeply troubling portrait of the culture of the streets in the Philadelphia ghetto during the Reagan years.

Michael Beschloss and Strobe Talbott, *At the Highest Levels* (1993). A dramatic narrative of the last years of the Cold War, based on detailed interviews with American and Soviet participants.

Susan Bibler Coutin, *The Culture of Protest: Religious Activism and the U.S. Sanctuary Movement* (1993). Examining foreign policy from the grass roots, sympathetically portrays the meanings that participants in the sanctuary movement gave their actions.

Thomas Byrne Edsall and Mary D. Edsall, *Chain Reaction: The Impact of Race, Rights, and Taxes on American Politics* (1991). Argues that the Democratic party has systematically alienated its working-class supporters.

Frances Fitzgerald, *Way Out There in the Blue: Reagan, Star Wars, and the End of the Cold War* (2000). A detailed analysis of the technical weaknesses and political appeal of strategic missile defense.

Elliot Liebow, *Tell Them Who I Am: The Lives of Homeless Women* (1993). A sensitive depiction of "street people" and "bag ladies" as complex individuals coping with personal problems and economic crisis.

Kevin Phillips, *Boiling Point: Democrats, Republicans, and the Decline of Middle-Class Prosperity* (1992). Expresses the belief that the economic policies of the Reagan and Bush administrations systematically damaged working- and middle-class families.

Lillian Rubin, *Families on the Fault Line: America's Working Class Speaks about the Family, the Economy, Race, and Ethnicity* (1994). Interviews with American families about their efforts to cope with economic and social change.

Garry Wills, *Reagan's America: Innocents at Home* (1987). A biography critical of Reagan's ideas but insightful about his personality.

COMPLACENCY AND CRISIS: 1993-2004

I'm a firefighter for the FDNY [Fire Department New York]. I had gotten off the night before.... My friend woke me up early that morning to borrow my car to take his sick cat to the vet.... I was up so I went to my local bagel store for my coffee and paper.... when I heard a lady scream a plane had hit the Trade Center.... I thought since it was a beautiful day that perhaps a Cessna with the pilot having a heart attack had accidentally done this.... I ran home to put the TV on.... as soon as I saw what damage was done I knew this wasn't any Cessna.... my God people were jumping... phone rang it was a fellow from my station and he hadn't turned his TV on yet.... I screamed to him to turn his #*#* TV on....

When the second plane hit.... I said goodbye and told him I was going in.... I jumped in my car and was off to the races.... the highway was closed.... but open for us.... I had the gas pedal to the floor as I headed toward the city looking out my window I see both towers burning.... when I hear a rumble and see the south tower #2 fall.... I have to get my gear so I pull off the highway going down the on ramp.... arriving at the firehouse everyone's in shock and we know we gotta get there now to help.... as we're getting ready to leave the 2nd tower fell.... we commandeer a bus and we're off....

We arrived at a staging area and then finally got the ok to go in.... who's in charge?... Shoes, papers, and dust are everywhere.... we wait til [building] 7 collapses.... chief gets us into the site by going thru the financial center and bam there we are.... pieces of the outside wall sticking out of the highway.... cars on fire... buses gutted.... I saw numerous acts of courage that day both civilian and uniformed.... the looks on the faces of the people coming out of the city that day will haunt me forever... everyone was the same color.... dust white.... women crying.... men

423

crying. . . . we must never forget the men and women that died that day. . . . their sacrifice will live
on for generations to come. . . .

—John McNamara

John McNamara Story #400, The September 11 Digital Archive, 13 April 2002,
http://911digitalarchive.org/stories/details/400.

JOHN MCNAMARA was one of the many off-duty New York City fire fighters who
rushed to the World Trade Center after the terrorist attack on September 11, 2001.
Hijacking four commercial jetliners, the terrorists crashed one plane into the Pentagon and
one into each of the twin towers of the World Trade Center, high 110-story buildings that
housed fifty thousand workers at the peak of the workday. Like John McNamara, tens of
millions of Americans were jolted out of morning routines by riveting television coverage of
the burning towers and watched in horror as first one tower and then the other disintegrated into itself. September 11 was the occasion for terror and courage. Passengers on the
fourth plane fought the hijackers and made sure that it crashed in the Pennsylvania mountains rather than hitting a fourth target. Altogether, 479 police officers, fire fighters, and other
emergency workers died in the collapse of the towers. Thousands of volunteers rushed to
assist rescue efforts or contribute to relief efforts. As of November 2003, the confirmed total
of victims was 2,752 in New York, 184 at the Pentagon, and 40 in Pennsylvania.

The attacks, masterminded by the Al-Qaeda network of Muslim extremists, ended a
decade of prosperity at home and complacency about the place of the United States in the
world. In their aftermath, as Americans noticed millions of Muslim neighbors and tried to
balance civil liberties against national security, they realized how diverse the nation had
become. For most of the 1990s, prosperity allowed politics to focus on social issues, such as
health care and education, as well as on bitterly partisan, but often superficial, battles over
personalities and presidential behavior. However, the terrorists attacked buildings that were
the symbols of the nation's economic and military power. The aftermath of the attacks deepened a business recession that had followed a decade of growth spurred by new technologies. At the same time, the vulnerability of the targets undermined Americans' sense of
security and isolation from world problems, underscored the global reach of terrorism, and
made understanding its sources more necessary than ever.

KEY TOPICS

Moderate policies and conservative reactions during the Clinton administration.

Broadening participation in American politics.

Information technologies and economic prosperity.

New policies under President George W. Bush.

Terrorist attacks and a dangerous world.

THE POLITICS OF THE CENTER

In Bill Clinton's race for president in 1992, the "war room" was the decision center where
Clinton and his staff planned tactics and countered Republican attacks. On the wall was a
sign with a simple message: "It's the economy, stupid." The short sentence was a reminder
that victory lay in emphasizing everyday problems that George Bush had neglected.

• CHRONOLOGY •

1969	First version of Internet (ARAPnet) launched.	2000	George Bush defeats Al Gore Jr. in nation's closest presidential election.
1980	CNN begins broadcasting.	2001	Congress passes massive ten-year tax reduction.
1991	World Wide Web launched.		U.S. refuses to agree to Kyoto Treaty to limit global warning.
1992	Bill Clinton elected president.		
1993	Congress approves the North American Free Trade Agreement (NAFTA).		Terrorists crash airliners into World Trade Center and Pentagon.
	Congress adopts Family Leave Act.		U.S. military operations eliminate Taliban regime in Afghanistan.
1994	Independent Counsel Kenneth Starr begins investigation of Bill and Hillary Clinton.		Congress passes U.S. Patriot Act to combat domestic terror.
	Paula Jones files sexual harassment lawsuit against Bill Clinton.	2002	United States and Russia agree to cut number of deployed nuclear warheads.
	Republicans sweep to control of Congress.		Congress creates Department of Homeland Security.
	Federal government temporarily shuts down for lack of money.		United Nations Security Council passes resolution requiring Iraq to allow open inspections of weapons systems.
1995	United States sends troops to Bosnia.		
1996	Clinton wins a second term as president.		
1998	Paula Jones lawsuit dismissed.	2003	U.S. and British troops invade Iraq and topple government of Saddam Hussein.
	House of Representatives impeaches Clinton.		
1999	Senate acquits Clinton of impeachment charges.		Supreme Court upholds limited forms of affirmative action in university admissions.
	United States leads NATO intervention in Kosovo.		

Clinton promised economic leadership and stressed the need for private investment to create jobs. He promised to reduce government bureaucracy and the deficit, touted the value of stable families, and talked about health care and welfare reform. His message revealed an insight into the character of the United States in the 1990s. What mattered most were down-to-earth issues, not the distant problems of foreign policy that seemed to have little urgency with the end of the Cold War. As voters worried about the changing economy and its social consequences, they were eager for leaders who promised practical responses. The mid-1990s brought erratic swings between the two major parties, but the most reliable position was the center. As had happened time and again, the nation's two-party system punished extremes and rewarded practical leaders who claimed the middle of the road with such issues as economic growth.

Bill Clinton's election in 1992 and reelection in 1996 showed the attraction of the political center. The later 1990s and the beginning of the new century also suggest that national politics may be stabilizing around a relatively even balance between political parties and partisan agendas, somewhat like the years from 1876 to 1896. In his first inaugural address in January 1993, Clinton pledged "an end to the era of deadlock and drift and a new season of American renewal." What he found in his first four years in office was an equilibrium that resulted in narrow, bipartisan victories and defeats. In 1996, voters showed that they liked the nation's break from an activist government by keeping the balance of a Democratic White House and Republican Congress, and the presidential election of 2000 proved the closest in history.

The Election of 1992: A New Generation

Every fifteen to twenty years, a new group of voters and leaders comes to power, driven by the desire to fix the mess that the previous generation left behind. The men and women who came of age during World War II learned to accept the need to struggle and to expect success. Their attitudes shaped the Cold War, dynamic conservatism, the New Frontier, and foreign policy under Johnson and Nixon. The conservative agenda for Ronald Reagan's and George Bush's administrations arose from the disillusion and crises of the late 1960s and 1970s, shaping leaders who believed that the answer was to turn the nation's social and economic problems over to the market while asserting America's influence and power around the world.

The mid-1990s brought another generation into the political arena. The members of "Generation X" came of voting age with deep worries about the foreclosing of opportunities. They worried that previous administrations had ignored growing economic divisions and let the competitive position of the United States deteriorate. The range of suggested solutions differed widely—individual moral reform, a stronger labor movement, leaner competition in world markets—but the generational concern was clear.

This generational change made 1992 one of the most volatile national elections in decades. A baby boomer and successful governor of Arkansas who was not widely known nationally, Democrat Bill Clinton decided that George Bush was vulnerable when more senior Democrats opted to pass on the contest. His campaign for the nomination overcame minimal name recognition, accusations of womanizing, and his use of a student deferment to avoid military service in Vietnam. Clinton made sure that the Democrats fielded a full baby boomer (and Southern) ticket by choosing as his running mate the equally youthful Tennessean Albert Gore Jr., who had served in the Senate for two terms and was widely known for his book on the environment, *Earth in the Balance*.

Bush, the last politician of the World War II generation to gain the White House, won renomination by beating back the archconservative Patrick Buchanan, who claimed that the last twelve years had been a long betrayal of true conservatism. The Republican National Convention in Houston showed how important cultural issues had become to the Republican party. The party platform conformed to the beliefs of the Christian right. Buchanan delivered a startling speech that called for right-thinking Americans to crusade against unbelievers. Buchanan's divisive comments were a reminder of the multiple ways that religious belief was reshaping American politics.

The wild card was the Texas billionaire Ross Perot, whose independent campaign started with an appearance on a television talk show. Perot loved flip charts, distanced himself from professional politicians, and claimed to talk sense to the American people. He also tried to occupy the political center, appealing to the middle of the middle-class—small business owners, middle managers, and professionals, who had approved of Reagan's antigovernment rhetoric but distrusted his corporate cronies. In May, Perot outscored both Bush and Clinton in opinion polls, but his behavior became increasingly erratic. He withdrew from the race and then reentered after floating stories that he was the target of dark conspiracies.

Bush campaigned as a foreign-policy expert. He expected voters to reward him for the end of the Cold War, and he ignored anxieties about the nation's direction at home. His popularity had surged immediately after the victory of the Persian Gulf War, only to fall rapidly as the country became mired in a recession. In fact, voters in November 1992 ranked the economy first as an issue, the federal budget deficit second, health care third, and foreign policy eighth. Clinton hammered away at economic concerns, appealing to swing voters, such as suburban independents and blue-collar Reagan Democrats. He presented himself as the leader of new, pragmatic, and livelier Democrats. He put on sunglasses and

Despite personal flaws, Bill Clinton was enormously effective as a political campaigner.

played the saxophone on a late-night talk show. His campaign theme song came from Fleetwood Mac, a favorite rock group of thirty-something Americans: "Don't stop thinking about tomorrow. . . . Yesterday's gone. Yesterday's gone."

Election day gave the Clinton-Gore ticket 43 percent of the popular vote, Bush 38 percent, and Perot 19 percent. Clinton held the Democratic core of Northern and Midwestern industrial states and loosened the Republican hold on the South and West. Millions who voted for Perot were casting a protest vote for "none of the above" and against "politics as usual" rather than hoping for an actual Perot victory. Clinton ran best among voters over 65, who remembered FDR and Harry Truman, and voters under 30.

Policing the World

Although Clinton was much more interested in domestic policies and the election had hinged on the economy, he inherited an expectation that the United States could keep the world on an even keel and counter ethnic hatred. During the administration's first years, U.S. diplomats helped broker an Israel-PLO (Palestinian Liberation Organization) accord that gave Palestinians self-government in Gaza and the West Bank, only to watch extremists on both sides undermine the accords and plunge Israel into a near-civil war by 2002. The United States in 1994 used diplomatic pressure to persuade North Korea to suspend building nuclear weapons, temporarily calming a potentially explosive trouble spot. The world also benefited from a gradual reduction of nuclear arsenals and from a 1996 treaty to ban the testing of nuclear weapons.

Elsewhere in the world, Clinton used military power with caution. Given the national distaste for overseas entanglements, he responded far more effectively than critics expected. He inherited a U.S. military presence in Somalia (in northeastern Africa) because of a post-election decision by George Bush; he withdrew American forces when their humanitarian mission of guarding food relief to starving Somalis was overshadowed by the need to take sides in a civil war. Clinton intervened decisively in Haiti to restore an elected president.

Bosnia and Kosovo Clinton reluctantly committed the United States to a multinational effort to end bloody civil war in ethnically and religiously divided **Bosnia** in 1995. In the early 1990s, the former Communist nation of Yugoslavia, in southeastern Europe, fragmented into five independent nations: Slovenia, Montenegro, Croatia, Bosnia, and Yugoslavia (the name retained by the predominantly Serbian nation with its capital at Belgrade). Bosnia, divided both ethnically and religiously between Christians and Muslims, erupted in bitter civil war. Christian Serbs, who were supported by Belgrade, engaged in massacres and deportations of Muslim Bosnians with the goal of creating "ethnically clean" Serbian districts. Too late to stop most bloodshed, NATO eventually intervened in 1995. U.S. and European troops enforced a brittle peace accord and a division of territory into Bosnian and Serb sectors under a shaky federated government.

The American military revisited the same part of Europe in 1999, when the United States and Britain led NATO's intervention in **Kosovo**. The overwhelming majority of people in this Yugoslav province were ethnic Albanians who have chafed under the control of the Serb-controlled Yugoslav government. When a Kosovar independence movement began a rebellion, Yugoslav president Slobodan Milosevic responded with brutal repression that threatened to drive over 1 million ethnic Albanians out of the province. To protect the Kosovars, NATO in March 1999 began a bombing campaign that targeted Yugoslav military bases and forces in Kosovo. In June, Yugoslavia agreed to withdraw its troops and make way for a multinational NATO peacekeeping force with 50,000 troops from Britain, France, Germany, Italy, the Netherlands and the United States, marking a measured success for U.S. policy.

The Reinvention of NATO   In order to satisfy Russia, the peacekeeping force that entered Kosovo in June was technically a U.S. operation, but it was a reinvented NATO that negotiated with Yugoslavia. Fifty years earlier, the North Atlantic Treaty Organization had been created for three purposes. The first was to unite non-Communist nations of Western Europe in an alliance against the Soviet Union. The second was to formally commit the United States and Canada to the defense of Western Europe by placing substantial U.S. military forces in Europe. The third was to establish a framework that would make the rearmament of West Germany acceptable to other European nations. For the next forty years—until the collapse of Eastern European Communism—NATO coordinated Western European defense planning and remained a foundation stone of United States foreign policy.

The new NATO is a product of the new Europe of the 1990s. A key step was expansion into the former Soviet sphere in Eastern Europe. At the anniversary summit in 1999, NATO formally admitted Poland, Hungary, and the Czech Republic. Over the objections of Russia, the action erased the last vestige of the buffer of satellite nations that the Soviet Union had created after World War II. Three years later, NATO agreed to give Russia a formal role in discussions about a number of its policy decisions, further eroding the barriers of the Cold War.

Clinton's Neoliberalism

Domestic policy attracted Clinton's greatest interest, and his first term can be divided into two parts. In 1993–1994, he worked with a slim Democratic majority in Congress to modernize the American economy, taking advantage of an economic upturn that lasted for most of the decade. In 1995 and 1996, however, he faced solid Republican majorities, the result of an unanticipated Republican tide in the November 1994 elections.

The heart of Clinton's agenda was efforts to make the United States economy more equitable domestically and more competitive internationally; these goals marked Clinton as a **neoliberal** who envisioned a partnership between a leaner government and a dynamic private sector. Steps to "reinvent" government cut federal employment below Reagan administration levels. A new tax bill reversed some of the inequities of the 1980s by increasing taxes on the well-off (the top 1.2 percent of households). At the other end of the income scale was expansion of the Earned Income Tax Credit, a Nixon-era program that helped lift working Americans out of poverty. An improved college student-aid program spread benefits to more students by allowing direct federal loans. The National and Community Service Trust Act created a pilot program for a domestic Peace Corps. In early 1993, Clinton pushed through the Family and Medical Leave Act, which provided up to twelve weeks of unpaid leave for workers with newborns or family emergencies and had been vetoed twice by George Bush.

The 1994 crime bill demonstrated the nation's delicate political balance. The bill was as much symbolic as practical, designed to make Democrats look tough before the 1994 elections. It included money to help localities hire more police officers, funded crime-prevention programs, and banned certain kinds of assault rifles. Conservatives disliked prevention programs that they caricatured as "midnight basketball." Liberals thought that the bill ignored the problem of racial bias in the court system. A compromise passed only because Clinton managed to recruit moderate Republicans to make up for defecting Democrats.

Clinton's biggest setback was the failure of comprehensive health-care legislation. The goals seemed simple at first: containment of health-care costs and extension of basic medical insurance from 83 percent of Americans under age 65 to 100 percent. In the abstract, voters agreed that something needed to be done. So did individuals like the 25-year-old photographer's assistant who found herself facing cancer surgery without savings or health insurance: "I work full-time, and because it's a very small business, we don't get any benefits. . . . It just devastated everybody financially. And that shouldn't happen. That's the American dream that's lost."

Clinton appointed his wife, Hillary Rodham Clinton, to head the health-care task force. Many found this an inappropriate role for a first lady, while others distrusted her preference for a substantial government role. The plan that emerged from the White House ran to 1,342 pages of complex regulations, with something for everyone to dislike. Senior citizens worried about limits on Medicare spending. Insurance companies did not want more regulations. Businesses did not want the costs of insuring their workers. Taxpayers liked the idea of wider medical insurance coverage but not the idea of paying for it through higher taxes or rationing of medical services. Thus the reform effort went nowhere.

If Reagan avoided blame for mistakes, Clinton in his first two years in office seemed to avoid credit for successes. Despite his legislative accomplishments, the press emphasized his difficulty in reaching decisions. Perhaps because he sometimes started with absolute statements and positions, what might look in another leader like a willingness to compromise looked like waffling in Clinton. Both the president and his wife attracted extreme and bitter hatred from the far right, of a sort previously reserved for Franklin and Eleanor Roosevelt and the Kennedy family. Indeed, Hillary Rodham Clinton became a symbol of discomfiting changes in American families.

Contract with America and the Election of 1996

Conservative political ideology and personal animosity against the Clintons were both parts of the background for an extraordinary off-year election in 1994, in which voters defeated dozens of incumbents and gave Republicans control of Congress. For most of 1995, the new Speaker of the House, Newt Gingrich of Georgia, dominated political headlines as he pushed the **Contract with America**, the official Republican campaign platform for the 1994 elections, which called for a revolutionary reduction in federal responsibilities.

Clinton laid low and let the new Congress attack environmental protections, propose cuts in federal benefits for the elderly, and try to slice the capital-gains tax to help the rich. As Congress and president battled over the budget, congressional Republicans refused to authorize interim spending and forced the federal government to shut down for more than three weeks between November 1995 and January 1996. Gingrich was the clear loser in public opinion, both for the shutdowns and for his ideas. Democrats painted Gingrich and his congressional allies as a radical fringe who wanted to gut Medicare and Medicaid, undermine education, punish legal immigrants, and sell off national parks—core values and programs that most Americans wanted to protect. Democrats, of course, proclaimed themselves the defenders of national values.

After the budget confrontations, 1996 brought a series of measures to reward work—a centrist position acceptable to most Americans. The minimum wage increased. Congress made pension programs easier for employers to create and made health insurance portable when workers changed jobs. After tough negotiations, Clinton signed bipartisan legislation to "end welfare as we know it." The new program of **Temporary Assistance to Needy Families (TANF)** replaced Aid to Families with Dependent Children (AFDC). TANF had strict requirements that aid recipients be seeking work or be enrolled in school, and it set a time limit on assistance. By 2001, the number of public-assistance recipients had declined 58 percent from its 1994 high, but there are doubts that many of the former recipients found jobs adequate to support their families.

Clinton's reelection in 1996 was a virtual replay of 1992. His opponent, Robert Dole, represented the World War II generation of politicians. The Republican party was uncertain whether to stress free markets or morality. The party tried to paper over its uneasy mix of traditional probusiness and socially moderate country-club Republicans, radical proponents of unregulated markets, and religious conservatives increasingly active in politics. Evangelicals dominated many state parties, but they made many traditional party regulars uncomfortable and carried few statewide elections. The Republicans thus displayed many of the internal fractures that characterized American society as a whole.

Because the nation was prosperous and at peace, and because Clinton had claimed the political center, which allowed him to sound like Dwight Eisenhower, the results were never in doubt. Clinton became the first Democratic president to be elected to a second term since Franklin Roosevelt. The Clinton-Gore ticket took 70 percent of the electoral votes and 49 percent of the popular vote (versus 41 percent for Dole and 9 percent for a recycled Ross Perot). Clinton easily won the Northeast, the industrial Midwest, and the Far West; Hispanic voters alienated by anti-immigrant rhetoric from the Republicans helped Clinton also take usually Republican states, such as Florida and Arizona.

The election confirmed that voters liked the pragmatic center. They were cautious about the radical free-market advocates on the extreme right, showing little interest in having Republicans actually put the Contract with America into practice. They were equally unimpressed by liberal advocates of extensive entitlements on the European model. What voters wanted was to continue the reduction of the federal role in domestic affairs that began in the 1980s without damaging social insurance programs.

The Dangers of Everyday Life

Part of the background for the sometimes vicious politics of mid-decade was a sense of individual insecurity and fear of violence that coexisted with an economy that was booming in some sectors but still leaving many Americans behind. The solutions, however, seemed inadequate. The liberal response of tighter limitations on the acquisition of firearms could not stop every irrational individual. The conservative response of harsher and mandatory prison terms was equally futile to prevent irrational actions.

Random Violence and Domestic Terrorism One after another, headlines and news flashes proclaimed terrifying random acts of violence. The greatest losses of life came in

Waco, Texas, and Oklahoma City. On April 19, 1993, federal agents raided the fortified compound of the Branch Davidian cult outside Waco after a fifty-one day siege. The raid triggered a fire, probably set from inside, that killed more than eighty people. On the second anniversary of the Waco raid, Timothy McVeigh packed a rented truck with explosive materials and detonated it in front of the federal office building in downtown Oklahoma City. The blast collapsed the entire front of the nine-story building and killed 169 people, presumably as revenge against what McVeigh considered an oppressive government.

Other acts of violence seemed even more pointless. A national manhunt in 1997 captured Ted Kaczynski, the so-called Unabomber, who since 1978 had mailed more than a dozen bombs to college professors and airlines as protest against an industrialized economy. In April 1999, two high school students in Littleton, Colorado, took rifles and pipe bombs into Columbine High School to kill twelve classmates, a teacher, and themselves; schools in Arkansas and Oregon experienced similar terror from gun-wielding students. In the fall of 2001, random sniper attacks on patrons of gas stations and minimarkets paralyzed the Washington, DC area until suspects were apprehended. The cumulative impact was a heightened sense of personal insecurity that compounded the psychological impact of the attacks of September 11, 2001.

Gun Control Workplace assassins, schoolroom murders, and domestic terrorism invigorated efforts to monitor access to firearms. The Brady Handgun Violence Prevention Act, passed in 1994, took its name from James Brady, President Reagan's first press secretary, who was seriously injured in the 1981 attempt to kill the president. The act set up a waiting period and background checks for purchases of firearms from retailers, pawnshops, and licensed firearm dealers. Congress also debated detailed restrictions on certain types of weapons, such as assault rifles, and particularly lethal types of ammunition and discovered that police forces and urban residents tended to line up in favor, and rural representatives in opposition.

Gun control was political dynamite, for Americans have drastically differing understandings of the Second Amendment, which states: "A well regulated militia, being necessary to the security of a free State, the right of the people to keep and bear arms, shall not be infringed." The powerful National Rifle Association, the major lobby for gun owners and manufacturers, now argued that the amendment establishes an absolute individual right. Until the 1980s, in contrast, federal courts consistently interpreted the amendment to apply to the possession of weapons in connection with citizen service in a government-organized militia, and federal courts have yet to strike down any gun control law for violating the Second Amendment.

Crime and the War on Drugs Conservatives, including many gun-ownership absolutists, put their faith in strict law enforcement as the best route to pubic security. The 1990s saw numerous states adopt "three strike" measures that drastically increased penalties for individuals convicted of a third crime. One result was an explosive growth of the prison industry. Mandatory minimum sentencing caused Louisiana's prison population to grow by 50 percent between 1994 and 2001. Mississippi legislation that severely restricted the possibility of parole caused an even greater jump in the state's prison population from 10,700 in 1994 to 37,700 in 2001. States diverted funds from education and health care to build and staff more prisons. The number of people serving sentences in state and federal prisons grew from 316,000 in 1980 to 740,000 in 1990 and 1,321,000 in 2000, with another 631,000 being held in local jails.

The war on drugs, begun in the 1980s, was the biggest contributor to the prison boom. As the drug war dragged on through the 1990s, the federal government poured billions of dollars into efforts to stop illegal drugs from crossing the Mexican border or from landing by boat or airplane in the Southeast. The United States intervened in South American nations that produced cocaine, particularly Peru and Colombia, aiding local military efforts to uproot crops and battle drug lords. In 2002, the United States was edged perilously close to full involvement in a Colombian civil war. Meanwhile, aggressive enforcement of domestic laws against drug possession or sales filled American prison cells. The antidrug campaign fell most heavily on minorities. Connecticut, for example, required mandatory sentences for selling or possessing drugs within two-thirds of a mile of a school, day-care center, or public housing project. Because these criteria encompassed nearly all the neighborhoods in Hartford and New Haven with large minority populations, minority offenders arrested on drug charges were nine times more likely than white offenders to end up in jail.

In fact, crime fell steadily for a decade after reaching a peak in 1991. The rate of violent crime (murder, rape, robbery, aggravated assault) fell by 31 percent from 1991 to 1999, including a 37 percent drop in number of murders. The rate of major property crimes (burglary, larceny-theft, and motor vehicle theft) fell by 27 percent over the same period. Easing fears combined with escalating costs to cause some states to rethink the reliance on prison terms. California voters adopted a measure that provides for treatment rather than prison for many drug offenders. A handful of states adopted measures legalizing marijuana for medical use. Other states, ranging from Mississippi to Connecticut to North Dakota, softened some of their sentencing laws.

Debating the Death Penalty Governor George Ryan of Illinois was elected in 1998 as a conservative Republican. In January 2003, this small-town businessman emptied death row in the Illinois prison system by commuting the death sentences of 167 convicted murderers to prison terms of life or less. His action followed a moratorium on executions that he had proclaimed three years earlier. He asserted that his review of individual cases had led him to doubt the justice of the death penalty system as a whole, which he said is "haunted by the demons of error—error in determining guilt and error in determining who among the guilty deserves to die." Ryan's extraordinary action reflected a wider uncertainty about the fair application of capital punishment that came from cases in which the new technique of DNA testing showed mistaken convictions, from revelations about incompetent defense attorneys assigned to penniless defendants, and from evidence of malfeasance by prosecuting attorneys in withholding evidence that might have exonerated defendants accused of murder.

Specific discussion of flaws in the application of the death penalty reveals basic disagreements about the best approach to public order. Thirty-eight of the fifty states impose the death penalty, although seven have not carried out an execution since 1976. The majority of Americans have accepted capital punishment as a flawed but necessary defense for society. In the presidential campaign of 2000, George W. Bush cited the record number of executions that had taken place in Texas while he was governor as evidence of his toughness against crime. He was confident, he said, that "everybody who has been put to death has been guilty of the crime charged."

In contrast, a passionate minority think that capital punishment is a tool so bent and blunted that it is worse than useless. The opponents muster both practical and religious arguments. They point out that the deterrent effect of capital punishment is weak at best; murder rates are often higher in death penalty states than in states without the penalty. They cite not only specific mistakes but also the disproportionate numbers of African Americans and Latinos who have received the death penalty, a far higher percentage than whites charged with the same crimes. The nation's Roman Catholic bishops in 1999 joined with the National Council of Synagogues to condemn the death penalty as contrary to teachings about the sanctity of human life. The debate about capital punishment exemplifies the fault lines that divide Americans as they try to balance the demands of justice and public order. On one question after another, we share the goal of a prosperous and just society, but we often find it difficult to agree on the best road to that end as we argue strenuously about conservative and liberal policies

Morality and Partisanship

If the economy was the fundamental news of the later 1990s, Bill Clinton's personal life was the hot news. In 1998 and 1999, the United States was riveted by revelations about the president's sex life, doubts about his integrity, and debates about his fitness for high office. Years of rumors, innuendoes, and law suits culminated in 1999 in the nation's second presidential impeachment trial. To his enemies, Clinton's behavior seemed one more example of disregard for law and morality, while his supporters found the questions they raised to be nothing but partisan politics.

The attacks on President Clinton were accompanied by unprecedented assaults on the reputation of Hillary Clinton, attacks which showed that tension over social values remained an important dimension of American life. Both her active role in shaping policy and her stands on social issues made her a symbol of changes and values in American families that distressed many conservatives. Talk-show hosts and ultraconservative activists tried repeatedly to link her to scandals and wrongdoing.

Clinton's problems began in 1994 with the appointment of a special prosecutor to investigate possible fraud in the **Whitewater** development, an Arkansas land promotion in which Bill and Hillary Clinton had invested in the 1980s. The probe by Kenneth Starr, the independent counsel, however, expanded beyond Whitewater into a wide-ranging investigation that encompassed the firing of the White House travel-office staff early in 1993, the suicide of White House aide Vincent Foster, and the sexual behavior of the president. Meanwhile, Paula Jones had brought a lawsuit claiming sexual harassment by then-governor Clinton while she was a state worker in Arkansas. The investigation of Whitewater brought convictions of several friends and former associates of the Clintons, but no evidence pointing directly at either Bill or Hillary Clinton themselves.

The legal landscape changed in January 1998, when allegations surfaced about an affair between the president and Monica Lewinsky, a former White House intern. Lewinsky admitted to the relationship privately and then to Starr's staff after the president had denied it in a sworn deposition for the Paula Jones case. This opened Clinton to charges of perjury and obstruction of justice. Although a federal judge dismissed Jones's suit in April, the continued unfolding of the Lewinsky affair treated the nation to a barrage of personal details about Bill Clinton and to semantic debates over what exactly constituted a "sexual relationship." The affair certainly revealed deep flaws in Clinton's character and showed his willingness to shade the truth. Newspaper editorials, radio talk shows, and politicians debated whether such flaws were relevant to his ability to perform his Constitutional duties.

In the fall of 1998, the Republican leaders who controlled Congress decided that Clinton's statements and misstatements justified the Constitutional process of impeachment. In December, the Republican majority on the House Judiciary Committee recommended four articles of impeachment, or specific charges against the president, to the House of Representatives. By a partisan vote, the full House approved two of the charges and forwarded them to the Senate. The formal trial of the charges by the Senate began in January 1999 and ended on February 12. Moderate Republicans joined Democrats to assure that the Senate would fall far short of the two-thirds majority required for conviction and removal from office. Article 1, charging that the president had perjured himself, failed by a vote of 45 to 55. Article 2, charging that he had obstructed justice, failed by a vote of 50 to 50.

· · · OVERVIEW · · ·

PRESIDENTIAL IMPEACHMENT

Andrew Johnson, 1868	Charges	Failure to comply with Tenure of Office Act, requiring Congressional approval to fire cabinet members.
	Political Lineup	Radical Republicans against Johnson; Democrats and moderate Republicans for him.
	Actions	Tried and acquitted by Senate.
	Underlying Issues	Johnson's opposition to Republican plans for reconstruction of Southern states after the Civil War.
Richard Nixon, 1974	Charges	Obstruction of justice in Watergate investigation; abuse of power of federal agencies for political purposes; refusal to recognize Congressional subpoena.
	Political Lineup	Democrats and many Republicans against Nixon.
	Actions	Charges approved by House committee; Nixon resigned before action by the full House of Representatives.
	Underlying Issues	Nixon's construction of a secret government and his efforts to undermine integrity of national elections.
Bill Clinton, 1999	Charges	Perjury and obstruction of justice in the investigation of sexual misconduct allegations by Paula Jones.
	Political Lineup	Conservative Republicans against Clinton; Democrats and some moderate Republicans for him.
	Actions	Tried and acquitted by Senate.
	Underlying Issues	Republican frustration with Clinton's ability to block their agenda; deep concern about Clinton's character and moral fitness for presidency.

Why did Congressional Republicans pursue impeachment to the bitter end? It was clear by the end of 1998 that a majority of Americans strongly disapproved of Clinton's conduct but did not think that his personal behavior merited removal from office (see Overview table, "Presidential Impeachment"). The 1998 election, which reduced the Republican majority in the House and resulted in the resignation of Newt Gingrich, confirmed the opinion polls. At the same time, 25 to 30 percent of Americans remained convinced that Clinton was a disgrace whose presence in the White House demeaned the nation. It was not so much that they disliked his policies, which were often quite conservative, but that they felt that his personal flaws and sins made him unfit to lead and represent the nation and deprived him of the moral authority necessary to inspire its people. In other words, although anti-Clinton people were a powerful force within the Republican party and impeachment was certainly motivated by politics, it was also another battle in America's continuing culture wars.

A NEW ECONOMY?

Within months of the impeachment trial, Americans had a new worry. In the closing months of 1999, many Americans stocked up on canned food, kerosene, powdered milk, ammunition, and cash. They were preparing to survive, not foreign invasion or natural disaster, but rather the possible collapse of the global computer network. Europeans called the problem the "millennium bug," Americans, the "Y2K" problem (for Year 2000). In the early years of computers, memory space was precious, causing programmers to designate dates with only the last two digits of the year (thus, "82" for 1982). In the mid-1990s, many realized that such programs might treat the year 2000 as 1900, or choke in electronic confusion, throwing information systems into chaos. Paychecks might be miscalculated, automatic-teller machines might crash, electric power grids might fall apart. While a small army of programmers worked to rewrite and repair the software, the media offered a steady diet of dire stories that urged preparations . . . just in case.

In fact, almost nothing happened. The software patches worked. Americans on the evening of December 31, 1999, could watch the progression of millennium celebrations and fireworks from Singapore to Rome and then to London as midnight swept westward across the globe. Since civilization did not collapse in Asia and Europe, North Americans could let midnight arrive with a sigh of relief.

In larger perspective, the Y2K worries illustrate how much the American economy had changed in even the previous decade, and how mysterious the changes seemed. More than ever, it was a global economy. And, unlike any time in the past, it was an economy that depended on electronic computing to manage and transmit vast quantities of data. The impacts of the electronic revolution were still being absorbed into the structures and routines of everyday life as Americans put Y2K behind them and looked to a new century.

The Prosperous 1990s

From 1992 through 2000, Americans enjoyed nine years of continuous economic expansion. Unemployment dropped from 7.2 percent in 1992 to 4.0 percent at the start of 2000 as American businesses created more than 12 million new jobs. Key states like California rebounded from economic recession with new growth driven by high-tech industries, entertainment, and foreign trade. The stock market soared during the nineties; rising demand for shares in established blue-chip companies and new **Internet** firms swelled the value of individual portfolios, IRA accounts, and pension funds. The rate of homeownership rose after declining for fifteen years. Prosperity also trickled down to Americans at the bottom of the economic ladder. The proportion of Americans in poverty dropped to 12 percent in 1999, and the gap between rich and poor began to narrow (slightly) for the first time in two decades.

The economic boom was great news for the federal budget. Tight spending and rising personal income turned perennial deficits into surpluses for 1998, 1999, and 2000. Reduced borrowing by the U.S. Treasury resulted in low interest rates, which further fueled corporate expansion and consumer spending. Both political parties anticipated a growing surplus for the next decade and debated whether to offer massive tax cuts, to buy down the national debt, or to shore up Social Security and Medicare. In 1997, Clinton signed a deficit-reduction bill that seemed to promise fiscal stability.

Behind the statistics were substantial gains in the efficiency of the American economy. International rivals, especially Japan, experienced severe economic slumps in the mid-1990s. In the United States, in contrast, by the end of the decade the productivity of manufacturing workers was increasing more than 4 percent per year, the highest rate in a generation. Part of the gain was the payoff from the painful business restructuring and downsizing of the 1970s and 1980s. Another cause was improved efficiency from the full incorporation of personal computers and electronic communication into everyday life and business practice.

It remains to be seen whether the growth of the 1990s marked the beginning of a new wave of sustained economic expansion like the earlier waves triggered by technological innovation. In the past, such waves have followed fifty-year cycles that begin with a thirty-year period of rapid expansion followed by two decades of consolidation and slow growth. From 1945 to 1974, for example, the automobile and aerospace industries helped Europe, Japan, and the United States enjoy an era of sustained growth that was followed by two decades of painful economic readjustment and problems. In the later 1990s, fast-growing information-based industries such as electronic communications, software, biotechnology, and medicine may have jump-started another era of prosperity, although many individual technology companies failed in 2001 and 2002, dragging down the stock market.

The Service Economy

At the beginning of the twenty-first century, the United States was an economy of services. As fewer Americans drove tractors and toiled on assembly lines, more became service workers. The service sector includes everyone not directly involved in producing and processing physical products. Service workers range from lawyers to hairstylists, from police officers who write traffic tickets to theater employees who sell movie tickets. In 1965, services already accounted for more than half of American jobs. By the 1990s, their share rose to more than 70 percent.

Service jobs vary greatly. At the bottom of the scale are minimum-wage jobs held mostly by women, immigrants, and the young, such as cleaning people, child-care workers, hospital orderlies, and fast-food workers. These positions offer little in terms of advancement, job security, or benefits. In contrast, many of the best new jobs are in information industries. Teaching, research, government, advertising, mass communications, and professional consulting depend on producing and manipulating information. All of these fields have grown. They add to national wealth by creating and applying new ideas rather than by supplying standardized products and services.

The information economy flourishes in large cities with libraries, universities, research hospitals, advertising agencies, and corporate headquarters. New York's bankers and stockbrokers made Manhattan an island of prosperity in the 1980s. Pittsburgh, with major universities and corporate headquarters, made the transition to the information economy even while its steel industry failed. A good benchmark of a brain-powered economy is whether more than a quarter of the adults (people aged 25 or over) have finished college. The District of Columbia, with its high-priced lawyers and lobbyists, ranked first in 1999, with 42 percent. Next was Colorado (39 percent), followed closely by Maryland, Connecticut, Minnesota, Virginia, and Massachusetts.

The rise of the service economy had political consequences. Rapid expansion of jobs in state and local governments triggered popular revolts against state taxes that started in 1978 with passage of California's Proposition 13, which limited property taxes, and continued into the 1990s. Another growth industry was health care. Spending on medical and health services amounted to 12 percent of the gross domestic product in 1990, up from 5 percent in 1960. The need to share this huge expense fairly was the motivation for Medicare and Medicaid in the 1960s and the search for a national health insurance program in the 1990s.

The High-Tech Sector

The epitome of the "sunrise" economy was electronics, which grew hand-in-glove with the defense budget. The first computers in the 1940s were derived in part from wartime code-breaking efforts. In the 1950s, IBM got half its revenues from air defense computers and guidance systems for B-52 bombers. "It was the Cold War that helped IBM make itself the king of the computer business," commented the company president Thomas J. Watson. Employment in computer manufacturing rose in the mid-1960s with the expansion of mainframe computing. Large machines from IBM, Honeywell, NCR, and other established corporations required substantial support facilities and staff and were used largely by universities, government agencies, and corporations. In the 1970s, new companies began to compete with smaller, specialized machines for purposes such as word processing.

One cluster of firms sprang up outside Boston around Route 128, benefiting from proximity to MIT and other Boston-area universities. California's **Silicon Valley**, north of San Jose, took off with corporate spinoffs and civilian applications of military technologies and benefited equally from proximity to Stanford University. Invention of the microprocessor in 1971 kicked the industry into high gear. The farmlands of Santa Clara County, California, became a "silicon landscape" of neat one-story factories and research campuses. In 1950, the county had 800 factory workers. In 1980, it had 264,000 manufacturing workers and 3,000 electronics firms. Related hardware and microchip factories spread the industry throughout the West, to such cities as Austin, Phoenix, Portland, Boise, and Salt Lake City, creating "silicon prairies," "silicon forests," and "silicon deserts" to complement California's original Silicon Valley.

The electronics boom was driven by extraordinary improvements in computing capacity. At the start of the microcomputer era, Intel cofounder Gordon Moore predicted that the number of transistors on a microchip would double every eighteen months, with consequent increases in performance and drops in price. "Moore's Law" worked at least to the opening of a new century as producers moved from chips with 5,000 transistors to ones with 50,000,000. The practical results were vastly increased capacities and portability of computers. The "portable" Osborne and Apple of the early 1980s were suitcase-sized packages with limited hard drives and tiny random access memories for running programs. Twenty years later, when students and business travelers pulled out their laptops at every opportunity, the first generation of personal computers were as outmoded as a Spanish galleon in an age of supertankers.

The computer industry generated an accompanying software industry as a major component of information technology employment (see American Views: "Creating and Working in the New Economy"). Every computer needed a complexly coded operating system, word-processing programs, spreadsheet programs, file-reading programs, Internet browsers, and, of course, games. Seattle-based Microsoft parlayed an alliance with IBM into a dominant position that eventually triggered federal antitrust action. Other software firms rose and fell with innovative and then outmoded programs. Software writing skills also spawned a new world of multimedia entertainment. A sequence of new films, such as

Creating and Working in the New Economy

Like many other American industries, the booming information technology sector that employed millions of workers by the 1990s started with a few key ideas and innovators. Bill Gates and Paul Allen, the founders of software giant Microsoft Corporation, talk about their early encounters with computers as high school students and the origins of Allen's idea of a "wired world" in the early 1970s. Following their interview are the reflections of a worker in the huge high-tech industry at the end of the 1990s.

> What do the experiences suggest about the pace of change in the high technology economy?
>
> What do they suggest about the process of technological innovation and industrial change?
>
> How do high-tech workers cope with the pace of change in their industry, and what are the implications for their jobs?

Bill Gates, Paul Allen, and the Seeds of the Personal Computer Revolution

GATES: Our friendship started [in high school] after the mothers' club paid to put a computer terminal in the school in 1968. The notion was that, of course, the teachers would figure out this computer thing and then teach it to the students. But that didn't happen. It was the other way around. There was a group of students who kind of went nuts.

ALLEN: The teletype room was full of rolled-up paper-tape programs and manuals and everything else. Between classes, or whenever any of us hard-core computer types had a spare period, we would congregate there.

GATES: We were always scrounging free computer time. One year a student's mother arranged for us to go downtown to a new commercial center. We didn't have to pay for the time as long as we could find bugs in their system and report them. . . .

ALLEN: At the end of every school day, a bunch of us would take our little leather satchel briefcases and ride the bus downtown to the computer center. Bill and I were the guys that stayed the latest, and afterward we'd eat pizza at this hippie place across the street. . . .

GATES: The event that started everything for us business-wise was when Paul found an article in 1971 in an electronics magazine. . . . about Intel's 4004 chip, which was the world's first microprocessor. Paul comes up and says "Whoa" and explains that this microprocessor thing's only going to get better and better. . . .

ALLEN: I remember having pizza at Shakey's in Vancouver, Washington, in 1973, and talking about the fact that eventually everyone is going to be online and have access to newspapers and stuff and wouldn't people be willing to pay for information on a computer terminal.

Susie Johnson, Computer Chip Layout Designer

I design the layout of computer chips for Cirrus Logic in Austin, Texas. We're what they call a "chip solutions company." . . . [Laughs] Right now, we're laying out audio chips that go into computers and improve the sound of the speakers. I saw a demo of them recently. They had a regular PC with those regular little speakers and it sounded very weak. Then they put our chip in there, and the speakers sounded like this huge stereo. It was pretty wild.

My job is I'm given a schematic of the chip by the engineers, and it's basically just a bunch of symbols-triangles and rectangles with lines going in and out of them. Each symbol represents a device on the chip that hooks up to something else, and each of these little devices is designed to perform some function electronically. . . . I translate this technical information into the way the chip will actually look—how all this information will be contained in this tiny space. I draw it out using a computer program. It's mostly an automated process. In the past, I'd draw the devices by hand, but the chips I'm working on now are too complicated for that. . . .

(continued)

I did lots of different jobs before—I was a waitress and I worked in a bunch of stores. . . . So I was wanting to change. . . . I certainly didn't think that I could do this, but one night I came into work with my ex-husband and he let me do some simple layout, and I thought, this is really cool, I want to try it. So I took a couple of classes at Austin Community College—an electrical design class and an integrated circuit layout class—so I'd understand a little more of the theory angle. . . . I've been doing this for three years. I have no plans to stop. I love it. . . .

There is some art to it. You could take one of these audio chips and give it to five different layout people and it would probably come back five different ways, you know? It's not all automated. Different people will put different things next to each other.

The way I think of it is I'm making little tiny highways for electrons. Some people say it's like New York City on a postage stamp. And it is! I mean, there are so many devices that I have to put into a tiny space. The one I was working on last week had over a hundred thousand. . . .

Sometimes there's problems that the computer catches and can't fix. I'm not sure why that happens, but it's the toughest part of the job. The computer will tell you what area of the chip the problem's in, but you have to go within that area yourself and find the problem and correct it. Like if something is too close to something else, then it needs to be moved over. . . . I think it's kind of fun. You have to figure it out, you have to be a detective. . . .

The Matrix (1999), repeatedly pushed the possibilities of combining computer simulation and live action.

Personal computers and consumer electronics became part of everyday life in the 1990s. Automakers built computers into their cars to diagnose engine problems; high-end models added global positioning systems for drivers too hurried to unfold a map. New buildings came with "smart" climate control systems that were touted as self-regulating. Busy people replaced their appointment books with handheld personal organizers. In 2002, 74 percent of adults reported that they had Internet access at home or work, up from 45 percent in 2000 and 14 percent in 1996, and nearly all of them had used it in the previous month. It took radio thirty-eight years and television thirteen years before 50 million Americans tuned in; the Internet reached the same level of use in four years. Children aged 10 to 14 used computers more frequently than any other age group, and nine out of ten could access the Internet at home or at school. The most networked state was Alaska, where computers helped to make up for vast distances and isolating winters. Close behind were New Hampshire, Washington, Utah, and Oregon.

The electronics boom was part of a larger growth of "high-technology" industries. If "high tech" is applied to industries that devote a substantial portion of their income to research and development, it also covers chemicals, synthetic materials, cosmetics, aircraft and space satellites, drugs, measuring instruments, and many other products. Pharmaceuticals, medical imaging and diagnosis, bioengineering, and genetic engineering were all areas of rapid advance in the 1990s with momentum for the future. In fundamental ways, they were all examples of activities based on the acquisition and processing of information.

An Instant Society

On June 1, 1980, CNN Cable News Network gave television viewers their first chance to watch news coverage twenty-four hours a day. Newscasters Bernard Shaw and Mary Alice Williams brought instant information to an initial audience of 1.7 million subscribers;

a decade later, CNN had hundreds of millions of viewers in more than seventy-five countries. Business executives in Zurich, college students in Nairobi, and farmers in Omaha, all tuned in to the version of world events pulled together in CNN's Atlanta headquarters. CNN made a global reputation with live reporting on the prodemocracy protests of Chinese students in Beijing in 1989. When American bombs began to fall on Baghdad in January 1991, White House officials watched CNN to find out how their war was going.

Fourteen months after CNN went on the air, another new cable channel, MTV: Music Television, started broadcasting and had an immediate impact. By the time it reached the key New York and Los Angeles markets in January 1983, MTV's round-the-clock programming of music videos had created a new form of popular art and advertising. With its own programming aimed at viewers aged 18 to 34, MTV inspired Nickelodeon for kids and VH-1 for baby boomers.

CNN, MTV, and the rest of cable television reflected both the fragmentation of American society in the 1980s and 1990s and the increasing dependence on instant communication. As late as 1980, ordinary Americans had few shared choices for learning about their nation and world: virtually identical newscasts on NBC, CBS, and ABC and similar stories in *Time* and *Newsweek*. Fifteen years later, they had learned to surf through dozens of cable channels in search of specialized programs and were beginning to explore the Internet. Hundreds of magazines for niche markets had replaced the general-circulation periodicals of the postwar generation. Vast quantities of information were more easily available, but much of it was packaged for a subdivided marketplace of specialized consumers.

The electronic society in the 1990s also learned to communicate by email and to look up information on the **World Wide Web**. No longer did messages need the delays of the postal system or the costs of long-distance telephone calls. Students could avoid inconvenient trips to the library to look up information in books because it was so much quicker to search the Web. (Many of the data for this section on the new economy were compiled in just that way.) The United States was increasingly a society that depended on instant information and expected instant results.

The Internet grew out of concerns about defense and national security. Its first form in 1969 was ARPANET (for Advanced Research Projects Administration, part of the Defense Department), intended to be a communication system to survive nuclear attack. As the Internet evolved into a system that connected universities and national weapons laboratories, the Pentagon gave up control in 1984. Through the 1980s, it was used mainly by scientists and academics to share data and communicate by email. The World Wide Web, created in 1991, expanded the Internet's uses by allowing organizations and companies to create Web sites that placed political and commercial information only a few clicks away from wired consumers. Addresses with the.com suffix (pronounced "dotcom") soon outnumbered those with edu, .gov, and .org. The equally rapid expansion of bandwidth and modem capacities allowed Web pages filled with pictures and graphics to replace the text-only sites of the 1980s. By the start of the new century, Web surfers could find vast quantities of material, from Paris hotel rates to pornography, from song lyrics to stock prices.

Instant satisfaction was one of the principles behind the boom of dotcom businesses in 1998, 1999, and 2000. Many were services that repackaged information for quick access. Others were essentially on-line versions of mail order catalogs, but capable of listing hundreds of thousands of items. Still others were instant delivery services designed to save consumers a trip to the video store or minimart. Although many of the dotcom companies crashed in 2001, they can be viewed as extensions of ongoing trends in retailing and services. Americans in 2000 spent 48 cents on meals out for every 52 cents spent on food to eat at home, paying for the convenience of quick meals without preparation and cleanup time. Automatic-teller machines had been a convenience when introduced in the early 1980s, but they were a necessity twenty years later when Americans expected to be able to pull cash from their bank accounts 168 hours a week rather than finding a bank open perhaps 30 hours a week.

Mobile telephones or "cell phones" were part of the same instant society. They exploited underutilized radio bands and communication satellites to allow wireless conversations among "cells" or geographic areas linked by special microwave broadcasting towers. Technological changes again drove demand. The chunky car phone built into a vehicle gave way to sleek handheld devices the size of *Star Trek* communicators. Wireless phone companies originally sold their phones as emergency backups and business necessities, just as wired telephones had been sold in the first years of the twentieth century. The 5 million cell phone subscribers of 1990 had exploded to 109 million in 2000 and 128 million in 2002. The phone had become ubiquitous, beeping in concerts and classrooms, in buses and on street corners. In the disaster of September 11, 2001, portable phones utilizing satellite links offered some final communications from passengers on hijacked airlines.

In the World Market

Instant access to business and financial information accelerated the globalizing of the American economy. Expanding foreign commerce had become a deliberate goal of national policy with the General Agreement on Tariffs and Trade (GATT) in 1947. GATT regularized international commerce after World War II and helped secure one of the goals of World War II by ensuring that world markets remained open to American industry. The Trade Expansion Act in 1962 had authorized President Kennedy to make reciprocal trade agreements to cut tariffs by up to 50 percent to keep American companies competitive in the new European Common Market. Although both measures were aimed at trade with Europe, they also helped expand American commerce across the Pacific.

With the help of national policy and booming economies overseas, the value of American imports and exports more than doubled, from 7 percent of the gross domestic product in 1965 to 16 percent in 1990—the largest percentage since World War I. Americans in the 1970s began to worry about a "colonial" status, in which the United States exported food, lumber, and minerals and imported automobiles and television sets. By the 1980s, foreign economic competitiveness and trade deficits, especially with Japan, became issues of national concern.

The effects of international competition were more complex than "Japan-bashers" acknowledged. Mass-production industries, such as textiles and aluminum, suffered from cheaper and sometimes higher quality imports, but many specialized industries and services such as Houston's oil equipment and exploration firms thrived. Globalization also created new regional winners and losers. In 1982, the United States began to do more business with Pacific nations than with Europe.

More recent steps to expand the global reach of the American economy were the **North American Free Trade Agreement (NAFTA)** in 1993 and a new worldwide GATT approved in 1994. Negotiated by Republican George Bush and pushed through Congress in 1993 by Democrat Bill Clinton, NAFTA combined 25 million Canadians, 90 million Mexicans, and 250 million U.S. consumers in a single "common market" similar to that of western Europe. GATT cut tariffs among 100 nations. A larger free-trade zone was intended to open new markets and position the United States to compete more effectively against the European Community and Japan. The agreement may have been a holdover from the Bush years, but it matched Clinton's ideas about reforming the American economy.

NAFTA was a hard pill for many Democrats, and it revived the old debate between free traders and protectionists. Support was strongest from professional businesses and industries that sought foreign customers, including agriculture and electronics. Opponents included organized labor, communities already hit by industrial shutdowns, and environmentalists worried about lax controls on industrial pollution in Mexico. In contrast to the nineteenth-century arguments for protecting infant industries, new industries now looked to foreign markets, while older and uncompetitive firms hoped for protected domestic markets. The readjustments from NAFTA have tended to produce obvious pain in the form of closed factories or farms made unprofitable by cheaper imports, while its gains are less visible—a new job here, larger sales there. Evidence from the early years favored NAFTA supporters, indicating that few manufacturing jobs relocated to Mexico.

The **World Trade Organization (WTO)**, which replaced GATT in 1996, became the unexpected target of a global protest movement. Seattle officials, committed to promoting Seattle as a "world class" city, lobbied hard to get the 1999 WTO meeting. With finance and foreign affairs ministers and heads of government expected to attend, it would give Seattle world attention. Instead, it gave the city a headache. Fifty thousand protesters converged on the meeting, held from November 30 to December 4, 1999. Most demonstrators were peaceful, but several hundred started a rampage through the downtown that triggered massive overreaction by unprepared police.

The battle of Seattle was part of an international movement. It was preceded by similar disturbances around an earlier WTO meeting in Geneva, Switzerland, and was followed by large demonstrations against the International Monetary Fund in Washington in 2000 and against a WTO meeting in Genoa, Italy, in 2001. Protesters were convinced that the WTO is a tool of huge transnational corporations that tramples on local labor and environmental protections in the name of "free trade" and benefits only the wealthy nations and their businesses. WTO defenders pointed to the long-term effects of open trade in raising net production in the world economy and thereby making more wealth available for developing nations. Opponents asserted, in turn, that such wealth never reaches the workers and

Protests against the WTO have united environmentalists and labor unions, interests that are often in opposition over domestic issues.

farmers in those nations. American opponents demanded that U.S. firms, such as sportswear companies that make their products overseas make sure that those overseas workers have decent living conditions and wages.

BROADENING DEMOCRACY

Closely related to the changes in the American economy were the changing composition of the American people and the continued emergence of new participants in American government. Bill Clinton's first cabinet, in which three women and four minority men balanced seven white men, recognized the makeup of the American population and marked the maturing of minorities and women as distinct political constituencies. The first cabinet appointed by George W. Bush in 2001 included four minority men and four women, one of whom was Asian American. In both administrations, the new prominence of women and minorities in the national government followed years of growing success in cities and states.

Americans in 2000

The federal census for the year 2000 found 281,400,000 Americans in the 50 states, District of Columbia, and Puerto Rico (and probably 2 to 3 million more residents were not counted). The increase from 1990 was 13.2 percent, or 32,700,000. It was the largest ten-year population increase in U.S. history, evidence of the nation's prosperity and its attractiveness for immigrants. One-third of all Americans lived in four states: California, Texas, New York, and Florida. These were the key prizes in presidential elections. Their regulations and consumer preferences conditioned national markets for products ranging from automobiles to textbooks.

As leadership opportunities for African Americans have increased in recent decades, they have gained positions of influence in a growing range of activities. In the field of foreign policy, for example, President George W. Bush chose Colin Powell as secretary of state and Condoleezza Rice as national security advisor. Here Powell (2nd from left) and Rice (right) observe a White House meeting between Bush and United Nations Secretary General Kofi Annan.

The West grew the fastest. The superboom states were Nevada (66 percent growth), Arizona (40 percent), Colorado (31 percent), Utah (30 percent), and Idaho (29 percent). Fast growth implies young populations, and the states with the lowest average ages were also Western: Utah, Alaska, Idaho, and Texas. The Southwest and South also had the fastest growing metropolitan areas. Las Vegas topped them all with an increase of 83 percent. Among large metro areas with over 500,000 people in 2000, all twenty of the fastest growing of were in the West and Southeast.

In contrast, parts of the American Midwest grew slowly. Rural counties in Appalachia and across the Great Plains continued to empty out as fewer and fewer

Americans were needed for mining and farming or for the small towns associated with those industries. No state lost population, but North Dakota and West Virginia had ten-year gains of only 1 percent.

Another important trend was increasing ethnic and racial diversity. Hispanics were the fastest growing group in the American population. Indeed, the number of Hispanics in 2000 (35.2 million) surprised many officials and matched the number of African Americans. Although immigrants concentrated in the coastal and border states, Hispanics and Asian Americans were also spreading into interior states. Both Asians and Hispanics who had been in the United States for some time showed substantial economic success. Non-Hispanic white people are now a minority in California (at 47 percent), as well as in the District of Columbia, Hawaii, and New Mexico.

The changing ethnicity of the American people promised to be increasingly apparent in coming decades. Immigrants tend to be younger adults who are likely to form families, and birth rates have been particularly high among Hispanics and Asian Americans. The result is a sort of multiethnic baby boom. In 1972, at the peak of the post–World War II baby boom, 80 percent of elementary and high school students were non-Hispanic white children. By 1999 the figure was 63 percent and falling. Over the coming decades, the effects of ethnic change will be apparent not only in schools but also in the workplace, popular culture, and politics.

Women from the Grass Roots to Congress

The increasing prominence of women and family issues in national politics was a steady, quiet revolution that bore fruit in the 1990s, when the number of women in Congress more than doubled. In 1981, President Reagan had appointed Arizona judge Sandra Day O'Connor to be the first woman on the United States Supreme Court. In 1984, Walter Mondale chose New York Congresswoman Geraldine Ferraro as his vice presidential candidate. In 1993 Clinton appointed the second woman to the Supreme Court, U.S. Appeals Court judge Ruth Bader Ginsburg. Clinton appointee Janet Reno was the first woman to serve as attorney general and Madeleine K. Albright the first to serve as secretary of state. In 2001, George W. Bush continued to break new ground by naming Condoleezza Rice as his national security advisor.

Political gains for women at the national level reflected their growing importance in grass-roots politics. The spreading suburbs of postwar America were "frontiers" that required concerted action to solve immediate needs like adequate schools and decent parks. Because pursuit of such community services was often viewed as "woman's work" (in contrast to the "man's work" of economic development), postwar metropolitan areas offered numerous opportunities for women to engage in volunteer civic work, learn political skills, and run for local office. Moreover, new cities and suburbs had fewer established political institutions, such as political machines and strong parties; their politics were open to energetic women.

The entry of more women into politics has been a bipartisan affair. Important support and training grounds are the League of Women Voters, which does nonpartisan studies of basic issues, and the National Women's Political Caucus, designed to support women candidates of both parties. Most women in contemporary politics have been more liberal than men—a difference that political scientists attribute to women's interest in the practical problems of schools, neighborhoods, and two-earner families. But women's grass-roots mobilization, especially through evangelical churches, has also strengthened groups committed to conservative social values.

Regional differences have affected women's political gains. The West has long been the part of the country most open to women in state and local government and in business. Many of the same skills learned from politics were also useful as women played a growing role as independent business proprietors. Several Western states granted voting rights to women before the adoption of the Nineteenth Amendment. Westerners have been more willing than voters in the East or South to choose women as mayors of major cities and as members of state legislatures.

In 1991, the nomination of Judge Clarence Thomas, an African American, to the U.S. Supreme Court ensured that everyone knew that the terms of American politics were changing. Because of his conservative positions on social and civil rights issues, Thomas was a controversial nominee. Controversy deepened when law professor Anita Hill accused Thomas of harassing her sexually while she had served on his staff at the U.S. Civil Rights Commission. The accusations led to riveting hearings before a U.S. Senate committee. Critics tried to discredit Hill with vicious attacks on her character, and the committee failed to call witnesses who could have supported her position. The public was left with Hill's plausible but unproved allegations and Thomas's equally vigorous but unproved denials. The Senate confirmed Thomas to the Supreme Court. Partisans on each side continued to believe the version that best suited their preconceptions and agendas.

Whatever the merits of her charges, Hill's badgering by skeptical senators angered millions of women. In the shadow of the hearings, women made impressive gains in the 1992 election, which pushed women's share of seats in the fifty state legislatures above 20 percent (it was 22 percent in 1999). The number of women in the U.S. Senate jumped from two to six (and grew further to six Democrats and three Republicans after November 1996). In 2000, Hillary Rodham Clinton won a Senate seat from New York (see Figure 14-1). Her husband had appointed women to 37 percent of the five hundred or so high-level jobs in the White House and federal departments. That is far higher than Jimmy Carter's 15 percent or Lyndon Johnson's 4 percent, and also above George W. Bush's 26 percent.

Women have influenced national politics as voters as well as candidates and cabinet members. Since the 1980s, voting patterns have shown a widening gender gap. Women in the 1990s identified with the Democratic party and voted for its candidates at a higher rate than men. The reasons include concerns about the effects of government spending cuts and interest in measures to support families rather than conservative rhetoric. This gender gap has helped keep Democrats competitive and dampened the nation's conservative swing.

Minorities at the Ballot Box

The changing makeup of the American populace also helped black and Latino candidates for public office be increasingly successful. After the racial violence of the 1960s, many black people had turned to local politics to gain control of their own communities. The first black mayor of a major twentieth-century city was Carl Stokes in Cleveland in 1967. The 1973 election brought victories for Tom Bradley in Los Angeles, Maynard Jackson in Atlanta, and Coleman Young in Detroit. By 1983, three of the nation's four largest cities had black mayors. In 1989, Virginia made Douglas Wilder the first black governor in any of the fifty states since Reconstruction.

The election of a minority mayor was sometimes more important for its symbolism than for the transfer of real power. Efforts to restructure the basis of city council elections, however, struck directly at the balance of power. Most midsized cities had stopped electing city councils by wards or districts during the first half of the twentieth century. Voting at large shifted power away from geographically concentrated ethnic groups. It favored business interests who claimed to speak for the city as a whole, but who could assign most of the costs of economic growth to older and poorer neighborhoods. In the 1970s, minority leaders and community activists realized that a return to district voting could convert neighborhood segregation from a liability to a political resource. As amended in 1975, the federal

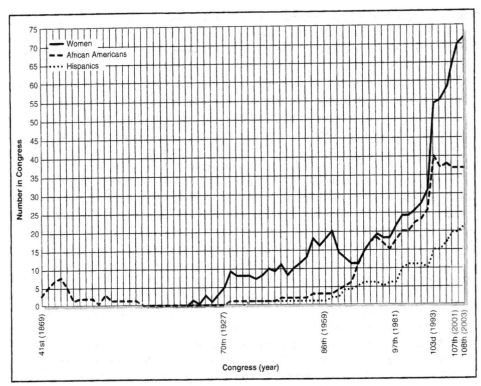

FIGURE 14-1   Minorities and Women in Congress, 1869–2001
The number of African Americans, Hispanics, and women serving in the House of Representatives and Senate increased rapidly in the 1980s and early 1990s and more slowly in the middle 1990s. The increases reflected changing attitudes, the impact of the Voting Rights Act, and decades of political activism at the grass roots.

Voting Rights Act allowed minorities to use the federal courts to challenge at-large voting systems that diluted the impact of their votes. Black Americans and Mexican Americans used the act to reestablish city council districts in the late 1970s and early 1980s in city after city across the South and Southwest.

The political rebalancing meant that local leaders faced strong pressures to assure equitable distribution of the benefits and burdens of growth. Newly empowered minorities began to press for a fair share of an expanding economic pie. In San Antonio and Denver, for example, young Hispanic politicians brought new ideas into city government in the 1980s. Henry Cisneros of San Antonio defeated a representative of the downtown establishment in 1981, and in Denver, Federico Peña ousted a sixteen-year incumbent with the help of an army of volunteers. Both men ran on platforms of planned growth and later served in Clinton's cabinet. Progressive African-American mayors in the 1990s included Dennis Archer in Detroit and Andrew Young in Atlanta, leaders who won on positive platforms of growth and equity and who mended fences with business leaders. Meanwhile, Washington state elected a Chinese American as governor, and Hawaii elected Japanese-American, native Hawaiian, and Filipino-American governors.

At the national level, minorities gradually increased their representation in Congress. Ben Nighthorse Campbell of Colorado, a Cheyenne, brought a Native American voice to the U.S. Senate in 1992. The number of African Americans in the House of Representatives topped forty after 1992, with the help of districts drawn to concentrate black voters. Even after a series of Supreme Court cases invalidated districts drawn with race as the "predominant factor," however, African Americans held most of their gains, while the number of Latino members rose to 22 by 2003 (see Figure 14-1).

In struggling for political influence, recent immigrants have added new panethnic identities to their national identities. In the nineteenth century, English-speaking Americans looked at European immigrants from widely separated regions and backgrounds and saw "Italians" or "Jews." In turn, newcomers found economic and political strength by making common cause across their differences, molding identities as ethnic groups within the U.S. context. Newer immigrants have gone through a parallel process. Hispanic activists revived the term *Chicano* (derived from Mexicano) to include both recent Mexican-American immigrants and Latinos whose families had settled in the Southwest before the American conquest in 1848. Great gaps of experience and culture separated Chinese, Koreans, Filipinos, and Vietnamese, but they gained political recognition and influence if they dealt with other Americans as "Asians." Native Americans have similarly downplayed tribal differences in efforts to secure better opportunities for Indians as a group.

Rights and Opportunities

The increasing presence of Latinos and African Americans in public life highlighted a set of troublesome questions about the proper balance between equal rights and equal opportunities. Was government justified in seeking to equalize outcomes as well as starting points? More broadly, was the United States to be a unitary society in which everyone assimilated to a single culture and adhered to a single set of formal and informal rules? Or might it be a plural society in which different groups accepted different goals and behaviors? The debates at the end of the twentieth century replayed many of the questions that European immigration had raised at the century's beginning.

Illegal Immigration and Bilingual Education One issue has been the economic impact of illegal immigration. Advocates of tight borders assert that illegal immigrants take jobs away from legal residents and eat up public assistance. Many studies, however, find that illegal immigrants fill jobs that nobody else wants. Over the long run, high employment levels among immigrants mean that their tax contributions through sales taxes and Social Security taxes and payroll deductions more than pay for their use of welfare, food stamps, and unemployment benefits, which illegal immigrants are often afraid to claim for fear of calling attention to themselves. Nevertheless, high immigration can strain local government budgets even if it benefits the nation as a whole. Partly for this reason, 60 percent of California voters approved **Proposition 187** in 1994, cutting off access to state-funded public education and health care by illegal immigrants. The mostly white supporters of the measure said that it was about following the rules; Hispanic opponents saw it as racism.

A symbolic issue was the degree to which American institutions should accommodate non-English speakers. Referendums in Alaska (1996) and Utah (2000) raised to twenty-six the number of states that declared English their official language. The measures ranged from general statements to specific prohibitions on printing forms and ballots in multiple languages. California voters in 1998 banned bilingual public education, a system under which children whose first language was Spanish or another "immigrant" tongue were taught for several years in that language before shifting to English-language classrooms. Advocates of bilingual education claimed that it eased the transition into American society, while opponents said that it blocked immigrant children from fully assimilating into American life.

Affirmative Action A more encompassing issue was a set of policies that originated in the 1960s as **affirmative action**, a phrase that first appeared in executive orders issued by Presidents Kennedy and Johnson. The initial goal was to require businesses that received federal contracts to "take affirmative action to ensure that applicants are employed, and that employees are treated during employment without regard for their race, creed, color, or national origin." By the 1970s, many states and cities had adopted similar policies for hiring their own employees and choosing contractors and extended affirmative action to women as well as minorities. Colleges and universities used affirmative action policies in recruiting faculty and admitting students.

As these efforts spread, the initial goal of nondiscrimination evolved into expectations and requirements for active ("affirmative") efforts to achieve greater diversity among employees, students, or contractors. Government agencies began to set aside a small percentage of contracts for woman-owned or minority-owned firms. Cities actively worked to hire more minority police officers and fire fighters. Colleges made special efforts to attract minority students. The landmark court case about affirmative action was **University of California v. Bakke** (1978). Allan Bakke was an unsuccessful applicant to the medical school at the University of California at Davis. He argued that the university had improperly set aside sixteen of one hundred places in its entering class for minority students, thereby engaging in reverse discrimination against white applicants. In a narrow decision, the U.S. Supreme Court ordered Bakke admitted because the only basis for his rejection had been race. At the same time, the Court stated that race or ethnicity could legally be one of several factors considered in college and university admissions as long as a specific number of places were not reserved for minorities.

In 1996, California voters took grass-roots action, approving a ballot measure to eliminate state-sponsored affirmative action. One effect was to prohibit state-funded colleges and universities from using race or ethnicity as a factor in deciding which applicants to admit. In the same year, the Supreme Court let stand a lower court ruling in *Hopwood v. Texas*, which had forbidden the University of Texas to consider race in admission decisions. The number of black freshmen in the University Texas dropped by half in 1997 and the number of black and Hispanic acceptances among first-year law students by two-thirds. The results were similar at the University of California at Berkeley, where the number of black acceptances among entering law students dropped from twenty to one.

Affirmative action has come under such close scrutiny and attack because it is a lightning rod for disagreements about the character of American society. The problem is that the goal of diversity seems to conflict with the fundamental American value of individual opportunity. In opinion polls, a majority of Americans reject the idea that past injustice and unequal opportunity can justify special consideration for all members of a group. Instead, they believe that individual merit and qualifications should be the sole basis for getting into school or getting a job, and that such factors as SAT scores and civil-service exams can measure those qualifications. Others argue that the merit system is severely flawed, that students from poor families lack the advantages at home and at school that give upper-middle-class and wealthy students a head start for success. Affirmative action, they argue, helps to level the field. Nevertheless, many minorities worry that affirmative action undermines their own success by suggesting that they received jobs or contracts by racial preference rather than merit.

The nation surely benefits when members of minority groups are able to build successful businesses. Both cities with large minority populations and suburbs with few minorities benefit when members of all groups are serving on their police forces and working in their classrooms. Students benefit when they interact with people of diverse backgrounds and opinions in the course of their studies. In 2003, the Supreme Court affirmed the basic principle of affirmative action in two cases involving admission to the University of Michigan. Aided by supporting statements filed by major corporations and by members of the U.S. military, the Court found that promoting ethnic and racial diversity among students constitutes a compelling state interest, and it narrowly approved tailored affirmative action programs that weigh race and ethnicity along with other admissions criteria on an individual basis.

EDGING INTO A NEW CENTURY

On the evening of November 7, 2000, CBS-TV made a mistake that journalists dread. Relying on questions put to a sample of voters after they cast their ballots in the presidential contest between Albert Gore Jr. and George W. Bush, the CBS newsroom first projected that Gore would win Florida and likely the election, then reversed itself and called the election for Bush, only to find that it would be days or even weeks before the votes in several pivotal states, including Florida, could be certified.

The miscue was reminiscent of the premature *Chicago Tribune* headline in November 1948 that proclaimed "Dewey Beats Truman" when the actual results were the reverse. The inability to predict the outcome in 2000 was also an indication of the degree to which Americans were split down the middle in their political preferences and their visions for the future. The United States entered the twenty-first century both divided and balanced, with extremes of opinion revolving around a center of basic goals and values.

The 2000 Election

On November 8, 2000, the day after their national election, Americans woke up to the news that neither Republican George W. Bush nor Democrat Albert Gore Jr. had secured a majority of votes in the electoral college. For the next five weeks, they woke to the same news. Although Gore held a lead in the popular vote (about 340,000 votes out of more than 100 million cast), both candidates needed a majority in Florida to secure its electoral votes and the White House. After protracted protests of voting irregularities and malfunctioning voting equipment, politically divided Floridians engaged in an on-again–off-again recount in key counties. The U.S. Supreme Court finally preempted the state process and ordered a halt to recounting on December 12 by the politically charged margin of 5 to 4. The result was to make Bush the winner in Florida by a few hundred votes and the winner nationwide by 271 electoral votes to 267 (see Map 14-1).

The heart of the controversy involved how to read Florida's punch-card ballots. Americans learned a new word, *chad*, for the little paper ovals that get punched out. How should election officials count dangling chads that were partially detached? What should they do with ballots where the chad was dimpled but not punched through? Until the Supreme Court put an end to the discussion, teams of officials struggled through recounts. Both parties put their own spin on the process. Republicans framed the issue as "following the rules," while Democrats framed it as "making every vote count."

It is difficult to know who "really" won Florida. There is good evidence that African-American voters, who strongly favored Gore, were turned away in disproportionate numbers because of technical challenges to their registration. In one county, a ballot with a particularly poor design probably caused several thousand mistaken votes for a minor candidate rather than Gore. Overseas absentee ballots, likely to favor Bush, were counted despite their frequent failure to meet the criteria for legitimate votes. But recounts by teams of newspaper reporters came to different conclusions about who might have won, depending on what criteria were used to accept or reject disputed punch card ballots. In the aftermath, each side could claim to have won, but the Supreme Court ruling and Bush's inauguration made the point irrelevant.

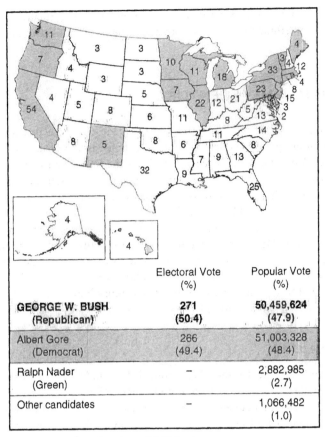

	Electoral Vote (%)	Popular Vote (%)
GEORGE W. BUSH (Republican)	**271** **(50.4)**	**50,459,624** **(47.9)**
Albert Gore (Democrat)	266 (49.4)	51,003,328 (48.4)
Ralph Nader (Green)	–	2,882,985 (2.7)
Other candidates	–	1,066,482 (1.0)

MAP 14-1 The Election of 2000

In the nation's closest presidential election, Democrat Al Gore was most successful in the Northeast and Far West, while George W. Bush swept the South and won most of the Great Plains states. Green Party candidate Ralph Nader took most of his votes from Gore, and, in a twist of irony, helped swing the election to Bush.

The outcome of the election showed a nation that was paradoxically divided around a strong center. The votes showed basic differences between the parties. Gore appealed especially to residents of large cities, to women, to African Americans, and to families struggling to make it economically. Bush appealed to people from small towns, to men, and to members of households who had benefited the most from the prosperity of the Clinton era. These were divisions that had marked the two parties since the 1930s, and their persistence was a reminder of the nation's diversity of opinions and values. The nation also divided regionally, with Gore strong in the Northeast, upper Midwest, and Pacific Coast, Bush was favored in the South, Ohio Valley, Great Plains, and Rocky Mountain states.

At the same time, both Bush, governor of Texas and son of President George Bush (1989–1993), and Gore, vice president for the previous eight years, targeted their campaigns at middle Americans. Each offered to cut taxes, reduce the federal government, and protect Social Security, differing in the details rather than the broad goals. In trying to claim the political middle, they reflected the successful political message of the Clinton administration. Voters also shaved the Republican control of Congress to razor-thin margins, further undermining any chance of radical change in either a conservative or a liberal direction. To those on the political left and right who had hoped for new directions for the nation, it looked like a formula for paralysis; for the majority of Americans, it looked like stability.

Reaganomics Revisited

Despite sophisticated exit polls and computer-based voting models, the 2000 presidential election was too close to call in the hours—and then the weeks—after the voting ended. The *Chicago Sun-Times* reflected the suspense and confusion in the news media, trying four different headlines as the lead see-sawed between George W. Bush and Albert Gore Jr.

Despite the message of stability, the Bush administration took the return to executive power as opportunity to tilt domestic policy abruptly to the right. In effect, the new administration decided it had a mandate for change and acted boldly to implement its goals. Following the example of Ronald Reagan, Bush made massive tax cuts the centerpiece of his first months in office. By starting with proposals for ten-year cuts so large that two generations of federal programs were threatened, Bush and congressional Republicans forced the Democrats to "compromise" on reductions far higher than the economy could probably support. The resulting cuts to income taxes and estate taxes were projected to total $1,350 billion over the decade, with one-third of the benefits going to families earning more than $200,000. The federal deficit for 2003 was $374 billion, with the deficit for 2004 projected even higher, undoing the careful political balancing and fiscal discipline of the Clinton administration. Nevertheless, the administration seemed likely to achieve its goal of making the tax cuts permanent after the 2002 elections confirmed a Republican majority in Congress.

The Bush team also moved quickly to deregulate the economy. It opened many of the environmental and business regulations of the previous two decades to reconsideration—from arsenic standards in drinking water to protections for wetlands to the pollution controls required of electric utilities. In many cases, the administration proposed to rely on the market through voluntary compliance and incentives to replace regulations. Vice President Dick Cheney developed a new production-oriented energy policy in consultation with energy companies but not with environmental or consumer groups. The administration failed to secure congressional approval for oil drilling in the Arctic National Wildlife Refuge in the far north of Alaska but crafted development-friendly policies for other federal lands. Collapse of the energy-trading company Enron in a hailstorm of criticism over deceptive accounting and shady market manipulations to create an energy crisis in California in early 2000 slowed the push to deregulate. In turn, Enron proved to be the first of many companies that had to restate earnings in 2002, depressing the stock market and raising questions about the ethics of big business and business accounting practices. Stock market declines and the evaporation of retirement savings for many workers raised doubts about the solidity of the 1990s boom and helped hold down economic growth for the third year.

Education policy, a centerpiece of Bush's image as an innovator when governor of Texas, was another legislative front. Tough battles with Congress resulted in compromise legislation, reminiscent of the 1990s, that included national testing standards, as Bush wanted, balanced by more federal funding. More important for both education and religion was the narrow decision by the Supreme Court in *Zelman* v. *Simmons-Harris* (2002) to uphold the use of taxpayer-funded assistance, or vouchers, to help students attend religious schools. By declaring that both religious and secular institutions can compete for government money as long as it is channeled through individuals who decided how to spend it, the court continued a two-decade trend to narrow the constitutional prohibition on the "establishment of religion."

Downsized Diplomacy

Strong conservatives had long criticized subordinating U.S. authority and freedom of action to international agreements. The new Bush administration heeded this criticism and brought a revolutionary approach to foreign affairs. The administration repeatedly adopted unilateral or bilateral policies in preference to the complexities of negotiations with an entire group of nations.

In his first eighteen months, Bush opted out of a series of treaties and negotiations on global issues, sometimes after years of careful bargaining. In each case he pointed to specific flaws or problems, but the goal was to reduce restrictions on U.S. business and its military. The administration undercut efforts to implement the Convention on Biological Warfare because of possible adverse effects on drug companies. It refused to sign on to efforts to reduce the international trade in armaments, declined to acknowledge a new International Criminal Court that is designed to try war criminals, and ignored an international compact on the rights of women in deference to cultural conservatives. Most prominently, it refused to accept the Kyoto Agreement, aimed at combating the threat of massive environmental change through global warming resulting from the carbon dioxide released by fossil fuels, dismissing a growing scientific consensus on the problem.

In the field of arms control, Bush entered office with the intention of ending the 1972 treaty that had limited the deployment of antimissile defenses by the United States and Russia in order to stabilize the arms race. The treaty had been a cornerstone of national security policy. Despite the objection of Russia, however, he formally withdrew from the treaty in December 2001. In its place he revived Ronald Reagan's idea of a Strategic Defense Initiative with proposals for new but unproven technologies to protect the United States against nuclear attacks by "rogue states." This argument was supported in 2002 by North Korea's revelation that it was pursuing a nuclear weapons program, even though it had agreed not to do so in 1994.

Bush also decided not to implement the START II treaty, which had been one of the major accomplishments of his father's term as president. In its place, he worked directly to improve relations with Russia and negotiated a bilateral agreement to reduce substantially the number of nuclear warheads that Russia and the United States actively deploy for potential use. A new U.S. policy that explicitly claimed the right to act militarily to preempt potential threats confirmed the go-it-alone approach.

PARADOXES OF POWER

The United States in the twenty-first century faced the paradox of power: The enormous economic, military, and technological capacity that allowed it to impose its will on other nations did not extend to an ability to prevent anti-American actions by deeply enraged individuals.

In the 1990s, the U.S. economy had surged while Japan's stagnated, Europe marked time, and Russia verged on economic collapse. The American economy in the early twenty-first century was twice the size of Japan's; California alone had economic capacity equal to France or Britain. America's lead was nurtured by research and development spending equal to that of the next six countries combined. The American military budget exceeded the total military spending of the next dozen nations. The United States had the world's only global navy and a huge edge in military technology.

But the United States remained vulnerable. Terrorist attacks by Islamic radicals killed nineteen American soldiers at military housing in Saudi Arabia in 1996 and seventeen sailors on the destroyer *Cole* while in port in the Arab nation of Yemen in 2000. Bombs at the U.S. embassies in Kenya and Tanzania in 1998 killed more than 200 people. These bombings followed the detonation of explosives in the basement garage of the World Trade Center in New York in February 1993, killing six people. New acts of terror remained a constant threat—realized in an appalling manner on September 11, 2001.

9/11/01

The men who hijacked four commercial jetliners on the morning of September 11 were part of the Al-Qaeda network of terrorists coordinated by Osama Bin-Laden. A Saudi Arabian businessman who had turned against the United States because of its role in the Gulf War and its support for Israel, Bin-Laden was probably the brains behind the attacks on the U.S. military and diplomats overseas and the earlier blast at the World Trade Center. Operating from exile in Afghanistan, he now masterminded the new and spectacular assault. The first hijacked plane hit the North Tower of the World Trade Center at 8:46 A.M. eastern time, and the second plane hit the South Tower at 9:30. As flames billowed upward, the South Tower disintegrated at 10:05 and the North Tower at 10:28. Each building took only 10 seconds to fall in on itself, but television replays burned the image into the national memory.

Fire fighters work in the rubble of one of the World Trade Center towers soon after its destruction on September 11, 2001.

The events of September 11 were an enormous shock to the American people, but worries about escalating terrorism were not new. Security specialists such as Defense Secretary William Cohen had been sounding the alarm through the 1990s. The U.S. Commission on National Security/21st Century, appointed by President Clinton, had included detailed warnings in its February 2001 report, although the new administration had ignored its recommendations to reorganize federal homeland security. The problem, however, has been to connect broad concerns to specific threats. After September 11, there were reports of information-gathering failures by the FBI and CIA, many of which were confirmed in the 2004 report of a commission appointed by President Bush. However, it is always enormously difficult to separate and correlate key points in the vast flood of information that flows through law-enforcement and intelligence agencies. Experts call this the problem of discerning real "signals" in the "noise" of information. It is much easier to read the warnings after an event has occurred than to pick out the essential data before the unexpected happens—something as true about the attack on Pearl Harbor, for example, as about the attack of 9/11.

Security and Conflict

On September 12, President George W. Bush called the Pentagon and World Trade Center attacks "acts of war." Three days later, Congress passed a Joint Resolution that gave the president sweeping powers "to use all necessary and appropriate force against those nations, organizations, or persons he determines planned, authorized, committed, or aided the terrorist attacks that occurred on September 11, 2001." Only one member voted against the resolution—the same level of agreement that the nation showed after December 7, 1941.

The government response in the United States was a hodgepodge of security measures and arrests. Air travelers found endless lines and stringent new screening procedures, watched over by army reservists called to duty by the president. Members of Congress and journalists received letters containing potentially deadly anthrax spores, heightening fears of biological warfare (the source of the letters still remains a mystery). Federal agents detained more than one thousand terrorist suspects, mostly men from the Middle East, releasing some but holding hundreds without charges, evidence, or legal counsel. President Bush also declared that "enemy combatants" could be tried by special military tribunals, although domestic and international protest caused the administration to agree to more legal safeguards than originally planned. Congress passed the **Patriot Act** (*P*roviding *A*ppropriate *T*ools *R*equired to *I*ntercept and *O*bstruct *T*errorists) in late October 2001, which gave federal authorities substantial new capacity to conduct criminal investigations, in most measures for the next three to five years. These included the power to request "roving" wiretaps of individuals rather than single telephones; obtain nationwide search warrants; tap information in computerized records; and to detain foreigners without filing charges for up to a week.

These measures raised a number of concerns about the protection of civil liberties, as noted by the several dozen members of Congress who voted against the act. Since 2001, the act has been subject to increasing criticism for threatening basic constitutional and political rights.

In November 2002, Congress approved a massive reorganization of the federal government to improve security at home. The new Department of Homeland Security includes the Immigration and Naturalization Service, Customs Service, Coast Guard, Secret Service, federal airport security workers, bioterrorism experts, and many others. With 170,000 employees, it is the second-largest federal agency, after the Defense Department, but it still leaves unsolved the problem of an ineffective FBI and CIA.

In contrast to suppression of dissent during World War I or the internment of Japanese Americans in World War II, Americans in 2001 and 2002 were careful on the home front. The leaders and supporters of the War on Terror reacted to dissenting voices, particularly those from a pacifist tradition, with caustic remarks rather than repression. Censorship has consisted of careful management of the news and stonewalling requests under the Freedom of Information Act rather than direct censorship of speech and the press. Violations of civil liberties have affected individuals rather than entire groups. President Bush made an important gesture soon after September 11 by appearing at a mosque and arguing against blanket condemnation of Muslims. Ethnic profiling has resulted in heightened suspicion and surveillance of Muslims, selective enforcement of immigration laws on visitors from twenty Muslim nations, and detention of several hundred U.S. residents of Middle Eastern origin, rather than incarceration of entire ethnic groups.

In the months after 9/11, the military response overseas focused on Afghanistan, where the ruling Taliban regime was harboring Bin-Laden. Afghanistan had been wracked by civil war since it had been invaded by the Soviet Union in 1979. The Taliban, who came to power after Soviet withdrawal and civil war, were politically and socially repressive rulers with few international friends. American bombing attacks on Taliban forces began in early October 2001, and internal opposition groups within Afghanistan threw the Taliban out of power by December. Bin-Laden, however, apparently escaped with the aid of mountainous terrain and the confusion of war, leaving the United States with an uncertain commitment to rebuild a stable Afghanistan. The Al-Qaeda network and sympathetic groups remained active around the world with bombings in places as distant as Indonesia and Kenya.

Iraq and Conflicts in the Middle East

Even while the United States was intervening in Afghanistan, the administration was expanding its attention to other nations that supported or condoned anti-American terrorists or had the capability to produce chemical, biological, or nuclear weapons of mass destruction. George Bush named North Korea, Iran, and Iraq as an "axis of evil" for these reasons and then focused on Iraq. After the Gulf War, Iraq had grudgingly accepted a United Nations requirement that it eliminate such weapons but had gradually made UN inspections impossible. Such resistance caused Bush to reject the previous policy of containing and isolating Iraq and to make the overthrow of Iraq's ruthless dictator, Saddam Hussein, the center of foreign policy. In effect, he declared one small, and possibly dangerous nation to be the greatest menace that the United States faced. In the meantime, North Korea created a further crisis by actively pursuing its atomic weapons program with the threat of additional war.

In addition to the direct fallout from the Persian Gulf War, background to deep-seated tensions in the Middle East included U.S. support of Israel amid deterioration of relations between Israel and the Arab Palestinians in territories occupied by Israel since 1967. The United States has consistently backed Israel since the 1960s. The cornerstones of American policy have been the full endorsement of Israel's right to exist with secure borders and agreement on the right of Palestinians to a national state—in effect, a policy of coexistence. The United States had helped broker an Israel-Egypt peace agreement in 1977 and agreements pointing toward an independent Palestinian state in the 1990s. But it has repeatedly found that hardline Israeli governments have taken advantage of U.S. support since the 1980s in Lebanon to the present.

In 2001–2002, the United States watched from the sidelines as the Israeli-Palestinian agreements for transition to a Palestinian state fell apart. Palestinian extremists and suicide bombers and an Israeli government that favored military responses locked each other into a downward spiral that turned anti-Israel demonstrations into civil war. The result for many Arabs has been to identify the United States as an enemy of Arab nations and peoples, despite formal U.S. policy. The deep and seemingly unsolvable Israel-Palestinian conflict helps to explain anti-American terrorism among Arabs, and sometimes other Muslims.

In the spring and summer of 2002, the administration escalated threats of unilateral intervention to change the Iraqi regime and began preparations for a second war in the Persian Gulf region. On October 10, Congress authorized preemptive military action against Iraq. However, international pressure from unenthusiastic allies and from other Arab nations persuaded Bush to place diplomacy ahead of war and devote two months making his case at the United Nations. On November 8, the UN Security Council unanimously adopted a compromise resolution whose effect was to give Iraq three and a half months to allow full and open inspections before military action might be considered. In the following months, UN inspectors searched Iraqi military sites while the United States built up forces in the Middle East in preparation for possible war. On March 17, 2003, Bush suspended further diplomatic efforts and on March 19 began a full scale U.S.–British invasion of Iraq.

The Iraq War was a military success. Heavy precision bombing disrupted the communications and command systems for Iraq's armed forces, which were unable to sustain a coordinated defense. The technological capacities of the American armed forces overwhelmed

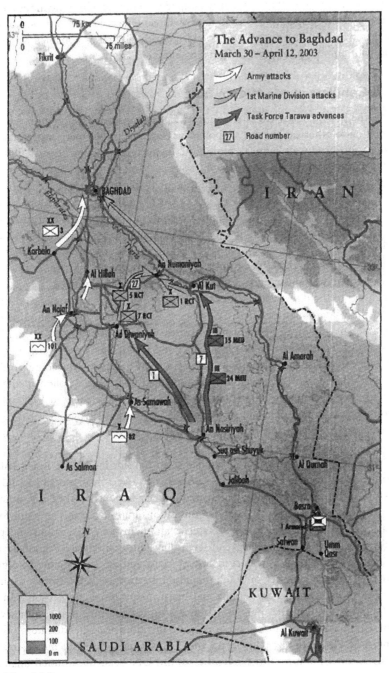

MAP 14-2

their opposition. Coalition forces encountered substantial pockets of resistance from Iraqi army units up to division size, but the battles failed to stop the steady push northward from the Persian Gulf. The U.S. took control of Baghdad without the door-to-door fighting that many had feared. On May 1, 2003, President Bush was able to declare that U.S. and British forces now controlled Iraq and that major combat operations in Iraq were over.

Peace proved more difficult than war. Reconstruction of damaged bridges, roads, water systems, and electrical systems took longer than expected. Saddam Hussein remained at large for several months before being captured. A new U.S.-sponsored governing council for Iraq was too unwieldy to be effective. Meanwhile, American troops and relief workers were the continuing targets of car bombs, booby-trapped highways, and mortar attacks, and similar guerilla resistance, which killed hundreds of Americans compared to 138 during the actual invasion.

The aftermath of the war also created political problems for George Bush. A systematic search found no stockpiles or active production facilities or stockpiles for chemical, nuclear, or biological weapons of mass destruction, refuting one of the basic justifications for the war. Congress in November 2003 approved $87 billion for reconstruction and ongoing military occupation in Iraq, but the request triggered substantial criticism of administration policy. So did the extension of military enlistments and the continuing necessity to mobilize National Guard and reserve units because of the need to keep an occupying army or more than 100,000 in Iraq. Pictures and reports of torture and humiliation of Iraqis held by U.S. forces violated the American sense of decency. Reporting in June 2004, the national commission investigating the World Trade Center disaster found no significant ties between Saddam Hussein and al-Qaeda, undercutting another argument that had been used in favor of the war. With support from the United Nations, a new interim Iraqi government assumed sovereignty on June 28, 2004 as a step toward free elections. However, the country was still struggling to recover from the economic effects of war and to achieve a semblance of political stability and unity. With American forces remaining in large numbers, many Iraqis viewed the United States as an invader rather than a liberator.

CONCLUSION

If there was a dominant theme that ran through the changes and challenges of the 1990s and early 2000s, it was interconnection. The Internet, email, and cell phones brought instant communication. The national economy was more and more deeply engaged with the rest of the world through trade, investment, travel, and immigration. Corporate mismanagement affected far more people than before because of pensions and savings invested in the stock market.

The nation's growing diversity—closely connected to its internationalized economy—was reflected in the political gains of African Americans and Hispanics, as well as women. The same diversity fueled battles over affirmative action and language politics. It underlay the effort to increase security against terrorism without endangering the civil liberties of Muslim Americans.

Despite what some might have wished, Americans also found that they could not always isolate the nation from the problems and conflicts that wracked much of the rest of the world. The Clinton administration joined international peacekeeping efforts in Bosnia and Kosovo. The Bush administration chose to ignore several international agreements, but still sought United Nations approval for action against Iraq.

The events of September 11, 2001 sparked a renewed sense of national unity, at least in the short run. Stories of heroism were inspiring, whether by emergency workers, by ordinary men and women who helped each other escape from the World Trade Center, or by passengers who kept the fourth airplane from its target. So was the outpouring of volunteers and contributions for rescue and relief efforts. As the nation slowly settled back into routines and then approached another presidential election contest between George W. Bush and Democrat John Kerry, however, the question remained whether Americans could sustain a new sense of unity and inclusiveness under the pressures of economic uncertainty, threats of terrorism, and war.

Review Questions

1. Was the American political system more polarized and divided in 1992 than in 1980? How did religiously conservative Americans understand issues of foreign relations and economic policy? How did religiously liberal Americans understand these same issues? What was the gender gap in national politics in the 1990s? Why were Republicans unable to appeal to most black and Hispanic voters in 1992?

2. What were Bill Clinton's major policy accomplishments? Do these represent "liberal," "moderate," or "conservative" positions?

3. What was the Contract with America? What are other examples of a conservative political trend in the 1990s?

4. What issues were involved in Clinton's impeachment? How does the impeachment compare with the challenges to Presidents Andrew Johnson and Richard Nixon?

5. Did the American economy undergo fundamental changes in the 1990s? What has been the impact of the computer revolution? Of the growing importance of world markets?

6. What new directions did George W. Bush establish for U.S. domestic and foreign policy?

7. How did the terrorist attacks of September 11, 2001 change life inside the United States? How did ordinary Americans respond at the time and since the attacks?

Key Terms

Affirmative action *447*

Bosnia *427*

Contract with America *429*

Internet *435*

Kosovo *428*

Neoliberal *428*

North American Free Trade Agreement (NAFTA) *441*

Patriot Act *454*

Proposition 187 *447*

Silicon Valley *437*

Temporary Assistance for Needy Families (TANF) *430*

University of California v. *Bakke* *448*

Whitewater *433*

World Trade Organization (WTO) *442*

World Wide Web *440*

Recommended Reading

William C. Berman, *From the Center to the Edge: A History of the Clinton Presidency* (2001). An assessment of the Clinton administration in historical perspective.

Thomas Friedman, *The Lexus and the Olive Tree* (1999). A positive assessment of the increasing integration of the world economy.

William Langewiesche, *American Ground: Unbuilding the World Trade Center* (2002). The story of the clearance and rehabilitation efforts at the World Trade Center after September 11.

William Mitchell, *E-Topia: Urban Life, Jim, But Not As We Know It* (2000). An evaluation of the impacts of new electronic communications on the American economy and society.

Richard A. Posner, *An Affair of State: The Investigation, Trial and Impeachment of President Clinton* (1999). An evenhanded account of the Clinton-Lewinsky scandal that finds few heros.

BIBLIOGRAPHY

Chapter Two

The Ferment of Reform

Karen Blair, *The Clubwoman as Feminist: True Womanhood Redefined, 1868–1914* (1980)

John W. Chambers, *The Tyranny of Change* (1980)

Ellen Chesler, *Woman of Valor: The Life of Margaret Sanger* (1992)

Nancy Cott, *The Grounding of Modern Feminism* (1987)

Robert Crunden, *Ministers of Reform* (1982)

Susan Curtis, *A Consuming Faith: The Social Gospel and Modern American Culture* (1991)

David B. Danbom, *The World of Hope: Progressives and the Struggle for an Ethical Public Life* (1987)

Melvyn Dubofsky, *We Shall Be All: A History of the Industrial Workers of the World* (1969)

Susan A. Glenn, *Daughters of the Shtetl* (1990)

Eric Goldman, *Rendezvous with Destiny* (1952)

Alan Kraut, *The Huddled Masses: The Immigrant in American Society, 1880–1921* (1982)

George Marsden, *Fundamentalism and American Culture* (1980)

Henry May, *Protestant Churches and Industrial America* (1949)

Kathy Peiss, *Cheap Amusements: Working Women and Leisure in Turn-of-the-Century New York* (1986)

Daniel T. Rodgers, *Atlantic Crossings: Social Politics in a Progressive Age* (1998)

Nick Salvatore, *Eugene V. Debs: Citizen and Socialist* (1982)

Anne Firor Scott, *Natural Allies: Women's Associations in American History* (1991)

Elliott Shore, *Talkin' Socialism: J.A. Wayland and the Role of the Press in American Radicalism* (1988)

Margaret Spruill Wheeler, *New Women of the New South* (1993)

Reforming Society

Paul Boyer, *Urban Masses and Moral Order in America* (1978)

Mina Carson, *Settlement Folk: Social Thought and the American Settlement Movement* (1990)

Elizabeth Clapp, *Mothers of All Children: Women Reformers and the Rise of Juvenile Courts in Progressive Era America* (1998)

Peter Coleman, *Progressivism and the World of Reform* (1987)

Ruth H. Crocker, *Social Work and Social Order* (1992)

David Danbom, *The Resisted Revolution: Urban America and the Industrialization of Agriculture* (1979)

Allen F. Davis, *Spearheads of Reform: The Social Settlements and the Progressive Movement* (1968) and *American Heroine: The Life and Legend of Jane Addams* (1973)

Alan Derickson, *Workers' Health, Workers' Democracy* (1988)

Lyle Dorsett, *Billy Sunday and the Redemption of Urban America* (1991)

Nancy S. Dye, *As Equals and as Sisters: Feminism, the Labor Movement, and the Woman's Trade Union League of New York* (1980)

Ellen Fitzpatrick, *Endless Crusade: Women, Social Scientists, and Progressive Reform* (1990)

Noralee Frankel and Nancy S. Dye, *Gender, Class, Race, and Reform in the Progressive Era* (1991)

Victoria Getis, *The Juvenile Court and the Progressives* (2000)

Elliott Gorn, *Mother Jones: The Most Dangerous Woman in America* (2001)

Samuel Haber, *Efficiency and Uplift: Scientific Management in the Progressive Era* (1964)

Morton Keller, *Regulating a New Society: Public Policy and Social Change in America, 1900–1930* (1994)

Molly Ladd-Taylor, *Mother-Work: Women, Child Welfare and the State, 1890–1930* (1994)

Kriste Lindenmeyer, *A Right to Childhood: The U.S. Children's Bureau and Child Welfare* (1997)

William A. Link, *The Paradox of Southern Progressivism* (1992)

Roy Lubove, *The Progressives and the Slums* (1962) and *The Struggle for Social Security, 1900–1935* (1986)

Martin Melosi, *Garbage in the Cities: Refuse, Reform, and the Environment* (1981)

Robyn Muncy, *Creating a Female Dominion in American Reform, 1890–1935* (1991)

Daniel Nelson, *Frederick W. Taylor and the Rise of Scientific Management* (1980)

Elizabeth Anne Payne, *Reform, Labor, and Feminism: Margaret Dreier Robins and the Women's Trade Union League* (1988)

Barbara Sicherman, *Alice Hamilton: A Life in Letters* (1984)

Anne Huber Tripp, *The I.W.W. and the Paterson Silk Strike of 1913* (1987)

Nancy Woloch, *Women and the American Experience* (1984)

Moral Crusades and Social Control

John Burnham, *Bad Habits: Drinking, Smoking, Taking Drugs, Gambling, Sexual Misbehavior, and Swearing in American History* (1993)

Mark Connelly, *The Response to Prostitution in the Progressive Era* (1980)

John Dittmer, *Black Georgia in the Progressive Era* (1977)

Richard Hamm, *Shaping the Eighteenth Amendment* (1995)

Louis Harlan, *Booker T. Washington: The Wizard of Tuskegee* (1983)

John Higham, *Strangers in the Land: Patterns of American Nativism* (1963)

K. Austin Kerr, *Organized for Prohibition: A New History of the Anti-Saloon League* (1983)

Jack Temple Kirby, *Darkness at the Dawning: Race and Reform in the Progressive South* (1972)

David Langum, *Crossing Over the Line: Legislating Morality and the Mann Act* (1994)

Linda O. McMurry, *To Keep the Waters Troubled: The Life of Ida B. Wells* (1998)

Ruth Rosen, *The Lost Sisterhood: Prostitutes in America, 1900–1918* (1982)

David Rothman, *Conscience and Convenience: The Asylum and Its Alternatives in Progressive America* (1980)

Cassandra Tate, *Cigarette Wars: The Triumph of "The Little White Slaver"* (1999)

James Timberlake, *Prohibition and the Progressive Movement* (1963)

Chapter 3

Reforming Politics and Government

John M. Allswang, *The Initiative and Referendum in California, 1898–1998* (2000)

Peter H. Argersinger, *Structure, Process, and Party* (1992)

Jean H. Baker, ed. *Votes for Women* (2002)

Kathleen Barber, *Proportional Representation and Electoral Reform in Ohio* (1995)

John D. Buenker, *Urban Liberalism and Progressive Reform* (1973)

Allen F. Davis, *American Heroine: The Life and Legend of Jane Addams* (1973)

Ellen Carol DuBois, *Harriot Stanton Blatch and the Winning of Woman Suffrage* (1997)

Thomas Goebel, *A Government By the People: Direct Democracy in America, 1890–1940* (2002)

Sara Hunter Graham, *Woman Suffrage and the New Democracy* (1996)

Dewey Grantham, *Southern Progressivism* (1983)

Melanie S. Gustafson, *Women and the Republican Party* (2001)

William F. Holmes, *The White Chief: James Kimble Vardaman* (1970)

Robert D. Johnston, *The Radical Middle Class: Populist Democracy and the Question of Capitalism in Progressive Era Portland, Oregon* (2003)

Jack Temple Kirby, *Darkness at the Dawning: Race and Reform in the Progressive South* (1972)

J. Morgan Kousser, *The Shaping of Southern Politics* (1974)

Richard C. Lower, *A Bloc of One: The Political Career of Hiram W. Johnson* (1993)

Richard L. McCormick, *From Realignment to Reform: Political Change in New York State* (1983)

Michael E. McGerr, *The Decline of Popular Politics* (1986)

Thomas Pegram, *Partisans and Progressives* (1992)

Steven L. Piott, *Giving Voters a Voice: The Origins of the Initiative and Referendum in America* (2003)

John F. Reynolds, *Testing Democracy: Electoral Behavior and Progressive Reform in New Jersey* (1988)

Martin Schiesl, *The Politics of Efficiency: Municipal Administration and Reform in America* (1977)

David P. Thelen, *The New Citizenship: Origins of Progressivism in Wisconsin* (1972)

—— *Robert M. La Follette and the Insurgent Spirit* (1976)

Nancy Unger, *Fighting Bob La Follette: The Righteous Reformer* (2000)

Robert F. Wesser, *Charles Evans Hughes: Politics and Reform in New York State* (1967)

James E. Wright, *The Progressive Yankees: Republican Reformers in New Hampshire* (1987)

Theodore Roosevelt and the Progressive Presidency

John M. Blum, *The Republican Roosevelt* (1954)

H. W. Brands, *T.R.: The Last Romantic* (1997)

David Burton, *The Learned Presidency: Theodore Roosevelt, William Howard Taft, Woodrow Wilson* (1988)

Kathleen Dalton, *Theodore Roosevelt: A Strenuous Life* (2002)

William H. Harbaugh, *Power and Responsibility: The Life and Times of Theodore Roosevelt* (1961)

Samuel P. Hays, *Conservation and the Gospel of Efficiency: The Progressive Conservation Movement* (1962)

Morton Keller, *Regulating a New Economy* (1990)

Gabriel Kolko, *The Triumph of Conservatism* (1963)

Edmund Morris, *Theodore Rex* (2002)

George E. Mowry, *The Era of Theodore Roosevelt* (1958)

Robert Mutch, *Campaigns, Congress, and Courts: The Making of Federal Campaign Finance Law* (1988)

Elizabeth Sanders, *Roots of Reform: Farmers, Workers, and the American State* (1999)

Martin Sklar, *The Corporate Reconstruction of American Capitalism* (1988)

Mark David Spence, *Dispossessing the Wilderness: Indian Removal and the Making of the National Parks* (1999)

Donald Worster, *Rivers of Empire: Water, Aridity, and the Growth of the American West* (1985)

Taft and the Tensions of Progressive Politics

Donald F. Anderson, *William Howard Taft: A Conservative's Conception of the Presidency* (1968)

Judith Icke Anderson, *William Howard Taft: An Intimate History* (1981)

Paolo Coletta, *The Presidency of William Howard Taft* (1973)

Julie Greene, *Pure and Simple Politics: The American Federation of Labor and Political Activism, 1881–1917* (1998)

James Holt, *Congressional Insurgents and the Party System* (1967)

Richard Lowitt, *George W. Norris: The Making of a Progressive* (1963)

James Penick Jr., *Progressive Politics and Conservation: The Ballinger-Pinchot Affair* (1968)

Stephen Ponder, *Managing the Press: Origins of the Media Presidency* (1999)

William G. Ross, *A Muted Fury: Populists, Progressives, and Labor Unions Confront the Courts* (1994)

Norman Wilensky, *Conservatives in the Progressive Era: The Taft Republicans of 1912* (1965)

Woodrow Wilson and Progressive Reform

John M. Blum, *Woodrow Wilson and the Politics of Morality* (1956)

Kendrick A. Clements, *Woodrow Wilson* (1987)

John Milton Cooper Jr., *The Warrior and the Priest: Woodrow Wilson and Theodore Roosevelt* (1983)

John Gable, *The Bull Moose Years: Theodore Roosevelt and the Progressive Party* (1979)

Lewis L. Gould, *Reform and Regulation: American Politics, From Roosevelt to Wilson* (1996)

August Hecksher, *Woodrow Wilson* (1991)

Arthur Link, *Woodrow Wilson and the Progressive Era* (1954)

James Livingston, *Origins of the Federal Reserve System* (1986)

David Brian Robertson, *Capital, Labor, and State: The Battle for American Labor Markets from the Civil War to the New Deal* (2000)

David Sarasohn, *The Party of Reform: Democrats in the Progressive Era* (1989)

Daniel Stid, *The President as Statesman: Woodrow Wilson and the Constitution* (1998)

John A. Thompson, *Woodrow Wilson* (2002)

Jeffrey K. Tulis, *The Rhetorical Presidency* (1987)

Melvin Urofsky, *Louis D. Brandeis and the Progressive Tradition* (1981)

Chapter 4

Roots of Imperialism

David L. Anderson, *Imperialism and Idealism: American Diplomats in China, 1861–1898* (1985)

Stuart Anderson, *Race and Rapprochement: Anglo-Saxonism and Anglo-American Relations, 1895–1904* (1981)

Patrick J. Hearden, *Independence and Empire: The New South's Cotton Mill Campaign, 1865–1901* (1982)

Patricia R. Hill, *The World Their Household: The American Woman's Foreign Mission Movement and Cultural Transformation, 1870–1920* (1985)

Michael H. Hunt, *Ideology and U.S. Foreign Policy* (1987)

Matthew Frye Jacobson, *Barbarian Virtues: The United States Encounters Foreign Peoples at Home and Abroad* (2000)

Edmund Morris, *The Rise of Theodore Roosevelt* (1979)

Emily S. Rosenberg, *Spreading the American Dream: American Economic and Cultural Expansion, 1890–1945* (1982)

Ronald Spector, *Admiral of the New Empire* (1974)

William Widenor, *Henry Cabot Lodge and the Search for an American Foreign Policy* (1980)

William A. Williams, *The Roots of the Modern American Empire* (1969)

The Spanish-American War

Richard Challener, *Admirals, Generals, and American Foreign Policy, 1889–1914* (1973)

Graham A. Cosmas, *An Army for Empire: The United States Army and the Spanish-American War* (1971)

John Dobson, *Reticent Expansionism: The Foreign Policy of William McKinley* (1988)

Willard B. Gatewood Jr., *Black Americans and the White Man's Burden, 1898–1903* (1975)

Lewis L. Gould, *The Spanish-American War and President McKinley* (1982)

David F. Healy, *U.S. Expansionism: The Imperialist Urge in the 1890s* (1970)

Gerald Linderman, *The Mirror of War: American Society and the Spanish-American War* (1974)

Joyce Milton, *The Yellow Journalists* (1989)

H. Wayne Morgan, *America's Road to Empire: The War with Spain and Overseas Expansion* (1965)

Julius W. Pratt, *Expansionists of 1898* (1936)

David R. Trask, *The War with Spain in 1898* (1981)

Anti-Imperialism

Robert L. Beisner, *Twelve Against Empire: The Anti-Imperialists, 1898–1900* (1968)

Thomas J. Osborne, *Empire Can Wait: American Opposition to Hawaiian Annexation, 1893–1898* (1981)

Daniel B. Schirmer, *Republic or Empire: American Resistance to the Philippine War* (1972)

E. Berkeley Tompkins, *Anti-Imperialism in the United States: The Great Debate, 1890–1920* (1970)

Imperial Ambitions: The United States and East Asia, 1899–1917

Charles S. Campbell, *Special Business Interests and the Open Door Policy* (1951)

Warren I. Cohen, *America's Response to China* (1989)

John M. Gates, *Schoolbooks and Krags: The United States Army in the Philippines* (1973)

Michael H. Hunt, *The Making of a Special Relationship: The U.S. and China to 1914* (1983)

Akira Iriye, *Pacific Estrangement: Japanese and American Expansion, 1897–1911* (1972)

Walter LaFeber, *The Clash: A History of U.S.-Japan Relations* (1997)

Thomas McCormick, *China Market: America's Quest for Informal Empire* (1967)

Stuart Miller, *Benevolent Assimilation: The American Conquest of the Philippines, 1899–1903* (1982)

Paul Varg, *The Making of a Myth: The United States and China, 1897–1912* (1968)

Richard E. Welch, *Response to Imperialism: The United States and the Philippine-American War* (1979)

Imperial Power: The United States and Latin America, 1899–1917

Howard K. Beale, *Theodore Roosevelt and the Rise of America to World Power* (1956)

Jules Benjamin, *Hegemony and Development: The United States and Cuba, 1890–1934* (1977)

Bruce Calder, *The Impact of Intervention: The Dominican Republic During the U.S. Occupation of 1916 to 1924* (1984)

Raymond Carr, *Puerto Rico: A Colonial Experiment* (1984)

Arturo Morales Carrion, *Puerto Rico* (1983)

John M. Cooper Jr., *The Warrior and the Priest: Woodrow Wilson and Theodore Roosevelt* (1983)

John Eisenhower, *The United States and the Mexican Revolution, 1913–1917* (1993)

David F. Healy, *Drive to Hegemony: The United States in the Caribbean, 1898–1917* (1988)

James Hitchman, *Leonard Wood and Cuban Independence, 1898–1902* (1971)

Walter LaFeber, *Inevitable Revolutions: The United States in Central America* (1993)

———— *The Panama Canal* (1990)

Jack C. Lane, *Armed Progressive: General Leonard Wood* (1978)

Lester Langley, *The Banana Wars: An Inner History of the American Empire, 1900–1934* (1983)

David McCullough, *The Path Between the Seas: The Creation of the Panama Canal* (1977)

Allan R. Millett, *The Politics of Intervention: The Military Occupation of Cuba, 1906–1909* (1968)

Louis A. Perez Jr., *Cuba Under the Platt Amendment, 1902–1934* (1986)

Chapter 5

General Studies

John Whiteclay Chambers II, *The Tyranny of Change* (1992)

John M. Cooper Jr., *Pivotal Decades: The United States, 1900–1920* (1990)

Otis L. Graham Jr., *The Great Campaigns: Reform and War in America* (1971)

Ellis W. Hawley, *The Great War and the Search for a Modern Order* (1992)

Michael J. Lyons, *World War I: A Short History* (1994)

Neil Wynn, *From Progressivism to Prosperity: World War I and American Society* (1986)

Diplomacy of Neutrality, War, and Peace

Lloyd Ambrosius, *Woodrow Wilson and the American Diplomatic Tradition* (1987)

Thomas A. Bailey and Paul B. Ryan, *The Lusitania Disaster* (1975)

Kathleen Burk, *Britain, America, and the Sinews of War* (1985)

John Coogan, *The End of Neutrality* (1981)

John M. Cooper Jr., *The Vanity of Power: American Isolationism and the First World War* (1969)

———— *Breaking the Heart of the World: Woodrow Wilson and the Fight for the League of Nations* (2001)

David S. Foglesong, *America's Secret War Against Bolshevism: United States Intervention in the Russian Civil War, 1917–1920* (1995)

Ross Gregory, *The Origins of American Intervention in the First World War* (1971)

Burton I. Kaufman, *Efficiency and Expansion: Foreign Trade Organization in the Wilson Administration* (1974)

Thomas J. Knock, *To End All Wars: Woodrow Wilson and the Creation of the League of Nations* (1992)

N. Gordon Levin Jr., *Woodrow Wilson and World Politics: America's Response to War and Revolution* (1968)

Lawrence W. Levine, *Defender of the Faith: William Jennings Bryan, The Last Decade* (1965)

Arthur S. Link, *Woodrow Wilson and the Progressive Era, 1910–1917* (1954)

Ernest R. May, *The World War and American Isolation, 1914–1917* (1966)

David W. McFadden, *Alternative Paths: Soviets and Americans, 1917–1920* (1993)

Daniel M. Smith, *The Great Departure: The United States and World War I* (1965)

Ralph A. Stone, *The Irreconcilables* (1970)

John A. Thompson, *Woodrow Wilson* (2002)

Arthur Walworth, *Wilson and the Peacemakers* (1986)

The Military

A. E. Barbeau and Florette Henri, *The Unknown Soldiers: Black American Troops in World War I* (1974)

Nancy Bristow, *Making Men Moral: Social Engineering During the Great War* (1996)

John Whiteclay Chambers II, *To Raise an Army* (1987)

John Garry Clifford, *Citizen Soldiers: The Plattsburgh Training Camp Movement* (1972)

Edward M. Coffman, *The Hilt of the Sword: The Career of Peyton C. March* (1966)

Frank Freidel, *Over There: The Story of America's First Great Overseas Crusade* (1964)

Gerald W. Patton, *War and Race: The Black Officer in the American Military* (1981)

Laurence Stallings, *The Doughboys: The Story of the AEF, 1917–1918* (1963)

David Trask, *The AEF and Coalition Warmaking, 1917–1918* (1993)

Frank E. Vandiver, *Black Jack: The Life and Times of John J. Pershing* (1977)

Wartime Economy and Society

William J. Breen, *Uncle Sam at Home: Civilian Mobilization, Wartime Federalism, and the Council of National Defense, 1917–1919* (1984)

Thomas Britten, *American Indians in World War I: At Home and at War* (1997)

Valerie Connor, *The National War Labor* (1983)

Robert D. Cuff, *The War Industries Board: Business-Government Relations During World War I* (1973)

David Danbom, *The Resisted Revolution: Urban America and the Industrialization of Agriculture* (1979)

Maurine Weiner Greenwald, *Women, War, and Work: The Impact of World War I on Women Workers in the United States* (1980)

Florette Henri, *Black Migration: The Movement North, 1900–1920* (1975)

Paul Koistinen, *Mobilizing for Modern War: The Political Economy of American Warfare, 1865–1919* (1997)

Frederick C. Luebke, *Bonds of Loyalty: German–Americans and World War I* (1974)

Joseph A. McCartin, *Labor's Great War: The Struggle for Industrial Democracy and the Origins of Modern American Labor Relations, 1912–1921* (1997)

Elliot M. Rudwick, *Race Riot at East St. Louis, July 2, 1917* (1964)

John A. Thompson, *Reformers and War: American Progressive Publicists and the First World War* (1987)

Stephen L. Vaughn, *Holding Fast the Inner Lines: Democracy, Nationalism, and the Committee on Public Information* (1980)

Wartime Dissent and Repression

Christopher Gibbs, *The Great Silent Majority: Missouri's Resistance to World War I* (1989)

Kathleen Kennedy, *Disloyal Mothers and Scurrilous Citizens: Women and Subversion During World War I* (1999)

Robert Morlan, *Political Prairie Fire: The Nonpartisan League, 1915–1922* (1955)

H. C. Peterson and Gilbert Fite, *Opponents of War, 1917–1918* (1957)

William Preston Jr., *Aliens and Dissenters: Federal Suppression of Radicals, 1903–1933* (1963)

Harry N. Scheiber, *The Wilson Administration and Civil Liberties* (1960)

James Weinstein, *The Decline of Socialism in America* (1967)

Postwar Conflict

David Brody, *Labor in Crisis: The Steel Strike of 1919* (1965)

Stanley A. Coben, *A. Mitchell Palmer, Politician* (1963)

Burl Noggle, *Into the Twenties: The United States from Armistice to Normalcy* (1974)

Athan Theoharis and John Stuart Cox, *The Boss: J. Edgar Hoover and the Great American Inquisition* (1988)

William M. Tuttle Jr., *Race Riot: Chicago in the Red Summer of 1919* (1970)

Chapter 6

General Studies

John D. Hicks, *Republican Ascendancy, 1921–1933* (1960)

William Leuchtenberg, *The Perils of Prosperity* (1958)

Michael E. Parrish, *Anxious Decades: America in Prosperity and Depression, 1920–1941* (1992)

Geoffrey Perrett, *America in the Twenties* (1982)

Economic Developments

Jo Ann E. Argersinger, *Making the Amalgamated: Gender, Ethnicity, and Class in the Baltimore Clothing Industry* (1999)

Irving L. Bernstein, *The Lean Years: A History of the American Worker, 1920–1933* (1960)

James J. Flink, *The Automobile Age* (1988)

Alice Kessler-Harris, *Out to Work: A History of Wage-Earning Women* (1982)

Roland Marchand, *Advertising the American Dream* (1985)

Stephen Meyer, III, *The Five Dollar Day: Labor Management and Social Control in the Ford Motor Company* (1981)

Ronald W. Schatz, *The Electrical Workers* (1983)

Susan Smulyan, *Selling Radio: The Commercialization of American Broadcasting, 1920–1934* (1994)

Susan Strasser, *Satisfaction Guaranteed: The Making of the American Mass Market* (1989)

Leslie Woodcock Tentler, *Wage-Earning Women: Industrial Work and Family Life in the United States, 1900–1930* (1979)

Robert H. Zieger, *American Workers, American Unions* (1994)

Politics and Government

David Burner, *Herbert Hoover: A Public Life* (1979)

———, *The Politics of Provincialism* (1967)

Douglas B. Craig, *After Wilson: The Struggle for the Democratic Party* (1992)

Ellis W. Hawley, ed. *Herbert Hoover as Secretary of Commerce* (1981)

Walter LaFeber, *Inevitable Revolutions: The United States in Central America* (1984)

Allan J. Lichtman, *Prejudice and the Old Politics: The Presidential Election of 1928* (1979)

Richard Lowitt, *George W. Norris: The Persistence of a Progressive* (1971)

Donald R. McCoy, *Calvin Coolidge* (1967)

Robert Murray, *The Politics of Normalcy* (1973)

Robert D. Schulzinger, *The Making of the Diplomatic Mind* (1975)

Eugene P. Trani, and David L. Wilson, *The Presidency of Warren G. Harding* (1977)

Joan Hoff Wilson, *American Business and Foreign Policy, 1920–1933* (1968)

———, *Herbert Hoover: Forgotten Progressive* (1975)

Cities and Suburbs

Sarah Deutsch, *No Separate Refuge: Culture, Class, and Gender on an Anglo-Hispanic Frontier in the American Southwest* (1987)

Juan Garcia, *Mexicans in the Midwest, 1900–1932* (1996)

David Goldfield, *Cotton Fields and Skyscrapers* (1982)

Peter Gottlieb, *Making Their Own Way: Southern Blacks' Migration to Pittsburgh, 1916–1930* (1987)

David Gerard Hogan, *Selling 'em by the Sack: White Castle and the Creation of American Food* (1997)

Kenneth T. Jackson, *Crabgrass Frontier: The Suburbanization of the United States* (1985)

Earl Lewis, *In Their Own Interests: Race, Class, and Power in Twentieth-Century Norfolk, Virginia* (1991)

Gilbert Osofsky, *Harlem: The Making of a Ghetto* (1968)

Ricardo Romo, *East Los Angeles: History of a Barrio* (1983)

John C. Teaford, *Cities of the Heartland* (1993)

William Worley, *J. C. Nichols and the Shaping of Kansas City* (1990)

Society and Culture

Charles C. Alexander, *The Ku Klux Klan in the Southwest* (1965)

Kathleen M. Blee, *Women and the Klan: Racism and Gender in the 1920s* (1991)

Paul Carter, *Another Part of the Twenties* (1977)

William H. Chafe, *The American Woman: Her Changing Social, Economic, and Political Roles* (1972)

Norman Clark, *Deliver Us from Evil: An Interpretation of American Prohibition* (1976)

Stanley Coben, *Rebellion Against Victorianism* (1991)

Nancy F. Cott, *The Grounding of American Feminism* (1987)

Lynn Dumenil, *The Modern Temper: American Culture and Society in the 1920s* (1995)

Sara M. Evans, *Born for Liberty: A History of Women in America* (1989)

Stuart Ewen, *Captains of Consciousness: Advertising and the Social Roots of the Consumer Culture* (1976)

Paula Fass, *The Damned and the Beautiful: American Youth in the 1920s* (1977)

Fred Hobson, *Mencken: A Life* (1994)

Nathan Huggins, *Harlem Renaissance* (1971)

Kenneth T. Jackson, *The Ku Klux Klan in the City* (1967)

Bruce B. Lawrence, *Defenders of God: The Fundamentalist Revolt against the Modern Age* (1989)

Lawrence W. Levine, *Defender of the Faith: William Jennings Bryan, the Last Decade, 1915–1925* (1965)

David L. Lewis, *When Harlem Was in Vogue* (1981)

Nancy Maclean, *Behind the Mask of Chivalry: The Making of the Second Ku Klux Klan* (1994)

Lary May, *Screening Out the Past: The Birth of Mass Culture and the Motion Picture Industry* (1980)

Leonard Moore, *Citizen Klansmen: The Ku Klux Klan in Indiana* (1991)

Robyn Muncy, *Creating a Female Dominion in American Reform* (1991)

Kathy H. Ogren, *The Jazz Revolution* (1989)

Elizabeth A. Payne, *Reform, Labor, and Feminism: Margaret Dreier Robins and the Women's Trade Union League* (1988)

Kathy Peiss, *Hope in a Jar: The Making of America's Beauty Culture* (1998)

Benjamin G. Rader, *American Sports: From the Age of Folk Games to the Age of Spectators* (1983)

Robert Sklar, *Movie-Made America: A Cultural History of American Movies* (1994)

Judith Stein, *The World of Marcus Garvey* (1986)

David Wiggins, *Sport in America* (1995)

Chapter 7

The Stock Market Crash and the Depression

David T. Beito, *Taxpayers in Revolt* (1989)

Ron Chenow, *The House of Morgan* (1990)

John Kenneth Galbraith, *The Great Crash: 1929* (1989)

John Garraty, *The Great Depression* (1986)

Susan Estabrook Kennedy, *The Banking Crisis of 1933* (1973)

Maury Klein, *Rainbow's End: The Crash of 1929* (2001)

Hard Times in Hooverville

Michael Bernstein, *The Great Depression* (1987)

Julia Kirk Blackwelder, *Women of the Depression: Caste and Culture in San Antonio* (1984)

Sean Dennis Cashman, *America in the Twenties and Thirties* (1989)

William H. Chafe, *The American Woman, 1920–1970* (1972)

Nancy F. Cott (ed.), *No Small Courage: A History of Women in the United States* (2000)

Elizabeth Faue, *Community of Suffering & Struggle: Women, Men, and the Labor Movement in Minneapolis, 1915–1945* (1991)

Robin D. G. Kelley, *Hammer and Hoe: Alabama Communists During the Great Depression* (1990)

Alice Kessler-Harris, *In Pursuit of Equity: Women, Men, and the Quest for Economic Citizenship in 20th-Century America* (2001)

Robert McElvaine, *The Great Depression: America, 1929–1941* (1984)

William Mullins, *The Depression and the Urban West Coast, 1929–1933* (1991)

Mark Reisler, *By the Sweat of Their Brow: Mexican Immigrant Labor in the United States* (1976)

George J. Sanchez, *Becoming Mexican American: Ethnicity, Culture, and Identity in Chicano Los Angeles, 1900–1945* (1993)

Lois Scharf, *To Work and to Wed: Female Employment, Feminism, and the Great Depression* (1980)

John Shover, *Cornbelt Rebellion: The Farmers' Holiday Association* (1965)

Richard White, *"It's Your Misfortune and None of My Own": A New History of the American West* (1991)

Herbert Hoover and the Depression

David Burner, *Herbert Hoover: A Public Life* (1979)

Roger Daniels, *The Bonus March* (1971)

Martin L. Fausold, *The Presidency of Herbert C. Hoover* (1985)

David E. Hamilton, *From New Day to New Deal: American Farm Policy from Hoover to Roosevelt* (1991)

Donald Lisio, *The President and Protest* (1974)

Albert Romasco, *The Poverty of Abundance: Hoover, the Nation, the Depression* (1965)

Jordan A. Schwartz, *Interregnum of Despair* (1970)

T.H. Watkins, *The Hungry Years: A Narrative History of the Great Depression in America* (1999)

Gwendolyn Mink, *The Wages of Motherhood: Inequality in the Welfare State, 1917–1942* (1995)

Catherine Stock, *Main Street in Crisis: The Great Depression and the Old Middle Class on the Northern Plains* (1992)

Susan Ware, *Holding Their Own: American Women in the 1930s* (1982)

Donald Worster, *Dust Bowl* (1979)

———, *Rivers of Empire* (1985)

Melvyn Dubofsky, *The State and Labor in Modern America* (1994)

The Election of Franklin D. Roosevelt

James MacGregor Burns, *Roosevelt: The Lion and the Fox* (1956)

Geoffrey Ward, *A First Class Temperament: The Emergence of Franklin Roosevelt* (1989)

Chapter 8

Launching the New Deal

Anthony J. Badger, *The New Deal: The Depression Years, 1933–1940* (1989)

Irving Bernstein, *Turbulent Years: A History of the American Worker, 1933–1941* (1970)

Edward C. Blackorby, *Prairie Rebel: William Lemke* (1963)

Alan Brinkley, *Voices of Protest: Huey Long, Father Coughlin, and the Great Depression* (1982)

David Conrad, *The Forgotten Farmers: The Story of the Sharecroppers in the New Deal* (1965)

Donald H. Grubbs, *Cry from the Cotton: The Southern Tenant Farmers Union and the New Deal* (1971)

Ellis Hawley, *The New Deal and the Problem of Monopoly* (1966)

William Leuchtenburg, *The FDR Years* (1995)

Leo P. Ribuffo, *The Old Christian Right: The Protestant Far Right from the Great Depression to the Cold War* (1983)

Albert Romasco, *The Politics of Recovery: Roosevelt's New Deal* (1983)

Theodore Saloutos, *The American Farmer and the New Deal* (1982)

Arthur M. Schlesinger, Jr., *The Coming of the New Deal* (1958)

T. Harry Williams, *Huey Long* (1969)

Consolidating the New Deal

John Allswang, *The New Deal and American Politics* (1978)

Kristi Andersen, *The Creation of a Democratic Majority* (1979)

Edward D. Berkowitz, *America's Welfare State* (1991)

Roger Biles, *A New Deal for the American People* (1991)

Gerald Gamm, *The Making of New Deal Democrats* (1989)

Colin Gordon, *New Deals: Business, Labor, and Politics in America* (1994)

Donald R. McCoy, *Landon of Kansas* (1966)

George McJimsey, *Harry Hopkins* (1987)

The New Deal and American Life

Jo Ann E. Argersinger, *Toward a New Deal in Baltimore: People and Government in the Great Depression* (1988)

Joseph L. Arnold, *The New Deal in the Suburbs* (1971)

John Barnard, *Walter Reuther and the Rise of the Auto Workers* (1983)

Roger Biles, *The South and the New Deal* (1994)

Lisabeth Cohen, *Making a New Deal: Industrial Workers in Chicago* (1990)

Elizabeth Faue, *Community of Suffering and Struggle: Women, Men, and the Labor Movement in Minneapolis* (1991)

Sidney Fine, *Sitdown: The General Motors Strike of 1936–1937* (1969)

Steven Fraser, *Labor Will Rule: Sidney Hillman and the Rise of American Labor* (1991)

James Gregory, *American Exodus: The Dust Bowl Migration and Okie Culture in California* (1989)

David G. Gutierrez, *Walls and Mirrors: Mexican Americans, Mexican Immigrants, and the Politics of Ethnicity* (1995)

Laurence C. Kelly, *The Assault on Assimilation: John Collier and the Origins of Indian Policy Reform* (1983)

Nelson Lichtenstein, *The Most Dangerous Man in Detroit: Walter Reuther and the Fate of American Labor* (1995)

Richard Lowitt, *The New Deal and the West* (1984)

Gwendolyn Mink, *The Wages of Motherhood: Inequality in the Welfare State, 1917–1942* (1995)

Bruce Nelson, *Workers on the Waterfront* (1988)

Harvard Sitkoff, *A New Deal for Blacks* (1978)

Douglas L. Smith, *The New Deal in the Urban South* (1988)

Catherine Stock, *Main Street in Crisis: The Great Depression and the Old Middle Class on the Northern Plains* (1992)

Patricia Sullivan, *Days of Hope: Race and Democracy in the New Deal Era* (1996)

Graham Taylor, *The New Deal and American Indian Tribalism* (1980)

Susan Ware, *Beyond Suffrage: Women in the New Deal* (1981)

———, *Holding Their Own: American Women in the 1930s* (1982)

Donald Worster, *Dust Bowl* (1979)

———, *Rivers of Empire* (1985)

Robert Zieger, *The CIO, 1935–1955* (1995)

———, *John L. Lewis* (1988)

Ebbing of the New Deal

Alan Brinkley, *The End of Reform: New Deal Liberalism in Recession and War* (1995)

Wayne Cole, *Roosevelt and the Isolationists, 1932–1945* (1983)

Robert Dallek, *Franklin Delano Roosevelt and American Foreign Policy, 1932–1945* (1979)

Kenneth S. Davis, *FDR: Into the Storm, 1937–1940* (1993)

Melvyn Dubofsky, *The State and Labor in Modern America* (1994)

Waldo Heinrichs, *Threshold of War: Franklin D. Roosevelt and American Entry into World War II* (1988)

Mark Leff, *The Limits of Symbolic Reform: The New Deal and Taxation* (1984)

Deborah E. Lipstadt, *Beyond Belief: The American Press and the Coming of the Holocaust, 1933–1945* (1986)

James T. Patterson, *Congressional Conservatism and the New Deal* (1967)

———, *The New Deal and the States* (1969)

Charles H. Trout, *Boston, the Great Depression, and the New Deal* (1977)

Chapter 9

The Politics of War

Wayne S. Cole, *Roosevelt and the Isolationists* (1983)

Robert Dallek, *Franklin D. Roosevelt and American Foreign Policy, 1932–1945* (1979)

Justus D. Doenecke, *Storm on the Horizon: The Challenge to American Intervention, 1939–1941* (2000)

Akira Iriye, *Power and Culture: The Japanese-American War, 1941–1945* (1981)

Warren Kimball, *The Juggler: Franklin Roosevelt as Wartime Statesman* (1991)

David Reynolds, *From Munich to Pearl Harbor: Roosevelt's America and the Origins of the Second World War* (2001)

James Schneider, *Should America Go to War? The Debate over Foreign Policy in Chicago, 1939–1941* (1989)

Military Operations

Anthony Beevor, *Stalingrad* (1998)

John D. Chappell, *Before the Bomb: How Americans Approached the Pacific War* (1997)

John Keegan, *Six Armies in Normandy; From D-Day to the Liberation of Paris* (1982)

Samuel Eliot Morrison, *The Two-Ocean War: A Short History of the United States Navy in the Second World War* (1963)

Gordon Prange, *At Dawn We Slept: The Untold Story of Pearl Harbor* (1981)

Ronald H. Spector, *Eagle against the Sun: The American War with Japan* (1985)

David Syrett, *The Defeat of the German U-Boats: The Battle of the Atlantic* (1994)

Barbara W. Tuchman, *Stillwell and the American Experience in China, 1911–1945* (1970)

Gerhard Weinberg, *A World at Arms: A Global History of World War II* (1994)

The Experience of War

Stephen Ambrose, *Citizen Soldiers: The U.S. Army from the Normandy Beaches to the Bulge to the Surrender of Germany, June 7, 1944–May 7, 1945* (1997)

Craig M. Cameron, *American Samurai: Myth, Imagination, and the Conduct of Battle in the First Marine Division, 1941–1951* (1994)

Michael Doubler, *Closing with the Enemy: How GIs Fought the War in Europe, 1944–1945* (1994)

Paul Fussell, *Wartime: Understanding and Behavior in the Second World War* (1989)

Harold P. Leinbaugh, and John D. Campbell, *The Men of Company K: The Autobiography of a World War II Rifle Company* (1985)

William Manchester, *Goodbye Darkness: A Memoir of the Pacific War* (1980)

Harrison Salisbury, *The 900 Days: The Siege of Leningrad* (1969)

Peter Schrijvers, *The Crash of Ruin: American Combat Soldiers in Europe During World War II* (1996)

E. B. Sledge, *With the Old Breed at Peleliu and Okinawa* (1981)

Mobilizing the Home Front

John M. Blum, *V Was for Victory: Politics and American Culture During World War II* (1976)

Thomas Doherty, *Projections of War: Hollywood, American Culture, and World War II* (1994)

Marilynn Johnson, *The Second Gold Rush* (1993)

Clayton Koppes, and Gregory Black, *Hollywood Goes to War* (1987)

Nelson Lichtenstein, *Labor's War at Home: The CIO in World War II* (1983)

Gerald Nash, *The American West Transformed: The Impact of the Second World War* (1985)

Wesley P. Newton, *Montgomery in the Good War: Portrait of a Southern City, 1939–1946* (2000)

Richard Polenberg, *War and Society: The United States, 1941–1945* (1972)

Richard Rhodes, *The Making of the Atomic Bomb* (1986)

William M. Tuttle, *Daddy's Gone to War: The Second World War in the Lives of America's Children* (1993).

Harold Vatter, *The U.S. Economy in World War II* (1985)

Women and the War Effort

Karen Anderson, *Wartime Women: Sex Roles, Family Relations, and the Status of Women during World War II* (1981)

D'Ann Campbell, *Women at War with America: Private Lives in a Patriotic Era* (1984)

Susan Hartmann, *The Home Front and Beyond: American Women in the 1940s* (1982)

Amy Kesselman, *Fleeting Opportunities: Women in Portland and Vancouver Shipyards during World War II and Reconversion* (1990)

Judy Barrett Litoff, *We're in This War Too: World War II Letters of American Women in Uniform* (1994)

Racial Attitudes and U.S. Policy

Roger Daniels, *Concentration Camps U.S.A.: Japanese Americans and World War II* (1971)

John Dower, *War Without Mercy: Race and Power in the Pacific War* (1986)

Dominic J. Capeci, Jr., *Race Relations in Wartime Detroit: The Sojourner Truth Controversy of 1942* (1984)

David S. Wyman, *The Abandonment of the Jews: America and the Holocaust, 1941–1945* (1984)

Chapter 10

Foreign and Military Policy

John L. Gaddis, *The United States and the Cold War* (1992)

Greg Herken, *The Winning Weapon: The Atomic Bomb in the Cold War, 1945–1950* (1980)

Michael Hogan, *Cross of Iron: Harry S Truman and the Origins of the National Security State, 1945–1954* (1998)

Hogan, Michael. *The Marshall Plan* (1987)

Walter Le Feber, *America, Russia, and the Cold War* (1985)

May, Ernest R., ed., *American Cold War Strategy: Interpreting NSC–68* (1993)

Thomas G. Paterson, *On Every Front: The Making of the Cold War* (1979)

Richard Rhodes, *Dark Sun: The Making of the Hydrogen Bomb* (1995)

Michael Schaller, *The American Occupation of Japan* (1985)

Herbert F. York, *The Advisors: Oppenheimer, Teller and the Super* (1976)

Vladislav Zubok, and Constantine Pleshkanov, *Inside the Kremlin's Cold War: From Stalin to Khrushchev* (1996)

Korean War

Bruce Cumings, *The Origins of the Korean War* (1981, 1990)

Rosemary Foot, *The Wrong War: American Policy and the Dimensions of the Korean Conflict, 1950–1953* (1985)

D. Clayton James, *Refighting the Last War: Command and Crisis in Korea, 1950–1953* (1992)

Burton I. Kaufman, *The Korean War: Challenges in Crisis, Credibility, and Command* (1986)

William Stueck, *The Korean War: An International History* (1995)

Society and Politics at Home

Steven Gillon, *Politics and Vision: The ADA and American Liberalism* (1987)

Eric F. Goldman, *The Crucial Decade and After: America, 1945–1960* (1960)

Alonzo Hamby, *A Man of the People: A Life of Harry Truman* (1995)

Barbara M. Kelly, *Expanding the American Dream: Building and Rebuilding Levittown* (1993)

Donald R. McCoy and Richard Ruetten, *Quest and Response: Minority Rights and the Truman Administration* (1973)

Joanne Meyerowitz, ed., *Not June Cleaver: Women and Gender in Postwar America* (1994)

James Patterson, *Mr. Republican: A Biography of Robert A. Taft* (1972)

Gregory Randall, *America's Original G.I.: Town Park Forest, Illinois* (2000)

Graham White and John Maze, *Henry A. Wallace: His Search for a New World Order* (1995)

Gwendolyn Wright, *Building the Dream: A Social History of Housing in America* (1981)

Red Scare

David Caute, *The Great Fear* (1978)

Richard Fried, *Nightmare in Red: The McCarthy Era in Perspective* (1990)

Robert Griffith, *The Politics of Fear: Joseph R. McCarthy and the Senate* (1970)

Stanley Kutler, *The American Inquisition* (1982)

Michael Paul Rogin, *The Intellectuals and McCarthy: The Radical Spectre* (1967)

Ellen Schrecker, *No Ivory Tower: McCarthyism and the Universities* (1986)

Athan Theoharis and John Stuart Cox, *The Boss: J. Edgar Hoover and the Great American Inquisition* (1988)

Chapter 11

The Eisenhower Presidency

Stephen E. Ambrose, *Ike's Spies: Eisenhower and the Espionage Establishment* (1981)

Robert Bowie and Richard Immerman, *Waging Peace: How Eisenhower Shaped an Enduring Cold War Strategy* (1998)

H. W. Brands, *Cold Warriors: Eisenhower's Generation and American Foreign Policy* (1988)

Robert Divine, *Eisenhower and the Cold War* (1981)

Mary Dudziak, *Cold War Civil Rights: Race and the Image of American Democracy* (2000)

Fred Greenstein, *The Hidden-Hand Presidency: Eisenhower as Leader* (1982)

Walter Hixson, *Parting the Curtain: Propaganda, Culture and the Cold War* (1997)

Richard Immerman, *The CIA in Guatemala: The Foreign Policy of Intervention* (1982)

Chester Pach, *The Presidency of Dwight David Eisenhower* (1991)

William B. Pickett, *Eisenhower Decides to Run: Presidential Politics and Cold War Strategy* (2001)

Science, Politics, and Society

Barbara Clowse, *Brainpower for the Cold War: The Sputnik Crisis and the National Defense Education Act* (1981)

Robert Divine, *The Sputnik Challenge* (1993)

Andrew Grossman, *Neither Dead nor Red: Civil Defense and American Political Development During the Early Cold War* (2001)

Robert Kleidman, *Organizing for Peace: Neutrality, the Test Ban, and the Freeze* (1993)

Laura McEnaney, *Civil Defense Begins at Home: Militarization Meets Everyday Life in the Fifties* (2000)

Walter McDougall, *The Heavens and the Earth: A Political History of the Space Age* (1985)

Jane Smith, *Patenting the Sun* (1990)

M. Costandina Titus, *Bombs in the Backyard: Atomic Testing and American Politics* (1986)

Allan Winkler, *Life under a Cloud: American Anxiety about the Atom* (1993)

The Politics of Growth

Carl Abbott, *The New Urban America: Growth and Politics in Sunbelt Cities* (1986)

Elizabeth Fones-Wolf, *Selling Free Enterprise: The Business Assault in Labor and Liberalism, 1945–1960* (1994)

Kenneth Jackson, *The Crabgrass Frontier* (1985)

Kim McQuaid, *Uneasy Partners: Big Business in American Politics, 1945–1990* (1993)

William L. O'Neill, *American High: The Years of Confidence, 1945–1960* (1986)

Mark Rose, *Interstate: Express Highway Politics* (1990)

Jon Teaford, *The Rough Road to Renaissance: Urban Revitalization in America* (1990)

Family Life and Culture

Glenn Altschuler and David Grossvogel, *Changing Channels: America in TV Guide* (1992)

Wini Breines, *Young, White and Miserable: Growing Up Female in the 1950s* (1992)

Thomas Doherty, *Teenagers and Teenpics: The Juvenilization of American Movies in the 1950s* (rev. ed.: 2002)

Daniel Horowitz, *Vance Packard and American Social Criticism* (1994)

Andrew Jamison and Ron Eyerman, *Seeds of the Sixties* (1994)

Eugenia Kaledin, *Mothers and More: American Women in the 1950s* (1984)

Elaine Tyler May, *Homeward Bound: American Families in the Cold War Era* (1988)

Leila Rupp and Verta Taylor, *Survival in the Doldrums: The American Women's Rights Movement, 1945 to the 1960s* (1987)

Jessica Weiss, *To Have and To Hold: Marriage, the Baby Boom, and Social Change* (2000)

William Whyte, *The Organization Man* (1956)

The Early 1960s

Michael Beschloss, *The Crisis Years: Kennedy and Khrushchev, 1960–1963* (1991)

David Burner, *John F. Kennedy and a New Generation* (1988)

Lawrence Freedman, *Kennedy's Wars: Berlin, Cuba, Laos, and Vietnam* (2001)

James Giglio, *The Presidency of John F. Kennedy* (1991)

Robert Alan Goldberg, *Barry Goldwater* (1995)

Elizabeth Cobbs Hoffman, *All You Need Is Love: The Peace Corps and the Spirit of the 1960s* (1998)

Doris Kearns, *Lyndon Johnson and the American Dream* (1976)

Edward Moise, *Tonkin Gulf and the Escalation of the Vietnam War* (1996)

James T. Patterson, *America's Struggle against Poverty, 1900–1985* (1986)

Rick Perlstein, *Before the Storm: Barry Goldwater and the Unmaking of American Consensus* (2001)

Mark Stern, *Calculating Visions: Kennedy, Johnson, and Civil Rights* (1992)

Peter Wyden, *Bay of Pigs: The Untold Story* (1979)

Struggles for Equal Rights

Rudolfo AcuZa, *Occupied America: A History of Chicanos* (1988)

Taylor Branch, *Parting the Waters: America in the King Years, 1954–1963* (1988)

Eric Burner, *And Gently He Shall Lead Them: Robert Parris Moses and Civil Rights in Mississippi* (1994)

David Chappell, *A Stone of Hope: Prophetic Religion and the Death of Jim Crow* (2003)

Robert J. Cottrol, Raymond T. Diamond, and Leland B. Ware, *Brown v. Board of Education: Caste, Culture and the Constitution* (2003)

Claybourne Carson, *In Struggle: SNCC and the Black Awakening of the 1960s* (1981)

William Chafe, *Civilities and Civil Rights: Greensboro, North Carolina, and the Black Struggle* (1980)

John Dittmer, *Local People: A History of the Mississippi Movement* (1994)

John Egerton, *Speak Now Against the Day: The Generation before the Civil Rights Movement in the South* (1994)

David Garrow, *Bearing the Cross: Martin Luther King Jr. and the Southern Christian Leadership Conference* (1986)

Roger Goldman and David Gallen. *Thurgood Marshall: Justice for All* (1993)

David Halberstam, *The Children* (1998)

Elizabeth Huckaby, *Crisis at Central High: Little Rock, 1957–1958* (1980)

Richard Kluger, *Simple Justice: The History of Brown v. Board of Education* (1976)

Charles Marsh, *God's Long Summer: Stories of Faith and Civil Rights* (1998)

Kay Mills, *This Little Light of Mine: The Life of Fannie Lou Hamer* (1993)

Charles Payne, *I've Got the Light of Freedom: The organizing Tradition and the Mississippi Freedom Struggle* (1995)

Harvard Sitkoff, *The Struggle for Black Equality: 1954–1992* (1992)

Chapter 12

War in Vietnam

Christian Appy, *Working-Class War: American Combat Soldiers and Vietnam* (1993)

Albert Auster and Leonard Quart, *How the War Was Remembered: Hollywood and Vietnam* (1988)

Robert Buzzanco, *Masters of War* (1996)

Frances Fitzgerald, *Fire on the Lake* (1972)

George Herring, *America's Longest War* (1986)

David W. Levy, *The Debate over Vietnam* (1991)

William Shawcross, *Sideshow: Kissinger, Nixon, and the Destruction of Cambodia* (1979).

Robert Schulzinger, *A Time for War. The United States and Vietnam, 1941–1975* (1997)

Neil Sheehan, *A Bright Shining Lie: John Paul Vann and America in Vietnam* (1988)

Brian Van De Mark, *Into the Quagmire: Johnson and the Escalation of the Vietnam War* (1991)

Lynda Van Devanter, *Home Before Morning* (1984)

Tom Wells, *The War Within: America's Battle over Vietnam* (1994)

Marilyn Young, *The Vietnam Wars, 1945–1990* (1991)

The Revolt of the Young

Terry Anderson, *The Movement and the Sixties* (1995)

Wini Breines, *Community and Organization in the New Left, 1962–1968* (1982)

Sara Evans, *Personal Politics: The Roots of Women's Liberation in the Civil Rights Movement and the New Left* (1979)

Todd Gitlin, *The Sixties: Years of Hope, Days of Rage* (1987)

Marty Jezer, *Abbie Hoffman: American Rebel* (1992)

James Miller, *"Democracy Is in the Streets": From Port Huron to the Siege of Chicago* (1987)

Charles Perry, *The Haight-Ashbury* (1985)

William Rorabaugh, *Berkeley at War* (1989)

Kirkpatrick Sale, *SDS* (1973)

Minority Rights and Minority Separatism

Paula Giddings and Cornel West, *Regarding Malcolm X* (1994)

Peter Mathiesson, *In the Spirit of Crazy Horse* (1983)

Russell Means, *Where White Men Fear to Tread* (1995)

Felix Padilla, *Puerto Rican Chicago* (1987)

Donald Parman, *Indians and the American West in the Twentieth Century* (1994)

Piri Thomas, *Down These Mean Streets* (1967)

William L. Van Deburg, *New Day in Babylon: The Black Power Movement and American Culture, 1965–1975* (1993)

Foreign Policy in the 1970s

James A. Bill, *The Eagle and the Lion: The Tragedy of American-Iranian Relations* (1988)

Raymond Garthoff, *Détente and Confrontation* (1985)

Walter Isaacson, *Kissinger: A Biography* (1992)

Walter Le Feber, *The Panama Canal: The Crisis in Historical Perspective* (1978)

Robert Litwak, *Détente and the Nixon Doctrine* (1984)

Keith Nelson, *The Making of Détente* (1995)

William B. Quando, *Camp David: Peacemaking and Politics* (1986)

Robert Schulzinger, *Henry Kissinger: Doctor of Diplomacy* (1989)

Gaddis Smith, *Morality, Reason, and Power* (1986)

Strobe Talbot, *Endgame: The Inside Story of SALT II* (1979)

Watergate and Politics in the Nixon Years

Stephen E. Ambrose, *Nixon: Ruin and Recovery, 1973–1990* (1991)

Dan T. Carter, *The Politics of Rage: George Wallace, the Origins of the New Conservatism, and the Transformation of American Politics* (1996)

John Robert Greene, *The Limits of Power: The Nixon and Ford Administrations* (1992)

Joan Hoff, *Nixon Reconsidered* (1994)

Stanley Kutler, *The Wars of Watergate* (1990)

Kevin Phillips, *The Emerging Republican Majority* (1969)

Richard Scammon, and Ben Wattenberg, *The Real Majority* (1973)

Michael Schudson, *Watergate in American Memory: How We Remember, Forget, and Reconstruct the Past* (1992)

Bob Woodward and Carl Bernstein, *All the President's Men* (1974)

Jimmy Carter and His Presidency

Jimmy Carter, *Keeping Faith: Memoirs of a President* (1982)

Betty Glad, *Jimmy Carter, In Search of the Great White House* (1980)

Erwin C. Hargrove, *Jimmy Carter as President: Leadership and the Politics of the Public Good* (1988)

Charles O. Jones, *The Trusteeship Presidency: Jimmy Carter and the United States Congress* (1988)

Burton I. Kaufman, *The Presidency of James Earl Carter, Jr.* (1993)

William Lee Miller, *Yankee from Georgia: The Emergence of Jimmy Carter* (1978)

Environmental Politics

Robert Gottlieb, *Forcing the Spring: The Transformation of the American Environmental Movement* (1993)

Samuel Hays, *Beauty, Health, and Permanence: Environmental Politics in the United States, 1955–1985* (1987)

Kirkpatrick Sale, *The Green Revolution: The American Environmental Movement, 1962–1992* (1993)

Economic Change

Barry Bluestone and Bennett Harrison, *The Deindistrialization of America* (1982)

David Callao, *The Imperious Economy* (1982)

Peter Davis, *Hometown: A Contemporary American Chronicle* (1982)

William Robbins, *Hard Times in Paradise* (1984)

Milton Rogovin and Michael Frrisch, *Portraits in Steel* (1993)

William Serrin, *Homestead: The Glory and Tragedy of an American Steel Town* (1992)

Studs Terkel, *Working* (1972)

Chapter 13

Economic Change: Opportunity and Inequality

Frank Beam and Gillian Stevens, *American's Newcomers and the Dynamics of Diversity* (2003)

Barbara Ehrenreich, *Fear of Falling: The Inner Life of the Middle Class* (1989)

Frank Levy, *The New Dollars and Dreams: American Incomes and Economic Change* (1998)

Ann Markusen, et al. *The Rise of the Gunbelt: The Military Remapping of Industrial America* (1991)

Hobart Rowan, *Self-Inflicted Wounds: From LBJ's Guns and Butter to Reagan's Voodoo Economics* (1994)

Daphne Spain, and Suzanne Bianchi, *Balancing Act: Motherhood, Marriage and Employment Among American Women* (1996)

James B. Stewart, *Den of Thieves* (1991)

Ida Susser, *Norman Street: Poverty and Politics in an Urban Neighborhood* (1982)

Sharon Zukin, *Loft Living: Culture and Capital in Urban Change* (1982)

African-American Experiences

Pierre Clavel and Wim Wiewel, eds. *Harold Washington and the Neighborhoods* (1991)

Daniel Coyle, *Hardball: A Season in the Projects* (1993)

Mitchell Duneier, *Slim's Table: Race, Respectability and Masculinity* (1992)

Andrew Hacker, *Two Nations: Black and White, Separate, Hostile, Unequal* (1992)

Steven F. Lawson, *In Pursuit of Power: Southern Blacks and Electoral Politics* (1985)

William Julius Wilson, *The Truly Disadvantaged* (1987)

The New Conservatism

William Bennett, *The De-Valuing of America: The Fight for Our Culture and Our Children* (1992)

Lee Edwards, *The Conservative Revolution: The Movement That Remade America* (1999)

John Ehrman, *The Rise of Neo-Conservative Intellectuals and Foreign Affairs, 1945–1994* (1995)

J. David Hoeveler, Jr., *Watch on the Right: Conservative Intellectuals in the Reagan Era* (1991)

Michael Katz, *The Undeserving Poor: From the War on Poverty to the War on Welfare* (1989)

Linda Kintz, *Between Jesus and the Market: The Emotions That Matter in Right-Wing America* (1997)

Irving Kristol, *Neoconservatism: The Autobiography of an Idea* (1995)

Theodore J. Lowi, *The End of the Republican Era* (1995)

Charles Murray, *Losing Ground: American Social Policy, 1950–1980* (1984)

Politics, Society, and the Mass Media

R. Serge Denisoff, *Inside MTV* (1988)

Don Flournoy, *CNN World Report: Ted Turner's International News Coup* (1992)

Todd Gitlin, *Watching Television* (1987)

Andrew Goodwin, *Dancing in the Distraction Factory: Music Television and Popular Culture* (1992)

Nicolaus Mills, *Culture in an Age of Money* (1990)

Military and Foreign Policy

Dana H. Allin, *Cold War Illusions: America, Europe, and Soviet Power, 1969–1989* (1998)

David Cortright, *Peace Works: The Citizen's Role in Ending the Cold War* (1993)

Theodore Draper, *A Very Thin Line* (1991)

Lawrence Freedman and Efraim Karsh, *The Gulf Conflict, 1990–1991: Diplomacy and the New World Order* (1993)

Aaron L. Friedberg, *In the Shadow of the Garrison State: America's Anti-Statism and the Cold War* (2000)

John L. Gaddis, *Now We Know: Rethinking Cold War History* (1997)

Stephen Graubard, *Mr. Bush's War* (1992)

 ed., Michael J. Hogan, *The End of the Cold War: Its Meaning and Implications* (1992)

Christian Smith, *Resisting Reagan: The U.S. Central American Peace Movement* (1997)

Robert W. Tucker and David C. Hendrickson, *The Imperial Temptation: The New World Order and America's Purposes* (1992)

Daniel Wirls, *Buildup: The Politics of Defense in the Reagan Era* (1992)

Politics and Politicians in the 1980s

Martin Anderson, *Revolution* (1989)

William Berman, *America's Right Turn: From Nixon to Bush* (1994)

Michael Duffy and Dan Goodgame, *Marching in Place: The Status Quo Presidency of George Bush* (1992)

John Robert Greene, *The Presidency of George Bush* (2000)

Steven M. Gallon, *The Democrats Dilemma: Walter F. Mondale and the Liberal Legacy* (1992)

Haynes Johnson, *Sleepwalking Through History: America in the Reagan Years* (1991)

William Pemberton, *Exit with Honor: The Life and Presidency of Ronald Reagan* (1997)

Peggy Noonan, *What I Saw at the Revolution: A Political Life in the Reagan Era* (1990)

Michael Schaller, *Reckoning with Reagan: American and Its President in the 1980s* (1992)

John W. Sloan, *The Reagan Effect: Economics and Presidential Leadership* (1999)

David Stockman, *The Triumph of Politics: How the Reagan Revolution Failed* (1986)

Chapter 14

The New Economy

Manuel Castells, *The Internet Galaxy: Reflections on the Internet, Business, and Society* (2001)

Robert Gilpin, *Global Political Economy* (2001)

Tracy Kidder, *The Soul of a New Machine* (1981)

John Micklethwait and Adrian Wooldridge, *A Future Perfect: The Challenge and Hidden Promise of Globalization* (2000)

Everett Rogers, *Silicon Valley Fever* (1984)

Peter Calthorpe and William Fulton, *The Regional City* (2001)

William Riebsame, et al. *Atlas of the New West* (1997)

Hal Rothman, *Neon Metropolis: How Las Vegas Started the Twenty-First Century* (2002)

America at War

Williamson Murray and Robert Scales, Jr., *The Iraq War: A MIlitary History* (2003)

Bob Woodward, *Bush at War* (2002)

CREDITS

INDEX